THE ASIAN AMERICAN EDUCATIONAL EXPERIENCE

THE ASIAN AMERICAN EDUCATIONAL EXPERIENCE

A Source Book for Teachers and Students

Edited by
Don T. Nakanishi *and* Tina Yamano Nishida

ROUTLEDGE
NEW YORK LONDON

Published in 1995 by

Routledge
29 West 35th Street
New York, NY 10001

Published in Great Britain by

Routledge
11 New Fetter Lane
London EC4P 4EE

Library of Congress Cataloging–in–Publication Data

The Asian American educational experience: a sourcebook for teachers and students / edited by Don T. Nakanishi and Tina Yamano Nishida.
     p. cm.
  Includes bibliographical references and index.
  ISBN 0-415-90871-x   ISBN 0-415-90872-8 (pbk.) :
  1. Asian Americans—Education.   I. Nakanishi, Don T.
II. Nishida, Tina Yamano.
LC2632.A85   1994
371.97'073—dc20
                                     94-16361
                                       CIP

British Library Cataloging-in-Publication Data also available.

Contents

Acknowledgments

WE WOULD LIKE TO EXPRESS our gratitude to the faculty, staff, and students of the UCLA Asian American Studies Center and the UCLA Graduate School of Education for their commitment to this project. We are particularly grateful to *Amerasia Journal* of the UCLA Asian American Studies Center, which annually compiles a thorough bibliography of publications in Asian American studies under the direction of Glenn Omatsu, the associate editor. These bibliographies were indispensable in developing a specialized one focusing on recent Asian/Pacific American educational research for this book.

We would like to extend our warmest regards to our families for providing us with extraordinary and continuous support to undertake and complete this project. We also would like to pay very special tribute to Jayne Fargnoli, the sociology and education editor, and Anne Sanow, editorial assistant, of Routledge, Inc. for their amazing patience and genuine dedication to the publication of this book.

And finally, we owe our greatest debt to the stellar group of scholars, educational policy analysts, and writers whose works on a number of significant dimensions of the Asian/Pacific American educational experience are showcased in this anthology. We believe readers of this book will concur with us that these works provide ample evidence of the contributions and future promise of the emerging field of Asian/Pacific American educational research.

Growth and Diversity: The Education of Asian/Pacific Americans

Don T. Nakanishi

INTRODUCTION

DURING THE PAST TWO DECADES, there has been an unprecedented growth and diversification of the Asian/Pacific American population. From California to New York and from Minnesota to Texas, Asian/Pacific Americans have had an impact on educational institutions at all levels. Elementary and secondary schools that are located in urban regions with long-established Asian/Pacific American communities such as Los Angeles, as well as those serving recently created ones such as Lowell, Massachusetts, have faced educational challenges that are both new as well as decades old. Issues of language and cultural adjustment and maintenance, differences in academic performance levels, inadequate presentation of the Asian/Pacific American experience in textbooks and curricula, and anti-Asian violence in schools, among other issues, have confronted teachers, administrators, parents, and Asian/Pacific American community leaders alike. At the same time, a highly publicized and prolonged controversy over allegations of admissions quotas against Asian/Pacific American applicants to many of the country's most competitive undergraduate institutions, the vigorous efforts by students and professors to establish Asian American studies programs, and several major lawsuits dealing with faculty tenure and promotion have underscored a number of issues of access and representation of Asian/Pacific Americans at America's colleges and universities.

In recent years, a body of research has begun to emerge to document, to analyze, and to offer practical and policy-oriented recommendations on the contemporary and historical educational experiences and issues of Asian/Pacific Americans. Approached through the theoretical perspectives and methodological tools of multiple disciplines—psychology, history, Asian American studies, anthropology, sociology, law, political science, and many subfields within educational research—this upsurge in scholarship has served to alleviate a longstanding paucity of studies on Asian/Pacific American educational topics. Although many factors contributed to this neglect, perhaps the most influential was the wide acceptance of the simple monolithic view of Asian/Pacific American academic prowess, and the labeling of Asian/Pacific Americans as "whiz kids," or model minorities. Indeed, in many of the most highly regarded comparative studies of minority students (Ogbu, 1978; Astin, 1982), Asian/Pacific Americans were not included in the data collection and analysis because they were not deemed "educationally disadvantaged" like other groups of color. This lack of a sustained and rigorous body of empirical and theoretical literature has had many lamentable, albeit often unintended, consequences. For example, there is much to suggest that the Asian American undergraduate admissions quotas controversy might not have escalated and become so explosive if there had been a body of knowledge that all parties to the dispute could have used to test or verify their largely unfounded assumptions and assertions about Asian/Pacific American college applicants. Instead, much of this controversy evolved in a virtual scholarly vacuum.

This book is intended to provide an array of readers—those who teach, counsel, or work with Asian/Pacific American students and their families, as well as those who are interested in undertaking research on or offering courses on Asian/Pacific American educational topics—with a collection of many of the most important, provocative, and practical recent studies from the emerging field of Asian/Pacific American education research. The articles span the entire length of the academic pipeline from elementary schooling to higher education, and also capture the deep historical roots of the actions taken by Asian/Pacific Americans to secure equal educational opportunities. Although the focus is on Asian/Pacific Americans, it will be evident that many of their educational experiences and struggles have had a wider, multifaceted impact on a range of academic policies and practices. For example, the 1974 United States Supreme Court lawsuit of *Lau v. Nichols*, which was filed by thirteen non-English-speaking Chinese American schoolchildren against the San Francisco Board of Education, remains as the landmark bilingual education case, and arguably was the most important educational civil rights decision since *Brown v. Board of Education* (Wang, 1976). Likewise, the high court's unanimous 1989 ruling in *E.E.O.C. v. University of Pennsylvania* involved allegations of racial and sexual discrimination in the denial of tenure for Rosalie Tung, an Asian/Pacific American woman professor of management at the Ivy League institution (Carmody, 1989; Minami, 1989). This far-reaching decision led many institutions of higher education to make unprecedented changes in their policies and procedures regarding the rights of faculty to gain access to confidential documents during formal promotional reviews.

Although research on the educational experiences of Asian/Pacific Americans can be traced back many decades, particularly to the early studies of intelligence focusing on second-generation Chinese and Japanese American schoolchildren (Yeung, 1921; Graham, 1926; Darcie, 1926; Strong, 1933), the increased number of works in recent years has been dramatic. In 1971, for example, when the University of California, Davis, Asian American studies program compiled the first-ever annotated bibliography of the then-existing works on Asian Americans, it identified less than fifteen articles, books, or reports on Asian American educational topics (Fujimoto, Swift, and Zucker, 1971). In contrast, for this sourcebook, Tina Yamano Nishida has compiled an annotated bibliography on recent Asian/Pacific American educational research from 1980 to 1993, and has listed and described over three hundred readily accessible articles, books, and other publications. Over twice as many other works, chiefly dissertations, theses, and investigatory reports that are more difficult to locate except at specialized research collections such as the UCLA Asian American Studies Center Reading Room and Library,* were not included. This augmentation of research on Asian/Pacific American educational topics parallels a similar growth in other areas of inquiry in Asian American studies. For example, the University of California, Davis, bibliography project located about 2,000 articles, books, and other publications that had ever been written on Asian Americans prior to 1971. On the other hand, the most recent annual bibliography on Asian American studies, compiled by *Amerasia Journal*, identified over 2,100 works that were published in 1992 alone (Omatsu, 1992).

The expansion of scholarly, policy, and pedagogical attention on Asian/Pacific American educational issues is occurring during one of the nation's most significant

---

*UCLA Asian American Studies Center Reading Room and Library, 2230 Campbell Hall, University of California, Los Angeles, CA 90024-1546.

periods of demographic and sociopolitical changes, in which the Asian/Pacific American population has been transformed in multiple ways. Since these demographic trends are projected to continue for decades to come, it would be well to provide an overview of these major shifts in the population characteristics of Asian/Pacific Americans, and their educational and social ramifications. After doing so, the articles in this collection will be introduced.

THE IMPACT OF THE GROWTH AND DIVERSITY OF THE ASIAN/PACIFIC AMERICAN POPULATION ON EDUCATIONAL INSTITUTIONS

Asian/Pacific Americans* are the country's fastest-growing group, having doubled during each of the past two decades from 1.5 million nationally in 1970 to 3.5 million in 1980, and finally to 7.2 million in 1990. Recent projections estimate that Asian/Pacific Americans will continue to increase to 11 million by 2000, and to nearly 20 million by 2020 (Fawcett and Carino, 1987; LEAP and UCLA Asian American Studies Center, 1993). This substantial increase can be attributed in large measure to the Immigration Act of 1965 (which eliminated the discriminatory quota provisions of the Immigration Act of 1924), the Indochinese Refugee Resettlement Program Act of 1975, and the Refugee Act of 1980. These latter two legislative measures permitted the migration and entry of close to 1 million refugees from Southeast Asia. In reversing a four-decade longitudinal trend, Asian/Pacifics now represent the largest group of legal immigrants to the United States. For example, between 1931 and 1960, when the provisions of the 1924 National Origins Act were in effect, 58 percent of the legal immigrants were from Europe, 21 percent from North America, 15 percent from Latin America, and the smallest portion, 5 percent, were from Asia. However, this situation was nearly the opposite by the reporting period, 1980 to 1984. Legal immigration from Europe had decreased to 12 percent of the overall total, North America to 2 percent, while Latin America had increased to 35 percent and Asian immigration had substantially increased to 48 percent of the country's total legal immigrants (United Way, 1985).

By extension, the growth in enrollment of Asian/Pacific Americans in America's schools and colleges has been substantial. They represent, for example, the fastest-growing ethnic group in the country's college-going population. Nationally in fall 1976, there were 150,000 Asian/Pacific American undergraduate and graduate students in higher educational institutions (Carnegie Foundation for the Advancement of Teaching, 1987). A decade later, in fall 1986, there were almost three times as many, or 448,000 Asian/Pacific American enrollees (Carnegie Foundation for the Advancement of Teaching, 1987). By 1992, there were 637,000 Asian/Pacific American undergraduate and graduate students (Chronicle of Higher Education, 1993). Similarly, elementary and secondary-school districts across the country from major metropolitan regions such as Philadelphia and Minneapolis to suburban and rural communities such as Falls Church, Virginia, and La Crosse, Wisconsin, have witnessed a dramatic growth in Asian/Pacific American students. Between 1980 and 1990, the school-age population of Asian/Pacific Americans who were between five and nineteen years of age nearly doubled nationally from 929,295 to 1,761,901

---

*In this book, the term *Asian/Pacific Americans* will be defined in a manner similar to that of a fact-finding report issued by the Asian/Pacific American Education Advisory Committee of the Office of the Chancellor of the California State University (1990): "Asian/Pacific Americans are defined as immigrants, refugees, and the U.S.–born descendants of immigrants from Asia, including Pakistan and the countries lying east of it in South Asia, Southeast Asia, East Asia, and the Pacific Islands" (p. 1).

(LEAP and UCLA Asian American Studies Center, 1993). Recent population projections estimate that the Asian/Pacific American age sectors for both elementary-secondary schooling and higher education will continue to increase from now until 2020, with the school-age population of five to nineteen years of age more than doubling to over 3 million nationally during the next three decades (LEAP and UCLA Asian American Studies Center, 1993).

During the decade from 1970 to 1980, and continuing into the 1990s, the Asian/Pacific American population also dramatically shifted from being largely American born to predominantly foreign born, as a result of this upsurge in international migration. For example, according to the 1980 census, 63.1 percent of all Asian/Pacific Americans in Los Angeles County were foreign born; with 92.9 percent of the Vietnamese, 85.9 percent of the Koreans, 72.8 percent of the Filipinos, and 70.3 percent of the Chinese having been born outside the United States (UCLA Ethnic Studies Centers, 1987). In marked contrast, 10.4 percent of the county's white residents, 2.4 percent of the African Americans, and 45.5 percent of the "Spanish-origin" population were foreign born (UCLA Ethnic Studies Centers, 1987). Nationally, in 1990, 64 percent of all Asian/Pacific Americans were born abroad. Recent population projections estimate that the percentage of foreign-born Asian/Pacific Americans will remain in the majority for several decades to come (LEAP and UCLA Asian American Studies Center, 1992). This significant demographic shift to a largely foreign-born population has had many educational ramifications, particularly in terms of issues of linguistic and social adjustment and maintenance, which are addressed by many articles in this volume.

California, with a population of over 3 million Asian/Pacific Americans in 1990, is the state with the largest population of Asian/Pacific Americans. Forty percent of the Asian/Pacific Americans in the United States live in California. By extension, over 40 percent of all Asian/Pacific Americans who are enrolled in American higher educational institutions attend a college or university in California. Large numbers of Asian/Pacific American college students can also be found in New York (which now has the nation's second largest population of Asian/Pacific Americans), and followed in rank order by Illinois, Hawaii, and Texas. In 1992, these five states accounted for nearly 65 percent of all Asian/Pacific American college students. (Chronicle of Higher Education, 1993). And although nearly two-thirds of the Asian/Pacific American population in the United States remained concentrated in the Pacific region, the recent growth of this population clearly has been national in scope. Whereas in 1970, for example, there were 1.5 million Asian/Pacific Americans in the entire country, by 1990 there were over 2 million who lived solely in states bordering the Atlantic Ocean (LEAP and UCLA Asian American Studies Center, 1993). The increases in enrollment for local school districts, as well as colleges, from Massachusetts to Virginia to Florida have been dramatic. Kiang and Lee have noted that "[i]n Lowell, Massachusetts—a city with fewer than a hundred Cambodian residents in 1980 that now represents the second largest Cambodian community in the country—the influx was so rapid that between 35 and 50 new Cambodian and Lao children were entering the Lowell public schools *each week* during 1987" (Kiang and Lee, 1993). Likewise, there has been a substantial increase in the numbers of Asian/Pacific American students at both private and public colleges on the East Coast, particularly in the City and State University of New York systems and Ivy League colleges.

The Asian/Pacific American population, as many of the articles in this book describe and analyze, should not be conceptualized as a single, monolithic group. It has become an extremely heterogeneous population, with respect to ethnic and national origins, cultural values, generation, social class, religion, and other socially differentiating characteristics. In 1970, for instance, Japanese Americans were the largest Asian/Pacific American ethnic group. By 1980, however, both Chinese Americans (812, 178) and Filipino Americans (781,894) surpassed Japanese Americans (716,331); and other Asian/Pacific groups, such as Asian Indian Americans (387,223), Korean Americans (357,393), and Vietnamese Americans (245,025) grew rapidly as well through immigration. By 1990, both Chinese Americans (1,645,472) and Filipino Americans (1,406,770) had grown to be nearly twice as large as Japanese Americans (847,562), who experienced relatively little immigration from Japan and a gradually declining birth rate. The other three major Asian/Pacific American groups—Asian Indian Americans (815,447), Korean Americans (798,849), and Vietnamese Americans (614,547)—also recorded substantial population gains by 1990. By 2000, it is projected that Japanese Americans will fall further down the population scale, with practically all other major Asian/Pacific American groups outnumbering them, and Filipino Americans replacing Chinese Americans as the largest Asian/Pacific American ethnic group (LEAP and UCLA Asian American Studies Center, 1993). Although this ethnic diversity among Asian/Pacific Americans is apparent in many local school districts, particularly in major metropolitan regions such as Seattle, it is extremely visible at colleges and universities, especially in the form of student organizations and activities. At UCLA, for example, there were more than sixty different Asian/Pacific American student organizations in 1993, which reflected the ethnic diversity of the student population.

Diversity among Asian/Pacific Americans is also evident in terms of other characteristics. Educational attainment levels for different groups of Asian/Pacific Americans, for men versus women, and for different generations show substantial variations. For example, 1980 census data revealed that nearly 25 percent of all Asian/Pacific Americans, age twenty-five years and over, have less than a high school degree, and some groups have large numbers who have very little formal schooling (UCLA Ethnic Studies Centers, 1987). Nearly a quarter of all Vietnamese and Guamanian women, in the working age group of twenty-five to forty-four years of age, have less than eight years of schooling. Similarly, while nearly 40 percent of the Chinese and Asian Indian women of the same age category are college graduates, one out of ten Chinese and one out of ten Asian Indian women, twenty-five to forty-four years of age, have eight years or less of formal education (UCLA Ethnic Studies Centers, 1987). At the same time, there is a greater percentage of Asian/Pacific Americans living below the federal poverty level than the non-Hispanic, white population. In 1990, the poverty rate for Asian/Pacifics was 12.2 percent compared to 8.8 percent for non-Hispanic whites (LEAP and the UCLA Asian American Studies Center, 1993). The poverty rates for groups like the Hmongs, Laotians, and Cambodians are over 60 percent (LEAP and the UCLA Asian American Studies Center, 1993).

There are many significant, and often unrecognized, educational implications of these wide disparities in income and educational levels. Asian/Pacific American students, for instance, are often excluded from being considered for equal-opportunity admissions programs, as well as special retention, tutoring, and counseling activities at higher educational institutions because the prevalence of social and economic disadvantages among Asian/Pacific Americans are usually not acknowledged (Bagasao and Suzuki, 1989; Escueta and O'Brien, 1991; Asian/Pacific American Education Advisory Committee, Office of the Chancellor, 1990). However, when poverty and other forms of social disadvantage are addressed by colleges, the results can be quite startling. At UCLA, for instance, Asian/Pacific American applicants who come from very-low-income households or are first-time college-goers in their families are given the same consideration for admissions as other applicants who come from similar backgrounds. In 1993 Asian/Pacific Americans comprised nearly a third of all students who were part of the university's Academic Advancement Program, which seeks to enhance the retention and graduation rates of students from historically excluded and low-income groups.

Finally, within any particular Asian/Pacific American group such as Chinese Americans, the within-group differences can be quite pronounced, reflecting different historical waves of immigration and different segments of a class hierarchical structure. Nee and Nee, in their classic ethnographic study of San Francisco's Chinatown, *Longtime Californ'* (1974), provide a revealing socio-historical analysis of such within-group diversity among Chinese Americans. Hirschman and Wong (1981) use census data to rigorously examine within-group differences in socioeconomic achievement among immigrant and United States–born Chinese, Japanese, and Filipinos. Similarly, Ima and Rumbaut, in an article in this collection, describe the academic implications of major differences in educational and social backgrounds between the so-called first wave and second wave of Southeast Asian refugees and their children. The first wave of 130,000 refugees came in 1975 and were primarily urban, educated Vietnamese with prior American contacts and some familiarity with English. The "second wave" arrived after 1978, and included "much greater proportions of lowland Lao and highland Hmong from Laos, Khmer survivors of the 'killing fields' of Cambodia, Chinese Vietnamese and Vietnamese 'boat people,' and rural and less educated persons." As a result, they write that, "the adaptation by the school-age children of these refugee groups reflects crucial differences in time of arrival and social class background" (Ima and Rumbaut, 1989).

Finally, although more in-depth analyses are available elsewhere (Nakanishi, 1991; 1993) it is important to at least briefly note that these demographic shifts coincided with the growing political maturity and influence of Asian/Pacific Americans during the past two decades. Perhaps at no other period in the history of Asian/Pacific Americans in the United States have so many individuals and organizations participated in such a wide array of political and civil rights activities, especially in relation to the United States political system but also related to the affairs of their ancestral homelands in Asia. In traditional electoral politics, what had come to be taken as a common occurrence in Hawaii, namely the election of Asian/Pacific Americans to public office, suddenly became a less than surprising novelty in the so-called mainland states with the election and appointment of Asian/Pacific Americans to federal, state, and local positions, including school boards and college governing bodies, in California, Washington, New York, and elsewhere (Nakanishi, 1991). And perhaps most significantly, the Asian/Pacific American population came to demonstrate that it, too, had resources and talents—organizational, financial, or otherwise—to advance its specific concerns in a variety of policy and political arenas, and to confront issues that potentially were damaging to its group interests. Two widely reported community-based campaigns of the 1980s and 1990s were illustrative of this new collective determination: (a) the successful drive by Japanese Americans to gain redress and reparations for their World War II incarceration in 1988; and (b) the national movement to appeal and overturn the light sentences that were given to two unemployed Detroit auto workers who, in 1982, used a baseball bat to kill a Chinese American named Vincent Chin. (The two men mistook Chin for a Japanese and, therefore, someone who was viewed as having taken away their jobs [Nakanishi, 1991]). As we shall see in several of the articles in this collection, particularly those dealing with the controversies over undergraduate admissions, faculty representation, and bilingual education, the overall upsurge in the political participation of Asian/Pacific Americans during the past two decades dovetailed with their efforts to mobilize around educational concerns and issues.

These are the broad dimensions of the contemporary Asian/Pacific American population—a large, continuously and rapidly growing, increasingly assertive and yet significantly diverse population that is projected to reach 20 million by the year 2020. The dramatic growth and diversification of the Asian/Pacific American population during the past two decades, as well as the likely continuation of many of these demographic trends in years to come, will have a significant bearing on their educational experiences. As a result, the emerging field of Asian/Pacific American educational research unquestionably has a full, compelling, and yet highly exciting agenda of topics that should be examined in the future. This collection of articles demonstrates the enormous promise, as well as importance, of this area of inquiry.

THE ASIAN/PACIFIC AMERICAN EDUCATIONAL EXPERIENCE: THE ORGANIZATION OF THE BOOK

The articles in this book are divided into four interrelated parts. The first two parts, which deal with historical studies and critiques of the controversial model minority view of Asian/Pacific Americans, are intended to provide two important frames of reference for understanding the contemporary educational experiences of the Asian/Pacific American population. In the latter two parts, the articles focus specifically on issues relating to elementary-secondary schooling and higher education. An annotated bibliography of recent works on Asian/Pacific American educational research concludes this book.

HISTORICAL PERSPECTIVES ON THE SCHOOLING OF ASIAN/PACIFIC AMERICANS

The articles in Part I are intended to provide an understanding of the historical legacy of contemporary educational issues facing Asian/Pacific Americans. They provide informative insights on how Asian/Pacific Americans, like other American ethnic and racial groups, have been long concerned about educational issues, and how they have pursued a variety of strategies to seek equal educational opportunities. The articles also serve to dispel the potentially unwarranted view that the educational issues that Asian/Pacific Americans have raised and pursued in recent years are unique, and tied solely to the demographic transformations they have undergone during the past two decades.

All of the articles are written from a "new" approach in historical studies of American race relations, which analyzes not only what laws and actions were taken against Asian/Pacific Americans, but also how they responded to these discriminatory and exclusionary measures (Ichioka, 1971). They are written by historians and educational scholars. They include Wollenberg's insightful article on how the Chinese and Japanese immigrant communities responded to the efforts of the pre–World War II anti-Asian movements in California to exclude and segregate Chinese and Japanese American children from the state's public schools, as well as Wang's engaging insider's history of the landmark *Lau v. Nichols* bilingual education lawsuit. The article by Hawkins, in many respects, parallels that of Wollenberg's, and provides a richly textured analysis of the actions taken by the Japanese immigrant community in Hawaii to maintain control of its community-based Japanese language schools in the face of opposition by the *haole* (white) power elites. Finally, historian Yu uses archival documents found in China to examine a decades-long effort that continues to this day, in which Chinese immigrants and their descendants in the United States have provided financial donations to build thousands of elementary and secondary schools in China, and to support that country's drive toward modernization. Other groups of Asian/Pacific Americans have also provided similar forms of contributions to assist in development activities in their ancestral homelands.

ACADEMIC ACHIEVEMENT AND THE MODEL MINORITY DEBATE

The four articles in Part II challenge the widely prevalent and highly influential view that Asian/Pacific Americans are a model minority, which is based on generalizations made from their seemingly high overall group-level academic achievement levels and higher-than-average median household incomes. The articles describe the shortcomings of the model minority interpretation in explaining the social status and quality of life of the diverse Asian/Pacific American population in American society, and delineate the often harmful educational and social ramifications of this perspective. The articles are written by leading educational policy analysts and social scientists, and offer a wealth of provocative insights and empirical information on one of the most long-standing debates in scholarly and policy analyses of Asian/Pacific Americans. The articles by Chun and Suzuki are classic treatments of the topic, while those by Sue and Okazaki, as well as Barringer, Takeuchi, and Xenos are the most important and insightful of the most recent writings on the debate.

ELEMENTARY AND SECONDARY EDUCATIONAL ISSUES

Part III contains an array of highly informative and engaging articles that are intended to capture the extraordinary dimensions of diversity of contemporary Asian/Pacific American schoolchildren and their families that are now having an impact on America's elementary and secondary schools. Topics ranging from bilingual education to parental involvement in schools are addressed, and several in-depth case studies are included on groups and sectors of the Asian/Pacific American student and parent population that rarely receive focused attention, such as Khmer refugees and Pacific Islanders. The part begins with Pang's superb, multifaceted article on the educationally relevant aspects of diversity among the nation's Asian/Pacific American schoolchildren, and is followed by Ima and Rumbaut's pioneering comparative study of fluent-English-proficient and limited-English-proficient Southeast Asian refugee students. Smith-Hefner offers a rigorous and provocative analysis of the attitudes and behavior of Boston-area Khmer refugee parents toward native language maintenance and adjustment, while Cheng shares a number of effective strategies on how to address the learning needs of limited-English-proficient Asian/Pacific American students. Finally, Wong and Mau provide comparative analyses of different cohorts of Asian/Pacific American high school students. Wong uses "High School and Beyond" data to compare the academic achievement levels, extracurricular pursuits, and college aspirations of White, Chinese, Filipino, and Japanese American students. Mau, on the other hand, provides one of the first-ever studies of Hawaiian, Samoan, and Filipina high school woman students, and the array of potential barriers of social class, culture, and gender, as well as those that are school based, that may affect their academic performance.

HIGHER EDUCATIONAL ISSUES

The articles in Part IV focus on major issues and controversies that have emerged in recent years dealing with the access, representation, and influence of Asian/Pacific Americans in American higher educational institutions. Written by many of the most recognizable scholars, commentators, and policy experts on Asian/Pacific American higher education issues, the articles cover a range of topics from the Asian/Pacific American admissions controversy to anti-Asian sentiments and violence on college campuses. The part begins with two excellent overviews—one by Hsia and Hirano-Nakanishi, and the other by Escueta and O'Brien—of the major demographic trends and other differentiating characteristics of the growing presence of Asian/Pacific Americans, particularly as undergraduate and graduate students, at higher educational institutions. The next three works examine several major aspects of the admissions controversy. Nakanishi investigates why the debate escalated, and became a major national focus of governmental and media attention, while Wang provides an in-depth analysis of how admissions policies and procedures, especially at the University of California, were deliberately changed against Asian/Pacific American applicants. Sue and Abe, on the other hand, provide a rigorous comparative examination of a major point of contention of the admissions controversy dealing with the predictive value of high school grades, college entrance examination scores, and other measures in estimating college performance. The findings of their study, which was commissioned by the

College Board, go against common practice in college admissions evaluations. The articles by Hune and Chan, respectively, provide informative and provocative commentaries on the goals of the field of Asian American Studies and of ethnic studies requirements. Finally, this section concludes with an investigatory essay by Morse on an ugly episode of anti-Asian behavior at the University of Connecticut, which unfortunately has been repeated at numerous colleges across the country; and civil rights attorney Minami's extremely insightful and practical analysis on the difficulties that Asian/Pacific American professors, as well as women and those of other groups of color, often face in tenure and promotional reviews, and how some of them have fought back to assert their rights.

The annotated bibliography on recent Asian/Pacific American educational research, stretching from 1980 to 1993, compiled by Tina Yamano Nishida, concludes the collection.

REFERENCES

Asian and Pacific American Education Advisory Committee, Office of the Chancellor, The California State University. 1990. *Enriching California's future: Asian/Pacific Americans in the CSU*. Long Beach, Calif.: Author.

Astin, Alexander. 1982. *Minorities in American Higher Education*. San Francisco: Jossey-Bass.

Bagasao, Paula, and Bob H. Suzuki, eds. 1989. Asian and Pacific Americans: Behind the myths. *Change* (November/December).

Carmody, Deirdre. 1989. Secrecy and tenure: An issue for high court. *New York Times*, December 6: B8.

Carnegie Foundation for the Advancement of Teaching. 1987. "Minority access: a question of equity." *Change*, (May/June): 36.

Chronicle of Higher Education. 1993. College enrollment by racial and ethnic group, selected years. *Chronicle of Higher Education*. August 25: 13.

Darcie, Marvin L. 1926. The mental capacity of American-born Japanese children. *Comparative Psychological Monograph*. 3:5. 89 pp.

Escueta, Eugenia, and Eileen O'Brien. 1991. Asian Americans in higher education: Trends and issues. *Research Briefs*. American Council on Education 2:4: 1–11.

Fawcett, James T., and Benjamin V. Carino, ed. 1987. *Pacific Bridges*. Staten Island, N.Y.: Center for Migration Studies.

Fujimoto, Isao, Michiyo Yamaguchi Swift, and Rosalie Zucker, eds. 1971. *Asian in America: A selected annotated bibliography*. Davis Calif.: Asian American Research Project, University of California, Davis.

Graham, Virginia T. 1926. The Intelligence of Chinese Children in San Francisco. *Journal of Comparative Psychology*. 6:1: 43–71.

Hirschman, Charles, and Morrison G. Wong. 1981. Trends in socioeconomic achievement among immigrant and native-born Asian Americans, 1960–1976. *Sociological Quarterly*. Vol. 22: 495–514.

Ichioka, Yuji. 1971. A Buried Past: Early Issei Socialists and the Japanese Community. *Amerasia Journal*. 1:2: 1–25.

Ima, Kenji, and Ruben G. Rumbaut. 1989. Southeast Asian Refugees in American Schools: A Comparison of Fluent-English Proficient and Limited-English Proficient Studies. *Topics in Language Disorders*. 9:3: 54–77.

Kiang, Peter N., and Vivian Wai-Fun Lee. 1993. Exclusion or contribution? Education K-12 policy. In LEAP and the UCLA Asian American Studies Center, *The state of Asian/Pacific America: Policy issues to the year 2020*. Los Angeles: LEAP and the UCLA Asian American Studies Center: 25–48.

LEAP and the UCLA Asian American Studies Center. 1993. *The state of Asian/Pacific America: Policy issues to the year 2020*. Los Angeles: LEAP and the UCLA Asian American Studies Center.

Minami, Dale. 1990. Guerrilla war at UCLA: Political and legal dimensions of the tenure battle. *Amerasia Journal.* 16:1: 81–207.

Nakanishi, Don. 1991. The next swing vote? Asian/Pacific Americans and California politics. In Byran Jackson and Michael Preston (eds.). *Racial and Ethnic Politics in California.* Berkeley, Calif.: Institute for Governmental Studies: 25–54.

Nakanishi, Don. 1993. Surviving democracy's "mistake": Japanese Americans and the enduring legacy of executive order 9066. *Amerasia Journal.* 19:1: 7–35.

Nee, Brett, and Victor Nee. 1974. *Longtime Californ': A Documentary Study of an American Chinatown.* Boston: Houghton Mifflin.

Ogbu, John. 1978. *Minority Education and Castle.* New York: Academic Press.

Omatsu, Glenn. 1992. 1992 Annual selected bibliography, *Amerasia Journal.* 18:3: 81–189.

Strong, Edward K. 1933. *Vocational Aptitude of Second-Generation Japanese in the United States.* Stanford, Calif.: Stanford University Press.

UCLA Ethnic Studies Centers. 1987. *Ethnic Groups in Los Angeles: Quality of Life indicators.* Los Angeles: Author.

United Way, Asian/Pacific Research and Development Council. 1985. *Pacific Rim Profiles: A Demographic Study of the Asian/Pacific Profile in Los Angeles county.* Los Angeles: United Way.

Wang, Ling-Chi. 1976. Lau v. Nichols: History of a struggle for equal and quality education. In Emma Gee, et al., eds. *Counterpoint.* Los Angeles: Regents of the University of California and the UCLA Asian American Studies Center.

Yeung, Kwok T. 1921. The intelligence of Chinese children in San Francisco and vicinity. *Journal of Applied Psychology.* 5:3: 267–74.

HISTORICAL PERSPECTIVES ON THE SCHOOLING OF ASIAN/PACIFIC AMERICANS

"Yellow Peril" in the Schools (I)

Charles M. Wollenberg

IN 1885 A COMMITTEE of the San Francisco Board of Supervisors made a study of the "Chinese Quarter and the Chinese in San Francisco." The committee estimated that 722 children lived in Chinatown, most of them born in the United States and thus American citizens. Nevertheless, the supervisors believed that the children were as Chinese "as if they had been born in the province of Canton," speaking little or no English and rarely having contact with white people. The committee also claimed that Chinatown's youth lived amidst immorality and debauchery: "the painted harlots of the slums and alleys, the women who are bought and sold to the slavery of prostitution, are surrounded by children." Given this situation, the question addressed by the supervisors was whether "the doors of our school-house are to be opened to admit children reared in such an atmosphere?" And if Chinese were allowed in the schools, "what result will follow . . . will assimilation begin and race mixture begin?" As far as the committee was concerned, the answers were obvious: Chinese in the public schools would be a disaster for the city. "Guard well the doors of our public schools that they do not enter. For however stern it might sound, it is but the enforcement of the law of self-preservation, the inculcation of the doctrine of true humanity and an integral part of the iron rule of right by which we hope presently to prove that we can justly and practically defend ourselves from this invasion of Mongolian barbarism."[1]

What brought on this remarkable display of racist rhetoric was an attempt the previous September by Joseph and Mary Tape to enroll their eight-year-old daughter Mamie in Spring Valley School. Although Joseph Tape was a native of China, he had lived in San Francisco for fifteen years and he and his wife described themselves as "Christian, Americanized" Chinese. Their daughter Mamie had been born in the United States and spoke English far better than Chinese.[2] But the principal of the school, Miss Jennie Hurley, refused to admit the child, explaining that San Francisco Board of Education policy prohibited Chinese from attending the city's public schools. The Tapes did not let the matter drop and appealed for assistance to the Imperial Chinese Consulate in San Francisco. On October 4, 1884, Consul General Frederick A. Bee wrote city school Superintendent Andrew J. Moulder that the refusal to enroll Mamie was "as inconsistent with the treaties, constitutions and laws of the United States, especially so in this case as the child is native-born, that I consider it my duty to renew the request to admit the child and all other Chinese children resident here who desire to enter the public schools under your charge."[3]

Of course, this was not the first time that Superintendent Moulder had confronted the

From *All Deliberate Speed.* Berkeley: University of California Press (1978): 28–81. Reprinted with permission of the Regents of the University of California and the University of California Press.

issue of non-whites in California public schools. Twenty-five years earlier he was the State Superintendent of Public Instruction who had recommended that "Negroes, Mongolians and Indians" be prohibited from attending public schools with white children. As we have seen, the state legislature accepted that recommendation in 1860, but by 1884 the California school law no longer allowed local districts to refuse admittance to students on account of race.[4] The courts had established the principle of "separate but equal," but since 1880 the legislature had denied districts the right to practice it. Nevertheless, by 1884 San Francisco had been totally excluding Chinese from the public schools for more than a decade. Mamie Tape was about to change that situation, but her case can only be understood in the context of the larger history of Chinese education in California.

UNWELCOMED SOJOURNERS

Mamie was one of more than 75,000 Chinese living in California in the early 1880s. They constituted the state's largest foreign-born group and the largest non-white minority. They had fled economic and political chaos in the region surrounding the southern Chinese city of Canton. At first the immigrants were attracted to California by the prospect of wealth in the gold fields, then by employment on railroads, farms and in urban shops and factories. During the 1850s alone, California's Chinese population increased from 800 to nearly 35,000.[5] The immigrants initially were well received, but by the early 1850s, they already were being regarded as "yellow barbarians" and potential economic rivals. In 1852 the legislature levied a "foreign miners tax" aimed specifically at the Chinese, and three years later white miners in Shasta County circulated petitions calling for an end to Chinese immigration. As aliens, the Chinese were unable to vote or hold political office, and in 1854 the state Supreme Court ruled that they were covered by the law which prohibited blacks and Indians from testifying in court against whites. The justices reasoned that Indians and Chinese were "Mongolians"; thus laws applying to one group applied to the other.[6]

   Initially, the question of Chinese children in public schools did not arise, since most of the immigrants were young men who planned to make their fortunes in California and return to China. If married, they left wives and children at home. As late as 1860, the bulk of the Chinese laborers were concentrated in the mining regions, with El Dorado and Calaveras counties having the largest populations. But though it had fewer Chinese than these mountain counties, San Francisco was California's Chinese capital. It was the chief point of arrival and departure to and from the Orient, headquarters for the most powerful Chinese merchants and labor contractors and seat of a number of Chinese regional, social and economic associations. The city was also an outpost of Chinese culture: a Cantonese opera company performed in San Francisco as early as 1852 and by 1854 San Francisco had its first Chinese-language newspaper.[7]

   A few wealthy Chinese families settled in the city, and by 1857 they were asking the Board of Education to provide a school for their children. In August 1859 the board agreed, and in September California's first Chinese public school opened for business on the corner of Stockton and Sacramento Streets.[8] But the institution was never a favorite project of city school Superintendent James Denman. In April 1860, Denman visited the facility and found only three children and seven adults in attendance. On the basis of this experience, he questioned "the justice and propriety of expending public funds to sustain this school when those for whom it was established manifest so little interest in availing themselves of its advantages." The superintendent claimed "the prejudices of caste and religious idolatry are so indelibly stamped upon their [the Chinese] character and existence," that the task of teaching them was "almost hopeless." Denman protested the expenditure of tax money on the Chinese school, "while 400 or 500 children of our own folks were excluded for lack of room."[9]

Nevertheless, the Board of Education felt some responsibility to the city's Chinese population. In October 1860, the school was reorganized as a night institution in order to make classes more convenient for Chinese workingmen who wished to learn English. By May of 1861 total enrollment was 65 (39 adults, 21 boys and 5 girls) but average daily attendance was only 20. Denman's successor, George Tait, claimed that the school "deserved notice, if not for good results manifested, at least to express our admiration of the philanthropy which suggested its organization." Tait admitted that classes were given in a "gloomy basement," but he believed that such facilities "were not repugnant to Mongolian tastes and habits."[10]

The next superintendent, John Pelton, was not so sanguine. He called for construction of an adequate schoolhouse, since only a small portion of the taxes paid by San Francisco Chinese into the school fund were being spent on the Chinese school. Pelton called this situation "a striking instance of taxation without representation,"[11] but he failed to persuade the board to build the new schoolhouse. However, he was successful in obtaining the dismissal of the teacher, Preceptor Lanctot, after Chinese businessmen complained about the strong Christian bias in his teaching methods and materials. In 1866 Lanctot was replaced by a Mr. Dye, whose approach apparently was a bit more secular. Three years later, Dye resigned after twice being refused a pay raise, and Lanctot took up his old post.[12]

In the same year, 1869, James Denman was again elected superintendent. He soon reinstituted his campaign against the Chinese school, pointing out that most of the students were young men who wished to learn English to get better-paying jobs. "I question the legality and propriety of expending the public funds to educate these young men, while we have not the means to furnish suitable accommodations for the large numbers of our own children constantly applying for admission." Denman also observed that in 1870 the legislature deleted the word "Mongolian" from the state school law, so that while districts still were required to provide education for "African and Indian children," no specific mention was made of Chinese or "Mongolians." The superintendent interpreted this to mean that the legislature "had repealed the law authorizing the establishment of Chinese schools," and that San Francisco had no obligation to continue support of such an institution.[13] (In his analysis of the legal situation, Denman ignored the fact that in 1868 the United States signed a treaty with China which assured Chinese children living in America the right to attend public schools.) The Board of Education accepted the superintendent's recommendation, and on February 14, 1871, the Chinese school was closed, not to be reopened until the court decision in the Tape case, fifteen years later.[14]

MISSIONARY SCHOOLS

But this did not mean that Chinatown was left without educational institutions. One of the arguments used by Denman and the board for closing the public school was that it duplicated several private programs sponsored by Christian missionary organizations. By 1871, Presbyterians, Baptists, Methodists, Episcopalians and Congregationalists all provided some form of English-language instruction in Chinatown. As early as 1853, Reverend William Speer, a Presbyterian with Chinese missionary experience, had opened a Chinese Chapel at Stockton and Sacramento streets. The chapel was supported by contributions from San Franciscans of all denominations and by grants from the Presbyterian Board of Missions. Its basement housed the Chinese public school after 1857, and Speer actively protested discrimination against the immigrants and lobbied on their behalf in Sacramento.[15]

Speer's activities established precedents for the missionaries who came after him. They also defended the Chinese from harassment and legal discrimination, and established schools for the immigrants, not only in San Francisco, but in Sacramento, Stockton, Oakland and other California communities.

By 1876, Methodist Reverend Otis Gibson estimated that 5,500 California Chinese were enrolled in classes sponsored by various Christian denominations. Twenty-five hundred attended evening programs and another 3,000 were in Sunday schools, though Gibson admitted that average attendance was only about one-third of total enrollment. He claimed that the classes acquainted the Chinese with "the spirit and genious of our institutions," and encouraged them to "adopt our higher form of civilization and purer faith."[16] But most missionaries probably would have agreed with the Conference of the Methodist Episcopal Church that "the great majority of the Chinese are content with the merest smattering of English . . . as soon as they are able to read the simplest sentences and speak and write a few words of broken English, they find remunerative employment which takes them away from school."[17]

The missionary schools were not above using these pecuniary motives of the immigrants for Christian purposes. According to the Congregationalist California Chinese Mission, "that desire to learn the English language is still our principal fulcrum in the effort to lift the Chinese into the light of Christian life. We could bait our hook with the bait of the English primer and make the primer speak to them of Christ."[18] And occasionally the tactic worked: a few of the students not only became proficient in English, but also devout Christians. Lau Choy, prize scholar at the San Francisco Presbyterian school, wrote that the original Chinese "emigrated to China not long after Noah had left the Ark . . . by and by they turned more to evil, and forgot the will of God . . . those heathen Chinese still keep on their idolatrous and wicked course."[19]

CHINESE LANGUAGE SCHOOLS

For Chinatown residents who wished an educational program less hostile to traditional Chinese culture, instruction could be found at one of several Chinese language schools. Legend has it that the first of these institutions was founded in the 1850s by an exiled leader of the unsuccessful T'ai p'ing Revolt. By the 1870s, several small language schools were operating in San Francisco, each conducted by a master who claimed to be a recognized Chinese scholar. Tuition was four or five dollars per month, and unlike the missionary classes, students were exclusively school-aged children.[20]

In 1884 the most important of the Chinese-language schools was established by the "Six Companies." The "Companies" actually were organizations comprised of people who had immigrated from particular districts of the Canton region. In 1862 the separate groups formed a coalition officially known as the Chinese Consolidated Benevolent Association, or, unofficially, the "Six Companies." The association was dominated by San Francisco's most powerful Chinese merchants and labor contractors, and became "the supreme organ of social control for California's Chinese." It took on a number of quasi-governmental functions, including low-cost education (tuition as low as fifty cents per month for needy parents).[21] The school was totally committed to teaching traditional Chinese culture and values. It attempted to operate as if it were located in China, hiring teachers with recognized Chinese degrees and licenses and offering a curriculum identical with that of Chinese institutions. In effect, its students were being trained to pass the traditional examinations for entrance into lucrative professions and public positions in China. It was an education based on the assumption that Chinatown's youth would someday return to their "homeland."[22]

But neither these traditional Chinese institutions nor the largely adult missionary schools provided what "Americanized" Chinese parents such as the Tapes wanted: a normal American public education for their children. In 1877 1,300 Chinese residents petitioned the state legislature, calling for "the establishment of separate schools for Chinese children and for universal education." The petitioners claimed that in San Francisco alone Chinese had been taxed $147,000 for educational purposes, yet the money had been used for schools benefiting "children of Negroes and white people, many of the latter being foreigners from European countries, while our youth have been excluded from participation in the benefit." The petition estimated that 3,000 Chinese school-aged children in California were being deprived of public education, and asked the legislature to amend the school law "so that our children may be admitted into public schools, or what we would prefer, that separate schools may be established for them."[23] The petition was supported by many Protestant missionaries. Reverend Gibson already had called for a "compulsory school" for Chinese children so that they would not grow up with the "vices" of their parents.[24] Presbyterian Reverend H. H. Rice said the Chinese "must be educated or excluded and I do not believe it is possible to exclude them."[25]

"THE CHINESE MUST GO"

Many white Californians disagreed with Reverend Rice on both counts. Not only was there little support for allowing Chinese to enter public schools, but in 1877 the movement to end Chinese immigration was at its height. The state's Chinese population more than doubled between 1860 and 1880 and in the latter year it constituted nearly 10 percent of California's total population. Since a very high proportion of the immigrants were male laborers, the Chinese comprised far more than 10 percent of the state's work force, and they were becoming concentrated in San Francisco. Mining and railroad construction was declining; thus an ever-increasing percentage of the immigrants were moving into urban occupations. Whereas Mother Lode mining counties contained the bulk of the Chinese population in the 1860s, by 1880 San Francisco not only had a larger Chinese population than any other county, it contained more than 25 percent of all Chinese in the state.[26]

While San Francisco's Chinese population steadily increased during the 1870s, the city's economy was hardhit by nationwide depression. Large numbers of white workingmen were unemployed, and traditional racial prejudice was aggravated by competition for scarce jobs. The result was a more militant anti-Chinese movement than ever before existed. In 1876 "anti-Coolie clubs" and labor organizations merged into the Workingman's Party, which campaigned on the slogan "the Chinese Must Go." Republican and Democratic politicians adopted similar stands, and the new state constitution of 1879 reflected the anti-Chinese crusade. In 1882 Congress banned further Chinese immigration to the United States, the first instance of substantial immigration restriction in the nation's history.[27]

Such an atmosphere not only ruled out public schools for San Francisco Chinese, it made the private educational efforts of the missionaries more difficult than ever before. Defenders of the Chinese such as Reverend Gibson were criticized by politicians and threatened by mobs of white workingmen. During an "anti-Coolie procession" in November 1876, Gibson had the honor of being hung in effigy twice: once by the Ninth Ward Club and again by the Tailor's Protective Union.[28] The Presbyterian mission claimed that attendance at the Chinese evening school was dropping because students found "it not only was unpleasant but dangerous for them to be out in the evening."[29] The Congregationalists noted that the anti-Chinese movement was creating a counter anti-American feeling in Chinatown, and as late as 1890, the Methodists explained that "daily instances of brutal ill-treatment at the hands of white people tends to alienate their [the Chinese] minds and make them sullen and bitter towards us."[30]

TAPE V. HURLEY

Such, then, was the general state of Chinese-white relations in 1884, when San Francisco School Superintendent Moulder received Consul General Bee's letter protesting the exclusion of Mamie Tape from the city's public education system. Moulder sought advice from State Superintendent of Public Instruction William T. Welcher, and Welcher pointed out that the California constitution declared Chinese to be "dangerous to the well-being of the state." He saw no reason why San Francisco should have "to undergo the expense of educating such people."[31] Thus fortified with support from the state level, City Superintendent Moulder informed Bee that "I must decline to admit Chinese resident here to the schools."[32] On October 21, 1884, the Board of Education ratified Moulder's actions, though not before one board member commented that "if the Chinese may sometime be allowed to vote, they certainly ought to be educated." But majority board opinion apparently was summed up by another member who claimed that he "would rather go to jail than allow a Chinese child to be admitted to the schools."[33]

Subsequent court action raised precisely that possibility. On November 14, 1884, the superintendent and all members of the board were required to appear in Municipal Court before Judge Maguire "to show cause why the daughter of Joseph Tape, an Americanized Chinese, should not be allowed to enter the public schools."[34] And on January 9, 1885, Maguire issued a decision requiring Principal Hurley to enroll Mamie Tape at Spring Valley. The judge noted that the state education laws specifically provided that public schools be open to "all children," and, "to deny a child of Chinese parents entrance to the public schools would be a violation of the laws of this state." Moreover, since Mamie was an American citizen, deserving of equal protection of the laws by virtue of the Fourteenth Amendment, it was also a violation of the Federal Constitution. Finally, the judge believed it was "unjust" to levy a "forced tax on Chinese parents to help maintain our schools, and yet prohibit their children born here from education in those schools." When a former board member pointed out to the court that school policy required the dismissal of Principal Hurley if she enrolled Mamie at Spring Valley, Maguire warned that the entire Board of Education would find itself in contempt if such a policy were enforced.[35]

State Superintendent Welcher described the decision as a "terrible disaster . . . Shall we abandon the education of our children to provide that of the Chinese who are thrusting themselves upon us?" Andrew J. Moulder claimed that Judge Maguire's ruling "meets with the disapproval of nearly every citizen," and requested the board to appeal the case to the State Supreme Court.[36] The board agreed, but on March 3, 1885, the high court unanimously upheld the earlier decision. Like Maguire, the justices found no legal basis for the exclusion of Chinese children. It was true that state law provided that schools could bar "the vicious, the filthy and those having contagious and infectious diseases," but these conditions had to be determined on an individual basis and "without regard to race, color or nationality."[37]

However, neither the Supreme Court nor Judge Maguire had challenged the doctrine of "separate but equal." They had only said that Chinese children had a right to public education, and since no existing state laws prohibited Chinese from going to school with whites, Mamie Tape must be enrolled in Spring Valley School. But the legal way was still open for the legislature to provide for segregated, all-Chinese institutions, and this fact was clearly recognized by Superintendent Moulder. On January 23, apparently convinced that Maguire's decision was going to be upheld, Moulder prevailed upon San Francisco assemblyman William F. May to introduce A.B. 268, a bill allowing school districts to establish separate facilities for "Mongolians."[38] Moulder telegrammed May after hearing of the Supreme Court action on March 3, and urged that A.B. 268 be passed immediately. The superintendent was now in a race to establish a separate Chinese school before Mamie Tape had to be accepted at Spring Valley. On March 4, May informed Moulder that the bill had passed the Assembly by a vote of 63 to 1. Superintendent Moulder, along with Board President Ira Hoitt, immediately left for Sacramento for some hurried lobbying, and on March 5 the State Senate suspended its rules and unanimously passed a law similar to the May Bill.[39]

Meanwhile, the Board of Education established a committee to find a site for the new Chinese school, and on April 1, the committee recommended leasing a building at Jackson and Stone streets for $60 per month. (One part of the structure could be sublet for $25, so net monthly cost to the taxpayers was only $35). One board member called for defiance, claiming that "if we have love for our fellowmen, the Caucasian race, if we have any regard for the 50,000 children that the sovereign-voice of the people has placed in our charge for two years, we should cry 'HALT!' " However, the rest of the board approved the committee recommendation, and the staff hurriedly prepared for the new school's opening.[40] On April 7, Mamie Tape appeared at Spring Valley School with her parents and attorneys, but Miss Hurley informed the girl that she needed a certificate of vaccination and medical examination before she could enroll. By the time Mamie completed these requirements, the new Chinese school was open for business, and she was forced to attend that institution.[41]

Outside of San Francisco, the Tape case seemed to have substantial effect only in Sacramento County. In 1893 the city of Sacramento established a segregated Chinese school and in the early twentieth century, three small communities in the delta region of the Sacramento River formed separate "Asiatic schools" for both Chinese and Japanese. But elsewhere in California, small numbers of Chinese children went to mixed institutions, if they attended public schools at all. In 1929 the State Department of Education found only one all-Chinese public school in California (in San Francisco) and three combined Chinese-Japanese schools, all in Sacramento County.[42]

"Separate But Equal" in Chinatown

In 1902 San Francisco's policy of segregating Chinese children was challenged in court when attorneys for Wong Him asked the Board of Education to allow their client to attend Clement School instead of being forced to enroll in the Chinese institution. The court refused, ruling "that it is well settled that the state has the right to provide separate schools for the children of different races, and such action is not forbidden by the Fourteenth Amendment to the Constitution, provided the schools so established made no discrimination in the educational facilities which they afford."[43] The existence of San Francisco's segregated, Chinese school and the doctrine of "separate but equal" were thus legally reaffirmed.

By this time, the Chinese school had certainly disproved Superintendent Moulder's 1885 prediction that the institution would not last six months due to the disinterest of Chinese parents.[44] Instead, it grew and thrived. The 1906 earthquake and fire destroyed the building but it was quickly reconstructed. In 1915 a new enlarged schoolhouse was built, and by 1920 the school's enrollment totaled 854 students.[45]

Gradually the rigid segregation policy broke down. As early as 1905, the Board of Education was forced to let Chinese youths attend regular city high schools when Chinese parents threatened to boycott the elementary school and cause a substantial loss of state financial aid. In 1918 parents of a seven-year-old Chinese boy were told their son could enroll in a "mixed" school if they claimed he was of Japanese descent. They refused, but the following year the boy was admitted to the school, no questions asked. The child of a wealthy

Chinese merchant living in one of the city's finest residential districts also was refused admittance to one neighborhood school, but was admitted to another a few blocks away.[46]

In 1921 a Chinese-American educator called for an end to San Francisco's segregation policy, noting that it "has not been so rigidly enforced." She claimed that Chinese students would not lower the educational level of white schools, since, on the average, they scored about as well on I.Q. tests as white children.[47] Fifteen years later the "Chinese school" no longer officially existed, though "Commodore Stockton School" had more than 1,000 students, all of them of Chinese ancestry. However, another 700 Chinese children attended Jean Parker and Washington Irving schools, institutions which also enrolled at least some white students.[48] A 1947 study of anti-Chinese feeling in San Francisco concluded that the formal policy of school segregation no longer existed. Commodore Stockton was still 100 percent Chinese, "but that is because of its location."[49]

The expansion of public education in Chinatown during the twentieth century had profound effects on the missionary and language schools. Traditionally the missions emphasized assimilation into the American way of life (and religion) by teaching immigrants English (along with a good dose of Christianity). But as fewer and fewer new immigrants arrived and American-born Chinese children began regularly attending public school, the educational need seemed to be for Chinese-language instruction for Chinese-Americans. By 1935 five Protestant denominations and the Catholic Church provided after-school Chinese-language programs for children. Only the Catholics established a full-scale English-language elementary school to compete with public institutions. The Six Companies school also had to adjust to the new situation. Its Chinese-language classes had to be offered after public school hours and on Saturday. Chinese-American children often resented the long hours they were forced to spend in language classes, and no longer could anyone pretend that the Six Company school's program remotely matched that of comparable Chinese institutions. According to Calvin Lee, the result was that second- and third-generation Chinatown residents spoke Chinese with a "chop suey type of dialect with a liberal dose of English thrown in."[50]

In the years after World War II overt discrimination against Chinese declined, though it certainly did not disappear. Many middle-class Chinese-Americans moved out of Chinatown and into integrated neighborhoods on Russian and Telegraph hills or into the Richmond and Sunset districts. The makeup of school enrollments in these neighborhoods soon reflected the new Chinese social and geographic mobility. But thousands of other people of Chinese descent, many of them desperately poor, remained in Chinatown. And they were joined by a new flow of humanity from Asia resulting from the liberalized immigration laws of the 1960s. In 1971 Chinese parents bitterly protested federal court-ordered integration plans that required busing children out of Chinatown. Two years later, in the case of *Lau v. Nichols*, the United States Supreme Court ruled that San Francisco was obligated to provide special school programs for Chinese-speaking students, a decision which also had important implications for California's Spanish-speaking school population.[51] How San Francisco could meet this obligation without concentrating some Chinese children into "racially unbalanced" schools was an unanswered question, and on its face, the 1973 court decision seemed potentially in conflict with the 1971 integration order.

But none of these problems were foreseen by the *Evening Bulletin* reporter who was in attendance on the sunny morning of April 13, 1885, when Rose Thayer, "a bright teacher," opened the doors of San Francisco's new Chinese school. The first students to appear were Mamie Tape and her younger brother Frank. The reporter noted that both Tapes seemed "bright and talk English as well as most children in the public schools." Frank did not have the traditional Chinese queue and Mamie wore her hair in typical schoolgirl braids. A few minutes later, four "bright Chinese lads" appeared, wearing "their queues and distinctive style of clothing." The Tapes had never attended school before and soon became restless with the lesson, but the other children were products of missionary classes and were well prepared for the scholastic routine. During recess Frank and Mamie played on their roller skates, and one of the other boys almost fell out of a second-story window. Consul General Bee arrived to inspect the premises, and according to the *Bulletin* was "so pleased with its appearance that . . . he regretted he was not a child himself, that he might become a member of her class."[52]

However, Mary Tape, mother of Mamie and Frank, was not nearly so complimentary. On April 15, 1885, two days after the school began operations, Mrs. Tape wrote to the Board of Education, protesting the fact that her children "were compelled to attend a school set apart exclusively for Chinese."[53] The board simply acknowledged receipt of the letter and tabled the matter. As far as board members were concerned, "separate but equal" was now the rule for San Francisco's Chinese schoolchildren.

NOTES

1. San Francisco Board of Supervisors, *Report of the Special Committee on the Condition of the Chinese Quarter and the Chinese in San Francisco* (San Francisco, 1885), 59–62.

2. San Francisco *Evening Bulletin*, Jan. 15, 1885.

3. *Ibid.*, Oct. 23, 1884.

4. *General School Law of California* (San Francisco, 1880), 14.

5. Thomas Chinn (ed.), *A History of the Chinese in California, a Syllabus* (San Francisco, 1969), 19–21; William Hoy, *The Chinese Six Companies* (San Francisco, 1942), 1.

6. Chinn, *Chinese in California*, 24–25; Elmer Clarence Sandmeyer, *The Anti-Chinese Movement in California* (Urbana, 1939), 42–47.

7. Chinn, *Chinese in California*, 10.

8. Francis Yung Chang, "A Study of the Movement to Segregate Chinese . . ." (Stanford, 1936), 260–261; Lee Stephen Dolson, "The Administration of the San Francisco Public Schools, 1847 to 1947" (Ph.D. Dissertation, University of California, Berkeley, 1964), 121.

9. Chang, "Study," 267; William W. Ferrier, *Ninety Years of Education in California: 1846–1939* (Berkeley, 1937), 103.

10. San Francisco Department of Public Schools, *Twelfth Annual Report of the Superintendent of Public Schools* (San Francisco, 1864), 31–32; Dolson, "Administration," 121.

11. *Annual Report of the Superintendent of Public Schools for the Year Ending October 15, 1867* (San Francisco, 1867), 55.

12. Chang, "Study," 287–288. Lanctot was popular enough to receive a watch as a gift from his students. Gunther Barth, *Bitter Strength: A History of the Chinese in the United States, 1850–1870* (Cambridge, 1964), 172.

13. Chang, "Study," 291; Sandmeyer, *Anti-Chinese Movement*, 50.

14. *Evening Bulletin*, Feb. 15, 1871; Chang "Study," 292.

15. Barth, *Bitter Strength*, 159–171; William Speer, *An Answer to the Common Objections to Chinese Testimony and an Earnest Appeal for their Protection by our Law* (Pamphlet, San Francisco, 1857).

16. Otis Gibson, *The Chinese in America* (Cincinnati, 1877), 176–177, *Report of the Presbyterian Mission to the Chinese in California* (San Francisco, 1881), 5–16.

17. *Report of the Chinese Mission to the California Conference of the Methodist Episcopal Church* (San Francisco, 1889), 9.

18. *Eleventh Annual Report of the California Chinese Mission* (San Francisco, 1887), 11.

19. *Report of the Presbyterian Mission*, 6–7.

20. Chinn, *Chinese in California*, 68.

21. Hoy, *Six Companies*, 1–29.

22. Chinn, *Chinese in California*, 65, 68–69. For later history of the language schools see, Yi Ying Ma, "Effects of Attendance at Chinese Language Schools Upon San Francisco Children" (Ed.

D. Dissertation, University of California, Berkeley, 1945), 4–13; and Kim-Fong Tom, "Function of the Chinese Language School," *Sociology and Social Research* (July–Aug., 1941), 557–561.

23. *To the Honorable Senate and the Assembly of the State of California* (Petition, San Francisco, 1887); Mary Roberts Coolidge, *Chinese Immigration* (New York, 1909), 436.

24. Otis Gibson, *Chinaman or White Man, Which?* (San Francisco, 1873), 29.

25. *Chinese Immigration, the Social, Moral and Political Effect of Chinese Immigration, Testimony Taken Before a Committee of the Senate of the State of California* (Sacramento, 1876), 161.

26. Sandmeyer, *Anti-Chinese Movement*, 17–19; Ping Chiu, *Chinese Labor in California 1850–1880* (Madison, 1963), xi.

27. Sandmeyer, *Anti-Chinese Movement*, 64–94; Chinn, *Chinese in California*, 24–27; Alexander Saxton, *The Indispensable Enemy: Labor and the Anti-Chinese Movement in California* (Berkeley, 1971), 113–156.

28. Gibson, *Chinese in America*, 381–383.

29. *Report of the Presbyterian Mission*, 5.

30. *Report of the Chinese Mission to the California Conference of the Methodist Episcopal Church* (San Francisco, 1890), 3–4; *Abstract Report of the Chinese Mission* (San Francisco, 1892), 2.

31. *Evening Bulletin*, Oct. 22, 1884; Chang "Study," 308–309; Cloud, *Education in California*, 45.

32. *Evening Bulletin*, Oct. 22, 1884.

33. *Ibid.*

34. *Ibid.*, Nov. 13, 1884.

35. *Ibid.*, Jan. 10, 1885; Chang, "Study," 311–312.

36. *Evening Bulletin*, Jan. 15, 1885; Chang, "Study," 314–316.

37. Tape v. Hurley, 66 California Reports 473–475 (1884–1885).

38. Chang, "Study," 320–324.

39. *Evening Bulletin*, Mar. 5, Mar. 19, 1885.

40. *Ibid.*, Apr. 2, 1885.

41. *Ibid.*, Apr. 14, 1885; Chang, "Study," 325–331.

42. Winfield J. Davis, *History and Progress of the Public School Department of the City of Sacramento, 1849–1893* (Sacramento, 1895), 141; *Biennial Report of the State Department of Education for the School Year Ending June 30, 1929–June 30, 1930* (Sacramento, 1932) Part 2, 75.

43. Wong Him v. Callahan, 119 Federal Reporter, 381–383 (1903); Coolidge, *Chinese Immigration*, 436.

44. Chang, "Study," 333.

45. Mary Bo-Tze Lee, "Problems of the Segregated School for Asiatics in San Francisco," (M.A. Thesis, University of California, Berkeley, 1921) 2–7; Coolidge, *Chinese Immigration*, 78–79.

46. Lee, "Problems," 4–7.

47. *Ibid.*, 18; Also see Virginia Taylor Graham, "The Intelligence of Chinese Children in San Francisco," *Journal of Comparative Psychology* (Feb. 1926), 43–71.

48. California State Emergency Relief Administration, *Survey of Social Work Needs of the Chinese Population of San Francisco, California* (San Francisco, 1935), 35.

49. Ruth Hall Whitfield, "Public Opinion and the Chinese Question in San Francisco, 1900–1947" (M.A. Thesis, University of California, Berkeley, 1947), 86.

50. Relief Administration, *Survey*, 35–37; Calvin Lee, *Chinatown, U.S.A.* (New York, 1965), 45–46.

51. *Johnson v. San Francisco Unified School District* 339 Federal Supplement 1315 (1971); *Lau v. Nichols* 93 Supreme Court Reporter 2786 (1972–73).

52. *Evening Bulletin*, Apr. 14, 1885.

53. *Ibid.*, Apr. 16, 1885.

"Yellow Peril" in the Schools (II)

Charles Wollenberg

"THE ENTIRE PROCEEDING was carried out in strict accordance with the pre-arranged programe," reported the *San Francisco Chronicle*. "All parties to the controversy observed strict courtesy toward each other." The *Chronicle* was referring to the confrontation that took place at San Francisco's Redding School on the morning of January 17, 1907, between ten-year-old Keikichi Aoki and Principal M. A. Deane. Keikichi, accompanied by representatives of the United States Attorney's office, requested admission to the school. Deane refused and referred the matter to Board of Education President L. F. Walsh, who explained that "because of state law providing for an Oriental school, this boy cannot be admitted." Walsh then read the relevant portions of Section 1662 of the Education Law, which allowed school districts to establish separate educational institutions for "children of Mongolian or Chinese descent" and required that if such an institution were established, such children "shall not be admitted to any other school." Then Keikichi and his party climbed into their carriages and went home.[1]

What had occurred at Redding School that morning was a legal ritual to establish a test case determining whether San Francisco and the State of California had the right to force Japanese children to attend segregated schools. Ultimately, the case of *Aoki v. Deane* was dismissed, for the controversy was settled out of court by political means. But in the process, the nation experienced its most serious school segregation conflict prior to the 1950s and weathered a major diplomatic crisis, the first in a long series of such crises which eventually led to war between the United States and Japan. *Aoki v. Deane*, the case that was dismissed rather than decided, is part of the strange career of "separate but equal" in California. It also is an important chapter in the extraordinary story of the Japanese in California public education, a story which stretches from San Francisco's Redding School to tarpaper classrooms behind barbed wire at the Tule Lake and Manzanar relocation centers.

YELLOW PERIL

The presence of Japanese children in California schools did not become a major concern until the first decade of the twentieth century. While tens of thousands of Chinese poured into California after 1850, the Japanese government kept severe restrictions on out-migration. In 1880 only 148 Japanese lived in the United States, but five years later Japan loos-

From *All Deliberate Speed*. Berkeley: University of California Press (1978): 28–81. Reprinted with permission of the Regents of the University of California and the University of California Press.

ened its emigration restrictions. American entrepreneurs in Hawaii began to use Japanese labor, and companies were formed in Japan to stimulate emigration. At the same time, California employers were feeling the effects of Chinese exclusion, and Japan was seen as a new source of cheap Asian labor. By 1890 the number of Japanese in the United States had grown to about 2,000; in 1900 the figure (excluding the recently annexed Hawaii) was nearly 25,000; and by 1910 it exceeded 72,000, with 41,000 Japanese living in California alone.[2]

The Japanese immigrants naturally inherited much of the anti-Orientalism that had long been directed against Chinese. Organized labor worried about job competition and low wages, and bigots proclaimed a new "yellow menace." The courts ruled that Japanese, like Chinese, were ineligible to become naturalized citizens. But for many years anti-Japanese feeling was overshadowed by the anti-Chinese hysteria. California worried that Chinese immigration might begin again, since the Exclusion Act of 1882 had to be renewed every ten years. Not until 1902 was it made "permanent."[3]

By this time, San Francisco had had its first anti-Japanese protest meeting. In 1900 Mayor James D. Phelan, Stanford Professor Edward A. Ross and labor leader Walter MacArthur were among speakers at a rally calling for extension of immigration exclusion to Japan. In 1901 San Francisco's new Union Labor Party included anti-Japanese planks in its platform, and in 1904 the American Federation of Labor, meeting in San Francisco, also called for an end to Japanese immigration.[4] The response of leaders of the Japanese community was the formation of a Japanese Association of America to represent the interests of the new immigrants.[5]

Most Californians probably rooted for underdog Japan at the outset of the Russo-Japanese War in 1904, but by the beginning of 1905 a series of stunning victories changed the Japanese image into both an international and domestic menace. On February 23, the *San Francisco Chronicle* ran a banner, page one headline proclaiming, "JAPANESE INVASION THE PROBLEM OF THE HOUR." "Once the war with Russia is over," the *Chronicle* claimed, "the brown stream of Japanese immigration is likely to become an inundating torrent."[6] Throughout the spring of 1905 the newspaper carried on a lurid anti-Japanese campaign, and on May 7 it announced that city trade union leaders were sponsoring a mass meeting to "protest against the Jap peril." The next day Lyric Hall was jammed with what the *Chronicle* described as "men with hardened muscles and determined faces." Speakers such as Olaf Tveitmoe and P. H. McCarthy of the Building Trades Council and Andrew Furuseth of the Sailor's Union castigated the Japanese as a threat to native American workers. The meeting voted to form an Anti-Japanese League with Tveitmoe as president.[7] Ironically, Tveitmoe, McCarthy and Furuseth were all immigrants themselves—from Sweden, Ireland and Norway.

According to the *Chronicle*, Japan was "sending her worst" to California; however, the bulk of the newcomers were in fact energetic members of farming families from the Hiroshima region.[8] To a greater degree than the Chinese, Japanese laborers coming to California were planning to become permanent residents and eventually raise a family in their new homeland. Many had worked in Hawaii before travelling to the mainland and thus had some familiarity with American customs. Unlike the Chinese, Japanese immigrants were coming from a country that was rapidly modernizing along Western industrial lines. Harry Kitano has noted that Japan "had many practices which matched those in America at the end of the century." It can be argued that the Japanese were better prepared than the Chinese, indeed than most immigrant groups of that era, to adjust to the social and economic realities of early twentieth-century California.[9]

One of the practices that Japan and California shared was an extensive public education system. By the turn of the century, four years of education were mandatory in Japan and another four years were available without cost. As a result, the Japanese may well have been the best-educated immigrant group ever to come to America, with over 90 percent of them literate in their own language. Adults averaged nearly eight years of schooling, a higher figure than for the average Californian.[10] The new Japanese residents had long experience with public education and believed it could promote their economic and social well-being. These values were passed to their children.

"Yellow Peril" in the Schools

On April 2, 1905, the *Chronicle* noted the presence of such children in San Francisco schools. The paper claimed that many of the Japanese children had trachoma, "one of the most terrible and infectious diseases of the eye." It quoted a school doctor as saying that it was "a rare thing to see a Jap who did not show some traces of trachoma." In addition, the *Chronicle* believed that many of the Japanese students were young men in their twenties who were enrolled in elementary grades to learn English. The paper claimed that these "over aged and diseased" immigrants were "allowed by mistaken liberality of the law to attend the public schools and sit side by side with native American children."[11] On the latter point, at least, the *Chronicle* was correct; unlike the Chinese, Japanese children were attending integrated neighborhood schools in San Francisco.

As early as 1901, the Union Labor Party had called for segregation of Japanese students, but after the party won control of San Francisco city government, the issue was forgotten.[12] By 1905 the Board of Education and school administration were firmly under Union Labor control, since all board members had been appointed by Mayor Eugene Schmitz. Albert Roncovieri, the superintendent of schools, was a trombone player in the mayor's orchestra, and Aaron Altmann, board president in 1906, was the brother-in-law of Abe Reuf, the Union Labor political boss. In the spring of 1905, probably because of the *Chronicle*'s articles and the general increase in anti-Japanese feeling, the board felt it necessary to reaffirm its commitment to Japanese segregation. On May 5 it passed a resolution favoring separate schools for Japanese students, "not only for the purpose of relieving the congestion at present prevailing in our schools, but also for the higher end that our children should not be placed in any position where their youthful impression may be affected by association with pupils of the Mongolian race."[13]

However, the board's action was only a resolution in principle; board members explained they did not have the money to establish separate schools in practice. Thus for another year, until the earthquake and fire of April 18, 1906, Japanese continued to attend integrated schools throughout the city. But anti-Japanese feeling hardened during the aftermath of the earthquake, as Japanese families were forced into predominantly white neighborhoods because their former homes had been destroyed. During the spring and summer of 1906, Japanese in San Francisco were often harassed and assaulted. Japanese-owned restaurants and businesses were subjected to boycotts and vandalism, and although Japan sent more relief funds to the city than all other foreign nations combined, Japanese scientists inspecting the earthquake damage were stoned by white youths.[14]

Segregation Order

In August the Anti-Japanese League requested the Board of Education to put its school segregation policy into effect, but again the board pleaded a lack of funds.[15] However, when school opened in September, Superintendent Roncovieri discovered that so many Chinese earthquake refugees had left the city that enrollment in the temporary "Chinese School" was below expectations. The superintendent informed the board that the Chinese School had enough room to accommodate the city's ninety-three Japanese students and the much smaller number of Korean school children. On Thursday, October 11, the board resolved that "principals are hereby directed to send all Chinese, Japanese, and Korean children to the Oriental Public School situated on the south side of Clay Street, between Powell and Mason Streets, on and after Monday, October 15, 1906."[16]

Almost all Japanese parents refused to obey the board resolution, choosing to keep their children at home rather than accept segregation. While most Korean children did appear at the Oriental School on October 15, only two Japanese did so, and one of those withdrew after talking to the Japanese Consul in San Francisco.[17] On October 18 the Secretary of the Japanese Association, Goroku Ikeda, appeared at a Board of Education meeting and asked the board to rescind its decision. If it did not, Ikeda threatened, San Francisco's Japanese would take legal action. Also appearing were two Methodist missionaries, Miss Margaret Lake and Dr. Herbert Johnson. Dr. Johnson handed the board members a resolution criticizing their decision passed by the Interdenominational Mission Congress then meeting in Oakland, and he claimed the segregation order was "unjust, unwise, un-American, untimely, un-Christianlike and unfair."[18] Five days later Japanese Consul K. Uyeno wrote a formal letter of protest. While he disassociated his government from the threat of legal action, he expressed "the deep-seated conviction that this action of your honorable board constitutes a species of discrimination which is offensive to the Japanese national spirit."[19]

By the time Uyeno's letter had been written, leaders of San Francisco's Japanese community had adopted a strategy which was to have profound effects on the future relations between the United States and Japan. They determined to use public opinion in Japan to combat discrimination in California. Secretary Ikeda of the Japanese Association and lawyer Misuji Miyakawa apparently wired several leading Tokyo newspapers about the problems in San Francisco and urged other Japanese parents in the city to do likewise.[20] On October 20 the *Mainichi Shimpo*, a Tokyo daily owned by a member of the Japanese legislature, called on its readers to "Stand up. Our countrymen have been HUMILIATED on the other side of the Pacific. Our boys and girls have been expelled from the public schools by the rascals of the United States, cruel and merciless like demons."[21] Other newspapers followed suit and on the twenty-second the American ambassador in Tokyo informed Washington that a potential crisis was at hand.

INTERNATIONAL CRISIS

On October 25, Japanese Ambassador to the United States, Viscount Aoki, visited Secretary of State Elihu Root for a "prolonged discussion." After the meeting, Aoki met with newsmen and left no doubt that the situation was serious. Although he denied that he had filed a formal protest, the ambassador strongly asserted that the Treaty of 1894 governing commercial relations between Japan and the United States accorded Japanese children the right to go to the same schools as anyone else. Aoki claimed that "the fact that Japanese children, because of their nationality, are segregated in special schools and not permitted to attend the ordinary public schools constitutes an act of discrimination carrying with it a stigma and odium which it is impossible to overlook." "After all the years of friendship between the two nations," Aoki lamented, "it seems too bad that the poor innocent Japanese school children should be subjected to such indignities."[22]

The attitude of the Japanese government was duly noted by Japanese-language newspapers in San Francisco. The *Japanese American* was sure that "every resident Japanese backed by the sympathetic outburst at home, will participate in the struggle with that vigor and tenacity that won us the heights of Hansha and the impregnable redoubts of 208-meter

Hill" (during the Russian War). The *Soko Shimpo* bitterly criticized "the most unjustifiable treatment at the hands of the unscrupulous elements in California."[23] On the evening of October 25, San Francisco's Japanese community held a protest meeting at Jefferson Square Hall. More than 1,200 people crowded the auditorium "to suffocation" and heard speeches by leaders of the Japanese Association, Japanese businessmen and Protestant clergymen. Misuji Miyakawa, the only Japanese lawyer eligible to appear before federal courts in the United States, announced that he and a well-known San Francisco attorney, Charles Fickert, had brought suit against the board action earlier that afternoon and asked for moral and financial support. Both were granted, and the meeting voted to "emphatically oppose" the segregation order and delegate the Japanese Association as spokesman for the community.[24]

The international crisis and the active resistance of local Japanese finally convinced the San Francisco press that the school segregation issue was important news. The *Bulletin* had not even bothered to cover the Board of Education's October 11 resolution, and the *Examiner* and the *Call* had mentioned the item in small stories on page 11. The *Chronicle* gave the matter somewhat more space, but on page 16.[25] However, after October 25, the controversy often received front-page treatment and occasionally even banner headlines. On the twenty-seventh, the *Chronicle* wrote its first editorial on the subject, claiming the "only way to maintain permanent friendship between Japan and America is to keep the two races apart." Ten days later the paper assured its readers that "whatever the status of the Japanese children while young and uncontaminated, as they grow older they acquire the distinctive character, habits and moral standards of their race, which are abhorrent to our people." The *Call* was more direct: "we are not willing that our children should meet Asiatics in intimate association . . . That is 'race prejudice' and we stand by it."[26]

One of the arguments most often used by defenders of the segregation policy was that most of the Japanese students were "over aged." Superintendent Roncovieri claimed that "ninety-five percent of the so-called children are young men . . . we object to an adult Japanese sitting beside a twelve-year-old school girl, and if this be prejudice, we are the most prejudiced people in the world."[27] In fact, only sixty-five of the ninety-three Japanese students were boys, and of this total, only two were twenty years or over. There also were charges of gross immorality and disruptive conduct by Japanese students, but even Superintendent Roncovieri admitted that "no complaint of bad conduct on the part of a Japanese scholar has ever come to my knowledge." Board President Altmann claimed "nothing can be said against the general character and deportment of the Japanese scholars."[28]

The segregation policy was criticized by Presidents Benjamin Ide Wheeler of the University of California and David Starr Jordan of Stanford. Los Angeles School Superintendent E. C. Moore said he "bitterly regretted" the decision. Superintendent Roncovieri's attempt to obtain support for San Francisco's stand at a meeting of school administrators in San Diego was voted down decisively. Even a San Francisco teacher defended the Japanese students as "examples of industry, patience, unobtrusiveness, obedience and honesty," and a member of the Board of Education admitted the Japanese students "have been able so successfully to compete with our white children as to win from the latter class medals that were intended for the children of our taxpayers."[29]

FEDERAL INTERVENTION

On October 31 the first serious attempt to resolve the conflict began when President Theodore Roosevelt's personal emissary, Secretary of Commerce and Labor Victor Metcalf, arrived in the Bay Area. Metcalf was a native of Oakland and on good terms with prominent San Franciscans. Although he was supposed to be only gathering information for the President, Metcalf tried to persuade the board to rescind its decision. Before he left for San

Francisco, the secretary visited the White House and Roosevelt was reported to have pointed to a lawn where his sons were playing football with the dark-complexioned children of the Turkish ambassador. "Is there anything wrong with that?" the President was supposed to have asked Metcalf.[30] But however much Roosevelt might have opposed segregation in principle, his actions in the San Francisco case were primarily motivated by expediency. He had not spoken out against separate schools for blacks in the South, nor during the entire San Francisco incident did he defend the right of the Chinese to attend integrated schools, although the treaty rights of Chinese citizens to education in the United States were at least as strong as those of the Japanese. Clearly the difference was that Japan was a strong power which had demonstrated its military might, and Roosevelt was determined not to let the action of the San Francisco School Board endanger friendly relations with such a power.[31]

Metcalf's mission did have a calming effect on Japanese opinion, but it failed to change educational policy in San Francisco. He asked Olaf Tveitmoe to reverse the stand of the Anti-Japanese League on grounds of national interest, but Tveitmoe later claimed "I could not betray the State of California and its citizens, even at the request of the President of the United States."[32] Metcalf argued that the Treaty of 1894 obligated San Francisco to treat Japanese children in the same manner as it treated children of European immigrants, but Board President Altmann contended "If there is a violation of treaty rights between two governments, the fault is not ours; it is with the legislature which passed the law."[33]

The next move was President Roosevelt's, and he made it in spectacular fashion on December 4, 1906. That was the day of his annual address to Congress, and Roosevelt devoted a portion of the speech to the San Francisco controversy. He condemned the ill-treatment of Japanese citizens and promised to uphold Japanese treaty rights with "all the forces, military and civil, of the United States which I may lawfully employ . . ." The President also recommended that Congress pass legislation allowing Japanese to become naturalized citizens. But he saved his strongest language for a condemnation of San Francisco's school policy: "to shut them [the Japanese] out of the public schools is a wicked absurdity."[34] Roosevelt announced that he had ordered the Attorney General to take court action against the Board of Education, and the next day United States Attorney Robert Devlin met with Board President Altmann to begin preparation of what was to become the case of *Aoki v. Deane*.[35]

The speech was joyfully received by representatives of the Japanese government. Ambassador Aoki gave it his full approval and Consul Uyeno claimed that "sentiment is practically universal among the ten thousand Japanese in San Francisco that the recommendations made by the President constitute the most rational solution of the American-Japanese problems yet attempted." As to rumors of war between the two countries, Uyeno felt that after Roosevelt's speech, there was "not the slightest chance" of such a conflict.[36]

But the President won few friends among white Californians. Of the major California newspapers, only the Los Angeles *Times* had anything favorable to say about Roosevelt's remarks on the school issue. The *Chronicle* called it an "astonishing outburst" while the kindest thing the *Call* could say was that the speech was based on a "misapprehension."[37] For many Californians the issue was no longer segregation of the Japanese, but states' rights. The President was threatening to use federal power to interfere with state and local control of the schools. Governor George Pardee, like Roosevelt a Republican, made it clear that the operation of the schools was the "prerogative and privilege" of the state, and he also emphasized that he favored "separate schools for the Japanese as well as any other alien and unmixing people."[38] The California congressional delegation "deeply resented" the President's message, and one member claimed he had "begged" Roosevelt not to make the speech. Republican Congressman Joseph Knowland of Oakland commented that "it is a good thing that this message did not become public before the election, for if it had we [Republican] candidates might have suffered."[39]

Two weeks later California received another blow from Washington when Roosevelt released Secretary Metcalf's report *The Japanese in San Francisco*. Metcalf pointed out that Japanese children were hardly overrunning San Francisco schools; out of a total of more than 28,000 students in the city, there were only ninety-three Japanese, attending twenty-three of the city's seventy-two schools. He claimed that all teachers he talked with believed that the Japanese were "among the very best of their pupils, clean in their persons, well behaved and remarkably bright." The Secretary agreed that "overaged" students should be separated from younger children, but advised that this be done for all nationalities, not just Japanese. In sum, Metcalf could find no justification for the segregation of San Francisco's Japanese schoolchildren.[40] For his trouble, the California Federation of Labor branded Metcalf a "betrayer" and declared his report "unworthy of credence."[41]

AOKI V. DEANE

Meanwhile, U. S. Attorney Devlin was methodically preparing the government's test case against the San Francisco Board of Education. The earlier court action brought by the Japanese community was set aside so that a single, definitive decision would be achieved. On January 17, after the prearranged confrontation between Keikichi Aoki and Principal Deane at Redding School, Devlin filed his brief in both Federal District Court and the State Supreme Court. He did not attack "separate but equal" per se but pointed out that Section 1662 of the school law did not specifically mention Japanese, only "Chinese and Mongolians." Devlin asserted that Japanese were not "Mongolians" but a "separate race"; thus the law did not provide for the segregation of Japanese. He further argued that the Oriental School was located so far from many Japanese homes that requiring the children to attend the Clay Street facility was, in fact, depriving them of their right to education. Finally, Devlin made a creative attempt to justify federal intervention in local educational affairs. At the time of statehood, California's initial establishment of a public education system was financed by a fund created by the sale of federal lands granted to the state; thus, Devlin claimed that the federal government had a legitimate interest in the operation of California's school system.[42]

But Devlin's key argument rested on the treaty-making powers of the federal government. The Treaty of 1894 between Japan and the United States provided that "the citizens or subjects of each Contracting Party shall enjoy in the territories of the other the same privileges, liberties and rights, and shall be subject to no higher imposts or charges in those respects than native citizens or subjects of the most favored nation." San Francisco did not segregate children of European immigrants, and so Japanese were being treated in a discriminatory fashion in comparison with citizens of other "favored nations." Since the Constitution provides that treaties have the force of federal law, and since state and local governments cannot act in violation of federal law, Devlin argued that San Francisco could not segregate Japanese children and deprive them of their treaty rights as citizens of "the most favored nation."[43]

Devlin's arguments were answered point by point by City Attorney William Burke. Burke was hardly a dispassionate advocate. He told the citizens of San Francisco that he was "inalterably opposed to ANY concession" and would work to keep the city's children "uncorrupted by contaminating influences that would be but the natural result of Oriental invasion." In court Burke argued that California law and popular usage clearly included Japanese in the broad term "Mongolian"; thus the segregation statute applied in this case.

He denied that the fourteen blocks between the Aoki home and the Oriental School constituted a prohibitory distance for Keikichi to walk. While admitting that the state education system originally had benefited from federal land grants, Burke claimed that the total value of those grants was minuscule compared to the amount of state and local resources spent on the schools since the 1850s.[44]

On the key issue of treaty rights, Burke pointed out that the Treaty of 1894 never specifically mentioned the right to education. But even if the treaty could be inferred to grant Japanese such a right, to say that this prohibited segregation would be "repugnant to the fundamental principles of government." The City Attorney cited a long list of cases, including *Ward v. Flood* and *Plessy v. Ferguson*, in which the courts had ruled that state-enforced segregation did not violate the Constitution, and he pointed out that the establishment and operation of public schools was clearly one of the powers reserved under the Constitution for the states. Thus, to say that the Treaty of 1894 prevented California from segregating Japanese was to claim that a treaty could override the constitutional powers of a state. Clearly, Burke argued, this was not true; the federal government cannot "cede away the constitutional right of a state by treaty."[45]

The case attracted national attention and even became a bone of contention between rivals in the Ivy League. The *Yale Law Journal* claimed the "Japanese have a grievance" based on their status as a "most favored nation."[46] This position seemed in accord with Consul Uyeno's statement that if the Board of Education segregated "pupils of all foreign nationalities . . . there would be no objection."[47] On the other hand, the *Harvard Law Review* argued that since the courts had allowed states to segregate the schoolchildren of non-white American citizens, to deny California the right to segregate Japanese aliens would be granting Japanese "a greater right or privilege than citizens of this country possess."[48] This point was also recognized by California Congressman Everis A. Hayes. In a speech before the House, Hayes observed that if California could not segregate children of Japanese citizens, southern states could not segregate black Jamaicans who were British citizens.[49]

The legal arguments were endlessly debated in the press and in Congress, but by January it was clear that Theodore Roosevelt hoped for a diplomatic rather than judicial solution to the San Francisco controversy. Apparently some members of his administration, including Secretary of State Root, had doubts about the strength of the government's legal case. Also the slow court proceedings would drag out a worrisome diplomatic crisis. What Roosevelt had in mind was winning Japanese acceptance to a treaty ending immigration of laborers to the United States in return for San Francisco rescinding its segregation order.[50] By February 1, even the *Chronicle* seemed willing to accept such a compromise. The real issue, the paper claimed, was immigration, and the "presence of ninety or one hundred small Japanese children scattered throughout the public schools does no harm to anyone."[51] However, the Japanese government refused to sign such a treaty unless the United States granted Japanese aliens the right to become naturalized citizens. Roosevelt knew this condition could never get through Congress: thus, he resorted to winning Japanese acceptance to executive orders and informal agreements limiting immigration, rather than a formal treaty.

THE BIG STICK

By the end of January the President apparently felt agreement with the Japanese government was possible, and he invited Superintendent Roncovieri and Board of Education President Lawrence Walsh to Washington for negotiations. Roncovieri and Walsh refused to go unless the President invited the entire board and Mayor Schmitz. Roosevelt reluctantly agreed, and on February 3 a large San Francisco delegation left for the nation's capital.[52] Also on the train was Misuji Miyakawa, the lawyer who brought the original legal challenge against the board. He was going to Washington as a correspondent for a San Francisco Japanese newspaper, but the *Call* believed that the "shrewd, young attorney" would play an "active and important" role. Miyakawa had lobbied on behalf of Japanese immigrants with congressmen in the past, and he had important contacts in Japan. He was in a position to disrupt an agreement by reinstituting his original suit. He claimed San Francisco's Japanese "are not in favor of a compromise" on the segregation issue, and he did not quite dismiss the continuing rumors of war: "only the ignorant among our people regard it as a possibility—at this time."[53]

Key man in the San Francisco delegation was Mayor Schmitz. Most of the other members of the group were his appointees and political associates. Schmitz already was under indictment for graft, and he may have hoped to recoup his political fortunes by resolving a diplomatic crisis. However, he found the political sledding precarious. His enemies were convinced he had gone to Washington purely as a political ploy, while his friends on the Anti-Japanese League were afraid he was selling them out. On February 10, Olaf Tveitmoe wired the mayor "Morning papers announce in big headline that 'Schmitz deserts labor for Japs . . .' Sovereign rights must not be bartered away . . . California is whiteman's country, not a Caucasian graveyard."[54] Nevertheless, on February 15 the San Francisco delegation agreed to rescind the segregation policy in return for Roosevelt's commitment to negotiate a "gentleman's agreement" with Japan ending immigration of laborers to the United States mainland. In addition, Roosevelt promised to issue an executive order prohibiting Japanese laborers from entering the mainland from Hawaii, Mexico or Canada and agreed to dismissal of the *Aoki v. Deane* case.[55]

By March 13 both sides of the bargain had been kept, and Mayor Schmitz was celebrating what he called a "great victory."[56] But the San Francisco press was not so euphoric. The *Call* greeted news of the agreement with the headline "SCHMITZ RAISES THE FLAG OF SURRENDER," while the *Examiner* proclaimed "SCHMITZ ADMITS SURRENDER ON JAPANESE QUESTION." The *Chronicle* said the mayor had surrendered on the "great fundamental principle whose establishment is of far more consequence than the presence or absence of a few Japanese children in our schools . . . the right of the Federal Government to interfere in the management of our schools . . ."[57]

To a limited degree, the *Chronicle* was correct. In 1907 and again in 1909 and 1911, Presidents Roosevelt and Taft "interfered" with political processes in California to prevent the legislature from passing anti-Japanese bills which would upset the diplomatic balance. Included was legislation amending Section 1662 to name specifically the Japanese as a group which could be subjected to school segregation, thus ending the argument about what, exactly, was a "Mongolian." In 1909 such a bill actually passed the Assembly, but Governor Gillett and Speaker Stanton used their influence to persuade the legislators to reconsider and eventually defeat the measure.[58] However, in 1913 Governor Hiram Johnson did nothing to stop passage of an Alien Land Law, a notably unsuccessful attempt to prevent Japanese from purchasing agricultural land in California.[59]

AGAIN THE YELLOW PERIL

By this time it was clear that the Gentleman's Agreement of 1907 had not "solved" the problem of Japanese immigration. While the flow of unskilled laborers was stopped, the agreement had not applied to wives and family members of Japanese already living in the United States. After 1907 an increasing number of Japanese women, many married by proxy to California Japanese, immigrated to the United States. This, through the natural course of events, created a boom in the population of second-generation Japanese Americans

(*Nisei*), who by virtue of birth were American citizens. The total *Issei* (first generation) and Nisei population in California increased from 41,000 to over 71,000 between 1910 and 1920, and the number of Nisei alone grew from 4,500 to nearly 30,000. By 1930 half the people of Japanese ancestry in California were Nisei and nearly 40,000 of them were under seventeen years of age.[60]

These statistics, along with the diplomatic conflicts between the United States and Japan which followed World War I, had by 1919 created a new phase of the anti-Japanese movement in California. A new Japanese Exclusion League was formed, this time not only with organized labor backing, but also strongly supported by the American Legion and the Native Sons and Daughters of the Golden West. Chief spokesman of the new crusade was Valentine S. McClatchy, member of the family which published the Sacramento and Fresno *Bees*, the most influential newspapers in the Central Valley. In 1920 California voters approved by a three-to-one margin an initiative measure which futilely tried to close the "loopholes" in the Alien Land Law, and in 1924 Congress banned all further immigration from Japan.[61]

The leaders of the new campaign became increasingly concerned about the growing number of young Japanese Americans in California schools. In 1920 Governor William Stevens noted that "the fecundity of the Japanese race far exceeds that of any other people we have in our midst." As a result, "in many of the country schools . . . the spectacle is presented of having a few white children acquiring their education in classrooms crowded by Japanese. The deepseated and often outspoken resentment of white mothers to this situation can only be appreciated by those people who have struggled with similar problems."[62]

JAPANESE-LANGUAGE SCHOOLS

V. S. McClatchy was particularly worried that the loyalty of the Nisei to the United States was being undermined by private Japanese-language schools. Such schools had been established during the first decade of the twentieth century, and by 1918 there were already 80 of them scattered around the state. Fifteen years later the total had grown to 220, and more than 65 percent of all Nisei youth were attending the schools for an average of about three years. Like the Chinese-language schools, classes were held in the late afternoons and on Saturdays, and tuitions were low. Policy usually was established by elected boards from the local Japanese community, and the schools often were informally linked with chapters of the Japanese Association.[63]

But unlike the early Chinese schools, the Japanese institutions were not training children to return to Asia. As early as 1913, the Japanese Education Association, an organization of language-school teachers, emphasized that the role of the schools was to help the Nisei fit into the American way of life. It was necessary for the young Japanese Americans to be able to communicate with their Issei parents so that family cohesiveness and discipline would not disappear. But the schools were "not intended to perpetuate the traditions and moral concepts of Japan."[64] Most also taught English to very small children in order to prepare them for public school, and some language schools purposely hired whites to teach these English classes. According to one Nisei educator, the "ultimate aim" of the schools was to make "good American citizens out of the children of Japanese parentage." Parents and teachers should "feel proud of educating and turning out good American citizens of their race."[65]

There is much evidence that language schools in fact taught very few Nisei to speak acceptable Japanese, let alone to absorb Japanese culture or nationalism. Distinguished Japanese educator Yamato Ichihashi of Stanford believed the Nisei "idealize America." They preferred to speak and read English and found American schools more rewarding than the language school. The latter did serve a social function of bringing Nisei youth together, and to some degree, separating them socially from their white contemporaries. But even the social programs of the schools were often assimilationist in character, for example, athletic teams in various American sports. One former student claimed he went to the school not for the language classes, which he hated, but to play on the basketball team.[66]

While a few Issei parents sent their children back to Japan for part of their education, most apparently were satisfied with the assimilationist philosophy of the language schools. In fact, Japanese adults themselves took great advantage of educational programs to aid their adjustment to California life. They attended English-language classes provided by public schools, Protestant missionary groups, the language schools or the Japanese Association.[67] In Los Angeles, private sewing schools for Issei women became popular during the 1920s, and the Nanka Ladies Tailoring School, run by the wife of a Japanese Protestant clergyman, in 1923 had more than seventy students. According to U.S.C. graduate student Gretchen Tuthill, the women were "able to produce any dress they may see in a picture without using a commercial pattern." "The only drawback," Tuthill claimed, was "the attitude of the husbands . . . Apparently, the men are afraid the women will get too independent as a result of their additional knowledge."[68]

But in spite of the predominantly assimilationist teachings of Japanese educational efforts in California, V. S. McClatchy still worried about the language schools. "The real purpose of the schools," he said, "is to teach Japanese ideals and loyalty and to make dependable Japanese citizens of the young Japanese children for whom are claimed, by birth, all rights of American citizenship."[69] The 1921 legislature established qualifications for language-school teachers and set standards to assure that textbooks did not reflect un-American values. In 1923 a bill abolishing the schools passed the legislature but was vetoed by Governor Richardson. Four years later, the United States Supreme Court ruled that a Hawaii statute controlling language schools was unconstitutional, and the ruling also had the effect of killing the 1921 California law. But since 1918, the Japanese Educational Association had been rewriting texts to "Americanize" them, and after 1927 many language schools continued to use the former state standards as criteria for teacher selection.[70]

JAPANESE IN THE PUBLIC SCHOOLS

The 1921 legislature also finally succeeded in amending Section 1662 specifically to name Japanese as a group eligible for segregation. However, only four small Sacramento County school districts—Courtland, Isleton, Walnut Grove and Florin—took advantage of the law to establish separate "oriental schools," (some of them for both Japanese and Chinese). In all four districts Japanese were a majority of the school population.[71] When asked why his town separated the schools, one Florin resident answered, "That's easy. Race prejudice. It got so my daughters went mostly with Japanese girls. The principal was letting Japs crowd our boys off the grammar school team just because they could play better baseball. The town around us began to razz our kids because of that . . . Well we couldn't stand for it any longer, so we separated our schools."[72]

But in 1929 there was a total of only 575 Japanese students in the segregated schools of Courtland, Isleton, Walnut Grove and Florin. Elsewhere throughout the state about 30,000 Nisei children attended integrated schools, and by 1930 they had achieved a remarkable scholastic record. The average California Japanese-American over twenty had completed twelve years of schooling, a higher figure than that for the general population.[73] In some towns Nisei students received so many awards at graduation exercises that white parents objected. Reginald Bell of Stanford University concluded that Nisei secondary-school students received substantially more "As" and "Bs" and fewer "Cs" and "Ds" and "Fs" than other students.[74] Marvin Darsie, also of Stanford, found that ten-to-thirteen year-old Nisei scored an average of 91 on the Stanford-Binet test as compared with 99 for white children. Darsie believed the eight-point differential was due entirely to the Nisei's difficulty with the English language. The test showed the Japanese-Americans inferior only in those mental processes "based on meanings or concepts represented by the verbal symbols of the English language." In other portions of the test, the Japanese-Americans were "at least equal and possibly superior."[75]

The findings of the social scientists coincided with the impressions of California teachers. Harry Kitano has observed that by 1930 teachers had come to accept the stereotype of the "ideal Japanese child and his wonderful cooperative parents."[76] A Los Angeles teacher claimed "we always like to have one or two Japanese children in our classes as an example to the other children . . ." To reinforce the favorable picture, the Nisei juvenile delinquency rate in Los Angeles County was less than one-third that of white children.[77] By 1929 even V. S. McClatchy had to admit that the young Japanese-Americans were "fine specimens physically and mentally, a credit to their race and to this country."[78]

But McClatchy also observed that the Nisei were subject to continuing discrimination. He believed this simply proved the wisdom of his earlier efforts to win Japanese exclusion, but his description of the Nisei as "American citizens in rights but a group set apart" was an accurate portrayal of the status of most Japanese-Americans in California public schools.[79] One Nisei youth, educated before World War II, remembered that in his hometown school "we did not mix with the Caucasians very much. We did not speak to the Caucasian girls at all." Another young man recalled that at the small multiracial elementary school he attended "there was no talk of race as everyone was the same." But as he went on to high school, the students separated themselves socially and the members of the Japanese Student Club "did everything by themselves." They organized a football and basketball team, the "Delta Lancers," and played in Nisei athletic leagues. In 1940 this particular youth was chosen "Typical Nisei Boy" at a statewide convention of Japanese students. Still another young man remembered that there was "little race consciousness" on the bus which took white and Nisei teenagers who had grown up together to the local high school, "but most of us went our own ways once we got on the school grounds."[80]

There were, of course, exceptions to the rule of social separation. One Nisei youth became a star on the high-school basketball team and "expanded out of the Nisei group."[81] In Fresno the predominantly white soccer team unanimously elected a Japanese-American as team captain, and in Santa Monica in 1942, after Japanese were informed they would soon have to report to "relocation centers," white high-school student body officers resigned en masse and turned their offices over to a slate of Nisei students.[82]

CLASSROOMS BEHIND BARBED WIRE

The relocation centers were, of course, the results of President Roosevelt's executive order of February 1942 requiring all people of Japanese ancestry who lived on the Pacific coast of the United States to move to camps established in the interior of the country. Over 70,000 of the more than 100,000 evacuees were California residents, and the majority were American-born Nisei. Thus, the War Relocation Agency (WRA) bureaucracy that operated the camps found itself responsible for the education of more than 25,000 American schoolchildren. Almost overnight the WRA had to create a school system equivalent to that of a small city, and by the very nature of relocation, it was a racially segregated system. It was in the camps that the great mass of Nisei children experienced school segregation for the first time.

By September 1942 schools were operating in eight of the ten original camps, but the operations were hardly without problems. In Manzanar, a camp located in California's Owens Valley, east of the Sierra Nevada, a WRA report described classes held in "unpartitioned recreational barracks without any lining on the walls or heat of any kind. Within two days a cold wave combined with dust storms at the center had forced the schools out of operation until the barracks could be lined and stoves could be installed." Initially, there were severe shortages of textbooks, instructional equipment and even furniture. "In the first weeks many of the children had no desks or chairs and for the most part were obliged to sit on the floor . . ."[83] The WRA hoped that schools in the two California camps, Manzanar and Tule Lake in Modoc County in the northeastern part of the state, would be integrated into the normal California school system and thus be eligible for state textbooks and financial aid. But this arrangement was ruled illegal by State Attorney General Earl Warren, and the Manzanar and Tule Lake schools, like those in other states, remained under federal control. Fortunately, the Los Angeles Board of Education donated thousands of used books, which helped to relieve shortages of texts. Even so, the schools never had sufficient instuctional materials and equipment, particularly for shop and laboratory classes.[84]

Another item in short supply was qualified teachers. The WRA was determined to hire only people who were eligible to obtain credentials in states in which the camps were located. By 1943 the agency had managed to hire 557 white teachers and about 25 evacuees. But the WRA was never able to find enough qualified faculty, and hundreds of evacuee "teaching assistants" were hired to help in the classrooms.[85] Despite all the problems, schools were in full operation at all camps by the spring of 1943. By this time the agency also was operating a successful program allowing Nisei formerly enrolled at West Coast colleges to finish their education at institutions in other parts of the country.

The schools were planned according to the best precepts of "progressive education" as understood by WRA bureaucrats.[86] Lester Ade, agency director of education, defined the main purpose of the schools as preparing students "for reabsorption into normal community life and for return to outside schools." Thus the WRA took pains to assure that all schools were accredited by the states in which the centers were located and that full college prep curricula were established at all camp high schools. Ade also claimed the schools were to become community centers, a "background for community participation of various types . . . an institution with which people were familiar, and which served as a connecting link with the cherished past . . ." In conformance with these ideals, the WRA encouraged formation of local PTA chapters and established parental advisory boards. But actual control of the schools remained in the hands of camp authorities.[87]

The WRA educational program was supposed to promote "an understanding of American ideals, institutions and practices"; thus, the schools had a full range of student activities. Student government ("to permit participation in the democratic process"), athletic teams, drama, art and music programs, debating teams all existed as they might in any large American school system.[88] Jeanne Wakatsuki Houston describes *Our World*, in 1943–44 Manzanar High Yearbook: "In its pages you can see school kids with armloads of books, wearing cardigan sweaters and walking past rows of tar paper shacks. You see chubby girl yell-leaders, pom-poms flying as they leap with glee. You read about the school play called *Growing Pains* . . . the story of a typical American home . . . with Soji Katamayer as George McIntyre, Takuda Ando as Terry McIntyre and Mrs. McIntyre played by Kigako Nagai . . ."[89]

The inconsistency between these "typical" American schools with their "progressive" ideals and the reality of camp life surrounded by barbed wire and armed guards was not lost on Nisei students. When school opened at the camp in Rohner, Arkansas, in September 1942, a student chalked the words "Jap Prison" on the tar paper wall.[90] Young people, particularly *Kibei*, American-born children who had been educated in Japan, were active in the protest movement against the WRA administration and Japanese-American Citizens League leaders who cooperated with WRA authorities. The protests became intense in 1943 after the government distributed questionnaires to evacuees which, in effect, asked them to declare allegiance to the United States. Most camp residents were willing to make such a declaration, but several thousand who refused to do so were transferred with their families to Tule Lake, which became a "segregation center" for "renunciants" and other "trouble-makers."[91]

The new status of Tule Lake had a profound effect on its school system. The educational program was disrupted by massive movements of people in and out of the camp. Some of the most militant "renunciants" pulled their children out of WRA institutions and began independent Japanese-language schools. A board was elected to run the language schools, and a major campaign was instituted to persuade Tule Lake parents to send their children to the new institutions. Unlike earlier language schools in California, the Tule Lake schools were training children to return to Japan after the war, and one was even called "The Greater East Asia Co-Prosperity School." By the beginning of 1945 language school enrollment at Tule Lake was about 4,300 as opposed to 2,300 children in the WRA schools (obviously, there were many dual enrollments). However, by the summer of 1945 a reaction against the hardline leaders apparently set in among Tule Lake parents, and language-school enrollment began to drop. The Japanese school board became more cooperative with camp authorities, and the Greater East Asia school was renamed the Tule Lake Language School. Nevertheless, after the war, more than 2,000 Tule Lake residents chose to be repatriated to Japan.[92]

CUTTING THE BARBED WIRE

In 1944 the WRA began encouraging evacuees to leave the camps and resettle in areas outside of the West Coast zone. WRA schools provided students with information on the resettlement program to take home to their parents and adult and vocational courses were started to prepare people for an end to camp life. By early 1945, about 3,000 children of resettled parents had left camp schools, and the total WRA school enrollment by the end of the spring semester of 1945 was about 5,000 less than it had been in the fall of 1944.[93] The success of the resettlement program and the impending end of the war convinced WRA officials not to plan to reopen the schools in September 1945 (except at Tule Lake). Some parents protested, claiming that it would take them many months to resettle or return home and that their children would be deprived of an education in the meantime.[94] But student opinion may have been better expressed by a photograph in *Valedictorian 1945*, Manzanar High's last yearbook. It showed a forearm and hand, squeezing a pair of pliers whose cutting edges were wrapped around a piece of barbed wire.[95]

The camp schools, with their rhetoric about community participation and democratic ideals, can be viewed as flagrant examples of institutional hypocrisy. The facilities, equipment, materials and probably a good portion of faculties were second-rate at best. But one alumnus, Dr. Harry Kitano of UCLA, believes that in some respects this first experience with segregated schooling was stimulating for Nisei students. Young Japanese-Americans for the first time had a chance to be the "big man" or "most popular girl" on campus, and this allowed them to develop a new sense of self-confidence and assertiveness.[96] Also, at least some learning went on at the camp schools. Jeanne Wakatsuki Houston remembers a Manzanar teacher "who was probably the best teacher I've ever had—strict, fair-minded, dedicated to her job. Because of her, I was, academically at least, more than prepared to keep up with my peers."[97]

The return of the Nisei to California public schools after World War II was often a difficult social, if not educational, process. But throughout the state, it was a process that occurred in an integrated setting. By 1962 Dr. Kitano found that the assimilation of Japanese-American students was proceeding rapidly, with the ironic effect that academic achievement and grade-point average were declining somewhat. According to Kitano, "With the breakdown of the ethnic community and increasing opportunities to participate in the broader one, the behaviors of the group are changing from typically Japanese to American. The current *Sansei* [third] generation offers an example where behaviors are now approaching the American middle class in terms of achievement and social participation."[98]

In the 1970s some Sansei youth turned away from assimilation and tried to find an identity in an Asian American or "Third World" context. But it is still true that no immigrant group has used the public schools more effectively than the Japanese. Excellence in educational achievement was often gained at great psychological and cultural cost, but it allowed the Nisei partially to offset the crippling blows American society dealt them. In this, the WRA schools played a role. Relocation shattered home life and even much of family life, but public school life, even with its contradictions and hypocrisy, continued in the camps. It provided a link and an avenue of return to life outside the barbed wire. Back in 1906, during the San Francisco controversy, Goroku Ikeda of the Japanese Association claimed that Japanese children were "endeavoring to assimilate themselves" and "obtain an education so that they might be good citizens."[99] Forty years later, as they emerged from the camps, most Nisei still were committed to those goals.

NOTES

1. *San Francisco Chronicle*, Jan. 18, 1907.

2. Yamato Ichihashi, *Japanese in the United States* (Stanford, 1932), 64, 97; Harry H. L. Kitano, *Japanese Americans: Evolution of a Sub-Culture* (Englewood Cliffs, N. J., 1969), 13–17.

3. Roger Daniels, *The Politics of Prejudice: the Anti-Japanese Movement in California and the Struggle for Japanese Exclusion* (New York, 1970), 20–21.

4. *Ibid.*, 21–23; Ichihashi, *Japanese*, 229–233.

5. Michinari Fujita, "Japanese Associations in America," *Sociology and Social Research* (Jan.–Feb., 1929), 211–216.

6. *Chronicle*, Feb. 23, 1905.

7. *Ibid.*, May 7, May 8, 1905; Daniels, *Politics*, 27–28.

8. *Chronicle*, Feb. 23, 1905.

9. Kitano, *Japanese Americans*, 11.

10. *Ibid.*, 23–24; Edward Strong, *The Second Generation Japanese Problem* (Stanford, 1934), 186; Yamato Ichihashi, *Japanese Immigration* (San Francisco, 1905), 41–42.

11. *Chronicle*, Apr. 2, 1905.

12. Arthur G. Butzbach, "The Segregation of Orientals in the San Francisco Schools" (M.A. Thesis, Stanford, 1934), 15–16.

13. *Ibid.*, 21–22; *Chronicle*, May 7, 1905; Ruth Haines Thompson, "Events Leading to the Order to Segregate Japanese Pupils in the San Francisco Public Schools" (Ph.D. Thesis, Stanford, 1931), 49.

14. United States Senate, *Japanese in the City of San Francisco, California: From the President of the United States Transmitting the Final Report of Secretary Metcalf* (U.S. Senate, 59th Congress, 2nd Session, Document 147, Washington, 1906), 9–16; George Kennan, "The Japanese in the San Francisco Schools," *Outlook*, June 1, 1907, 246–247; Raymond Leslie Buell, "The Development of the Anti-Japanese Agitation in the United States," *Political Science Quarterly* (Dec. 1922), 621.

15. Thomas Bailey, *Theodore Roosevelt and the Japanese-American Crisis* (Stanford, 1934), 28.

16. *Chronicle*, Oct. 12, 1906; San Francisco *Call*, Oct. 12, 1906; San Francisco *Examiner*, Oct. 12, 1906.

17. *Outlook*, Nov. 3, 1906.

18. *Chronicle*, Oct. 19, 1906; *Call*, Oct. 19, 1906.

19. *Chronicle*, Oct. 25, 1906.

20. Bailey, *Theodore Roosevelt*, 47–48; *Call*, Feb. 3, Feb. 4, 1907; Butzbach, "Segregation," 28.

21. Bailey, *Theodore Roosevelt*, 50; *Chronicle*, Oct. 25, 1906.

22. Bailey, *Theodore Roosevelt*, 62–65; *Chronicle*, Oct. 26, 1906; *Call*, Oct. 26, 1906.

23. U. S. Senate, *Japanese*, 22–23.

24. *Chronicle*, Oct. 26, 1906; *Call*, Oct. 26, 1906.

25. *Chronicle*, Oct. 12, 1906; *Call*, Oct. 12, 1906; *Examiner*, Oct. 12, 1906; Bailey, *Theodore Roosevelt*, 72–75.

26. *Chronicle*, Oct. 27, Nov. 6, 1906; *Call*, Dec. 1, 1906.

27. William Inglis, "The Width of a School Bench," *Harpers Weekly*, Jan. 19, 1907, 83–84.

28. U. S. Senate, *Japanese*, 4–5; Kennan, "Japanese," 249–250.

29. Kennan, "Japanese," 250–251; Bailey, *Theodore Roosevelt*, 77–79; *Outlook*, Dec. 26, 1906.

30. *Chronicle*, Oct. 30, Nov. 1, 1906.

31. Daniels, *Politics*, 35; Bailey, *Theodore Roosevelt*, 320.

32. *Proceedings of the First International Convention of the Asiatic Exclusion League of North America* (Seattle, 1908), 67.

33. *Chronicle*, Nov. 2, 1906.

34. *Ibid.*, Dec. 5, 1906.

35. *Call*, Dec. 5, 1906; *Examiner*, Dec. 5, 1906.

36. *Chronicle*, Dec. 8, Dec. 11, 1906; *Call*, Dec. 7, 1906; Bailey, *Theodore Roosevelt*, 95.

37. *Chronicle*, Dec. 5, 1906; *Call*, Dec. 5, 1906.

38. *Call*, Dec. 6, 1906; *Examiner*, Dec. 6, 1906; Bailey, *Theodore Roosevelt*, 96–100.

39. *Chronicle*, Dec. 5, 1906.

40. U. S. Senate, *Japanese*, 2–18.

41. *Call*, Dec. 24, 1906; *Minutes of the Japanese and Korean Exclusion League* (San Francisco, Feb. 1907), 7–8.

42. *Keikichi Aoki v. M. A. Deane. Petition for Writ of Mandate* (Supreme Court of the State of California, San Francisco, 1907), 1–13; *Chronicle*, Jan. 18, 1907.

43. *Aoki v. Deane*, 1–13.

44. William Burke, *Japanese School Question* (San Francisco, 1907), 1–14.

45. *Ibid.*

46. Edwin Maxey, "Exclusion of Japanese Children From the Public Schools of San Francisco," *Yale Law Journal* (Dec. 1906), 90–93.

47. *Chronicle*, Dec. 20, 1906.

48. "Rights of the Japanese in California Schools," *Harvard Law Review* (Feb., 1907), 338–339.

49. Everis A. Hayes, *The Treaty-Making Power of the Government and the Japanese Question* (Washington, 1907), 7–8.

50. *Chronicle*, Dec. 16, 1906; *Call*, Feb. 3, 1907; Bailey, *Theodore Roosevelt*, 139, 320.

51. *Chronicle*, Feb. 1, 1907.

52. *Ibid.*, Feb. 3, 1907; *Call*, Feb. 2, 1907; *Examiner*, Feb. 4, 1907.

53. *Call*, Feb. 3, Feb. 4, 1907.

54. *Minutes of the Japanese and Korean Exclusion League* (San Francisco, Mar., 1907), 4–5; Walton Bean, *Boss Ruef's San Francisco* (Berkeley, 1952), 182–183.

55. Bailey, *Theodore Roosevelt*, 139–149.

56. *Chronicle*, Mar. 14, 1907.

57. *Call*, Feb. 16, 1907; *Examiner*, Feb. 16, 1907; *Chronicle*, Mar. 15, 1907.

58. Bailey, *Theodore Roosevelt*, 120, 308–310; Daniels, *Politics*, 47.

59. Daniels, 58–62.

60. Strong, *Second Generation*, 68; Ichihashi, *Japanese*, 97–100; Reginald Bell, *Public School Education of Second Generation Japanese in California* (Stanford, 1934), 7.

61. Daniels, *Politics*, 82–105; Raymond Leslie Buell, "Again the Yellow Peril," *Foreign Affairs* (Dec. 15, 1923), 295–309.

62. California State Board of Control, *California and the Oriental* (Sacramento, 1920), 9.

63. Bell, *Public School*, 17–26; Ichihashi, *Japanese*, 327–328; Marian Svensrud, "Attitudes of the Japanese Towards Their Language Schools," *Sociology and Social Research* (Jan.–Feb., 1933), 259–264.

64. Bell, *Public School*, 17–26; Kitano, *Japanese Americans*, 24–26; Gretchen Tuthill, "A Study of the Japanese in the City of Los Angeles" (M.A. Thesis, University of Southern California, 1924), 56–59.

65. Sakae Tsuboi, "The Japanese Language School Teacher," *Journal of Applied Sociology* (Nov.–Dec., 1926), 163–165.

66. Ichihashi, *Japanese*, 347–349; Kitano, *Japanese Americans*, 25; Dorothy Swaine Thomas, *The Salvage* (Berkeley, 1952), 212.

67. Tuthill, "Study," 40–43; Fujita, "Japanese Associations," 217–218.

68. Tuthill, "Study," 43–45.

69. Valentine S. McClatchy, *California's Language Schools* (Sacramento, 1922), 2.

70. *Ibid.*, 4–5; Bell, "Public School," 23–24; Svensrud, "Attitudes," 261.

71. Bell, *Public School*, 65–67; Strong, *Second-Generation*, 199–201.

72. Ichihashi, *Japanese*, 351–352.

73. Strong, *Second-Generation*, 186.

74. Bell, *Public School*, 37–60.

75. Marvin Darsie, *The Mental Capacity of American-Born Japanese in California* (*Comparative Psychology Monographs*, No. 15, Baltimore, 1926), 84–85.

76. *Ibid.*, 87; Kitano, *Japanese American*, 23–24.

77. Tuthill, "Study," 52; Strong, *Second-Generation*, 179.

78. Valentine S. McClatchy, *The Japanese Problem in California* (San Francisco, 1929), 8–9.

79. *Ibid.*, 9.

80. Thomas, *Salvage*, 159–160, 185, 213.

81. *Ibid.*, 159.

82. Elliot G. Mears, *Resident Orientals on the Pacific Coast* (New York, 1927), 366.

83. United States War Relocation Authority (WRA), *Second Quarterly Report* (Washington, 1942), 17–18; *Quarterly Report: October 1 to December 31, 1942* (Washington, 1943), 14.

84. WRA, *First Quarterly Report* (Washington, 1942), 27; *Second Quarterly Report*, 30.

85. WRA, *Semi-Annual Report: January 1 to June 30, 1943* (Washington, 1943), 30.

86. Dorothy Swaine Thomas, *The Spoilage* (Berkeley, 1946), 37.

87. WRA, *Education Program in War Relocation Centers* (Washington, 1945), 1–2.

88. *Ibid.*, 1, 12; WRA, *Semi-Annual Report January 1—June 30, 1944* (Washington, 1944), 39–40.

89. Jeanne Wakatsuki Houston and James D. Houston, *Farewell to Manzanar* (Boston, 1973), 87.

90. Edward Spicer et al., *Impounded People* (Tucson, 1959), 123.

91. *Ibid.*, 180.

92. *Ibid.*, 180, 275; WRA, *Semi-Annual Reports July 1–December 31, 1943*, 74; *January 1—June 30, 1945*, 37, 52–53.

93. WRA, *Semi-Annual Reports, January 1–June 30, 1944*, 40; *January 1–June 30, 1945*, 37–38.

94. Spicer, *Impounded*, 256.

95. Houston, *Farewell*, 115.

96. Kitano, *Japanese Americans*, 38.

97. Houston, *Farewell*, 90.

98. Kitano, "Changing Achievement Patterns or the Japanese in the United States" *Journal of Social Psychology* (Dec. 1962), 263–264.

99. *Chronicle*, Oct. 19, 1906.

2

Politics, Education, and Language Policy: The Case of Japanese Language Schools in Hawaii

John N. Hawkins

IN CULTURALLY DIVERSE SOCIETIES, national language policy, especially as it relates to the function of schooling, is one of the most complex and at times emotionally charged educational issues. Traditionally, the bulk of research on this controversial issue has focused on the psychological or linguistic dimensions of multilingual education.[1] In recent years, new studies are appearing that attempt to account for the larger social context in which language policy is formulated. Other studies are directing their attention to the thousands of recent bilingual and multilingual programs that have emerged outside of North America, often in the wake of intense social unrest.[2] Indeed, debates on the positive and negative aspects of bilingual or multilingual educational policy are worldwide. Viewed on an international scale, the complexity of issues concerning intergroup ethnic relations, and language policy specifically, are sharply apparent.[3] Hence, reinterpretations of existing data as well as case studies analyzing the influence of political, economic, and social forces on the formation of education and language policy are sorely needed. This case study of the early Japanese language schools in Hawaii is one attempt to meet such a need.

The study will focus on the political struggle of the Japanese immigrant community in the early twentieth century to maintain their autonomous Japanese language schools in the face of strong opposition from the Hawaiian Territorial Government, controlled by the *haole* (white) elite.

After a long, drawn-out judicial process, the Japanese immigrant community won their case. This study will not examine, however, the legal aspects of the conflict, but will trace instead the intense period of political mobilization preceding the legal victory. Both proponents and opponents of the Japanese language schools mobilized their respective forces to maximize their access to educational policy making. Because the conflict was eventually decided in favor of the Japanese language schools, examining the political reasons for this policy outcome may shed light on language policy formation in general.

At the outset it is necessary to clarify some terms and concepts that are already referred to above and often used in analyzing language policy formation and the politics of education. Central to such study is the significant question of who has access to the formal and informal political institutions to change, modify, and adapt other institutions and resources. According to Lutz, there are three basic characteristics of educational decision making involving subordinate and dominant groups: 1) politics and power are integral to understanding any given educational decision; 2) power holders tend to maximize their own

From *Amerasia Journal* 5:1 (1978): 39–56. Reprinted with permission of the Regents of the University of California and the UCLA Asian American Studies Center.

values and interests; and 3) subordinate groups, despite democratic and ideological exhortations to the contrary, are seldom represented politically in an equitable manner.[4] While these observations are not surprising, they represent the social and political conditions which existed in Hawaii at the turn of the century. During this period, in general, the *haole* elite utilized their monopoly on formal political and economic institutions to promote their own values and interests at the expense of the numerous subordinate populations (Hawaiians, Portuguese, Pilipino, Japanese, Korean, Chinese). These conditions and their concrete manifestations led supporters of the Japanese language schools to begin a process of political mobilization and participation in an effort to gain access to and ultimately influence the educational decision making.

What do we mean by mobilization and participation? Mobilization suggests participation, and several authors have insisted that regardless of how the politics of education is conceptualized (ranging from systems theory to psychological models), the interlinking thread inherent in all models is the degree of participation present and visible in the people involved.[5] Yet participation is a deceptive and elusive phenomenon. To "participate" politically conjures up images of actors playing roles in the numerous voluntary associations normally associated with politics and decision making, yet this range of possibilities is vague. In order to equate participation with a "share in the power" of decision making in education, we must distinguish between conventional concepts of participation (which Schermerhorn terms activation)[6] and the use of critical resources in the direct interests of the group attempting to influence policy making. In this case, supporters of Japanese language schools succeeded in mobilizing a critical number and variety of resources directly related to the preconditions mentioned above.[7] This form of participation (not simply numbers of actors, since many Japanese did not support the struggle) was crucial to mounting an effective campaign around the issue of control of the language schools. Additional minimum conditions from the perspective of the subordinate group included a shared target of hostility (the Territorial Government and the *haole* elite),[8] feelings of grievance and hardship, and a sense of collective oppression. In addition, an organizational base was available along two horizontal lines: traditional lines of ethnicity and secondary group lines of occupation and religion.

The terms "subordinate group" and "dominant group" are, of course, generalizations useful only to describe general patterns of relations. The Japanese community was never wholly united in support of the language schools, and the *haole* sector of the population experienced internal dissension as well. On the Japanese side, one major Japanese newspaper, and especially its editor (Kinzaburo Makino of the *Hawaii Hochi*), provided much of the leadership toward preserving the language schools and was backed by much of the Buddhist clergy. The Japanese Consul General's office and the other major Japanese newspaper, *Nippo Jiji*, wavered and at times opposed the struggle. On the American side, both newspapers and their editors, specifically Allen of the *Star Bulletin* and Irwin of the *Advertiser*, were vocal in their opposition to the schools. They were backed by Territorial Government officials associated with the Department of Public Instruction as well as elected officials in the legislature and the Governor's office. However, labor and plantation interests were at times opposed to the government's efforts to regulate the schools. Despite these apparent divisions in both communities (and we shall discuss them in more detail), they were in fact two different communities, overlapping very little institutionally, with separate communications channels and separate social organizations.

These characteristics of Hawaiian society during the early 1900s and the concepts of mobilization and participation as discussed above provide a loose framework for analyzing some salient aspects of the politics of educational decision making, especially as this process relates to cultural diversity and language policy.

JAPANESE LANGUAGE SCHOOLS IN HAWAII: A BRIEF SURVEY

In the following sections we will first examine the social and political context in which the language schools developed, and second, look at the mobilization efforts of the parties involved to acquire or maintain control over the schools. The history and characteristics surrounding the rise of the language schools were important factors in convincing the Territorial Government that they must be regulated and ultimately abolished.

Following a major period of Japanese immigration to Hawaii in the late 19th century and the subsequent rise of a new second generation, the Japanese community developed independent, private language schools which were designed to promote a sense of community through the study of Japanese culture and language, as well as to perpetuate Japanese culture and values.[9] The first schools were founded in the late 1800s on Maui and in Honolulu by both Buddhist and Christian representatives.[10] Although initially the schools were strongly tied to formal religious organizations, independent schools eventually dominated. Of the 181 Japanese language schools established in Hawaii by 1934, 76 percent were independent, 22 percent Buddhist, and 2 percent Christian.[11] Reverend Okumura's school in Nuuanu, considered by some as the model, included the following items in the school regulations: "The purpose of this school is to give children Japanese education . . . the subjects taught are reading, calligraphy, and composition. In addition, moral education and physical education will be given. Textbooks used for reading will be those approved by the Japanese Ministry of Education."[12] Children in these early schools observed major Japanese holidays and were at those times absent from the American public schools, which according to law they were required to attend. They bowed to the Emperor's picture, sang the Japanese national anthem, and studied the Imperial Rescript on Education.[13] This type of instructional activity continued down to 1915. As a result of increasing criticism by American educational authorities, from 1916 onward most schools made efforts to discard the image of being a separate educational track. They changed their names from Japanese Elementary Schools to Japanese Language Schools and discontinued use of Japanese Ministry of Education instructional materials; a period of curricular reform began.[14]

An umbrella organization, the Japanese Education Association, was founded in 1914 and included both Christian and Buddhist representatives (led by Okumura and Imamura respectively). Both groups within the Japanese community recognized the need for curriculum reform, and in 1915 a distinguished group of Japanese educators met to formulate a revision plan (Rev. Okumura, Bishop Imamura, Professor Haga of Tokyo University, R. Tsunoda of Honpa Hongwanji). Later, in 1916, Japanese Consul General Rukuro Moroi spearheaded a Central Educational Association which worked in cooperation with the Territorial Government to standardize the curriculum. At this early date a slight rift occurred within the Japanese community when Okumura introduced a new issue apart from the question of curriculum revision. Essentially, he suggested that all Japanese Language Schools be converted into independent schools under the joint supervision of American and Japanese educators. The Central Commission eventually disbanded. In any case, the revised texts that appeared after 1916 were "Hawaiianized versions" of the previous materials. These revisions made by the Japanese schools can be seen as a political strategy to relieve the pressure from American authorities.[15] Concomitantly, the revised curriculum may also be viewed as a reflection of the changing worldview of the Japanese immigrants toward themselves, from sojourners to settlers with a political and economic status in Hawaii.

Apart from the criticism directed against the curriculum, the schools drew little attention from authorities in the Territorial Government and expanded steadily. By 1917, the majority of Japanese school-age children attended the public schools during the day and the Japanese Language Schools in the late afternoon and on weekends. The end of World War I brought a high degree of national chauvinism to Hawaii which, coupled with rising suspicion of the Japanese community in the 1920s (related in some measure to Japan's actions in China), created conditions for the conflict around the issue of control and regulation of the language schools. An additional factor raised repeatedly by the *haole* elite was the role played by Japanese strike leaders in the 1909 and especially the 1920 sugar plantation strikes. Even though the latter strike was broken and the leaders publicly humiliated the specter of a unified and mobilized Japanese labor force alarmed Hawaii's dominant groups, who viewed the language schools as an institutional organizational base of un-Americanism. An editorial in the *Star Bulletin* somewhat hysterically warned against "the priests of Asiatic paganism who were in an unholy alliance with foreign language school teachers and Japanese editors to control the industrialism of Hawaii."[16] One underlying cause for the tension that developed between the dominant leadership in Hawaii and the Japanese was fear on the part of the *haole* elite that the Japanese were getting out of hand economically and politically. The Buddhist temples and the language schools were considered the most dangerous manifestation of this trend.[17]

Throughout the struggle over regulation of the schools, Japanese supporters of the schools, particularly the *Hawaii Hochi*, maintained that the basic problem was the religious differences between Buddhist and Christian communities. Supporters of regulatory legislation, however, argued that religion had nothing to do with the struggle and instead stressed institutional and pedagogical problems related to the language schools. Despite some outward displays of religious tolerance, the record of *haole* antagonism toward non-Christian religions coupled with anti-foreign sentiment during this period made it easier for government officials and American educators to attack the language schools. The Territorial Government could and did interfere often on educational matters, and educational agencies in Hawaii increasingly saw the Japanese Language Schools as obstacles to their attempts to inculcate American values and attitudes in Japanese as well as other ethnic groups (especially Chinese and Koreans, who also maintained separate language schools).[18]

By 1919, legislation and proposals began to appear, calling for the certification of teachers on the basis of "ideals of democracy and knowledge of English."[19] This represented the first of several moves to monitor and limit the number of Japanese teachers (the majority of whom spoke only Japanese) and thereby further regulate the schools. The following excerpt from the Judd proposal appeared in the 4 January 1919 edition of the *Pacific Commercial Advertiser* and elaborated on additional preconditions for teacher certification in any school, public or private:

> To prescribe certain qualifications for school teachers and for the purpose of safeguarding American citizenship in the Territory of Hawaii. Be it enacted by the legislature of the Territory of Hawaii. *Section 1*. No person shall serve as a teacher in any school, without first having obtained a certificate from the Department of Public Instruction. . . . Before issuing a certificate to any teacher, the department shall satisfy itself that such teacher possesses ideals of democracy and has a knowledge of the English language, American history, and methods of government. . . . *Section 3*. The department may revoke a certificate, when satisfied that the holder thereof is unable to qualify under Section 1 of this Act. . . . *Section 4*. Whoever shall serve as a teacher, without first having obtained such certificates, shall be punished by a fine.

Other legislation was introduced to abolish the schools entirely, but such efforts were haphazard and immediately opposed by leaders in the Japanese community. The Japanese response to the Judd proposal (January 1919), and later the Andrews bill (March 1919), was attacked by the *Advertiser* and American officials as "intemperate." The Japanese community was warned that such an attitude might result in further regulatory legislation. In fact, the Japanese response was quite temperate and consisted of petitions, mass meetings (Asahi Theatre, 10 March 1919), and a formal request from the Japanese Education Association (Ryuhei Mashimo) to officials requesting that the bills be withdrawn. The Hongwanji Educational Home Committee also submitted a formal resolution. Consequently, till 1920 all such acts, including the Lyman proposal, which was more strongly phrased, were either tabled or defeated.[20] These measures were the first overt efforts to wrest control of the schools from the Japanese and met with the first instance of mobilized opposition. A "veritable flood of petitions" was sent to the legislature, Japanese workers on the plantations threatened to leave their jobs, and even the Chinese and Korean communities supported efforts to defeat the measures.[21]

Both sides had, however, made their positions clear. The Territorial Government realized that a planned, concerted effort was required to obtain control of the language schools. The Japanese community had, on the other hand, realized that only through effective mobilization could they influence educational decision making. The lines were thus drawn between those (including some Japanese) who increasingly favored control or abolition of language schools—accompanied as rapidly as possible with total assimilation of the Japanese into American society—and those, primarily in the Japanese community, who argued for cultural preservation and saw the language schools as the principal vehicle to achieve this goal.

The crisis accelerated during the period from 1919 to 1921. The defeat of the Judd and Andrews bills encouraged the Governor to invite the United States Commissioner of Education to investigate all public and private schools in the Territory in order to build a base for elimination of the private language schools. The 1920 labor strike also had the effect of inflaming opinion against the Japanese. Irwin of the *Advertiser* (he was also Territorial Attorney General) charged that teachers in the Japanese Language Schools had taken an active role in the strike, and McNally of the *Star Bulletin* argued that the previous bills had been defeated because of fear of further labor unrest. Both newspapers implied that a lobby group composed of labor and plantation interests had convinced the legislature of the danger of abolishing the separate schooling system for the Japanese, and of the need to maintain them. Legislation to eliminate the schools would adversely affect labor conditions, they argued, since the Japanese would become Americanized to the point where they would acquire the skills and abilities which would allow them to leave the fields for more lucrative and professional occupations. Members of this sector of the business community clearly were firm believers in the transformational power of education and sought to isolate the Japanese (and other Asian laborers) from the mainstream educational system, and by extension, from access to political and economic power. Here we see one example of the split in the *haole* community over regulation of the Japanese Language Schools.[22]

Reportedly at the request of the Chamber of Commerce, the Territorial Attorney General, Harry Irwin, drafted a proposal which was presented at a special session of the Territorial legislature on 20 November 1920. This proposal urged the total abolition of all foreign language schools and was the harshest legislation yet presented.[23] The response by moderate members of both the Territorial Government and the Japanese community was a compromise proposal known as Act 30. This measure, and what the Japanese later considered to be a betrayal of its contents, led to an open struggle and eventually a complicated legal battle over the issue of control of the Japanese Language Schools.

THE STRUGGLE FOR CONTROL OF THE JAPANESE LANGUAGE SCHOOLS

Educational officials, government authorities, and other leading members of the Territory of Hawaii set the stage for the legislative struggle that was to follow by a variety of both direct and indirect means. Direct efforts were made to remove the financial base of the language schools by such organizations as the Committee of the Japanese Section of the Hawaiian Evangelical Association. This committee passed a resolution to discontinue plantation owners' subsidies to Japanese Language Schools operated by non-Christian organizations (i.e., the majority Buddhist schools).[24] Meanwhile, a series of media reports and statements ultimately removed any doubt regarding the overall goals of American society and the specific function of schooling as viewed by the Territorial Government and other opinion leaders in the *haole* elite. An annual government report issued in 1919 stated: "There can neither be national unity in ideals nor in purpose unless there is some common method of communication through which may be conveyed the thought of the nation. All Americans must be taught to read and write and think in one language; this is a primary condition to that growth which all nations expect of us and which we demand of ourselves."[25] The report goes on to lament a democracy which allows multi-language instruction in the schools and added that the machinery for effective Americanization is to be found in public education. The Territorial Superintendent was no less direct. Henry Kinney urged voters to support legislation aimed at controlling the Japanese Language Schools and declared that those Japanese who supported the schools were "troublemakers and agitators."[26] He predicted that the language schools would eventually die, killed off by second- and third- generation Japanese who would not attend: "The task of the Department of Public Instruction is to weld the large Japanese factor . . . into an integral part of our American body politic."[27] Eliminating the language schools was the first step. Other non-governmental institutions followed this lead and some, such as the YMCA, took active steps to promote the Americanization of the Japanese as quickly as possible.[28]

Supporters of the language schools at this time were represented primarily by the Hawaii Kyoiku Kai (Hawaii Education Association, also known as Japanese Education Association) founded in 1914.[29] The Association had been forewarned of the potential dangers of stressing cultural preservation and language integrity by Japanese Consul General Arita. In 1916, the Association began to revise the curriculum to remove clauses overtly stressing Japanese citizenship. A parallel move to separate the language schools from religious affiliation also took place.[30] However, these compromise actions had little effect as several bills introduced in 1919–1920 proposed either the abolishment or regulation of the language schools. The Japanese community responded with a series of volatile mass meetings during which race discrimination was denounced, petitions were drawn up and presented to a wide range of government authorities (including President Wilson), and appeals were made through the Japanese language newspapers (*Hawaii Hochi* and *Nippo Jiji*) to the community to fight the legislation.[31] The first signs of a split in the Japanese community emerged at this time. Increasingly, the language of protest shifted to suggestions that perhaps the existence of the language schools would actually promote Americanization and that for this reason the Territorial Government should retreat from its position on elimination of the schools. By 1920, however, the Japanese community was effectively mobilized and able to call mass meetings that were well attended, as well as reach organized labor groups and utilize the Japanese language media as an information channel.[32]

In the face of such widespread mobilization by the Japanese, Territorial Government officials, especially the Office of the Superintendent of Public Instruction, did not expect to successfully promote legislation that would entirely abolish the language schools. They were successful, however, in introducing and eventually signing into law the compromise measure, Act 30. The committee which drafted the measure included both moderate government officials and moderate members of the Japanese community. The Act stated that the government and the Office of the Superintendent of Public Instruction would be allowed to: "Regulate and not to prohibit the conducting of foreign language schools and the teaching of foreign languages; but to regulate the same so that the Americanism of the pupils be promoted."[33] The measure thus satisfied a broad segment of both communities, the *haole* elite who were concerned about the Americanism of Japanese youngsters, and the Japanese community who were now assured that the schools would not be eliminated but only "regulated." However, in a move that retriggered the conflict, American members of the committee proposed and added a clause to Act 30 that restricted the student enrollment in language schools to students who had reached the third grade of the public schools.[34] The Japanese members of the committee first opposed this action and then reluctantly agreed to support the entire document. Thus, it became obvious that the original intention of eliminating the schools was still in the minds of the American members of the committee, who justified their actions in the following manner:

> Practically all of the pupils are American citizens [second generation], and almost none of them will return to Japan to become Japanese residents or subjects. We shall hold these children more and more to American standards of manners, conduct, speech and habits of thought. We should be unjust to them if we allowed them to be surrounded by preventable alien influence, and forced them to enter the competitive American life under the resulting handicap. . . . Assume if you choose, that the Japanese educational, social and political system is superior. The fact remains that there is a place for both civilizations, and the place for Japanese civilization is in Japan, not in the United States. In the interests of social harmony and good will, it is inexpedient that we should have, as a permanent institution, a system of schools managed and taught by aliens, even with the best of intentions on their part. We believe that the proper answer to the desire of Americans of oriental ancestry to learn the language of the orient is by offering instruction therein in the public schools, and charging tuition if necessary.[35]

Apart from the patronizing tone of the statement, it was clearly out of spirit with the original intent of Act 30, at least from the Japanese point of view. After all, they had complied with the certification and licensing requirements, had formed a joint committee to revise the curriculum, and had compromised on a variety of other issues. Despite disapointment, frustration, and outrage at what some members of the Japanese community believed to be a betrayal of their trust, in a compromise solution the Act was signed into law and became effective 1 January 1923.

Dissension in the Japanese community took place over the course of what future action, if any, ought to be taken. The possibilities ranged from complete acquiescence to mass protest and violence. One group, supported and encouraged by the Japanese Consul General and several prominent members of the Japanese community, urged the community not to fight the issue at this time but to assure government officials that they would Americanize as quickly as possible and reorganize the language schools accordingly. They argued that only through this method could the language schools be saved from complete elimination. Japanese Premier Hara and a number of other high officials in Japan also supported Americanization. Japanese in Hawaii were encouraged by this group to eliminate their "pagan" ways, give up persistent customs and manners (e.g., "noisy festivals and wrestling tournaments that disrupt the quiet Sundays") and generally "forget the idea of Japanese and always think and act from the point of view of the American people."[36] One prominent leader in the Japanese community challenged Japanese in Hawaii to become American in all ways except physical features and suggested that those parents who wanted their children to preserve Japanese manners and customs (including language) send them to Japan permanently.[37] It is difficult to determine from existing sources how widespread these sentiments were. Support for Act 30 and rapid Americanization clearly existed. Among officials of the Japanese government (the consulate in Hawaii and officials in Japan), fifty *nisei* (second generation) students at the University of Hawaii signed a petition in support of the

Act, and seven of sixteen members of the committee appointed by the Superintendent's office to revise the curriculum of the language schools supported the legislation.[38] In addition, one of three Japanese language newspapers supported the Act.

The forces in the community opposed to the Act realized that the dissension over the issue of litigation seriously retarded the momentum that had built up since the Territorial Government began introducing regulatory legislation. The range of opinion was wide. One prominent Buddhist priest (Ninryo Nago) commented that the cultural differences between Japanese and Americans were simply too great and probably irreconcilable. For this reason he opposed control or elimination of the language schools on the grounds that it would be disastrous to the cultural integrity of Japanese in Hawaii. In fact, he stated, Japanese should look to Japan for identity and security, and if a choice should ever have to be made in terms of loyalty, it should be made in favor of Japan.[39] Others were more hopeful that a less extreme position could be found. The Japanese Society of Hawaii, a large umbrella organization of Japanese public opinion, met several times and reached the conclusion that further protest was necessary; that the language schools should be supported. At the same time, their argument shifted to emphasize the positive role the schools could play in creating good American citizens (not necessarily "Americanized," however). Moreover, they took the position that if the schools were eliminated, social disorder could result, especially among Japanese youth. Here we see one of the first important expressions of a threatened sanction to both the non-Japanese and Japanese communities in Hawaii: youth violence. Their opinion was formulated in a petition and sent to the Superintendent of Public Instruction, along with the veiled threat that enforcement of the Act could lead to social chaos.[40] The Japanese media (primarily the *Hawaii Hochi* and *Hawaii Shinpo*) directed their attention to the Japanese community itself.[41] In a series of articles from February to May 1923, the *Hawaii Hochi* encouraged the community to fight the legislation and stand up for their rights. Writers played on the theme of "manhood" and derided those who succumbed to the Territorial Government's actions as "weak Japanese." Other writers were more vehement, suggesting that those Japanese who submitted to the legislation should be despised as *chorinbo*, or outcasts.[42] Editorials encouraged Japanese labor to apply pressure on the Sugar Planter's Association and reminded the Association of the 1920 strike and the potential danger of a similar strike over the school issue. The paper urged a frontal assault against the Territorial Government, extending from formal litigation to pressure on the labor community and the educational establishment.[43] All of these plans sufficiently alarmed the Government, the *haole* elite, and the sugar plantation owners for whom the labor strike of 1920 was still a fresh memory. The situation was described by Governor Farrington as "delicate." Other influential *haoles* urged the Governor to proceed with caution, and the entire situation was "touchy."[44] So while the Japanese community was clearly divided over the issue of further protest, the opponents of the schools, primarily government officials and educators, were also beginning to waver. The combined threats of labor unrest (in actuality more in the minds of the *haole* elite than most Japanese), youth violence, and social instability within the Japanese community had the effect of weakening support for Act 30 and regulation of the language schools in general.

Although the initial response of the Japanese community toward the idea of formal legal action was not widespread, (only eleven out of one hundred and thirty language schools voted to join a lawsuit), a test case was entered. As litigation proceeded and community pressure grew in favor of fighting the Act, more schools joined, so that by August 1923 eighty-seven supported the test case.

Prior to the signing of Act 30, the legal firm of Lightfoot and Lightfoot, representing the Japanese Society of Hawaii, filed a brief with the Governor's office challenging the constitutionality of the new regulations. The Hawaii Circuit Court tried the case, and the constitutionality of Act 30 was upheld by Judge James Banks. In the meantime, a landmark case, *Meyers* v. *Nebraska*, was decided in favor of an elementary school teacher who taught the subject of reading in German. The Nebraska State Supreme Court had originally upheld a state ruling prohibiting "teaching any subject to any person in any language other than the English language." In this case there was clearly no religious argument; the State of Nebraska instead focused on the foreign language threat to order and stability. The Supreme Court of the United States finally reversed the ruling in 1923, on the grounds that it violated the 14th Amendment.

In Hawaii by 1925, eighty-four of a hundred and forty Japanese Language Schools joined the litigants. The Japanese community was able to raise over $25,000 to fight the case. On 21 February 1927 the United States Supreme Court finally decided in favor of the Japanese language schools. The judgment of the Court was particularly harsh toward Territorial officials. After detailing the various attempts to control the language schools, the court ruled: ". . . all are parts of a deliberate plan to bring foreign language schools under a strict governmental control for which the record discloses no adequate reason." Both parties avoided the religious issue and focused instead on loyalty, stability, and threats to the state.[45] The seven-year effort to preserve the schools and to maintain autonomous control over the curriculum and administration was successful. This was an impressive example of a clearly subordinate group effectively mobilizing available resources, coping with a damaging split in the mobilization effort, and finally emerging victorious.

Twenty years later, in 1947, an attitudinal survey revealed that although first- and second-generation Japanese generally agreed that the preservation of the language schools was a positive development, considerable disagreement existed regarding other aspects of the language school issue. The disagreement as revealed in the questionnaire was directly correlated with generation and had little to do with other measures (e.g., occupation, sex, religion, education, etc.). First-generation Japanese favored the schools for most of the reasons stated earlier (knowledge of Japanese was essential to maintain linkages between generations, the schools promoted goodwill and assisted in the Americanization process, moral training in the schools was important for community solidarity, and so on). However, the statements of second-generation Japanese were more critical. The schools, they charged, caused far too much stress in children (one of the earlier *haole* arguments), and in fact hindered Americanization the schools were too small and run inefficiently; curricular objectives were not coordinated with the public schools, creating confusion in the child; and the language schools generally did a poor job of teaching the language.[46]

On the surface it might appear that the preservation of Japanese Language Schools was the result of well-argued litigation and an equitable judicial system. And in fact it was through the courts that supporters of the language schools were finally able to gain access to the educational decision-making structure. Yet the road to the first test case, as we have seen, was long and arduous. An earlier point stressed the importance of mobilization as the key to access, and the court action, while critical, could not have occurred had not other conditions been present. What were these conditions and what judgments can be made in relation to language policy formation in general? We cannot generalize on the basis of one case study; nonetheless, in the case of the language schools, at least two sets of conditions seemed to be present.

First, the attempt by the Territorial Government to regulate and eliminate the foreign language schools was only one of many such efforts to maintain dominance over the many subordinate ethnic groups in Hawaii. This attempt came, however, at a time when the Japanese realized the political resources available to them and were also aware of their ability to mobilize these resources. Control of language schools was an issue that prompted the Japanese community to increasingly participate and mobilize in opposition to the dominant elite. A mobilization effort of this kind is not necessarily the result of conscious leadership, at least at the beginning.[47] In the Hawaii case it is difficult to isolate individual leaders, aside from Makino of *Hawaii Hochi*, who from the start agitated for struggle on the language issue. Rather, we see larger organizations and institutions (the Buddhist church, the Japanese media, the Hawaii Education Association, labor groups, etc.) responding to a perceived threat, and later duplicity on the part of the *haole* elite. As the struggle progressed, the Japanese were able to mobilize power resources and threaten sanctions, satisfying the preconditions of mobilization as we have discussed.[48] This combination of activities (inter- and intra-group struggle, intensive participation, mobilization of available resources, and the threat of sanctions) laid the basis for the successful court action that was to come.

Second, the dominant group in Hawaii (the *haole* elite) had increasingly experienced a lessening of social control over the Japanese as well as other subordinate ethnic groups. The success of Japanese labor organizers in the early 1900s (culminating in the 1909 strike which was 100 percent Japanese), and the joint Japanese-Pilipino strike in 1920 contributed to the alarm the *haole* elite were beginning to feel about their own ability to maintain control over the industrial and political institutions of the Territory. On another level, the Territorial Government was having increasing difficulty dealing with higher-level officials in Washington, upon whose legitimacy they depended. Attempts to convince Washington officials to lift immigration laws at this time (1920s) in order to allow more Chinese labor into the islands (an action designed to weaken Japanese labor solidarity and control) ran into severe difficulties.[49] In short, the Japanese endeavor was aided by the weakening social control of the *haole* elite.

This dual set of circumstances—political mobilization of the oppressed group and weakening of social control on the part of the dominant elite—appears to be the essential element in the Japanese community's maintaining control of the language schools. The implications of this study for language policy formation in general is probably limited to experiences that are at least somewhat similar in context. Yet clearly the institutional survival of the language schools and the opening of access to educational decision making were directly related to the politics of mobilization and participation by a subordinate group. This experience, along with subsequent struggles, contributed to the eventual emergence of a more equitable political and economic relationship between the Japanese and *haoles* in Hawaii.

NOTES

1. Joshua A. Fishman, *Bilingual Education: An International Sociological Perspective* (Rowley, Mass., 1976), 108.

2. Kellman's study suggests that depending upon the kind of attachment that groups and subgroups may have to the national system, language can either serve an integrative or disintegrative function. Herbert C. Kellman, "Language as Aid and Barrier to Involvement in the National System," *Conference on Language Planning and Processes, East West Center*, Honolulu (1969). Additional recent cross-national studies include: Alfa Ibrahim Sow, *Languages and Linguistic Policies in Black Africa: The Experience of UNESCO* (Paris, 1977); M. L. Marasinghe, "Some Problems Associated with a Language Switchover in the Third World," *Law and Modernization*, No. 4 (1978); Istvan Fodor and Claude Hagege, *Language Reforms of the Past and in the Developing Countries* (Hamburg, Germany, 1978).

3. Fishman, 1976; Bernard A. Spolsky and Robert L. Cooper, eds., *Case Studies in Bilingual Education* (New York, 1977).

4. Frank Lutz, "Methods and Conceptualizations of Political Power in Education" in J. Scribner, ed., *The Politics of Education* (Chicago, 1977), 33.

5. Kjell Eide, "Participation and Participatory Planning in Educational Systems," in *Participatory Planning in Education* (Paris, 1974); Lutz, "Methods and Conceptualizations of

Political Power in Education"; R. A. Schermerhorn, *Comparative Ethnic Relations: A Framework for Theory and Research* (New York, 1970).

6. Schermerhorn, *Comparative Ethnic Relations*, 130.

7. Hubert M. Blalock, *Toward a Theory of Minority-Group Relations* (New York, 1967), 110–112.

8. Anthony Oberschall, *Social Conflict and Social Movements* (New Jersey, 1973), 120. The term "*haole* elite" refers to those Caucasians who constituted an elite group, around 5 percent of the population in 1900, of American or British background. Of primarily missionary or business background, they sought and acquired political and economic control of the islands by the 1920s. A small core of families dominated the inner group of all *haoles* (in 1935 about 20 percent of the population). For a detailed analysis of the role of the *haole* elite in Hawaii see: Lawrence H. Fuchs, *Hawaii Pono: A Social History* (New York, 1961).

9. Koichi Glenn Harada, "A Survey of Japanese Language Schools in Hawaii" (M.A. thesis, University of Hawaii, 1934), 33; John E. Reinecke, "Feigned Necessity: Hawaii's Attempt to Obtain Chinese Contract Labor, 1921–1923" (M.A. thesis, University of Hawaii, 1967), 32.

10. Reverend Yonichi established the Buddhist Hongwanji mission in 1887, and Reverend Okumura founded the Nuuanu Japanese Church in 1890: both were bases for the eventual proliferation of Japanese language schools: Harada, "A Survey of Japanese Language Schools in Hawaii," 42; Katsumi Onishi, "A Study of the Attitudes of the Japanese in Hawaii Toward the Japanese Language Schools" (M.A. thesis, University of Hawaii, 1948), 7.

11. Harada, "A Survey of Japanese Language Schools in Hawaii," 42.

12. Hawaii Nihonjin Iminshi Kauko Iinkai, ed., *Hawaii Nihonjin Iminshi* (Honolulu, 1964), 232.

13. Hawaii Nihonjin Iminshi Kauko Iinkai, ed., *Hawaii Nihonjin Iminshi*, 232. The Imperial Rescript was promulgated on 30 October 1890 and became the basic statement of official educational aims in Japan. Stressing filial piety, harmony, and morality, it was essentially a neo-Confucian pedagogical statement: Herbert Passin, *Society and Education in Japan* (New York, 1965), 151.

14. *Ibid.*, 232–233.

15. Louise H. Hunter, *Buddhism in Hawaii* (Honolulu, 1977), 99.

16. Fuchs, *Hawaii Pono*, 219.

17. Reinecke, "Feigned Necessity," 34.

18. *Ibid.*

19. *Ibid.*, 37.

20. Harada, "A Survey of Japanese Language Schools in Hawaii," 63; Hunter, *Buddhism in Hawaii*, 109.

21. Reinecke, "Feigned Necessity," 39.

22. Hunter, *Buddhism in Hawaii*, 110.

23. Hawaii Nihonjin Iminshi Kauko Iinkai, ed., *Hawaii Nihonjin Iminshi*, 235–238.

24. *Ibid.*, 228–229.

25. *Advertiser*, 4 January 1919.

26. *Advertiser*, 13 March 1919.

27. *Ibid.*

28. For example, the YMCA published English language books for plantation workers and established special classes with the expressed desire to further the Americanization process: *Advertiser*, 6 January 1919.

29. Onishi, "A Study of the Attitudes of the Japanese," 15.

30. *Ibid.*, 16.

31. *Advertiser*, 11 March 1919; *Advertiser*, 12 March 1919.

32. *Ibid.*

33. Reinecke, "Feigned Necessity," 398.

34. *Ibid.*, 400.

35. *Ibid.*, 399.

36. Takie Okumura and Umetaro Okumura, *Hawaii's American-Japanese Problem* (Honolulu, 1927), 9.

37. *Ibid.*, 17.

38. Reinecke, *"Feigned Necessity,"* 390.

39. *Hawaii's Buddhism* (Honolulu, February 1923).

40. *A Brief Survey of the Foreign Language School Question* (Honolulu, 1923), 14.

41. The Superintendent's office regularly had selections of the Japanese newspapers translated in order to keep abreast of sentiment in the Japanese community.

42. Reinecke, "Feigned Necessity," 402.

43. *Hawaii Hochi*, 23 February, 20 March, 21, 23, 25, 28 April, 3 May 1923.

44. Reinecke, "Feigned Necessity," 401–402.

45. Harada, "A Survey of Japanese Language Schools in Hawaii"; Onishi, "A Study of the Attitudes of the Japanese." *Meyers* v. *Nebraska*. Supreme Court of the United States, 1923. 262 U.S. 390, 43 S.Ct. 625; 67 L.Ed. 1024, 281–286. *Farrington* v. *Tokushige*. Supreme Court of the United States, 1927. 465 U.S. 273, 284–299.

46. Onishi, "A Study of the Attitudes of the Japanese."

47. This point is made by Oberschall, *Social Conflict and Social Movements*, 146–148.

48. Schermerhorn, *Comparative Ethnic Relations*, 130.

49. Fuchs, *Hawaii Pono*, 228–229.

3 Chinese American Contributions to the Educational Development of Toisan 1910–1940

Renqiu Yu

BACKGROUND OF EDUCATION IN TOISAN

CHINESE AMERICANS have always maintained a close relationship with their emigrant homeland. Since the 1850s, the majority of Chinese in the United States have sent remittances to support their families and relatives in China. They also sent money to establish schools, orphanages, hospitals, and other public institutions. In the Pearl River delta of Guangdong Province, from which the majority of Chinese emigrated, the economic and cultural influences of Chinese Americans on local communities are still quite visible. One outstanding example is the highly developed educational institutions of Toisan (Taishan) County, which have been supported by Chinese Americans for many decades.

From the middle of the nineteenth century, it is estimated that 80 percent of the Chinese who emigrated to the United States were from Toisan. Most of these emigrants were poor peasants displaced by political and social turmoil, famine, and poverty caused by the disintegration of the traditional agrarian economy due to foreign imperialist penetration of China.[1]

With large-scale emigration, overseas remittances became an increasingly important part of Toisan's economy.[2] According to rough estimates of local Toisan historians, yearly remittances from America to Toisan from the turn of the century to 1949 (exclusive of the war years, 1937–1944), exceeded the annual value of the county's agriculture output. In the 1920s and the early 1930s, remittances to Toisan from America constituted one-eighth of the national remittances which China received from abroad.[3]

Remittances were used by Toisan families first for necessities. After meeting basic living expenses, any remaining money was spent for the children's education. Chinese parents hoped that through education their children would become scholar-officials, a traditional ideal.

As more emigrant families were able to afford schooling for their children, the number of schools in Toisan increased. Before 1910, education took two forms. One form was the *sisuk* (*shishu*) in which scholars were hired by one or more families to teach their children. Pupils were taught the rudiments of Chinese classical works in classrooms located usually in one of the pupil's homes or in the local Confucian temple. The tutors were paid regularly, often on a monthly basis, either in cash or rice and meat. Sisuk flourished in villages of large emigration in part because remittances could be used to pay the tutors.[4]

From *Amerasia Journal* 10 (1983): 47–72. Reprinted with permission of the Regents of the University of California and the UCLA Asian American Studies Center.

After finishing their studies in sisuk, pupils who did well would take competitive examinations for *siyuen* (*shuyuan*) or academies of classical learning. Students studied the essential works of Confucian philosophy, poetry, calligraphy, and the writing of the "eight-legged essay" in preparation for examinations to enter the government bureaucracy. Those who passed the national examinations would be appointed to administrative positions in the central, provincial, or local governments. Those who failed either went back to the siyuen to review for the next examinations or to the countryside to work as a sisuk tutor.

Before the 1860s, Toisan had only five siyuen. Six more were established in 1869. By the turn of the century, the *Sunning Yunchi* (*Xinning Xianzhi*) or *Toisan Gazetteer* recorded more than twenty siyuen in most of the major towns of the county. Again remittances played an important role in providing for the students' tuition and board. Because of this educational system, it is estimated that about 90 percent of the adult males in the county were more or less literate by 1910.[5]

After the birth of the Republic of China in 1911, the government embarked on the development of a modern educational system which would teach about democracy, modern industry, trade, and agriculture rather than prepare students in the classics. The reform movement also called for the building of new elementary schools. As a result, by 1920 there were 104 elementary schools, two middle schools (one junior high, one women's teachers middle school), one trade school, and one women's elementary school in the county. Except for the Toisan County Middle School and the Toisan County Women's Teachers School, which were publicly financed by the local government, all other schools were privately funded and administered. U.S. Toisanese provided most of the financial support for the private schools.

During this period, the local government ordered each clan or village to allocate a portion of its ancestral lands for the construction of its own school. The school movement was supported by advocates of educational reform but encountered stormy opposition from some traditional clan leaders. Beleaguered by stubborn infighting and meager funds, many schools turned to the U.S. Toisanese to carry out their school building plans.

Fund-raising was divided into two stages. In the first stage, village and clan leaders held discussions on how to obtain money for the school, and often took the lead in donating money. At the same time wealthy persons such as shopkeepers, merchants, and the relatives of overseas Chinese were persuaded to donate. The local clan elite, who usually controlled the village remittance agencies, knew each family's financial capability. The second stage consisted of donation campaigns targeted at the Toisanese especially in the United States, which will be discussed in detail later in the essay.

Despite increased school building following the establishment of the Republic, three major factors hindered educational reform until after 1920. First, several gangs of bandits terrorized the county from 1913 onwards.[6] They robbed mainly American returnees and wealthy merchants and later kidnapped teachers and pupils for ransom. In 1922, for example, the united Lee, Wong, and Woo (Li, Huang, and Wu) clans' Nam Chuen (Nancun) school in the Sze Kou (Sijiu) region were attacked. Two teachers and fifteen pupils were taken hostage and held for half a year. A ransom of $10,000 for the two teachers and $2,700 per student was demanded and paid.[7]

Second, the fierce machinations and competition of local elites for control of schools hampered new construction and the implementation of reforms. These elites regarded building a school in their village or region as a means to enhance their power in the local community. Infighting forced some schools to shut their operations after only one or two years.

Third, during World War I the exchange rate of the American dollar to the Chinese dollar declined. U.S. Toisanese were reluctant to remit their hard-earned monies to Toisan because of the decline in buying power.

The next two decades constituted a golden age for the educational development of Toisan and the building of schools. A "reforming, vitalizing, and universalizing" educational reform movement was begun. Under the leadership of Lau Choi Po (Liu Zhaipu), a reformer and supporter of Sun Yat-sen, Toisan was granted status as an autonomous county under the Revolutionary Guangdong Government. Autonomy empowered the county government to promote educational reform. From 1922 to 1926, the county education bureau directed its efforts to closing down private elementary schools and organizing and building modern schools. The number of old-style elementary schools decreased while modern schools increased dramatically. By 1920, there were four middle schools in the county, rising to eleven, including two vocational schools, by 1928.

The case of vocational schools illustrates the significance of overseas donations and of American returnees in the county's development. In 1928, the first telecommunication school in Guangdong province, the Jaiwa (Zhaihua) vocational school was founded through the fund-raising efforts of Wong Jaiwa (Huang Zhaihua). Wong, who went to the United States at the age of fifteen, graduated from Columbia University and returned to Toisan in 1927. He began the campaign to establish the telecommunication school while teaching English in the Toisan Middle School. The vocational school trained many technicians for the county's transportation and telephone companies.[8]

In addition, the number of elementary schools in the county jumped rapidly from 104 in 1920 to about 1,000 in 1928. Most of these 1,000 village elementary schools were built and controlled by members of a single clan. There were also other types of elementary schools such as the united clan or regional schools built by several clans in the same region. School size varied from the small village clan school of twenty pupils and one teacher for three grades to the united clan school with several hundred pupils and several dozens of teachers. The size of a school depended on the number of children of school age in the area, and the amount of financial support garnered from the U.S. Toisanese.

In the 1920s and 1930s, massive donation movements aimed at the U.S. Chinese were launched with successful results. During this period, the number of Toisan schools, including elementary and middle schools, was three to four times greater than those in neighboring emigrant counties such as Hoiping (Kaiping), Shuntak (Shunde), Sunhui (Xinhui), and Chungshan (Zhongshan). Until World War II, and thereafter until 1949, Toisan schools continued to obtain financial aid from the U.S. Chinese, much of it to rebuild schools which had been destroyed by the Japanese.[9]

MOTIVATIONS OF DONATING SCHOOL FUNDS

In order to understand why Chinese emigrants financially supported schools in Toisan over many decades, we must examine the political and historical circumstances both in China and America.

THE EDUCATIONAL REFORM MOVEMENT AND THE EMIGRANT HOPE OF MODERNIZING CHINESE SOCIETY

Shortly after the first Chinese emigrants entered America, a number of laws and ordinances were enacted to restrict and finally to exclude them.[10] Although Chinese Americans contributed greatly to the development of the American West, they were treated harshly by the U.S. government and by the dominant society. Discriminated against and persecuted, the Chinese were denied naturalization. Exploited by American capitalists, they were limited to certain occupations such as laundries, restaurants, and domestic services. Isolated from the mainstream of American life, they were confined for the most part to ghettos in large cities, so-called Chinatowns. The Chinese in America were not only denied their legal rights by the U.S. government, but also lacked the protection of the Qing government, the last of the feudal Chinese dynasties.

Beginning in the 1840s, successive defeats of the Qing imperial armies in wars with Britain, France, and Japan had rendered the dynasty impotent. By the end of the nineteenth century, progressive Chinese intellectuals, searching for a way to save China from further penetration, proposed political and economic reform, rebuilding of the army, and the importation of advanced Western technology. At the same time, scholars, especially those who had received their higher education in Japan or the West, demanded a complete overhaul of the educational system.

The advocates of educational reform regarded it as vital to the future of China. They strongly criticized the traditional examination system for destroying the health of young people and blocking the development of a national spirit. If the Chinese adhered to traditional educational and social institutions, they warned, the people would inevitably become the slaves and subordinates of foreign powers.[11]

Confronting pressures from within and without, the Qing government was forced to accept demands for educational reform. In 1898, the emperor issued decrees to abolish the traditional essays, calligraphy, and poetry required for the *fokoi* (*keju*) examination. In 1903, for the first time in Chinese history, an imperial school charter was published which provided a uniform school code for the nation. In 1905, the central government established a board of education to administer nationwide educational reform. In the following year, each province and county formed its own education committee to help build modern schools under its own jurisdiction.[12] After the Republican Revolution of 1911, the construction of modern schools was facilitated.

The founding of the Republic in 1911 raised the hopes of U.S. Chinese for a modern nation-state. By supporting the reform movement, they believed that their contributions to China would eventually be rewarded. In addition, the U.S. Chinese hoped that a powerful China would assist them in bettering their lot in America. They were especially influenced by the idea "develop education to save China."

The modern Chinese education movement influenced the people of Toisan on both sides of the Pacific. As early as 1908, a number of progressive Toisan scholars founded an "Education Association" in order to promote modern education and reform Toisan's politics, economy, and society.[13] Their organ, the *Sunning* magazine (*Xinning Zazhi*) published many editorials, commentaries, and articles to promote the educational development of the county. From 1911 to the 1930s, almost every issue of the magazine included articles or news discussing and reporting various education issues.

The U.S. Chinese had great expectations for the educational institutions in their home county. One U.S. Toisanese presented a perspective in 1925 that reflected the sentiments of his fellow countymen. In an article urging the U.S. Chinese to contribute to educational development in the county, Lau Ying Lun (Liu Yinlun) stated that education was the basis of democratic politics and economic development in a modern country, which was proven by the experience of the advanced Western nations. In order to modernize China, it was necessary to universalize education. Since the economic situation of Toisanese in the U.S. was relatively better than that of people inside China, Lau reasoned, the U.S. Chinese should donate money to advance education in Toisan. Modern schools would develop human resources for industry and agriculture, and provide jobs for people. Lau stated in a painful tone, "Our descendants will have a means to survive in our native place. They will not, as we did, have to go to foreign countries and become slaves to other nations just for survival." He emphasized that donating to local Toisan schools was a way to save China from the imperialist powers and contribute to the nation.[14]

The Emigrant Desire to Provide Welfare and Improve the Education of Their Kin in Toisan

Before World War II, the majority of Chinese in the United States were poor, single, able-bodied men. Because of U.S. exclusion laws, they could not bring wives and children with them. Chinatowns remained "bachelor societies" for many decades. Deeply concerned about their families' welfare in Toisan, many of these emigrants regularly remitted hard-earned savings towards the education of their children.[15] Some emigrants, in light of their impoverished experiences in America, hoped that their children with an education would find decent jobs and remain in China.[16] Other emigrants, even though they planned for their children to later join them, still wanted to provide them with an education. In Toisan, many sons of emigrants were called "*yi sai jau*" (*er si zu*) or fops because of their extravagant behavior. Living on remittances from America, these young men became gamblers, alcoholics, and drug addicts.[17] Distressed at hearing shameful stories of their sons, emigrants hoped that a well-administered school would educate their children in correct behavior. One emigrant from the Holong (Helang) region, to cite an example, wrote a letter to the head of the Wenjiang school along with his donation, saying, "My son is now studying at your school . . . I would be grateful to you if you give him earnest teachings and strict discipline. It is my hope that my son will become a useful man. . . ."[18]

The Emigrants' Desire to Expand the Influences of Their Clan in the Local Community

Numerous researchers of Chinese communities in the United States suggest that people from Guangdong had very strong regional and kinship ties.[19] In 1854, Toisan emigrants in the United States founded their own district association, the Ning Yung Association (Ningyang Huiguan), which had the largest membership of any U.S. Chinese district associations. According to one observer's account, in 1876 the Ning Yung Association had 75,000 members.[20] This indicates that people from Toisan exceeded over half of the total Chinese population then in the United States (111,971).[21] With such a large membership, the Ning Yung Association became the most powerful of the seven Chinese district associations and had a bigger voice in the Chunghwa Chung Association (Zhonghua Huiguan), which was the collective organization of all Chinese district associations in America.

Of Chinese Americans from Toisan, about 10,000 bearing the surname Yee (Yu) did not join the Ning Yung Association because of disputes with Toisanese of other surnames. Instead they joined together with the people of Hoiping and Yanping (Kaiping and Enping) to form the Haapwo Association (Hehe Huiguan) with the Yees constituting about half the membership.[22]

In addition to the district associations, Toisan people also established clan organizations. The clan organizations were usually organized by people of the same surnames, such as the Yee Fongchoitong (Yu Fengchaitang), by the Yee clan; the Muisih Gongsoh (Meishi Gongsuo), by the Moy (Mei) clan; the Leisih Gungsoh (Lishi Gongsuo), by the Lee (Li) clan; and so forth. To counteract the power of large clans, several smaller clans would combine. For example, the Lau (Liu), Quon (Guan), Cheung or Jeong (Zhang), and Chow (Zhao) organized the Lung Gong Gungsoh (Longgang Gongsuo) in America and functioned as one clan.[23] Like the district associations, the main functions of the clan associations were to take care of new immigrants and settle disputes among members. The clan organizations were strong and historically controlled some of the smaller Chinatowns, such as the Lee clan, which dominated Philadelphia; the Yee clan in Pittsburgh; the Moy clan in Chicago; the Quon clan in Sacramento, and so on.[24] The U.S. Toisanese district and clan organizations played a very important role in maintaining relations with Toisan and promoting educational development there.

Before the 1930s, the Ning Yung Association always invited gentry from Toisan to act as the association president.[25] Although the presidents did not hold real power because of their ignorance of Chinatown affairs, they greatly influenced support for construction projects in their home county.[26] For example, at the first annual conference of the Ning Yung Association in 1928, new regulations clearly stated the organization's purpose was "to protect Ning Yung Association members' interests in America and to promote public welfare constructions in Toisan."[27] The Toisan clan organizations also encouraged their members to donate to their own clan's public welfare in Toisan.

Many clans regarded building modern schools as an important measure of the clan's development. Especially after the educational reform movement of the 1920s, having a modern school became one criterion for judging a clan's prestige. A letter regarding school fund donation reflects this tendency in Toisan. The Gee (Zhu) clan in Hoiyin (Haiyan) region stated worriedly that, "Education is related to the prospects of a country. It is also true to a clan. . . . We Gee people now have only few small schools, it's such a great shame! If we do not make efforts to develop our clan's education, our children will become illiterate and incompetent, and our clan will disappear. . . ."[28]

Table 1 shows that of the total 1,122 schools in the county in 1931, 1,113, or 99.2 percent, were private schools. Only nine schools, or .8 percent, were public schools. The overwhelming majority of the private schools were clan schools.

FUND-RAISING METHODS

From the beginning of the modern educational reform movement in Toisan in 1908, the planners of schools would send *gwin chak* (*juance*) or *yuen bou* (*yanbu*) known as money-collecting booklets, to U.S. Chinese communities. The booklet was a kind of roster of donors with the stated purpose of collecting money for building schools. After receiving the booklets, U.S. clan members were persuaded to donate, and their names were added to the roster. The booklets were eventually sent back to Toisan along with the collected money. After the construction of a school, the names of donors were carved on a "memorial stone tablet" extolling the donors' deeds and spirits and placed in front of or inside the school.

Many clan or village elementary schools were built in this way. For example, as early as 1913, the Kwong Tai (Guangda) School in Kwong Tai village received 20,000 Chinese silver dollars from the U.S. Toisanese from Kwong Tai and built a two-storied Western-styled school building.[29] In 1915, after ten years of construction, the Chung Ying

Table 1. Number of Schools, Students, and Teachers in Taishan, 1931

Type of School	Public Schools	Students	Teachers	Private Schools	Students	Teachers
Middle School	1	737	50	4	597	73
Middle Teachers School	2	973	72	3	257	35
Vocational School				2	315	23
Nurse School	1	18	10			
Kindergarten	1	46	3			
Elementary School	4	1,190	45	1,104	71,858	2,517
Total	9	2,964	180	1,113	73,027	2,648

Source: Taishan County Government Bulletin, vol. 3, June 1931.

(Zhongying) School was founded in Tikhoi (Dihai), supported by the powerful Toisanese Yu Fungchoitong.[30] Even the county public school, the Toisan County Middle School, which suffered from insufficient funds, considered the possibility of collecting money from overseas Chinese communities.[31]

During the period of the 1920s and the early 1930s, sending money-collecting booklets to the United States was still the primary method that most civilian-administrated schools utilized to collect school funds. However, several new features of the *chaufoon* (*choukuan*) or fund-raising movement appeared with the rise of the educational reform movement.

One of the most common and effective methods was to publish a magazine. From the 1920s on, several dozen clan or regional magazines were published in Toisan, performing a key function in the overseas school fund-raising movements. The vast majority of the magazines were related to the construction of schools. The editors and contributors of the magazines were usually school teachers and members of the education committees. Some magazines were published solely for the purpose of building schools and collecting school funds.[32] These magazines discussed the financial difficulties of construction; compared clan schools; and criticized conservatives opposed to reform. More importantly, overseas fellow countrymen were urged to donate and have their names and the amount of their donations published.

As the educational reform movement progressed in Toisan, education committees in various regional villages devoted their efforts to collect a large amount of money to establish a Western-style school building. Rural modern elementary schools built in Toisan before the 1920s were usually located in Confucian temples or other temples such as *Kwantai* (*Guandi*). At these temples, sacrificial rites often hampered the regular school activities.[33] Moreover, these temples were old and shabby, and vulnerable to rains and winds. Many elementary schools were forced to shut down due to dilapidated building conditions.[34] School planners in the 1920s thus tried to collect as much money as possible to establish durable and permanent buildings.

To encourage donors, a variety of rewards were created. Carving the donors' names on a "memorial stone tablet" was popular. Donors' names were published in local clan or village magazines and some schools erected monuments with porcelain pictures of donors (which were manufactured in Japan).[35]

For those U.S. Chinese whose donations exceeded the usual amount, special rewards were designed. For example, the Toisan County Middle School designated twelve different rewards for donors according to the amount of their donations. Porcelain pictures of those who donated more than fifty dollars were displayed in a memorial hall. Ten sizes of porcelain pictures ranging from four to twenty-six square inches were developed according to the amount of the donation. Those who donated over $15,000 were granted two permanent tuition waivers for their children or relatives, while donors of $10,000 received one permanent tuition waiver, and donors of $5,000 were granted one tuition waiver for ten years only. Every donor of over one hundred dollars received a memorial button and every donor of over five dollars had his name carved in a memorial hall. Those who donated less than five dollars had their names published in local magazines or newspapers, as well as newspapers published in America, such as *The Chinese World* in San Francisco. When the school building was completed, all donors received a memorial booklet.[36]

Other schools devised different types of rewards. If one individual donated a large amount of money to a school, a memorial tower or hall would be built in his name. If a school was built solely by one individual's contribution, the school would be named after the person, such as the Bakhing Elementary School in Daosan (Doushan) region. Built with the contributions of a Chinese American bourgeois, Chin Bakhing (Chen Boxin), the school still exists.

The rewards for school fund donors were supported both by the county and the provincial government. The education department of Guangdong Province issued a regulation in 1927 encouraging donations from individuals inside and outside China.[37] Chinese consulates abroad and local officers in China were responsible for investigating and reporting on overseas donors. Although the rewards to donors bestowed by the education department of Guangdong Province were only medals or certificates of merit, they were greatly valued as patriotic symbols.

To strengthen the belief among Chinese donors abroad that their donations would be used to build schools, Toisan people developed school building preparatory committees to handle the processes of collecting, receiving donations, and building schools. The members of the committees might include education reformers and prominent clan or village leaders in local communities who also enjoyed a reputation among clan members in the United States. The duties of the school building preparatory committees included: 1. the formation of a detailed plan for the school building; 2. the collection of school funds in the local community and the U.S. Chinese community; 3. registration of donors and distribution of rewards according to the amount of contributions; and, 4. the purchase of construction materials and supervision of the construction of the school. Upon the school's completion, a board of directors would be established to manage the school's operation. If the school had a shortage of funds, the directors would initiate another campaign to solicit money from the U.S. Toisanese.

The inclusion of many American returnees on the school building preparatory committees and the boards of directors greatly facilitated the building of schools. First, the returnees themselves were donors, and second, they could act as a bridge between the local people and the U.S. Toisanese, persuading them to donate when they returned to America.

Generally speaking, the returnees were more than willing to devote their efforts to their hometowns' educational development as well as to other public welfare facilities. They actively promoted the development of Toisan's educational institutions. In 1926, the returnees founded an Overseas Chinese Club to raise funds for the Toisan County Middle School in the Chinese communities of North and South America.[38]

Other Toisan institutions also supported the building of schools. For example, when the Toisan County Middle School was expanding its campus in 1924, it obtained the support of the Sunning Railway Company in the form of 20 percent discounts for one year on the transportation of building materials. Similarly, the Toisan Bricklayers' Association waived its "construction fee" which was usually levied on all construction within the boundaries of the county.[39]

CLAN SCHOOL FUND-RAISING CAMPAIGN IN THE UNITED STATES

Fund-raising activities in the United States took two forms. Toisanese clan organizations for several decades launched regular fund-raising campaigns among their members after receiving the money-collecting booklets from Toisan. The second form was more fascinating. The Toisan County public schools or the civilian regional united schools would send fund-raising representatives to America to launch donation movements with the support of the Ning Yung Association and clan organizations. Fund-raising of this nature mainly took place in the late 1920s and early 1930s.

In most cases, booklets from Toisan were necessary to arouse clan members to donate. But some clan organizations would collect and send money back to Toisan to build clan schools on their own initiative, especially when their clan's educational institutions were fewer than that of others.

After receiving money-collecting booklets from Toisan, the clan usually formed a school fund-raising committee comprised of prominent leaders, who acted as the supervisors, and volunteers, who acted as fund-raising advisors. Their duties were to encourage clan members to donate, to collect money, and to make a roster of donors. Because the U.S. Toisanese were dispersed throughout the United States, committee members were usually sent to the towns or cities where clan members resided.[40]

The two major clan methods of raising funds consisted of "membership" donations and "free will" donations. The first required every member of a clan to donate a set amount of money, usually five dollars.[41] In most cases, an individual was willing to donate the amount. Unwilling members might have their shops boycotted and were ostracized by clan members. In addition to a clan donation, everyone was encouraged to donate more to enchance the school fund, the "free will" donation. An extensive examination of donors rosters indicates that over half of the donors gave more than the minimum required.[42]

The donations were consolidated by the school fund-raising committee and sent back to the clan in Toisan. In the 1910s, donations were sent directly to the county. But from the 1920s on, the U.S. Chinese preferred to send the money to Hong Kong and entrust their clan members there to supervise the usage of the collected school fund. Their reluctance to entrust the funds to the local elites in Toisan stemmed from their experiences with campaigns such as the abortive Dwunfan (Duanfeng) School building.

In 1905, Moy clan members in America from the Dwunfan region initiated a fund-raising campaign to build a clan school in Toisan. The campaign amassed thirty thousand Hong Kong dollars and the clan sent the funds to Toisan. Unfortunately, the money caused fierce bickering and competition among the local elites. Each village tried to have the school built in its own region. The conflicts lasted for several years with no school constructed. Eventually the money was returned to the Moy people in the United States. Some U.S. Toisanese refused to take back their donations or threw the money to the ground; others swore angrily at the local elites whose selfishness had aborted the plans for the school.[43]

This episode gave the Moy people and other clan organizations in the United States a negative impression of the local elites. The U.S. Toisanese preferred to entrust their donations to the Hong Kong Toisan Businessmen's Association to supervise construction. As a consequence, during the educational reform movement of the 1920s, the Toisan people organized many "education committees" and "school building preparatory committees" to strengthen the donors' confidence. Nonetheless, it was not until 1932, almost thirty years after the Moy clan's first raised funds, that a middle school was built. The Dwunfan Middle School was one of the most splendid school buildings in the county.[44]

The U.S. Toisanese commonly sent representatives to oversee the building of larger clan or united regional schools. Representatives from America joined the school building preparatory committees as supervisors. Due to the great traveling expenses incurred which were subtracted from the donations, only one or two representatives were sent. Sometimes the responsibility was entrusted to people who were traveling to Toisan.[45] However, the representative supervised only the construction of the schools. After attending the inauguration ceremony, he would return to America, leaving the management of the school to a board of directors.

THE NING YUNG ASSOCIATION AND THE PUBLIC SCHOOL FUND-RAISING MOVEMENTS IN THE UNITED STATES

Compared to the fund-raising movements for clan schools, the campaign organization for the county public schools or the civilian regional united schools was more complex. In the late 1920s and the early 1930s, the three Toisan County public middle schools, The Toisan

County Middle School, The Toisan County Teachers' School, and the Toisan Women's Teachers' School, adopted the method of sending fund-raising representatives to America to raise funds. The civilian regional schools which included the Hong Wo (Kanghe) School and the Chisan (Jishan) Middle School also employed this method.[46] Because the Toisan County Middle School occupied a top position in the county educational system and its fund-raising movement in America was typical, this section will discuss the characteristics of the middle school's 1930 fund-raising campaign.

The Toisan Middle School, founded in 1909, was known as the *chui gou hok fu* (*zhuigao xuefu*) or the academic high of Toisan. Though its main source of finances was the county government's educational fund, its school buildings were built completely with the funds of Toisanese in the United States and Canada. In 1926, with the support of the Canadian Toisanese, the middle school constructed its first set of buildings.[47] In 1929, in response to the need of the many graduates from the newly developed junior high schools, the middle school set up a senior high section. The next year, the school launched a massive fund-raising campaign in U.S. Toisanese communities, in order to establish separate school buildings for a senior high section and to establish a permanent general operations fund.

Vital to the campaign was the selection of a fund-raising representative who had prestige in the local community and who possessed characteristics respected by the U.S. Toisanese. The fact that the Toisan County Middle School decided to send its principal to America for two years illustrates the importance of the position.

An important issue was how and by what means to solicit donations. Before going to America, the principal, Wong Tit Jang (Huang Tiezheng), developed a school building proposal with details on the expansion plan, the need for support from overseas countrymen, the amount of money needed, and the number of classrooms, student and teacher dormitories, and teaching facilities the donations could support (see Table 2). He wrote personally to the Ning Yung Association in San Francisco and its branches in other cities one month before he departed, stating the purpose of his trip and his hope that they would help him. He stressed that the school was the best in the entire Toisan school system and that the school's expansion was the hope of local people and also of fellow countrymen abroad. Although the county government was responsible for the school's finances, it lacked the funds to develop the school. Wong noted that the county government always delayed paying out its school fund and that it was in debt to the school. Thus, he stated, the only way the school could expand was to seek assistance from overseas. He urged the U.S. Toisanese, with their "long, glorious tradition of contributing to the development of the hometown," to contribute again to the school.[48]

Before Wong's departure, a variety of county organizations wrote support letters to the Ning Yung Association and other associations. Those who wrote included: the Toisan branch of the Guomindang (the nationalist party), and the Toisan County Autonomous Committee; the Businessmen's Association of Toisan, the Overseas Chinese Association of Toisan, and the Education Association of Toisan; the Chin, Wong, Yee, Lau, Lee, and Quon-Cheung-Chow clan organizations; the Toisan Student Association, and the Association of Toisan County Middle School Alumni.[49]

In addition, one letter was signed on behalf of the entire county and another on behalf of all the students and teachers of the Toisan County Middle School. It should be noted that even the head of the county, Lee Hoi Wan (Li Haiyun), wrote a letter to the Ning Yung Association and the Chinese Six Companies stating specifically that Principal Wong's campaign had been examined and endorsed by the county government.

Upon his arrival in San Francisco in October 1930, Wong went first to the Ning Yung Association to seek help. After the meeting, the association formulated a fund-raising char-

Table 2. Fund-raising Plan of the Taishan County Middle School, 1930[1]

A.	*Construction and Facilities* (Figures in Chinese dollars)	
	Senior High School Building	
	a. Common classroom	45,000
	b. Teacher's Training classroom	45,000
	c. Trade classroom	50,000
	d. Engineering classroom	15,000
	e. Agricultural classroom	60,000
	f. Student dormitory	80,000
	Library	150,000
	Science Center	100,000
	Sports Center	50,000
	Music and Art Center	40,000
	Young Overseas Chinese School	20,000
	Model Elementary School	25,000
	Kindergarten	20,000
	Spare-time School	20,000
	Dining Room	30,000
	Student's Shop and Bank	50,000
	Skill Training Factory	100,000
	Products Exhibition Room	20,000
	A large lounge	10,000
	Teacher and Staff Dormitory	15,000
	Memorial Hall and Clock Tower	40,000
	Overseas Chinese Guest House	15,000
B.	*Funds*	
	Permanent School Management Fund	1,000,000[2]
	Poor Students Tuition Waiver Fund	100,000[3]

[1]Fund-raising period was from January 1931 to December 1932. Two million Chinese dollars was equivalent to 500,000/American dollars.

[2]Funds were deposited in a bank, earning an annual interest of about 50,000 dollars which could be used only for school management.

[3]This amount was not in the original proposal. Money and interest could only be used for tuition waiver and for stipends to poor students. The amount per student ranged from five to thirty dollars per semester.

Source: Taizhong Banyuekan (Taizhong biweekly), vol. 31/32 (Taishan, 1931).

ter and established a general committee in San Francisco and branches in cities such as Portland, Seattle, Chicago, Boston, and New York.

The charter reveals the detailed organization of the fund-raising campaign. It consisted of twenty-one clauses related to the responsibilities and organization of committees for fund-raising; methods of collecting, depositing, and remitting the funds; and detailed items of different rewards for donors, etc. The charter stipulated that all donations should be remitted to the general committee in San Francisco and deposited in the American Trust Company. The money was drawn and remitted to Toisan only after the committee for the building of the middle school's senior high section mailed its budget to the general committee in San Francisco and after the signature of two-thirds or more members of the general committee had been obtained. The charter indicates that the Toisanese were very concerned about possible corruption in the course of fund-raising. One provision ruled that in cases of graft any person in America or China could be charged in court and his property confiscated as compensation.[50]

After the establishment of committees, Wong began his fund-raising travels to various cities. Accompanied by representatives of the general committee, he arrived in a city where the local fund-raising committee and the Ning Yung Association branch would usually host a welcome banquet. There Wong would state the purpose of his trip and urge his fellow countrymen to donate. The leaders of the Ning Yung Association branch or of the clan organizations, who were usually the wealthy merchants, then responded with a public donation to the school. The elites usually donated several hundred or even thousands of dollars.[51]

During his stay in a city, the principal and his committee went on a door-to-door campaign. If the donor gave more than fifty dollars, Wong requested a photo in order to make a porcelain picture. After each campaign, Wong mailed the donor roster to San Francisco to publish in *The Chinese World*, and sent the donations to the general committee in San Francisco.

From December 1930 to November 1932, *The Chinese World* frequently published the rosters of donors to the Toisan County Middle School. Examination of the rosters shows the majority of donors gave the obligatory five dollars. Thus it appears that except for a handful of wealthy merchants, most of the U.S. Toisanese belonged to the laboring class of laundrymen, cooks, domestic workers, restaurant workers, and so on.[52] Spurred by patriotism to donate to the home county's educational development, they were, however, limited by their incomes. Moreover, the Great Depression which began in 1929 severely reduced the employment of Chinese Americans.[53] Under the circumstances, the total amount of donations which the Toisan County Middle School expected—half a million U.S. dollars—seemed too high and the school building plan too ambitious.

Despite their limited financial capability, the U.S. Toisanese managed to donate $240,000.[54] By the end of 1932, Wong returned to China. Because the funds were far less than expected, the school reduced its construction plans, and eliminated plans for a permanent school management fund and a tuition waiver fund for poor students. Construction was finished in 1936, with the addition of a female student dormitory; a senior section teaching building; a library, museum, and memorial hall; and cemented roads, gardens, pools, and lampposts.[55] Although the school did not fully realize its original plans, its new buildings were the best in the county.

CONCLUSION

The massive U.S. Toisanese donation movement for building modern schools in Toisan occurred in an era of rising nationalism in China. Seeking to abolish foreign oppression, the Chinese on both sides of the Pacific sought to modernize China. The fund-raising movements were a response to the drive "to help education to save China." In Toisan, an extensive education reform movement corresponding to national educational policy developed in the 1920s. One aspect of this movement was to obtain financial aid from the U.S. Chinese utilizing a variety of methods. In America, the powerful Ning Yung Association, along with other clan organizations, actively promoted fund-raising efforts.

Over a period of almost forty years, between the 1910s and the 1940s, the U.S. Toisanese donated a great deal of money to build or rebuild schools in Toisan. Chinese emigrants in other places, such as South America and Southeast Asia, also contributed to a lesser degree.

The substantial, continuing financial aid of the U.S. Toisanese during the county's education reform movement in the 1920s made it possible to realize one of the movement's objectives: to universalize primary education in Toisan. Although schools were fewer in areas with less emigration, modern elementary schools could be found throughout the county. As a result, most children of school age were attending school, a great achievement in those times. Universal primary education created a large pool of students from which the middle schools could select. The Toisan County Middle School, therefore, could select the best graduates from elementary schools and train many excellent students. Many of its graduates of the 1930s and 1940s went to other parts of China, and became professors, musicians, engineers, doctors, and even chancellors and deans of universities.[56]

However, it should be noted that the development of middle schools in the county did not keep pace with the growth of elementary schools. Table 1 indicates that there were 73,048 pupils in elementary schools in 1931. But there were only 2,879 students in middle schools (junior and senior high schools, middle teachers' schools, and vocational schools). This seems to indicate that the middle schools could only absorb about 4 percent of the elementary school graduates. As a result, many graduates of elementary schools had to go to other places, such as Guangzhou, to seek middle education opportunities.

Table 1 also shows that in 1931 there were only four public elementary schools, while 1,104 village elementary schools were private. Of these private elementary schools, all were clan schools except for a few united clan schools. Indeed, many clan elementary schools built imposing buildings and hired qualified teachers. However, some clan elementary schools did not meet the academic standards established by the Department of Education of Guangdong Province. Every school had to apply for accreditation with local education authorities who were responsible for examining the academic standards of schools.[57] If the local education bureau approved a school's application, it would become a "registered school," officially sanctioned to operate. Denial of an application relegated the school to "unregistered" status. In 1919, 312, or 29 percent of the total schools in the county were unregistered. According to the accounts of the *Taishan Chun Po* of the 1920s, all these unregistered schools were clan schools. In theory unregistered schools should have been closed, but because they filled some gaps in the school system, the Department of Education allowed them to continue.

Another weakness in the Toisan educational system was the lopsided distribution of schools. Most of the schools with good equipment, sound school buildings, and qualified teachers were built in regions of higher emigration. Table 3 shows that in regions 2–11, where many Toisanese emigrated to the United States, schools were proportionately more numerous than in regions 12–19, where fewer people had emigrated to the United States or had gone to Southeast Asia.

The influence of U.S. Toisanese upon the county's educational development was mainly to provide great financial support for building ample, handsome school buildings. Overseas Chinese had little, if any, influence on Toisan's education in terms of curriculum or policy making. The whole county educational system followed the Guangdong provincial education regulations and national education decrees. Moreover, the U.S. Toisanese had only a general understanding of the kind of education necessary for the political and economic progress of the nation. Preoccupied with their own survival in America, they did not develop clear and systematic plans for modern educational development in Toisan. Nonetheless, without the school buildings and monetary support from the Chinese in America, modern educational reform in the county could not have been carried out.

In addition, by developing schools, the Toisanese abroad hoped to promote the growth of industry and agriculture in the county. They ultimately failed to realize their goal due to the complex relationship among the local bureaucracy, feudalism, foreign competition, etc., which is another topic in itself.

If the U.S. Toisanese wanted to develop industry and agriculture, why didn't they invest in them directly? Why did they actively fund schools but reluctantly invest in industry and agriculture?

Actually, at the turn of the century the U.S. Toisanese had made several investment attempts in Toisan. In 1910, an emigrant returned to the county with modern equipment

Table 3. Comparison of the Registered and Unregistered Schools in Taishan, 1929

Region	Registered	Unregistered	Total
1. Taichen	200	70	270
2. Chonglou	85	10	95
3. Gongyi	70	20	90
4. Xinchang	70	10	80
5. Dihai	50	25	75
6. Haiyan	40	35	75
7. Dufu	35	25	60
8. Shanhe	40	25	65
9. Beisha	40	30	70
10. Haikou	40	15	55
11. Chaojin	40	5	45
12. Nafu	5	30	35
13. Shangzhe	20	4	24
14. Guanghai	20	0	20
15. Xin'an	9	1	10
16. Shuzai	8	0	8
17. Shangchuan	1	7	8
18. Xiachuan	3	0	3
19. Zaimen	2	0	2
Total:	778	312	1090
Percentage:	71%	29%	100%

Source: The Taishan County Government Bulletin, Taishan, 1929, pp. 91–92.

and set up Toisan's first textile mill.[58] The products of the mill, however, could not compete with textiles imported from abroad. In the same period, Chin Yee Hee (Chen Yixi) had accumulated one and a half million U.S. dollars from his fellow countrymen to build the Sunning Railway, one of the three railways in China operated and built with private capital before 1949. From the construction of the first part of the railway, begun in 1906, the railway company suffered from chronic indebtedness. It was not until 1922 that the railway's shareholders received any dividends. Moreover, the Guangdong government's attempt to nationalize the civilian-administered railway in 1926 met with strong protest from local and overseas Toisanese.[59] Due to the railway's bureaucratic and fiscal problems, especially after the Great Depression, the U.S. Toisanese believed that economic investment in the county was a losing proposition.

In ensuing years, the Japanese invasion of Guangdong and World War II were factors which also hampered further large-scale investments by the U.S. Toisanese.

This essay suggests that historical research on Chinese Americans can be expanded by considering the political, social, and economic factors which exist in both China and America. Due to the long-term irregular relationship between the People's Republic of China and the United States, it has been difficult until recently for scholars in Chinese American studies to utilize local data in China. Attempting to fill this gap, the essay has utilized emigrant language materials to explore some of the factors which led to the development of school building and education in Toisan.

Further research would benefit from a closer examination of political and social conditions in Chinese American communities and in the broader society which affected the ability of the U.S. Chinese to contribute to the development of a modern education system in their emigrant homeland.

NOTES

(Chinese terms in the text are transliterated in Cantonese, with *pinyin* following. Footnotes are in *pinyin*.)

1. See June Mei, "Socio-economic Origins of Emigration: Guangdong to California, 1850–1882," *Modern China* 5:4 (1979), 463–501.
2. Betty Lee Sung, *The Story of the Chinese in America* (New York, 1971), 11–20.
3. *Taishan Xianzhi* (Taishan gazetteer), (Taishan, 1962).
4. *Ibid.*
5. Liu Xiaoyun, "The Plan to Rebuild Taishan," *Xinning Zhazhi* (Xinning magazine), 12 (Taishan, 1912).
6. *Taishan Xianzhi* (Taishan, 1962).
7. *Xinning Zhazhi*, 19 (1922), 10 (1923).
8. "Huang Zhaihua: A Patriotic Overseas Chinese," *New Siyi*, compiled by the Siyi Association, 3 (Hong Kong, 1980).
9. One example was that the Beishui Forth School obtained about 20,000 American dollars from the Tan clan members in the United States to rebuild itself in 1946. See *Beishui Disi Guomin Xiaoxue xiaokan* (The Beishui Forth School magazine), 1, (Taishan, 1947).
10. Thomas W. Chinn, ed. *A History of the Chinese in California* (San Francisco, 1976), 23–26.
11. Chen Qitian, *Jindai Zhongguo jiaoyu shi* (A history of modern China's education), (Taiwan, 1969), 70–74.
12. Chen Qingzhi, *Zhongguo jiaoyu shi* (A history of education in China), (Shanghai, 1936), 583–584.
13. *Taishan Xianzhi* (Taishan, 1962).
14. Liu Yinlun, "Pleading Fellow Countrymen from Taishan to Donate to Schools to Save China," *The Chinese World* (San Francisco), 21 July 1925.
15. Paul Siu, *The Chinese Laundryman, A Study of Social Isolation*, Ph. D. dissertation, University of Chicago, 1953, 158.
16. *Fengchai Yuekan* (Fengchai monthly), 37 (Taishan, 1946).
17. *Taishan Xianzhi* (Taishan, 1962).
18. *Wenjiang Yuebao* (Wenjiang monthly), 2–3 (Taishan, 1926).
19. Stanford Lyman, *Chinese Americans* (New York, 1974), 39–42.
20. Li Gui, *Huanyou diqiu xilu*, 3, 28–29.
21. Mary R. Coolidge, *Chinese Immigration* (New York, 1909), 498.
22. Liu Boji, *Meiguo Hwaqiao shi* (A history of the Chinese in the United States of America), (Taiwan, 1976), 172.
23. Rose Hum Lee, *The Chinese in the United States of America* (Hong Kong, 1960), 174.
24. *Ibid.*, 173–174.
25. Liu Boji, 174.
26. Liang Qichao, *Xindalu you ji* (Travels in the new world), (Taiwan, Wende Press, 1959).
27. The Proceedings of the First Convention of the Ning Yung Benevolent Association in America (San Francisco, 1928).
28. *Zhiyang Yuekan* (Zhiyang monthly), 8 (Taishan, 1946).
29. *Taishan Xianzhi* (Taishan, 1962).
30. *Fengchai Yuekan* 16 (Taishan, 1947).
31. *Ersi nian lai zhi Taizhong* (The Taishan county middle school in the past twenty years), (Taishan, 1928), 2.
32. See *Wenjiang Yuebao* (monthly publication of the Huang clan, first published in 1924); *Kanghe Yuekan* (a regional school magazine, 1926); *Zhouxin*, (publication of the Huang clan, 1929); *Dongken Yuekan* (monthly publication of the Li clan, 1927); *Xicun Yuekan* (monthly publication of the Kuang clan, 1930); and the *Yinchuan Yuekan* (monthly publication of the Chen clan, 1926), etc.
33. *Juzheng Yuebao* (Juzheng monthly), 5 (Taishan, 1930).
34. *Taishan Chun Po* (Taishan morning news), 3–12 (Taishan, 1921).

35. The earliest record of making porcelain pictures for school fund donors is in Lei Zhepu, *Shongxia shuxueji*, 3 (Taishan, 1923).

36. *Taizhong Banyuekan* (Taishan county middle school biweekly), 31–32 (Taishan, 1931).

37. *Xicun Yuekan*, "The School-building Special Issue, 1930." Includes the Regulation of Encouraging Donations to Building Schools of the Education Department of Guangdong province.

38. *Linghai Yinhang Ribao* (daily news published by a bank), 1:7 (Taishan, 1926).

39. *Taizhong xinxiaoshe dianji jiyanlu* (Taishan, 1926).

40. *Fengchai Zhongxue mujuan jijin zhengxin jiyance* (A commemorative book of fund-raising movement for Fengchai middle school), (San Francisco, 1949).

41. *The Chinese World* (San Francisco), 19 May 1925.

42. See *Kanghe Yuekan*, 3 (Taishan, 1930); *Fengchai Zhongxue mujuan jijin zhengxin jiyance*, (San Francisco, 1949); *Taishan Chun Po* (Taishan, 1922); and *Xinning Zhazhi* (Taishan, 1926–28).

43. *Duanfeng Zhongxue xiaokan*, a special issue of the Duanfeng middle school magazine, (Taishan, 1944).

44. *Duanfeng Zhongxue xiaokan*, 5 (1946).

45. *Yinchuan Yuekan*, 1 (Taishan, 1926).

46. *Juzheng Yuebao*, 5:2 (Taishan, 1930).

47. *Taishan Xianli Zhongxuexiao gailan*, (Taishan, 1926).

48. *Taizhong Banyuekan*, 31/32, (Taishan, 1931).

49. *Ibid.*

50. *Ibid.*

51. *The Chinese World* (San Francisco), 15 October 1932.

52. Kung Shien-woo, *Chinese American Life: Some Aspects of their History, Status, Problems, and Contributions* (Westport, Connecticut, 1973), 180.

53. "Meizhou jingji konghuang yu juankuan zi kunnan (The economic depression in America and difficulties in donating money)," *Juzheng Yuebao*, 5 (Taishan, 1930).

54. *The Chinese World* (San Francisco), 14 November 1932.

55. The records on the Memorial Pavilion for the U.S. Taishanese fund-raising for the Taishan County Middle School senior high section, 1936.

56. Interview with Wu Zhengquan, an old teacher of the Taishan County First Middle School (its predecessor was the Taishan County Middle School) on 28 December 1981. Wu gave the author a list of important alumni working in various parts of China.

57. The regulation was included in *Xicun Yuekan*, in its special school building issue, 1930.

58. *Taishan Xianzhi*, (Taishan, 1962).

59. Liu Yuzun, Cheng Luxi, and Zheng Dehua, "*Huaqiao, Xinningtielu yu Taishan*" (Overseas Chinese, the Xinning Railway, and Taishan) *Zhongshan Daxue Xuebao* (Journal of Zhongshan University), 4, (Guangzhou, 1980).

4 Lau v. Nichols: History of a Struggle for Equal and Quality Education

L. Ling-Chi Wang

ON JANUARY 21, 1974, the Supreme Court of the United States decided in the case of *Lau v. Nichols* that the failure of the San Francisco Unified School District (SFUSD) to provide special assistance to nearly 2,000 Chinese American students who do not speak English denies them "a meaningful opportunity to participate in the public educational program" and thus violates regulations and guidelines issued by the Secretary of Health, Education and Welfare (HEW) pursuant to Section 601 of the Civil Rights Act of 1964.[1] Recognizing the special educational needs and rights of limited English-speaking students for the first time in the history of the United States, the Supreme Court held that:

> ... there is no equality of treatment merely by providing students with the same facilities, textbooks, teachers, and curriculum; for students who do not understand English are effectively foreclosed from any meaningful education.

To expect limited English-speaking students to know English before they can effectively participate in the educational program, the Court declared, "is to make a mockery of public education." Addressing itself directly to the plight confronting non-English-speaking students, the Supreme Court Justices unanimously concluded, "We know that those who do not understand English are certain to find their classroom experience wholly incomprehensible and in no way meaningful." The Supreme Court sent the case back to the U.S. District Court in San Francisco with an order that "appropriate relief" be fashioned by the SFUSD and that it be subject to the approval of the court.

The purposes of this article are to trace briefly the history and issues leading to the Supreme Court victory, and the ensuing community struggle first, for the right to fashion the "appropriate relief" mandated by the Supreme Court and secondly, for the right to have quality bilingual-bicultural education for students of all language and cultural backgrounds.[2] The long struggle for the right to an equal and quality education and for community control of the school provides valuable insight and understanding into the nature and working of American legal and educational institutions and gives clues to future strategies for bringing about institutional and systemic changes in America.

HISTORY OF LAU V. NICHOLS

On March 25, 1970, Kinney Kinmon Lau and 12 non-English-speaking Chinese American students, over half of them American-born, filed suit in Federal District Court in San

From *Counterpoint* by Emma Gee, et al. (eds.) Los Angeles: Regents of the University of California and the UCLA Asian American Studies Center, 1976, pp. 240–259. Reprinted with permission of the Regents of the University of California and the UCLA Asian American Studies Center.

Francisco against Alan Nichols, president of the San Francisco Board of Education on be-half of nearly 3,000 Chinese-speaking students.[3] Their class action suit alleged that Chinese-speaking children were not receiving the kind of education to which they are entitled in the SFUSD because they needed special help in English. The denial of such an education, ac-cording to their parents, "doomed them to become dropouts and to join the rolls of the un-employed."[4] The plaintiffs asked the Federal District Court to order the Board of Education to provide special English language classes with bilingual teachers, asserting that laws en-acted by both Congress and the California State Legislature demonstrated the need for bilin-gual teachers. Without bilingual teachers, the plaintiffs contended that even special instruction in English would be a fruitless gesture: students would merely parrot teachers rather than learn English.

The suit was not developed in a vacuum; it was the last resort after all known chan-nels for seeking equal educational opportunity had been exhausted. For a number of years, the Chinese American community had tried innumerable meetings, heated negotiations, documented studies, peaceful and violent demonstrations, and concrete proposals to rec-tify the educational deprivation suffered by the limited English-speaking Chinese American students.[5] While the number of new immigrants entering the school system continued to escalate each year by leaps and bounds since 1962, these good faith efforts of the Chinese American community resulted invariably in token gestures. For example, no formal spe-cial language program existed in the elementary and secondary schools before 1966. In that year, the first pilot program of teaching English as a Second Language (ESL) was estab-lished. The program provided 40 minutes of ESL class each day for *some* of the limited English-speaking Chinese students. For the remainder of the day, they were required to at-tend regular classes taught only in English and compete helplessly and hopelessly with their English-speaking peers in all subject areas.[6] In San Francisco, this approach is known as the "ESL-pullout" or "one-a-day ESL bitter pill."

In the following year, the school district identified 2,456 limited English-speaking Chinese students and appropriated $88,016 to establish hastily a Chinese ESL Program, misnamed the Chinese Bilingual Education Program, staffed mostly by non-bilingual ESL teachers. Again, many Chinese-speaking students did not even get the minimal benefit of one ESL class a day. In 1968–69, the budget for the program was increased to $280,469, but the ongoing ESL program was found to be "woefully inadequate" according to SFUSD's own report, which was issued in February 1969. That report with the pretentious title of *The Education Equality/Quality Report* indicated that the program lacked ESL teachers (only 14 full-time teachers in elementary schools and 4 in junior high), an inadequate in-service teachers training program and a "language specialist on the administrative level to design an effective program that can be implemented in an orderly manner throughout all grade levels." The report also noted that ESL materials were "virtually non-existent beyond the beginning level" and that there was no personnel assigned to develop materials and cur-riculum. In spite of such mild self-indictment, the report dealt exclusively with ESL classes: it made no reference to the use of Chinese language as a medium of instruction and the need for the Chinese-speaking students at all grade levels to learn and progress academi-cally in other subject areas in a language they understood while they were in the process of acquiring English-language proficiency. Worse yet, the ESL program is always seen as an added program to the existing, regular school curricula, hence an added burden.

Illustrative of the indifferent attitude in San Francisco was the school district's ac-knowledgement of the following facts found by the Federal Court on May 28, 1970:[7]

1. 2,856 Chinese-speaking students in SFUSD needed special instruction in English.
2. Of these, 1,790 received no special help or instruction at all, not even the 40-minute ESL a day.

3. Of the remaining 1,066 who did receive some help, 623 received help on a part-time basis and 433 on a full-time basis.
4. Only 260 of the 1,066 receiving special instruction in English were taught by bilingual teachers.

Only one-fourth of the limited English-speaking Chinese students were getting help in English, most by non-bilingual teachers, and little or no help in other subject matters. Students were placed arbitrarily into classrooms by ages, irrespective of English-language proficiency and achievement in subject areas. The negative and demoralizing effects of this repressive approach were fully recognized by the school district. In a report issued in 1969, the school district freely admitted:

> When these (Chinese-speaking) youngsters are placed in grade levels according to their ages and are expected to compete with their English-speaking peers, they are frustrated by their inability to understand the regular work. . . . For these children, the lack of English means poor performance in school. The secondary student is almost inevitably doomed to be a dropout and another unemployable in the ghetto.[8]

Paralleling the deteriorating situation in the school district was the accelerating juvenile delinquency rates in the 1960s in the Chinese community. According to data released by the San Francisco Police Department, the juvenile delinquency rate for Chinese between 1964 and 1969 rose by 600%.[9] The school data admitted openly in the Federal Court and the police records clearly and directly related to the plight of these students.

During the District Court hearing on *Lau v. Nichols*, the school district acknowledged the grave needs of these children to receive special instruction, but vigorously contended that such needs did not constitute legal rights because they were provided the same educational setting offered to other children throughout the district. A bilingual education program, according to the attorney representing the school district, would be offered only "gratuitously," as personnel permitted, rather than as a matter of right and duty.

In its decision, the Federal District Court agreed with the school district and denied the limited English-speaking Chinese students any relief.[10] The Court expressed sympathy for the Chinese American students, but concluded that their rights to an education and to equal educational opportunities had been satisfied as "they received the same education made available on the same terms and conditions to the other tens of thousands of students in the SFUSD." It is important to point out that, though the Chinese American students contended that the "surface equality" of identical textbooks, teachers and classrooms afforded no education to non-English-speaking children, the Federal District Court ruled that the school district had no legal duty to rectify this situation.

The Chinese-speaking students appealed the decision to the U.S. Court of Appeals for the Ninth Circuit.[11] Their contention that the lower court decision should be reversed was supported by the United States Government, which filed an *amicus curie* (friend of the court) brief. However, a three-judge panel, in a two-to-one decision, affirmed the lower court order on January 8, 1973, and accepted the school district's argument that its responsibility to non-English-speaking children "extends no further than to provide them with the same facilities, textbooks, teachers and curriculum as is provided to other children in the district."[12] The panel further observed that the problems suffered by the Chinese American children were "not the result of law enacted by the state. . . . but the result of deficiency created by [the children] themselves in failing to learn the English language."

The implications of the appellate court decision were devastating: "surface equality" was ruled adequate and legal and the language deficiency of the non-English-speakers, as if they knew *no* language at all and possessed neither culture nor knowledge, was self-created and self-imposed. In other words, if they happened to be Native Americans, Chicanos, or immigrants from non-English-speaking countries, they were entitled to attend schools, but they had no right to expect the same educational benefits as the English speakers.

Faced with this disastrous decision, the Chinese American students petitioned the U.S. Supreme Court to take their case and reverse the appellate decision. On June 12, 1973, the Supreme Court granted the petition to hear the case and oral arguments were heard on December 10, 1973, again with the support of the U.S. Government and a number of national organizations representing educators and ethnic communities.[13]

Finally, on January 21, 1974, after nearly four long years of litigation, the U.S. Supreme Court delivered its *unanimous* decision which directly refuted both the position and language of the lower courts:

> . . . There is no equality of treatment merely by providing students with the same facil-
> ities, textbooks, teachers and curriculum; for students who do not understand English
> are effectively foreclosed from any meaningful education.

The limited English-speaking students, according to the Supreme Court decision, must be able to participate effectively in the classroom and they must receive an education that is both "meaningful" and "comprehensible." This could be achieved only through bilingual-bicultural education.

The significance of the *Lau v. Nichols* decision nationwide was immediately felt.[14] Not since the *Brown v. Board of Education* decision in 1954 which outlawed school segregation was there such an important decision on education handed down by the Supreme Court. There are, according to the U.S. Office of Education, approximately five million schoolchildren in the United States covered by the decision.[15] Congress immediately amended in August 1974 the bilingual education law by expanding Federal involvement in bilingual education[16] and the U.S. Department of H.E.W. announced in January 1975 its plan to conduct *Lau* enforcement activities nationwide to assure equal educational opportunity for the limited English-speaking students.[17] Nine "*Lau* Centers" were established under Title IV of the Civil Rights Act of 1964 to assist school districts across the United States to develop bilingual educational programs to meet the *Lau* mandate.[18] To help identify the precise number of children of limited English-speaking ability, H.E.W. initiated a project in June 1975 to develop language survey instruments.[19] States such as Massachusetts, Illinois, Texas, New Jersey and Colorado now have state laws mandating bilingual education for students of limited English-speaking ability.[20] To date, all court decisions which have applied and interpreted *Lau v. Nichols* have all concluded that *Lau* requires bilingual-bicultural education to overcome the deprivations suffered by the limited English-speaking children.[21] Similarly, in a first nationwide report on bilingual-bicultural education, the U.S. Commission on Civil Rights urged on May 13, 1975, that bilingual-bicultural education be provided for students of limited English-speaking ability.[22]

Beyond the impact on public education, the *Lau* decision has long-range legal implications on both the effectiveness and quality of government-sponsored social and legal services now provided to non-English-speakers across the nation. For example, the new Voters Rights Act of 1975 cited *Lau v. Nichols* as one of the bases for extending voting rights to non-English-speaking citizens.[23] Other issues will undoubtedly follow in the near future.

With a decision as far-reaching and significant as *Lau v. Nichols* on the future of education for limited English-speaking children, one naturally expected the SFUSD, the defendant in the case, to respond promptly and creatively to the educational needs of children from various language and cultural backgrounds, especially when the school district now had a chance to reorder its priorities and develop a meaningful educational plan in response to the Supreme Court mandate. As mentioned above, the Court remanded the case back to the Federal District Court in San Francisco and the SFUSD was expected to submit an "appropriate" educational plan for court approval. Unfortunately, the SFUSD acted as if it were under no court order for a long time. When confronted by communities in San Francisco to respond, it reacted with arrogance and contempt. It is to this phase of community struggle that we now turn.

COMMUNITY STRUGGLE FOR THE RIGHT TO FASHION REMEDY

Perhaps the most important educational and political development in San Francisco after the Supreme Court remanded the case back to the Federal District Court was the long struggle between the entrenched and unyielding school administration and the increasingly politicized minority communities over initially, *who* should be responsible for drawing up the "appropriate relief" plan mandated by the Court and subsequently, *what* is educationally and legally "appropriate" and "effective." The stuggle was predicated on the desire of the communities to have some control over the education of their children and a prevailing distrust of the school administration and Federal District Court's ability to define what was educationally important to their children. On the one hand, the school administration wanted to provide only the minimum required, meaning least costly, and above all, no parental and community input or interference if possible. On the other hand, the minority language communities in San Francisco, long alienated by a white-dominated political process and an irresponsive school bureaucracy, had no confidence in the school administration's competence and willingness to formulate an effective plan that would meet the educational and cultural needs of their children. What follows therefore is a sketch of how San Francisco community organizations and parents fought the school administration by forming a strong coalition of minority communities and won the right to fashion a citywide master plan for the education of the students from different language and cultural backgrounds, what they eventually defined as the most appropriate and effective response to the *Lau* mandate, and how they collectively won what was generally conceded to be a political impossibility for any minority group in San Francisco, the approval of the master plan by the Board of Education, the governing body long plagued by factionalism, indecisiveness and ineffectiveness.

In order to understand the gradual unfolding of the remedy phase of the *Lau v. Nichols* decision, it is essential to begin with a brief description of the San Francisco situation in terms of its diverse but declining population, overall language needs of its school population and the school administration's response prior to the *Lau* decision.

SCHOOL POPULATION CHARACTERISTICS

San Francisco as a city has long been known to be cosmopolitan. In addition to her Italian and Irish populations which long dominated San Francisco politics, there are numerous white ethnic groups and a rapidly increasing minority population. Like many old cities in the U.S., the population of San Francisco has been decreasing since 1950. Population figures of the city for the last three decades are: 775,357 in 1950, 740,310 in 1960 and 715,674 in 1970. Paralleling the population decline has been the rapid disappearance of manufacturing industries and sharp increases in white collar and service occupations, reflecting the new role of San Francisco as a headquarter for large corporations and a tourist/convention favorite.[24] According to one estimate, San Francisco had a population of 681,200 in 1973. (For the ethnic composition in that year, see Table 1.[25])

In absolute numbers and percentages, the white population has been declining rapidly while the opposite trend prevails for the minority groups, especially the Asian groups. In

Table 1. Ethnic Composition of the City of San Francisco, 1973

	Number	% of Total
White	361,300	53.0%
Asian American	117,500	17.2
Chinese	64,800	9.5
Filipino	38,000	5.6
Japanese	11,800	1.7
Korean	2,900	0.4
Black	99,000	14.5
Spanish surname	90,400	13.3
Other non-white	9,900	1.5
Native American	3,100	0.5

spite of these trends. the white population continues to have almost full control of the city's elected offices, appointed positions, and bureaucracies.[26]

A look at the school population reveals the same trends. In the 1973–1974 school years, the year of the Supreme Court decision, the SFUSD had a total student enrollment of 78,023, kindergarten through twelfth grade (see Table 2).[27]

Among the "Other non-whites" are Samoans, Arabs, Hindi, Burmese, Vietnamese, Pacific Islanders and others. This means that 73.1% of the students in the school district are from minority backgrounds, as compared to five years ago when the school district had only 58.9% minorities. In spite of such high percentage of minority school population, the administration of the SFUSD continues to be totally controlled by whites. Of the seven persons on the Board of Education, only two are from minority backgrounds, one Black and one Spanish-surname. This political reality of course has a tremendous bearing on the struggle for equal and quality education for students of limited English-speaking ability, as we shall soon see.

LIMITED ENGLISH-SPEAKING STUDENTS IN SFUSD

The dramatic decline of white student population and sharp increase of minority students, due largely to Chinese, Filipino and Korean immigration account for the changing student composition. In fact, court records on *Lau v. Nichols* showed an average net gain of 80 limited English-speaking students per month or 960 a year in 1969–1970. In 1969, the school district reported 5,269 limited English-speaking children. The number increased to 9,084 in 1973, or an increase of 72.4% in four years. Among these 9,084, 3,457 are Chinese, 2,980

Table 2. Ethnic Composition of the San Francisco Unified School District, 1973–74

	Number	% of Total
White	21,001	26.9%
Asian American	19,728	25.3
Chinese	12,315	15.8
Filipino	5,715	7.3
Japanese	1,304	1.7
Korean	394	0.5
Black	23,794	30.5
Spanish surname	11,131	14.3
Other non-white	2,103	2.7
Native American	266	0.3

Spanish-speaking, 1,519 Filipino, 202 Japanese, 179 Samoans, and 747 other languages.[28] Both immigration policy and government statistics to date point to a continuation of the patterns established since 1965.[29] In other words, the school district must reasonably expect the number of limited English-speaking children to increase steadily at approximately the same rate as in the past ten years.

In spite of this well-established trend, the school district reported a total of 6,511 limited English-speaking students in April 1974, an unexpected and unexplained drop of 29% in one year.[30] According to school data, 2,330 Chinese, 1,860 Spanish-speaking, 1,076 Filipino, 187 Koreans, 151 Samoans, 124 Japanese and 782 other languages made up the 6,511 figure. Subsequently, in a testimony before the Ways and Means Committee of the California State Assembly on December 10, 1974, Raymond del Portillo, Director of Bilingual Education Division of the SFUSD, gave new data which further reduced the 6,511 total to 4,911 limited English-speaking students, representing a net reduction of almost 100% between 1973 and 1974.[31] The unexplained reduction from 9,084 in 1973 cast serious doubts on both the results and methods of the annual state-mandated survey of students of limited English-speaking ability and raised questions on the intention and political implications of the reduction.[32] A closer examination of the raw data indicated that the initial computation in May 1974 yielded a figure slightly above 9,000—a figure more consistent with the well-established trend of the previous few years.

The conflicting figures underscore the importance of developing a more objective, reliable yardstick to conduct the annual census. For the time being, the method and figures are highly suspect. A check on the enumeration methods revealed that figures were arrived at by totalling the subjective judgment of some 2,500 classroom teachers, a method of questionable standardized character and scientific value. A culturally unbiased and linguistically sound device for detecting language proficiency must be developed to assess those students and to make precise determination of student placement and to devise the appropriate educational program best suited to their needs. If such a standardized device or test could not be formulated for each of the language groups in the near future, the increasingly favored method, and recently incorporated into the new Federal law on bilingual education, ought to be utilized. Instead of relying solely on individual teachers' impressions as has been done in San Francisco and elsewhere, a series of simple questions on each child's home language is used to provide the preliminary identification of his or her language proficiency.[33] A more thorough linguistic and academic assessment then follows. This method, in fact, was used by the SFUSD in 1972 and the outcome showed that there were 20,000 students whose primary languages were other than English.[34]

DISTRICT EFFORTS TO MEET THE NEEDS IN 1974

What was the SFUSD's response to the needs identified prior to the development of a new remedy as a result of *Lau*? In this section, these efforts will be examined in terms of the educational programs set up, the allocation of district funds for these programs, and the hiring of qualified bilingual personnel.

Regarding the educational programs available to limited English-speaking students, see Table 3 for the spring 1974 survey.[35] Of the 6,510 limited English-speaking students in 1974, 2,953 were getting the 40-minute ESL Pullout classes a day, and 2,853 were getting no assistance at all. Therefore, of the conservatively estimated 6,510 in 1974, only 704 were getting the full benefit of bilingual-bicultural education programs; the rest were getting either minimal or no benefit whatsoever.

As for the cost of providing these ESL programs for the limited English-speaking students, the data in Table 4 comes from the Division of Research in March 1974. The SFUSD figures on the surface show a substantial increase of expenditures towards the spe-

Table 3. Programs for Limited English-speaking Students

	ESL	BBE*	No Help	Total
Chinese	1,138	193	1,000	2,331
Spanish-speaking	604	454	802	1,860
Pilipino	524	49	503	1,076
Japanese	70	4	50	124
Korean	144	2	41	187
Samoan	50	2	98	150
Other Languages	423	0	359	782
Total	2,953	704	2,853	6,510

*Bilingual-Bicultural Education

cial education of the limited English-speaking students, from $809,168 in 1968–1969 to $2.4 million in 1973–1974, excluding the $982,390 from various State and Federal sources. To the school district, the $2.4 million was an additional cost beyond the funds already allocated for the education of the 6,510 limited English-speaking students. In other words, as long as the 6,510 students were occupying classrooms bodily every day during school hours, the district was required to provide full-time teachers and other costs for these classrooms regardless of their ability to communicate with and provide an education for these students. Since almost all the teachers present in these classrooms were non-bilingual, it would not be difficult to understand why the U.S. Supreme Court found such classroom experience "wholly incomprehensible and in no way meaningful." In other words, funds were being spent on these students and in these classrooms, but no benefit was being derived from such expenditures.

The $2.4 million spent on hiring administrators and ESL teachers was considered by the school district as *additional costs* or burden, an argument soundly rejected by the Supreme Court. A closer examination of how the district channeled its funds into the various programs reveals that only a small portion of this $2.4 million was spent in support of some of the State- and Federally funded bilingual program and the rest was used for hiring of teachers for the ESL Pullout and the ESL-oriented newcomers programs.[36] Such additional ESL teachers were necessary because the regular classroom teachers for the 6,510 students did not know how to teach English as a second language. Simple logic requires us to draw the conclusion that, if the classrooms occupied by the 6,510 limited English-speaking students were assigned bilingual teachers, the Supreme Court would not have found the school district in violation of the rights of these students and there would have been no need to have the floating ESL teachers creating an additional financial burden on the school district.

Table 4. Cost of ESL Programs for Limited English-speaking Students

Administration of Bilingual Office	$ 50,688
Chinese Program	975,122
Spanish Program	948,414
Pilipino Program	283,282
Japanese Program (Bilingual)	40,290
ESL Program at McAteer High	140,338
Total: District Programs	2,438,134
Total: Federal & State Funded Programs	982,391
GRAND TOTAL [All Programs]	$3,420,525

Whatever funds made available to start any bilingual program in the SFUSD, therefore, have consistently come from non-district sources, as the data from the Division of Research in March 1974 clearly show. For example, the district operated four bilingual-bicultural programs in that year:[37]

Chinese Bilingual Program (1-6): Federal
Chinese Bilingual Program (7-9): State
Spanish Bilingual Program (K-6): Federal
Japanese Bilingual Program (K-3): Fed. & District

The district's contribution to these bilingual programs was limited to one teacher, not necessarily with bilingual competency, for each Federally or State-funded bilingual class.

It is clear from the above analysis that the SFUSD has no commitment to provide bilingual-bicultural education for students of limited English-speaking ability.[38] The District would set up a bilingual program only on the condition that either the State or the Federal government provides the necessary funds. As a result of such policy, programs are set up not on the basis of needs and sound planning; they are established because certain Federal or State funds for various purposes happen to be available.[39] Programs, therefore, proliferate as funds flow in from different and varying sources and for assorted purposes, and programs may be abruptly terminated if their funding sources dry up.

Closely related to the effectiveness of any program designed for students of limited English-speaking ability is the availability of teachers who can communicate with students in languages they understand. That of course is the heart of education. The need for bilingual/bicultural teachers is self-evident. In 1974, the SFUSD employed more than 10,000 persons, serving its 73,040 students. Five years before that, it had 6,206 employees, serving 93,204 students. Of the 1974 employees, 4,572 are teachers, reflecting a net gain of 174 teachers, from 4,398 in 1969–1970 school year.[40] In terms of teacher-student ratio, this meant one teacher for every 24.5 students, or a drop from 25.4 five years before. As for the ethnic composition of the teaching staff, a recent survey shows the following: 73% White, 11% Black, 5% Spanish-surname, 6% Chinese, 2% Japanese, 2% Filipino and 1% Native American—a completely reverse proportion to the ethnic composition of the student population.

On account of the declining student enrollment in recent years, virtually no new teachers were hired in the past few years, except those hired with funds from Federal and State sources. Herein lies the difficulty of recruiting and hiring qualified bilingual teachers desperately needed to provide the kind of education needed by students of limited English-speaking ability. With most school districts in the nation facing virtual bankruptcy and being forced to lay off teachers, San Francisco is no exception; most of the minority teachers recruited in the past few years undoubtedly will be the first to be let go. This will have adverse effects on the few bilingual programs now operating in the SFUSD. It would indeed be a tragedy if teachers were to be pitted against minority teachers and communities.

This sketchy program and budget analysis demonstrates clearly a serious contradiction between district policy and action. On March 16, 1972, the Board of Education committed itself to provide bilingual-bicultural education to students of limited English-speaking ability.[41] The above review indicates that less than 10% of such students are receiving bilingual-bicultural education, over 30% are getting no help at all, and the remainder (55.3%) are deriving only minimal benefit, one out of six classes a day, through the ESL Pullout program.

Furthermore, the Board, through its budgetary decisions, has consistently failed to commit district funds for bilingual-bicultural education. Instead, it has allowed bilingual-bicultural programs to exist mostly on Federal and State funds. In 1974, the school district contributed less than 3% of its own $148 million budget toward bilingual-bicultural programs. Faced with these glaring contradictions, we must inevitably conclude that the district has thus far assigned a very low priority to the educational needs of children of limited English-speaking ability.

Perhaps the most disturbing part of this analysis is the indifference shown in the budget decisions. The school enrollment dropped 21.6% in the five-year period before 1974. However, there was no comparable decline in the number of students of limited English-speaking ability; in fact, that number increased over the same period. Within this same period, the district budget increased from $120 million to $148 million a year, or the cost per student rose a spectacular 58%, from $1,286 to $2,035. If we use a rough estimate of 10,000 limited English-speaking students in the district, the amount of money appropriated for meaningful bilingual education programs in 1974 should have been at least $20 million instead of the $2.4 million cited above. If the students of limited English-speaking ability are not getting the full benefit of public education, as the Supreme Court ruled, then it is clearly the responsibility of the Board to make sure that they do, and to see that district funds are used properly to achieve the kind of educational results expected by the Court.

CREATION OF THE CITIZENS TASK FORCE

With these kinds of political and educational conditions existing in San Francisco, it was not surprising that the communities with most to gain—the Chinese, Filipino, Japanese, Korean and Spanish-speaking communities—greeted the Supreme Court decision with jubilation and great expectation while the San Francisco Board of Education reacted with a typical evasive, non-committal statement and inaction.

In a press statement issued on February 5, 1974, Eugene Hopp, President of the Board of Education, expressed "hope" to work with the community on a program to be submitted for approval to the Federal District Court. He said that the Board "will probably propose a Committee of the Whole hearing to provide a means of communication for the parents." The district staff, according to Hopp, was directed to proceed with "a study of the problem along with an inventory of the present program and then develop a program to present to court." The hearing did not take place until January 28, 1975, a year later; even then, it was used as a parliamentary maneuver to delay a decision on the master plan submitted to the Board on January 7, 1975, by the Citizens Task Force on Bilingual Education. However, the study and program mentioned in the press release were initiated immediately under strict secrecy and revealed on April 15, 1974, at a meeting of a group of 44 parents and citizens called in by Raymond Del Portillo, Director of Bilingual Education, to rubber stamp the proposed program by the district staff. Needless to say, no community group, parents or teachers were consulted in the formulation of the program. In fact, the school administration ignored any community offers of assistance or input. To make the situation worse and more divisive, someone was spreading a rumor that the Chinese community was trying to use the court decision to seize control of the district's bilingual funds and programs.[42] The rumor greatly incited fear among the Spanish-speaking parents active in the cause of bilingual education and effectively frustrated various ethnic groups from working together for a common cause.[43]

The first community organization to take an active part in leading the fight for full community control of the formulation of the plan was Chinese for Affirmative Action (CAA), a community-based civil rights organization with extensive experience in dealing with education and employment problems facing the Chinese in San Francisco.[44] Through a series of consultations and meetings within the Chinese community, a two-page position paper was developed by early February 1974 and formally transmitted to the Board of Education on February 15.[45] The position paper contained a list of concrete school problems related to the *Lau v. Nichols* decision and a series of recommendations to the Board of Education for consideration. Essentially, the heart of these recommendations was a proposal that the Board appoint a Citizens Task Force on Bilingual Education "to develop a city-wide master plan for bilingual education for the purposes of (a) complying with the order of the U.S. Supreme Court, (b) submitting it to the U.S. District Court for approval and (c) meeting the educational needs of *all* limited English-speaking students otherwise not covered by the original order."[46] According to the proposal, the Task Force would not be made up of just Chinese Americans, but representatives from the various languages in San Francisco. The position paper further outlined the responsibilities of the Citizens Task Force.

The Board of Education, not surprisingly, ignored the letter. On March 19, 1974, another letter was sent to the Board of Education, reiterating the recommendations and at the same time requesting information on "the specific steps the Board planned to take to implement the Supreme Court mandate."[47] Again the letter was ignored.[48] This perhaps is the most arrogant expression of the Board's utter contempt of community organizations.

It is important to point out here that CAA did not work in isolation. Over a thousand copies of the position paper were sent to individuals and community organizations throughout the city for support and endorsement. In addition, CAA also sent letters to both state and Federal government officials, urging their support and intervention to assure community participation in the planning process and quality education in the final plan. By early May, or three months after the *Lau* decision, many community organizations and civic leaders had endorsed the recommendations and sent letters to the Board of Education urging the same. Among them were: the San Francisco Human Rights Commission, Coalition for Effective Schools, Asian Education Caucus and some school district bilingual education advisory committees. In addition, almost all of the state and federal elected officials representing San Francisco and many television and radio stations joined in a concerted effort to urge the Board to set up the Citizens Task Force. The only opposition came from a very small handful of high-level school administrators who stubbornly hung on to the secret plan then under way and flatly refused to deal with the broadly supported community proposal.

The demand of parents and community organizations received unexpected, indirect support from the California State Superintendent of Public Instruction, Dr. Wilson Riles, who told the press in Washington, D.C., that the performance of the San Francisco school system was "an embarrassment" to him as the head of the California school system.[49] Riles was referring to the fact that the San Francisco school district spent more money per capita than most school districts in California, but its reading and achievement levels were consistently the lowest in the state.[50] His remark received extensive headline coverage in San Francisco for a few days and generated public outcries for improvement of the school system.[51] The bad publicity lent credence to the community demand for the creation of a Citizens Task Force and for some voice in the future of the children in San Francisco.

As outside and citywide pressures mounted rapidly and the administration tried frantically to complete its secret plan, the April 15 meeting was suddenly called by Del Portillo. Forty-four parents and citizens known to be interested in bilingual education were asked to "advise" the district on "the overall planning and coordination of the programs that (would) serve the needs of non-English-speaking and limited English-speaking students in San Francisco."[52] At that meeting, the invited citizens, already angry about the poor performance of their schools and the Board's indifference and arrogance, were told that they constituted the "Special Advisory Committee on *Lau v. Nichols*" and were presented a 53-page "preliminary Report to Dr. Lane DeLara on Bilingual/ESL/Newcomer Staff Response to Implications of *Lau v. Nichols*," dated April 3, 1974.[53] The report, prepared by an Anglo administrator, included a narrow interpretation of the Supreme Court decision, descriptions and costs of some 15 existing ESL/Bilingual programs, a series of recommendations, and a timeline which anticipated the presentation of a final plan to the Board of Education on May 14, 1974—29 days after the April 15 meeting!—for adoption. The plan, put together in utmost secrecy, essentially called for the maintenance and slight expansion of the *status quo* to meet the *Lau* mandate. According to the time line, the Director of Bilingual Education was to submit the whole package to the Superintendent Steven Morena on April 26, 11 days after the April 15 meeting. In other words, the parents and citizens were invited that night to rubberstamp the plan prepared in secret by a white school administrator. It soon became clear to most of those present at the meeting that the complete silence that greeted the community proposal was part of an overall school strategy to keep parents and communities affected by the *Lau* decision out of the planning process. In fact, according to reliable sources inside the school administration, the strategy further called for the same delaying tactics so effectively employed by segregated school districts across the nation in their response to the *Brown v. Board of Education* decision of 1954. The 44 parents and citizens were called in to legitimatize the proposed plan. Many felt insulted by the treatment accorded them by the school administration.[54]

After a long discussion and some serious conflicts among the various language groups, the majority of those invited eventually decided to reject the responsibility assigned the group by the school administration and demanded instead that the Board of Education reconstitute the multilingual-multiracial group into a viable Citizens Task Force charged with the responsibility of developing a master plan to respond to the *Lau* decision.

Because of the Board's failure to respond to the community proposal, a coalition of community organizations, prior to the April 15 meeting, arranged a press conference for April 16 to publicly protest the Board's continuing disregard of the educational needs of at least 10,000 students of limited English-speaking ability and to reiterate the demand for a Citizens Task Force to develop the master plan. During the press conference, CAA specifically made the following charges against the Board of Education.[55]

1. The Board has taken no action and made no plan to effectively meet the mandate of the Supreme Court.
2. The Board, to date, has made no attempt on its own to solicit ideas and inputs from parents and concerned citizens as to how the Board could best meet the mandate of the Court.
3 The Board has so far ignored innovative ideas and concrete proposals from concerned citizens and parents groups.
4. The Board has been deliberately kept ignorant on what its own staff is doing or not doing and has been effectively shut off from activities at State and Federal levels relative to the *Lau* decision.[56]
5 The Board has even failed to comply with a simple State Education Code, requiring the District to conduct annual census of students of limited and non-English-speaking background by April 1 each year.[57]
6. The Board's inaction already has caused the school system to lose a rare opportunity to seek available Federal funds for bilingual education and has placed the District in a position most vulnerable to lose all its existing Federally funded programs due to non-compliance with Title VI of the Civil Rights Act of 1964 and the order of the U.S. Supreme Court.[58]

CAA further warned that it might seek a contempt citation against the Board of Education and/or sue the School District for damage. The press conference was covered extensively by local media.

On April 22, the Clerk of Federal Judge Lloyd Burke unexpectedly phoned the Board of Education and conveyed the judge's intention to have a court hearing on June 28 on *Lau v. Nichols*. In addition, the judge asked that any plans for complying with the Supreme Court order be filed with the Clerk of the District Court "no later than 10 days prior to the date of the Court hearing," namely June 18, 1974. The surprise phone call led George Kreuger, representing the School Board, to demand that "whatever plan is to be presented to the Court" be submitted to his office no later than June 3. This meant that the school district had only a few weeks to complete, review and adopt a plan before June 3. The task became particularly difficult when the citizens group put together by Del Portillo on April 15 refused to be used by the school district and demanded full participation in the formulation of the master plan.

As pressure continued to build from all sides, the U.S. Department of Health, Education and Welfare on April 9 asked the U.S. Department of Justice to represent the U.S. Government to intervene as a party plaintiff in Burke's Court in San Francisco on the ground that the outcome of the San Francisco case would have national implications. A motion to intervene was filed in May and Judge Burke promptly scheduled a hearing on the motion for May 17, creating a crisis situation for the school administration.[59] Furthermore, the school district needed to have some kind of response to the motion before the Court by May 17 instead of the originally scheduled June 28 hearing.

It was largely due to these pressures that the Board finally allowed a resolution creating a Citizens Task Force to appear on its agenda and reluctantly approved it on May 14, 1974. According to the resolution, the Citizens Task Force on Bilingual Education was to develop "a master plan for bilingual education with special emphasis being given to designing a program in response to the *Lau v. Nichols* decision."[60] The resolution specifically called for cooperative effort between the Task Force and the Office of the Superintendent in the development of the master plan. As we shall see later, the Superintendent misguided the Task Force, his staff, and the attorneys representing the Board, the U.S. Government and the plaintiffs by rewarding their good faith and hard work with contempt and insults.

At the same Board meeting on May 14, the Board also authorized $15,000 to retain the Center for Applied Linguistics "to provide technical assistance in the preparation of a master plan to be presented to the Board and the Court in the case of the *Lau v. Nichols* decision."[61]

The two resolutions adopted by the Board proved to be a life-saver for the school district in the May 17 hearing before Judge Burke. During the May 17 hearing, the Judge granted the Government's motion to intervene and approved an agreement reached by the attorneys representing all parties that the Board-created Citizens Task Force would develop the master plan cooperatively with the Superintendent's Office, Center for Applied Linguistics, plaintiffs and the U.S. Government. The Judge further cancelled the June 28 court date indefinitely as long as all parties were working cooperatively in good faith.[61] Another court date would be set when the master plan was ready for court review.

The four-month struggle for control over the development of the master plan finally came to an end with a victory for the communities and parents in San Francisco. That of course was just the beginning of an uphill battle. For the next eight months, the Citizens Task Force on Bilingual Education worked hard and cooperatively with the staff of the Superintendent and the Center for Applied Linguistics to come up with a 700-page master plan for bilingual-bicultural education, as mandated by the Board resolution and approved by the District Court. When the plan was completed and transmitted to the Superintendent, he first publicly disclaimed any responsibility to the formulation of the plan and then attempted to prevent the approval of the plan by the Board. When that became impossible, he altered and mutilated the plan to the point of totally destroying it. Once again, the parents and communities found themselves in a fight against the Superintendent and the Board to restore the full master plan. Finally, a compromised version of the master plan was approved by the Board on March 25, 1975, and its implementation was set for September 1975.

In the next two sections, we shall describe first the work of the Citizens Task Force and then the struggle with the Superintendent and his deputy, Lane De Lara.

WORK OF THE CITIZENS TASK FORCE

Following the decision of the Board of Education, the Superintendent appointed fifty parents and citizens from the entire cross-section of the San Francisco community to the Task Force. Not only were the Chinese, Filipino, Japanese and Spanish-speaking communities significantly represented, the white and black communities were also included among the appointees. In addition, to assure continuous input from the Board of Education, each Board member named a personal representative to the Task Force, pursuant to the same resolution establishing the Task Force.

With the consent of the Superintendent's Office, the Task Force decided in June to reconstitute itself to increase its effectiveness and efficiency and to assure fair and adequate representation by all parties and communities concerned with the plight of the students from different language and cultural backgrounds. The reorganization called for five representatives from each of the Chinese, Filipino, Japanese and Spanish-speaking communities and provisions for five additional seats for representatives of other language groups, such as Samoan, Korean, Hindi, etc., not included among the original fifty approved by the Superintendent.[62] Of the five from each language group, two were to be parents with children in existing bilingual programs, one parent with a child in the SFUSD and two representatives of the language community at large. Unfortunately, despite active solicitation by the Task Force, only one of the five vacant seats for other languages was filled. Also, only six of the seven Board members appointed their representatives to the Task Force. Each Task Force member was allowed to designate an alternate. The Task Force also elected Richard Cerbatos, a Filipino American parent, to be its chairman.

The Task Force, therefore, had a total membership of twenty-seven. Even though the Task Force was created to address itself solely to the needs of limited English-speaking students in the SFUSD as required by the U.S. Supreme Court, the composition of the Task Force reflected in fact the ethnic composition of the total enrollment and displayed a kind of sensitivity normally not shared by the dominant white society.[63]

Two types of committees were formed within the Task Force. First, there were ethnic or language caucuses designed to deal with the particular needs and interests of each language or cultural group and to facilitate a direct link between the Task Force and each of the language communities. These caucuses held neighborhood public meetings to assess educational needs of their communities and to establish goals and objectives within each language community.[64] These meetings conducted by the caucuses became a vital means of community education and mobilization, both indispensable for the successful struggle for bilingual-bicultural education against the school administration.

The second type of committee on the Task Force performed many concrete tasks throughout the planning process. For example, each report or document prepared for the Task Force by the Center for Applied Linguistics was first scrutinized by such a committee and then brought before the Task Force with recommendations for further scrutiny and approval. Sometimes, the Task Force approved something in principle and authorized one of these committees to work out the details. Without exception, each of these committees was represented by at least one person from each language caucus. The task-oriented committee eventually became an effective tool of the Task Force for dealing with specific problems related to the master plan, such as school integration, facility utilization, school personnel, budget, etc.[65]

Besides the four language caucuses and the task-oriented committees, a Steering Committee, also consisting of one representative from each caucus, was set up to provide planning directions and strategies, to represent the Task Force in various capacities, including public relations, to develop preliminary policy recommendations and to carry out the mandates of the Task Force. Without exception, all decisions of the Steering Committee were subject to the final approval of the full Task Force.

Even though all meetings were conducted publicly, the Task Force was particularly concerned about the input of teachers who eventually would have the sole responsibility of implementation of the master plan within each classroom. A Teachers Advisory Committee to the Task Force was set up to promote a formal and continuous basis for active participation of classroom teachers. Many of the active teachers were members of minority teacher organizations and of either the American Federation of Teachers (AFT) or California Teachers Association (CTA). The advisory committee had access to all documents of the Task Force. Teachers were also urged to attend all meetings of the Task Force: a number did with considerable regularity. The full Task Force met regularly once every two weeks with caucus and committee meetings between regular Task Force meetings. Minutes of all meetings were kept and all full Task Force meetings were taped.[66]

The Task Force, of course, had many problems to overcome. To begin with, it was the first time that such a coalition of minority communities had come together to work on a common cause. Prior to this, communities were separated and preoccupied by the school administration through a continuous proliferation of powerless community advisory committees for every little project or program in the school district. The scheme instilled mutual suspicion among minority communities and forced each committee to be protective of its own project or program. It was therefore rather difficult, especially at the beginning, for the Task Force with all major language communities represented to work together without factionalism and suspicion. On numerous occasions, the Task Force almost became another victim of the divide-and-conquer strategy of the school administration. Fortunately, a desire to work for the common good of all facilitated considerable give and take among Task Force members and solidified the coalition as work progressed from month to month. The strong coalition became the most important single factor in the Task Force's subsequent struggle against both the school administration and the Board. Secondly, it took months for the professional staff of the Center for Applied Linguistics and the Citizens Task Force to arrive at a good working relation because of different interests and conflicting expectation.[67] For example, the Center understood its contractual requirement to extend no further than a description of *how* to devise a master plan, while the Task Force expected the consultants to deliver a master plan with specific data on student assignments, teacher and budgetary allocation, curriculum and facilities needed. Thirdly, the district staff assigned to work with the Task Force was never given clear directions, full authority and sufficient resources by the Superintendent. This often created tension between the Task Force and the staff, especially with regard to access to district data considered to be either confidential or controversial.

These were some of the major problems with which the Task Force had to reckon in almost every meeting. But, in the final analysis, the Task Force did succeed in forming a viable coalition of minority communities and managed to work cooperatively with the Center and the Superintendent's staff in completing the master plan for bilingual-bicultural education. The question now is: Will the Superintendent and the Board of Education approve the master plan fashioned by the Task Force with the assistance of the Center and the district staff? Before we answer this question, it is necessary to mention a few words about the substance of the master plan itself.

MASTER PLAN FOR BILINGUAL-BICULTURAL EDUCATION

In early December 1974, as the planning process was coming to an end, the Task Force, based on the working papers of the Center and projected work to be completed by both the Task Force and the staff of the Superintendent, decided that the master plan would consist of three components:

1. An "Abstract" of the master plan to include not only a detailed summary of the entire master plan, but also the following documents: (a) Description of the work of the Task Force, (b) History and interpretations of the *Lau v. Nichols* decision, (c) Needs assessment and District 68 efforts to date, and (d) Rationale of the master plan.[68]
2. The master plan consists of documents prepared by the Center for Applied Linguistics and revised and approved by the Task Force.[69]
3. Implementation or administrative details of the master plan to be completed by the Task Force and the Superintendent's staff before February 25, 1975.[70]

What follows is a concise summary of the master plan without the details of Component 3.

Essentially, the master plan criticizes the existing approaches of the district as "totally inadequate and ineffective" and calls for a comprehensive, full-time bilingual-bicultural education program of the maintenance type for *all* children of limited English-speaking ability.[71] The plan also invites active participation of English-dominant and English-monolingual students to achieve real integration and to promote peer learning in a truly multilingual and multi-cultural setting.[72] The master plan or Component 2, in four volumes, but summarized in 55 pages in the "Abstract," includes chapters on the system, the student, staff training, curriculum and materials, counseling and assessment, community, management, and research and evaluation.[73]

Bilingual-bicultural education is defined as a full-time program of instruction in which two languages, one of which must be English, are used as media of instruction with full appreciation of the history and cultural heritage of these children.[74] The program is also designed to develop and reinforce their self-esteem and to foster a legitimate pride in and development and maintenance of both languages and cultures.[75] Furthermore, the master plan recommends that as many bilingual schools at the elementary and secondary levels as needed for each of the major language groups in San Francisco—Chinese, Filipino, Japanese and Spanish—be established to provide full bilingual-bicultural programming, and to serve as assessment, resource, and training centers for satellite bilingual-bicultural classes in other schools throughout the city. For language groups with small numbers of limited English-speaking students, the master plan recommends that they be provided bilingual support wherever they are enrolled.

This, in essence, is the master plan.

COMMUNITY STRUGGLE FOR APPROVAL OF THE MASTER PLAN

As mentioned above, Component 2 of the master plan prepared by the Center for Applied Linguistics provides only the necessary steps to be taken by the school district to implement a bilingual-bicultural education program: it does not provide details such as prospective time lines for attainment of measurable goals in the development of curriculum, the employment of objective test instruments, the assignment of students, and the full utilization of district bilingual teachers. Obviously no plan is complete without these details; hence Component 3 is necessary. By November 1974, the Task Force recognized that such data must be included in the final plan and must be supplied by the Task Force with fullest co-operation of the Superintendent's top aides. Moreover, in order to achieve implementation of the master plan by fall 1975, it was necessary for the Task Force to have all the details in the plan no later than the end of February 1975, when the budgetary, personnel and pro-grammatic planning process for the following academic year was to begin by the Board of Education.

It was largely due to this dilemma that the Task Force decided in November 1974 that the following steps would be taken to complete the master plan and to have it included in the budgetary deliberation of the Board scheduled in February:[76]

1. Submit the "Abstract" of the master plan or Component 1 to the Superintendent and the Board in early January so that the school district can mobilize its staff to supply the necessary details for the implementation of the plan, and so that addi-tional technical details could be secured for inclusion in Component 3, scheduled to be completed by February 24, 1975.
2. As soon as the Board approved the master plan in principle, the Center for Applied Linguistics would complete the revisions of the working papers and the Task Force would work closely with the Superintendent's top aides to fill in the details of the master plan.
3. The Board of Education to submit the final master plan to the Federal District Court for further scrutiny. (The schedule allowed plenty of time for the Court to examine the plan and to call in expert witnesses to validate the appropriateness of the plan).
4. Upon the approval of the plan by the Board and the District Court, the Task Force would work with district staff to begin preparation for the fall and would conduct extensive community education and preparation to assure parental awareness and participation. (During this time, the monolingual English-speaking students would be actively recruited to participate in the bilingual-bicultural education program).

The above four steps and schedule were considered by the Task Force and the dis-trict staff assigned to work with the Task Force to be realistic and workable. When the at-torneys for the school district, plaintiffs and the U.S. Government met on December 17, 1974, they too agreed to these same steps subsequently confirmed in a December 31 letter from the U.S. Department of Justice to the school district attorney.[77] Since Del Portillo was designated by the Superintendent to be his personal representative to work with the Task Force and every recommendation, including the above steps, developed by the Task Force met his approval, it was natural for the Task Force to expect no difficulty in following the four steps and meeting the schedule outlined above. That turned out to be a false assump-tion on the part of the Task Force. In fact, it required even more time, energy, manpower and community pressure to just achieve the first step than the creation of the Task Force. As a result, the Task Force was unable to adhere to the original schedule. What follows is a brief sketch of the struggle that took place after January 9, 1975, when Component 1, an 80-page document, entitled, "Response to the Mandate of *Lau v. Nichols* by the San Francisco Unified School District: An Abstract of the Master Plan for Bilingual-Bicultural Education," was transmitted to both the Superintendent and the Board.

Shortly before the completion of the "Abstract," the Task Force decided that it would be useful to have a preliminary meeting with the Superintendent himself to brief him di-rectly on what to expect from the Task Force and to get his suggestions on how to get the Abstract approved by the Board as fast as possible and how the second step could be best carried out administratively. The meeting took place on January 7 in the Superintendent's Office. It was a friendly meeting and the Superintendent was very pleased with the progress made by the Task Force and his representative, Del Portillo. As for the content of the master plan, he said that as long as Del Portillo had no problem with it, he would have none either. When asked how to best seek the approval of the master plan in principle by the Board, he suggested that the Task Force should include a draft of the resolution it wanted at the time of official delivery of the "Abstract." On the question of getting a head start on the second step to be taken, the Superintendent volunteered to make arrangements personally for the Task Force: appointments were made for the Task Force to meet with Margerie Levy, Director of Desegregation and Integration, on January 9, Milton Reiterman, Associate Superintendent of Administration, on January 10 and 14, Lyle Eckert, Director of Budget, on January 17 and Fred Kennedy, Director of Personnel, on January 22. The Superintendent further agreed to present the "Abstract" to the Board on January 21, the first anniversary of the *Lau v. Nichols* decision and to set February 25 for the completion of the final master plan with all the necessary implementation details to be supplied by those persons with whom he made appointments for the Task Force. As far as the Task Force was concerned, the meeting with the Superintendent was a complete success.

In accordance with the instruction of the Superintendent, the Task Force officially transmitted the "Abstract" of the master plan together with the requested draft of a resolution approving the master plan in principle on January 9 to the Superintendent and the seven members of the Board of Education. The "letter of transmittal" called the master plan "realistic and necessary" and commended "the cooperation and expert assistance rendered by both the staff of the Center for Applied Linguistics and of the Superintendent's Office." The Task Force promised a detailed implementation plan "no later than February 24, 1975" and requested the Superintendent to provide "technical information and clerical support" to complete the planning process on time.

On January 13, the Task Force met again with the Superintendent to discuss the "Abstract" and to work out the procedures and strategy for the Board's approval of the draft resolution prepared by the Task Force and Del Portillo. At this meeting, the Superintendent brought with him his deputy, Lane DeLara. Essentially, the resolution called for the Board to approve the basic concepts embodied in the master plan with the understanding that the detailed master plan would be forthcoming "no later than Feb. 24, 1975." The resolution would also direct the Superintendent "to commit all such departments as will be necessary to work in cooperation with the Bilingual Department to complete the implementation of the master plan." Again, the Superintendent was very pleased with the work of the Task Force and promised the Task Force that he would present the proposed resolution to the Board on January 21 for the first reading and the final reading on January 28.[78] The Task Force told the Superintendent that the communities would turn out en masse on January 28 to support the approval of the resolution. He again repeated his commitment to assist the Task Force in getting the necessary data between then and February 24.

Something drastic, however, happened soon after the January 13 meeting and led the Superintendent to reverse his earlier cooperative posture: he abruptly and unilaterally decided not to present the "Abstract" and the resolution on the January 21 meeting of the Board, even though he repeatedly had promised the Task Force that he would do so. Moreover, he did not even inform the Task Force of his decision. A subsequent telephone conversation with his secretary and a newspaper article in the San Francisco *Examiner* on January 20 indicated that nothing on the master plan would be on the Board's agenda and no plan was under way to present the "Abstract" and the resolution in future Board meetings. Just as peculiar and abrupt was the complete inaccessibility of the Superintendent. It was as if an iron curtain had descended between the Task Force and the Superintendent.

Lane DeLara, the Deputy Superintendent, a hardline, anti-bilingual education administrator, became the stone wall separating the Task Force from the Superintendent and from the Board.[79] Del Portillo, now working directly under DeLara, suddenly lost his enthusiasm and effectiveness and became rather inaccessible and uncooperative. There was no mistake that DeLara was very much in charge of the school administration. He was determined not to let the master plan go before the Board and not allow any staff member to render any assistance to the Task Force without his authorization.[80]

Faced with this unexpected and insurmountable barrier erected by DeLara, the Steering Committee met hastily on January 18 to develop an alternative way to present both the "Abstract" and the resolution to the Board and to devise a plan to mobilize the communities to begin to exert pressure on the Board. It was decided at the meeting that the Task Force would flood the Office of the Superintendent with phone calls on January 20 and 21 to remind him of his earlier promise of cooperation. If that failed, at least one Board member would be asked to introduce the resolution as the first reading on January 21. John Kidder, one of the seven Board members, was asked to introduce the resolution over the objection of DeLara and apparently some Board members as well.

Through parliamentary maneuvers, the resolution was unexpectedly referred to a Committee of the Whole Board for public hearings on January 28, meaning no action could be taken by the Board on that date. About 500 persons from the various communities turned out as planned in January to urge prompt approval of the proposed resolution. The Task Force further sought and received letters of support from numerous civic organizations throughout the city and elected officials at all levels. The two State Senators representing San Francisco made personal appearances to express their support of the master plan. From the questions raised by Board members and the Superintendent, it appeared that none had read the "Abstract" and most reacted with total indifference and distrust; in fact, the Superintendent surprised the Task Force and some Board members by publicly disassociating himself completely from the proposed master plan and the work of his personal representative, Del Portillo, on the Task Force. Before the long and frustrating night was over, an amendment by Sam Martinez to delay the second reading of the resolution until February 25 and two substitute resolutions by Eugene Hopp and Zuretti Goosby were introduced; the former would have watered down the original resolution to such generalities that it could hardly have been implemented, while the latter would have had the effect of burying the entire master plan.[81] The way the discussion took place between the Superintendent and the Board that night, the U.S. Supreme Court decision, the work of the Task Force, the meetings with the Superintendent on January 7 and 13 and the agreement among the attorneys of the three parties involved could just as well have not existed!

Precisely what led the Board members to do what they did is still unknown. DeLara, a staunch opponent to bilingual education and ethnic studies, clearly had a hand in it. One thing that was clear, the Board could not possibly have come to an agreement in its next meeting on February 4 with four out of the seven Board members locked in three conflicting resolutions and a disruptive amendment. Given this situation, DeLara could have effectively blocked the Task Force from moving forward and could have easily controlled the divided Board. It was equally clear that the Task Force and community organizations had to adopt one single strategy and lobby each Board member separately before the February 4 meeting. The Task Force met on January 30 to assess the situation and decided not to push for the original resolution introduced by Kidder because the four votes needed could not be firmly secured. Besides, Kidder himself was having doubts about the resolution.[82] Instead, the Task Force decided to concentrate its effort on putting some teeth into the Hopp substitute resolution. The plan therefore called for some modification of the Hopp resolution and intensive lobbying of the other six Board members.

On February 3, Hopp accepted some of the modifications proposed by the Task Force. At the Board meeting on February 4, the Board unanimously adopted the modified Hopp resolution, over the strong protest of a small handful of white mothers representing the P.T. A.[83] The resolution approved the concept of bilingual-bicultural education for children of limited English-speaking ability, imposed a February 25 deadline for "the entire report" on the master plan and authorized the Superintendent "to commit the staff needed for implementation no later than September 1975."[84] Even though the language of the resolution was vague, both the Task Force and the U.S. Department of Justice independently arrived at the same interpretation: the Superintendent was required by the Board to complete the details of the master plan by February 25, and to implement it by September 1975.[85]

On February 5, 6 and 7, the Task Force repeatedly called the Superintendent to set up a meeting to delineate the specific tasks to be completed before the February 25 deadline mandated now by the Board and to work out a time line for the completion of the final master plan. These phone calls, however, failed to reach the Superintendent. So, on February 7, a registered letter was sent to the Superintendent, requesting a meeting with the Task Force on February 10. To make sure that the Board was fully aware of what was happening to its own resolution, the Task Force sent a letter to all the Board members on February 6, reiterated the importance of completing the master plan on schedule and indicated the difficulty it was having in getting an appointment with the Superintendent. On February 10, the Task Force was told by the Superintendent's secretary that he would be out of town that day. Another letter was sent to reiterate the importance of having the meeting if the Task Force was to complete the master plan by February 25 as the Board resolution called for. The letter requested a meeting the following day. On February 11, the chairman of the Task Force personally went to the Superintendent's Office at 8:30 a.m. to see if he could catch the Superintendent on his way to his office and get an appointment to see him on February 12. He was allowed only to talk with his secretary who relayed the following message: the Superintendent would meet with the Task Force on February 13 at 8 a.m., he considered the February 4 resolution to be a request for a "final report" on February 25, *not* the final master plan, and he understood "the final report" of the Task Force to be the basis for him to draw up his own master plan.[86] In short, the Task Force did its work for nothing: the Superintendent would devise his own master plan! To make the situation even more incredible was the sudden and unexpected departure of Del Portillo for an indefinite period of vacation!

When the meeting took place on February 13, the Task Force submitted two supplementary documents, entitled, "Models for Bilingual-Bicultural Education Schools" and "Recommendations for Elementary Bilingual Classroom Models," both designed to assist district staff in filling in facts and figures necessary for completion of the master plan. The Superintendent and his deputy, DeLara, however, reiterated his interpretation of the February 4 resolution. When Task Force members told him to stop playing games, he "angrily stomped out of the meeting without a word" barely ten minutes into the meeting. The meeting ended soon after.

On the next day, the Task Force sent the Superintendent a letter, accusing him of "using the unprofessional-like and insulting walk-out tactic" and of unilaterally undoing "ten months of intensive study and planning conducted by the Board-created, Board-appointed Task Force, by Board-hired outside consultants, and by his own personal representatives." The Task Force said, "Our goodwill and strict compliance with Board resolutions apparently was naivete on our part; our good faith effort was rewarded with insult and rejection. The Superintendent clearly abused our trust . . . and was in violation of the Federal Court approved agreement on May 16, 1974." The Task Force told the Superintendent that it would not allow "one man's defiance and obstruction to prevent it

from fulfilling its mandates from the Board and the Supreme Court. . . . The Task Force intends to proceed with the limited and incomplete data it has accumulated to date and to
work with whoever on his staff is willing to cooperate with us." That same day, the
Superintendent called the chairman of the Task Force to apologize for his behavior a day
before, but there was no change in his position regarding cooperation with the Task Force.

By then, the Task Force had only ten days left to prepare the final master plan without the assistance of vacationing Del Portillo. On February 20, the Task Force wrote the
President of the Board and informed her that the Task Force was getting "neither oral nor
written communication from the Superintendent or his staff." However, the Task Force
would make every effort to submit the final master plan on February 25. No staff person
was willing to help without an authorization from the Superintendent or his deputy.[87] Even
though the Task Force kept the Board fully informed of all its frustrating attempts to work
with the Superintendent, not once did any member of the ineffective and incompetent Board
offer to bring the Superintendent and the Task Force together to carry out the mandate of
the Board.

When the Board actually met on February 25, it was not surprising that the Task Force
was unable to submit the final master plan, Component 3. The school administrators made
sure that the Task Force had no access to the data needed to complete the plan. Instead,
only Component 2, as revised by the Task Force, was submitted. As pointed out earlier,
Component 2 was summarized in the "Abstract." It contained only the framework of the
master plan.

The failure of the Task Force of course was a victory for the Morena-DeLara clique.
The originally planned timetable for completion of the planning process was completely
upset. Worse yet, the commitment and ability of the Board to implement the master plan
by fall 1975 became increasingly uncertain as the Morena-DeLara delaying tactic became
more effective. The Task Force was exhausted and demoralized. Fortunately, the Task
Force, having gone that far, was determined not to let two indifferent and irresponsible
school administrators block its mandate from the Supreme Court and its commitment to
fight for equal educational opportunity for thousands of children in San Francisco.
Moreover, the U.S. Department of Justice began to realize that its agreement on the timetable
with the district staff was not being met. On February 12, the Justice Department wrote the
school district, "A timetable is necessary so that the plaintiffs can insure appropriate review in time for implementation for the Fall 1975 semester. We are concerned that any further delay in the presentation of the master plan will jeopardize implementation for this
Fall." The letter concluded with a demand for a new timetable for the presentation of the
master plan to the U.S. Government. When it became obvious that the Board was not going
to abide by its earlier commitment on a February 25 deadline, the Justice Department tele-
phoned on February 21 and 24 and wrote on February 25, requesting a new timetable again.

By the end of February, two possible courses of action emerged from the Task Force.
On the one hand, the Task Force would bypass the Superintendent and continue to press
the Board of Education for the approval of the master plan and its February 4 commitment
to implement the plan by September 1975. On the other hand, the Task Force would seek
possible legal action to remove the stalemate. Once again, task-oriented committees of the
Task Force were formed to work on the two areas. Board members were contacted and resolutions were drafted for Board members.

On March 4, 1975, Board member Sam Martinez introduced a new resolution "to accept the full master plan with the understanding that it is subject to further revision and
final approval of the Board" and to set the March 25 date for the final approval of the master plan. The resolution was approved on March 11 in time for the meeting with the frus-

trated attorney of the Justice Department on March 13. At that meeting, the Board and staff agreed that "to be properly evaluated the master plan must include sufficient detail such as student and teacher assignment, and timeline projections" and that "this information and the master plan with all modifications would be available on March 25, 1975."[88]

The deadline required by the March 11 resolution and agreed upon by both DeLara and the Justice Department's representative on March 13 was ignored again for the third time. Instead of completing the entire master plan with "sufficient detail" by March 25 as promised, DeLara, acting in behalf of the Superintendent, introduced unexpectedly on March 18 another resolution that presumed to approve the master plan and commit the school district to the maintenance of the *status quo*, the very conditions that led the Supreme Court to find the San Francisco school system "a mockery of public education." The resolution called for the approval of the master plan without the necessary data, and under the following major conditions: (1) "top priority" be given to instruction of English using the bilingual-bicultural techniques, (2) all recommendations for administrative changes be deleted (meaning, maintenance of existing structure), (3) community council's role be "advisory in nature" (meaning, no power of decision), (4) recommended expansion of staff "be held in abeyance" (meaning, no staff increase), (5) recommended bilingual schools to be given "additional study" (meaning, no bilingual schools), (6) existing methods of instruction be continued for another year (meaning, continue the sink-or-swim and ESL Pullout approaches), and (7) bilingual education be considered a "compensatory education program."[89]

The resolution was promptly and soundly denounced by a chorus of community spokesmen as "deceptive, insulting and arrogant" and branded as "an irresponsible product of a lame-duck superintendent."[90] Some wanted the resolution rejected, others demanded summary removal of the Superintendent, and none spoke in support of the resolution. By the end of the Board meeting, the Superintendent's resolution was dead.

Capitalizing on the unpopular sentiment against the Superintendent's ill-conceived and ill-intended resolution, the Task Force and community organizations once again organized its multi-ethnic, task-oriented committees to mount yet another intensive campaign for the approval of the master plan. Up until then, the Board had made only the following decisions: approval of the concept of bilingual-bicultural education and commitment to implementation of a master plan by September 1975 on February 4, 1975, and acknowledgement of the receipt of the "Abstract" on March 11. In other words, the Board had yet to approve the master plan, with or without the details required. Instead of introducing a substitute resolution, the Task Force and community organizations decided to work with Board members on a major revision of the Superintendent's resolution.[91] After intensive lobbying between March 18 and 25 and the editorial support of the San Francisco *Examiner* on March 24, the Board finally agreed on March 25 to a series of amendments which deleted highly objectionable clauses 5, 6, and 7, substantially modified clauses 2, 4 and 6 of the Superintendent's resolution, and added the following provisions: "the plan for implementation shall include prospective time lines for attainment of measurable goals in the development of curriculum, the employment of objective test instruments, the assignment of students, and the full utilization of District bilingual teachers. That on or before May 15, 1975, the Superintendent shall provide the Board with necessary data to implement the Master Plan by September 1975." The amended resolution, however, still changed considerably the master plan submitted by the Citizens Task Force and the Center for Applied Linguistics. However, it retained the bilingual-bicultural education of the maintenance type,[92] mandated extensive reassignment of administrative responsibilities beyond the existing Bilingual Education Department, allowed expansion of staff, required existing ESL and Newcomer programs to be modified to comply with the master plan, called for aggressive pursuit of state and federal funds "to supplement the District's effort," and included all provisions in the master plan not mentioned or unaltered by the resolution.

The approval of the master plan of course did not mean that its implementation would be guaranteed in September 1975. The Board's inability to make its staff carry out its policy decision is a rule rather than exception;[93] the Superintendent's ability to withhold vital information from the Board and to prevent the Board from making sound decisions and long-range plans is obvious. The distrust and division among Board members render the Board ineffective and vulnerable to staff manipulation. The reality of the situation in the San Francisco school district therefore requires laborious and independent monitoring of the implementation of the master plan, to see to it that all provisions are carried out faithfully.

Returning to the mandate of the March 25 resolution, the Superintendent once again ignored the May 15 deadline.[94] Actually, the data requested by the Board was submitted to DeLara, but it was withheld from the Board as of this writing.[95] This is another example of the defiance of the Superintendent and his deputy and the Board's inability to do anything about it. The administration's tactic has been to do the minimal and to delay the transmittal of the master plan to the Federal Court until it could no longer be carried out in September 1975.

Fortunately, the U.S. Department of Justice took the necessary step toward the implementation of the approved master plan. As if he knew that the May 15 deadline would again be ignored by the Superintendent, J. Stanley Pottinger, Assistant U.S. Attorney General, filed pleadings on April 29 at the Federal District Court seeking "the information that is necessary for the plan's implementation."[96] He reminded the school district that the questions in the interrogatories were "similar to those I presented in my letter of October 16, 1974, which have not been fully answered."[97] The school district was given 30 days to answer 23 very extensive questions. If these questions were answered adequately, they would have provided the very information the Task Force had tried in vain to obtain since January 1975. The Justice Department further expressed its desire to meet with both the plaintiffs' attorney and the attorney representing the school district to evaluate the master plan and the answers to the interrogatories.

Between November 1974 and April 1975, the U.S. Department of Justice was repeatedly given false promises and misinformation. Numerous attempts were made in February and March 1975 to either kill the master plan or significantly modify it into either an ESL plan or an ethnic studies program. It was not until March 25, 1975, that the Board reluctantly approved the master plan with some minor modification. It was the result of months of intensive lobbying and pressures from all sides. The resolution approving the master plan also called for its implementation by September 1975.

The master plan was subsequently submitted to the Federal Court for further scrutiny and approval. No decision to date has been reached by the Court, and in the meantime, the school administration failed to carry out the Board resolution, calling for the implementation of the master plan in September last year. According to the 1975 figures released by the school district, only 931 out of 5,258 limited English-speaking students at the elementary level were receiving BBE called for by the master plan, 2,820 were getting the inappropriate, inadequate ESL program and 1,507 were getting nothing. No figures were available for the secondary students. There is no way to ascertain the quality and effectiveness of these programs now in operation.

In terms of district funds committed to meet the needs of the limited English-speaking students, there was budget increase from $2.4 millon in 1974 to $2.5 million in 1975. The $2.5 million represents about 2% of the total district budget; the meager increase was not even sufficient to cover the cost of living increase. However, Federal and state funds for BBE increased sharply from $982,000 to about $2 million between 1974 and 1975.

It is clear that the district is still not putting its own resources into BBE programs and is depending almost solely on Federal and State hand-outs to support BBE now mandated by the Supreme Court. The school administration continues to ignore the Supreme Court decision, H.E.W. guidelines and the master plan approved by the Board of Education.

CONCLUSIONS

The struggle of the Chinese American students and parents in San Francisco, as lengthy and often-times as hopeless as it may seem, points to the importance of fighting for the legal right of equal and quality education on all fronts and at various levels. We are just beginning to understand the full legal and educational ramifications of the *Lau v. Nichols* decision nationwide. Socially and politically, the decision should begin to alter public sentiment against non-English languages and non-WASP cultures in American society on the one hand and to instill pride, instead of shame and self-hatred, in one's own language and culture on the other hand. But no significant change of public attitude will take place unless established institutions and policies are continuously pressured by community groups to meaningful and systematic changes. This means coordinated and persistent, rather than isolated, efforts in the struggle to achieve equal rights. The experience of the Chinese American indicates the limitations of relying solely on legal remedy: political and legislative actions at the local, state and Federal levels must go hand in hand with litigation. In fact, well-planned political and community actions are most crucial in times of legal setback and bureaucratic resistance.

Secondly, sound strategy for institutional changes could only come out of thorough and correct analysis of a situation. The decision to avoid seeking the "appropriate remedy" through litigation in the Federal Court and to have the master plan fashioned solely by parents is basically sound because Federal Court and the ineffective and irresponsive Board of Education should not be placed in a position of determining what type of education could best benefit students of limited English-speaking ability and because the divided and powerless minority communities had a rare opportunity to be united as a political force in San Francisco through working on a common cause. The many months spent mobilizing the communities and fighting for the right to develop the master plan and to have bilingual-bicultural education are in fact vital to raising the political and legal consciousness of the communities and to forming a solid political coalition never before existing in San Francisco. Instead of being divided and working against each other, the strategy brought the communities together to work for their common interests.

Thirdly, the difficulties and barriers the parents in San Francisco had to go through to secure what they are legally entitled to demonstrated clearly whose interests are being best served by the public school system in the U.S. Throughout the struggle, the school administration displayed arrogantly not the slightest interest in responding to the educational needs and legal rights of students from different language and cultural backgrounds. In fact, legal and political pressures failed to persuade the school administration to modify its posture. Morena, DeLara and company could care less that a substantial portion of students was receiving no education, inferior education or dropping out of schools and turning the school system into a "mockery of public education" and a national disgrace. The school administration sees itself protecting and serving the interests and needs of those who are white and those who come from an upper socio-economic background. To the administrators, the interests and needs of the poor, the non-English-speaking and non-white are secondary, if not negligible. Moreover, the political and administrative structure of the school system is set up to facilitate maximum participation and reinforce the interests of the rich and the powerful and to prevent and frustrate effective minority participation. The ability of Morena and DeLara to stall and ignore community pressure single-handedly is a perfect example of the biased nature of the structure of our public educational system.

Finally, the short-term, small gains in the long struggle for bilingual-bicultural education made by the Task Force and the minority communities in San Francisco should not be construed as a lasting victory. Even as this article is being completed, there are indications everywhere that the master plan will be largely ignored or deliberately destroyed through faulty implementation and uncooperative administration. Therefore, to assure lasting equality of educational opportunity, the class bias in public educational services and decision-making processes must be removed. As long as there is no fundamental change in the existing political structure, the distribution of power and resources, and educational priorities, the problems encountered in this study will continue to exist and inequality and exploitation of the poor and the minorities will not only be tolerated but pursued with vigor. Similarly, bilingual-bicultural education as effective and appropriate as it may be, will be rendered useless and given no chance to survive in an environment that is both intolerant and hostile to the needs and interests of the students of different language and cultural backgrounds.

The *Lau* decision has made important contributions toward recognizing the rights of non-English-speaking Americans and has helped put together a strong coalition of minority communities in San Francisco, California, and nationwide to fight for meaningful change in our social institutions. However, like *Brown v. Board of Education*, these changes will not come easy and fast. Persistence and unity among the ignored and oppressed thus far seem to be the key to any successful struggle.

NOTES

1. Supreme Court of the United States, Slip Op. No. 72–6520. The full text of the Supreme Court opinion is reprinted in *A Better Chance to Learn: Bilingual-Bicultural Education*, pp. 207–212, published by the U.S. Commission on Civil Rights, Clearinghouse Publication No. 51, May 1975; also in *A Synthesis of Theories and Research on the Effects of Teaching in First and Second Languages: Implications for Bilingual Education*. Austin, Texas: National Educational Laboratory Publishers, June 1974. Title VI of the Civil Rights Acts of 1964 provides: "No person in the United States shall, on the ground of race, color, or national origin be excluded from participation in, be denied the benefits of, or be subjected to discrimination under any program or activity receiving Federal financial assistance." (42 U.S.C. 2000 d). The regulations promulgated by the Secretary of HEW under this statute include 45 C.F.R. 80.3(b)(1). The specific passage cited by the Supreme Court opinion is: "Where inability to speak and understand the English language excludes national origin-minority group children from effective participation in the educational program offered by a school district, the district must take affirmative steps to rectify the language deficiency in order to open its instructional program to these students." (35 *Fed. Reg.* 11595; July 10, 1970; popularly known as the "May 25, 1970 Memo"). For the full text of this important memo, see the Commission on Civil Rights' report, pp. 204–206.

2. A small section of this paper is based on this writer's article in *Amerasia Journal*, Vol. 2:2 (Fall 1974), pp. 16–45. Another section of this paper is based on the writer's contribution to the "Abstract" of the San Francisco Unified School District's master plan, to be discussed later in this paper. I am indebted to Edward Steinman, attorney for *Lau* plaintiffs, for his assistance in the legal section of this paper.

3. For significant papers in *Lau v. Nichols*, see *Equal Educational Opportunity: Hearings before the Select Committee on Equal Educational Opportunity, the U.S. Senate*, Part 9B, pp. 4715–4754. 92nd Congress, 1st Session, 1971.

4. Press Statement of the Plaintiffs, March 25, 1970.

5. Many community committees and school-appointed committees worked diligently for years to rectify the situation, but very little was accomplished. Among the committees actively working for better education for the Chinese prior to the lawsuit were: Education Committee of the Chinatown-North Beach District Council, Chinese Bilingual Education Advisory Committee, Title VII Chinese Bilingual Education Advisory Committee, Board appointed Bilingual Advisory Committee and the Rosenberg Education Committee. The complaints and aspirations of the Chinese community are best represented in a statement distributed during a rain-soaked demonstration on February 14, 1969 in front of the school board headquarters at 135 Van Ness Avenue. (Paul Jacobs and Others, *To Serve the Devil*, Vol. 2, pp. 158–160. New York: Random House, 1971). The most violent outburst of student and parental anger and frustration erupted on February 27, 1969 in an open confrontation with Superintendent Robert Jenkins in a jam-packed auditorium of the Commodore Stockton Elementary School in Chinatown. (See *East-West Chinese American Weekly*, March 5, 1969 and the *San Francisco Chronicle*, February 28, 1969). The distrust and frustration culminated in the long school boycott and protest in 1971–72 when a citywide school busing program was initiated. Needless to say, the SFUSD offered the Chinese community no educational programs relevant to her needs. Min S. Yee, "Busing Comes to Chinatown," in *Chinese-Americans: School and Community Problems*, pp. 69–74. Chicago: Integrated Education Associates, 1972.

6. SFUSD had never undertaken any planning study on the educational needs of limited English-speaking students in the district, even though it always had a sizeable non-English-speaking population. All the classes set up for immigrant children were remedial in nature and had the sole objective of Americanization. The *Lau* decision and the push of the parents and communities forced the SFUSD to conduct its first comprehensive planning on the problem.

7. It is important to point out that the data was collected by the school district in December 1969, and no objective standards were developed to collect the data. The subjective judgment of individual classroom teachers was the basis of the survey. Moreover, placement of these students into the few special English classes was generally arbitrary and was not based on specially designed testing procedures or ascertainable standards. Outside of these special English classes, most of the Chinese-speaking students, who needed help in English, were placed in regular classes that were taught only in English. They could not adequately compete with their peers, and this led to eventual frustration, discouragement, resentment, truancy, delinquency and dropout. For some of the educational problems of the Chinese students in San Francisco, see the writer's testimony in *Equal Educational Opportunity: Hearings before the Select Committee on Equal Education Opportunity of the U.S. Senate*, Part 9A, pp. 4229–4235. 92nd Congress, 1st Session, 1971.

8. SFUSD, *Pilot Program: Chinese Bilingual*, p. 3A, May 5, 1969.

9. For some data and brief discussion on education and delinquency among the Chinese students in San Francisco, see reference in footnote 7.

10. U.S. District Court for the Northern District of California, Civil No. C-70 627 LHB Order, May 26, 1970. An important passage of the order reads as follows: "This Court fully recognizes that the Chinese-speaking students involved in this action have special needs, specifically the need to have special instruction in English. To provide such special instruction would be a desirable and commendable approach to take. Yet, this Court cannot say that such an approach is legally required. On the contrary, plaintiffs herein seek relief for a special need—which they allege is necessary if their rights to an education and equal educational opportunities are to be received—that does not constitute a rights which would create a duty on defendants' part to act. These Chinese-speaking students—by receiving the same education made available on the same terms and conditions to the other tens of thousands of students in the San Francisco Unified School District—are legally receiving all their rights to an education and to equal educational opportunities. Their special needs, however acute, do not accord them special rights above those granted other students. Although this Court and both parties recognize that a bilingual approach to educating Chinese-speaking students is both a desirable and effective method, though not the only one, plaintiffs have no right to a bilingual education. Again, this Court is in no position to mandate that such instruction must be given by bilingual Chinese-speaking teachers; though desirable, there is no legal basis to require it."

11. For relevant legal papers for the appeal, see Note 3.

12. *Ibid*. The appellate court further observed that the problems suffered by the children were "not the result of law enacted by the state . . . but the result of deficiencies created by the (children) themselves in failing to learn the English language." As Edward Steinman, attorney for the plaintiffs, correctly pointed out, "Such a statement . . . not only suggests that the 'sins' of the fathers be visited upon the children; it further labels the child 'sinful' for not absorbing on his own, the language of the society into which he has been cast." He called such legal opinion "incredible." "Testimony of Edward Steinman before the Committee on Ways and Means of the California State Assembly," December 10, 1974.

13. For the legal brief of the United States before the Supreme Court in the *Lau* case, see *Bilingual Education Act: Hearings before the General Subcommittee on Education of the Committee on Education and Labor, U.S. House of Representatives*, pp. 10–19. 93rd Congress, 2nd Session, 1974. Other national organizations are: Childhood and Government Project, National Educational Association, California Teachers Association, San Francisco Lawyers' Committee for Urban Affairs, Center for Law and Education of Harvard University, Efrain Tostado, Mexican American Legal and Educational Fund, American G.I. Forum, League of United Latin American Citizens, Association of Mexican American Educators, Puerto Rican Legal Defense and Educational Fund, and ten Chinese American community organizations in San Francisco: among them is Chinese for Affirmative Action, which played an active part in the case.

14. The national significance of the *Lau* decision is attested by the prompt decision by Congress to conduct a series of public hearings, from March 12 to May 10, 1974 on the effects of that decision on local school districts and the states. For the record of the hearings, see *Ibid*. The decision was cited among the bases for a new bilingual education legislation by both houses of Congress. See *Education Amendments of 1974: Report . . . of the Committee on Labor and Public Welfare, U.S. Senate*, pp. 44–49. 93rd Congress, 2nd Session, Report No. 93–763, March 29, 1974; *Elementary and Secondary Education Amendments of 1974: Report . . . of the Committee on Education and Labor, U.S. House of Representatives*, p. 69. 93rd Congress, 2nd Session, Report No. 93–805, February 21, 1974; *Education Amendments of 1974: Conference Report*, pp. 147–154. 93rd Congress, 2nd Session, Report No. 93–1026, July 22, 1974.

15. Testimony of Frank Carlucci, Under Secretary of HEW, on March 28, 1974 before the General Subcommittee on Education of the Committee on Education and Labor. *Op. cit.*

16. Public Law 93–380. For the new regulations on Title VII of ESEA, see *Federal Register*, 40:49, March 12, 1975.

17. Chief State School Officers in 26 states were asked by the Office for Civil Rights (OCR) of HEW to help assure that some 333 school districts are providing equal educational opportunity to national origin minority students. This is a follow-up effort of a policy established in the "May 25, 1970 Memo," requiring school districts receiving Federal funds "to rectify the language deficiency and open instructional programs" to national origin minority students who face language barriers. Of the 333 districts, 157 are in California. These school districts were to complete an HEW Form OS 53–74 or the "*Lau* Form," within 45 days. Compliance review is now underway. For a criticism of this latest OCR effort, see a paper by this writer delivered at the 4th International Conference on Bilingual-Bicultural Education, Palmer House, Chicago, May 22, 1975, entitled, "Federal Response to the *Lau v. Nichols* Decision: A Critical Assessment of HEW's Policies and Actions."

18. The *Lau* centers are now being set up pursuant to Section 503 of the *Education Amendments of 1972* (Public Law 92–318) and pursuant to the authority contained in Title IV of the Civil Rights Act of 1964, 78 Stat. 246, as amended (42 U.S.C. 2000 c-2000c-9). For a description of the regulations and guidelines for the *Lau* centers, see *Federal Register*, 40:52 (March 17, 1975), pp. 12244–12250. These are centers designed to assist local school districts in meeting the requirements of *Lau*. A total of nine centers would be established with a total funding of $3.7 million for fiscal year 1975. See *East-West Chinese American Weekly*, April 9, 1975.

19. A preliminary study is being conducted by the Center for Applied Lingusitics through a contract with the National Center for Educational Statistics of HEW.

20. The Massachusetts, Texas and Illinois bilingual education laws could be found in *A Better Chance to Learn*, pp. 217–244. In 1973, the National Advisory Council on the Education of Disadvantaged Children conducted a nationwide survey on state legislation on bilingual education.

The result of the survey could be found in *Education Legislation, 1973: Hearings before the Subcommittee on Education of the Committee on Labor and Public Welfare, U.S. Senate*, Part 7, pp. 2578–2584. 93rd Congress, 1st Session, October 31, 1973. The California Legislature is considering similar legislation. The most important bill is SB 7, sponsored by Senator George Moscone of San Francisco. The bill passed the Senate on June 26, 1975 and was referred to the Assembly for further deliberation. Meanwhile, the California Advisory Committee of the U.S. Commission on Civil Rights held a two-day hearing on bilingual education in Sacramento on June 26 and 27, 1975. The Committee is expected to issue a report with recommendations soon.

21. *Serna v. Portales New Mexico School District*: The U.S. Court of Appeals for the Tenth Circuit ruled on July 19, 1974 that bilingual-bicultural education is the only appropriate remedy under the *Lau* decision. In *Aspira v. Board of Education of the City of New York*, the Federal District Court on August 29, 1974 relied on the *Lau* decision in sanctioning the immediate implementation of a complete bilingual-bicultural education program for nearly 200,000 Spanish-speaking Puerto Rican children in New York City. Similarly, the *Keyes v. Denver Unified School District* case held on April 9, 1974 that bilingual-bicultural education is required by *Lau*. The Federal Court in *Keyes* held the *Lau* decision demonstrates that it is ineffective to require non-English-speaking children to learn a language with which they are unfamiliar, and at the same time acquire normal basic learning skills which are taught through the medium of that unfamiliar language. For the Denver plan for remedy, see Jose A. Cardenas, *An Education Plan for the Denver Public Schools*. National Education Task Force de La Raza, San Antonio, Texas, January 21, 1974; also by the same author, *Addendum to the Intervenor's Education Plan for the Denver Public Schools*. Congress of Hispanic Educators, February 1974. It is important to point out also that in the 20 educational plans negotiated by the OCR in its enforcement effort of the May 25 Memo, all required bilingual-bicultural education. For a detailed description of one of these compliance reviews of HEW, see the example of the Beeville Independent School District in Texas. *Education of the Spanish-Speaking: Hearings before the Civil Rights Oversight Subcommittee of the Committee on the Judiciary, U.S. House of Representatives*, pp. 41–67. 92nd Congress, 2nd Session, June 1972.

22. U.S. Commission on Civil Rights, *A Better Chance to Learn*. See also, Illinois Advisory Committee to the U.S. Commission on Civil Rights, *Bilingual-Bicultural Education—A Privilege or a Right?*, May 1974. The Commission report attracted national attention, e.g., *S.F. Examiner*, May 13, 1975 ran a long report by the Associated Press; *Washington Post*, May 14, 1975.

23. *Voting Rights Act Extension: Report of the Committee on the Judiciary*, pp. 20–21. 94th Congress, 1st Session, House Report No. 94–196, May 8, 1975. The pending legislation on bilingual court systems in the U.S. (S. 1724 and H.R. 7728) is probably going to be the next major reform based on *Lau v. Nichols*.

24. In 1953, San Francisco had 158,817 or 40.8% of the San Francisco Bay Area's 230,186 industrial jobs. But in 1975, it has 140,002 or 24.96% of the 420,764 industrial jobs in the Bay area. However, the city's white-collar jobs in areas such as banking, insurance, general administration and retailing increased substantially as were the jobs related to tourism and convention business. See San Francisco Department of City Planning, *Commerce and Industry: Industrial Trends: Report Containing Background Information for the Commerce and Industry Element of the Comprehensive Plan of San Francisco*, May 1975. For earlier trends, see *San Francisco Industrial Trends* by the City Planning Department, October 1968. See also, *Yerba Buena: Land Grab and Community Resistance in San Francisco* by Chester W. Hartman, pp. 158–183. San Francisco: Glide Publications, 1974. For a discussion on the tourist-convention industry in San Francisco, see *San Francisco Convention and Visitor Study*, Parts 1 and 2 by Herbert H. Oestreich and Dirk J. Wassenaar, Institute for Business and Economic Research, School of Business, San Jose State College, San Jose, California, May 1971 and August 1972.

25. State of California, Employment Development Department, Northern California Employment Data and Research, "Ethnic Groups, Veterans and the Handicapped in San Francisco," June 1974.

26. For data on the under-representation of minorities in city government, see "Survey of San Francisco Commissions, Agencies and Boards" in Minutes of the San Francisco Human Rights Commission meeting on January 23, 1975. On minority participation in educational institutions, see

forthcoming "Study of Employment Discrimination against Asian Americans in the San Francisco-Oakland SMSA: Educational Institutions" by Asian, Inc., San Francisco. On the politics of San Francisco, see Chester Hartman, *op. cit.*, pp. 28–89 and Frederick M. Wirt, *Power in the City: Decision Making in San Francisco*. Berkeley and Los Angeles: University of California Press, 1974.

27. San Francisco Unified School District, "Selected Data for Study in the Challenge to Effect a Better Racial Balance in the San Francisco Public Schools, 1973–1974." This report is issued every year. The changing composition of enrollment discussed in this section is based on data accumulated in the last six years.

28. San Francisco Human Rights Commission, "Status Report: Bilingual Education in the San Francisco Public Schools, 1973–74 Academic Year," November 7, 1974. See also, *English Programs for Speakers of Other Languages* by Frances Noronha, Program Evaluator, Division of Research, SFUSD, July 1974.

29. *Annual Reports* of the Immigration and Naturalization Service, U.S. Department of Justice, 1960–1974. Also, U.S. Department of HEW. Office of Special Concerns. *A Study of Selected Socio-Economic Characteristics of Ethnic Minorities Based on the 1970 Census*; Vol. II, "Asian Americans." HEW Publication No. (OS) 75–121, July 1974. For the impact of Chinese immigration on San Francisco, see San Francisco Bay Area Social Planning Council, *Working Papers of Background Information on the Study of San Francisco's Chinese Newcomers*, San Francisco, June 1970.

30. Percentage derived by comparing the data in the Human Rights Commission reports for 1973 and 1974. See Note 28.

31. Del Portillo, Raymond, Director of Bilingual Education, SFUSD, "Testimony Given at the Ways and Means Committee, California Legislature," December 10, 1974.

32. *San Francisco Examiner*, January 9, 1975. The number of limited English-speaking students in a school district is now a politically and legally sensitive issue since the *Lau* decision. School districts are required by the California law to conduct such a census at the beginning of each year. To avoid embarrassment and being cited for non-compliance, many school districts in California have been using highly questionable methods of conducting the annual survey and vastly reduced the actual numbers of limited English-speaking students to the minimal.

33. According to the definition of "limited English-speaking student" in the new Title VII law, self-identification method could be used initially to identify the students. The preliminary survey could then be refined and collaborated by more sophisticated instruments, teacher assessment and direct observations.

34. Data supplied by Del Portillo. The 20,000 figure is of course quite different from the official 6,611 figure given by the district. It is understandable that school districts prefer not to use this method of survey.

35. See Note 28.

36. Both Federal and state guidelines require that classroom teachers in any Federal or state-supported bilingual program be paid by the local district. Under these guidelines, SFUSD had to hire bilingual teachers for the few bilingual programs funded by the state and Federal government. Otherwise, most of the teachers are non-bilingual. For an example of violation of this Federal guideline, see "$3.5-million Shocker at School Board," *San Francisco Chronicle*, June 25, 1975.

37. SFUSD, "Preliminary Report to Dr. Lane DeLara on Bilingual/ESL/Newcomer Staff Response to Implications of *Lau v. Nichols*," April 3, 1974.

38. There were actually 1,454 students enrolled in the various bilingual-bicultural programs in the SFUSD. Of these, 704 were limited English-speaking, the remainder was made up of mostly black and white students. Such mixture in bilingual programs is required by state and Federal guidelines to achieve school integration. Both Title VII of ESEA and AB 2284 prohibit linguistic and racial isolation. For problems involving bilingual education and school integration, see *San Francisco Examiner*, May 11, 1974; "Board of Education Exempts Many Bilingual Students from School Bus Program," *San Francisco Examiner*, June 12, 1974.

39. In 1974–75, Federal sources for bilingual education are: $631,994 from ESAA Bilingual Set-aside, $198,056 from ESAA, $493,608 from Title VII of ESEA, $275,000 from CETA. State sources are: $187,946 from AB 2284 and $72,036 from AB 116.

40. "School Costs Rose As Enrollment Fell," *San Francisco Chronicle*, November 22, 1974. Cf. "San Francisco Staff Still Outnumbers Teachers," *San Francisco Chronicle*, March 16, 1972.

41. Board Resolution No. 23-16-Sg 5. The resolution was recommended by a Board-appointed Bilingual Advisory Committee following a massive protest by Chinese parents and students from the Marina Junior High School. Unfortunately, adoption of a good policy statement means very little in San Francisco.

42. The unfounded rumor was probably based on a well-established practice of the school district: yield only to pressure. The Supreme Court decision obviously was presumed to be a major pressure on the Board and would make the Chinese needs appear more urgent and visible. Also, the attempt to organize a Citizens Task Force made up of all ethnic groups happened to have come out of the Chinese American community first. This may have been presumed as a threat. Individuals and organizations with vested interests in the *status quo* naturally saw the formation of a citizens task force a threat as well.

43. The SFUSD responded only to community pressure. For example, in 1966–67, the district appropriated $190,000 to the Chinese only. In 1967–68, when the Spanish-speaking community put pressure on the Board, $61,132 was given to a Spanish ESL program. It was not until 1971–72 when the Filipino community first received $145,651 for its ESL program. Under pressure in 1972–73, the Board allocated $41,000 to start a Japanese bilingual program. S.F. Human Rights Commission, *op. cit.*

44. CAA has long been active in the field of education and employment. Many members of CAA too have long advocated bilingual-bicultural education of both Chinese immigrants and Chinese Americans.

45. The position consisted of two parts: description of current problems and recommendations to the Board.

46. For details of this recommendation, see the position paper.

47. Letter of CAA to Board of Education, March 19, 1974.

48. In a letter, dated February 27, 1974, to J. Stanley Pottinger, Assistant Attorney General of the U.S., CAA recommended four specific courses of action to be undertaken by the government. The fourth recommendation sought Federal intervention in San Francisco. Also on February 27, 1974, CAA requested Dr. Wilson Riles, State Superintendent of Public Instruction, to assist San Francisco parents in their effort to come up with solutions to school problems related to *Lau*.

49. "San Francisco Schools Are Bad, Riles Says," *San Francisco Chronicle*, March 20, 1974; "Riles Indicts San Francisco Schools," *San Francisco Examiner*, March 20, 1974.

50. *Ibid.*

51. "Angry San Francisco Parents Ask State for Help," *S.F. Chronicle*, March 23, 1974; "Angry Board Members Talk: Why Schools Don't Improve," *S.F. Examiner*, March 21, 1974. After months of public outcries and intensive, behind-the-scene maneuvers, the Board finally accepted the recommendation of Riles early this year which called for the appointment of a blue-ribbon commission to see what could be done to improve the school system from the management point of view. The appointment of the commission is like declaring the school district a disaster area, in need of outside and state assistance.

52. Letter of Del Portillo to Advisory Committee members, April 5, 1974.

53. Actually, the first draft of this plan was completed in total secrecy as early as February 15, 1974. The draft, entitled, "Bilingual/ESL/Newcomer Staff Response to Implementation of *Lau v. Nichols*," was apparently prepared under Lane DeLara's direct supervision, following Hopp's press statement of February 4. However, most Board members were unaware of the existence of this report until they were told of it in mid-April 1974.

54. Most of the parents and citizens had had considerable experience in dealing with the school bureaucracy. Most knew immediately what the district staff was up to. But there were a few defenders of the district staff as expected. *S.F. Examiner*, April 16, 1974 and *S.F. Chronicle*, April 17, 1974.

55. *S.F. Examiner*, April 16, 1974; *S.F. Chronicle*, April 17, 1974. Prior to the press conference, the *S.F. Examiner* gave a special coverage on the problems of getting a public response to *Lau* from the school district: "Schools Dragging Bilingual Feet," *S.F. Examiner*, April 15, 1974.

56. For example, the Board of Education was not informed by the Superintendent of a letter,

dated March 11, 1974, from Edward Aguirre, Regional Commissioner of the U.S. Office of Education, informing the SFUSD that it was "ineligible for funding under the Emergency School Aid Act" because of the Supreme Court decision on *Lau*. In fact, DeLara transmitted a request for a waiver of the ineligibility to the Office for Civil Rights on March 20, again without the Board's knowledge. Another example is the Board's total ignorance of Federal funds available for Chinese bilingual education curriculum development. The SFUSD was asked to submit a proposal, but no such proposal was submitted. Funds for this project are now awarded to the Berkeley Unified School District for Asian bilingual curriculum. Still another example is the Board's unawareness of the decision by the U.S. Department of Justice to intervene in the *Lau* case at the U.S. District Court when it considers remedies for *Lau*. The school district eventually was granted a waiver on the ground that a plan was being developed. *S.F. Chronicle*, May 2, 1974.

57. *California Education Code*, Section 5761.3.

58. See Note 56.

59. Three documents were filed by the Department of Justice: "U.S.'s Notice of Motion and Motion for Leave to Intervene as Party Plaintiff," "U.S.'s Memorandum of Points and Authorities in Support of Motion for Leave to Intervene," and "Complaint in Intervention." John B. Rhinelander, General Counsel of U.S. Department of HEW to J. Stanley Pottinger, Assistant Attorney General, April 9, 1974 letter included among these legal documents.

60. Board Resolution No. 44-23A5, May 14, 1974.

61. Board Resolution No. 44-9A2, May 1974.

62. "*Lau v. Nichols*: the Legal Struggle for Bilingual Education," *S.F. Examiner*, May 27, 1974. For an excellent series of nine articles on bilingual education in San Francisco, see *S.F. Examiner*, May 27–31, 1974. For a rare and sympathetic coverage on bilingual education by the *S.F. Chronicle*, see "Learning Barrier in San Francisco Schools," *S.F. Chronicle*, August 19, 1974. Since the *Lau* decision, the *Examiner* has done no less than thirty articles related to the case and to bilingual education. *Chronicle*, on the other hand, has done about four or five articles.

63. Exclusion of minority participation is a long established tradition in San Francisco. As a result of the civil rights movement of the 1960s, token minority representation is sometimes tolerated. See Note 24. Allegations that the Task Force had no white representatives were totally false and hypocritical.

64. There are four ethnic or linguistic caucuses: Chinese, Filipino, Japanese and Latino. As a rule, each caucus invited community participation beyond the members of the Task Force. It organized and took part in numerous community events dealing with education and bilingual education.

65. In 1971, in the case of *Lee v. Johnson*, the SFUSD was ordered by the Federal District Court to integrate through an extensive busing program based solely on race, rather than socio-economic backgrounds and educational and language needs. If the master plan was to be implemented, it must conform with the integration order. The Task Force, therefore, had to meet with the staff of the Office of Desegregation and Integration (D & I). Similarly, the forced closing of many schools under the Field Act requirements (earthquake safety measures) necessitated relocation of thousands of students and programs. Again, the Task Force had to meet with the staff dealing with facility utilization, Office of Association Superintendent of Administration.

66. Minutes and tapes of Task Force meetings are kept in Del Portillo's office.

67. Center for Applied Linguistics, an internationally renowned center for linguistic research, is located in Arlington, Virginia. The Task Force was to provide input to the Center and working papers prepared by the Center. Unfortunately, because of the distance between San Francisco and Washington, it was difficult for Center staff to be present in all meetings of the Task Force. Moreover, messages and recommendations of the Task Force had to be relayed through the Superintendent's staff to the Center. Oftentimes the Task Force asked that the tapes of meetings be sent to the Center; but apparently none had been sent. Communication, therefore, was one of the major problems.

68. This component was officially transmitted to the Superintendent and all members of the Board on January 9, 1975. Acknowledgement of the receipt of this component was not made by the Board officially until March 11, 1975 in a resolution No. 53-4A6. See *Minutes of Regular Meeting of Board of Education*, March 11, 1975, pp. 17–19.

69. This component, as presented to the Board, is not the totality of the master plan. The back-

ground papers in Component 1 are not included. A number of working papers, documents and recommendations from the Center were included in the master plan, but not fully explained. Also, the details in Component 3 were absent in Component 2. The Board of Education officially accepted this component with Component 1 in Board Resolution No. 53-4A6 on March 11, 1975.

70. The Task Force, district staff, Center for Applied Linguistics and U.S. Department of Justice all agreed that the master plan could not be carried out without Component 3. Yet this is one component that the Superintendent most stubbornly refused to cooperate and complete. In spite of repeated demands by the Board in resolutions adopted on February 4, March 11 and 25, the Superintendent ignored the demand for this component. As of this writing, June 15, the Superintendent has yet to comply.

71. Unlike the transitional bilingual-bicultural education program, the master plan calls for a program which utilizes the student's native language and culture in instructing, maintaining and developing all the necessary skills in the second language and culture. The end result is a student who can function, totally, in both languages and cultures. For extensive discussion on various types of bilingual education program, see William F. Mackey, "A Typology of Bilingual Education," in *Bilingual Education in a Binational School*, pp. 149–171. Rowley, Mass.: Newbury House Publishers, 1972; Valencia, Atilano, *Bilingual-Bicultural Education: A Perspective Model in Multi-cultural America*. Albuquerque, N.M.: Southwestern Cooperative Educational Laboratory Inc., April 1969; Fishman, Joshua, and John Lavas, "Bilingual Education in Socio-linguistic Perspective," *TESL Quarterly*, IV:3 (Sept. 3, 1970), pp. 215–22; Cornejo, Ricardo J., *op. cit.*, pp. 31–38; Kjolseth, Rolf, "Bilingual Education Programs in the U.S.: For Assimilation or Pluralism?" in *The Language Education of Minority Children: Selected Readings*, pp. 94–121, edited by Bernard Spolsky. Rowley, Mass.: Newbury House Publishers, 1972; Troike, M. and R., *A Handbook on Bilingual Education* (Revised Edition), pp. 24–31. Washington, D.C.: Teachers of English to Speakers of Other Languages, 1971.

72. See Note 38 on integration requirements and also Note 65.

73. SFUSD, Center for Applied Linguistics and Citizens Task Force on Bilingual Education, "A Master Plan for Bilingual-Bicultural Education in the SFUSD in Response to the Supreme Court Decision in the Case of *Lau v. Nichols*," February 25, 1975.

74. This definition is consistent with both state and Federal laws' definition. See Component 1, pp. 18 and 19.

75. For a detailed discussion on this point, see U.S. Commission on Civil Rights, *A Better Chance to Learn*, pp. 30–47.

76. "No Bilingual Student Aid Plan," *S.F. Examiner*, August 8, 1974. This article explains also why the Task Force could not possibly complete an implementable plan for September 1974.

77. Letter of J. Stanley Pottinger to the SFUSD, December 31, 1974.

78. The Superintendent's promise again was very firm. DeLara sat through the meeting without saying much. The only assurance the Superintendent wanted from the Task Force was that the Board be given a chance to review the plan without debates in news media. The Task Force agreed fully and subsequently refused to speak with reporters about the substance of the plan. However, the *S.F. Examiner* managed to secure a copy through district sources and reported about the master plan on January 20, 1975.

79. DeLara's reputation as a hard-line anti-bilingual administrator was well known. On May 31, 1974, he was quoted in the *S.F. Examiner* as admitting frankly he preferred instruction in English "pure and simple" as a way to satisfy the high court's demand to provide a "meaningful education" to non-English-speaking youngsters. He said, "If the primary objective is to teach the youngster English and get him into the mainstream, then I think ESL is a much more effective and efficient way to do it." He also claimed that bilingual education was too costly to the district.

80. Reliable district sources told this writer. In spite of U.S. Government's request, no action was taken to complete the plan. "Bilingual Plan Asked," *S.F. Examiner*, January 27, 1975.

81. Kidder Resolution No. 51-21A12 of January 21. See *Minutes of Regular Meeting of the Board of Education, January 21, 1975*, pp. 18–19; Martinez Resolution No. 51-21A13 of January 21. See *Minutes*, p. 20; Hopp Resolution No. 52-4A11 of January 21; and Goosby Resolution No.? of January 21, 1975. Even though circulated copies of Hopp and Goosby resolutions were dated

January 21, official minutes of the Board indicated no such motions were made. Moreover, the same official minutes did not show that the Kidder resolution was referred to the Committee of the Whole. In fact, the minutes of January 21 reads as follow: "Commissioner Kidder moved adoption of the following resolution which was seconded by Commissioner Dr. Goosby and held over to the next Board meeting pursuant to Paragraph 15.4 of Board Policy P120" (p. 18). The Martinez resolution too was held over to the next meeting, which was January 28, 1975. It is interesting to note that the beginning statement in the official minutes of January 28 reads: "President Mrs. Abrahamson stated that the Board convened at the regularly scheduled hour of 7:00 p.m., and will adjourn at 8:00 p.m., in order to convene as a Committee of the Whole for the purpose of discussion of the Abstract of the Proposed Master Plan for Bilingual Education" (p. 1). Obviously, the resolutions of Hopp and Goosby were not introduced on January 21 and the resolutions of Kidder and Martinez were not referred to the Committee of the Whole as claimed by the President.

82. Kidder was under pressure from advocates of integration who presumed that the bilingual education plan would undermine the already defunct integration program and set up a separate bilingual school system with the SFUSD.

83. The small handful of white parents wanted to have a chance to address the board, but they were cut off abruptly. From private conversations and public statements of this small, but extremely active group of PTA mothers, one could easily identify their major concerns: preservation of what was left of the integration program, fear of a potential separate bilingual school system, presumed high cost of the master plan, and fear that approval of the master plan would mean reallocation of school priorities which gave top priority to their children. Their concerns were brought out and debated publicly in a series of confrontations with minority communities at the meetings of the San Francisco Human Rights Commission, dating back to Nov. 1974. See minutes of the Commission in January, February and March 1975.

84. Board Resolution No. 52-4A11, Feb. 4, 1975: "Resolved, that the Board of Education approves the concept of Bilingual/Bicultural education; further be it resolved, that the Board requests the Superintendent to commit the staff needed for implementation no later than September, 1975; further be it resolved, that the final plans or whenever options are arrived at, be presented to the Board for public appraisal and Board approval; further be it resolved, that the *entire report* be provided the Board no later than February 25, 1975."

85. Task Force letter to the Board, February 6, 1975 and Justice Department's letter to the SFUSD, February 12, 1975.

86. Citizens Task Force for Bilingual Education, "Report by the Steering Committee," February 12, 1975, p. 2.

87. Note 80.

88. Board Resolution No. 53-4A6. *Minutes of Regular Meeting of Board of Education, March 11, 1975*, pp. 17 and 18.

89. Board Resolution No. 53-18S-p. 1.

90. "Morena v. Task Force on Bilingual Education," *S.F. Chronicle*, March 19, 1975; "Citizens Task Force's Attack: Bilingual Program Denounced," *Examiner*, March 19, 1975.

91. This decision was based on a realistic understanding of the relations between the Board and the Superintendent, and between the Superintendent and the communities. Actually, a substitute resolution was going to be prepared. But it was decided that such a resolution could not bring in the necessary four votes on the Board. Amendments to the Superintendent's resolution were proposed. However, the Board accepted some and rejected some.

92. Martinez amendments No. 53-25A6. *Minutes of Regular Meeting of the Board on March 25, 1975*, pp. 21–22. Goosby's attempt to further water down the amendments was defeated (Resolution No. 53-25A7). *S.F. Examiner*, March 26, 1975. *Chronicle* reporter was apparently not present or unaware of what resolution was passed because it came out with this headline, "Bilingual Policy Unchanged," a reference to the Superintendent's original resolution (*S.F. Chronicle*, March 26, 1975).

93. The Board has been accused repeatedly for interfering with the school administration. Morena in particular made this accusation. The accusation was supported by the commission set up by Riles to improve the San Francisco school system. There is some truth to this accusation. However,

the cause of Board interference is probably due to the Board's inability to force the Superintendent to carry out its policies. As a result, Board members find themselves intervening in many administrative matters and repeatedly bargaining with the Superintendent on just about anything. Often time, the Superintendent successfully divides the Board by trading favors with Board members and helping the pet projects of each member.

94. This is just another example of the inability of the Board to make its Superintendent comply with its policy decision!

95. Sources from within the school administration informed this writer that the data was indeed submitted to the Deputy Superintendent.

96. The relevant legal documents are: "Plaintiff-intervenor's Request to Defendants for Admissions," and "Interrogatories of Plaintiff-intervenor to Defendants."

97. Letter of Justice Department to the SFUSD, April 29, 1975.

II ACADEMIC ACHIEVEMENT AND THE MODEL MINORITY DEBATE

5 The Myth of Asian American Success and Its Educational Ramifications

Ki-Taek Chun

INTRODUCTION

THERE IS A widely shared belief that Asian Americans not only have overcome the bondage of racial discrimination, but also have become a successful model minority worthy of emulation by other minorities. Asian Americans are said to be better educated, to be earning as much as any group, to be well assimilated, and to manifest low rates of social deviance. This contention seems firmly entrenched because it is allegedly supported by scientific, empirical research.

The following essay examines the empirical basis of this success contention against its historical background, and explores its ramifications. It explores the way in which the popular belief of Asian American success has come into prominence in order to arrive at a sociopolitical understanding of the contention. It critically evaluates the empirical basis, exposing the shaky, untenable ground on which the thesis of Asian American success stands, and illustrates some of the major consequences of this success myth. The essay demonstrates that the premise of Asian American success is in urgent need of reassessment by educators.

The first part of three parts (Section 2) will trace the ascendance of the Asian American success theme in the second half of the 1960s, at a time when the nation was agonizing over its civil rights turmoils and their aftermath. The portrayal of Asian Americans as a hardworking, successful group was usually accompanied by invidious comparisons to Blacks, as if to suggest that the industrious docility Asian American style was the solution to racial discrimination.

The second part (Section 3) will critically examine the nature of the alleged scientific research basis and show that the available evidence does not warrant the popular belief in Asian American success. A major argument will be that typical indicators of success, such as education and income, have not been properly adjusted for extraneous factors. (For income, for example, variables such as the number of wage earners, the education of wage earners, and the type of occupation must be considered.) Numerous research journal articles and monographs that use either 1970 census or more recent regional statistics will be examined.

Based on a review of diverse sources, the third part of this essay (Section 4) will il-

From *IRCD Bulletin* (Winter/Spring 1980): 1–12. Reprinted with permission of ERIC Clearinghouse on Urban Education, Teachers College, Columbia University.

lustrate several consequences of the success myth and pursue their educational ramifications. It will be shown that:

1. Asian Americans, their youths in particular, resent the success contention as a device of political exploitation.
2. A pattern of occupational segregation for Asian Americans delimits the range of occupational aspirations and choices of Asian Americans youths.
3. Asian Americans experience a sense of lost identity and attribute this feeling to the pressures of assimilation and to their ancestors' concern for survival.

THE "SUCCESS" MYTH: ITS EVOLUTION AND PREVALENCE

It was in the 1960s—when the plight of Black Americans was occupying the nation's attention as it tried to cope with their assertive demands for racial equality—that two of the nation's most influential print media presented to the American public a portrait of Asian Americans as a successful model minority. The portrait created a glowing image of a population that, despite past discrimination, has succeeded in becoming a hardworking, uncomplaining minority deserving to serve as a model for other minorities.

At that time, when the nation was still groping for solutions to its racial unrest, the portrayal of Asian Americans as a successful minority seemed to serve a need; the image quickly caught on and dominated the stage for years. Despite objections, this image is still prevalent today. It has seeped deep into the thinking of policy makers and the general public, and has become a firmly entrenched belief among commentators and social scientists. It is visible everywhere—in the mass media, in social commentaries, in social science literature, and even at the high levels of our Federal government. In a 1966 *New York Times* essay "Success Story, Japanese American Style," sociologist William Peterson categorically states "By any criterion of good citizenship that we choose, the Japanese Americans are better off than any other group in our society including native-born whites. . . . Even in a country whose patron saint is the *Horatio Alger* hero, there is no parallel to this success story" (pp. VI-20).

The same year, *U.S. News and World Report* featured an article entitled "Success Story of One Minority Group in U.S." It begins:

> At a time when Americans are awash in worry over the plight of racial minorities. . . .
> At a time when it is being proposed that hundreds of billions be spent to uplift the Negroes and other minorities. . . . The Nation's 30 thousand Chinese Americans are moving ahead on their own—with no help from anyone else. . . . Winning wealth and respect by dint of his own hard work. [1966: 73]

The article portrays Chinese Americans as an industrious, hardworking, uncomplaining group willing to "do something" instead of "sitting around moaning."

Such depictions of success have circulated widely in newspapers and magazines since that time. A 1970 *New York Times* article, "Japanese Joining Hawaii's Elite," describes the rise of Japanese Americans in Hawaii to positions of leadership as businessmen, lawyers, doctors, teachers, and members of government (p. 17)

A 1971 *Newsweek* article presents an updated version of the global success portrait of Japanese Americans under the forceful title "Success Story: Outwhiting the Whites" (p. 24), while a 1975 *Time* magazine article, "The Americans of Japanese Ancestry: Fast Rising Sons," notes that "Americans of Japanese ancestry . . . have flourished in the islands [Hawaii] and now dominate [the islands'] politics" (p. 26). A similar theme appears in a 1977 *Los Angeles Times* article entitled "Japanese in U.S. Outdo Horatio Alger." Not only does the theme become repetitious, but it acquires momentum with each repetition: the article concludes: "despite great odds, Japanese Americans have become the most successful racial minority in U.S. history" (p. I-1). In a similar vein, a 1978 *Washington Post* article "Korean Americans: Pursuing Economic Success" (p. 1) recapitulates the theme that through hard work, success can be won even by the latest of the immigrant groups, the Korean Americans.

The portrayal of Asian Americans as a successful model minority has not been limited to the mass print media: A close parallel has evolved in the social science literature. In a paper comparing "the position of U.S. Orientals with that of U.S. Negroes," Makaroff notes that "for Niseis [second-generation Japanese Americans] race discrimination against them is virtually nonexistent today. They mingle freely and easily with white Americans, and there are practically no professional jobs that are not held by them" (1967: 311). He draws a sweeping conclusion:

> . . . practically none of them live in poverty, and many of them even have highly paid professional jobs. Moreover, juvenile delinquency and adult crime are virtually unheard of among them. Despite their bitter . . . background of racial discriminations and persecutions, the second generation Japanese Americans are now accepted as clean, decent, and law abiding citizens in all American communities. [p. 314]

During the same year, a more data-based research paper (Varon 1966) was published. Basing her conclusions on the demonstration of upward changes in educational attainment and occupational status of the Japanese Americans between 1950 and 1960, Varon asserts that Japanese Americans no longer constitute a "minority" in the sense that minority status carries with it the connotation of exclusion from full participation in the life of the society.

The significance of Varon's study lies in the frequency with which her conclusions have been cited by other researchers as a major reference. Petersen (1971: 120) cited Varon approvingly in what, as will be noted presently, has become one of the two most influential references in the field. Varon's conclusions also provided a context for a comparative study of minorities (Jiobu 1976) from which the following points are drawn:

> For present purposes, the major point is that Asian Americans, particularly the Japanese, have achieved substantial gains and have appeared to be exceptions to the traditional argument that prejudice and discrimination by the majority retard the social economic achievements of the minority . . . Asian Americans have attained more in the way of economic advancement while Chicanos and Blacks remain minorities in Varon's sense of the term. [1976: 25]

Thus, there emerges from Varon's work and its subsequent citations a consistent image of Asian Americans no longer occupying a minority status, but fully participating in American society with its attendant economic benefits.

The ascendancy of Asian Americans as a model minority reached its peak with the publication of two important books, *Japanese Americans: The Evolution of a Subculture* by Kitano (1969) and *Japanese Americans: Oppression and Success* by Petersen (1971). Petersen reiterated his contention that Japanese Americans are better off than any other segment of American society, including native-born Whites, and that they, unlike other minorities with a history of oppression, "have realized this remarkable progress by their own almost unaided effort" (p. 4). Kitano also views the evolution of Japanese Americans as an unmistakable success story, citing the high income and educational levels (1969: 1) of Japanese Americans, whose "most optimistic dreams have been surpassed" (1969: 147). The 1976 revision of his book shows little change in its view.

Kitano and Petersen are key references in the field, and continue to exert influence on the contemporary scene. It was on the basis of their work that, in 1975, Sowell drew the following conclusions:

> Japanese Americans have been the most successful nonwhite immigrant group in America, whether success is measured in income, education, and similar achievements or in low rates of crime, mental illness, and other forms of social pathology. [1975 b: 92–93, 255]

Editors Marden and Meyers in their volume, *Minorities in American Society*, asked whether Asian Americans "are still a minority in any other sense than numerical" (1973:410). The book's coverage of Japanese Americans had relied almost exclusively on Kitano and Petersen. Slawson, in a commentary on Asian Americans, once again repeats the success portrait (1979:53), basing his depiction not on the work of Kitano and Petersen, but on the secondary source of Marden and Meyers, who relied on Kitano and Petersen. It is tempting to predict a citation of Slawson as the basis of yet another version of the success portrait. Perhaps this is the way a myth is propagated.

The assertion that Asian Americans are a successful group had become, by the early 1970s, an established "fact"—leading some social scientists to state that "the success of Chinese and Japanese is a matter of record" (Sue and Kitano 1973:92). Contemporary examples of this ingrained belief are readily discernible in the work of many prominent authors (e.g., Glazer 1978:xii; Petersen 1978:65–106; and Sowell 1978:212–237).

It is clear that both Kitano and Petersen, and many others who rely on them, accept the success of Japanese Americans as an undisputed fact. Their interest lies in being able to account for that success by identifying elements of the subculture responsible for it.

> The Japanese Americans ought to be a central focus of social studies. This is a laboratory case of an exception . . . we might find a means of isolating some of the elements of this remarkable culture and grafting it onto plants that manifestly need the pride, persistence and the success of our model minority.

So writes Kitano, quoting Petersen's 1966 *New York Times* article (1969:2).

What emerges is an evolving process of reification: first, a portrait of success is rendered; that image of success is reified into a reality deemed beyond dispute; then a search begins for the success-inducing elements in the reified reality. Such a search is epistemologically futile, but that is not the topic of this essay. For our purpose, however, it is important to recognize that the success literature has failed to explicate the sociopolitical context by which Asian Americans were suddenly propelled into a success group worthy of emulation.

Compared to the 1960s, we are now in a period of enhanced political sensitivity, and to dwell excessively on earlier studies from a period past would be counterproductive. Accordingly, our purpose here is not so much to criticize the success literature of the 1960's as to demonstrate how we have become easy victims of the success myth. Several other authors have expressed similar concerns in recent years (Hune 1977; Suzuki 1977a).

EXAMINATION OF EMPIRICAL EVIDENCE

THE INDICATORS OF SUCCESS

All myths die hard, if ever, but what makes the myth of Asian American success so invincible and contagious is the generally accepted belief that it is based on scientific, empirical research evidence. Therefore, an examination of the empirical evidence becomes crucial.

This section evaluates available evidence to ascertain whether or not the alleged evidence indeed supports the contention of Asian American success.

As a preliminary, it might be helpful to place into a larger context those indicators—education, occupation, and income—that have traditionally been used as measures of success, remembering the contextualist perspective* that "context defines meaning and meaning shifts with its context." Social statistics become useful only when one understands the social and political context in which—and the purpose for which—they are being used. What is appropriate for one purpose could be misleading and even abusive for another. Therefore, before using any set of statistics, one should first determine its appropriateness for the specific purpose. For example, in order to use the median grade completed as an indicator of how well a minority group is doing, one must consider such related questions as the distribution of grades completed among group members, distribution of specializations, cost of education vis-à-vis family income, and rewards of education in terms of occupation and wage. The reasons for this are simple. If members of a minority group view education as the only means of social mobility and invest heavily in their children's college education at a disproportionate sacrifice to family finances, should that college education be regarded necessarily as a sign of success of this group? It might reflect a story of disproportionate sacrifices for college education or of society's delimiting mobility structure. If college graduates of a minority group make, say, as much as high school graduates of the majority group, is college graduation a sign of success or an indictment of wage inequity? If members of a minority group, believing that certain desirable occupations are practically closed to them, choose a second or third best occupation open to them, shouldn't it be regarded more as an indication of painful resignation to limited occupational opportunity? If a large number of highly educated professionals emigrate from a foreign nation, thus raising the educational level of the ethnic group to which they belong, is it proper to say that the group is successful since it has a high level of educational attainment? The point here is simply that the level of educational attainment is open to multiple interpretations. As such, unless it is accompanied by statistics that clarify its meaning by placing it in a proper context, the use of educational attainment as a solitary indicator of success is highly suspect.

The use of broad occupational categories as an indicator of success is likewise crude. To argue that a minority is doing as well as the majority solely because of its proportion of white-collar workers in the labor force, is overly simplistic, unless one is prepared to accept the proposition that the position of a clerk typist is equivalent to that of a company president or a mid-level staff member to an administrative chief.

The use of household income as a success indicator is also fraught with problems unless methodological controls are incorporated to avoid interpretive ambiguity. Consider a typical husband-wife, two-wage earner situation. For those families whose total income is about the national average, the two wages are likely to be the result of financial necessity,

---

*Contextualism, as it was originally expounded by Stephen Pepper in his 1942 classic, *World Hypotheses*, refers to an epistemological framework. It provides a unique frame for the analysis and understanding of occurrences in the natural and man-made worlds; and through the provision of unique frames, it constrains the kinds of questions to be asked, models to be applied, and analyses to be adopted. Contextualism holds that the purpose of an inquiry is to understand the total meaning of an event, occurrence, or phenomenon, and that an analysis or inquiry is meaningful only in terms of its utility for some purpose, that is, only when connected to the context in which it is being used. Contextualism is not a fancy name for old wine, as Jenkins (1974) has so persuasively shown; indeed, it has profound ramifications for the conduct of social sciences as demonstrated in an elegant exposition by Sarbin (1977).

entailing sacrifice and hidden cost to household maintenance. If minority families earn close to the national average when both spouses work, whereas non-minority families achieve this standard through a single wage earner, must we accept the conclusion that this minority is doing well just because families of this group make as much as the national average?

The value of household income depends on family size or on the composition of those who rely on the income in part or in whole. The size of the nuclear family is known to vary across racial and ethnic groups, and the extent of informal extended family systems may also vary across groups. One may also consider income from other than wages (e.g., stocks and bonds, inheritance, assistance from parents or relatives). Ownership of property and assets contributes heavily to economic well-being, but it is not reflected in wage income.

Similarly, high income may be a result of longer work hours or sacrificed weekends. It follows that for the household income to be a usable index for purposes of group comparison, one has to make adjustments for the number of wage earners and the number of hours worked. In addition, since education is known to be a substantial contributor to occupational mobility as well as higher income, the level of wage income should be adjusted at least for wage earner's education. Since salary levels vary across occupation and minority groups differ from the majority in their profiles of occupational distribution, it is only logical that wage income should be adjusted for occupational type as well as educational level. (Similar concern for various decontaminations appears in a perceptive footnote of Gee's 1976 essay, Footnote 4, pp. 11–12.)

In addition, it must be noted that until recently, assimilation rather than pluralism has been the dominant perspective of our society. This has hindered the public from recognizing explicitly that the quintessence of well-being is subjective: The well-being of a group should be gauged by how the members of the group themselves feel about their own lot. As for Asian Americans, the labelling of success has been imposed from without; how Asian Americans themselves feel about their own status has been ignored. Since their efforts at materialistic sustenance were prompted by the pressures of Americanization against the backdrop of legally-imposed discrimination, and since they feel locked into a second-class citizenship bound by a "thin gray line" of subtle discrimination, Asian Americans would find it frivolous to be called successful by others. The comfort of secure subsistence and the pride of education may well be overshadowed by the resignation to a second-class status or by the denial of one's heritage and, hence, identity. Viewed from this contextualist perspective, it is evident that the success label should be withheld until the context in which it is used and its ramifications are fully recognized.

THE LITERATURE OF SUCCESS

The empirical literature that allegedly supports the success contention reveals two trends. The 1960s literature generally drew conclusions in support of the success argument, despite its failure to incorporate the type of methodological controls described earlier in this section. A few studies from this period contradicting the success theme have remained unnoticed, if not ignored, by the main body of the 1960's and subsequent success literature. Several studies published in the 1970's using the 1970 census data indicate the status of Asian Americans to be incongruent with that suggested by the stereotype of success or the dominant literature of the 1960's. Curiously, however, the current success literature has neither noticed nor refuted the contraindicative studies of the 1970's: There is a mutual disregard between the success contention and its counterevidence.

As indicated in Section 2, one of the two initial salvos for what was to become a campaign of Asian American success was the 1966 *New York Times* article by Petersen. He based his general argument on 1) the higher level of educational attainment in 1960 (12.2

years for the Japanese compared to 11.0 for Whites), 2) the higher occupational attainment in 1960 (56 percent of the Japanese in white-collar jobs compared to 42 percent of Whites), and 3) low rates of crime and delinquency. The other salvo, the 1966 *U.S. News and World Report* article, was less data-oriented but rested on the same type of evidence.

In her influential paper using the census data of 1950 and 1960, Varon (1967) compares urban Japanese Americans with their White counterparts in educational attainment and occupational status and bases her conclusions—that Japanese Americans could no longer be termed minority members or be classified with Blacks or Mexican Americans—on findings of increased urban population, high educational level, and improved occupational status.

An analysis of the industrial classifications of the 1960 census leads Yuan (1969) to show a shift in occupational trends of Chinese Americans away from the "traditional" jobs such as laundry workers and small restaurant owners toward professional fields. In noting that the predicted as well as observed disappearance of certain low-prestige jobs will create a new occupational image of Chinese Americans, the author implies that such disappearance would be an indication of Chinese Americans' improving status.

In a 1965 study based on an analysis of the 1940 to 1960 trends, Schmid and Nobbe (1965a) examined education, occupation, and income of nonwhite races and compared them with that of their White counterparts. They report what by now must have acquired a familiar ring: 1) a greater proportion of college graduates among Chinese and Japanese Americans than among the total White population, 2) Japanese Americans ahead of Whites in terms of median grade completed, and 3) a greater proportion of Chinese and Japanese Americans in white-collar occupations (see Figures 3,4,5 and Tables 3 and 4). There is however, an interesting twist to the Schmid and Nobbe paper: as a caveat, the authors note that Chinese and Japanese Americans lag behind Whites in income despite their lead in educational status, and mention discrimination as a possible factor (p. 918). The authors neither elaborate on this point, nor pursue the ramifications of this differential return on education, even though, had they placed emphasis on the income differential, they could have argued from the same finding that rather than enjoying the rewards of higher educational attainment, Asian Americans were suffering from inequity and societal constraints.

Kitano's statement: "Common measures of success find the Japanese on the 'right' side of the ledger. Both [their] income and education levels are high" (1969:1) is without direct supporting documentation. References to education in this book pertain to such topics as school segregation in the early 1900's, employment discrimination for qualified Japanese teachers before World War II, and the quality of education in the relocation camps during the war, but not to whether education brings about commensurate return in the form of appropriate jobs and income.

Petersen's book (1971), already noted as one of the two major works along with Kitano's, presents a similar problem. Recognizing education as the main key to material success, Petersen cites the study by Schmid and Nobbe (1971:113), adding one qualifier to his overall success interpretation: "at least as of that date [1959], a considerable discrimination persisted, since a group with qualifications that should have demanded larger salaries in fact earned less on the average" (pp. 120–122). However, the discussion of Schmid and Nobbe is left inconspicuous and is overshadowed by the prevailing theme of "phenomenal economic and social success," as exemplified by the title of a key chapter, "Six Times Down, Seven Times Up." Consistently, these studies fail to account or adjust for extraneous variables, thus leaving the indicators of educational attainment and income susceptible to misleading interpretations.

Before we move on to the 1970's, we must highlight a study by Fogel (1966) that provides an instructive contrast to Schmid and Nobbe (1965 a and b) in its perspective and interpretation. In "The Effects of Low Educational Attainment on Income: A Comparative Study of Selected Ethnic Groups," Fogel uses the 1960 census data to evaluate education in terms of how it converts into income for selected minority groups. His guiding premise is that since schooling has substantial income value for those who obtain it, high levels of education should lead to desirable occupations with greater earnings, increased chances for promotion, and relative stability (pp. 22–23). Finding that a given number of years of education has less value for the members of the "disadvantaged" minority population, he concludes that income benefits derived from educational investment for Asian Americans have been lagging and deficient for at least 20 years—i.e., 1940 to 1960 (pp. 36 and 38, Table 6). His interpretation and conclusions, unlike those of Varon (1967) and Schmid and Nobbe (1965 a and b), contradict the overall success interpretation of the 1960 census data. In particular, he demonstrates that the income picture of Asian Americans, when adjusted for education, does not imply success. Had one incorporated additional controls such as occupational type, tenure, upward mobility, and the number of wage earners, the glitter of success that many reported in the 1960's would have disappeared even more rapidly. Unfortunately, this study remained unnoticed by Kitano (1969 and 1976), Petersen (1971), and the authors of other success literature.

The social science studies of the 1970's, as a whole, indicate that the socioeconomic status of Asian Americans is nowhere near the level of success conveyed by the stereotype. They also show that lumping all Asian Americans into one category is oversimplistic; it covers up serious differences among Asian American groups. And, within each group, there are socioeconomic differences: laborers working long hours in restaurants or garment factories; Nobel laureates in science; and representatives and senators in the U.S. Congress. If they are sometimes called "Americanized" model members of Asian descent, their immigrant counterparts are viewed as foreign, unacculturated, and unassimilable. Just as there are educated individuals who emigrated with financial resources or professional skills after the 1965 liberalization of the immigration quota, there are pensioners who emigrated as laborers before the Depression and were forced to remain single (because of past immigration restrictions) and who now quietly live out the remainder of their lonely lives on Social Security.

A study by Wilber, Jaco, Hagan, and deFierro (1975) based on the 1970 census data is a curious exception to the 1970's studies. Although the authors provide a glowing picture of Asian American success, a closer examination of their data reveals something different. For example, the participation rate for the "services" category occupation is three and four times higher for Filipino and Chinese males than for White males (i.e., 20.3 and 25.1 vs. 6.4 percent), but the rate for such categories as "managers, sales, crafts, and operatives" is lower for Chinese, Japanese, Koreans and Filipino men (p. 60). Nevertheless, the authors conclude that "Oriental men are concentrated heavily in white-collar occupations. Japanese, Chinese, and Korean men compare favorably with white men in this respect" (p. 59).

Their study also shows that at every level of education from none to post-graduate, Chinese, Korean, and Filipino males make less than their White counterparts. For Japanese American males, the pattern is slightly different—they make more than Whites through the high school level, but less above the high school level. Thus, all Asian American males with more than high school education make less than their White counterparts (Wilber, et al. 1975:141, Table 6.06). Yet, they conclude that

> the pattern of similarities in the earnings of Orientals and whites by 1970 takes on special significance, since it suggests that being nonwhite in the U.S. is not tantamount to economic hardship. Moreover, with the exception of Filipino men, Oriental men and women tend to average earnings as high as or higher than comparable whites. [p. 161]

Almost half of the Asian Americans on the mainland (48 percent) are concentrated in the four metropolitan areas of San Francisco, Los Angeles, New York, and Chicago, and the income of the metropolitan area residents is known to be higher than the national average or that in non-metropolitan areas. Accordingly, either an adjustment for metropolitan residency or separate analysis for metropolitan residents is essential to appraise the extent of economic well-being of Asian Americans. This point has been recognized by Owan (1975) and, in recent analyses of the 1970 census data, Cabezas (1977), Cabezas and Yee (1977), and Moulton (1978). These studies highlight how misleading the national aggregate data can be. According to Owan, for instance,

> The Chinese male median income was considerably lower than the white, Negro, and Spanish-origins in all the metropolitan areas except for Long Beach-Los Angeles; also their median income for Boston and New York were the lowest median income recorded among all groups in 1969. [1975:31–32]

Furthermore, Chinese and Filipino males all had lower median incomes than their White counterparts in the six metropolitan areas included in Owan's tabulation (p. 31, Table 1). This certainly contradicts the overall impression given by aggregate comparisons, $10,010 and $9,318 for Chinese and Filipino American families against $9,596 for the national median.

Moulton's tabulation reveals similar results for individual income. That is, Asian American males (Chinese, Japanese, Korean, and Filipino) had median individual incomes lower than that of Whites in Chicago, Los Angeles, New York, and San Francisco (1978:B-68, Table 10A). He further notes "A comparison with the incomes of black men shows that Chinese and Filipino men are no better off in their earning power" (p. B-67).

The ratio of Asian American to White male earnings computed by Cabezas tells the same story. All Asian American males—Chinese, Japanese, and Filipino Americans (Korean Americans are not included in his analysis)—had lower incomes than Whites in the four metropolitan areas. Similarly, all three groups of Asian American females had incomes lower than White females, with the exception of Filipino females in Chicago and New York (Cabezas 1977:3, Table 3).

Had adjustment been made for education in these studies, the income differential would probably have been even greater. A recent report by the U.S. Commission on Civil Rights (1978), *Social Indicators of Equality for Minorities and Women*, bears out this prediction by showing that the extent of income inequality becomes more pronounced after differences in education have been taken into account (p. 54, Table 4.3). For example, Japanese Americans in the period 1969–75 are shown to make more than Whites, but after adjustment has been made for education, they actually earn less than Whites with similar qualifications (p. 54, Table 4.3).

The study by Cabezas and Yee (1977) on the employment patterns of Asian Americans in the San Francisco-Oakland area is instructive. Through an analysis of the 1970 census data and the 1970 and 1975 data compiled by the Equal Employment Opportunity Commission on employment in large private industries, the authors show a grim picture of Asian American employment. Through meticulous tabulations, they demonstrate that

1. Asian Americans are underrepresented in the manager/administrator categories across all 132 industries studied (except for 3 industries that can be explained in terms of such idiosyncratic industry characteristics as the preponderance of ethnic restaurants and laundries) (pp. 134–136, Tables 2 and 3).
2. The rate of their labor-force participation is substantially below parity except in such industries as apparel products, where they are operatives (i.e., seamstresses);

banking and insurance, where they are clerical workers; eating and drinking places, where they are service workers (i.e., waiters and waitresses); and hotels and health services, where they are mostly food and cleaning service workers (p. 83, also Fig. C-7, C-38, C-40 to C-44, C-46).

3. Their employment rate is low in high-wage industries, but high in low-wage industries (p. 83, Fig. 12).

4. The family income of Chinese, Japanese, and Filipino Americans is lower than that of Whites, and the proportion of Asian American families below poverty level larger than that of Whites (p. 139 and Table 4).

5. The proportion of Asian American families with multiple wage earners exceeds that of Whites (p. 139 and Table 5), and the income of Asian American wage earners lags far behind that of their White counterparts (p. 139 and Table 6).

These findings hardly suggest a picture of occupational or economic success for Asian Americans, and the disparities uncovered by these authors would be grimmer if adjustment had been made for the higher level of educational attainment.

A recent report by the Civil Service Commission of the State of California (1976) indicates that Asian Americans in California's Civil Service are underrepresented in administrative, decision-making positions. Using the California portion of the 1970 census data, Jiobu (1976) demonstrates that the high educational attainment of Asian Americans is not being rewarded by commensurate income or occupation. Using the same data, Wong (1974) shows that at the intermediate level of education and experience, Chinese Americans are so well paid so as to compensate their underpay at the higher level. In fact, they are so well paid at the intermediate level that the average income for Chinese Americans is raised, thus obscuring the deficit at the higher level.

The employment situation of professional Asian Americans is equally grim. According to the Survey of Earned Doctorates conducted by the National Academy of Sciences (Gilford and Snyder 1977), more than 60 percent of all doctorate awardees have definite offers of employment at the time their degrees are awarded (e.g., 68 percent in 1973, 67 percent in 1974, 69 percent in 1975, and 63 percent in 1976). Over the four-year period from 1973 to 1976, the proportion of Asian American doctorate awardees with definite employment offers was always lower than that of Whites, Blacks, American Indians, Chicanos, and Puerto Ricans. In 1975, for instance, the proportions of male doctorates with definite employment at the time they received their degrees were 65.8 for Blacks, 66.5 percent for Chicanos, and 68 percent for Puerto Ricans, all higher than 62.7 percent for Whites—but for Asian Americans it was only 44.8 percent. As for Asian American female doctorates, in 1975 their proportion was 52.1 percent, the lowest of all female groups, compared to the 58.5 percent for all female doctorates (pp. 60–62, Table I-17).

The Survey of Doctoral Scientists and Engineers conducted by the National Research Council (Gilford and Snyder 1977) illuminates another side of the Asian American doctorates' employment status. Among the post-1970 doctoral scientists and engineers employed in institutions of higher education. Asian Americans received the lowest median annual salary in 1975 (pp. 80–81). Analysis of the American Council on Education data (1972–1973) led Sowell (1975a) to conclude:

> Orientals receive less than either blacks or whites with the same qualifications, and only the fact that Orientals have generally better qualifications than either of the other two groups conceal this. [p. 17]

Compared to the majority and to other minority groups, then, more Asian Americans go to college and ultimately earn their doctoral degrees; but upon graduation, fewer job opportunities are available to them, and even when they are employed, their salaries are lower. The emerging picture of Asian American doctorates is not one of success, but rather one of unrewarded effort and frustration.

Fields of specialization for Asian American doctorates reveal another problem. According to one National Science Foundation report on minorities and women (1977), in 1973 the proportion of employed Asian American doctorates exceeded that of the total population in such fields as engineering, mathematics, and physical sciences. On the other hand, in fields such as social sciences and psychology, the proportion of Asian Americans fell far below that of the total population, the greatest discrepancy being in psychology, 2.9 percent for Asian Americans compared to 11.5 for the total population (p. 6). The same trend is uncovered in a 1975 survey of doctoral scientists and engineers that showed, in terms of relative proportions, more Asian American doctoral scientists employed in engineering and biosciences but less in psychology and social sciences (Gilford and Snyder 1977:64). This trend exists among doctorates who received their degrees between 1973 and 1976 (Gilford and Snyder 1977:40).

A similar distribution of undergraduate majors is revealed at one of the nation's largest universities with heavy enrollment of Asian American students (Sue and Frank 1973). Although reliable data are not available, the same trend probably exists on other campuses. Thus, there seems a general trend of Asian Americans overconcentrating in a limited range of specializations such as engineering and biophysical sciences where quantitative, non-linguistic skills are at a premium, and of avoiding other fields like social sciences, humanities, and arts, whose primary vehicle for professional activities is either linguistic communication or interpersonal contacts,

If one of the shared goals of our society is to provide a full range of occupational opportunities, any barriers to this should become a matter of serious concern. Using a questionnaire survey of Chinese American youth in San Francisco, Wong (1977) observed that their occupational aspirations are influenced by their "fears of economic competition and racial prejudice, and the resultant discrimination" (p. 60). Occupational aspirations and choice are determined in part by the likelihood of success in the real world. Asian Americans may consider certain occupations and fields of specialization closed to them, and are resigned to a restricted range of occupational choices—pharmacy instead of medicine, business accounting rather than law, retail store ownership instead of corporate management, and so on. Such self-selection and self-restriction seem indeed to be at work (Wong 1977; Lan 1975).

EDUCATIONAL IMPLICATIONS

The revelation that the alleged success of Asian Americans is a false image standing on tenuous empirical ground has educational, research, and political implications. This section will pursue three facets of the educational implication: resentment against the success stereotype, self-limiting occupational aspirations, and sense of lost identity.

RESENTMENT AGAINST THE SUCCESS MYTH

When a group generally viewed as successful is not represented in the process of policy deliberation, which is often the case with Asian Americans, that group may inadvertently become a victim of inattention or even exclusion. By 1973, observers were already noting such consequences of the success image:

> The widespread belief that Asian Americans have somehow overcome prejudice and discrimination has given them a low priority in terms of attention and aid. For example, in hiring, in admissions to institutions of higher education, and in financial aid, Asians are often regarded as whites. [Kitano & Sue 1973:1]

> Clearly, many Asian Americans and Pacific peoples are invisible to the governmental agencies which are responsible for providing public services. Discrimination against Asian Americans and Pacific peoples is as much the result of omission as commission. [California State Advisory Committee 1975:58]

Hard evidence does not accompany these quotes or other references of similar nature (Hata & Hata 1976:11; New York State Advisory Committee 1977:28; Sue, Sue, & Sue 1975:906), and it is difficult to come by. But these sources demonstrate that many observers have felt Asian Americans suffer from inattention or exclusion.

In addition, observers on Asian American affairs feel that the propulsion of Asian Americans into a "model" minority status was a means of political exploitation. They charge that the success portrait was designed to divert attention away from the racial problems of our society, thus victimizing Blacks and Hispanics as groups which, unlike Asian Americans, have allegedly failed through their own fault to take advantage of the available opportunities.

> As the Black and Brown communities push for changes in our present system, the Oriental is set forth as an example to be followed—a minority group that has achieved success through adaptation rather than confrontation. [*Gidra* 1969:6]

Even some of those who, in the past, have contributed heavily to the Asian American success theme now profess the feeling that the image of Asian American success has been abused.

> The whites use us by saying to the others, Why can't you be like Japanese? The Chicanos and Blacks turn against us. [Kitano 1971:24]

This sense of not only being neglected but also used has made many Asian Americans resentful of the success myth; they charge that Asian Americans "are used as 'proof' of a racial equality that does not exist, and as showpieces of how docile acceptance of white supremacy is the key to success for non-white Americans" (Kim 1975b:140). Their sense of resentment and exploitation is discernible in a variety of sources, including such recent anthologies of Asian American writers as *Aiiieeeee!* (Chin, Chan, Inada & Wong 1974), "*Chink!*" (Wu 1972), *Counterpoint* (Gee 1976), and *Roots* (Tachiki, Wong, Odo & Wong 1971). In a thoughtful overview on Japanese Americans, Endo (1974) provides a cogent observation that a growing number of Japanese Americans take exception to what has rapidly become a stereotype of success and rebel against using a model minority notion as an "example to other racial and ethnic groups . . . on how progress should be made in American society" (p.203).

Given the besetting feeling of resentment among Asian Americans against being singled out as a model minority, we, as teachers, must first become aware of the tenuous nature of evidence upon which the success contention has stood, and then choose carefully the context in which ethnic intergroup comparisons and the status of Asian Americans are presented to our students. To portray Asian Americans as a successful minority (however well-intentioned) would intensify distrust among resentful students and would undermine our credibility as teachers. In the long run, students would benefit from understanding how Asian Americans have come to be viewed as a successful model minority and from inquiring into the general question of how the well-being of a group should be assessed. Subjective evaluation by the appraisees themselves should also have a legitimate place in appraising the status of well-being. It is patronizing and insensitive to expect a group to accept the evaluation of outsiders concerning its feeling about its own status.

Asian Americans are underrepresented in such occupations as journalism, law, and social sciences that require language skills and person-to-person contact, but are heavily concentrated in other fields where technical knowledge rather than linguistic and social skills are at a premium. This pattern of occupational segregation is evident at both undergraduate (Sue & Frank 1973) and doctorate (Gilford & Snyder 1977; National Science Foundation 1977) levels, and in private industries as well (Cabezas & Yee 1977).

If accepted uncritically, this pattern may perpetuate itself. Teachers and occupational counselors may come to believe that the existing pattern is a reflection of Asian Americans' aptitudes and preferences and they may unknowingly steer Asian American youths into those fields where there are role models and proof of occupational attainability.

Section 2 illustrated that the pattern of Asian American occupational choices does not necessarily reflect aptitude, but rather an adaptive response to the world of reality as they have experienced it—a preoccupying concern for survival rather than considerations of aptitude, preference, and open choice. This is substantiated by the fact that Asian American youths are apprehensive about "discrimination and biased economic competition" (Wong 1977:60), and that Asian Americans feel they are viewed by the management as good only for certain occupations and only for staff, not administrative, positions (Lan 1976:49–50). Although there is no firm evidence on how the occupational selection of Asian Americans is influenced by their perception of external constraints, it would be potentially prejudicial to assume that the existing pattern of occupational segregation is an undistorted reflection of their aptitudes and preferences.

Students need to be counseled into those fields where their aptitudes and aspirations would find optimal fulfillment. At the same time, Asian American students need to become aware of harsh reality, the reality that upward mobility becomes disproportionately blocked for them as they go up the ladder (Sung 1975; Lan 1976); that Asian Americans are perceived as suited only for staff positions and only for certain occupations; that they would be deprived of ethnic network and support systems if they were to enter the underrepresented fields. The recognition of these existing inequities and constraints, however, does not necessarily, and should not, lead to justification of continued occupational segregation.

ASSIMILATION AND SENSE OF LOST IDENTITY

As Endo (1974) has noted, the increasing resentment against the Asian American success stereotype grows in part out of a challenge to the very notion of success and the sinking realization that their success (if it exists at all) has exacted a hidden, but heavy, cost. Japanese and Chinese Americans in the past have been pressured into assimilating within an inflexible mold of Americanization (Suzuki 1977b:151) to avoid the anti-Oriental stereotypes and prejudices of American society. To achieve their present level of social acceptance, the Chinese have attempted to succeed through educational achievement, exemplary conduct, and, most importantly, accommodation (Yee 1973:104). For Japanese Americans, too, the strategy of survival in the dominant White society has been that of accommodation (Kurokawa 1969).

Asian Americans have reacted intensely against this pressure to assimilate. Third-generation Japanese Americans, for example, argue that although their parents had to work quietly to earn a place in American life and to be accepted as Americans, they are Americans by birthright, and should not need to make any extra effort to earn their right to belong here (Maykovich 1973b).

Accordingly, Kagiwada (1973) reproaches the prevailing studies on acculturation because they "perpetuate the view that the assimilation of ethnic individuals to the Euro-

American . . . culture is the acceptable . . . mode of adaptation to American society" (p. 162). He expresses an emerging theme among Asian American commentators when he notes that

> American society continues to restrict personal and group freedoms considerably more than is necessary by forcing the dominant perspective upon minority peoples and denying them the alternatives of viable ethnic life styles. As a result, many Japanese Americans as well as other ethnic youths find themselves facing what has been referred to as an identity crisis. [p. 162]

Recognition of these effects of the pressures of assimilation led Takagi (1973) to criticize assimilation as blatant racism and to call for the type of research that is capable of leading to the "development of an alternative theory" of ethnic relations (p. 156).

Other Asian American observers have also been concerned about the hidden, yet injurious, costs of their so-called success. They identify the hidden costs as behavioral overconformity (Hutchinson, Arkoff, & Weaver 1966), conservatism (Okimoto 1971), loss of social consciousness, (Yamamoto 1968), adoption of the dominant group's stereotypes resulting in a second-class mentality (Fong 1965; Weiss 1970), negative self-image (Sue & Sue 1971), and the sense of lost identity. The thrust of these concerns is that if the educational attainment and material comfort of Asian Americans, hard-earned through disproportionate sacrifice and overwork, represent "success" at all, that success has been motivated by concern for survival in an alien soil, has been molded by the dominant society's assimilationist cast, and has exacted its price in the form of restricted self-definition, i.e., ethnic identity. The combined force of the drive for acceptance and the pressure for assimilation has resulted in a continued effort to emulate and "out-Yankee the Yankees." Consequently, the "successful adaptation" of Asian Americans is hardly more than a gilded image with hidden costs. This context of assimilation also reveals the irony contained in statements like "the Chinese Americans are the most American of Americans while also being the most alien of aliens" (Block 1970) and "scratch a Japanese American and find a white Anglo-Saxon Protestant" (Kitano 1969:3). Asian Americans view their identity problems not so much as individual problems of psychological adjustment, but as inseparably linked to external forces of assimilative pressure and political expediency. The following quotes exemplify this attitude:

> In the past, Asians have seen an abandonment of their own identity as the price white society exacts for their socioeconomic success. [Kim 1975a:58]

> Too often, the plight of the Asian American is one of forced rejection of his own culture in favor of the dominant one in order to survive. This process of accommodation, which often appears under the guise of acculturation, has produced considerable psychological damage. [Asian American Political Alliance 1971:265]

> The Yellow Power movement has been motivated largely by the problem of self-identity in Asian Americans. . . . Now they [Asian Americans] are beginning to realize that this nation has a "White democracy" and yellow people have a mistaken identity. [Maykovich 1973b:1–2]

Others have made similar observations (Kuo 1979; Surh 1975). Iwasaki (1971) considers that "the search for . . . identity . . . is . . . a central problem in much of the [contemporary Asian American] literature" (p. 91). These manifestos and observations should not be regarded merely as expressions of radical youths. From a clinical perspective, a practicing psychiatrist notes:

The issue [is] the positive sense of identity. . . . Here is a problem which may be unrelated to personal psychodynamics and much more due to conflicts engendered by cultural differences and the illusion of the melting pot. [Yamamoto 1968:143]

Thus, the concern for ethnic identity seems to permeate the Asian American experience of today. It is significant that Asian Americans view their feeling of lost identity as resulting from the preemptive concern for survival and the pressures for assimilation. Once the theme of ethnic identity is recognized against such historical context, the "model" behavior traits of Asian Americans—unobtrusiveness, diligence, industriousness, and docility—take on a new meaning, and we are at once faced with the ultimate challenge: whether the education of our ethnic minority students should be guided by the assimilationist or pluralist persuasion. The question of assimilationism vs. pluralism bears on sociopolitical issues of deeper magnitude that defy simple solutions and fashionable suggestions. At the least, however, we must articulate alternative paradigms and their ramifications in order to bring the conflict under public scrutiny, and to allow reasonable choices to be made.

When examined closely, the image of Asian American success dissolves helplessly, baring strands of past discrimination, sacrifice and overwork, preoccupation with survival, and the disquieting feeling of lost identity. Asian Americans feel they have paid an injurious price for their so-called success. They feel trapped in the promised land as perennial second-class citizens, and they seethe with resentment at having been treated friviously at the expediency of shifting politics. Vacuous at best are the dichotomous idioms of success vs. failure and the rhetoric that a group is a success merely because it is faring better than other disadvantaged groups. Our newly gained perspective challenges us to develop a fresh orientation toward Asian Americans and to translate into practice the insights that emerge as we demolish the premise of Asian American success as a myth.

REFERENCES

Asian American Political Alliance. 1971. "Asian Studies: The Concept of Asian Studies." In *Roots: An Asian American Reader.* Amy Tachiki, Eddie Wong, Franklin Odo, and Buck Wong, eds. Pp. 264–265. Los Angeles: University of California, Asian American Studies Center.

Block, M. 1971. "Chinese in U.S. Seek an Identity: New Problems Arise for a Silent Minority." *Wisconsin State Journal,* Dec. 19.

Cabezas, Amado Y. 1977. *A View of Poor Linkage Between Education, Occupation and Earnings for Asian Americans.* The Third National Forum on Education and Work, February 2–4, 1977, San Francisco, California.

Cabezas, Amado Y., and Harold T. Yee. 1977. *Discriminatory Employment of Asian Americans: Private Industry in the San Francisco-Oakland SMSA.* San Francisco: ASIAN, Inc.

California State Advisory Committee to the U.S. Commission on Civil Rights. 1975. *Asian American and Pacific Peoples: A Case of Mistaken Identity.* 75 pp. ED 110 550.

Chinn, Frank, et al., eds. 1974. *Aiiieeeee!: An Anthology of Asian American Writers.* Washington, D.C.: Howard University Press.

Endo, Russell. 1974. "Japanese Americans: The 'Model Minority' Perspective." In *The Social Reality of Ethnic America.* Rudolph Gomez, Clement Cottingham, Jr., Russell Endo, and Kathleen Jackson, eds. Pp. 189–213. Lexington, Mass.: D.C. Heath.

Fogel, Walter. 1966. "The Effects of Low Educational Attainment on Incomes: A Comparative Study of Selected Ethnic Groups." *The Journal of Human Resources* 1: 22–40.

Fong, Stanley L. M. 1965. "Assimilation of Chinese America: Changes in Orientation and Social Perception." *American Journal of Sociology* 71:265–273.

Gee, Emma, ed. 1976. *Counterpoint: Perspectives on Asian America*. Los Angeles: University of California, Asian American Studies Center. 614 pp. ED 147 378.

Gee, Emma. 1976. Introduction to *Counterpoint*. Emma Gee, ed. Pp. 4–12. Los Angeles: University of California, Asian American Studies Center. ED 147 378.

Gidra. 1969. 1:6–7 (Quoted in Maykovich 1973a:167).

Gilford, Dorothy M., and Joan Snyder. 1977. *Women and Minority Ph.D.'s in the 1970s: A Data Book*. Washington, D.C.: National Academy of Sciences. 247 pp. ED 148 197.

Glazer, Nathan. 1978. *Affirmative Discrimination: Ethnic Inequality and Public Policy*. New York: Basic Books.

Hata, Donald Teruo, and Nadine Ishitani Hata. 1976. "Run Out and Ripped Off: A Legacy of Discrimination." *Civil Rights Digest* 9:3–11.

Hune, Shirley. 1977. *Pacific Migration to the United States: Trends and Themes in Historical and Sociological Literature*. Washington, D.C.: Research Institute on Immigration and Ethnic Studies, Smithsonian Institution.

Hutchinson, Sandra, Abe Arkoff, and Herbert B. Weaver. 1966. "Ethnic and Sex Factors in Classroom Responsiveness." *Journal of Social Psychology* 69–321–325.

Iwasaki, Bruce. 1971. "Response and Change for the Asian in America: A Survey of Asian American Literature." In *Roots: An Asian American Reader*. Amy Tachiki, et al. eds. Pp. 89–100. Los Angeles: University of California, Asian American Studies Center.

Jenkins, James J. 1974. "Remember That Old Theory of Memory?: Well, Forget It." *American Psychologist* 29:785–795.

Jiobu, Robert M. 1976. "Earnings Differentials Between Whites and Ethnic Minorities: The Case of Asian Americans, Blacks, and Chicanos." *Sociology and Social Research* 61:24–38.

Kagiwada, George. 1973. "Confessions of a Misguided Sociologist." *American Journal* 2:159–164.

Kim, E. H. 1975a. "Yellow English." *Asian American Review* 2:44–63.

———. 1975b. "The Myth of Asian American Success." *Asian American Review* 2:122–149.

Kitano, Harry H. L. 1969. *Japanese Americans: The Evolution of A Subculture*. New Jersey: Prentice-Hall. (Revised edition, 1976.)

———. 1971. "Success Story: Outwhiting the Whites." Quoted in *Newsweek*, June 21, p. 24.

Kitano, Harry H. L., and Stanley Sue. 1973. "The Model Minorities." *Journal of Social Issues* 29:1–9.

Kuo, Wen H. 1979. "On the Study of Asian Americans: Its Current State and Agenda." *Sociological Quarterly* 20:279–290.

Kurokawa, Minako. 1969. "Acculturation and Childhood Accidents Among Chinese and Japanese Americans." *Genetic Psychology Monograph* 79:89–159.

Lan, Dean. 1976. *Prestige with Limitations: Realities of the Chinese-American Elite*. San Francisco: R&E Research Associates. 84 pp. ED 138–654.

Los Angeles Times. 1977. "Japanese-U.S. Outdo Horatio Alger." October 17, pp. I–1.

Makaroff, Julian. 1967 "America's Other Racial Minority: Japanese Americans." *Contemporary Review* 210:310–314.

Marden, Charles F., and Gladys Meyer. 1973. *Minorities in American Society*. New York: Van Nostrand.

Maykovich, Minako K. 1973a. "Political Activation of Japanese American Youth." *Journal of Social Issues* 29:167–185.

———. 1973b. *"Yellow Power: Search For New Identity*. Paper delivered at the 68th Annual Convention of the American Sociological Association, Aug. 28, 1973.

Moulton, David M. 1978. "The Socioeconomic Status of Asian American Families in Five Major SMSAs." In *Summary and Recommendations: Conference on Pacific and Asian American Families and HEW-Related Issues*. Pp. B-24–107. Washington, D.C.: U.S. Government Printing Office.

National Science Foundation. 1977. *Women and Minorities in Science and Engineering*. Washington, D.C.: National Science Foundation. 56 pp. ED 147 098.

New York State Advisory Committee to the U.S. Commission on Civil Rights. 1977. *The Forgotten Minority: Asian Americans in New York City*. 56 pp. ED 156 784.

New York Times. 1970. "Japanese Joining Hawaiian's Elite." October 24, pp. 17.

Newsweek. 1971. "Success Story: Outwhiting the Whites." June 21, pp. 24–25.

Okimoto, Daniel. 1971. "The Intolerance of Success." In *Roots: An Asian American Reader.* Amy Tachiki, et al. eds., Pp. 14–19. Los Angeles: University of California.

Owan, Tom. 1975. *Asian Americans: A Case of Benighted Neglect.* National Conference of Social Welfare, May 13, 1975, San Francisco, California. 77 pp. ED 159 254.

Pepper, Stephen C. 1942. *World Hypotheses.* Berkeley: University of California Press.

Petersen, William. 1966. "Success Story: Japanese American Style." *The New York Times,* January 9, pp. VI–20.

———. 1971. *Japanese Americans: Oppression and Success.* New York: Random House.

———. 1978. "Chinese Americans and Japanese Americans." In *American Ethnic Groups.* Thomas Sowell, ed. Pp. 65–106. Washington, D.C.: Urban Institute.

Sarbin, Theodore R. 1977. "Contextualism: A World View for Modern Psychology." In *Nebraska Symposium On Motivation, 1976.* Alvin W. Lanfield, ed. Pp. 1–41. Lincoln, Nebraska: University of Nebraska Press.

Schmid, Calvin F., and Charles E. Nobbe. 1965a. "Socioeconomic Differentials Among Nonwhite Races." *American Sociological Review* 30:902–922.

———. 1965b. "Socio-economic Differentials Among Nonwhite Races in the State of Washington." *Demography* 2:549–566.

Slawson, John. 1979. *Unequal Americans: Practices and Politics of Intergroup Relations.* Westport, Conn.: Greenwood.

Sowell, Thomas. 1975a. *Affirmative Action Reconsidered.* Washington, D.C.: American Enterprise Institute for Public Policy Research. 53 pp. ED 130 570.

———. 1975b. *Race and Economics.* New York: David McKay.

———. 1978. "Ethnicity in a Changing America." *Daedalus* 107:213–237.

State of California. 1976. *The Status of Asian and Filipino Employees in the California State Civil Service.* Sacramento: Personnel Board, State of California.

Sue, Derald W., and Austin C. Frank. 1973. "A Typological Approach to the Psychological Study of Chinese and Japanese American College Males." *Journal of Social Issues* 29:129–148.

Sue, Stanley, and Harry H. L. Kitano. 1973. "Stereotypes as a Measure of Success." *Journal of Social Issues* 29:83–98.

Sue, Stanley, and Derald W. Sue. 1971. "Chinese-American Personality and Mental Health." *Amerasia Journal* 1:36–49.

Sue, Stanley, Derald W. Sue, and David W. Sue. 1975. "Asian Americans as a Minority Group." *American Psychologist* 30:906–910.

Sung, Betty Lee. 1975. *Chinese American Manpower and Employment.* Springfield, Virginia: National Technical Information Service (PB No. 246259). 373 pp. ED 117 378.

Surh, Jerry. 1975. "Asian American Identity and Politics." *Asian American Review* 2:151–166.

Suzuki, Bob H. 1977a. "Education and the Socialization of Asian Americans: A Revisionist Analysis of the 'Model Minority' Thesis." *Amerasia Journal* 4:23–51.

———. 1977b. "The Japanese-American Experience." In *In Praise of Diversity: A Resource Book for Multicultural Education.* Milton J. Gold, Carl A. Grant, and Harry N. Rivlin, eds. Pp. 139–162. Washington, D.C.: Association of Teacher Educators.

Tachiki, Amy, et al., eds. 1971. *Roots: An Asian American Reader.* Los Angeles: University of California, Asian American Studies Center.

Takagi, Paul. 1973. "The Myth of 'Assimilation in American Life.' " *Amerasia Journal* 2:149–158.

Time. 1975. "The A.J.A.s: Fast-Rising Sons." October 20, p. 26.

U.S. Commission on Civil Rights. 1978. *Social Indicators of Equality for Minorities and Women.* Washington, D.C. 166 pp. ED 159 290.

U.S. News and World Report. 1966. "Success Story of One Minority Group in U.S." December 26, p. 73.

Varon, Barbara F. 1967. "The Japanese Americans: Comparative Occupational Status, 1960 and 1950." *Demography* 4:809–819.

Washington Post. 1978. "Korean-Americans: Pursuing Economic Success." July 13, p. 1.

Weiss, M. S. 1970. "Selective Acculturation and the Dating Process: The Patterning of Chinese-Caucasian Interracial Dating." *Journal of Marriage and The Family* 32:273–278.

Wilber, George L., et al. 1975. *Minorities in the Labor Market*, Vol. II: *Orientals in the American Labor Market*. Springfield, Virginia: National Technical Information Service (PB-250 418). 207 pp. ED 128 643.

Wong, Harold H. 1974. *The Relative Economic Status of Chinese, Japanese, Black and White Men in California*. Ph.D. dissertation, Department of Economics, University of California at Berkeley.

Wong, James L. 1977. *Aspirations and Frustrations of the Chinese Youth in the San Francisco Bay Area: Aspersions upon the Societal Scheme*. San Francisco: R&E Research Associates. 137 pp. ED 167 645.

Wu, Cheng-Tsu, ed. 1972. *"Chink!"* New York: World Publishing.

Yamamoto, Joe. 1968. "Japanese American Identity Crisis." In *Minority Group Adolescents in the United States*. Eugene B. Brody, ed. Pp. 133–156. Baltimore: Williams and Wilkins.

Yee, Albert H. 1973. "Myopic Perceptions and Textbooks: Chinese Americans Search for Identity." *Journal of Social Issues* 29:99–133.

Yuan, D. Y. 1969. "Division of Labor Between Native-born and Foreign-born Chinese in the United States: A Study of Their Traditional Employment." *Phylon* 30:160–169.

6 Education and the Socialization of Asian Americans:
A Revisionist Analysis of the "Model Minority" Thesis

Bob H. Suzuki

FROM YELLOW PERIL TO MODEL MINORITY

THE POPULAR CONTEMPORARY image of Asian Americans as the "model minority" is of relatively recent vintage and the result of an amazingly rapid transformation in the American public's consciousness that has taken place only over the past decade or two. Paradoxically, during some 150 years preceding this period, Asians in this country were usually depicted by dehumanizing stereotypes that conjured up visions of invading "yellow hordes."[1] They were also victims of some of the most repressive, vicious and humiliating acts of racism ever directed against any minority group, acts which have been well documented.[2]

The change toward a more positive image became particularly noticeable in the mid-1960's in the wake of the Watts riot and amid growing discontent among blacks and other minorities. Around this time articles began appearing in the popular press calling attention to the seemingly phenomenal success of Asian Americans. One of the first of these articles appeared in the *New York Times* under the heading, "Success Story, Japanese-American Style." It was written by sociologist William Peterson, whose glowing account was epitomized in the following oft-quoted passage:

> By any criterion of good citizenship that we choose the Japanese-Americans are better than any other group in our society, including native-born whites . . . Even in a country whose patron saint is the Horatio Alger hero, there is no parallel to this success story.[3]

This was followed shortly afterwards by an article in *U.S. News & World Report* entitled, "Success Story of One Minority Group in the U.S.," which offered these observations:

> At a time when it is being proposed that hundreds of billions be spent to uplift Negroes and other minorities, the nation's 300,000 Chinese-Americans are moving ahead on their own—with no help from anyone else. . . . In crime-ridden cities, Chinese districts turn up as islands of peace and stability. . . .[4]

While paying homage to their past tribulations, both articles praised the two Asian American minorities for overcoming their adversities through the particular strengths of their cultural backgrounds, and strongly implied that Asian Americans had finally succeeded in becoming accepted into white, middle-class society through their hard work, uncomplaining perseverance and quiet accommodation.

From *Amerasia Journal* 4 (1977): 23–51. Reprinted with permission of the Regents of the University of California and the UCLA Asian American Studies Center.

The initial reaction of most Asian Americans to these ostensibly flattering reports was doubtlessly quite positive in view of their past experience as scapegoats for the lurid purveyors of "yellow journalism."

However, coincidentally and perhaps inevitably, the late sixties marked the beginning of a movement among Asian Americans toward greater ethnic consciousness and sociopolitical activism.[5] Many of these activists took strong exception to these rosy views about the status of Asian Americans and did not find it fortuitous that these success stories were being widely publicized at a time when the country was facing a racial crisis of major proportions. The activists charged that the actual status of Asian Americans was being deliberately distorted to fit the "model minority" image in an attempt to discredit the protests and demands for social justice of other minority groups by admonishing them to follow the "shining example" set by Asian Americans.[6]

Yet, while pockets of poverty obviously existed in many Asian American communities, such as in the inner city Chinatowns, it did appear that many Asian Americans had managed to escape to the suburbs and had, indeed, achieved middle-class status. In fact, these impressions seem to be supported by the following findings of a recent study[7] based on the 1970 U.S. Census data:

1. The median years of schooling completed was 12.5 for Chinese, 12.5 for Japanese, and 12.2 for Pilipinos; compared to 12.1 for the U.S. population as a whole.
2. The median annual family income was $10,600 for Chinese, $12,500 for Japanese, and $9,300 for Pilipinos; compared to $9,600 for U.S. families as a whole.
3. The 1970 prevalence rates of outmarriage in the U.S. for ages 16–24 were Chinese males, 41%, females, 28%; Japanese males, 38%, females, 46%; Pilipino males, 49%, females, 50%. Moreover, Asian Americans who outmarry mainly chose white spouses.

However, as we shall see later in this paper, these figures are quite misleading and under closer analysis will lead to a very different interpretation of the socioeconomic status of Asian Americans. Moreover, even if one were inclined to accept such evidence at face value, Asian Americans have argued that the high psychological cost paid by middle-class Asian Americans for this apparent "success" has far outweighed the socioeconomic benefits.[8]

According to this point of view, over-anxious attempts by Asian Americans to gain acceptance have stripped them of their dignity and have caused many of them to suffer from severe psychological disorders characterized by lack of confidence, low self-esteem, excessive conformity and alienation. Thus, far from having succeeded in American society, the argument goes, Asian Americans continue to be victims of white racism, albeit insidiously subtle in form. However, such assessments were largely based on impressionistic evidence rather than on empirical data obtained by supposedly "objective" social science research.

Social scientists who have studied the upward mobility of Asian Americans have forwarded various theories in attempting to explain it and have arrived at different positions concerning the "model minority" thesis. Most of these theories lend support to this thesis; a few of them qualify the thesis by pointing to the attendant liabilities accrued by Asian Americans in attaining their current status; and at least one seems to reject the thesis outright. None of them, in my opinion, provide an adequate theoretical explanation which permits us to fully understand the complexities of the causal factors involved and the reasons for the emergence of conflicting interpretations.

Therefore, in this paper I will present an alternative theoretical analysis which will hopefully provide a more comprehensive critique of the "model minority" thesis. In particular, by more closely analyzing the available socioeconomic data. I will demonstrate that a basic contradiction exists between the educational attainments of Asian Americans and their incomes.[9] Despite their highly touted success, Asian American males still generally earn less than their white counterparts who have the same amount of education. The obvious question this raises is: Why does this disparity in incomes exist? At the same time, it is true that Asian Americans have achieved some degree of upward mobility in comparison with other minority groups. But given their previous status as an intensely despised pariah group, how did Asian Americans achieve even this limited mobility?

In attempting to answer these questions, the next section will review what has become known as the "revisionist interpretation" of American educational history.[10] This background provides the necessary perspectives for the third section of the paper in which the various theories mentioned above are re-examined. A series of propositions will then be forwarded as the basis for an alternative theory.

THE "GREAT SCHOOL LEGEND" REVISITED

Historians' claims to the contrary, men often learn more from the present about the past than from the past about the future. Common versions of the recent past have frequently proved deceptive guides to the future.[11]

The cogency of the observation made in the above-quoted passage by historian William L. Neumann was perhaps never more apparent than during the past decade of the sixties. The social upheavals of that period laid bare many of the contradictions between social rhetoric and social action in American society, and forced a profound re-examination of much of the conventional wisdom which, in many fields, including education, had been accepted as well-established bodies of "objective" knowledge.[12] Conflicts over such issues as school desegregation, community control and ethnic studies forcefully called attention to the deplorable state of education for minority children and led to the writing of a spate of books which severely criticized the atrocious conditions and practices that prevailed in most urban inner-city schools.[13]

Liberal reformers tended to attribute the educational failure of minority children both to their "disadvantaged" environments and to incompetent, uncaring, mindless or racist individual educators within the system.[14] From their perspective, the obvious remedies were to compensate for the disadvantages of minority children and to replace or retrain the "defective" educators. They saw little need for fundamental structural changes in the existing educational system; once their proposed correctives were carried out, they saw the system functioning as well for minorities as it did for others. However, by the late 1960's, when it was becoming clear that the massive infusion of Federal funds for compensatory education programs was not having the expected effects, the cures claimed for the proposed remedies were looking more and more like empty promises.[15]

About this time the so-called deficit hypothesis was forwarded to explain the ineffectiveness of these programs. The proponents of this hypothesis argued that the source of the problem lay in the "culture of poverty" in which minority children grew up and on which the schools had little influence, thus neatly placing the blame on the victims themselves.[16] Moreover, since the problem seemed peculiar to minorities, especially blacks, it then became a "racial problem." The hypothesis was carried to its vulgar extremes by the "new eugenicists" led by Arthur Jensen, William Shockley and others, who claimed to have scientific evidence showing that the educational failure of black children was primarily due to their genetic inferiority in intelligence.[17]

Almost concurrently an alternative school of thought was being developed by a group of revisionist historians. These revisionists rejected the conventional interpretation of

American educational history, which generally portrayed the public school system as the institution primarily responsible for the democratization of American society. This conventional history—labeled the "Great School Legend" by Colin Greer[18]—saw the schools not only educating the masses to produce an informed, enlightened electorate, but also serving as the "great equalizer" by giving all children, no matter how humble their backgrounds, an equal chance to succeed and realize the American dream.[19] Historians of this bent tended to view blacks and other minorities as simply the last of the various ethnic groups to migrate to the urban centers. According to this "immigrant analogy," once these minorities were assimilated to white middle-class norms, they would eventually follow the same path toward upward mobility taken by the white ethnic groups who had preceded them.[20]

However, the revisionists could not reconcile this optimistic version of history with the crisis facing urban inner-city schools. This interpretation could not explain for them why the schools had failed so disastrously for minority children unless they accepted both the racist assumption of the "deficit hypothesis" and the improbability of an almost overnight deterioration of school conditions. These apparent contradictions led a number of revisionist historians over the past few years to undertake studies which have led to a very different interpretation of American educational history.[21] Three of these studies will be reviewed here to provide a cursory outline of this revisionist interpretation.

One of the pioneering studies was Michael Katz's *Class, Bureaucracy & Schools: The Illusion of Educational Change in America*,[22] which examined the development of the public elementary schools between 1800 and 1885. During this period education in the United States gradually evolved from the early one-room rural or village community schools to the large, consolidated urban school systems which by 1885, according to Katz, were "universal, tax-supported, free, compulsory, bureaucratic, racist and class-biased."[23] Katz's thesis is that the development of this type of educational system did not just happen fortuitously, but was systematically promoted by powerful interests over other decentralized, locally controlled alternatives. He contends that in order to centralize power in their hands, these interests supported a dominant bureaucratic structure. Backed by these interests, the bureaucracy in turn utilized the schools to control and properly socialize the "unruly" working class.

Joel Spring continues Katz's critique in his book, *Education and the Rise of the Corporate State*,[24] which examines further developments in American education starting from around the turn of the century. This period, in which the rate of industrialization and urbanization reached a peak in the United States, also marked the closing of the frontier, the beginning of the massive immigration from Europe and the rise of large-scale industrial corporations. These rapid changes created severe problems of urban poverty and disorganization, violent labor conflicts, corporate monopolies and government corruption.

According to Spring, the solution to these problems was envisioned to be the corporate state, "not only because it was considered the most viable solution, but also because it supported the interests and actions of the emerging elite in business and labor unions."[25] These two powerful interest groups joined hands through an alliance of the American Federation of Labor, under the leadership of Samuel Gompers, and the National Association of Manufacturers. Spring argues that through the efforts of this alliance public education was shaped to meet the needs of the corporate state in two major ways. On the one hand,

> Education adopted the goal of training the type of man required by the new corporate organization. This meant teaching the student how to cooperate and work with others, and to accommodate to an educational hierarchical structure organized along the lines of a large corporation . . . On the other hand, education was viewed as only one institution working with others to assure the progress and efficient operation of the social

system. This meant that schools trained pupils in the specialized skills required by the new corporate organization.[26]

This ideology, Spring maintains, resulted in such educational innovations as vocational guidance, junior high schools, team sports, student government and other extracurricular activities—all of which were designed to sort and prepare working class children for their appropriate roles in the new industrial order.

Finally, to complete this outline of the revisionist interpretation, let us review Colin Greer's study, *The Great School Legend*.[27] One of the major points made by Greer is that if one accepts the revisionist version of the past, then one cannot accept the liberal reformers' assumption that schooling had previously served as a path to upward social mobility for white ethnic groups. To support this position, he cites considerable evidence which shows that many white ethnics failed to achieve middle-class status and that millions of them continue to live in poverty today. Those who succeeded, he contends, did so despite the schools which often actually worked to retard mobility. He believes that mobility among the children of European immigrants was tied primarily to their parents' occupational and/or socioeconomic status at the time of entry, and not to the schooling they received. Thus, he asserts, the current crisis in American schools cannot simply be viewed as a "black problem," but one that has also been experienced by white ethnic groups as well. Although he recognizes that racism has severely intensified the crisis for blacks and other minorities, he contends that the liberal reformers have been badly mistaken in treating it as an affliction affecting only the racial minorities, leading them to prescribe such remedies as compensatory education. He does not believe that such piecemeal reforms are capable of solving the problems since they are based on the faulty assumption that schooling leads to upward social mobility. On the contrary, he argues, the American educational system has largely served to maintain and legitimize the unequal, hierarchical class structure of American society—in which the racial minorities occupy the bottom rungs—by sorting out and socializing students for their appropriate positions in that structure.

Not surprisingly, the revisionist interpretation outlined above has elicited strong counterattacks from many quarters. The revisionists have been criticized for being overly presentist, distorting the facts to fit their thesis, overlooking contrary evidence, and oversimplifying interpretations of complex historical events, not to mention a host of other, more minor sins of commission and omission.[28] Nevertheless, even their critics give the revisionists due credit for rejuvenating interest in a field that was becoming stale, and for introducing a much-needed alternative perspective.

The new insights derivable from this perspective are well exemplified by the recently published study, *Schooling in Capitalist America*,[29] written by two economists, Samuel Bowles and Herbert Gintis. Since the results of their analysis are directly relevant to the critique of the educational attainments of Asian Americans presented in the next section, they will be briefly summarized here.

Bowles and Gintis challenge what must certainly be one of the most cherished beliefs about the American educational system—that of the "meritocratic thesis." According to this thesis, the educational system functions in such a way that those with innate intellectual abilities in our society are generally able to advance regardless of their socioeconomic background; or, to put it metaphorically, "The cream shall always (or almost always) rise to the top." More specifically, the thesis posits that the schools: (1) sort out (by means of IQ tests) those children with innate intellectual abilities, (2) send them on to additional years of schooling, (3) help them attain superior cognitive skills, and finally, (4) enable them to acquire higher paying jobs. Or, to put it somewhat differently, "The rich are rich because they're smart, and the poor are poor because they're dumb." This view has been strongly reinforced by studies conducted by educational economists who have shown that both the income and IQ of an individual are highly correlated with the number of years of schooling he has acquired.[30] In fact, the correlation of IQ with income is so high that education has sometimes been referred to as an "investment in human capital." Moreover, these studies also show that a person's childhood IQ is highly correlated with his socioeconomic background, which is another way of saying, "The rich tend to have smarter kids." Combining this with the previously mentioned correlation leads to the corollary that, "The rich get richer not only because they're smarter, but also because their kids are smarter too!"

Of course, such a dictum would not be swallowed whole by most people, least of all by the poor. However, the weight of conventional wisdom buttressed by empirical data has given it considerable credibility so that most people probably believe that the schools function to a large degree in accordance with the meritocratic thesis.

To challenge this thesis, Bowles and Gintis carried out detailed statistical computations on an extensive body of data on the socioeconomic characteristics of white males in the United States, aged 24–65 years, who were from nonfarm backgrounds and in the experienced work force.[31] Then through a rather ingenious analysis, they were able to arrive at the following two important results:

1. That on the average a person's income and level of cognitive skills (as measured by standard achievement tests) both depend strongly on and increase with the amount of education (years of schooling) he has acquired; however, his income is weakly dependent on his level of cognitive skills.
2. That on the average a person's income and childhood IQ both depend strongly on and increase with his family socioeconomic background; however, his income is weakly dependent on his childhood IQ.

The ingenuity of Bowles and Gintis' analysis is in showing that even though two variables depend strongly on a third, this does not necessarily mean that they depend strongly on each other. In the two results summarized above, quite the opposite is true. Usually the inference of strong dependency is drawn without proof, and thereby often leads to erroneous conclusions. This is precisely what happened in the case of the meritocratic thesis. The above results destroy the two link-pins which hold this thesis together by clearly showing that neither the attainment of superior cognitive skills by the more highly educated, nor the higher "innate intelligence" of those from higher socioeconomic backgrounds can explain their higher chances of economic success. Nevertheless, as pointed out by Bowles and Gintis, the meritocratic thesis has served to legitimize the unequal, hierarchical class structure of American society by creating the illusion that schooling could enable even the poor to achieve social advancement if they are blessed with the requisite intellectual endowments.

Since the first of the above results (i.e., that income depends weakly on cognitive skills) is particularly surprising, further interpretation may be helpful. Bowles and Gintis basically argue that while cognitive skills are important for most jobs, they are not scarce since they are usually produced in sufficient abundance through schooling and/or on the job and therefore are not important determinants of a person's income. Consequently, they contend, other criteria including race, sex, personality and credentials become the important determinants.[32]

The second result, though perhaps less startling, is also of major significance since it demolishes the arguments of the "new eugenicists" (i.e., Jensen, et al.) even before they begin by showing that their basic premise for embarking on studies into the heritability of IQ—i.e., that IQ is an important predictor of a person's future chances of economic success—is simply wrong.

By taking both of the above results together, one arrives at the conclusion that a person's income depends primarily on his educational level (years of schooling) and family socioeconomic background (SEB), and does not depend to any significant degree on either his level of cognitive skills or childhood IQ. While the dependency on family SEB is not surprising, the dependency on schooling may seem paradoxical since, as discussed above, it cannot arise through its development of cognitive skills in an individual. How, then, one may ask, does schooling influence a person's earning power?

According to Bowles and Gintis, this apparent paradox may be explained by the differentiation in such noncognitive traits as personality (e.g., motivation, perseverance, docility), modes of self-presentation (e.g., manner of speech and dress), and class loyalties between individuals of different educational attainments. They argue that these traits are differentiated among people according to their position in the class structure and tend to be reproduced from generation to generation through the socialization process that begins in the family.

> Thus, children of parents occupying a given position in the occupational hierarchy grow up in homes where child-rearing methods and perhaps even the physical surroundings tend to develop personality characteristics appropriate to adequate job performance in the occupational roles of the parents. The children of managers and professionals are taught self-reliance within a broad set of constraints; the children of production-line workers are taught conformity and obedience.[33]

These patterns, they further argue, are strongly reinforced by the schools through the structural correspondence that exists between the social relations of schools and those of production. This is most evident in the hierarchical structure of most schools in which there are vertical lines of authority from administrators to teachers to students, and in which students, like production workers, become alienated since they have little control over their education. This correspondence principle is further reflected in the social relations exhibited at different levels of schooling.[34]

Finally, the unequal financing of the schools results in similar differences between the social relations of working-class schools and those of schools in upper-income communities. Poorly financed schools in working-class communities must usually contend with overcrowded classrooms, deteriorating facilities and inadequate material and human resources, which force administrators and teachers to adopt rigid, authoritarian procedures and practices that tend to mirror those of the factory. On the other hand, well-financed schools can afford to hire more teachers and specialists, build facilities with open, flexible environments, and acquire the latest in innovative equipment and materials; thereby enabling administrators and teachers to individualize instruction and develop independence, self-initiative and other characteristics in children to prepare them for adequate job performance in the upper levels of the occupational hierarchy.

According to Bowles and Gintis's thesis, these aspects of schooling contribute to the reproduction of the unequal class structure of American society by reinforcing and inculcating noncognitive traits in students that are characteristic of their family SEB. The exceptional few who manage to move upward in the occupational hierarchy through their educational attainments gain this mobility not because of their increased cognitive skills, but primarily because their socialization through schooling has made them acceptable to employers for higher job status.

ASIAN AMERICANS AS THE "MODEL MINORITY": MYTH OR REALITY?

The revisionist interpretation of American educational history outlined in the previous section raises some profoundly disturbing questions regarding the widely acclaimed "success" of Asian Americans, particularly in view of the fact that they are one of the most highly educated ethnic groups in the country. Why have Asian Americans invested so heavily in education? What has been the effect of all this schooling on the socialization patterns of Asian Americans? Has it led to the class-differentiated socialization patterns posited by the revisionists? Or, have these patterns been significantly modified for Asian Americans as a result of their encounters with racism?

These and other questions posed earlier will be explored in this section as we examine various aspects of the "model minority" thesis. Previous theories that have attempted to delineate the causal factors leading to the current socioeconomic status of Asian Americans will be compared with each other and re-examined from the revisionist perspective within the context of three major propositions that will be presented as the basis for an alternative theory. The rationale behind each proposition will be discussed and supporting empirical data, when available, will also be presented.

Most of the previous theories that have been forwarded to account for the apparently phenomenal and anomalous rise in the socio-economic status of Asian Americans may be described as variants of the theory of "cultural determinism." Basically, this theory posits that the current status of Asian Americans is a logical outcome of their unique cultural characteristics. One of the earliest studies to forward such a thesis was that conducted by Caudill and DeVos on Japanese Americans who had resettled in Chicago after their release from detention camps at the end of World War II. They came to the conclusion that the acceptance and surprisingly successful adaptation of the Chicago Japanese was basically due to the compatibility between traditional Japanese and American middle-class values. Such characteristics as respect for authority and parental wishes, diligence, punctuality, cleanliness, neatness, self-discipline and high achievement motivation were seen by Caudill and DeVos as Japanese cultural attributes that were viewed favorably by members of the majority group, particularly employers.[35]

With minor modifications, Harry Kitano's study, *Japanese Americans: The Evolution of a Subculture*, generally reaffirms Caudill and DeVos's thesis. While he does not believe that Japanese and American middle-class values are the same, Kitano takes the position that the acculturation of Japanese Americans has been relatively successful because of the "functional compatibility and interaction" between the two value systems. Moreover, using sociologist Milton Gordon's model of assimilation, he concludes that Sansei and later generations of Japanese Americans will become increasingly assimilated both culturally and structurally to American middle-class society in the near future.[36]

Almost parallel theories have been forwarded to explain the success of Chinese Americans. Again, the importance of their unique cultural characteristics is emphasized in most of these theories. For example, Betty Lee Sung and Francis Hsu have both pointed to such cultural values and norms as family unity, respect for elders, respect for authority, industry, high value for education, and personal discipline as traits that have served the Chinese well in helping them succeed in American society.[37]

A variation in this repetitive theme was introduced by Ivan Light in his comparative study of entrepreneurship among the Chinese, Japanese and blacks in the United States. He attributes the success of small businesses in the Chinese and Japanese communities not only to the enterprising propensities of individuals, but also to the tradition of rotating credit associations that was widely practiced in these communities.[38] A similar theory was forwarded by William Peterson in a book that he wrote as a follow-up to his article in the *New York Times*. He also cites the supportive structure of the Japanese community as the major causal factor in the success of Japanese Americans, although his notions about the nature of this structure are both more general and less defined than Light's.[39]

Only after the rise of the Asian American movement in the late sixties did a few Asian

American scholars begin to question the validity of such "success" theories and to forward alternative explanations. For example, Stanley and Derald Sue argued that traditional Asian cultural values were not compatible, but strongly conflicted with American middle-class values.[40] In studies conducted on Chinese and Japanese students at the University of California at Berkeley, Sue found that:

> Because of their practical and applied approach to life problems, [Asian Americans] tend to be more intolerant of ambiguities and to feel much more comfortable in well-structured situations. Asian Americans also appear less autonomous and less independent from parental controls and authority figures. They are more obedient, conservative, conforming and inhibited.[41]

These results, he contended, were due to the fact that:

> Asian cultural values, emphasizing restraint of strong feelings, obedience, dependence upon the family, and formality in interpersonal relations, are being exhibited by these students. These values are in sharp contrast to Western emphasis on spontaneity, assertiveness, and informality.[42]

According to the Sues, such conflicts have led to serious psychological problems for Asian Americans.[43] Similar observations have been reported in other studies on both males and females of Chinese and Japanese ancestry.[44] Based on their clinical studies, the Sues present a typology of three personality types—the Traditionalist, the Marginal Man and the Asian American—which they propose as a possible framework for assessing the mental health problems of Asian Americans.

The Sues' theoretical framework has, in turn, been scathingly critiqued by Ben Tong, who contends that passive, conforming and acquiescent behavior was not at all characteristic of the early Chinese immigrants. He cites studies which indicate that the 19th century Cantonese peasants were "a worldly, rebellious and emotional lot."[45] According to Tong's alternative thesis, the personality traits exhibited by the progeny of these "bold and vigorous" Chinese pioneers resulted from the long history of racial oppression against the Chinese beginning with the rabid anti-Chinese movement in the latter half of the 19th century. He argues that in order to survive this movement, the Chinese were forced to adopt behavioral patterns that would not attract too much attention or elicit adverse reaction from the larger white society.[46]

Thus, Tong rejects the Sues' basic premise that the early Chinese immigrants brought traditional Chinese cultural values with them. He also takes them to task for their ahistorical approach to the mental health problems of Asian Americans and for proposing remedies that are bound to the narrow and basically conservative framework of conventional psychotherapy, without considering more radical alternatives.

Such alternatives are difficult to consider, however, given our present level of understanding of the various causal factors involved. The theories purporting to explain the "success" of Asian Americans and the ensuing debate over them seem to have created more confusion than clarity. It is my belief that our understanding of the issues can be clarified considerably by analyzing them through the revisionist perspective in conjunction with the three major propositions that constitute the basis for my alternative theory.

The first of these propositions may be stated thus:

> Proposition 1: The personality traits exhibited by Asian Americans are the result of a socialization process in which the schools play a major role through their selective reinforcement of certain cultural behavior patterns and inculcation of others that are deemed "appropriate" for lower-echelon white-collar wage workers.

This proposition is strongly suggested by the striking similarities in the personality traits of Asian Americans as described by the Sues and others[47] and those of individuals from working-class backgrounds as reported by other investigators.[48] Such traits as obedience, conformity, punctuality and respect for authority have been observed to characterize both groups. As discussed earlier, Bowles and Gintis have argued that these traits are produced in working-class children through their socialization in the family and the schools. The logical extension of their argument strongly suggests that similar influences may be at work in the personality development of Asian Americans.

The above-stated proposition differs in two respects from the thesis forwarded by the Sues. First of all, contrary to the Sues' thesis, the proposition postulates the transmission of only certain Asian cultural characteristics and implies, conversely, that certain others were suppressed and not transmitted. These suppressed characteristics may have been the very ones that Tong claims were the predominant traits of the early Chinese immigrants. Secondly, the proposition further implies that the personality traits are those sought by employers in lower-echelon white-collar wage workers, and in this respect, are quite compatible. This compatibility may, in fact, partly account for the upward mobility of Asian Americans. Although this proposition may appear to lead to a conclusion very similar to that of Caudill and DeVos and of Kitano, its interpretation and implications are actually quite different.

Furthermore, the first proposition is also not totally in accord with Tong's contention that the cultural behavior patterns of the early Chinese immigrants were completely transformed by the effects of racial oppression. Although it does imply that certain "undesirable" traits (such as rebelliousness) may have been suppressed through socialization, it also implies that certain other traits may have been reinforced and passed on. This would appear to be a more tenable position than Tong's. His thesis seems to over-emphasize the effects of the 125-year-long history of anti-Chinese oppression and to underestimate the rapid and powerful influence that schools and other social institutions can have on the socialization of children.

The past experiences of Southern and Eastern European ethnic groups clearly demonstrate the pervasive influence such institutions can have. Beginning in the late 1800's, the nativist movements directed against these groups culminated in the Americanization movement during the First World War and its aftermath when intensive efforts were mounted to "Americanize" the millions of new immigrants and their children through extensive educational programs.[49] As a result, millions of these "white ethnics" were forcibly and traumatically acculturated into the American mainstream. The almost total obliteration of the cultural identities of these ethnic groups, which are only now being painfully revived, attests to the outstanding success of the Americanization movement.[50]

Asian Americans have also suffered similar traumas of acculturation as so poignantly exemplified in the classic autobiography by Jade Snow Wong.[51] Her dilemma has been incisively analyzed by Chun-Hoon in terms of its contemporary relevance to the issues of cultural identity for Asian Americans.[52] This phenomenon is still observable today among families of recent Asian immigrants. "Cultural conflicts" frequently break out between the immigrant parents and their American-born and educated offspring, despite (or perhaps because of) the best efforts of the parents to maintain traditional cultural values.[53] Thus, while the blatant racism of the "yellow peril" era on which Tong focused so much attention undoubtedly had some effect, the more pervasive and insidious effect is more likely to be found in the subtle, implicit forms of contemporary racism, such as the socialization process to which children are subjected in the public schools.[54]

This brings us to the second major proposition of the paper, which more directly addresses the question of whether or not Asian Americans have indeed achieved the phenomenal success for which they have been so profusely extolled.

Proposition 2: Although they have attained high levels of education, the upward mobility of Asian Americans has been limited by the effects of racism and most of them have been channeled into lower-echelon white-collar jobs having little or no decision-making authority, low mobility and low public contact.

While this proposition appears to be in contradiction to the fact, cited in the introductory section, that both the Chinese and Japanese have higher median family incomes than do families in the population as a whole, it becomes plausible when the incomes of individuals rather than those of families are examined. Table 1 summarizes data from the 1970 U.S. Census on the median annual incomes of individuals, median years of schooling completed, and median ages of whites, blacks and the three major Asian subgroups by sex.

As seen from this table, the median incomes of Chinese and Pilipino males are only about 75 percent of the median income of white males in the U.S.; while that of Japanese males is about 10 percent above that of white males.

In the case of Japanese males, however, it should be noted that both their median years of schooling and median age are substantially greater than the corresponding medians for white males. Moreover, a large percentage of the Japanese are concentrated in areas where incomes are higher than average (such as California), or where the cost of living is higher than average (such as Hawaii). If adjustments were made for these demographic variables, the resulting "normalized" median income of Japanese males could fall considerably below that of white males.

Although such adjustments could not be computed from the available Census data, some indication of their effect may be seen in the results reported in a recent paper presented by Amado Cabezas.[55] In comparing the earnings of Asian and white males in the SMSA's of San Francisco, Los Angeles, Chicago and New York—cities with relatively high concentrations of Asian Americans, he found that the ratios between the median annual incomes of Chinese, Pilipino and Japanese males and those of white males were on the order of 0.5, 0.6 and 0.9, respectively.

If further adjustments could be made for the disparities in median years of schooling, these ratios would undoubtedly be even lower. Again, some indication of the effect of such adjustments may be seen in the results obtained by Betty Lee Sung for a study she conducted for the U.S. Department of Labor. Table 2 compares the relative earnings of whites, blacks and Chinese at different levels of education. The percentage of Chinese males earning $10,000 or more is seen to be consistently below that of white males at the same educational levels. In fact, the percentage figure for Chinese males is even below that of black males at the post-graduate level.

Table 1. Median Years of Schooling Completed and Median Age in 1970, by Race & Sex

Race	Population		Income*		Schooling+		Age	
	M	F	M	F	M	F	M	F
White	86,891,708	91,215,482	$6,772	$2,374	12.1	12.1	27.6	30.2
Black	10,728,182	11,821,633	4,067	2,002	9.4	10.0	21.0	23.7
Chinese	226,733	204,850	5,124	2,642	12.5	12.1	27.8	25.8
Japanese	271,453	316,871	7,471	3,200	12.6	12.4	29.6	34.3
Pilipino	183,175	153,556	4,971	3,476	11.9	12.8	28.3	24.5

*Persons 14 yrs. & older.; + Persons 25 yrs. & older.
Source: U.S. Bureau of the Census, 1970 Census of Population, *General Social and Economic Characteristics: U.S. Summary* PC(1)-C1; *Detailed Characteristics: U.S. Summary*, PC(1)-D1. Subject Reports: *Japanese, Chinese and Filipinos in the U.S.*, PC(2)-1G. In a number of cases, further computations using data from these sources were necessary in order to arrive at the tabulated medians.

Table 2. Percentage of Persons Earning $10,000 or More in 1969 by Educational Level, Race and Sex

Race	High School Graduates		College Graduates		Post-Graduates	
	M	F	M	F	M	F
White	32.5	2.4	59.6	10.2	67.1	27.7
Black	10.4	0.9	35.3	11.2	53.0	34.2
Chinese	20.9	2.6	38.3	9.3	50.9	13.3

Source: Betty Lee Sung *Chinese American Manpower and Employment*, Washington, D.C.: U.S. Dept. of Labor Manpower Administration (1975), Table 24

Finally, a general indication of the overall pattern for all three Asian subgroups may be seen in the results obtained by Urban Associates in a study conducted for the Department of H.E.W. A summary of these data is presented in Table 3, which tabulates the ratio of persons earning $10,000 or more to persons with 4 years of college or more for 1969 by race, age and sex. The ratios for white males are seen to be consistently higher than those for Asian males with the single exception of Japanese males in the age range 45–65 years old. Generally speaking, these data imply that white males without college degrees have a much higher chance of earning $10,000 or more than Asian males without college degrees; or, conversely, that Asian males with college degrees have a much lower chance of earning $10,000 or more than white males with college degrees.

The apparent contradiction between the relatively low median incomes of Asian males and the relatively high median incomes of Asian families may be explained primarily by the fact that a larger proportion of Asian families have two or more earners than do families in the general population.[56] Not only do a larger percentage of Asian wives work than wives in the population as a whole, but Asian families are also larger on the average and Asian children remain longer with the family and, therefore, contribute more to family income. Moreover, the higher median incomes of Asian families may be due to regional differences and, thus, more apparent than real. In fact, Fong and Cabezas in a recent paper show that in the San Francisco-Oakland SMSA, the mean incomes of Chinese, Pilipino and Japanese families all fall below that of white families.[57]

Another factor contributing to the higher median incomes of Asian families may be the higher median incomes of Asian females compared to their white counterparts (c.f., Table 1, 2 and 3). However, much of this additional income may be earned in low-status occupations, as indicated by Table 2, which shows that Chinese females have a better chance than white or black females of earning $10,000 or more only at the lower educational lev-

Table 3. Ratio of Persons Earnings $10,000 or More to Persons With 4 Years of College or More, 1969, by Race, Age and Sex

	25–34		35–44		45–64	
	M	F	M	F	M	F
White	1.5	0.1	2.4	0.3	3.1	0.5
Chinese	0.5	0.1	1.1	0.3	1.5	0.4
Japanese	0.9	0.1	1.8	0.4	3.4	0.8
Pilipino	0.5	0.1	0.9	0.2	2.2	0.3

Source: Urban Associates, Inc., *A Study of Selected Socio-Economic Characteristics of Ethnic Minorities Based on the 1970 Census*, vol. 2: Asian Americans, Washington, D.C.: Dept. of HEW, Office of Special Concerns (July 1974).

els, but not at the higher levels. Furthermore, the higher incomes of Asian females may again be due to regional differences and their incomes may actually fall below that of white females if comparisons were made on a regional basis.[58]

In any event, the above data indicate that gross disparities exist between the incomes of Asian males and those of white males, particularly if cohorts of equal educational attainment in regions of relatively high Asian American concentration are compared. Education obviously does not gain nearly as much earning power for Asian males as it does for white males. In fact, the preceding analysis indicates that Asian American males, on the whole, are under-employed, underpaid, or both; and that they have certainly not achieved middle-class status as measured by economic indices. Since their status is a good measure of the relative status of Asian Americans as a group, one must conclude that the celebration of their phenomenal "success" as the "model minority" is at best premature, and at worst, a devious deception.

What is suggested by the second proposition is that the contradiction described above between the educational attainments of Asian Americans and their incomes arises from the effects of racism and the relegation of Asian Americans to lower-echelon white-collar occupations. While these factors may have historical antecedents, which will be discussed later in conjunction with the third proposition, only their contemporary manifestations will be examined in the present discussion.

As mentioned earlier, racism against Asian Americans has assumed rather subtle, implicit forms. The institutionalized racism manifested in the "Anglo-conformity" orientation of most school systems—an inevitable result of centralized, bureaucratic control—has already been noted. Other related manifestations have been described in a perceptive essay by Watanabe.[59] In support of his assertion that Asian Americans exhibit a noticeable reticence and inability to express and assert themselves verbally, he cites data from the University of California at Berkeley showing that over half of the entering first-year Asian American students, twice the rate for entering students as a whole, failed to pass a required entrance examination which tested for basic competence in reading and composition. He believes that the verbal reticence of Asians, while partly due to cultural influences, is strongly reinforced by their encounters with American racism. Not only are Asian American students reluctant to call attention to themselves in class for fear of inviting ridicule or hostility, they are also alienated by the cultural incongruity of the Anglo-dominated and -oriented school system, thus further hindering the development of their basic verbal-linguistic skills.

There is also evidence of subtle and widespread employment discrimination against Asian Americans. Since the advent of the Asian American movement in the late sixties, Asian Americans have been less reluctant to protest against instances of perceived discrimination. Consequently in recent years numerous complaints have been filed by Asian Americans, mainly in civil service, who have charged that they have been continually passed over for promotion to supervisory positions by whites who had scored lower on the written civil service exams.[60] In cases that have been investigated, the usual explanation given is that the Asian American candidate did poorly on the oral interview compared to his white competitor, implying that Asian Americans do not have the requisite personality traits, such as aggressiveness, verbal fluency and self-confidence, to assume supervisory positions.

Even greater employment discrimination against Asian Americans appears to exist in the private sector. A survey of executives of 50 major corporations in California in 1970 revealed that few of them had ever employed Asians at the executive levels.[61] According to this survey, a general distrust of Asians prevailed along with a concern that their placement in executive positions would elicit adverse reactions from potential customers.

As posited by the second proposition, these various forms of discrimination have worked to channel large numbers of Asian Americans into lower-echelon white-collar jobs.

This hypothesis seems to be supported by some limited data compiled by Cabezas on the occupational scores of Asians and whites in three selected SMSA's. He shows that:

> Asian occupational scores are five to ten points lower than white scores among those with less than a high school education as well as for those with a high school education. And among those who have attended college, the Asian scores are 10 to 20 points lower, on the average.[62]

Furthermore, Cabezas also notes that as professionals, Asians tend to be accountants, dentists, engineers, nurses and health technicians, rather than attorneys, physicians, social scientists, or teachers; as managers, they tend to be self-employed, rather than buyers, managers, school or public administrators, or salaried managers; as salesworkers, they are mostly retail sales clerks, and not insurance agents, brokers, retail salespersons, or sales representatives; and, finally, as clerical workers, they are usually file clerks, typists and office machine operators, rather than receptionists or secretaries. Generally speaking, most of those jobs appear to be the type that have little or no decision-making authority, low mobility and low public contact.

While this completes our discussion of the first two propositions, we are still left with some unanswered questions. In particular, reasons have not yet been given to explain why Asians invested so heavily in education, why most of them entered lower-echelon white-collar occupations rather than semi-skilled or skilled blue-collar occupations, and why they acquired the particular type of training and socialization deemed appropriate for these jobs. These questions will be addressed in conjunction with the presentation of the third and last proposition.

> Proposition 3: The limited upward mobility of Asian Americans was achievable because of the demand for workers to fill lower-echelon white-collar jobs created by post–World War II expansion in the economy (technological/bureaucratic) coupled with the type of training and socialization Asians had acquired through both the home and extended schooling.

In order to provide a plausible rationale for this proposition, I shall briefly examine the historical experience of Asians in the United States, and the ways in which that experience may have influenced their outlook on American society, particularly their attitudes toward education.[63]

Due to discriminatory laws and practices, the early Asian immigrants were denied entry into craft and other unions and barred from employment in most white-owned businesses. As a consequence, they saw no future for themselves as blue-collar wage workers and were forced to become independent farmers or to open their own businesses and develop their own largely self-sufficient communities—the Chinatowns and Little Tokyos— which could meet most of the needs of the Asian populaces. However, as self-employed entrepreneurs occupying the lower rungs of the stratified system, most of them were forced to wage a continuous struggle against the harshest of conditions in order to eke out a living.[64]

In order to survive this ordeal, Asian parents probably felt it was necessary to inculcate their children with some of the more authoritarian aspects of traditional cultural values such as filial piety, respect for parental authority, obedience and self-discipline. At the same time, they doubtlessly hoped for a better way of life for their children. Since very few other options existed, they very likely saw schooling as one of the only avenues left for their children's upward mobility. This almost desperate faith in schooling was undoubtedly reinforced by the traditional veneration accorded to education in Asian societies. The schools, in turn, reaffirmed this faith by rewarding the compliance, good behavior, perseverance and docility of Asian children and by instilling in them the dream that everyone—no matter how humble their origins—had an equal chance to succeed in American society.

Due to their marginal position in the class structure outside the wage economy, we can speculate that the Asian entrepreneurial class, despite their low economic status, gradually developed an outlook on American society corresponding to that of a petit bourgeois. This outlook and their past experiences with the racism of white workers led them to shun possible futures for their children in blue-collar occupations, and, instead, to aspire toward white-collar professions for their children. However, the realities of racism imposed practical limits on these aspirations and led them to encourage their children to choose careers in lower-echelon white-collar occupational areas, especially in the technical-scientific areas.[65] These choices were undoubtedly also strongly influenced by the underdevelopment of their verbal-linguistic skills, which discouraged them from entering fields requiring high public contact, and by the advice and direction offered by teachers and guidance counselors.

Thus through this process we can hypothesize that Asian Americans came to acquire the values and skills that uniquely suited them for lower-echelon white-collar jobs. A high demand for masses of workers to fill such jobs was created in the two decades following World War II as a result of the enormous expansion in the technological/bureaucratic sectors of the economy.[66] Asian Americans were almost ideally prepared to meet this demand since so many of them had been trained in the appropriate areas. They were also probably viewed by employers as having the almost ideal personality traits for these jobs as a result of their socialization in the home and through their extended years of schooling. Moreover, given their relatively small numbers, they were no longer a serious competitive threat, particularly in the civil service sectors where there was a shortage of workers for low-paying jobs requiring specialized, technical skills.

CONCLUSIONS

Although the alternative theory just presented is only a tentative, preliminary synthesis and is presently supported by limited empirical evidence. I believe it provides a more comprehensive analysis of the "model minority" thesis than those provided by previous theories. In particular, it goes beyond the theory of cultural determinism and seeks to explain the behavioral patterns of Asian Americans not only in terms of their cultural values and norms, but also within the broader context of dynamical socio-historical forces and the larger social system. Moreover, by applying the revisionist perspective, it seriously challenges the widely accepted notion that Asian Americans have achieved middle-class status and have been almost completely assimilated into the American mainstream.

The raising of this challenge suggests that additional empirical evidence is needed to differentially assess the validity of the various theories. However, it also suggests that different theoretical perspectives on social processes can lead to very different interpretations and conclusions. In social science research we often find that the available empirical evidence is compatible with more than one theory. Consequently, conflicting theoretical explanations of social processes frequently emerge. Since empirical data are rarely sufficient to clearly determine which of the various theories is correct, such conflicting explanations tend to reflect the underlying value assumptions of their respective theoretical perspectives.[67]

Speaking quite generally, one can say that the perspective of the cultural determinists reflects what sociologists have referred to as the "consensus perspective"; whereas, the revisionist perspective reflects what they have referred to as the "conflict perspective."[68] The particular perspective adopted may influence not only the interpretations and conclusions of a research study, but also the methodology employed in the study. For example, the demographic and survey-type studies frequently conducted by consensus theorists would tend to be of doubtful validity to conflict theorists, who would be wary of accepting the data at face value without examining such factors as actual outcomes and conditions, unintentional effects and underlying causes. Instead, they would tend to rely more on field-based methods such as participant-observation, open-ended personal interviews and unobtrusive measures.[69]

These limitations of methodology should be kept in mind in future studies that attempt to assess the socioeconomic status of Asian Americans. Cold statistical data alone cannot tell the whole story. For example, many Asian Americans may be drawing relatively good wages, but find themselves trapped in monotonous, meaningless, dead-end white-collar jobs that stifle their creativity and potential. Their income figures alone would hardly reveal their personal agonies over frustrated ambitions, broken dreams and suppressed anger.

Furthermore, many Asian Americans do not fall into the category of lower-echelon white-collar wage worker to which the theory presented in this paper applies, but may still earn relatively good incomes by working long, exhaustive hours, often at menial tasks, as self-employed gardeners, shopkeepers or small farmers. For example, by working 10–12 hours per day and 6 days per week, many Asian American gardeners can make as much as $15,000 to $20,000 annually.

Finally, more caution should probably be exercised in interpreting certain statistical data, such as those showing high rates of out-marriage for Asian Americans cited at the beginning of this paper. Employing Gordon's model of assimilation, mentioned earlier in connection with Kitano's study, one may conclude that such rates are another indicator of how rapidly Asian Americans are being assimilated. However, as noted by William Newman, Gordon's model is derived from the consensus perspective and leads to the conclusion that assimilation is a linear, irreversible process.[70] Newman, on the other hand, adopting the conflict perspective, concludes that assimilation is neither irreversible nor inevitable. He points out that in interracial marriages the minority group partner may not necessarily assimilate into the majority group, and cites studies which show that the opposite process may often occur instead.[71]

The examples discussed above attempt to demonstrate the importance of a researcher's perspective in making interpretations about data. In general, as Newman and Schermerhorn have suggested, the consensus and conflict perspectives should be viewed in dialectical relationship to each other, rather than as two separate and unbridgeable schools of thought.[72] Since both order and conflict are ubiquitous in society, the relevance of a particular perspective may depend on the time, place and context in which the social process under examination is occurring. However, Newman has suggested that the conflict perspective may provide the most useful and meaningful framework for understanding intergroup relations in highly plural societies, such as the United States.[73] Yet the consensus perspective has predominated research in this field, for fairly obvious reasons, not the least of which may be the "safeness," acceptability and fundability of studies conducted from that perspective.

Hopefully, some of the concepts and ideas presented in this paper will begin to redress the balance, and more importantly, stimulate new directions of inquiry and analysis that can eventually contribute to the development of a more coherent theory and deeper understanding of the Asian experience in American society.

NOTES

1. Dorothy Jones, *The Portrayal of China and India on the American Screen, 1896–1955* (Cambridge, Mass., 1955); Stuart C. Miller, *The Unwelcome Immigrant: The American Image of the Chinese, 1785–1882* (Berkeley, 1969); Dennis Ogawa, *From Japs to Japanese: The Evolution of Japanese-American Stereotypes* (Berkeley, 1971).

2. See, e.g.: Mary Coolidge, *Chinese Immigration* (New York, 1909); Gunther Barth. *Bitter Strength: A History of the Chinese in the United States, 1850–1870* (Cambridge, Mass., 1964); Alexander Saxton. *The Indispensable Enemy: Labor and the Anti-Chinese Movement in California* (Berkeley, 1971); Roger Daniels, *The Politics of Prejudice: The Anti-Japanese Movement in California and the Struggle for Japanese Exclusion* (New York, 1967); Yamato Ichihashi, *Japanese in the United States* (New York, 1932/1969); Jacobus tenBroek, et al., *Prejudice, War and the Constitution* (Berkeley, 1968); Roger Daniels and Harry Kitano, *American Racism* (Englewood Cliffs, N.J., 1970), Michi Weglyn, *Years of Infamy: The Untold Story of America's Concentration Camps* (New York, 1976).

3. William Peterson. "Success Story, Japanese-American Style," *New York Times* 9 January 1966, 21.

4. "Success Story of One Minority Group in U.S.," *U.S. News & World Report* 26 December 1966, 73–76.

5. Paul Wong, "The Emergence of the Asian American Movement," *Bridge 2* (Sept./Oct., 1972). 33 39; Paul Jacobs et al., *To Serve the Devil: A Documentary Analysis of America's Racial History and Why It Has Been Kept Hidden* (New York, 1971). 2, 219–222.

6. Amy Uyematsu, "The Emergence of Yellow Power in America," in Tachiki, et al., *Roots: An Asian American Reader* (Los Angeles, 1971), 9–13; Lloyd K. Wake, "Shhh! An Asian American is Speaking," *Hokubei Mainichi* 24 February 1970.

7. Urban Associates, Inc., *A Study of Selected Socio-economic Characteristics of Ethnic Minorities Based on the 1970 Census*, II: "Asian Americans" (Washington, D.C.: Dept. of H.E.W., Office of Special Concerns, 1974).

8. "Precisely because Asian Americans have become economically secure, do they face serious identity problems. Fully committed to a system that subordinates them on the basis of non-whiteness. Asian Americans still try to gain complete acceptance by denying their yellowness. They have become white in every respect but color," Uyematsu. "Yellow Power," 9.

9. The term, Asian American, as used throughout this paper, refers to Chinese and Japanese living in the United States, the two largest Asian American subgroups. However, occasional references will be made to Filipinos, who constitute the third largest Asian American (or Pacific Island American, as many of them prefer to be called) subgroup, whenever information on this group is available.

10. The term, "revisionist," a term widely used among educational historians, refers here simply to an alternative perspective on American educational history.

11. William L. Neumann, *America Encounters Japan: From Perry to MacArthur* (Baltimore, 1963), 161.

12. Some of the critiques that have appeared in various fields include: Dell Hymes, ed., *Reinventing Anthropology* (New York, 1969); Alvin W. Gouldner, *The Coming Crisis of Western Sociology* (New York, 1970); Jurgen Habermas. *Legitimation Crisis* (Boston, 1973); Clarence J. Karier, et al., *Roots of Crisis: American Education in the Twentieth Century* (Chicago, 1973).

13. See, e.g.: Johnathan Kozol, *Death at an Early Age* (Boston, 1967); Charles F. Silberman, *Crisis in the Classroom* (New York, 1970).

14. C. Bereiter and S. Englemann, *Teaching Disadvantaged Children in the Pre-school* (Englewood Cliffs, N.J., 1966); Robert Rosenthal and Lenore F. Jacobson, *Pygmalion in the Classroom* (New York, 1968); J.L. Frost and G.R. Hawkes, eds., *The Disadvantaged Child: Issues and Innovations* (Boston, 1966); A. Harry Passow, et al., *Education of the Disadvantaged* (New York, 1967).

15. U.S. Commission on Civil Rights, *Racial Isolation in the Public Schools*, I (Washington, D.C., U.S. Government Printing Office, 1967); V. Cicirelli, et al., "The Impact of Head Start: An

Evaluation of the Effects of Head Start on Children's Cognitive and Affective Development," (Report presented to the Office of Economic Opportunity, Contract B89-4536, Westinghouse Learning Corporation/Ohio University, 1969); Michael J. Wargo, et al., "ESEA Title I: A Reanalysis and Synthesis of Evaluation Data from Fiscal Year 1965 Through 1970" (Palo Alto, American Institute for Research, 1972).

16. Critiques of the deficit hypothesis include: William Ryan, *Blaming the Victim* (New York, 1971); Charles A. Valentine, *Culture and Poverty: Critique and Counter-Proposals* (Chicago, 1968); Michael Cole and Jerome S. Bruner, "Cultural Differences and Inferences About Psychological Processes," *American Psychologist* 26 (1971), 867–876.

17. Arthur R. Jensen, "How Much Can We Boost IQ and Scholastic Achievement?," *Harvard Educational Review* 39 (1969), 1–123; William Shockley, "Dysgenics, Geneticity, and Raceology," *Phi Delta Kappan* (1972); R.J. Herrnstein, *I.Q. in the Meritocracy* (Boston, 1–73); H.J. Eysenck, *The IQ Argument* (New York, 1971), Leon Kamins, *The Science and Politics of I.Q.* (Hillsdale, N.J., 1974).

18. Colin Greer, *The Great School Legend: A Revisionist Interpretation of American Public Education* (New York, 1972).

19. Lawrence A. Cremin, *The Genius of American Education* (New York, 1965); Bernard Bailyn, *Education in the Forming of American Society* (New York, 1960); Ellwood P. Cubberley, *Public Education in the United States* (Boston, 1919).

20. Oscar Handlin, "The Goals of Integration," *Daedalus* 95 (1966), 2; J. Iverne Dowie, "The American Negro: An Old Immigrant on a New Frontier," in O.F. Ander, ed., *In the Trek of the Immigrant* (Rock Island, 1964).

21. Michael B. Katz, *Class, Bureaucracy & Schools: The Illusion of Educational Change in America* (New York, 1971); Joel H. Spring, *Education and the Rise of the Corporate State* (Boston, 1972); Martin Carnoy, ed., *Schooling in a Corporate Society* (New York, 1972); Karier, *Roots of Crisis.*

22. Katz, *Class, Bureaucracy & Schools.*

23. *Ibid.*, xx.

24. Spring, *Education and Corporate State.*

25. *Ibid.*, 1.

26. *Ibid.*, xii.

27. Greer, *Great School Legend.*

28. Marvin Lazerson, "Revisionism and American Educational History," *Harvard Educational Review* 43 (1973), 269–283; R. Freeman Butts, Public Education and Political Community," *History of Education Quarterly* 14 (1974), 165–183; J. Christopher Eisele, "John Dewey and the Immigrants," *History of Education Quarterly* 15 (1975), 67–85; Wayne J. Urban, Some Historiographical Problems in Revisionist Educational History: Review of "Roots of Crisis," *American Educational Research Journal* 12 (1975), 337–350; Floyd M. Hammack, "Rethinking Revisionism," *History of Education Quarterly* 16 (1976), 58–64.

29. Samuel Bowles and Herbert Gintis, *Schooling in Capitalist America: Educational Reform and the Contradictions of Economic Life* (New York, 1976).

30. Gary Becker, *Human Capital* (New York, 1964); Theodore Schultz, *The Economic Value of Education* (New York, 1963).

31. Bowles and Gintis, *Schooling in America*, 30, 110.

32. *Ibid.*, 114.

33. Samuel Bowles, "Getting Nowhere: Programmed Class Stagnation," *Society* 9 (1972), 48.

34. ". . . in education, lower levels (junior and senior high school) tend to severely limit and channel the activities of students. Somewhat higher up the educational ladder, teacher and community colleges allow for more independent activity and less overall supervision. At the top, the elite four-year colleges emphasize social relationships conformable with the high levels in the production hierarchy," Bowles and Gintis, *Schooling in America*, 132.

35. William Caudill and George De Vos, "Achievement, Culture and Personality: The Case of the Japanese Americans," *American Anthropologist* 58 (1956), 1102–26.

36. Harry Kitano, *Japanese Americans: The Evolution of a Subculture* (Englewood Cliffs, N.J., 1969).

37. Betty Lee Sung. *Mountain of Gold* (New York, 1967); Francis Hsu, *The Challenge of the American Dream: The Chinese in the United States* (Belmont, Ca., 1971).

38. Ivan Light, *Ethnic Enterprise in America: Business and Welfare Among Chinese, Japanese and Blacks* (Berkeley, 1972).

39. William Peterson, *Japanese Americans: Oppression and Success* (New York, 1971).

40. Stanley and Derald Sue, "Chinese-American Personality and Mental Health," *Amerasia Journal* 1, no. 2 (July 1971), 36–49.

41. Derald Sue, "Ethnic Identity: The Impact of Two Cultures on the Psychological Development of Asians in America," in Stanley Sue and Nathaniel Wagner, eds., *Asian Americans: Psychological Perspectives* (Palo Alto, Ca., 1973), 144.

42. *Ibid.*

43. Stanley and Derald Sue, "Chinese American Personality."

44. See, e.g.: W. Fenz and A. Arkoff, "Comparative Need Patterns of Five Ancestry Groups in Hawaii," *Journal of Social Psychology* 58 (1962), 67–273; Joe Yamamoto, "Japanese American Identity Crisis," in Eugene Brody, ed., *Minority Group Adolescents in the United States* (Baltimore, 1968); V.S. Sommers, "Identity Conflict and Acculturation Problems in Oriental-Americans," *American Journal of Orthopsychiatry* 30 (1960), 637–444: Melford Weiss, "Selective Acculturation and the Dating Process: The Patterning of Chinese-Caucasian Interracial Dating," *Journal of Marriage and the Family* 32 (1970).

45. Ben Tong, "Ghetto of the Mind: Notes on the Historical Psychology of Chinese America," *Amerasia Journal* 1, no. 3 (1971), 1–32.

46. *Ibid.*

47. Mamoru Iga, "The Japanese Social Structure and the Source of Mental Strains of Japanese Immigrants in the United States," *Social Forces* 25 (1957), 271–278; George DeVos and Kenneth Abbott. "The Chinese Family in San Francisco" (MSW dissertation, University of California, Berkeley, 1966).

48. Melvin Kohn, *Class and Conformity: A Study in Values* (Homewood, Ill., 1969); Richard C. Edwards, "Personal Traits and 'Success' in Schooling and Work," *Educational and Psychological Measurement* 35 (1975).

49. John Higham, *Strangers in the Land: Patterns of American Nativism, 1860–1925* (New York, 1972).

50. Michael Novak, *The Rise of the Unmeltable Ethnics* (New York, 1971).

51. Jade Snow Wong, *Fifth Chinese Daughter* (New York, 1950).

52. Lowell Chun-Hoon, "Jade Snow Wong and the Fate of Chinese-American Identity," *Amerasia Journal* 1, no. 1 (1971), 52–63.

53. I do not accept the popular thesis that these cultural conflicts arise because Asian children are socialized by the schools to become more independent, autonomous and individualistic. Quite to the contrary, they may simply become regimented and conform to a different set of rules, regulations and values promulgated by the schools. Worse yet, they may shift their loyalty and respect from their parents to authority figures in the schools. Such cultural conflicts may arise because in the process of "Americanizing" these children, the schools subtly denigrate the values and behaviors of their parents.

54. Mildred Dickeman ("Teaching Cultural Pluralism," in James Banks, ed., *Teaching Ethnic Studies: Concepts and Strategies* [Washington, D.C., 1973]) has described the racism implicit in the centralized, bureaucratic control of the schools. Randall Collins in ("Some Comparative Principles of Educational Stratification," *Harvard Educational Review* 47 (1977), 1–27) argues that such control devices have been used primarily in multi-ethnic societies by the dominant classes to preserve their privileged position.

55. Amado Y. Cabezas, "A View of Poor Linkages Between Education, Occupation and Earnings for Asian Americans" (Paper presented at The Third National Forum on Education and Work, San Francisco, 1977).

56. Urban Associates, *Characteristics of Ethnic Minorities.*

57. Pauline Fong and Amado Cabezas, "Economic and Employment Status of Asian-Pacific Women" (Paper presented to The Conference on the Educational and Occupational Needs of Asian-Pacific Women, San Francisco, 1976).

58. *Ibid.*

59. Colin Watanabe, "Self-Expression and the Asian American Experience," *Personnel and Guidance Journal* 51 (1973), 390–396.

60. Governor's Asian American Advisory Commission, "Report to the Governor on Discrimination Against Asians" (Based on hearings conducted in Seattle, Washington, 1973); California FEPC, "Chinese in San Francisco, 1970: Employment Problems of the Community as Presented in Testimony Before the California Fair Employment Practice Commission" (1970). San Francisco; California Advisory Committee, "Asian Americans and Pacific Peoples: A Case of Mistaken Identity" (Report to the U.S. Commission on Civil Rights, Los Angeles, 1975).

61. Tachiki, *Roots*, x.

62. Cabezas, "Linkages Between Education."

63. I am indebted to Prof. Paul Takagi of the University of California at Berkeley for suggesting and contributing his ideas to the development of this historical analysis.

64. Barth, *Bitter Strength*: Saxton, *Indispensable Enemy*; Daniels, *Politics of Prejudice*; Ichihashi, *Japanese in the United States*.

65. A study by R. Chu ("Majors of Chinese and Japanese students at the University of California, Berkeley for the past 20 years," Project Report, AS 150, Asian Studies Division, University of California, Berkeley, 1971), found that approximately 70 percent of American-born Chinese and Japanese males at the University of California at Berkeley matriculated in either engineering or the physical sciences.

66. Maurice Dobb, *Capitalism Yesterday and Today* (New York, 1962); James O'Conner, "The Expanding Role of the State," in R.C. Edwards, et al., *The Capitalist System* (Englewood, N.J., 1972); C. Wright Mills, *White Collar* (New York, 1956).

67. William E. Connolly and Glen Gordon, *Social Structure and Political Theory* (Lexington, 1974), 40–66.

68. Richard Schermerhorn, *Comparative Ethnic Relations* (New York, 1970).

69. Connolly and Gordon, *Political Theory*.

70. William Newman, *American Pluralism: A Study of Minority Groups and Social Theory* (New York, 1973).

71. *Ibid.*, 162–164.

72. Schermerhorn, *Ethnic Relations*.

73. Newman, *American Pluralism*.

7 Asian American Educational Achievements:

A Phenomenon in Search of an Explanation

Stanley Sue and Sumie Okazaki

GREAT CONCERN HAS been expressed over the educational achievements of American students in general and of ethnic minority students in particular. In 1984, Skinner wrote an article entitled "The Shame of American Education." Skinner's article lamented the educational mediocrity of American schools in terms of student achievements, motivational levels, and learning. Spence (1985), in her American Psychological Association Presidential Address, also noted the lack of excellence in schools, especially in fostering the learning of math and science. Indeed, there has been growing concern that Americans are falling behind students from other countries in educational achievements. The problems are particularly apparent in the schooling of ethnic minority students, such as Blacks, Hispanics, and American Indians, who show lower levels of educational attainments, grades, graduation rates, and school persistence (see California State Department of Education, 1986).

In ethnic minority research, one of the most remarkable phenomena has been the high educational achievements demonstrated by some Asian American groups over the last four decades. Although Asian Americans have been subjected to similar prejudice and discriminatory practices encountered by other ethnic minority groups, their educational attainments have been increasing. In this article we examine the achievements and two of the major explanations that have been proposed for the achievements of Asian Americans, involving possible hereditary or cultural advantages. The topic, of course, is highly controversial. Genetic explanations for racial or ethnic group differences in intelligence and achievements have generated intense debates. Even attributing Asian American achievements to cultural factors can result in disputes involving cultural "superiority" or deficits.

From the very outset, let us make four points. First, as a group, Asian Americans do demonstrate exceptional achievement patterns. However, Asian Americans represent a heterogeneous group with marked within- and between-group variations in a number of characteristics (Barringer, Takeuchi, & Xenos, 1990; Sue & Abe, 1988). We also know that the high achievement levels must be tempered. Asian Americans show not only high educational attainments but relatively higher proportions of individuals with no education whatsoever compared with Whites and ethnic minority groups (Sue & Padilla, 1986). Second, although there is growing interest in Asian American achievements, research findings have not been able to shed much light on the factors that account for the achievement levels. This fact is caused in part by the lack of research on the phenomenon and by the failure to clearly devise adequate or critical tests. Third, in the search for factors that influence achieve-

From *American Psychologist* 45 (1990):913–920. Copyright 1990 by the American Psychological Association. Reprinted by permission.

ment levels, single explanations cannot adequately account for the observed performance patterns. Thus, research on heredity, culture, child-rearing practices, educational experiences, and personality, among other topics, has yielded interesting but inconclusive results. Fourth, explanations for Asian American achievements must incorporate what we call *relative functionalism*. Although cultural explanations propose that achievement is a result of Asian cultural values that extol the virtues of education, or of cultural practices that maximize skills in gaining education, the concept of relative functionalism also considers the problems of achieving in noneducational types of endeavors—those that are not a clear and direct outcome of educational performance. Perceived limitations in mobility in these endeavors increase the relative value or function of education as a means of achieving success.

ACHIEVEMENT LEVELS

In recent years, a number of popular magazines have portrayed Asian Americans as extraordinary achievers: *U.S. News and World Report* (Asian Americans: Are They, 1984); *Newsweek* (A Formula for Success, 1984); *New York Times* (Why Asians Are Going, 1986); *Chronicle of Higher Education* (Asian Students Fear, 1986); *Los Angeles Times Magazine* (When Being Best, 1987); *Time* (The New Whiz Kids, 1987); *National Education Association Today* ("Whiz Kid" Image, 1988); and *Asian Week* (Probing Into, 1990). These periodicals have pointed to the high levels of educational attainments shown by Asian Americans and supported by empirical evidence.

As indicated in Table 1, Asians and Pacific-Islander Americans exceed the national average for high school and college graduates. The rate of graduation from colleges and universities are higher, whether men or women are considered or whether Asians are compared solely with Whites (Bureau of Census, 1983, 1984). Other indicators such as measures of pursuit of higher education and persistence also reveal a strong involvement in education. For example, 86% of Asian Americans versus 64% of Whites are found in some kind of higher education program, two years after high school graduation; and for those who entered a four-year university, 86% of Asian Americans stayed the following year, compared with 75% for Whites, 71% for Blacks, and 66% for Hispanics (Peng, 1988). Within the University of California system, which enrolls the largest number of Asians in the United States, fully 26% of Asian American high school students (not including for-

Table 1. Schooling Completed by Sex and Race/Ethnicity for Persons 25 Years or Older, 1980

Race/ethnicity	High school graduates (%)		4+ years college completed (%)	
	Men	Women	Men	Women
White	69.6	68.1	21.3	13.3
Black	50.8	51.5	8.4	8.3
Hispanic	45.4	42.7	9.4	6.0
AI/Alaskan	57.0	54.1	9.2	6.3
Asian/PI	78.8	71.4	39.8	27.0
Chinese	75.2	67.4	43.8	29.5
Filipino	73.1	67.4	32.2	29.5
Japanese	84.2	79.5	35.2	19.7
Korean	90.0	70.6	52.4	22.0
Asian Indian	88.8	71.5	68.5	35.5
Vietnamese	71.3	53.6	18.2	7.9

Note. AI/Alaskan = American Indian/Alaskan Native; Asian/PI = Asian/Pacific Islander. Bureau of the Census (1983, 1984).

eign students) in 1985 qualified for entry, whereas only 13% of non-Asian students did. Asians also had the highest proportion of students graduating within five years of entry: 63% compared with 61% for Whites, 43% for Blacks, 50% for Hispanics, and 46% for American Indians. These figures do not include foreign students. The high levels of educational achievements can also be seen in reports from the College Board. College-bound Asian American seniors (about 10% of them were foreign students) receive superior high school grades and consistently demonstrate higher Scholastic Aptitude Test scores on the mathematics (SAT-M) subscores, but lower English verbal (SAT-V) subscores than do White or all non-Asian students. For example, in 1989, Asian Americans achieved average scores of 409 on the SAT-V and 525 on the SAT-M compared with scores of 427 on the SAT-V and 476 on the SAT-M for all other students. The high school grade point average of Asian American students was also higher than those of all other students, 3.25 versus 3.08 (College Board, 1989). (For all students, women had slightly lower SAT scores than did men, but they had superior high school grades.) Hsia (1988) noted high achievements not only in these scores but also among the finalists and winners in the National Merit Scholarship Program, Presidential Scholars, and Westinghouse Science Talent Search Program. The evidence for high educational attainments is quite convergent.

EXPLANATIONS FOR THE ACHIEVEMENT PATTERNS

Is it possible to find a simple or parsimonious explanation for the achievement levels of Asian Americans? For example, we know that educational achievements of individuals are directly related to the social class of parents (Jencks, Crouse, & Mueser, 1983). Perhaps Asian Americans are "advantaged" in terms of socioeconomic standing and provide their children with special resources and opportunities. There is no strong evidence that this can explain the racial or ethnic differences. In a report by Arbeiter (1984) on college-bound seniors, the median parental income of Asian Americans was lower than that of Whites, $25,400 and $32,900, respectively; the educational attainments of the parents were comparable. Yet, Asian Americans were found to have higher high school grades and SAT-M scores than did Whites.

Perhaps some of the educational achievements can be accounted for by the inclusion of foreign students among the Asian Americans or by the inclusion of Asian immigrants who already have high levels of education and subsequently become naturalized American citizens or permanent residents. The available evidence does not support this possibility. Using data from the 1980 U.S. Census, Kan and Liu (1986) compared the percentage of native- and foreign-born individuals who had completed four years of college. Although there was a tendency for foreign-born individuals to have higher educational levels, perhaps because of immigration policies favoring the educated, American-born Asians exceeded American-born Whites in the proportion of those with four years of college education. Whites, 18%; Chinese, 42%; Japanese, 27%; and Koreans, 27%. Filipinos (15%) and Asian Indians (13%) born in the United States had somewhat lower percentages than did Whites.

HEREDITY

Is it possible that Asians are innately superior to Whites in intelligence? Consensus exists that the heritability of intelligence is high (Vernon, 1982). However, to fully address this question, it is necessary to demonstrate that Asian Americans are higher not only in educational attainments but also in intelligence and cognitive functioning. Unfortunately, few studies have compared these groups on intelligence measures. After examining studies on IQ test performances, Sowell (1978) concluded that Chinese and Japanese Americans equal or exceed the national average. In a review of intellectual test results for Chinese and Japanese Americans, Vernon also argued that these two groups were superior. However, sample sizes for the reviewed studies were small, and estimates were based on performance rather than on verbal tests, inasmuch as English is not the first language for many Asian Americans—a major limitation in making ethnic comparisons.

Because only small samples of Asian Americans are available, investigators have examined the question of racial differences in intelligence by studying overseas, or foreign, Asians. In 1977, Lynn calculated the mean IQ of Japanese in Japan from standardization studies of the Wechsler (1949, 1955) tests in Japan. Using only the performance subtests, he found that at every age level the Japanese children outperformed the Americans. He discounted other explanations such as test bias and environmental advantage. Lynn (1977) reasoned that because the tests were developed in the United States, it is unlikely that they would be biased in favor of the Japanese. Furthermore, at the time Japanese had lower per capita income than did Americans. Lynn concluded that heredity plays an important role in explaining the group differences. The conclusion was refuted by other investigators, especially Flynn (1982), who reanalyzed Lynn's data. He criticized Lynn for a variety of reasons, but particularly for not taking into account the yearly average gains in IQ that have occurred; the American norms used to compare with Japanese performances were established several years earlier. In addition, Flynn noted that Lynn vacillated between using Whites and all Americans (Whites and other ethnic minority Americans) as the standard by which to compare Japanese performances. By correcting for these factors, Flynn found little differences in IQ performance between Americans and Japanese. The debate between the two investigators has continued (see Flynn, 1987; Lynn, 1987). It has highlighted the methodological and conceptual problems in cross-national studies of intelligence and has revived the controversies regarding the meaning of intelligence, methods to estimate intelligence, and validity of instruments. In view of the problems, the hereditary perspective has received little empirical support.

The most extensive work on cross-national comparisons in intelligence has been conducted by Harold Stevenson and his colleagues (Stevenson & Azuma, 1983; Stevenson, Lee, & Stigler, 1986; Stevenson et al., 1985; Uttal, Lummis, & Stevenson, 1988). Stevenson et al. believe that Lynn failed to take into account the fact that the Japanese samples tended to have higher socioeconomic standing and a higher representation of urban than rural children than did the American samples from which the norms were constructed. Stevenson wanted to use a direct approach to comparing cognitive abilities. First- and fifth-graders in Japan, Taiwan, and United States were carefully selected and matched on demographic variables. Cognitive measures—verbal and performance tests—were devised with considerable attention to task equivalence and appropriateness for the different cultures and languages. Achievement tests for mathematics and reading were also constructed. Reliability for the measures was found to be generally good. Results on the cognitive measures revealed a few group differences on subtests, but no overall difference in intelligence. Distribution and variability of scores were similar for each sample. On mathematics achievement tests, Chinese performed well, whereas Americans had relatively low scores. Cognitive performance was a fairly good predictor of mathematics achievement scores but not of verbal scores. There were no general differences in cognitive functioning between the samples, and superiority of Asians in math was not attributable to higher levels of cognitive functioning among the Asian samples. Obviously, group differences in complex characteristics or behaviors such as intelligence may be attributed to the interaction of innate characteristics, cultural roots, and other environmental conditions (Greenfield & Childs, in press), but the hypothesis that Asians are genetically superior in intelligence would appear to be refuted by empirical data.

CULTURE

The other major explanation for the achievements of Asian Americans is cultural in nature. Cultural institutions, such as schools, may affect learning and performance. For example, in their extensive observations in the three societies, Stevenson, Lee, and Stigler (1986) found that U.S. schools spent less time on academic activities, U.S. teachers imparted less information, and there was less emphasis on homework in U.S. than in Chinese or Japanese schools. However, in explaining the achievements of Asian Americans, differences in school experiences cannot fully account for the high achievement levels of Asian Americans, especially those born and educated in this country.

The most popular cultural view is that Asian family values and socialization experiences emphasize the need to succeed educationally. Largely on the basis of anecdotal and observational evidence rather than on empirical findings, investigators have identified the following values or practices in Asian families that may promote educational achievements: demands and expectations for achievement and upward mobility, induction of guilt about parental sacrifices and the need to fulfill obligations, respect for education, social comparisons with other Asian-American families in terms of educational success, and obedience to elders such as teachers. From structured interviews with Asian American students, Mordkowitz and Ginsburg (1987) provided anecdotal support for a cultural interpretation involving family socialization for high achievements. The students reported that their families emphasized educational accomplishments, held high expectations for achievements, controlled the behaviors of the students, and considered schooling very important. Such anecdotal evidence about Asian culture and socialization practices must be tempered. Culture is a concept that has been used to explain all phenomena, but one that is difficult to define and to test.

A cultural interpretation proposes that socialization patterns and institutional practices within a culture can aid, be irrelevant to, or hinder educational pursuits. Hard work, respect for education, and the motivation to become educated, among other traits, foster academic success. In the cultural model, the research task is to identify relevant cultural values and practices and correlate them with educational attainments. Three implications are generated by the model, as shown in Table 2. First, cultural factors (e.g., child-rearing

Table 2. Contrasting the Cultural and Relative Functionalism Perspectives

Culture	Relative functionalism
Assumptions and predictions	
Cultural values can aid, be irrelevant to, or hinder educational pursuits. Asian American values foster educational achievements. Asian cultural values are directly related to educational achievements. With increased acculturation, educational achievements decline.	Asian Americans experience and receive limited mobility in noneducational areas of success. The greater the limitations in noneducational areas the more salient education becomes as a means for mobility.
Research tasks	
Identify relevant cultural values and correlate with educational achievement over time.	Examine perceptions of mobility in non-educational areas; correlate perceptions with educational pursuits and priorities.
Societal implications	
Inculcate in others those Asian American values that facilitate educational achievements.	In addition to cultural values, the status and situation of Asians in American society must be studied

Note. The relative functionalism perspective does not disagree with the assumptions, tasks, and implications of the cultural thesis. It simply adds another dimension to explain the achievements of Asian Americans.

practices, and socialization experiences characteristic of the cultural group) should correlate strongly with achievement levels. Second, with increased acculturation to mainstream American values (and extinction of Asian cultural values), achievement levels should diminish. Third, to improve educational attainments for all groups, Americans should selectively adopt certain Asian cultural values. Certainly, the American business community has explored alternative corporate practices, often modeling after the Japanese, who are perceived as being successful economic and business entrepreneurs.

Despite much anecdotal speculation, few rigorous studies have tested the cultural thesis, and available research provides little support. In examining possible cultural factors in achievements, Dornbusch and colleagues (Dornbusch, Prescott, & Ritter, 1987; Dornbusch, Ritter, Leiderman, Roberts, & Fraleigh, 1987; Ritter & Dornbusch, 1989) have recently reported on their ongoing investigations of thousands of high school students in California, including one of the largest population of Asian Americans ever surveyed. The project investigated the relation between family variables and academic achievement for various ethnic minority groups. Several interesting findings that have relevance for our discussion emerged from the rich data collected. First, Asian American students exhibited the highest grade point average among all groups, including Blacks, Latinos, Whites, and others. Second, on the basis of the responses to the questionnaires, students from the ethnic groups were compared on the type of family in which they had been reared: Parental communication patterns that foster unquestioning obedience to parents (authoritarian style), freedom for the child to choose what to do with minimal parental involvement (permissive), and expectations for mature behavior and encouragement of open two-way communications between parents and children (authoritative). Asian American students came from families high on authoritarian and permissive and low on authoritative characteristics, the opposite of White students. Their parents also had the lowest level of parental involvement among the groups studied. Third, for all groups and irrespective of social class, authoritarianism and permissiveness were inversely related, whereas parental involvement was directly related to academic achievements. (Parenting style, however, was a weaker predictor of grades for Asians than for Whites.) Thus, the very characteristics associated with the Asian American group predicted low academic achievements for all groups; yet, Asian American students had higher levels of academic achievements. The results suggest that although parenting styles may account for within-group achievement levels for Asian Americans, they fail to explain between-group differences (i.e., between Asian Americans and the other groups). The findings do not support the cultural hypothesis that Asian Americans differ from other groups in achievements because of differences in upbringing. Although ethnic differences in parenting styles do exist, they fail to account for the observed ethnic differences in achievements.

Other variables examined by the investigators did not reveal group differences. Asian American responses were not significantly different from the other groups on reasons cited for working hard, parental pressures for achievement, need for making parents proud, not embarrassing family, and sacrifices made by the family for educational pursuits, variables that have often been used and supported by anecdotal examples to explain Asian achievements. Only on one response was there a significant group difference: Asian Americans were more likely to believe that success in life has to do with the things studied in school. This belief was directly related to high school grades. The inability to find variables that could explain the success of Asian American students led the investigators to conclude that "Something associated with being Asian is having a positive impact on school performance independent of the family process variables that may work so well in predicting performance among Whites" (Ritter & Dornbusch, 1989, p. 7).

The findings, of course, do not invalidate a cultural explanation. Perhaps other family or socialization variables are important, singly or in combination, and more studies should be conducted. However, the difficulty in finding cultural factors that strongly correlate with Asian American achievements and that can serve as an explanation for differential achievement patterns is troublesome for such a widely held thesis. It is not that "culture" is unimportant. If one excludes genetic factors as a significant determinant of the higher levels of achievement attained by Asian Americans, then some features of the culture are likely to play an important role. Because not all cultural differences will be germane, the challenge is to determine those features that are relevant to educational achievement for that culture. The evidence suggests that proximal values such as the importance of study and working hard, rather than distal values and behaviors such as socialization practices, may be important predictors of achievement. Moreover, cultural values do not operate in a vacuum. By focusing on Asian cultural as well as hereditary explanations, important contextual factors in the larger society are ignored. We propose that cultural values are weakly related to achievement, inasmuch as cultural values are often too global, or distal to achievements. A better model would posit that cultural values or socialization patterns affect a mediator (a more proximal variable such as effort or motivation), which is likely to show a stronger correlation with achievements. The mediator is also influenced by other variables, besides culture, such as opportunities for advancement in other areas of life.

RELATIVE FUNCTIONALISM

The academic achievements of Asian Americans cannot be solely attributed to Asian cultural values. Rather, as for other ethnic minority groups, their behavioral patterns, including achievements, are a product of cultural values (i.e., ethnicity) and status in society (minority group standing). Using the notion of relative functionalism, we believe that the educational attainments of Asian Americans are highly influenced by the opportunities present for upward mobility, not only in educational endeavors but also in noneducational areas. Noneducational areas include career activities such as leadership, entertainment, sports, politics, and so forth, in which education does not directly lead to the position. To the extent that mobility is limited in noneducational avenues, education becomes increasingly salient as a means of mobility. That is, education is increasingly functional as a means for mobility when other avenues are blocked. Several propositions are apparent. First, similar to the cultural explanation, relative functionalism assumes that there is in any particular group a drive for upward mobility and that cultural values and practices can affect educational attainments. Second, when opportunities for upward mobility are limited or are perceived to be limited in other areas, educational achievements should increase. This is particularly true with groups that are culturally oriented toward education and have experienced academic success. Third, trying to change American educational values and practices in the direction of Asian values may result in only small increments in educational attainments, inasmuch as mainstream Americans have other avenues of mobility.

Table 2 contrasts the assumptions made by the cultural and relative functionalism perspectives. In the cultural interpretation, investigators traditionally assume that some ethnic groups have cultural values that match or fit the society in which they live. For example, in the classic book *Assimilation in American Life*, Milton Gordon (1964) argued that the extraordinary achievements of Jews in this country can primarily be explained by cultural, middle-class values such as thrift, sobriety, ambition, and ability to delay immediate gratification for long-range goals. Sue and Kitano (1973) have also found that many social scientists attribute the educational success of Chinese and Japanese Americans to cultural values that promote upward mobility in this country—values that emphasize hard work, family cohesion, patience, and thrift. However, many Asian values such as emphasis on the collective rather than on the individual, hierarchical role structures rather than egalitarian relationships, and respect for authority are not fully consistent with White, middle-class values (Hirschman & Wong, 1986). Another problem with the cultural explanation is that cultural values are not necessarily predictive of educational attainments. As noted by Ogbu and Matute-Bianchi (1986), the Chinese in China, presently and in the past, have not shown relatively high rates of educational attainments and literacy. This has led investigators to question why children of Chinese peasants do so well in American schools in contrast to their peers in China. Indeed, in mainland China, where intellectuals are under increased scrutiny, receive inadequate salaries, and find other jobs more financially rewarding, we see a decline in the proportion of students applying for admission into graduate programs in that country.

As argued by Steinberg (1981), cultural values interact with conditions in any particular society. In the case of Jews, he noted that

> In terms of their European background, Jews were especially well equipped to take advantage of the opportunities they found in America. Had Jews immigrated to an industrial society without industrial skills, as did most other immigrants, their rich cultural heritage would have counted for little. Indeed, a parallel situation exists today in Israel, where Jews immigrating from underdeveloped countries in North Africa typically lack the occupational and educational advantages of the earlier settlers, and despite the fact that all share the same basic religion, the recent immigrants find themselves concentrated at the bottom of Israeli society. Thus, in large measure Jewish success in America was a matter of historical timing. That is to say, there was a fortuitous match between the experience and skills of Jewish immigrants, on the one hand, and the manpower needs and opportunity structures, on the other. It is this remarkable convergence of factors that resulted in an unusual record of success. (p. 103)

In the case of Chinese and Japanese Americans, Suzuki (1977) has also taken issue with a cultural interpretation of their success. Although acknowledging that respect for education is a cultural value among these two groups, he also advanced the proposition that Asian Americans came to pursue education because of their status as a minority group. Many labor unions discriminated against Asians, refusing them union membership during the 1940s. In addition, technological advancements and an expanding economy after World War II required educated professionals and white-collar employees. Thus, one development limited occupational opportunities for manual laborers and the other placed a premium on professional-technical skills requiring advanced education. In such a situation, mobility through education took increased significance, above and beyond the contributions of Asian cultural values. Using a similar argument, Connor (1975) attributed the high educational attainments of Japanese Americans to the denial of opportunities to participate in social and other extracurricular school activities in the pre-World War II period. This also set the stage for emphasizing educational achievements.

For relative functionalism to be a viable explanation, at least three issues must be addressed. First, relative functionalism and the cultural thesis would predict decreasing educational achievements with acculturation of Asian Americans. However, each differs in the factors that account for decrements in performance. One proposes that increased opportunities for mobility make education a less preferred avenue for mobility, whereas the other assumes that a loss of cultural values is responsible for decreased achievement levels. Is there evidence that opportunities for mobility influence achievements? Second, relative functionalism assumes that limitations in mobility in noneducational endeavors influences educational levels. Is it possible that educational values and attainments affect interest or performance in noneducational means of mobility? Third, is there evidence that Asian Americans perceive or experience limitations in non-educational avenues for mobility?

Unfortunately, critical tests comparing the cultural and relative functionalism models have not been conducted. Dornbusch et al. (1987) and Ritter and Dornbusch (1989) have found that Asian American achievement levels tend to be inversely related to the number of generations in the United States, apparently supporting a cultural interpretation (i.e., decreased maintenance of Asian cultural values results in lower academic grades). With increased acculturation, it has been assumed that Asian values of hard work, discipline, and respect for education have eroded. However, an inverse relation between acculturation to American values and academic achievements is not incompatible with relative functionalism. Increased acculturation also results in more avenues for mobility. For example, Sue and Zane (1985) found that recent Chinese immigrants were significantly more likely than were acculturated Chinese to agree with the statement that their choices of academic majors were influenced by their English skills. These students had low English proficiency, averaging in the 18th percentile on the verbal portion of the Scholastic Aptitude Test. They confined their selection of majors to fields requiring quantitative skills (e.g., mathematics and computer sciences) rather those requiring more sophisticated English proficiency (e.g., social sciences and humanities). Increased English proficiency is likely to be related to knowledge of American society and ways of getting ahead, which may ultimately decrease the relative value of education as a means of mobility. In addition, it is highly likely that the recent immigrants perceive career limitations and, therefore, avoid those fields such as the social sciences and humanities, in which English facility and interpersonal skills specific to American society are needed. Mathematics and sciences are more likely to emphasize technical competence. Here we have an example of directing educational pursuits because of perceived limitations in certain career areas.

With respect to the other questions involving cause-effect (Do educational achievements limit interest or pursuit of noneducational endeavors, or do limitations in these endeavors influence educational pursuits?) and perceptions of limitations in noneducational avenues, no studies have directly examined the issues. Obviously, if Asian Americans perform well in education and consequently assume professional and technical positions, they may be more motivated to continue this pattern of mobility. They may even deemphasize activities in such areas as sports, the entertainment industry, and political positions because they have been successful in securing education-based careers. However, there is evidence from various sources that many Asian Americans perceive limitations in their career choices or upward mobility because of English language skills or social discrimination (Sue, Sue, Zane, & Wong, 1985). In a survey of Asian American students at the University of California, Berkeley, Ong (1976) found that respondents cited as reasons for obtaining an education (a) ability to make money, increasing the chances for a better job, and (b) the difficulty in finding other avenues for advancement because of discrimination. Hirschman and Wong (1986) have argued that "Education was a channel for the social mobility of Asians, partly because they were frozen out of some sectors of the economy" (p. 23). Hearings sponsored by the U.S. Commission on Civil Rights (1980) resulted in testimonies that documented restrictions in occupational mobility, especially for those without much education (Pian, 1980; Wang, 1980). The point is that education is perceived as a viable means for mobility, in view of limitations for success in other areas. Thus Asian Americans expend great efforts in attaining an education because they have been successful and also because without a strong educational background, their mobility is limited. Research strategies that focus on the relation between cultural values and education provide an incomplete picture.

If Asian Americans encounter and perceive restrictions in noneducational areas of mobility, as do other ethnic minority groups such as Blacks and Latinos, why do these other ethnic groups fail to adopt education as a means of mobility? Addressing this question—and that poses a real challenge—is beyond the scope of this article. It is worth noting that ethnic minority groups have different cultural backgrounds and different historical and contemporary experiences in the United States. Precisely because of the importance of the interaction between culture and minority group status, we maintain that cultural interpretations of the success of Asian Americans are inadequate.

More specifically, Ogbu and Matute-Bianchi (1986) have proposed that individuals develop folk theories of success (e.g., "If I get a good education, I will succeed in getting a good job and maintain a high standard of living" or "Even if I get a good education, people will discriminate against me"). Factors such as cultural values, discrimination, past success, beliefs in self-efficacy, availability of successful role models, and so on, influence the folk theories. Mickelson (1990) has found that although Blacks hold favorable *abstract* attitudes concerning the value of education, they are less likely than Whites to believe in the value of education in their own lives. As mentioned previously, Ritter and Dornbusch (1987) found that Asian Americans tended to believe that success in life has to do with the things studied in school. The folk theory for Asian Americans may be, "If I study hard, I can succeed, *and* education is the best way to succeed."

CONCLUSIONS

In trying to explain the educational success of Asian Americans, the tendency has been to compare and contrast genetic and cultural explanations. Because the evidence does not support a genetic interpretation, many have simply assumed that Asian cultural values, beliefs, and practices are responsible for their academic achievements. In contrast, we have suggested that the effects of culture have been confounded with the consequences of our society. Although culture is certainly an important factor in achievements, education has been functional for upward mobility, especially when participation in other arenas, such as sports, entertainment, and politics, has been difficult. One could argue that educational success, increased numbers of educated Asian role models, and limitations in mobility in other areas contribute to performance, above and beyond that which can be predicted from Asian cultural values.

Several implications can be drawn from our analysis. First, studies that examine the relation between cultural values and achievements may yield low correlations, inasmuch as achievement patterns are influenced by many factors. These factors may influence mediators of achievement such as motivation and effort. Second, attention should be paid to individual differences within the Asian populations. Although cross-national studies may provide significant insights for studies of Asian Americans, it should be recognized that the social context of overseas Asian and Asian Americans differs quite dramatically, particularly in majority-minority group status and in societal values and practices. Differences among Asian Americans are also important to consider. For example, Sue and Abe (1988) examined predictors of educational performance among thousands of Asian American and White students. Regression equations significantly differed not only between Asian Americans and Whites but between some of the different Asian groups (Chinese, Japanese, Koreans, Filipinos, and East Indians/Pakistanis). Dornbusch et al. (1987) have also found important differences in school acculturation and achievement patterns among various Asian American groups. Third, in predicting educational achievements, investigations into perceptions, expectancies, and beliefs over opportunities for other areas of mobility may be important. Perhaps the greatest problem in the research is the failure to study the phenomenon of mobility in general, because educational attainments may be strongly influenced by these other avenues for mobility. Finally, some have objected to the notion that Asian Americans are a "minority" group, precisely because they have become well educated. From our perspective, Asian Americans are indeed a minority group and their achievements can be fully understood only if attention is paid to their experiences in society.

REFERENCES

Arbeiter, S. (1984). *Profiles, college-bound seniors, 1984.* New York: College Entrance Examination Board.

Asian Americans: Are they making the grade? (1984, April 2). *U.S. News and World Report,* pp. 41–47.

Asian students fear top colleges use quota systems. (1986, November 19). *Chronicle of Higher Education,* pp. 1, 34–36.

Barringer, H. R., Takeuchi, D. T., & Xenos, P. C. (1990). Education, occupational prestige and income of Asian Americans: Evidence from the 1980 Census. *Sociology of Education, 63,* 27–43.

Bureau of the Census. (1983). *Asian and Pacific Islander population by state: 1980 Census of population* (Supplementary report PC80-1-C). Washington, DC: U.S. Department of Commerce.

Bureau of the Census. (1984). *Detailed population characteristics: 1980 Census of population* (PC80-1-D1-A). Washington, DC: U.S. Department of Commerce.

California State Department of Education. (Ed.). (1986). *Beyond language: Social and cultural factors in schooling language minority students.* Los Angeles: California State Department of Education, Evaluation, Dissemination, and Assessment Center.

College Board. (1989). *College-bound seniors: 1989 SAT profile.* New York: College Entrance Examination Board.

Connor, J. W. (1975). Changing trends in Japanese American academic achievement. *Journal of Ethnic Studies, 2,* 95–98.

Dornbusch, S. M., Prescott, B. L., & Ritter, P. L. (1987, April). *The relation of high school academic performance and student effort to language use and recency of migration among Asian- and Pacific-Americans.* Paper presented at the meeting of the American Educational Research Association, Washington, DC.

Dornbusch, S. M., Ritter, P. L., Leiderman, P. H., Roberts, D. F., & Fraleigh, M. J. (1987). The relation of parenting style to adolescent school performance. *Child Development, 55,* 1244–1257.

Flynn, J. R. (1982). Lynn, the Japanese, and environmentalism. *Bulletin of the British Psychological Society, 35,* 409–413.

Flynn, J. R. (1987). The rise and fall of Japanese IQ. *Bulletin of the British Psychological Society, 40,* 459–464.

A formula for success. (1984, April 23). *Newsweek,* pp. 77–78.

Gordon, M. (1964). *Assimilation in American life.* New York: Oxford University Press.

Greenfield, P., & Childs, C. P. (1991). Developmental continuity in bio-cultural context. In R. Cohen & A. Siegel (Eds.), *Context and development.* Hillsdale, NJ: Erlbaum.

Hirschman, C., & Wong, M. G. (1986). The extraordinary educational attainment of Asian Americans: A search for historical evidence and explanations. *Social Forces, 65,* 1–27.

Hsia, J. (1988). Limits on affirmative action: Asian American access to higher education. *Educational Policy, 2,* 117–136.

Jencks, C., Crouse, J., & Mueser, P. (1983). The Wisconsin model of status attainment: A national replication with improved measures of ability and aspirations. *Sociology of Education, 56,* 3–19.

Kan, S. H., & Liu, W. T. (1986). The educational status of Asian Americans: An update from the 1980 Census. *P/AAMHRC Research Review, 5 (3/4),* 21–24.

Lynn, R. (1977). The intelligence of the Japanese. *Bulletin of the British Psychological Society, 30,* 69–72.

Lynn, R. (1987). Japan: Land of the rising IQ. A reply to Flynn. *Bulletin of the British Psychological Society, 40,* 464–468.

Mickelson, R. A. (1990). The attitude-achievement paradox among Black adolescents. *Sociology of Education, 63,* 44–61.

Mordkowitz, E. R., & Ginsberg, H. P. (1987). Early academic socialization of successful Asian American college students. *Quarterly Newsletter of the Laboratory of Comparative Human Cognition, 9,* 85–91.

The new whiz kids. (1987, August 31). *Time* pp. 42–51.

Ogbu, J. U., & Matute-Bianchi, M. E. (1986). Understanding sociocultural factors: Knowledge, identity, and school adjustment. In California State Department of Education (Ed.), *Beyond language: Social and cultural factors in schooling language minority students* (pp. 73–142). Los
Angeles: California State Department of Education, Evaluation, Dissemination, and
Assessment Center.

Ong, C. (1976). *The educational attainment of the Chinese in America.* Unpublished manuscript,
University of California, Berkeley, Department of Anthropology.

Peng, S. (1988, April). Attainment status of Asian Americans in higher education. Paper presented
at the National Association for Asian and Pacific American Education (NAAPE) Conference,
Denver, CO.

Pian, C. (1980). Identification of issues. In U.S. Commission on Civil Rights (Ed.), *Civil rights issues of Asian and Pacific Americans: Myths and realities* (pp. 7–20). Washington DC: U.S.
Government Printing Office.

Probing into the success of Asian American students. (1990, January 26). *Asian Week*, p. 7.

Ritter, P. L., & Dornbusch, S. M. (1989, March). *Ethnic variation in family influences on academic
achievement.* Paper presented at the American Educational Research Association Meeting, San
Francisco.

Skinner, B. F. (1984). The shame of American education. *American Psychologist, 39*, 947–955.

Sowell, T. (1978). (Ed.) *Essay and data on American ethnic groups.* Washington, DC: Urban Institute.

Spence, J. T. (1985). Achievement American style: The rewards and costs of individualism. *American
Psychologist, 40*, 1285–1295.

Steinberg, A. (1981). *The ethnic myth: Race, ethnicity, and class in America.* Boston: Beacon Press.

Stevenson, H. W., & Azuma, H. (1983). IQ in Japan and the United States: Methodological problems
in Lynn's analysis. *Nature, 306*, 291–292.

Stevenson, H. W., Lee, S., & Stigler, J. W. (1986). Mathematics achievement of Chinese, Japanese,
and American children. *Science, 231*, 693–699.

Stevenson, H. W., Stigler, J. W., Lee, S., Lucker, G. W., Kitamura, S., & Hsu, C. (1985). Cognitive
performance and academic achievement of Japanese, Chinese, and American children. *Child
Development, 56*, 718–734.

Sue, S., & Abe, J. (1988). *Predictors of academic achievement among Asian American and White
students* (Report No. 88-11). New York: College Entrance Examination Board.

Sue, S., & Kitano, H. H. L. (1973). Stereotypes as a measure of success. *Journal of Social Issues, 29*,
83–98.

Sue, S., & Padilla, A. (1986). Ethnic minority issues in the United States: Challenges for the educational system. In California State Department of Education (Ed.), *Beyond language: Social
and cultural factors in schooling language minority students* (pp. 34–72). Los Angeles:
California State Department of Education, Evaluation, Dissemination, and Assessment Center.

Sue, S., Sue, D. W., Zane, N., & Wong, H. Z. (1985). Where are the Asian American leaders and top
executives? *P/AAMHRC Review, 4*, 13–15.

Sue, S., & Zane, N. (1985). Academic achievement and socioemotional adjustment among Chinese
university students. *Journal of Counseling Psychology, 32*, 570–579.

Suzuki, R. H. (1977). Education and the socialization of Asian Americans: A revisionist analysis of
the "model minority" thesis. *Amerasia Journal, 4*, 23–52.

U.S. Commission on Civil Rights. (Ed.). (1980). *Civil rights issues of Asian and Pacific Americans:
Myths and realities.* Washington, DC: U.S. Government Printing Office.

Uttal, D. H., Lummis, M., & Stevenson, H. W. (1988). Low and high mathematics achievement in
Japanese, Chinese, and American elementary-school children. *Developmental Psychology, 24*,
335–342.

Vernon, P. E. (1982). *The abilities and achievements of Orientals in North America.* New York:
Academic Press.

Wang, L. C. (1980). Federal exclusionary policy. In U.S. Commission on Civil Rights (Ed.), *Civil
rights issues of Asian and Pacific Americans: Myths and realities* (pp. 21–24). Washington,
DC: U.S. Government Printing Office.

Wechsler, D. (1949). *Wechsler Intelligence Scale for Children.* New York: Psychological Corporation.

Wechsler, D. (1955). *Manual, Wechsler Adult Intelligence Scale*. New York: Psychological Corporation.

When being best isn't good enough. (1987, July 19). *Los Angeles Times Magazine*, pp. 22–28.

"Whiz kid" image masks problems of Asian Americans. (1988, March). *National Education Association Today*, pp. 14–15.

Why Asians are going to the head of the class. (1986, August 3). *New York Times*, pp. 18–32.

8 Education, Occupational Prestige, and Income of Asian Americans

Herbert R. Barringer, David T. Takeuchi, and Peter Xenos

ASIAN AMERICANS have been labeled "model minorities" because it is presumed that they have attained "success" through education and high-income occupations. Although there is no question about the high educational levels of most categories of Asians in the United States, it is not clear whether Asian Americans have been able to translate their education into equivalent occupational prestige or income levels. Most careful research indicates that they have not, but some confusion exists in the literature, either because only a few ethnicities have been studied (usually Chinese and Japanese) or because insufficient attention has been paid to the differences that are due to the immigration histories of various groups. In addition, previous studies did not really investigate the reasons why higher levels of education may not be paying off for Asian Americans. The study presented here attempted to rectify these problems by examining as many ethnic groups as possible, by paying close attention to immigration variables, and by examining the relationships of education, occupation, and income.

THEORIES OF ADAPTATION

ASSIMILATION

The general role of education in the occupational achievement of immigrant minorities has long attracted sociologists. Assimilation theories (Gordon 1964, 1978; Park 1950) mostly assumed that education would help immigrants to become acculturated and subsequently to assimilate to some degree. Examples of research dominated by this viewpoint abound (Hurh and Kim 1984; Kitano 1976; Kuo 1977; Montero 1981; Montero and Tsukashima 1977; Peterson, 1971; Wang 1981; Yu 1977). Although all these studies focused on some variant of assimilation theory, it is noteworthy that most of them questioned some or all the outcomes one would expect of assimilation theory. Hurh and Kim, for example, found Koreans to be relatively unassimilated and were led to the concept of "adhesive adaptation," which is similar to "enclave." On the other hand, most of the assimilation studies found strong relationships between education and income or occupation, especially in the case of Japanese Americans.

HUMAN CAPITAL

Human capital theory even more directly asserts the positive role of education in the advancement of minorities. It asserts that success in school and high levels of formal educa-

From *Sociology of Education* 63 (1990):27–43. Copyright 1990 by the American Sociological Association. Reprinted by permission.

tion increase the prospects for better paying, higher status, and more satisfying employment (Berg 1969; Parsons 1968). This approach has dominated American educational policy toward minorities. Its advocates cite the high levels of both the educational achievement and economic success of Jews and Asian Americans in support of the theory (Peterson 1971; Sklare 1971; Sung 1967). Portes and Stepick (1985) stated that many of the positive aspects of human capital can be found in ethnic enclaves, a position disputed by Nee and Sanders (1987).

STRUCTURAL CRITIQUES

More recently, with structural theories dominating the literature, the role of education in the successful adaptation of migrants to American society has been questioned. Both Lieberson (1980) and Steinberg (1981) supported structural arguments by showing that the social and economic entry of a generation into American society preceded the high levels of formal education of its children. Bonacich and Cheng (1984) made a similar point with regard to Asian minorities, demonstrating that their immigration to the United States was tied to peripheral economic exploitation. The high levels of education of the children of these early immigrants came after their parents' initial adjustments. Earlier generations of sociologists had assumed that education, would eventually minimize the inequities confronting American minorities, but today, more often than not, we confront the question of continuing inequities, in terms of both educational achievement and the relationship between education and occupational and economic achievement (Bowles and Gintis 1976; Collins 1971; Mayes 1977; Ogbu 1978; Scimecca 1980).

Many of the structural criticisms of assimilation and human capital theories rest on studies of longtime resident minorities in the United States, especially blacks, Hispanics, and American Indians. Asian Americans have been considered different from these ethnic groups because of their comparatively high levels of education and high visibility as petite bourgeoisie and professionals. This view has led to explanations popularized by the terms "model minorities" (Kitano 1976) or "middlemen" (Bonacich 1973). In general, these theories assert that Asian Americans have benefited from selective immigration, relatively favorable entry conditions, and favorable "niches" in the host economy (Lieberson 1980). There can be little question that most Asian Americans are well educated (Hirschman and Wong 1986) and that they tend not to experience extreme residential segregation (Langberg and Farley 1985; Massey and Denton 1987), although some enclaves exist, notably among Chinese in New York and San Francisco (for an analysis of San Francisco, see Nee and Sanders 1987). However, there is an abundant literature that suggests that the higher levels of education of Asian Americans are not always translated into other measures of success.

STUDIES OF ASIAN AMERICANS' SUCCESS

Suzuki (1977), E. Wong (1985), and Woo (1985) all attacked the "myth" of the success of Asian Americans. The report of the U.S. Commission on Civil Rights (1978) demonstrated vividly that minorities and women were not receiving income returns on educational investment equivalent to those of white men. The commission reported that Chinese, Filipinos, and Japanese had higher educational levels than did other minorities, but that . . . "the greater educational attainment of the Asian American populations does not result in increased financial rewards compared to majority males, as would be expected if everything else were equal" (p. 26).

M. Wong (1980, 1982), Hirschman and Wong (1981, 1984, 1986), and Wong and Hirschman (1983) extended these concerns specifically to Asian Americans. Their studies all showed that Asian Americans are at a disadvantage in turning education into income, as are new immigrants and women; the only possible exception is Japanese, whom they suggested had "made it" as of 1975. Chiswick (1983), however, concluded that *American-born* Chinese and Japanese earned about the same income per year of education as did whites; Filipinos still experienced some economic deprivation. In the case of Hawaii, Fujii and Mak (1983) showed that as of 1975, all minorities were disadvantaged compared to whites, although they stated that all immigrants (except whites) were more disadvantaged than were the native born.

In summary, research seems to indicate that although some Asian Americans are better educated and better paid than are many other American minorities, there still may be a slippage between their relatively high educational levels and their equivalent occupations or incomes. The literature suggests that compared to whites, most Asian Americans seem to be overeducated for the occupations they hold. In addition, all the foregoing research suggests that we should tend carefully to the following:

1. There is an enormous variation among the different Asian American ethnic groups. Thus, these groups must be examined separately.
2. Each Asian American group is composed of both those who were born here (natives) and immigrants. The effects of nativity and period of immigration must be dealt with separately.
3. Gender differences may be as great or greater than interethnic differences.
4. The "success" of Asian Americans is often cited only in reference to professional occupations or business. The whole range of occupational categories needs to be examined.

IMPLICATIONS FOR RESEARCH

Several hypotheses are suggested by the previous discussion:

The assimilation hypothesis: The longer an immigrant group lives in the United States, the closer the income parity with whites, controlling for other variables known to affect income.

The human capital hypothesis: The higher the educational levels of *any* ethnic group, the greater the income parity with whites, controlling for other variables known to affect income.

The structural hypothesis: Differences exist between minorities and dominant members of the society in the relationship between length or residence and income and between education and income. Structural barriers prevent minorities from converting their length of residence or education into income parity with whites.

Many of the assertions of assimilation theory are untestable with census data. However, in general, there is a strong presumption that immigrants will come to resemble natives the longer they remain in the host society. It would also follow that Asian American natives should appear more similar to whites than to immigrants and that each succeeding generation should be more assimilated. This presumption is complicated, however, by the history of older Asian American cohorts. As Bonacich and Cheng (1984) pointed out, earlier immigrants, for the most part, were brought to the United States as cheap labor for the peripheral economy. Most were not well educated and faced fierce discrimination. The most recent immigrants were generally well educated before they entered the United States, and many were already integrated into the urban core economic sector (Gardner, Robey, and Smith 1985). Nevertheless, Moon (1986), citing Lieberson (1980), suggested that older cohorts of immigrants (Chinese and Japanese) should show more resemblance to whites than should the newer groups (Koreans, Vietnamese, and Asian Indians). This suggestion holds only for the native-born members because Chinese and Japanese as a whole would be affected by more recent immigrants.

It is apparent that many Asian Americans have high levels of education, although educational levels may vary according to ethnic group. Human capital theory holds that high levels of education should result in higher incomes. The structuralist critiques of assimilation and human capital theories suggest that education need not translate to higher levels of either occupation or income. Their arguments are generally based on the experiences of blacks and American Indian minorities, who also exhibit low educational levels overall. Asian Americans should provide an excellent test for these critiques because they are well educated, but nevertheless appear to gain fewer returns from education than do whites. Assuming that the recency of immigration does not explain this discrepancy completely, we should turn our attention to other explanations. The Wisconsin studies of achievement (Sewell, Haller, and Portes 1969; Sewell and Hauser 1975) suggest that the interrelationships of education, occupational prestige, and income may provide a key. We may ask if discrepancies in the education and income of Asian Americans are due to slippages between education and occupational prestige or between prestige and income. This is an important point for human capital advocates and critics alike: Is the problem one of not obtaining jobs commensurate with education or one of receiving lower salaries for the same jobs? The latter would be a case of exploitation or discrimination.

In pursuing these questions, we must examine other well-known determinants of income, such as age, work experience, occupational sector, time at work, and gender (Chiswick 1983; Hirschman and Wong 1981, 1984). Throughout, it is essential that each ethnic category of Asian Americans be examined separately, to avoid the common obfuscation caused by lumping all persons of Asian descent into one category (see, for example, Tienda and Lii 1987).

The 1980 census is extremely valuable to these ends. It allows us to incorporate data on the large number of immigrants from Asia who have entered the United States since the revisions of the immigration laws in the late 1960s and to examine, for the first time, sizable samples of Koreans, Asian Indians, and Vietnamese.

THE SAMPLE AND DATA ANALYSIS

The Asian American data used here are from a tape prepared by the Pacific/Asian American Mental Health Research Center from the 1980 Census 5% Public Use Sample (PUMS A). All households containing at least one Asian American were drawn from the PUMS A tape. This procedure eliminated households not containing Asian Americans, so we drew smaller samples of whites, blacks, and Hispanics from a composite of the PUMS A and B .1% tapes. The present research is based on a file that restricts the sample to ages 25–64, a convention enabling us to examine persons who presumably completed their formal education.[1] The term races refer to the census definition of race, except *Hispanic*, which includes all races. However, we drew samples in such a way that there are no overlaps between Hispanics and Asian Americans. Throughout, we employed the census definitions of *races*, though we prefer the term, *ethnicity*. It should be noted that the present samples represent population numbers (5 percent of the population) for Asian Americans only. Whites, blacks, and Hispanics were included for comparison purposes only; their samples, while random, are not proportional to the population on any consistent basis.[2]

The working files contained sample sizes ranging from approximately 20,000 (Chinese, Japanese, and Filipinos) to about 5,000 (Vietnamese, whites, blacks, and Hispanics). The exact numbers are presented in Table 1.

Table 1. Years of Education, by Race, 1980 (percentage)

Years of Education	Japanese	Chinese	Korean	Filipino	Asian Indian	Vietnamese	Black	Hispanic	White
None (no formal education)	0.5	4.7	2.2	0.8	1.4	4.7	0.9	3.7	0.5
1–6 (primary school)	1.2	8.4	5.4	6.9	3.1	11.6	8.9	21.9	3.5
7–11 (some middle school and some high school)	10.8	11.4	12.0	11.7	10.5	19.5	32.7	28.2	20.7
12 (high school degree)	37.0	19.6	29.1	19.1	13.4	29.7	33.2	25.1	39.9
13–15 (some college)	21.7	15.7	16.3	20.6	14.0	21.5	15.5	13.2	17.3
16 (college degree)	15.6	15.8	21.2	21.7	14.1	6.1	4.9	3.5	9.4
17–19 (some graduate school or more)	10.5	17.2	9.4	14.1	23.1	4.9	3.4	3.2	6.5
20 or more (doctorate or equivalent)	2.6	7.1	4.4	5.1	20.5	2.0	0.5	1.2	2.1
Total number	21,129	21,725	8,833	19,689	10,477	4,916	4,151	4,186	4,887

RESULTS

LEVELS OF EDUCATION

Table 1 shows the educational levels of Asian Americans, compared to whites, blacks, and Hispanics. As previous research indicated, all Asian American groups, except Vietnamese, are better educated than are whites. Hispanics, blacks, and Vietnamese exhibit the lowest levels of education. Note that Chinese, Koreans, Filipinos, and Asian Indians all are better educated than are Japanese, but Japanese are somewhat better educated than are whites. Asian Indians, in particular, stand out, since a high percentage (43.6 percent) of them have had graduate education. This high percentage is due to the selective immigration primarily of physicians and engineers.

A relatively high number of Chinese, Korean, Filipino, and Vietnamese individuals have had only a primary school education or less. These data reflect the state of education in Asia, since all these groups are predominantly immigrants who completed all or most of their education before coming to the United States (Barringer, Smith, and Gardner 1985, pp. 22–25). To put these data in perspective, note that as of 1980, only about 27 percent of Japanese were immigrants, but 75 percent of Chinese, 83 percent of Filipinos, 92.2 percent of Asian Indians, 93.7 percent of Koreans, and 98.2 percent of Vietnamese in the United States had immigrated to this country.

OCCUPATION AND EDUCATION

As Kan and Liu (1986) demonstrated, most Asian Americans are better educated for professional and executive occupations than are whites. Table 2 verifies this finding and extends the analysis to other occupational categories. Although the results vary somewhat, depending on which category we scrutinize, it appears generally true that Asian Americans (again except Vietnamese) are "overeducated" compared to whites for a wide variety of occupational categories. In this regard, Japanese most nearly approximate whites, but in lower prestige jobs, their educational levels are also one to two years higher than those of whites. Fluctuations in this table, plus important differences in the proportions holding specific occupations within each of these broad categories (not shown), suggest that an intensive study of actual occupations is badly needed (Barringer, Cho, and Xenos forthcoming; Xenos, Barringer, and Levin 1989).

Table 2 also displays the mean educational levels of men and women. As might be expected, men are generally better educated than are women (with the exception of blacks and Filipinos, for which the differences are minimal). The greatest differences appear for Chinese, Koreans, Asian Indians, and Vietnamese, which again reflects the large proportion of immigrants in these populations. The uniformity for Filipinos reinforces our earlier warnings about generalizations. Differences in education by gender are not great for whites—a fact that will take on special significance when we examine income.

OCCUPATIONAL SECTOR

Not unexpectedly, "core" employees are generally better educated than are those in the "periphery."[3] The differences are not great for most ethnicities, and there is no difference for whites. The differences appear the greatest for Chinese, Asian Indians, and Hispanics. As we shall see, incomes are generally much higher in the core than in the periphery, so the lack of educational differences is significant, as in the case of gender.

REGION OF THE UNITED STATES

There is some regional variation in educational attainment. We have not shown it here because it is small and has little effect on occupational prestige or income. Whites show little variation, but other ethnicities are best educated in the East and worst educated in the South and West. One exception is Chinese in the East. This anomaly *is* associated with a low income level. A little investigation and questioning led us to New York City, which

Table 2. Mean Years of Education, by Occupation, Sex, Occupational Sector, and Race[a]

Variable	Japanese	Chinese	Korean	Filipino	Asian Indian	Vietnamese	Hispanic	Black	White
Total population	13.28	13.06	13.15	13.56	15.28	11.11	9.75	11.01	12.32
Occupation									
Executive, administrative, managerial	14.71	14.76	15.19	15.41	16.33	13.86	13.28	13.22	14.10
Professional specialty	16.48	17.49	16.92	17.02	18.20	15.59	14.98	15.23	16.06
Technical and related support	15.02	16.40	16.00	15.56	16.83	14.30	13.36	12.92	13.55
Sales	13.28	13.16	13.77	13.82	14.33	11.18	11.51	12.10	12.84
Administrative support	13.40	14.02	13.93	14.52	14.54	12.88	12.14	12.48	12.57
Service—private household	10.98	8.37	7.42	9.53	9.47	6.69	7.26	9.46	10.39
Service—protective	13.75	13.07	12.84	13.25	13.73	12.42	11.70	12.40	12.74
Service–other	12.00	9.92	11.24	11.78	12.07	10.48	8.92	10.40	11.02
Farming, forestry, fishing	12.02	10.29	11.39	8.76	8.71	9.20	5.96	8.08	10.66
Precision production, craft	12.21	11.45	12.57	12.47	13.51	11.02	9.53	10.85	11.42
Operator, assembler, inspector	11.57	7.90	11.50	11.71	11.96	10.64	8.33	10.59	10.71
Transportation, equipment, material movers	11.88	11.90	13.02	11.15	12.91	10.45	9.29	10.59	10.88
Handlers, helpers, cleaners	11.73	10.67	11.67	10.37	11.91	9.84	8.36	9.94	10.30
Sex									
Male	13.93	13.86	14.87	13.60	16.58	12.15	9.99	10.89	12.61
Female	12.85	12.23	12.00	13.53	13.60	10.14	9.51	11.11	12.03
Occupational Sector									
Periphery	13.29	12.27	13.37	13.85	15.04	11.51	9.68	11.29	12.53
Core	13.75	14.94	13.76	14.22	16.52	12.17	10.62	11.55	12.54

[a]Occupation and occupational sector for those with wages or salaries only.

has a large enclave of Chinese. This community deserves an in-depth study. Since almost all Asian Americans reside in standard metropolitan statistical areas, we conclude that these differences are due to true regional variations that are perhaps explainable by concentrations of people in certain occupations.

PERSONAL INCOME

Turning to Table 3, one can observe the benefits in personal income that are attributable to various levels of education. The mean total income for all groups is shown at the bottom of the table. Asian Indians enjoy the highest personal incomes, followed by Japanese and whites. It is notable that Vietnamese exhibit the lowest incomes—even lower than those of blacks and Hispanics. Of the people with a middle-school education or lower (no education through Grade 9), as well as of those with various levels of high school and of those with some college, whites and Japanese clearly enjoy the greatest income advantage. For college graduates, Japanese, whites, and Hispanics have the greatest marginal increases in income.

Various levels of graduate education show considerable fluctuation, which is not comprehensible without knowing something about the actual degrees acquired or the occupations filled. Of those with 20 or more years of education, it appears that Japanese lose some of the advantages they demonstrated in other categories. Filipinos and Hispanics appear to gain considerably in this bracket, and Asian Indians begin to lose their relative advantage to whites. Notably, Japanese gain much less than do whites at this high level of education, the explanation of which will require a close examination of particular occupations. Note that the actual incomes of individuals with 20 or more years of education are highest for whites, followed by Filipinos, Koreans, and Asian Indians. Throughout this table, Vietnamese continue to demonstrate the lowest returns from education of all the groups studied. It is also clear that whites have a considerable advantage over all Asian American

Table 3. Marginal Increase in Income for Additional Education Completed, by Race, 1979[a]

Years of Education	Japanese	Chinese	Korean	Filipino	Asian Indian	Viet-namese	Hispanic	Black	White
Fewer than 12									
Total income	$11,187	$7,587	7,603	$9,124	$8,430	$7,309	$8,550	$8,827	$11,346
12 (high school)									
Total income	12,921	10,573	8,881	10,731	10,255	8,730	11,052	10,136	12,604
(marginal increase)	(1,734)	(2,985)	(1,278)	(1,607)	(1,824)	(1,421)	(2,502)	(1,309)	(1,258)
13–15									
Total income	14,036	12,408	11,401	11,865	11,046	9,454	12,346	11,690	14,095
(marginal increase)	(1,115)	(1,835)	(2,520)	(1,134)	(791)	(724)	(1,294)	(1,554)	(1,491)
16 (college)									
Total income	19,860	14,612	13,670	13,024	13,614	12,274	16,259	14,796	18,126
(marginal increase)	(5,824)	(2,204)	(2,269)	(1,159)	(2,568)	(2,820)	(3,913)	(3,106)	(4,031)
17–19									
Total income	18,144	16,841	20,005	16,179	17,951	14,203	15,387	15,919	20,183
(marginal increase)	(−1,716)	(2,229)	(6,335)	(3,155)	(4,338)	(1,929)	(−872)	(1,123)	(2,057)
20 or more									
(doctorate or equivalent)									
Total income	24,706	25,056	26,918	27,813	26,771	17,939	26,232	19,485	29,560
(marginal increase)	(6,562)	(8,215)	(6,913)	(11,634)	(8,819)	(3,736)	(10,845)	(3,566)	(9,377)
Mean total income	15,215	13,309	12,315	13,013	16,667	9,391	10,638	10,542	14,186

[a]Mean personal income (wages and salaries only).

groups except Japanese, especially in terms of the marginal income these groups attain for various levels of education.

Table 4 presents the means for years of schooling, age, occupational prestige, personal income, and number of weeks worked in 1979, by period of immigration and by nativity. Generally speaking, the newest immigrants are slightly less well educated than those who immigrated in the 1970–74 period. This trend could reflect a change in the later immigrants (more people who joined their families), or it could mean that the earlier immigrants received some education in the United States immediately after they immigrated. Japanese

Table 4. Mean Characteristics of Asian Immigrants and Natives, by Period of Immigration/Nativity

Ethnicity	Period of Immigration	Years of Education	Age (in Years)	Mean Occupational Prestige (Temme Score)	Personal Income (Wages and Salaries)	Weeks Worked in 1979	Number
Chinese							
Immigrants	1975–80	12.1	37.2	40.7	$7,946	25.9	5,291
	1970–74	13.0	37.2	44.2	11,797	36.5	3,908
	1965–69	13.4	39.3	46.1	14,333	38.8	3,229
	1960–64	13.2	41.8	46.4	15,837	39.8	1,560
	1950–59	12.8	45.6	46.7	16,663	38.9	1,476
	Before 1950	11.2	53.2	43.8	16,205	38.1	1,239
Natives		14.4	39.4	48.7	15,971	39.9	5,022
Filipino							
Immigrants	1975–80	13.3	37.9	39.0	9,074	31.4	5,050
	1970–74	14.4	37.0	44.7	13,588	40.9	4,941
	1965–69	14.4	39.6	46.4	15,643	42.1	3,427
	1960–64	13.8	41.0	46.5	15,846	41.1	1,123
	1950–59	13.3	45.0	43.4	15,494	39.1	1,175
	Before 1950	10.2	53.3	35.0	13,363	33.9	609
Natives		12.4	37.4	39.4	12,756	38.3	3,364
Korean							
Immigrants	1975–80	12.1	36.5	37.2	9,027	27.1	3,805
	1970–74	13.2	37.7	41.4	12,609	34.2	2,840
	1965–69	14.2	38.9	47.9	16,975	33.0	949
	1960–64	13.8	41.6	46.5	16,822	34.9	461
	1950–59	15.3	42.7	50.7	20,128	37.9	278
	Before 1950	13.5	52.2	44.3	17,425	23.0	31
Natives		13.4	41.7	45.0	15,909	37.0	469
Asian Indian							
Immigrants	1975–80	14.6	34.3	48.9	11,414	29.9	3,710
	1970–74	15.8	35.2	54.0	17,522	37.4	3,434
	1965–69	16.9	38.6	57.6	23,753	40.7	1,538
	1960–64	17.0	41.3	58.9	26,791	43.6	466
	1950–59	16.6	46.3	55.9	25,101	41.3	233
	Before 1950	12.5	53.1	48.7	18,739	28.5	57
Natives		12.2	46.5	41.9	11,396	26.6	1,039
Japanese							
Immigrants	1975–80	14.5	34.0	48.4	19,236	24.7	2,152
	1970–74	13.2	36.7	40.1	13,330	28.5	1,128
	1965–69	12.9	40.8	39.4	12,593	28.7	858
	1960–64	12.3	44.3	37.3	11,370	28.1	937
	1950–59	12.5	46.6	36.9	10,897	30.2	1,859
	Before 1950	12.1	53.4	39.6	13,602	33.8	187
Natives		13.5	43.8	44.5	15,656	40.2	14,008

are an exception, probably because recent immigrants (few in number) are mostly employees of large Japanese corporations located in the United States who can be expected to return to Japan after a tour of duty; thus, they are of little interest here. There appears to be little consistent difference in education between natives and immigrants, but, for the most part, immigrants seem to be better educated than are natives. Figures for blacks and whites are not shown because virtually all are native born.

Age differences are minimized in this table because the sample is restricted to ages 25–64. Nevertheless, the lack of large age differences between adjacent periods of immigration is striking. As we would expect, immigrant groups who have been in the United States longer are older, but there seems to be only a year or two difference between those who entered from 1975 to 1980 and those who arrived between 1970 and 1974. This age table also gives us a reasonably good idea about the average length of employment if we assume that employees are reasonably settled in a job by age 25. Of course, immigrants might have changed specific jobs, but, overall, job experience should be highly correlated with age. Occupational prestige is considerably lower for immigrants who entered between 1975 and 1980 than for all those who entered later.[4] After that period, prestige increases only gradually. Also, immigrants who entered in about 1965 or earlier appear to have higher prestige than do natives. Again, Japanese appear to be an exception for the reasons suggested earlier.

Personal income follows about the same pattern as occupational prestige, with immigrants who entered from 1975 to 1980 having much lower incomes than those who entered from 1970 to 1974. Each succeeding group of immigrants has a higher income, and, again with Japanese an exception, natives earn considerably less than do later immigrants. Note that groups with a high proportion of immigrants in the 1975–80 period have depressed overall mean incomes.

Weeks worked in 1979 is highly correlated with income, so it is not surprising that the pattern for this variable is about the same for immigrants as are the patterns for income, prestige, and education. The exception is that natives seem to work more weeks per year than do all immigrants.

On the face of it, these figures suggest that new immigrants (those immigrating from 1975 to 1980) have some initial adjustments to make, after which their education, occupational prestige, and income improve with the time they spend in the United States. We wish to emphasize that variations in income appear much greater and are more consistent than are variations in prestige and education. If we assume that similar prestige scores indicate similar occupations, it would appear that immigrants' occupations vary little by the length of time the immigrants spend in the United States. Their incomes do vary considerably, which suggests that when they first arrive, immigrants are paid less for similar occupations. We will return to this subject in our multivariate analysis.

It is possible, of course, that these cross-sectional data simply show different cohorts with different characteristics. However, the trends are so consistent that it seems unlikely. Also, from 1960 to 1980, there were no lengthy periods of change in the gross national product, employment, or other measures of economic growth in the United States that could correspond in any way to the patterns shown in Table 4. We suggest, then, that this table gives some tentative support for the assimilationist argument that Asian immigrants should improve their positions the longer they remain in this country. We also find some tentative support for Moon's (1986) contentions about "earlycomers" and latecomers from the data on natives (see also, Lieberson 1980). Chinese and Japanese natives have the highest incomes, with Koreans close behind. They are followed by Filipinos and Asian Indians, the newcomers.

After examining data from the 1980 census, Kan and Liu (1986) found a relative increase in the educational levels of Asian Americans that was at least partially attributable to the high educational levels of recent immigrants. They concluded, however, that relatively high proportions of Asian Americans in professional and managerial occupations are mismatched (overeducated), a finding noted earlier in the report of the U.S. Commission on Civil Rights (1978). It remains to be seen whether this mismatch results in proportionately lower incomes. We were curious about this phenomenon and decided to break down these categories in greater detail, especially with respect to class of worker.

Table 5 generally agrees with Kan and Liu, but it also reinforces what other data have shown, namely, that Japanese are better compensated for their education, while other Asian Americans generally are not. Again, Vietnamese are the least compensated. There is also a consistency across class of worker, except among self-employed professionals. Generally, self-employed workers are the best paid, followed by private-wage workers and governmental workers. It is surprising that Japanese are the best-paid self-employed executives

Table 5. Mean Years of Education and Personal Income, by Class of Worker, (Executives and Professionals), by Race, 1979[a]

Class of Worker	Japanese	Chinese	Korean	Filipino	Asian Indian	Viet-namese	Hispanic	Black	White
Executives, administrators, and Managers									
(number)	2,352	2,492	720	1,385	1,064	213	203	197	497
Private wage worker									
Mean years of education	14.9	15.3	15.4	15.5	16.7	14.1	13.3	13.2	14.1
Mean income	$23,918	$17,371	$18,375	$15,767	$20,489	$13,648	$16,239	$15,226	$21,826
Government worker (all)									
Mean years of education	15.1	16.2	16.2	15.5	16.5	14.0	14.2	13.7	14.7
Mean income	$19,698	$18,492	$15,530	$16,059	$16,728	$14,407	$17,789	$14,855	$18,801
Self-employed (all)									
Mean years of education	13.4	13.0	14.8	14.6	15.0	13.2	11.6	10.9	13.5
Mean income	$25,163	$16,635	$20,112	$21,241	$19,191	$14,104[b]	$19,078[b]	$8,498[b]	$22,533
Professional Specialty									
(number)	3,055	4,034	1,102	3,259	3,295	368	234	286	529
Private wage worker									
Mean years of education	16.0	17.4	16.6	16.7	18.0	15.6	14.0	14.7	15.4
Mean income	$18,195	$20,741	$19,120	$18,371	$22,698	$14,687	$14,659	$13,163	$17,378
Government worker (all)									
Mean years of education	16.7	17.5	17.2	17.0	18.3	15.6	15.7	15.6	16.4
Mean income	$17,384	$17,147	$21,002	$18,181	$20,268	$13,091	$12,519	$13,767	$15,051
Self-employed (all)									
Mean years of education	17.3	17.9	17.5	18.8	19.0	15.7	16.7	13.7	17.4
Mean income	$35,483	$36,438	$37,978	$46,314	$45,781	$22,635[b]	$26,754	b	$30,018
Total sample (number)	21,129	21,725	8,833	19,689	10,477	4,916	4,106	4,151	4,887

[a]Mean personal income (wages and salaries only).
[b]$N < 20$.

and administrators because it has been thought that few Asian Americans were in these categories. But what is of greater interest is that Asian American self-employed professionals
(again, except Vietnamese) earn much more than do whites. It seems that Asian Americans
have made their greatest gains in the professions, but Japanese are also doing well in executive and administrative occupations. The numerical representation of Asian Americans
in all these occupational categories is generally even, although Filipinos are somewhat underrepresented in executive and administrative occupations. In summary, Japanese are doing
well in high-prestige occupations, but other Asian Americans seem to be best off as self-
employed professionals.

MULTIVARIATE ANALYSIS

The analysis so far has suggested that Asian Americans do not receive income returns from
education that are equal to those of whites (although Japanese come close). We pointed to
the recency of immigration as a major contributor to the low income of immigrants and examined the effects of sex, occupational sector, occupation, age, and time worked, as well
as education and income. At this point, it is necessary to introduce all these variables simultaneously, to observe how they combine to affect income. For this purpose, we employed multiple classification analysis (MCA), since many variables of interest are not
continuous and education cannot be reduced to a dummy variable without losing information on returns in relation to credentials. Weeks worked in 1979 was introduced as a covariate because it is continuous and does not lend itself easily to categorization.

We should emphasize that the purpose of this analysis is not to maximize the predictions of mean income. Rather, we are interested in determining how well some of our
predictor variables hold up in a multivariate model when all variables are considered together. Because sex, sector, immigration, nativity, prestige, time worked, and education
have so far appeared to have effects on income, we shall pay special attention to those variables.

Table 6 abstracts all the necessary information from the MCAs. Blacks and Hispanics
are not shown because neither are particularly relevant at this stage of analysis. F ratios can
be compared within each ethnicity, but not across ethnicities because of differences in the
size of the samples. For comparisons among ethnic categories, we instead examine the adjusted beta coefficients. For example, education contributes more to variations in income
among Chinese than among Japanese or Filipinos. The diminished adjusted effects of education on income are due to occupational prestige, which intervenes between education
and income. We were concerned that part of this effect may be due to the artificial nature
of the Temme prestige scores, so at one point we substituted occupational categories themselves, with no discernible change.

Table 6 lists both η, a correlation measure indicating the independent relationship of
a predictor variable and income, and β, the regression coefficient, which gives the contribution of each independent variable adjusted for all other independent variables simultaneously. Because the number of cases is large, almost all values shown are statistically
significant. Also shown are the absolute dollar variations from the overall mean income associated with each category of each adjusted independent variable. After other predictors
were adjusted for gender, work in the industrial sector, period of immigration/nativity (except for whites), age, education, and prestige all retained considerable importance. Weeks
worked in 1979, as a covariate, showed consistently high F ratios. We did not analyze its
precise effects, but simply controlled for it. The overall model is quite effective in predicting mean income, with a multiple R of about .40, varying with ethnicity.[5]

Even after adjustment, income differentials between the sexes remain very high, especially for Japanese and whites. Among Japanese, for example, the income difference be-

Table 6. Multiple Classification Analysis of Determinants of Personal Income[a]

Variable/Statistic	Japanese	Chinese	Filipino	Korean	Asian Indian	Viet-namese	Whites
Weeks Worked, 1979 (covariate)							
F ratio	3298.2	4853.8	3382.1	1599.3	2389.2	1527.3	1147.7
Grand mean income	$15,230	$13,307	$13,180	$12,336	$16,689	$9,416	$14,166
Sex							
F ratio	2381.4	948.7	1096.8	308.1	240.6	170.3	615.9
Eta (unadjusted)	.45	.31	.26	.37	.35	.28	.47
Beta (adjusted)	.32	.19	.23	.21	.15	.19	.34
Deviation in dollars (adjusted)							
Male	$3,686	$1,866	$2,529	$2,591	$1,533	$1,161	$3,421
Female	−3,638	−2,312	−2,028	−2,272	−2,815	−1,476	−4,376
Industrial Sector							
F ratio	312.7	449.4	164.7	72.3	75.4	95.0	93.9
Eta (unadjusted)	.23	.29	.14	.15	.18	.21	.25
Beta (adjusted)	.12	.14	.09	.09	.08	.14	.13
Deviation in dollars (adjusted)							
Periphery	$−1,211	$−1,214	$−828	$−832	$−1,055	$−983	$−1,547
Core	1,412	1,892	940	1,384	1,126	895	1,427
Year of Immigration/Nativity							
F ratio	27.0	98.1	108.6	44.6	83.8	9.0	.03[b]
Eta (unadjusted)	.17	.29	.25	.28	.37	.13	.06[b]
Beta (adjusted)	.07	.13	.14	.15	.18	.08	.02[b]
Deviation in Dollars (adjusted)							
1975–80	$2,413	$−2,289	$−2,287	$−1,819	$−2,705	$−132	$−1,209
1970–74	1,046	−728	−162	300	170	129	−1,438
1960–69	−1	534	1,691	2,507	3,717	732	−546
Before 1960	−729	1,883	1,462	3,704	4,133	5,097	−183
Native	−242	1,048	381	1,846	−827	3,354	16
Age							
F ratio	328.0	156.7	53.9	17.0	42.3	6.6	45.7
Eta (unadjusted)	.15	.14	19	.21	.25	.08	.15
Beta (adjusted)	.21	.14	.09	.08	.11	.06	.15
Deviation in dollars (adjusted)							
25–34	$−3,263	$−1,664	$−970	$−1,037	$−1,610	$1	$−2,293
35–44	1,550	1,637	779	672	1,588	405	632
45–54	2,096	1,449	1,011	1,207	1,201	−330	1,931
55–64	1,375	518	−191	−378	446	−1,744	1,317
Education Completed							
F ratio	127.0	140.7	74.0	14.3	45.9	19.1	62.0
Eta (unadjusted)	.28	.37	.27	.36	.37	.31	.28
Beta (adjusted)	.15	.16	.12	.08	.13	.12	.21
Deviation in dollars (adjusted)							
1–3 years high school or less	$−1,945	$−2,323	$−1,349	$−1,061	$−2,491	$−479	$−2,487
Completed high school	$−1,383	−1,304	−1,215	−713	−2,251	−238	−866
Some college	−508	−651	−882	−503	−2,207	−371	−146
College graduate or more	2,389	1,936	1,312	1,268	1,297	1,830	4,349
Occupational Prestige							
F ratio	450.6	465.8	694.7	178.9	242.7	66.3	54.0
Eta (unadjusted)	.39	.46	.39	.44	.44	.34	.30
Beta (adjusted)	.22	.24	.29	.24	.23	.18	.16
Deviation in dollars (adjusted)							
Low (0–33)	$−3,080	$−2,901	$−2,796	$−2,257	$−4,232	$−917	$−1,901
Medium (34–51)	−716	−911	−1,218	−933	−2,978	−27	−340
High (51–88)	3,275	3,120	4,196	4,327	2,929	2,599	2,656
Multiple R	.651	.659	.603	.631	.646	.658	.668
Multiple R^2	.423	.435	.364	.399	.418	.433	.446
Number	15,225	16,005	15,113	5,616	7,654	3,101	3,437

[a]Personal income (wages and salaries only).

[b]Statistically insignificant at the .01 level.

tween men and women is about $7,300; the incomes of men exceeding the income of women by 63 percent. The sex differences are smaller for immigrant Asian American groups, but nevertheless remain impressive. The industrial sector differentiates income levels strongly for most ethnic groups, but for some reason is weak for Filipinos and Koreans. As we expected from previous analyses, recency of immigration retains salience after adjustment for Asian American groups with a large number of immigrants. It is least important for Japanese because there have been few recent immigrants and because of the character of recent Japanese immigrants. In the case of Vietnamese, the figures are hard to interpret because almost all immigrants had been in the United States for a short time as of 1980. In general, it appears that Asian American immigrants (except Japanese) receive low incomes during their first five years in the United States but later approach equity. Again, we must caution that these arguments are based on cross-sectional data. Finally, note that all Asian American natives receive less income than do immigrants who have been here a long time. Education remains a strong predictor of income. Only college graduates and postgraduates show any significant gains over the average because of the skewed distribution of income. White graduates, in particular, have a substantial income advantage over Asian Americans. Prestige, too, retains strong predictive power, about the same as gender.

After we account for other variables, it is clear that new immigrants (1975–80) suffer a large income loss for reasons not explained by this model. Although prestige, time worked, and educational levels are somewhat lower for new immigrants, these characteristics account for only part of the initially observed differences in income.

Curious about this phenomenon, we constructed another MCA to predict occupational prestige (Table 7). The predictor variables are the same, except for occupational prestige. When one compares the results of Tables 6 and 7, it is clear that gender, sector, age, and immigration/nativity have very small (though mostly statistically significant) effects on prestige. Education has a very powerful effect, as we would expect. These findings may be contrasted with those for income, for which education, gender, sector, immigration/nativity, age, and weeks worked all have strong adjusted effects. Accordingly, we suggest that the occupations held by Asian Americans are determined largely by their educational levels, not by the many other factors that we know shape income.

However, for given levels of occupational prestige, income varies considerably. For example, women are paid less than are men in similar occupations, perhaps, in part, because of such factors as pregnancy, but most of the difference remains unexplained (see the Appendix). We also know that the periphery pays less than does the core (which provided Bonacich and Cheng [1984] with a theory of exploitation and international migration). In the case of new Asian American immigrants, lower incomes are due, in part, to the fewer weeks they worked in a year, concentrations in the periphery, lower ages, less work experience, less education, and being in lower prestige occupations. Still, the very large difference in income by period of immigration cannot be explained by these variables. We would like to suggest here that new immigrants are also paid less for equivalent occupations, as is the case with women.[6]

CONCLUSION

Our results do not allow unequivocal tests of the hypotheses suggested by the assimilation, human capital, and structural theories discussed previously. However, they tend to support the structuralist arguments for the following reasons:

1. The *assimilation* hypothesis is generally not supported because native Asian Americans have not attained income equity with whites. In the case of more recent immigrants, there seems to be some evidence that a longer stay in the United

Table 7. Multiple Classification Analysis of Determinants of Occupational Prestige (Temme Score)

Variable/Statistic	Japanese	Chinese	Filipino	Korean	Asian Indian	Vietnamese	Whites
Weeks Worked, 1979 (covariate)							
F ratio	480.4	951.2	801.3	422.6	1,055.2	118.1	89.6
Grand mean prestige score	43.5	45.1	42.4	41.1	52.1	37.6	42.3
Sex							
F ratio	7.8	115.7	0.1[a]	169.9	15.6	3.8[a]	1.8[a]
Eta (unadjusted)	.16	.16	.01	.31	.23	.12	.05
Beta (adjusted)	.02	.06	.00	.14	.04	.03	.02
Deviation in prestige (adjusted)							
Male	0.29	1.0	0	2.6	0.6	0.4	−0.3
Female	−0.28	−1.1	0	−2.2	−0.9	−0.5	0.3
Industrial Sector							
F ratio	409.5	397.3	145.9	0.0[a]	9.5	17.8	18.7
Eta (unadjusted)	.18	.28	.11	.05	.08	.10	.04
Beta (adjusted)	.13	.12	.08	.00	.03	.06	.06
Deviation in prestige (adjusted)							
Periphery	−1.71	−1.5	−1.2	0	0.5	−0.9	−0.8
Core	2.24	2.6	1.4	0	−0.6	0.9	0.8
Year of Immigration/Nativity							
F ratio	55.3	39.1	110.2	69.5	7.4	5.4	0.8[a]
Eta (unadjusted)	.19	.17	.19	.24	.24	.13	.05
Beta (adjusted)	.10	.08	.14	.17	.05	.07	.02
Deviation in prestige (adjusted)							
1975–80	0.9	−1.9	−3.7	−2.8	−1.0	−0.3	−0.2
1970–74	−2.4	−0.6	−0.4	0.2	0.5	1.1	−2.2
1960–69	−3.1	0.1	2.0	4.2	1.3	3.8	−2.3
Before 1960	−3.1	2.1	2.7	5.0	0.3	−3.2	−0.3
Native	0.7	1.0	1.8	4.2	−1.2	4.0	0.1
Age							
F ratio	39.2	18.1	14.6	0.7[a]	6.5	4.0	14.0
Eta (unadjusted)	.21	.19	.18	.11	.14	.08	.08
Beta (adjusted)	.07	.04	.04	.01	.04	.05	.09
Deviation in prestige (adjusted)							
25–34	−1.1	−0.3	0	0	−0.7	−0.6	−1.7
35–44	1.4	1.2	0.8	0	0.9	1.0	1.0
45–54	0.9	−0.5	−0.6	0	−0.3	0.2	1.0
55–64	−.8	−0.6	−1.7	−1	1.0	0.8	0.4
Education Completed							
F ratio	2,024.3	2,767.4	2,240.1	612.8	1,028.3	350.9	591.3
Eta (unadjusted)	.55	.61	.56	.54	.57	.50	.55
Beta (adjusted)	.53	.56	.55	.45	.52	.47	.56
Deviation in prestige (adjusted)							
Less than high school	−10.8	−12.1	−13.5	−9.2	−17.3	−6.5	−9.1
Completed high school	−6.3	−7.2	−8.5	−6.4	−12.0	−3.2	−3.1
Some college	−.4	−1.7	−2.7	0	−7.4	2.7	2.3
Completed college or more	11.2	10.3	9.4	9.2	7.3	14.3	14.3
Number	17,749	18,895	16,645	7,206	8,844	3,833	4,089
Multiple R	.585	.643	.590	.585	.599	.516	.565
Multiple R²	.343	.413	.349	.342	.359	.266	.320

[a]Statistically insignificant at the .01 level.

States increases income, but it does not produce consistent equity when other variables are controlled.

2. The *human capital* hypothesis is rejected because the higher levels of education of Asian Americans are not translated into income parity with whites when other variables are accounted for.

3. The *structuralist* hypothesis is tentatively accepted because neither the length of residence nor the educational levels of Asian Americans produces income equity with whites when other factors are accounted for. The results of this investigation show that although the higher levels of education of Asian Americans result in higher occupational prestige scores, there is a slippage between these higher prestige scores and income, especially in the case of recent immigrants. We attribute this slippage to discrimination against new immigrants, which is consistent with the structuralist position.

The observation of the discrepancy between prestige and incomes is all somewhat complicated by the fact that Asian Americans do not form a coherent category. Rather, there appear to be at least four different types with different characteristics. First, Japanese are most similar to whites in socioeconomic characteristics; they have a long history of immigration but few recent immigrants. Second, Chinese, Koreans, Filipinos, and Asian Indians have a very large number of recent immigrants; members of these groups vary considerably in socioeconomic characteristics, depending on the period of immigration. Third, Vietnamese resemble blacks and Hispanics, with low educational levels and incomes. Fourth, native Asian Americans differ from both whites and recent immigrants.

Education appears to be a useful channel to occupational prestige and (more equivocally) to higher incomes for most Asian Americans, unlike the situation of resident underprivileged minorities, such as blacks, Hispanics, and American Indians. This observation does not apply to Vietnamese in 1980, for their situation appears worse than that of blacks or Hispanics. However, only Japanese seem to have reached essential equity with whites, and even that point can be disputed for particular data sets.

The remaining disparities between Asian Americans and whites appear to be accounted for, in part, by the very large number of recent immigrants among Chinese, Koreans, Filipinos, and Asian Indians and, ironically, by differences between whites and native Asian Americans. It is clear that recent immigrants are underpaid in their various occupational settings in much the same fashion as are women. This conclusion is based on data as of 1980, and, of course, the "deindustrialization" of the American economy that began just before the 1980 census may have made it more difficult for recent immigrants to achieve the economic success enjoyed by their immediate predecessors. Certainly, the data we examined indicate that Asian immigrants who have resided in the United States for a decade or two are enjoying excellent income returns on their education, competing handily with whites. These advantages are due, in large part, to their being professionals, especially those who are self-employed.

The data we presented here show that overall, Asian Americans are better educated than are whites. In the case of Japanese, it is difficult to find much evidence of income discrimination compared to whites. Chinese, Koreans, Filipinos, and Asian Indians all show smaller income advantages compared to their high levels of education, but, as we reported, this finding appears to be due mostly to the large proportion of recent immigrants in these ethnic categories. We think it is important that the disadvantages experienced by immigrants are similar to those experienced by women: They both appear to be paid less for equivalent occupations. It is true, of course, that some new immigrants enter the labor force in occupations that are beneath their educational capabilities, some tend to be drawn into the periphery, and some suffer the consequences of less time worked or less experience because they are young. However, many appear to find occupations that are commensurate with their education but are paid less than are dominant Americans or older immigrants for those positions. In this sense, they are similar to their early twentieth-century forbears, but it is hoped, for a shorter period of their lives.

It is obvious that Asian American women receive a much smaller income return on their education than do Asian American men—a situation they share with white women. Sex discrimination, in fact, appears to be equal to or greater than the discrimination experienced by new immigrants. This finding cannot be explained by education, weeks worked, occupational prestige, or recency of immigration.

Some of these findings do not disagree completely with the general expectations of assimilation theory, but neither do they suggest that Asian Americans have been assimilated, either structurally or politically. The census data tell nothing about the elite strata of American society, which apparently remains an exclusive network of dominant Americans. We feel more comfortable with the formulations of Kim and Hurh (1983) and of Ogbu (1978), who suggested that minorities may be forming separate "adaptive" communities. Asian Americans may have higher educational and income levels than do blacks, Hispanics, or American Indians, but it does not follow that they are more "assimilated." One may recall that Jews relearned this lesson most bitterly earlier in this century.

At the same time, in partial deference to human capital theory, it is true that Asian Americans (except Vietnamese) are better educated and have higher incomes than do blacks or Hispanics. The weakness of human capital theory appears to be that it makes too simplistic assumptions about the relationship of education to income, which needs to be articulated by the intervention of occupation (or occupational prestige).

Although our results seem to give some support for the structural theories of Bonacich and Cheng (1984), Lieberson (1980), or Steinberg (1981), those theories rest on historical analyses of previous generations of immigrants. As we pointed out earlier, many recent immigrants to the United States were already well educated and embedded in a capitalist international economic system before they immigrated, unlike the earlier Asian (and other) immigrants to the United States. Even so, very recent Asian immigrants show income losses that cannot be explained by ordinary predictors of income. Furthermore, by no means do all Asian immigrants fit these generalizations: Many continue to enter the United States without high educational or occupational skills, and their situations will bear close examination over the next decade. Vietnamese, in particular, should make an ideal test case for the proponents of structuralist and human capital theories.

Despite the weaknesses of human capital theory, it would nevertheless be foolhardy to disregard the general importance of education and occupation in determining income in contemporary American society. Many Asian Americans appear to have learned how to reap their combined rewards, despite other obstacles. However, an accurate assessment of their "success" requires that we also consider such factors as national origin, recency of arrival (for immigrants), nativity, gender, actual occupations obtained, and employment in the industrial sector. The failure to do so leads to overly simplistic stereotypes and unfortunate social policies.

APPENDIX

Although sex differences were not the principal focus of this article, we were asked about the effects of other variables on them. In response, we entered the variables "hours worked in 1979" and "marital status" (married or unmarried) into two additional MCA runs for Chinese and Japanese, respectively. With number of hours worked, weeks worked and age entered as covariates; the R^2 for Japanese was .430, compared to the original value of .423. For Chinese, the revised R^2 was .441, compared to the original .435. The added variables changed the beta for sex from .32 to .30 (for Japanese) and from .19 to .17 (for Chinese). The beta values for marital status itself were .12 for Japanese and .08 for Chinese. Both hours worked and marital status were statistically significant contributors to the equation, but neither changed the effects of sex appreciably, nor did they have much effect on the R^2. They had no effect on the variable "year of immigration." We conclude, therefore, that gender differences in income cannot be explained away by traditional predictors of income. The same is true of period of immigration. In the case of both recent Asian immigrants and of women, factors unmeasured in this study had adverse effects on income.

NOTES

1. This convention produces some obvious biases, as can be seen in average ages and in incomes and occupations. However, the purpose of this article is to examine the consequences of education, and this purpose is best served by limiting the sample to those who have completed their education and to those who have jobs and incomes. For a precedent, see Blau and Duncan (1967).

2. We decided to examine each race separately because of the size of these files. A composite file would have permitted us to enter race as a variable, but the cost of running it would have been prohibitive. Besides, research reported by Blau and Schwartz (1984) and Hirschman and Wong (1981, 1984) suggested that "race" as such would produce little in the way of direct effects. Readers may note some variation in the figures reported here compared to other sources. This difference is ordinarily due to different methods of recoding or specifying missing data and poses no problem for analytical purposes as long as the methods are consistent. However, "real" figures are best taken from official reports of the U.S. Bureau of the Census. Whether census figures are accurate representations is another question. One may question some data for good reasons. The language-ability items are particularly suspect, and certainly income reports may be biased downward.

3. *Sector* refers to the concepts of *core* and *periphery* that are similar to formal and informal sectors. The core is characterized by a sophisticated technology, is capital intensive, and generally denotes modern industry. The periphery is labor intensive, smaller scale, with a simpler technology; agriculture and service are examples. We used the scheme to reclassify subjects by industry of employment.

4. Occupational prestige is a complex measure that is based on a national prestige study, educational level, and income. The measure used in this article was developed by Temme (1975) and used in the 1978 report of the U.S. Commission on Civil Rights. Because the U.S. Bureau of the Census changed occupational codes for 1980, we obtained a matching of the 1970 and 1980 codes from the bureau. Some guesswork was entailed, so we trust these scores only for comparative purposes. Since we completed this task, Stevens and Cho (1985) adapted the Featherman-Stevens scores. We tried both and found that the Temme scores gave stronger correlations with income, so we retained that measure. Blau and Duncan (1967) discuss prestige scores in detail.

5. We do not discuss interactions here because first- and second-order interactions were very small, and nearly all were statistically insignificant. Those that were significant varied by ethnicity, making coherent discussion, much less modification of the overall model, unproductive.

6. Informants have told us that many firms in Silicon Valley make it a practice of hiring immigrant engineers in Asia at low salaries. Until recently, many interns and physicians in inner cities and in rural communities were Asian immigrants. Other examples abound.

REFERENCES

Barringer, H., S. N. Cho, and P. Xenos. Forthcoming. "A Fact Book of Koreans in the United States." Occasional Papers. Honolulu: Center for Korean Studies.

Barringer, H., P. Smith, and R. Gardner. 1985. "Income Attainment of Asian Americans: Evidence from the 1980 Census." Paper presented at the Annual Meetings of the Western Conference, Association for Asian Studies, Long Beach, CA, October 11 and 12.

Berg, I. 1969. *Education and Jobs: The Great Training Robbery.* New York: Praeger.

Blau, P., and O. D. Duncan. 1967. *The American Occupational Structure.* New York: John Wiley & Sons.

Blau, P., and J. E. Schwartz. 1984. *Crosscutting Social Circles: Testing a Macrostructural Theory of Intergroup Relations.* Orlando, FL: Academic Press.

Bonacich, E. 1973. "A Theory of Middlemen Minorities." *American Sociological Review* 38: 583–594.

Bonacich, E., and L. Cheng. 1984. "Introduction: A Theoretical Orientation to International Labor Migration." Pp. 1–56 in *Labor Migration under Capitalism: Asian Workers in the United States before World War II.* Berkeley: University of California Press.

Bowles, S., and H. Gintis. 1976. *Schooling in Capitalist America: Educational Reform and the Contradiction of Economic Life.* New York: Basic Books.

Chiswick, B. R. 1983. "An Analysis of the Earnings and Employment of Asian American Men." *Journal of Labor Economics* 1(2): 197–214.

Collins, R. 1971. "Functional and Conflict Theories of Educational Stratification." *American Sociological Review* 36:1002–1019.

Fujii, E. T., and J. Mak. 1983. "The Determinants of Income of Native and Foreign-born Men in a Multiracial Society." *Applied Economics* 15:759–776.

Gardner, R., B. Robey, and P. C. Smith. 1985. "Asian Americans: Growth, Change and Diversity." *Population Bulletin* 40(4):1–44.

Gordon, M. 1964. *Assimilation in American Life.* New York: Oxford University Press.

———. 1978. *Human Nature: Class and Ethnicity.* New York: Oxford University Press.

Hirschman, C., and M. G. Wong. 1981. "Trends in Socio-economic Achievement among Immigrant and Native-born Americans: 1960–1976." *Sociological Quarterly* 22(4):485–514.

———. 1984. "Socioeconomic Gains of Asian Americans, Blacks, and Hispanics: 1960–1976." *American Journal of Sociology* 90(3):584–607.

———. 1986. "The Extraordinary Educational Attainment of Asian Americans: A Search for Historical Evidence and Explanations." *Social Forces* 65(1):1–27.

Hurh, W. M., and K. C. Kim. 1984. *The Korean Immigrant in America: A Structural Analysis of Ethnic Conflict and Adhesive Adaptation.* Cranberry, NJ: Association of University Presses.

Kan, S., and W. Liu. 1986. "The Educational Status of Asian Americans: An Update from the 1980 Census." Pp. 1–12 in *Issues in Asian and Pacific American Education,* edited by N. Tsuchiya. Minneapolis, MN: Asian/Pacific American Learning Resource Center.

Kim, K. C., and W. M. Hurh. 1983. "Korean Americans and the 'Success' Image: A Critique." *Amerasia* 10(2):3–21.

Kitano, H. 1976. *Japanese Americans: The Evolution of a Subculture.* Englewood Cliffs, NJ: Prentice-Hall.

Kuo, W. H. 1977. "Assimilation among Chinese-Americans in Washington, D.C." *Sociological Quarterly* 18 (Summer):340–352.

Langberg, M., and R. Farley. 1985. "Residential Segregation of Asian Americans in 1980." *Sociology and Social Research* 70(1):71–75.

Lieberson, S. 1980. *A Piece of the Pie: Black and White Immigrants since 1880.* Berkeley: University of California Press.

Massey, D. S., and N. A. Denton. 1987. "Trends in the Residential Segregation of Blacks, Hispanics and Asians: 1970–1980." *American Sociological Review* 52:802–825.

Mayes, S. S. 1977. "The Increasing Stratification of Higher Education: Ideology and Consequence." *Journal of Educational Thought* 11(1):16–27.

Montero, D. 1981. "The Japanese Americans: Changing Patterns of Assimilation over Three Generations." *American Sociological Review* 46(6):829–839.

Montero, D., and R. Tsukashima. 1977. "Assimilation and Educational Attainment: The Case of the Second Generation Japanese-American." *Sociological Quarterly* 18:490–503.

Moon, C. 1986. "Year of Immigration and Socioeconomic Status: A Comparative Study of Three Asian Populations in California." *Social Indicators Research* 18:129–152.

Nee, V., and J. Sanders. 1987. "Limits of Ethnic Solidarity in the Enclave Economy." *American Sociological Review* 52:745–773.

Ogbu, J. 1978. *Minority Education and Caste: The American Status System in Cross Cultural Perspective*. New York: Academic Press.

Park, R. E. 1950. *Race and Culture*. Glencoe, IL: Free Press.

Parsons, T. 1968. "The Social Class as a Social System: Some of Its Functions in American Society." *Harvard Educational Review* (Reprint Series) 1:69–90.

Peterson, W. 1971. *Japanese Americans*. New York: Random House.

Portes, A., and A. Stepick. 1985. "Unwelcome Immigrants: The Labor Market Experiences of 1980 (Mariel) Cuban and Haitian Refugees in South Florida." *American Sociological Review* 50:493–514.

Scimecca, J. A. 1980. *Education and Society*. New York: Holt, Rinehart & Winston.

Sewell, W. H., A. D. Haller, and A. Portes. 1969. "The Educational and Early Occupational Attainment Process." *American Sociological Review* 34:82–96.

Sewell, W. H., and R. M. Hauser. 1975. *Education, Occupation and Earnings: Achievement in the Early Career*. New York: Academic Press.

Sklare, M. 1971. *America's Jews*. New York: Random House.

Steinberg, S. 1981. *The Ethnic Myth: Race, Ethnicity and Class in America*. Boston: Beacon Press.

Stevens, G., and J. H. Cho. 1985. "Socioeconomic Indexes and the New 1980 Census Occupational Scheme." *Social Science Research* 14(2):142–168.

Sung, B. L. 1967. *The Story of the Chinese in America*. New York: Macmillan Co.

Suzuki, B. H. 1977. "Education and Socialization of Asian Americans: A Revisionist Analysis of the 'Model Minority' Thesis." *Amerasia* 4(2):23–51.

Temme, L. V. 1975. *Occupational Meaning and Measures*. Washington, DC: Bureau of Social Science Research.

Tienda, M., and D. T. Lii. 1987. "Minority Concentrations and Earnings Inequality: Blacks, Hispanics and Asians Compared." *American Journal of Sociology* 93(1):141–165.

Tolbert, C., P. M. Horan, and E. M. Beck. 1979. "The Structure of Economic Segmentation: A Dual Economy Approach." *American Journal of Sociology* 85(5):1095–1116.

U.S. Commission on Civil Rights. 1978. *Social Indicators of Equality for Minorities and Women: A Report of the United States Commission on Civil Rights*. Washington, DC: U.S. Commission on Civil Rights.

Wang, J. 1981. "Korean Assimilation in the Multi-ethnic Setting of Hawaii: An Examination of Milton Gordon's Theory of Assimilation." Unpublished Ph.D. dissertation, University of Hawaii.

Wong, E. 1985. "Asian American Middleman Minority Theory: The Framework of an American Myth." *Journal of Ethnic Studies* 13(1):52–88.

Wong, M. 1980. "Changes in the Socioeconomic Status of the Chinese Male Population in the United States from 1960 to 1970." *International Migration Review* 14(4):511–524.

———. 1982. "The Cost of Being Chinese, Japanese, and Filipino in the United States: 1960, 1970, 1976." *Pacific Sociological Review* 25(1):59–78.

Wong, M. G., and C. Hirschman. 1983. "Labor Force Participation and Socioeconomic Attainment of Asian American Women." *Sociological Perspective* 26(4):3–46.

Woo, D. 1985. "The Socioeconomic Status of Asian American Women in the Labor Force: An Alternative View." *Sociological Perspective* 27(3):307–338.

Xenos, P., H. R. Barringer, and M. Levin. 1989. "Asian Indians in the U.S." Honolulu: East-West Population Institute.

Yu, C. 1977. "The Correlation of Cultural Assimilation of the Korean Immigrants in the United States." Pp. 167–176 in *The Korean Diaspora: Historical and Sociological Study of Korean Immigrants and Assimilation in North America*, edited by H. Kim. Santa Barbara, CA: ABC-Clio.

III

ELEMENTARY AND SECONDARY EDUCATIONAL ISSUES: THE CHALLENGES OF GROWTH AND DIVERSITY

9 Asian American Children:
A Diverse Population

Valerie Ooka Pang

To MANY TEACHERS, Asian American students seem to look and be alike—they are model minority students. Like many other stereotypes, this perception is easier believed than carefully examined. In fact, most Asian American students are neither "super brains" nor "gang members." They do represent many cognitive strengths and weaknesses, have diverse ethnic roots, live in many parts of the United States, and range from being newly immigrated to having roots over 200 years old.[1] Without basic knowledge of the diversity of the particular population, schools cannot provide an equal chance for all to develop their intellect and skills.[2]

Asian Americans encompass a number of highly diverse groups, including those of the Cambodian, Chinese, East Indian, Filipino, Guamanian, Hawaiian, Hmong, Indonesian, Japanese, Korean, Laotian, Samoan, and Vietnamese heritages. The U.S. Bureau of the Census included smaller Asian American groups within the category of all other Asians in the 1980 Census. These were Bangladeshi, Bhutanese, Bornean, Burmese, Celbesian, Cernan, Indochinese, Iwo-Jiman, Javanese, Malayan, Maldivian, Nepali, Okinawan, Sikkimese, Singaporean, and Sri Lankan.[3] In toto, they make up the fastest growing minority group in the United States. From 1970 to 1980, the Asian population increased by approximately 143 percent.[4] In 1985, Asian American population was estimated to be 5.1 million and projected to increase to 10 million by the year 2000, approaching four percent of the national population.[5] The 1984 Elementary and Secondary School Civil Rights Survey reported an Asian American student population of just about one million.[6] Taking into consideration birthrate and continued immigration, it may be safely surmised that the figure has further increased in more recent years.

Though the number of children who are of mixed parentage is not known, it is important to note that Asian American youth include a number of EurAsian Americans, Asian Latino-Americans, Asian Black-Americans, Asian Native-Americans, and others. Interracial marriages have been occurring since the first Filipino immigrants made Louisiana their home in 1763 and wed outside their ethnic community.[7] More recently, of course, there have been many mixed children conceived during the Vietnam war who were rejected both in Vietnam due to their White-American roots and in the U.S. because of their Vietnamese backgrounds.[8] Many families also include intraracial marriages among different Asian American groups. Thus, it is not uncommon for children to have both Chinese and Japanese roots or Filipino and Vietnamese heritages.

From *The Educational Forum* 55 (1990):49–65. Reprinted with permission of Kappa Delta Pi, an International Honor Society in Education.

Before getting into the general discussion of Asian American population, a word must be said about the label, "Oriental." Though this term is often used in education to identify students with Asian roots, its use in reference to U.S. citizens and residents ignores the negative connotations of an outgroup status, of foreigners, and perhaps even of "yellow peril." Asian Americans have resided in the United States for over 200 years, some being able to trace their roots back over ten generations. Also, soldiers from the Filipino-American community fought in the War of 1812.[9] It is more appropriate to call these people "Asian American" or, more inclusively, "Asian- and Pacific Islander-American."

FACTORS CONTRIBUTING TO DIVERSITY

ASIAN AMERICAN STUDENTS, NATIVE OR IMMIGRANT

An important variable when dealing with Asian American population is place of birth, American born or immigrant. The experiences of the two groups may differ greatly, and so does the manner in which they identify themselves. Though it is dangerous to overgeneralize across individuals within a group, American-born students are likely to be more highly assimilated into the mainstream,[10] especially those who do not reside in ethnic communities.[11] For example, many Japanese-American students who live in middle-class suburban neighborhoods[12] may not choose to identify themselves along ethnic lines.[13] Matute-Bianchi found such high school students from central California identify themselves through their school activities like student government and social clubs, rather than through ancestry. They did not want to engage in school activities that were ethnically tied. For example, though attempts had been made at one school to establish a club focusing on Japanese history, no students of Japanese descent joined the group.

However, many American-born, limited-English-proficient students may readily identify themselves through ethnic lines, and even boast, "I can be President of the United States." These children may come to school unable to speak English because they have spoken their ancestral languages all their lives. Kindergarten could be the very first setting requiring them to use English. On the other hand, many American-born students speak only English.[14] They can be categorized as being bicultural, and they may look positively at ethnic membership and life in an environment that mixes both mainstream and traditional Asian values.[15] These children may be family oriented, respect elders, and value education, while at the same time participate in mainstream, after-school activities such as football or ballet. They may not choose to take part in Asian American activities at school, but can be members of, for example, a local Buddhist temple, participating in ethnically specific activities in that context.[16]

Like their American-born counterparts, immigrant students clearly demonstrate a wide range of approaches to their background. There are highly assimilated ones who may feel compelled to blend into American society and so relinquish ancestral cultural values, behaviors, and traditions. They may, for example, refuse to speak their first language, and view their ethnic ties as obstacles to being accepted into the mainstream. In contrast, there are those who are extremely proud of their background. The parents of these children speak their ancestral language at home,[17] and children may attend a special Saturday or after-school language school built to ensure that the values, beliefs, and language of the originating culture remain in the community.[18]

Many from Asian countries have migrated to the United States in search of economic stability. Prior to 1965, Chinese-American, Filipino-American, Japanese-American, and Korean-American communities consisted of families who had long American roots, since immigration had been prohibited for the Chinese after 1882, the Japanese and Koreans after

1924, and the Filipinos after 1934 (the Filipino Exclusion Act).[19] With the Immigration Act of 1965, the numbers of Chinese, Korean, and Filipino immigrants dramatically rose. More recently, after the governments of South Vietnam, Cambodia, and Laos fell in 1975, there were thousands of Vietnamese, Chinese, Cambodians, and other Asian refugees who fled Southeast Asia because of political strife.[20] The largest proportion of the refugee population were Vietnamese with smaller numbers of Laotians, Chinese-Vietnamese, and Hmong refugees. They represented a large diversity in socioeconomic and educational levels.[21] Some were fluent English speakers and others had no English language skills at all. With all this influx, difficulties have sometimes developed between immigrant and American-born Asian students. Differences between the two categories of students, their values and feelings,[22] can affect their interactions at school.

POSSIBLE INTRAGROUP CONFLICTS

Many Asian Americans have found themselves with increasing feelings of marginality,[23] as the pressure of cultural assimilation can produce ambivalent feelings about ethnic group membership.[24] Marginality refers to conflicting attitudes that may develop when a member of a minority group finds himself or herself at cultural odds with the dominant society, and the marginal person can develop personality traits of insecurity, hypersensitivity, and excessive self-consciousness. Even within the Asian American population itself, those students whose families have old roots within the United States may not feel comfortable with new immigrant students. They may fear being identified with the immigrants who, they feel, are old fashioned, "nerds," or "weird" in dress and behavior. When new immigrants are being harassed by other students, the better established ones may feel the pressure to "join in" the mainstream so as not to be perceived as being associated with the newcomers. Or they may ignore the harassment, without trying to discourage the taunting. Educators should be aware of this possible area of conflict and not routinely choose other Asian Americans as buddies for immigrant students, assuming incorrectly that older ones can be of the most help to the new arrivals. Asking students to volunteer for this responsibility may reduce the potential for such conflict.

The second source of intragroup conflict may lie in the past, "old country" animosities. Many new immigrant students may find themselves placed in classes with others from groups that, historically, have been fierce enemies. Antagonism has cropped up in some school incidents involving Asian American students battling each other. In one instance, a teacher who had Vietnamese-American and Cambodian-American students learned about these animosities in a peer teaching situation. The Vietnamese-American student had lived in the United States for about seven years and spoke English well. The Cambodian-American student had been in the United States for only three years and was having some difficulties understanding the material. The teacher mistakenly assumed that they would be happy to work with each other, since they had similar refugee experiences. He asked the Vietnamese youth to help the Cambodian. Since such students generally have a high regard for teachers, they were rather reluctant to speak out, but the Vietnamese student explained diplomatically that he did not think the other student would accept his help. This greatly surprised the teacher, but the prediction of the student was confirmed when the Cambodian student said, "I do not want to accept help from a Vietnamese." These feelings were worked through, but even then it was difficult for the students who had been in adversary roles to view situations in a new light. These historical sentiments often come with new immigrants, and teachers need to be aware of such long-standing animosities.

Of course, immigrant and American-born youth may not generally form close friendships with each other. There can exist a mutual feeling of mistrust, reflecting a lack of understanding of each other's values and beliefs. Sometimes language barriers contribute to the distance. Those born in the U.S. who do not speak an ancestral language may feel unable to communicate with immigrants who are speaking a first language other than English. And, on their part, immigrant youngsters may not understand English sufficiently well to feel comfortable participating in peer group conversations. School staff should be sensitive to these possible sources of conflict in encouraging cooperative activities. Students with varied roots can be placed in small mixed groupings where personal experiences can help reduce prejudicial attitudes. Here, again, the danger of overgeneralizing is ever present, as the dynamics between groups are not always apparent. Teachers need to react to their Asian American students as individuals, and to understand how the differing experiences of these students can influence their behaviors in school.

SOCIALIZATION OF CHILDREN

Parental attitudes and child rearing practices definitely impact the development of children. Though quite a few studies have examined general tendencies of Asian Americans as one group, only two large projects could be located that compared varying practices within that large group. One study, conducted by Cabezas,[25] examined the early childhood development of 233 Asian American families (Chinese, Japanese, Korean, and Vietnamese) from the San Francisco-Oakland metropolitan area, focusing upon parent values, child rearing, and interactional styles. He found, in Asian American mothers born both here and overseas, a predominance of question-asking behavior in comparison to modelling, cueing, or direct commands, even though American-born ones showed a higher incidence than those born elsewhere. Chinese and Filipino mothers born overseas used more direct commands and were more authoritarian in their beliefs than the other mothers. In those families where mothers asked more questions, the children (preschool and primary grades) also responded with more questions and sought more verbal approval from their mothers. The results of this study seem to be in conflict with the belief that Asian American students do not have the verbal skills to involve themselves in an interactive school setting. An Asian American child's failure to participate may reflect a lack of encouragement to engage in interaction rather than lack of ability. If these children are not being consistently included in class discussions, they may feel reticent about participating because of strong respect for authority. If they go into the school with strong verbal interaction skills, but these skills are not being developed in classrooms, they could become less apt to participate as they progress through the educational system.

The second study was by Rumbaut and Ima, who examined parent-child relationships of the Southeast Asian American refugee community in the San Diego City Schools.[26] Extensive data were collected on 579 youth, while general comparative information was collected on 1,485 junior and senior high school students. Lao and Khmer parents were found to stress academic discipline and pressure youth to achieve less than Vietnamese, Chinese-Vietnamese, and Hmong parents. In addition, there was a less sense of obligation toward elders and parents in Lao and Khmer communities. Vietnamese, Chinese-Vietnamese, and Hmong parents had stronger parental controls and domination over their children, and they emphasized the importance of collective survival. In contrast, the Lao and Khmer, rural in origin and less educated, seemed to value a more individualistic adjustment to American life (e.g., in moving out as quickly as possible from shared living arrangements). Yet their communities also had a fatalistic point of view toward life, which seemed to manifest itself in the lack of an aggressively competitive attitude toward academic success. The Lao of the upper-class background are more likely to have migrated to France, and many of the Khmer elite were killed in Kampuchea. Therefore, many of the refugees who settled in the United States have had fewer resources and hold values that do not advance a strong desire for "success."

The Vietnamese-American community, in particular, seemed to have much more strict control over their children than Khmer and Lao parents, regardless of social class. Vietnamese-American students are more likely to feel familial obligation and to be competitive in school. In elite Vietnamese families, a complex bicultural manner of resolving conflicts with children was found—though the word of parents was highly respected, children were permitted in some instances to explain, in a polite tone, their perspective in the conflict situation. Parents wanted children to feel that they had some control over their own existence. Meanwhile, people in the Hmong community, whose agrarian roots did not include high levels of education, have adapted nicely to the American school system. The discipline parents have instilled in children, coupled with strong respect for authority, seemed to result in high levels of motivation in Hmong students. These students demonstrated great tenacity and discipline in their school work. Unfortunately, though many Hmong students do well in high school, very few continue studies on the college level. There is a great deal of pressure to have a family and many Hmong youth marry young. Of course, they then find it difficult to support a family with a high school degree.

SOCIOPSYCHOLOGICAL AND ACADEMIC NEEDS

SELF-CONCEPT AND PSYCHOLOGICAL NEEDS

To many school personnel, Asian American students appear to have fewer and less severe personal problems than other students. Though teachers are often aware of the academic problems of those from Southeast Asia, the needs of other students may not be readily apparent. It is easy for teachers to spot problems of language proficiency, but it is much more difficult to identify internal conflicts in students.

Needless to say, Asian American students must deal with the stresses of racism and the existence of conflicting cultural messages communicated by frequently portrayed images of Asian Americans. One of those images is the "model minority" classification, which can be accompanied by the belief that they are the students who raise the grading curve. They are usually not the football stars or cheerleaders, and they may be perceived as "nerds." Students who do well must cope with this social image, and it is not always an asset to stand out academically, to be considered "eggheads." Yet they oftentimes come from families in which education is highly valued. Parents will sacrifice material comfort in order to provide the best educational experience for their children.[27] Some parents expect not only "good" grades but also "exceptionally high" grades from their offspring. Thus, students who feel pressure from their families must deal with possible rejection from their peers.

On the other hand, there are Asian American children who are not intellectually gifted and cannot reach the high academic standards which parents or teachers have set for them. These students have a difficult time dealing with negative feelings of being a "loser." One *sansei* (third-generation Japanese-American) high school student said about himself, "My folks just gave up on me because I didn't get into college." Unfortunately, this message was also reiterated by his teacher, who told the student, "Your sister was an *A* student— how come you only get *C*'s? You're not trying." The model minority image can be a terrible liability for those students who are not academically inclined, especially when teachers assume that children from certain Asian American groups will be top achievers. These students are trying to deal with the powerful process of assimilation, and mixed messages regarding their acceptance into mainstream society can be a heavy burden for them to carry.

The impact of being a member of a visibly different minority group can also have a forceful effect on the fragile and developing self-image of children. The findings of a study examining the self-concept of Asian American youth show a disturbing pattern of generally lower levels of self-esteem than Caucasian and Black American youngsters.[28] Another study reported Vietnamese-American students to score lowest on overall self concept in comparison to non-Vietnamese Asian, Caucasian, Black-American, and Mexican-American students.[29] Similarly, Korean-American and Chinese-American students may not feel as positive about their physical self-image as Black- or White-American students.[30] In yet another study of the general self-concept of Japanese-American students in the fourth through sixth grades, lower physical self-concept scores were seen offset by high academic self-image scores to make the general scores less than revealing.[31] These findings may be surprising to many teachers who believe Asian American students are well-adjusted, competent students. Such studies point to the need for schools to take steps to help Asian American students develop more positive perceptions of themselves.

PARENTAL FACTOR IN TEST ANXIETY AND ACHIEVEMENT

The importance of parental support in Asian American families cannot be overestimated. For example, Pang found that the parent support felt by middle school students of Chinese, Filipino, Korean, and East Indian heritages was predictive of mathematics grades. However, these students were also more test anxious than their White-American counterparts, because of their desire to please their parents. The side effect of high parent expectations and need for approval may be test anxiety.[32] In comparison with their White-American peers, Asian American students report more support and encouragement from their parents. On their part, Asian American parents, more than the White-American parents, believed that their children try to please them. The socialization of Asian American students follows a complex interpersonal process that transforms into an intrapersonal one.[33] The need for approval through doing well becomes internalized, though children are typically unaware of the process. Besides, it may be the support Asian American children feel that helps them to diffuse, to an extent, the pressure of high parental academic expectations.

The role of parents in academic achievement was perceived as extremely important also by another group.[34] In contrast with CaucAsian Americans, Chinese-American mothers of sixth-grade students placed more responsibility for their children's poor performance in mathematics upon the training received at home. While acknowledging the training their children received at school to be critical, these mothers explained that it was the duty of parents to instill in their children the value of education. In addition, they lacked confidence in the school and felt it necessary to take an active part in remedying the shortcomings of the school. They revealed high academic expectations, stressing the importance of the child's effort. These studies display not only the prominence of parental attitudes and values in the academic process, but also the importance of child-rearing practices. Many Asian American students indeed come from family environments that emphasize schooling. In some cases, families take an active part in monitoring the progress of students.

ACADEMIC ACHIEVEMENT OF CHILDREN

Research on academic achievement of Asian American students has typically indicated high levels of scholarship, and, in fact, the popular press often labels them "whiz kids."[35] Unfortunately, this portrayal does not accurately reflect the actual achievement levels found across the group. The Admissions Testing Program of the College Board collected data for five years (1980–1985) on college-bound seniors. The 1985 sample included the responses of 1,052,351 high school seniors. There were 42,637 Asian American students, or four percent of all candidates, which was almost a 50 percent increase from the beginning of their study in 1980. The sample represented a broad spectrum of Asian communities. On the Scholastic Aptitude Test in 1985, the Asian American verbal mean score of 404 was below the national average of 431, but their mathematics mean of 518 was above the national average of 475.[36] The observed trend of Asian American children doing better in mathematics than in verbal areas had been reported earlier,[37] but the literature does not, unfortunately, indicate specific realms of strengths or weaknesses within these broad subject areas.

However, the Admissions Testing Program did provide information regarding the SAT reading comprehension and vocabulary subscores. On the reading-comprehension subscale, Asian Americans scored 40.7 in contrast to the White-American mean of 44.9. On the vocabulary subscale, the scores were 40.4 for Asian Americans and 45.0 for White-Americans.[38] In the questionnaire administered by the Admissions Testing Program, seniors were asked how many years they had studied mathematics. The Asian American mean was 3.89 years in contrast with the White-American mean of 3.72. The additional two months of instruction may be reflected in the difference in mathematics performance. Another reason may be the strong interest Asian American seniors show in mathematics and science. While 58.6 percent of these students indicated their intended area of study in college to be the biological or physical sciences, only 38.8 percent of the White-American seniors are the same. This probably means that more Asian American college-bound students had become interested at an earlier age, and engaged themselves in extracurricular activities that foster the development of the relevant knowledge and skills. In addition, if their parents indicated a preference for careers in mathematics and sciences, the children would be more likely to have pursued that route.

In English instruction on the other hand, the College Board study found almost the same number of years of study. The mean years of instruction were 3.97 for Asian Americans and 4.00 for White-Americans. In spite of the equivalence in the length of instruction, a lack of strong English-language skills obviously plagues many Asian American children. Of the 1985 Asian American high school seniors, those who indicated that English was not their best language had the SAT verbal median score of 272, a quite low figure even in contrast with others who reported English as being their best language. The latter's median was 434, still lower than the mean of 449 among White-Americans. The great number of recent Asian American immigrants, who have migrated to the United States in recent years, many of whose families have home languages other than English, may account for such findings. Program development in communication skills, both oral and written, for Asian American students is an area that must be addressed, a need Asian American seniors themselves perceived. Also, even though 73 percent rated themselves high on mathematics abilities, only 56 percent so rated themselves for oral expression (in comparison with 64 percent for all students).[39] Asian American students seem to have "communication anxiety"—they not only feel the inability to do well, but reveal a fear of writing and speaking. Such apprehension in itself may further induce them into more technical and scientific fields of study.

Some relevant information is currently gathered by a few, large school districts according to the specific Asian ethnic groups. Their data clearly show that there are both successful and failing Asian American students. For example, the Seattle School District's 1986–87 student population contained 19.5 percent Asian Americans or the total of 8,532. These were of nine heritages: Chinese, East Indian, Filipino, Japanese, Korean, Other Asian, Samoan, Other Southeast Asian, and Vietnamese.[40] This district defined students to be "at risk" if they scored below the 50th percentile on the California Achievement Test (1977 norms). These children are likely to score among the bottom third of students nationwide on a more recently developed test. Over 39 percent of the Asian American high school students, who took the California Achievement Test during the 1986–87 academic year, scored below the 50th percentile in reading. A similar pattern was found in 40.9 percent of Chicano/Latino students, but only 18.3 percent of White-American students were found "at risk." Table 1 provides a more complete description of the data including the results in language and mathematics.[41] Just as there were many students who were "at risk," many oth-

Table 1. Proportions of High School Students Scoring below the 50th Percentile on the California Achievement Test, 1986–1987*

Ethnic Group	Reading	Language	Mathematics
		Subject	
Asian American	39.8%	34.4%	20.5%
Japanese	12.8	12.1	11.3
East Indian	28.1	37.5	31.3
Korean	28.4	22.2	12.3
Chinese	29.2	23.9	8.1
Other Asian	34.2	42.5	37.5
Filipino	40.7	35.6	28.6
Vietnamese	55.7	46.4	15.8
Samoan	76.9	69.8	65.4
Southeast	79.1	65.1	36.7
American Indian	50.0	57.1	57.8
Black-American	54.9	59.8	58.6
Chicano/Latino American	40.9	41.9	41.8
White-American	18.3	23.4	25.4

*Source: Seattle Public Schools, "Data Profile District Summary" (Seattle: Author, September 1987). Adapted from pp. 85, 87, 89.

ers were dropouts. Table 2 presents details for Asian American youth.[42]

It is obvious that the education community should not facilely generalize when dealing with such a diverse population as Asian American youth. They are like any other group, some students doing well and others not doing so well. Each child should be treated as an individual. Needless to say, information of the type presented here should not be utilized to stereotype any of the subgroups of children within the Asian American population.

Similar patterns of academic achievement have also been found in the San Francisco School District. In the analysis of the May 1987 reading scores on the Comprehensive Tests of Basic Skills (CTBS) by youngsters in kindergarten through the eleventh grade, Japanese-American students had the highest mean percentile ranks, followed by Korean-Americans, Chinese-Americans and, finally, Filipino-Americans.[43] The details can be found in Table 3. Since there were many limited-English-proficient students in the district, the scores were recalculated for those who were proficient in English, based on oral and written assign-

Table 2. Proportions of Asian American High School Dropouts, 1985–1986*

Ethnic Group	Proportion
Asian American	11.0%
Japanese	5.1
Chinese	5.3
Korean	8.6
Other Asian	10.4
Filipino	11.0
Vietnamese	11.8
East Indian	12.7
Other Southeast	17.9
Samoan	34.6
White-American	16.1

*Source: Seattle Public Schools, "Data Profile District Summary" (Seattle: Author, September 1987). Adapted from p. 135.

Table 3. Mean Percentile Ranks of the CTBS Reading Scores, May 1987[*]

Ethnic Group	K	1	2	3	4	5	6	7	8	9	10	11
						Grade						
Asian American												
Japanese[†]	58[‡]	69	67	60	65	70	74	72	82	71	67	71
Korean[†]	53	64	60	52	59	60	49	62	47	47	36	50
Chinese	40	53	51	43	47	48	46	45	39	41	33	39
Filipino	50	57	49	42	49	45	37	39	37	32	35	34
White-American	67	56	68	57	69	69	70	73	77	68	71	73
American Indian[†]	52	40	36	46	59	63	68	64	50	41	50	35
Black-American	33	31	27	27	27	34	31	32	28	26	24	33
Hispanic-American	31	30	29	28	32	32	27	32	26	25	19	22

[*]Source: San Francisco Unified School District, "Districtwide (CTBS/U) Test Results" (San Francisco: Author, August 1987). Adapted from p. 28.

[†] At each grade level less than 60 students were tested.

[‡] The percentile rank of 50 represents the national average.

ments, class progress, and achievement at or above the 36th percentile on standardized tests. As seen in Table 4, the patterns for such subgroups were somewhat similar to those for the Asian American students in general. Thus, Japanese-American students again had the highest ranks, followed by Chinese-Americans and then Korean-Americans.[44] Meanwhile, Filipino students were recording mean ranks close to the national average.

Needless to say, it is as difficult to identify all the variables that affect achievement among Asian American students as it is among White-American students. There are, at least, some definite differences in relation to the varied background and experiential factors reviewed here. In my opinion, the literature on academic achievement does point to the need for the continuance of bilingual education for Asian American students. And it also points to a lack of research that carefully examines the needs of diverse Asian American

Table 4. Mean Percentile Ranks of the CTBS Reading Scores, May 1987, of English-Proficient Students[*]

Ethnic Group[†]	K	1	2	3	4	5	6	7	8	9	10	11
						Grade						
Asian American												
Japanese[†]	71[‡]	74	85	65	76	72	81	78	85	72	68	73
Korean[†]	55	68	69	63	70	68	63	73	67	65	59	59
Chinese	68	71	70	62	64	63	66	65	63	62	60	62
Filipino	56	62	55	52	56	53	46	50	48	44	50	47
White-American	68	57	70	59	70	70	71	74	78	70	71	76
American Indian[†]	52	42	35	48	59	63	69	67	50	41	50	35
Black-American	33	31	27	27	27	34	31	32	28	26	24	33
Hispanic-American	51	47	49	43	45	46	41	43	40	36	36	39

[*]Source: San Francisco Unified School District, "Districtwide (CTBS/U) Test Results" (San Francisco: Author, August 1987). Adapted from p. 36.

[†] The number (and proportion) of the "English-proficient" students varied from one group to another, as well as from one grade to another. Consult the cited source for details.

[‡] The percentile rank of 50 represents the national average.

groups in the area of language and reading skills.

The impact of ethnic prejudice as an influential factor on the socio-psychological development of Asian American children must also be addressed. There are enough reports of the frustrations Asian American students have in dealing with prejudicial attitudes and remarks. For instance, Kim found 30 percent of the Korean-American children she studied reporting discrimination at school in the form of harassment or name-calling.[45] Such incidents involved not only other students but also some school personnel. She recounted an incident in which a five-year-old boy said, "They [his classmates] call me Chinese!" Apparently, this child was disturbed by his Korean-American identity, and angry about his bicultural existence. Similar concerns were expressed by Japanese-American high school students in central California. They were upset because of the perceived image their peers had of Japanese-Americans.

> As one ninth grader said: "They [the school community] think we're all smart and quiet. We're not, but they think we are." Another student indicated that Japanese-American "students have a reputation for being really good in science and math." And another student said he was not particularly "good" in math but "the teacher expected me to do good in it."[46]

To understand the experiences of Southeast Asian American students in the San Diego City Schools in California, the district surveyed 521 junior high students and found strong resentment against Southeast Asian Americans. Approximately 30 percent of the non-refugee students made disturbing remarks such as:

> "Get rid of the Cambodians."
> "I think the Blacks and Whites get along great but it's the Vietnamese we can't stand."
> "Move some Nips to other schools."[47]

Southeast Asian American students gave suggestions on how to improve intercultural relationships. They wanted school staff to do something about, among others, the name-calling, as it often escalated into physical violence between Vietnamese and non-refugee students. Vietnamese-American students were greatly offended by derogatory remarks which abusers considered to be casual statements. In addition, some Southeast Asian American youth felt that some teachers were biased against them, making negative statements about Vietnam or giving them unfair punishment.

These biases found in school experiences can greatly affect the emerging bicultural identity of Asian American youth. The teaching staff must begin to understand the choices and dilemmas such students face in the cultural assimilation process and to assist them in developing the personal confidence and coping skills to deal with ethnic prejudice that they may encounter. Students may withdraw from the school community or fight back, verbally or physically, if they feel powerless to deal with prejudicial situations.

The inaccurate "model minority" myth and belief in the homogeneity of the Asian American student population have limited the development of educational programs that fully address their varied needs. New perspectives on these children should be adopted by school personnel.

One area of concern is self-concept of which a global view may not be sufficient to clarify their feelings of specific inadequacies. Asian American children may also suffer from test anxiety and pressures for high academic achievement. Some appear to be highly influenced by a desire to please their parents, an impetus potentially stronger than direct parental pressure. Additionally, teachers may be unconsciously contributing to the heightened anxiety in students by assuming most Asian American students to be high achievers. Another important concern is the inability of many school staff to recognize feelings of depression, frustration, and desperation in these students. Schools should consider instituting programs to help students and parents to understand better the pressures for high academic achievement and to assist highly anxious students to develop effective coping skills.

There is also the need for schools to institute educational programs to help Asian American children become confident in communication skills, both oral and written. Because these students often exhibit competencies in technical and scientific fields, school personnel may overlook their lower grades in English, creative writing, or composition. There are some Asian groups whose children are dropping out of school at a very high rate, and the effects can be devastating on the economic and political survival of their communities. In addition, there are high numbers of "at risk" students in certain groups to call for a balanced view of Asian American students and their families. Like any other group, they have strengths and needs. We are still saddled with an educational system that has difficulty dealing with children who come to school with varying values, languages, and motivational backgrounds. Understanding the great diversity within the group is crucial, otherwise their needs may continue to be overlooked. Creation of alternatives in curriculum, counseling, and instructional strategies demand a change in our attitudes toward, and knowledge of, these students. Asian American students cannot have equal educational opportunity when their educational experience is shaped by inaccurate information and naive beliefs.

NOTES

The author would like to acknowledge the generous financial support and warm encouragement of the Spencer Foundation and National Academy of Education in the development of this manuscript. In addition, the following individuals were instrumental in providing suggestions during the evolution of the article: Benjamin Bloom, Barbara Ballard, Mako Nakagawa, Fred Cordova, Margie Kitano, Dennis Mah, and Sandy Fujita.

1. Fred Cordova, *Filipinos: Forgotten Asian Americans* (Dubuque, Iowa: Kendall/Hunt Publishing Co., 1983).

2. Margie Kitano, "Early Education for Asian American Children," in *Understanding the Multicultural Experience in Early Childhood Education*, eds. Olivia Saracho and Bernard Spodek (Washington, D.C.: National Association for the Education of Young Children, 1983), pp. 45–66.

3. Robin W. Gardner, Bryant Robey, and Peter C. Smith, *Asian Americans: Growth, Change, and Diversity* (Washington, D.C.: Population Reference Bureau, 1985).

4. Bob Suzuki, "Asian Americans in Higher Education: Impact of Changing Demographics and Other Social Forces." (Paper presented at the National Symposium on the Changing Demographics of Higher Education, the Ford Foundation, New York, April 1988).

5. Jayjia Hsai, *Asian Americans in Higher Education and at Work*, (Hillsdale, N.J.: Lawrence Erlbaum Associates, 1988).

6. DBS Corporation, *Elementary and Secondary Civil Rights Survey 1984* (Washington, D.C.: Office for Civil Rights, U.S. Office of Education, June 1986; ERIC Document Reproduction Service No. ED 271 545).

7. Cordova, *Filipinos*.

8. Jean Carlin and Burton Sokoloff, "Mental Health Treatment Issues for Southeast Asian Refugee Children," in *Southeast Asian Mental Health: Treatment, Prevention, Services, Training and Research*, ed. Tom Owan (Washington, D.C.: U.S. Department of Health and Human Services, 1985; DSHS Publication No. ADM 85–1399), pp. 91–112.

9. Cordova, *Filipinos*.

10. Amado Cabezas, *Early Childhood Development in Asian and Pacific American Families:*

Families in Transition (San Francisco: Asian Inc., 1981).

11. David Sue, Derald Sue, and Diane Sue, "Psychological Development of Chinese-American Children," in *The Psychological Development of Minority Group Children*, ed. Gloria Powell (New York: Brunner/Mazel Publishers, 1983), pp. 159–166.

12. Harry Kitano, *Japanese Americans: The Evolution of a Subculture* (New Jersey: Prentice-Hall, 1976).

13. Maria Matute-Bianchi, "Ethnic Identities and Patterns of School Success and Failure among Mexican-Descent and Japanese-American Students in a California High School: An Ethnographic Analysis," *American Journal of Education* 94 (November 1986): 233–255.

14. Cabezas, *Early Childhood Development.*

15. David Sue and Derald Sue, "Chinese American Personality and Mental Health," *Amerasia Journal* 1 (Fall 1971): 95–98.

16. Matute-Bianchi, "Ethnic Identities."

17. Grace Guthrie, *A School Divided* (Hillsdale, N.J.: Lawrence Erlbaum Associates, 1985); Bok-Lim Kim, "The Korean-American Child at School and at Home." (Report of a project funded by the Administration for Children, Youth, and Families, U.S. Department of Health, Education, and Welfare, Washington, D.C., 1980).

18. Guthrie, *A School Divided.*

19. Bok-Lim Kim, *The Asian Americans: Changing Patterns, Changing Needs* (Montclair, N.J.: Association of Korean Christian Scholars in North America, 1978).

20. Shirley Hume, "U.S. Immigration Policy and Asian and Pacific Americans: Aspects and Consequences," in *Civil Rights Issues of Asian and Pacific Americans: Myths and Realities* (Washington, D.C.: U.S. Commission on Civil Rights, May 1979), pp. 283–291.

21. Ruben Rumbaut, "Mental Health and the Refugee Experience: A Comparative Study of Southeast Asian Refugees," in *Southeast Asian Mental Health: Treatment, Prevention, Services, Training and Research*, ed. Tom Owan (Washington, D.C.: U.S. Department of Health and Human Services, 1985; DSHS Publication No. ADM 85–1399), pp. 433–486.

22. Genevieve Lau, "Chinese American Early Childhood Socialization in Communication," Doctoral dissertation, Stanford University, 1988.

23. Sue and Sue, "Chinese American Personality."

24. Milton Gordon, *Assimilation in American Life* (New York: Oxford University Press, 1964).

25. Cabezas, *Early Childhood Development.*

26. Ruben Rumbaut and Kenji Ima, "The Adaptation of Southeast Asian Refugee Youth: A Comparative Study." (A report prepared for the U.S. Department of Health and Human Services, Family Support Administration, Office of Refugee Resettlement, Washington, D.C., January 1988).

27. Elliott Mordkowitz and Herbert Ginsburg, "The Academic Socialization of Successful Asian American College Students." (Paper presented at the Annual Meeting of the American Educational Research Association, San Francisco, April 1986).

28. Romeria Tidwell, "Gifted Students' Self-images as a Function of Identification Process, Race and Sex," *Journal of Pediatric Psychology* 5 (March 1980): 57–69.

29. Nguyen T. Oanh and William B. Michael, "The Predictive Validity of Each of Ten Measures of Self-Concept Relative to Teacher's Ratings of Achievement in Mathematics and Reading of Vietnamese Children and of Those from Five Other Ethnic Groups," *Educational and Psychological Measurement* 37 (Winter 1977): 1005–1016.

30. Theresa Chang, "The Self-Concept of Children in Ethnic Groups: Black American and Korean American," *Elementary School Journal* 76 (October 1975): 52–58; David Fox and Valerie Jordan, "Racial Preference and Identification of American Chinese, Black and White Children," *Genetic Psychology Monographs* 88 (November 1973): 220–286.

31. Valerie Ooka Pang, Donald Mizokawa, James Morishima, and Roger Olstad, "Self Concepts of Japanese-American Children," *Journal of Cross-Cultural Psychology* 16 (March 1985): 99–109.

32. Valerie Ooka Pang, "Test Anxiety and Mathematics Achievement as They Relate to Parental Values in Asian American and White American Students." (Paper presented at the Annual Meeting of the American Educational Research Association, San Francisco, March 1989).

33. Michael Cole, Vera John-Steiner, Sylvia Scribner, and Ellen Souberman, eds., *Mind in*

Society (Cambridge, Massachusetts: Harvard University Press, 1978).

34. Robert Hess, Teresa McDevitt, and Chang Chih-Mei, "Cultural Variations in Family Beliefs about Children's Performance in Mathematics: Comparison among People's Republic of China, Chinese-American, and Caucasian American Families," *Journal of Educational Psychology* 79 (April 1987): 179–188.

35. E.g., "The New Whiz Kids," *Time*, August 31, 1987, pp. 42–51.

36. Leonard Ramist and Solomon Arbeiter, *Profiles: College-Bound Seniors, 1985* (New York: College Entrance Examination Board, 1986). Pp. xix-xx, 36–45.

37. Susan Stodolsky and Gerald Lesser, "Learning Patterns in the Disadvantaged," *Harvard Educational Review* 37 (Fall 1967): 546–593.

38. Ramist and Arbeiter, *Profiles*.

39. Ibid, p. xix.

40. Seattle Public Schools, "Data Profile District Summary" (Seattle: Author, September 1987).

41. Ibid., pp. 85, 87, 89.

42. Ibid., p. 135.

43. San Francisco Unified School District, "Districtwide (CTBS/U) Test Results" (San Francisco: Author, August 1987) p. 28.

44. Ibid., p. 36.

45. Kim, *The Korean-American Child*.

46. Matute-Bianchi, "Ethnic Identities," p. 247.

47. Rumbaut and Ima, "The Adaptation, " p. 59.

10 Southeast Asian Refugees in American Schools:

A Comparison of Fluent-English-Proficient and Limited-English-Proficient Students

Kenji Ima and Rubén G. Rumbaut

THERE HAS BEEN a significant growth in the Asian and Pacific Islander communities in the United States, from less than 1% of the U.S. population in 1970 to 1.5% in 1980, to a projected 3% in 1990 and 4% in the year 2000—a fourfold increase in 30 years (see Gardner, Robey, & Smith, 1985). Asians are highly concentrated in a few states, notably California, Hawaii, New York, Illinois, and Texas. In California, as a result of both sharply increased immigration and natural increase. Asians/Pacific Islanders (APIs) currently constitute 7% of the state's population, with a projected growth to approximately 11% in the year 2000 (Bouvier & Martin, 1987). Moreover, they have already affected school enrollments well out of proportion to their numbers, since they tend to be a much younger population—especially the Southeast Asians. For example, while the median age of the general American population is 32 years, it is only 18 in the Vietnamese community (Rumbaut & Weeks, 1986). For these young new Americans, the acquisition of English-language competency is the principal obstacle that they must overcome in their educational adaptation; it is also a major challenge for their teachers in American public schools.

During the 1980s legal immigration into the United States has averaged about 600,000 persons annually, by far the highest level since the first decade of this century. In addition, 48% of all immigrants and refugees admitted in the 1980s have come from Asia, compared to fewer than 5% in any decade prior to the 1965 law that eliminated racial restrictions from U.S. immigration. Who would have predicted this consequence of the 1965 immigration law, especially the rapid growth of Filipino, Korean, Asian Indian, and other API populations? And who would have imagined that the 1975 defeat of U.S. policy in Vietnam would lead to a massive and still continuing flow of Southeast Asian refugees into this country?

The consequence for many schools is a significant increase of students with widely different languages, cultures, levels of literacy, social class backgrounds, and life experiences.

An estimated 3 to 5 million K-12 students in American public schools now speak a language other than English at home with over one million in California alone (First & Carrera, 1988). The 1987 language census by the California State Department of Education showed that 29% of all children in the state's public schools were language-minority students; of these, 613,222 were designated as limited-English-proficient (LEP) and 568,928 as fluent-English-proficient (FEP) students (Olsen, 1988).

From *Topics in Language Disorders* 9:3 (1989): 54–75. Reprinted with permission of Aspen Publishers, Inc. © 1989.

In the face of these changes, how well are schools prepared to cope with an increasingly diverse student population? In particular, what are the consequences of these changes for special education programs and service providers?

The *Lau v. Nichols* decision requires schools to take into account the student's home language, and because of the large numbers of Hispanic students the public's impression is that bilingual programs serve primarily Hispanics. Yet it may surprise many to discover that over 50% of all API children come from homes where a primary language other than English is spoken, and up to 90% of the most recent arrivals have no fluency in the English language (Chan, 1983).

Bilingual education services throughout the country have "yet to address adequately" the wide variety of Asian and Pacific Islands languages. The most advanced special education services have been extended only to Chinese speakers, not to Khmer, Hmong, Lao, or Vietnamese language groups (Siegel & Halog, 1986). If the teacher observes heightened anxiety, confusion about the "locus of control," withdrawal, or unresponsiveness in a language minority student, is it possible for the teacher to confidently determine whether or not the child is suffering from linguistic or acculturative stress, depression, a learning disability, or a combination of these conditions?

While many of the usual manifestations of learning problems may have their genesis in a variety of factors, most practitioners are ill-equipped to diagnose the source, thus leaving untended a large number of students who either remain underserved in the corner of a regular classroom or are moved to a special education program that may not have the resources or skills to deal with their linguistic and cultural backgrounds. One suspects that, given classrooms with a wide diversity of students, an untrained teacher may be tempted to refer a troubling Asian child to special education as a means of "getting rid of a problem" or, more commonly, to assume that the child's problem is solely one of second-language learning rather than a learning disorder. In light of the traditionally low prevalence of such students from Asian groups in the past, many teachers are now surprised to see "difficult" Asian children. These observations call for careful research, not only to identify possible learning disorders among linguistic minority students but also to identify the diverse learning styles and approaches that work for these populations. Within the larger context of Asian-American students, we see an ongoing debate on the appropriateness of teaching approaches, particularly as this population grows more diverse (Wong-Fillmore, 1985). Useful information on API groups cannot be adequately obtained by reviewing, for example, older materials on Japanese-American students that may or (more likely) may not be appropriate for new Asian groups such as the Khmer or the Lao.

This article focuses specifically on Southeast Asian LEP and FEP refugee students, and raises questions about the appropriateness of placing them among other Asian Americans. When policies based on ethnic or racial groups are entertained, the wide spectrum of Asians and Pacific Islanders—both the foreign-born and those born in the United States—tend to be lumped into a single category, presuming a homogeneity of background contexts and characteristics that in fact does not exist. Instead, we argue that there is a need to document and to recognize the extraordinary diversity of API groups, especially as it affects learning in general and language learning in particular. For the purposes of this article, we concentrate on five main Indochinese ethnic groups: the Khmer from Cambodia, the Lao and the Hmong from Laos, and the Chinese and Vietnamese from Vietnam. Their public image—particularly that of the Vietnamese—is often an extension of the "model minority" image associated with East Asian "brain drain" immigrants. It would be a mistake to accept this image, both because of the socioeconomic and ethnocultural diversity evident among the Southeast Asians themselves and because of fundamental differences between the immigrant and refugee experiences.

SOUTHEAST ASIAN REFUGEES IN THE UNITED STATES

The newest and the largest group of recently arrived Asians has been the Southeast Asians, a population that now includes nearly 900,000 refugees who have been admitted to the United States from 1975 to 1988, plus over 200,000 children born to these groups since their arrival (Rumbaut & Weeks, 1986). Many thousands remain in refugee camps overseas awaiting resettlement to the United States, and still others are being admitted under an "orderly departure program" directly from Vietnam. These refugees come from three countries, all former colonies of French Indochina, with widely different languages and ethnocultural traditions. There is not a single Indochinese language, nor are there dialectical variations of a single Indochinese language family. Additionally, the social composition of each refugee group has been shaped by their country's respective histories and by selective migration processes. Only 130,000 refugees, almost all Vietnamese, were evacuated to the United States in 1975 as part of a "first wave" comprising mostly an urban, educated elite with prior American contacts and some familiarity with English. Among the Cambodians the bulk of the educated class either fled to France (as did the Lao elites) or were killed by the Khmer Rouge during the forced deurbanization, massacres, and famine of the 1975–1978 Pol Pot period. However, most Indochinese refugees have in fact been resettled here since 1980. These more recently arrived "second-wave" refugees include much greater proportions of lowland Lao and highland Hmong from Laos, Khmer survivors of the "killing fields" of Cambodia, Chinese-Vietnamese and Vietnamese "boat people," and rural and less educated persons. Consequently, the adaptation by the school-age children of these refugee groups reflects crucial differences in time of arrival and social class background.

Unlike most Asian Americans who are born in the United States, foreign-born students—whether immigrants or refugees—must confront the immediate problem of English-language acquisition and acculturation to American ways of life. However, what typically distinguishes refugees from other immigrants are their motives for leaving and their persistent memories of the past, especially the acute sense of loss and trauma that often accompanies forced, unplanned, and sudden uprooting, and their inability to return to their homeland. The conditions of refugee exit and permanent resettlement in a country of asylum, sometimes after prolonged stays in transit camps, have long-term consequences for psychosocial adjustment that may be reflected in special acculturation and learning problems among school-age refugees. For example, a recent study of secondary-level Cambodian students revealed that half of them were experiencing emotional crises such as depression and posttraumatic stress disorder, reflecting the holocaust in Cambodia of the late 1970s (Kinzie, Sack, Angell, Manson, & Rath, 1986). Khmer youngsters who were too young to remember or who were born after that period may suffer indirectly through disrupted families and traumatized parents or guardians, who in many instances may be emotionally and physically incapable of providing adequate supervision.

The consequences of such traumas for refugee populations may thus include serious disruption of normal schooling, family life, and social support systems; emotional problems among both youth and parents; and a reduced readiness to devote time and effort to school. An assessment of Southeast Asian schoolchildren must, consequently, look beyond the usual linguistic and acculturative adjustments to more basic socioemotional problems that may be associated with their particular refugee experiences.

Although this general distinction between refugees and immigrants has important implications for educators, specific variations and exceptions occur. For example, Southeast Asian refugees who left in 1975 are likely to have been exposed to less severe trauma than those who left after 1978, and among the latter the Cambodians are likely to be more severely traumatized than the Laotians. Refugees from different social classes differ significantly in their coping resources and reactions to otherwise similarly stressful life events. Additionally, some individuals classified as "economic immigrants" or "illegal aliens" may have left their country under conditions every bit as traumatic as those of many second-wave Southeast Asians, such as escapees from civil wars in El Salvador and Guatemala. The latter are not defined as refugees by the U.S. government, primarily for political reasons. Thus an official designation of "refugee" does not necessarily signify a greater level of stress or trauma than that experienced by "immigrants." Furthermore, with the passage of time after arrival in the United States, the differences between refugees and immigrants tend to become gradually less significant, as the varying effects of the past recede before the common challenges of the future (Rumbaut, 1989). Nevertheless, especially during the first few years of residency in the United States, such differences are important to recognize since needs, motives, attitudes, and behaviors are likely to vary between immigrants and refugees.

SOUTHEAST ASIANS AND SPECIAL EDUCATIONAL SERVICES

Chan (1983), Cheng (1987a, 1987b), Dao and Grossman (1985), and Siegel and Halog (1986) lament the lack of trained bilingual personnel, informed monolingual personnel, and linguistically appropriate instruments for the identification of learning-handicapped Asian students, especially those who are submerged with other language-minority students. In examining the files of a random sample of Southeast Asian students from the San Diego Unified School District, we found that only 17 out of 579 students (3%) were classified as special education students, or roughly one-third of what one might have expected in the general student population. Reasons given for this presumed underrepresentation include lack of trained personnel in primary languages, preoccupation with transition into the regular English-language curriculum, lack of cultural understanding, and lack of parental cooperation. This phenomenon is commonly repeated in all districts with large numbers of API students, such as San Jose and San Francisco in California and Montgomery County in Maryland (Dao & Grossman, 1985). We remain ignorant of their special educational needs and are thus faced with questions as to whether or not Southeast Asians are truly underrepresented as recipients of special educational services.

Still, it seems premature to target 10% of the Southeast Asian student population for special educational services, since those who come to the United States are not representative of the total population of their home countries. The rule-of-thumb estimate that 10% of the general school-age population needs special educational services may not apply to the refugee population; the true rate is probably lower, owing more to compositional factors than to an inability to diagnose properly special educational needs among refugee students. Immigrant groups are likely to contain disproportionate numbers of individuals with above-average physical and mental competence and hardiness. This is due to (1) subjective self-selection, reflecting the often extraordinary effort, motivation, and resources required to leave one's homeland and to tackle the hardships of uprooting and transplantation; and (2) the objective selection criteria of U.S. immigration law, including those used by gatekeepers who are mandated to screen out social and mental incompetents, and a system of preferences that favors so-called brain drain immigration by professional and technical workers (combined with family reunification concerns).

In refugee camps in Southeast Asia, interviewers are required to identify individuals with excludable physical and mental disorders; persons thus eliminated from admission to the United States include individuals who would otherwise be identified for special education programs. Hence, in the absence of compelling data to the contrary, the assumption that 10% of the foreign-born student population requires special educational services may not be warranted.

Given the present lack of extensive experience with and knowledge of Southeast Asian students who may have special educational needs, we propose here to explore the differences and similarities between FEP and LEP Southeast Asian students—that is, those who have versus those who have not made the transition into regular English-language courses—as a basis for understanding their particular learning contexts and factors affecting their academic progress. Such an exploratory study lays the groundwork for establishing criteria for intervention with Southeast Asian LEP and potential special education students (Chan, 1983).

SAMPLES AND SOURCES OF DATA

The data for this article were drawn from the Southeast Asian Refugee Youth Study (SARYS), a comparative community study of the adaptation of Southeast Asian refugee youth (Rumbaut & Ima, 1988). The project was conducted during 1986–1987 in San Diego, California. Its aim was to examine both successes and problems of these refugee youth regarding their educational and occupational attainments and aspirations, their social adjustment, and their prospects for economic self-sufficiency. It was based on a combination of extensive survey research and school district data for a large sample of Southeast Asian students, plus intensive interviews with a smaller sample of refugee youth about their experiences and perceptions of schooling and the world of work, thus adding a qualitative ethnographic component to our quantitative analyses. These data form the basis of the findings reported.

Two sets of quantitative data are used in this article: (1) all linguistic minority students in the spring of 1987 who were either juniors or seniors in the San Diego Unified School District ($N = 5,472$), and (2) a random sample of secondary school (grades 7–12) Southeast Asian students in the same district ($N = 239$). Both data sets contain basic information on the students' age, gender, ethnicity, year in school, active/inactive status, and LEP/FEP language status, as well as two types of measures of educational attainment: the students' cumulative grade point average (GPA) and their CTBS (Comprehensive Test of Basic Skills) standardized achievement test scores.

The CTBS is a standardized test that is widely used throughout the United States to gauge the educational achievement of students in grades K-12, and its results provide data that may be compared nationally with other student groups at similar grade levels. It measures skills that are prerequisite to studying and learning in school—recognition, translation, interpretation, application, and analysis—and produces three composite indices of achievement: (1) *reading* (combining the Vocabulary and Comprehension subtests), (2) *language* (combining Language Expression and Language Mechanics subtests), and (3) *mathematics* (combining computation skills and mathematics concepts and applications). In this article we report student scores on these three composite indices.

The first data set identified above makes possible a comparative assessment of Southeast Asians versus all other non–Southeast Asian linguistic minority students. It cannot, however, distinguish among the various ethnic groups from Vietnam, Laos, and Cambodia that make up the Southeast Asian student population, since the school district does not specifically code such information. The second data set does permit a detailed comparison among Vietnamese, Chinese-Vietnamese, Lao, Hmong, and Cambodian (or Khmer) students. It is part of a larger longitudinal study of refugee households in San Diego—the Indochinese Health & Adaptation Research Project (IHARP)—which collected information on their social backgrounds, migration histories, social and economic adjustment, and physical and mental health (see Rumbaut, 1989).

By joining the extensive IHARP data on refugee parents and households with the school district's data on the academic performance of their children, we were able to identify a wide range of determinants of the educational attainment of these students. Interestingly, to obtain an indication of the generalizability of our data a comparison was made between the GPAs of the SARYS random sample of Vietnamese students in San Diego and those reported by Caplan, Whitmore, and Bui (1985) for Vietnamese students in five regions of the United States (Boston, Chicago, Houston, Orange County, and Seattle); the grade distributions for both samples were nearly identical.

A cautionary note should be emphasized here before proceeding to the results of our study. It is one thing to look at performance on standardized achievement tests and another thing to review performance in classes as reflected by GPAs; moreover, it is one thing to evaluate English-language reading proficiency levels and another to assess mathematics skills, especially of the foreign-born. Although all of these possible academic outcomes (GPA, reading and mathematics scores) are to some extent interrelated, they are not coterminous; that is, there will be some independence of these outcomes from each other. Thus the practitioner should not assume that test performance is equivalent to classroom performance or, for that matter, that mathematic and reading test performances may be substituted for one another.

In this article, we examine the differences between students who are classified as LEP and as FEP. In practice, those classified as LEP receive special language assistance (sometimes with the use of their home language), while those classified as FEP are assigned to regular classes without any assistance in their home language. In the school district of our Southeast Asian sample, a main criterion for transferring students from LEP status to FEP status is passing the reading portion of the CTBS at the 36th percentile level. This language status transition is one measure of school adjustment, and it seems to be particularly significant for those whose interests involve diagnosing and treating individuals with special linguistic learning problems. In California today an average of 50,000 LEP students are reclassified as FEP each year. Most of the reclassifications take place within three years after a student has entered the school system, and very few students remain designated as LEP beyond five years (Olsen, 1988).

There is considerable debate, however, over the meaning of the 36th percentile cutoff point for the classification of LEP and FEP students. It is an arbitrary cutoff point that can be raised or lowered depending on what percentage of the population one wishes to define as having "sufficient" English proficiency. Nevertheless, educators need to proceed on the basis of some objective standard, and this has been the accepted procedure for determining the transfer of LEP students into mainstream classes. There is, of course, no single "true" measure of the distinction between LEP and FEP; rather, as with the concept of literacy, there are multiple determinant criteria as well as a continuum of competence (Cook-Gumperz, 1986). Hence, as a method yielding merely a convenient dichotomy between levels of English reading proficiency, the 36th percentile remains a rough basis for bureaucratic decisions to mainstream students into regular classes; but since all students are assessed by the same criterion, LEP-FEP comparisons based on it are at least methodologically legitimate. In any case, on our bivariate analyses we will rely on this distinction in order to identify the principal background factors and other characteristics distinguishing LEP from FEP students; in our multivariate analyses we will then use the CTBS reading score as a continuous variable in order to estimate the independent effects of various predictors on the actual (not the arbitrary) level of measured English proficiency.

Additional reservations should be noted concerning the use of the reading scores, particularly since reading is a complex skill area that may require years before substantial fluency is likely to be achieved. Unlike the spelling, language mechanics, and especially the mathematics portions of the CTBS, we found that English reading vocabulary and comprehension scores remain low even for Southeast Asian students who are in mainstream classes; it appears to be the most difficult area of basic skills to master. Yoshioka (1929) reported over a half a century ago a similar pattern of high scores in mathematics but significantly low reading comprehension and vocabulary scores for another Asian sample (young second-generation Japanese Americans). Although reading scores improved over time among Japanese-American test takers, this was the last area to show improvement and the one in which improvement occurred over the most prolonged period. An important implication of these observations for Southeast Asian students is that the reading portion of the CTBS is a much poorer predictor of academic success (e.g., of GPAs) than is the mathematics component. Thus the assumption that test scores of Southeast Asians can be interpreted much as those of the general population born in the United States is problematic. These observations raise questions about the timing and level of English-language acquisition and direct attention toward identifying factors that may facilitate or inhibit the transition from limited English proficiency to fluent English proficiency among Southeast Asian refugee students.

RESULTS AND INTERPRETATIONS

Results will be reported in three parts. The first analysis relies on the data on language minority juniors and seniors ($N = 5,742$), and provides a comparison of the educational performance of LEP and FEP Southeast Asian students as a whole with that of other LEP and FEP ethnic groups. This is followed by an analysis of the smaller but randomly selected IHARP-SARYS sample of refugee students ($N = 239$), enabling us to compare the five major Southeast Asian ethnic groups with each other while again controlling for LEP versus FEP language status. Next we focus on a description of those social background characteristics of the refugee students that we found to be most significantly associated with language status and academic attainment. Finally, the results of a multivariate analysis are presented, focusing on those background factors that are independently predictive of our key dependent variable: English reading comprehension and vocabulary as measured by the CTBS achievement test. These results, taken together, should in turn help to delineate some criteria that service providers should consider in assessing these students and developing appropriate programs. Caution should be taken when interpreting the second set of data since the sample size is relatively small, which affects its statistical stability. Nevertheless, since this appears to be the only data file on Southeast Asians that includes a plethora of background variables as well as performance outcomes, it provides the best exploratory estimate to date of the academic progress of Southeast Asian students.

COMPARISONS BETWEEN SOUTHEAST ASIANS AND OTHER LINGUISTIC MINORITY STUDENTS

Table 1 provides an initial comparison of the academic performance of Southeast Asian and other language minority groups, broken down by ethnicity and LEP or FEP status. Among all ethnic groups, as is shown in Table 1, Southeast Asians are most likely to be LEP, reflecting their recent arrival in the United States. Although the popular image of the bilingual student is that of a student of Hispanic origin, on the whole Hispanics are more likely than Southeast Asian refugees to be native English speakers or classified as FEP. Hispanics (especially in California and the Southwest) include many United States–born Chicanos, whereas all Southeast Asian refugees by definition immigrated after 1975 (and most of them arrived in the United States only after 1980). Thus we found that only 28%

Table 1. Educational attainment of juniors and seniors with primary language other than English, by ethnicity and FEP-LEP status (San Diego 1986–87 junior-senior cohort, $N = 5,742$)

Ethnic groups	FEP or LEP	N	GPA*	CTBS Achievement Scores†		
				Reading	Language	Math
East Asians	FEP	144	3.02	5.97	6.86	7.39
	LEP	67	2.98	3.81	5.07	7.36
Southeast Asians	FEP	391	2.91	4.20	5.66	6.76
	LEP	1,006	2.34	2.54	3.60	5.06
Other immigrants	FEP	291	2.48	4.81	5.60	6.02
	LEP	136	2.52	3.97	4.97	5.74
Filipinos	FEP	660	2.56	5.08	6.25	6.35
	LEP	152	2.05	3.58	4.64	4.62
Hispanics	FEP	1,605	1.91	4.05	4.74	4.97
	LEP	1,204	1.85	3.12	3.66	4.10
Pacific Islanders	FEP	67	1.89	3.72	4.83	5.14
	LEP	19	1.80	2.58	4.09	4.92
Totals	FEP	3,138	2.30	4.45	5.38	5.72
	LEP	2,581	2.11	2.98	3.87	4.71

*GPA = cumulative grade point average excluding physical education.
†In stanine (STANdard scale of NINE units) scores. The mean stanine of the national norming population is 5, and the standard deviation is 2. A stanine of 1 reflects the lowest level (the bottom 4% of test scores nationally), a stanine of 5 is average (the middle 20%) and a stanine of 9 reflects achievement at the top 4% of scores nationally.

of Hispanic juniors and seniors in San Diego high schools were LEP, whereas two-thirds of Southeast Asian juniors and seniors were LEP. Moreover, examining only those with a primary home language other than English (and thus excluding Hispanic-origin students whose native language is English), we found that 43% of language-minority Hispanics were LEP in their junior and senior years, which is still well below the two-thirds of Southeast Asians who were classified as LEP.

Still, as Table 1 shows, despite their language handicap Southeast Asian students as a whole are receiving higher GPAs than all other students in San Diego high schools, with the exception of East Asians; they even have a higher GPA than the 2.33 average of white majority students. The "East Asians" category includes Chinese, Japanese, and Korean students. This grouping frequently includes children from "brain drain" immigrant families (such as those headed by a Taiwanese engineer) who, as a general rule, have not only received a quality education in their home country but have also had little disruption of their schooling. By contrast, many Southeast Asian students have seriously disrupted schooling histories and parents who are less likely to be well-educated professionals; in fact, a substantial number are the children of illiterate peasants and fishermen. Thus the comparatively high academic performance of East Asians is understandable, given these social class differences (see also Olsen, 1988).

The category "other immigrants" in Table 1 includes linguistic minority students who have immigrated from Europe, Iran, India, and Arab countries, and whose families, like those of many East Asian immigrants, include disproportionate numbers of professionals. Their high GPA thus probably reflects the selective migration pattern of families with highly educated parents. Filipinos exhibit GPAs just above the district average. Under the 1965 immigration law, admissions criteria for family reunification reasons have been used extensively by Filipinos, resulting in the immigration of less well educated individuals as well as persons from highly educated families. By contrast, Hispanics and Pacific Islanders have academic attainment patterns well below district norms. The socioeconomic composition of these groups is known to include a larger proportion of less well educated individuals and commensurately accounts, at least in part, for the students' lower GPAs and test scores.

The rank order of student CTBS achievement test scores parallels the GPA pattern, yet notable deviations emerge. On the whole, Southeast Asian students achieve above-average scores on the CTBS mathematics portion, but in reading they are significantly below average. In all three areas of the CTBS (mathematics, language, reading), as expected, Southeast Asian LEPs have lower scores than FEP students, yet the gap is greatest for both Southeast Asians and Filipino students, possibly reflecting a wider variation in social background characteristics. More notable is the fact that, in spite of their higher GPA, Southeast Asian LEP students have lower reading scores than those of Hispanic LEP students. Clearly the Southeast Asians excel in mathematics overall; they are in the top quartile nationally in mathematics computation. On the other hand, their reading vocabulary subtest scores place them in the bottom quartile nationally, reflecting their present difficulties with learning and becoming proficient in a new language, a new alphabet, and a new culture.

Indeed, the sequence of achievement indicated by these scores—and the pattern is the same for all ethnic groups—reflects a progression from the most culture- and language-bound basic skills tested (i.e., those requiring the greatest familiarity with the host culture), such as reading vocabulary, reading comprehension, and language expression, to the more easily memorizable and the least culture- and language-bound skill areas, such as spelling and language mechanics and mathematics applications and computation. Mathematics computation reflects the clearest example of objective, rule-bound skills; a vivid illustration of this is the fact that immigrants typically continue to "think in their native language" when carrying out operations such as addition, subtraction, multiplication, and division, even after they become completely fluent in English and reach the point where they "think in English" in routine conversations and interactions. Further observation of longitudinal data on CTBS tests taken by the Southeast Asian students in our sample suggests that mathematics achievement scores remain relatively stable over time, while achievement in reading and language skills undergoes significant improvement over time, as the refugees become increasingly proficient in English. That is, the English language-based achievement levels are not indicative of a static pattern, but one that appears to be improving fairly rapidly over time. The transition from LEP to FEP status does take time, of course, and is conditioned by diverse other factors, such as the level of previous education and literacy in one's native language.

These first observations reveal the following general conclusions: (1) Southeast Asian students are more likely to be LEP than other linguistic minority groups; (2) as expected, FEPs are doing better in all measures of academic achievement than are LEP students; (3) in spite of having proportionately more LEP individuals, Southeast Asians, as an aggregate, have above-average grades; (4) the level of academic achievement corresponds roughly to the socioeconomic composition of each group, such as the proportion of parents with more schooling; (5) while the Southeast Asian students' CTBS mathematics scores are above average, their reading scores are significantly below average. These observations, in turn, begin to provide a larger context for understanding the English language acquisition of Southeast Asian students.

It should be noted that language identification and assessment decisions, including the determination of LEP or FEP status, are made when the students first enter the public schools. LEP students are then reassessed periodically (usually on an annual basis). The initial assessment does not judge the students' competency in their primary language (including literacy skills in that language), but rather identifies the preferred language spoken at home if other than English. Data about the composition of the linguistic minority population, including such factors as country of origin, birth date, length of stay in the United

States, age upon entry into the United States, educational background, parental social class, and level of proficiency in non-English languages as well as in the English language, are typically not collected by the schools. While eventually a more precise delineation of the composition of each LEP population will be necessary to more accurately ferret out predictive factors, we have systematic data only for our Southeast Asian sample, which will be reported in the next section.

COMPARISONS OF EDUCATIONAL ATTAINMENT AMONG SOUTHEAST ASIAN GROUPS

Table 2 presents similar data on GPAs and CTBS achievement test scores for our random sample of Southeast Asian students in grades 7–12 ($N = 239$) broken down by each of the five major refugee ethnic groups as well as by FEP or LEP status. There is clearly considerable diversity in educational attainment among these groups. The Vietnamese have the highest GPAs; even when we control by language status. Vietnamese LEP students still exhibit very high GPAs (2.96) as well as mathematics scores. They are followed closely by the Chinese-Vietnamese, then the Hmong, the Khmer, and lastly the Lao. Surprisingly, Hmong students were found to have GPAs above those of majority white students; Khmer and Lao students had slightly lower GPAs than white Anglos, but still significantly higher GPAs than blacks, Hispanics, and Pacific Islanders. We ran a series of separate analyses to see whether their higher GPAs were due to possibly less demanding ESL (English as a Second Language) courses, but found that with the exception of the most recently arrived Khmer, whose GPAs in ESL courses were somewhat higher than those in mainstream courses, the pattern of high GPA attainment persisted across the ESL and regular curricula. Indeed, Hmong GPAs in regular English, mathematics, science, and social science courses were actually slightly higher than their GPAs in the ESL track.

Turning to CTBS reading scores, note that the rank order by ethnic group changes somewhat. The Vietnamese show the highest reading scores, followed by the Chinese-Vietnamese, the Khmer, the Lao, and last the Hmong (whose reading scores place them in the bottom quintile nationally). The particular difficulties that Hmong students exhibit in reading comprehension and vocabulary skills partly reflect the prevalent illiteracy and lack of education among their parents. Nonetheless, the Hmong students do much better in the more "mechanical" portions of the CTBS, such as spelling and, especially, mathematics

Table 2. Educational attainment of Southeast Asian refugee students in grades 7–12, by ethnicity and FEP-LEP status (IHARP-SARYS sample grades 7–12. $N = 239$)

Ethnic groups	FEP or LEP	N	GPA*	CTBS Achievement Scores†		
				Reading	Language	Math
Vietnamese	FEP	28	2.98	4.67	5.65	7.11
	LEP	26	2.96	3.36	4.91	6.80
Chinese-Vietnamese	FEP	26	3.33	3.92	5.91	7.58
	LEP	19	2.27	2.63	4.76	5.72
Hmong	FEP	21	3.03	3.50	5.00	6.26
	LEP	26	2.57	2.33	3.93	5.18
Khmer	FEP	9	3.10	3.94	4.59	5.78
	LEP	26	2.49	2.77	3.28	4.23
Lao	FEP	13	2.90	3.95	5.58	5.77
	LEP	45	2.48	2.39	3.59	5.39
Totals	FEP	97	3.08	4.04	5.47	6.67
	LEP	142	2.56	2.68	3.94	5.53

*GPA = cumulative grade point average, excluding physical education.
†In stanine scores.

computation. Hmong FEP students show mathematics scores well above the U.S. national average, and even Hmong LEP students' mathematics scores surpass the national average—a fact that demonstrates the considerable potential of these students and also helps to explain their high GPAs. Without a doubt, the Vietnamese and Chinese-Vietnamese FEP students exhibit a pattern of extraordinarily high achievement in mathematics, putting them as a group near the top 90% nationally. The Lao and especially the Khmer, by contrast, show much more modest mathematics skills, although still around the U.S. national average.

What explains the different patterns of educational attainment among these refugee groups and the rank order observed above with respect to their GPAs and CTBS scores? An answer to this question is made possible by the availability of our extensive IHARP data set, which contains comprehensive information about the migration and resettlement histories of the refugee students' families, socioeconomic backgrounds, and occupational and psychological adjustment in the United States. Some of the most important of these characteristics should be considered. The discussion is not intended to be exhaustive, but rather to help sketch a social context within which the educational progress of these refugee students can be better understood and appreciated.

BACKGROUND CHARACTERISTICS OF SOUTHEAST ASIAN STUDENTS

What are some of the characteristics of these refugee youths and their families? These parameters include temporal factors (e.g., how long these refugee families stayed in refugee camps overseas prior to their resettlement in the United States and how long they have been in the United States), socioeconomic factors (e.g., father's and mother's prior education, employment, and poverty levels in the United States), and family composition (e.g., the proportion of two-parent versus single-parent families among refugee students). Such characteristics have important implications that service providers might wish to take into account for evaluation and planning.

Overall, the Vietnamese students in our sample had been in the United States the longest, an average of nearly seven years as of fall 1985 (largely because of the presence among them of some "first-wave" students who came to the United States in 1975), although the majority of the Vietnamese did not arrive until 1980 or after. They are followed by the Hmong, the Lao, and the Chinese-Vietnamese, all of whom had been in the United States an average of nearly six years as of fall 1985. The Khmer, finally, were the most recently arrived group overall, with the students in our sample averaging just under 5 years in the United States as of 1985.

Adaptation to a new school or a new society takes, among other things, time. For refugee adults as well as children, time in the United States is clearly an important correlate of adaptive processes. On the average, FEP students had been in the United States a year and a half longer than LEP students. Additionally, FEP students had shorter stays in refugee camps than LEP students.

There is also great diversity in the social class backgrounds of these students' families. Overall, Vietnamese parents are much more educated, with an average of over nine years of education, followed by the Chinese-Vietnamese (nearly seven years), then the Khmer and the Lao (each averaging about five years), and lastly the Hmong (with a parental average of just above a first-grade education). LEP students in general had parents with fewer years of schooling than did FEP students—on the average, a two-year difference. In all groups, fathers had significantly higher levels of education than mothers. In all groups except the Vietnamese, the average level of education of mothers is less than sixth grade, with almost all Hmong mothers never having attended school.

The prevalent lack of education among the Hmong reflects the fact that about 90%

came from rural origins (most were slash-and-burn farmers from the Laotian highlands or guerilla fighters during the U.S. secret war in Laos in the 1960s and early 1970s). The Hmong language, moreover, was but an oral tradition until the 1950s, when missionaries developed a written notation for it based on the Roman alphabet; as a consequence, many Hmong adult refugees are illiterate not only in English but in any language, which tends to handicap further their children's development of literacy and reading skills in English.

PREDICTORS OF ENGLISH READING PROFICIENCY

All of these characteristics of Southeast Asian students, and of their parents and families, clearly affect their learning and educational progress. But which are more important? Bivariate correlations show strong and statistically significant differences between LEP and FEP students in all of the factors with the exception of student age. As the next step in our investigation, then, we move from a bivariate to a multivariate analysis to determine which of these factors emerge as the main predictors of the students English language status. Before proceeding, it should again be noted that the sample size is small ($N = 239$), a limitation that leads to small cell sizes when the Southeast Asian students are divided into the various ethnic groups. Therefore, the results are relatively unstable and should be taken as provisional and indicative of general trends rather than of definitive conclusions. Nevertheless, given the paucity of large data files on Southeast Asians, this initial analysis provides an early estimate of factors that shape their academic attainment.

Since transition from LEP to FEP status is governed by the students' reading skills as measured by the CTBS, we use their reading test scores as the dependent variable in the multivariate analysis that follows. Our purpose is to estimate how much of the variance in the students' CTBS reading scores can be predicted by selected background characteristics, and to determine the independent effect of each predictor variable while controlling for all of the other variables. In other words, this last analysis departs from a direct comparison between FEP and LEP students and examines factors that might predict the level of CTBS reading scores using a continuous rather than a dichotomous variable.

For our purposes here, we report the findings of a stepwise multiple regression procedure. Three main types of predictor variables were examined in the regression procedure: (1) ethnicity, (2) age and time in the United States, and (3) parents' socioeconomic status. In the first set we included dummy variables for Vietnamese, Lao, Khmer, and Hmong ethnicity (Chinese students were the reference group). In the second set we included the students' ages, years in the United States, and semesters in U.S. secondary schools. In the third set we included the parents' level of education, employment status, and level of poverty and welfare dependency. We also looked at household size and entered a dummy variable for parental composition of the students' homes to control for the effect of two-parent households.

Three variables emerged as the most significant predictors of the refugee students' CTBS reading scores: (1) parents' education, (2) years in the United States, and (3) age of the student. That is, the more educated the parents, the more time spent in the United States, and the younger the student, the greater the student's English reading skills when all the other variables in the equation are controlled. Interestingly, the IHARP study found that the same variables were also the key predictors of English reading and writing proficiency among Southeast Asian adults (see Rumbaut, 1989). Among the students, these three variables alone accounted for over 40% of the variance in the CTBS reading test scores. While that suggests that this parsimonious model has considerable explanatory power, it is well to note that more than half of the variance remains "unexplained" by the selected predictor variables, implying the existence of other causal factors not yet captured by our data. Still, the three factors taken together explained most of the difference in the students' English language status accounted for by the model. Once these variables were controlled, neither parental composition, household size, ethnicity, nor any of the other socioeconomic status measures (e.g., poverty and welfare dependency) was found to have a significant effect on reading scores.

DISCUSSION AND IMPLICATIONS

Teachers and other professionals responsible for the education of linguistic minority students face the formidable tasks of assessing their needs and designing services that will effectively meet those needs. Readers who are unfamiliar with Southeast Asian students may marvel at the complexity of their lives. If a lesson is to be learned from the study of Southeast Asian youth, it is that while their wide diversity of backgrounds and experiences may challenge or overwhelm our initial ability to comprehend them, over time we can come to recognize patterns and insights that deepen our understanding and guide our ability to provide appropriate services. One needs to take into account ethnicity and culture, family and social class background, age and time in the United States, the trauma of the refugee experience, the stress of acculturation processes, and the conditions of survival in this country—considerations that go well beyond questions of whether or not the child has a special learning problem or linguistic disorder. Southeast Asian refugee youth come into American schools with complex life histories that affect their educational attainment and need to be contextualized and understood by American educators. In this concluding section we will suggest some practical implications that follow from the results of our study.

INTERPRETING TEST SCORES AS A MEASURE OF ACADEMIC ATTAINMENT

Southeast Asian students in general do well in the mathematics component of the CTBS and also reasonably well in the more easily memorized English language skill areas such as spelling and language mechanics. In fact, especially for Vietnamese students, their high mathematics scores, averaging in the top quartile of all test takers, are indicative of a brighter than normal population. Not only do these high mathematics scores probably reflect a strong cultural support for mathematics, but they also suggest that refugee students in general are a highly selected group, both "internally" and "externally." Some Vietnamese parents, for example, did not send mentally retarded or less capable children to the United States because they reasoned that the high risks and costs of escape would not be worth the low probability that these children would succeed in America. All of this suggests that special learning problems manifested by refugee students may be due less to neurophysiological disorders than to linguistic, acculturative, socioeconomic, and temporal factors. Our additional observation that a very large percentage of recently arrived Southeast Asian students are LEPs reinforces an emphasis on language and culture as priority issues.

Reading scores are much less predictive of academic outcomes such as GPA than are the language, and especially the mathematics component of the CTBS (Rumbaut & Ima, 1988). Therefore, in assessing Southeast Asian students, practitioners who have access to test scores should pay special attention to mathematics achievement and to the more memorizable aspects of English language skills rather than to the more culturally problematic areas that test vocabulary, reading comprehension, and language expression. This is especially important for newly arrived refugees. Indeed, in separate multivariate analyses we found that CTBS mathematics scores alone account for nearly half of the variance in GPAs among Southeast Asian students, whereas reading scores are not significant predictors of GPA. This does not mean that the development of reading skills should be ignored, of course, but underscores the fact that mathematics scores are simply a more adequate indicator of future academic attainment. It should also be noted that standardized tests are time-limited. Therefore, the same students who might have trouble answering test items under time-limited conditions may be capable of performing academic tasks on regular classroom assignments that do not have similar time constraints. Additionally, we have found that reading scores, despite lagging behind both the language and mathematics areas, are the ones most likely to improve over time in the United States.

INTERPRETING PREDICTORS OF ENGLISH LANGUAGE PROFICIENCY

The level of parents' premigration education is a factor that refugee parents themselves use as an explanation for variations in Southeast Asian student performance. Although discovering precisely how the educational background of refugee parents becomes translated into the English reading skills of their children is an area for future investigation, Heath's work (1983) suggests that more educated parents provide a home learning environment that enhances their children's prospects for academic success regardless of the language employed at home—an observation that may apply to Southeast Asian students as well. For those students whose parents have little formal schooling, intervention will require the presence of bilingual/bicultural professionals or paraprofessionals who can bridge the gap between the home and the school and who can assist the parents to promote their children's success in school.

Time spent in the United States is clearly a crucial predictor of English proficiency. Those who have been in the United States longest have had the greatest opportunity to acquire competence in the new language, and this is reflected in their improving English reading test scores over time. Therefore, if a longtime-resident student manifests little improvement along with a pattern of low scores in this area of language achievement, then the possible existence of a learning disability or some other related condition becomes more plausible. By contrast, if a student has been in the United States only a short time and is experiencing difficulty in reading skills, it is not easy to ascertain whether or not that person is simply going through normal processes of second-language acquisition or experiencing other learning problems.

Moreover, this study confirms that foreign-born persons who are younger are more likely to acquire fluency in all areas of English language skills than are their older counterparts. Among refugee students who arrived at an older age, particularly after puberty, their academic problems are more likely to be a function of their greater difficulty in acquiring competence in the English language, all other things being equal, thus resembling adult language learning patterns more closely than those of younger children. It should be stressed that age at arrival is a critical variable, almost as predictive of English proficiency as are time in the United States and educational background, and especially with regard to whether a student arrived before or after the onset of puberty. In this regard, educators should be alerted to the need to distinguish between true age and official age in this population, because frequently refugee students are older than their officially listed age. Knowing their true age will give a better estimate of their language-learning problems and processes. Those entering American schools after puberty will generally present more problems, since they will have greater difficulty not only with learning the English language but also with acculturative stress and identity formation during the developmental transition of adolescence. Such problems will be mediated by the quality of the students' schooling in their home country (a function of parental social class) or during their refugee camp period (where high-quality education rarely occurs).

INTERPRETING ETHNOCULTURAL DIFFERENCES AMONG SOUTHEAST ASIAN REFUGEES

Southeast Asian refugees vary considerably, not only in their social class backgrounds and migration histories but also in their diverse ethnocultural orientations. Though our quantitative analysis above did not identify ethnicity as a major predictor of language status, its power was nevertheless recorded as a key predictor of other academic outcomes, especially of GPAs and mathematics scores. Vietnamese and Chinese ethnicity were significant positive predictors of GPA and mathematics achievement, while Khmer and Lao ethnicity were significant negative predictors; Hmong ethnicity reflected a weaker and less significant effect. The responses of Southeast Asian students to the teaching and learning situation vary by ethnicity and evidently reflect differences in cultural values, childrearing practices, learning styles, and modes of family organization. To amplify the cultural implications that were not evident in the quantitative data, we collected ethnographic and other qualitative information through interviews and field observations; this forms the basis of the following interpretations.

The cultures of Indo-Chinese societies have been shaped historically by two major cultural influences, the Indian and the Chinese (see Rumbaut & Ima, 1988, for a review of the scholarly literature). Both the Khmer and the Lao (Luangpraseut, 1987) have been more influenced by Indian civilization, whereas the Vietnamese and Chinese-Vietnamese (and the Hmong to a lesser extent) have been decisively influenced by Chinese and especially Confucian traditions. The Chinese model is based on vertically organized, hierarchical, patrilineal, highly disciplined extended-family systems that instill deeply felt norms of filial piety and ancestor worship. These norms of deference are part of a system of mutually reciprocated obligations, including the expectation of extraordinary parental self-sacrifice to ensure, in the U.S. context, that children will go as far as possible in pursuit of their education in order ultimately both to honor and support the parents financially, thus making good on the parents' investment (Duong, 1981; Huynh, 1987). Furthermore, this Confucian model reflects an adaptive style that is active, pragmatic, and instrumental, based on a work ethic of personal effort and an "internal locus of control" orientation to problem solving. This form of social organization creates a structure of pressures that results in disciplined and motivated effort on the part of students, greater responsiveness to teachers and rule-bound instruction, and a higher level of competitive academic achievement (Wong-Fillmore, 1985).

By contrast, the Lao and Khmer generally share a common religion (Theravada Buddhism) and common linguistic and cultural roots. Perhaps more importantly, they do not have the kind of patriarchal, patrilineal, extended-family system found in the Chinese model. Instead, family organization tends to be more nuclear, neolocal, bilateral, and matrifocal. Comparatively, where one finds extended families among the Lao and Khmer, they tend to reflect optional and individualistic rather than obligatory or deeply institutionalized commitments. Several of the Khmer respondents we interviewed, for example, illustrated this perspective by asserting their need to establish a household separate from their parents, thus reinforcing the idea of family relationships as conditional and voluntaristic, based on individual feelings rather than on collective obligations. In parent-child relationships, one finds looser social controls and filial piety norms among the Lao and Khmer, less discipline (including less parental pressure to achieve), and a weaker sense of obligation to parents and to status norms of material achievement. These features seem to result in a lower functional affinity between their cultural orientation toward authority and achievement and the relatively authoritarian and competitive nature of American public schools and work settings.

The Hmong occupy an intermediate position, largely because of the relative absence of social class resources among preliterate parents (although in those cases where Hmong parents had some educational advantage or other human capital, that difference was positively reflected in the children's attainment patterns). Instead, Hmong family and clan organizational resources may be more predictive of future self-sufficiency outcomes, despite the obstacles posed by the demography of this population as well as by the severely disadvantaged labor-market position of the first generation. Clan and family structure is manifested most notably in the discipline and attention that Hmong youth give to authorities, especially teachers. They are highly motivated to avoid negative sanctions and will go to great lengths to avoid shame and to protect their "face" and family name. Nevertheless, despite the promise they have shown through high school, Hmong youth face an array of other problems that may seriously undermine or diminish their potential for success, including their relative failure at present to make the transition to postsecondary schooling. This failure is due in part to early marriages (often coerced by parents) and early family formation, to the severe devaluation of girls by the Hmong patrilineal system, and to the lack of role models and the financial wherewithal to support the college education of children (see Rumbaut & Ima, 1988, for a detailed discussion).

Although these characterizations of the Chinese, Indian, and Hmong models of social life are themselves broad oversimplifications, they point to the necessity of recognizing the ethnocultural diversity of Southeast Asians and its effects on patterns of learning and educational attainment.

FINAL IMPLICATIONS

One result of the general lack of primary language knowledge and cultural understanding of Southeast Asians among American teachers and allied professionals is the confusion over assigning Southeast Asian students to special education programs. However, precisely because of the lack of clarity about the source and nature of refugee students learning problems, is it proper to assign them to special education classes? If there are no bilingual services available, then this may be a reasonable placement, if only because those students may be apt to receive more individual attention from teachers—all the more so if the specialist is informed about the range of possible sources of learning difficulties faced by refugee students (e.g., second-language acquisition, acculturation, trauma) and makes allowance for these as part of the services rendered. But if teachers simply operate on the assumption that they are dealing with linguistically disordered or special education students as traditionally defined, then there is cause to be skeptical of such a placement, for all of the reasons mentioned earlier.

An alternative to the referral of Southeast Asians directly to special education programs is a prereferral process that sorts out the various temporal and social factors (including second-language problems, acculturation, and traumatic refugee experiences) that may shape their learning problems, and does so *prior* to a decision to trigger the regular process of referral into special education. The necessary ingredients of such a process are a bilingual and bicultural staff capable of dealing with the ubiquitous communication problems (preferably a professional trained individual or at the least a paraprofessional bilingual specialist) and the availability of alternative services. At this prereferral stage the individual student can be diagnosed and, if his or her problem does not clearly require a speech-language pathologist or special education specialist, sent to alternative placements, thus obviating the need to rely on special educational programs that may lack appropriate resources or expertise. Despite these cautionary comments about the placement of Southeast Asians into special education programs, they are more likely to be left in bilingual and ESL classes on the assumption that theirs are primarily linguistic rather than special education problems. This trend is associated with the frequent observations of apparent underrepresentation of Southeast Asian LEP students in special education programs. Regardless of placement, unless the combination of language, cultural, and emotional stresses of refugee life is addressed, Southeast Asian students will continue to be underserved. It would be naive to assume that these students bring to the classroom the same general worldview and life experiences as their American teachers. Instead, as we have argued, their patterns of educational achievement in the United States are shaped by identifiable factors.

While the understanding of strangers is a difficult and often frustrating task, it is also clear that knowing the life histories and cultures of these newcomers will make a difference in providing quality education services. In the process it may deepen our understanding of ourselves and enhance the meaning, value, and quality of careers in American education.

REFERENCES

Bouvier, L. F., & Martin, P. L. (1987). *Population change and California's education system.* Washington DC: Population Reference Bureau, Inc.

Caplan, N., Whitmore, J. K., & Bui, Q. I. (1985). *Southeast Asia refugee self-sufficiency study: Final report* Ann Arbor: University of Michigan, Institute for Social Research.

Chan, K. S. (1983). Limited English speaking, handicapped, and poor. Triple threat in childhood. In M. Chu-Chang (Ed.), *Asian- and Pacific-American perspectives in bilingual education: Comparative research* (pp. 153–171). New York Teachers College Press.

Cheng, L. L. (1987a). *Assessing Asian language performance: Guidelines for evaluating limited-English-proficient students.* Rockville, MD Aspen Publishers.

Cheng, L. L. (1987b). Crosscultural and linguistic considerations in working with Asian populations. *Asha 29,* 33–37.

Cook-Gumperz, J. (1986). *The social construction of literacy.* Cambridge, Cambridge University Press.

Dao, M. & Grossman, H. (1985). *Identifying instructing and rehabilitating Southeast Asian students with special needs and counseling their parents.* Unpublished manuscript.

Duong, N. D. (1981). *A collection of papers in Vietnamese culture.* Houston: Indochinese Culture Center and Harris County Employment and Training Administration Youth Program.

First, J. M., & Carrera, J. W. (1988). *New voices: Immigrant students in U.S. public schools* Boston National Coalition of Advocates for Students.

Gardner, R. W., Robey, B., & Smith, P. C. (1985). Asian Americans: Growth, change, and diversity. *Population Bulletin, 40,* 1–44.

Heath, S. B. (1983). *Ways with words—Language, life, and work in communities and classrooms.* Cambridge, England: Cambridge University Press.

Huynh, D. T. (1987). *Introduction to Vietnamese culture.* San Diego: San Diego State University Multifunctional Resource Center.

Kinzie, J. D., Sack, W. H., Angell, R., Manson, S., & Rath, B. (1986). The psychiatric effects of massive trauma on Cambodian children. I. The children. *Journal of the American Academy of Child Psychiatry. 25,* 370–376.

Lau v. Nichols, 414 U.S. 563, 94 S.Ct. 786 (1974).

Luangpraseut, K. (1987). *Laos culturally speaking: Introduction to the Lao culture.* San Diego: San Diego State University Multifunctional Resource Center.

Olsen, L. (1988). *Crossing the schoolhouse border. Immigrant students and California public schools.* San Francisco: California Tomorrow.

Rumbaut, R. G. (1983). Mental health and the refugee experience. A comparative study of Southeast Asian refugees. In T. C. Owan (Ed.), *Southeast Asian mental health: Treatment, prevention, services, training, and research* (pp. 433–486). Rockville, MD: National Institute of Mental Health.

———. (1989). Portraits, patterns and predictors of the refugee adaptation process. In D. W. Haines, (Ed.), *Refugees as immigrants: Cambodians, Laotians and Vietnamese in America,* pp. 138–182: Totowa, NJ, Rowman and Lattlefield.

Rumbaut, R. G. & Ima, K. (1988). *The adaptation of Southeast Asian refugee youth. A comparative study.* Washington, DC: US Office of Refugee Resettlement.

Rumbaut, R. G. & Weeks, J. (1986). Fertility and adaptation: Indochinese refugees in the United States. *International Migration Review. 20* (2), 428–466.

Siegel, V., & Halog, I. (1986). Assessment of limited English proficient children with special needs. In N. Tsuchida (Ed). *Issues in Asian and Pacific American education* (pp. 13–20). Minneapolis, MN: Asian Pacific American Learning Resource Center.

Wong-Fillmore, L. (1985). Learning a second language: Chinese children in the American classroom. In J. E. Alatis & J. J. Staczek (Eds.). *Perspectives on bilingualism and bilingual education* (pp. 436–452). Washington, DC: Georgetown University Press.

Yoshioka, J. G. (1929). A study of bilingualism. *Journal of Genetic Psychology*, 36, 473–479.

11

Language and Identity in the Education of Boston-Area Khmer

Nancy J. Smith-Hefner

THE ISSUE OF native language maintenance has been a topic of considerable debate within the Khmer community of metropolitan Boston. Teachers and bilingual program coordinators report that many Khmer parents are not interested in Khmer language programs, insisting their children learn only English. However, many Khmer parents and community leaders express dismay at their children's loss of native language ability. These parents consistently emphasize that they want their children to study English, but they also want them to learn to read and write Khmer.

The debate has been influenced by state policies on education for linguistic minorities. In 1971, the commonwealth of Massachusetts passed the nation's first mandatory Bilingual Educational Act (Crawford 1989:33; Massachusetts Department of Education 1976). By state law, schools which have 20 or more children from a minority group whose native language is not English and who are limited English proficient must provide bilingual instruction for those children (MDE 1976:3). The program is a transitional one with most children moving into mainstream classrooms within 3 to 4 years. Although some school systems in metropolitan Boston continue to have difficulty securing qualified Khmer bilingual teachers, the overwhelming majority of limited English proficient Khmer children in area public schools (with 20 or more such students) are placed in bilingual classrooms and receive at least some instruction in Khmer (MDE 1988).

For the most part, however, Khmer parents played little role in the formulation of these bilingual programs. The general shape of Boston's programs was decided long before the arrival of ethnic Khmer, largely through the efforts of Hispanic and East Asian minorities. Today, teachers and administrators in Boston-area schools regularly complain that Khmer parents are little involved in their children's education; parental attendance at school functions and parent-teacher conferences, they note, is negligible. Communications between parents and non-Khmer educators have been complicated by language barriers and by parental reluctance to question school policy. Bilingual teachers, themselves ethnic Khmer, are often at a loss to explain what seem to be contradictory attitudes and behavior on the part of Khmer parents.

What, in fact, do Khmer refugee parents want for their children? How do Khmer perceive the role of their native language in the education of their children, and how do native-language attitudes correspond to the more general educational aspirations that Khmer parents hold for their children in this country?

From *Anthropology and Education Quarterly* 21:3 (1990): 250–268. Reproduced by permission of the American Anthropological Association. Not for further reproduction.

This article reports on ten months of observations and interviews with the parents and teachers of Khmer children attending a Boston public school with a large bilingual program. Research focused on the language attitudes of Boston-area Khmer as they relate to issues of social, moral, and political identity. Khmer attitudes toward the maintenance of their native language provide significant insight into their views on education. Interestingly, however, the research discovered that parents' decisions concerning their children's language learning and general education have less to do with language attitudes than they do Khmer notions of person, intelligence, and motivation. These notions are only implicit in Khmer discourse and behavior, and are thus often overlooked or misinterpreted by teachers and school officials. Moreover, in important respects, these ideas distinguish Khmer from other East and Southeast Asian immigrants.

The research thus underscores the importance of recognizing cultural variation in the educational attitudes of Asian immigrants. It also cautions against any approach that would see Southeast Asian refugees as a homogeneous category whose members share the same psychological response to their immigrant minority status, as suggested by the work of some cultural ecologists (Gibson 1987; Ogbu 1987; Ogbu and Matute-Bianchi 1986). More generally, it argues for the importance of understanding culturally informed ideals of person, identity, and behavior in the educational performance of ethnic minorities (Trueba 1988).

BOSTON'S CAMBODIAN COMMUNITY

Of a total of some 846,000 Southeast Asian refugees who have been resettled in the United States since 1975 and some 200,000 who have subsequently been born in this country (Haines 1989:2), approximately 35,474 have settled in Massachusetts. Of these, 18,335 are Cambodian (Massachusetts Office for Refugees and Immigrants 1988).

Cambodians began to arrive in Massachusetts in significant numbers in the early 1980s, as part of the third and most recent wave of Southeast Asian immigration to the United States. The different waves of Southeast Asian immigration roughly correlate with what are in fact substantial differences of socioeconomic standing among immigrant Vietnamese, Lao, Khmer, and Sino-Vietnamese. In general, the first refugees to arrive were more urban and better educated, while later arrivals, including those still coming today, tend to come from more rural and less well educated backgrounds (Kelly 1986:41; Strand and Jones 1985:35).

Although initial U.S. policy was to disperse Southeast Asian refugees throughout the country so as to avoid large, "unassimilable" enclaves, later policy recognized the social and psychological importance of ethnic communities in refugee adaptation, and designated a number of "cluster" communities. Boston was one such site (Ebihara 1985:135; Gordon 1987:164). According to 1988 estimates, the Khmer population in Boston (Suffolk County) is 5,362 (MORI 1988). In the 1988–89 school year there were over 450 Khmer-speaking children in the city's public school system (MDE 1988).

In recent years the flow of new Cambodian arrivals to the United States has diminished. Thai refugee camps remain seriously overcrowded, but countries of resettlement like the United States are accepting fewer and fewer refugees. U.S. immigration policy today is focused on family reunification, and Thai policies have effectively limited the number of Khmer allowed to leave the camps (Crossette 1988:17). At present, there is no possibility of bringing family members who are still in Cambodia to the United States, as the U.S. government does not recognize the Vietnamese-backed government of Hun Sen.

Although the number of new Khmer arrivals to the United States is decreasing, inmigration, the movement of Cambodians from one place to another within the state, as well as secondary migration, the movement of refugees initially settled in one state to another, has resulted in a growing concentration of Khmer in areas like the Merrimack valley region of Massachusetts (MORI 1988). Whereas Boston's population has diminished somewhat in the past five years, during the same time period the nearby cities of Lowell and Lynn have experienced significant increases in the number of Khmer children in their schools. Cambodians have moved to these areas for a variety of reasons. The most often-cited attractions include greater employment opportunities and a more reasonable cost of living, especially as regards housing. Now that these communities have become so large, an additional and important magnet drawing more Cambodians to the area is the size and vitality of the Khmer community itself.

Boston Khmer benefit from the social contacts and services available in these larger, adjacent Khmer communities. Many, for example, attend the Cambodian Buddhist temple in nearby Lynn. At the same time, Khmer from Lynn, Chelsea, Revere, and even Lowell, hold their weddings in Boston's Chinatown, and many shop and do business in Chinatown establishments.

THE STUDY

The research upon which this study is based was originally inspired by my earlier research on language and socialization in Southeast Asia (Smith-Hefner 1988), and, more specifically, some 18 months of informal discussion with Cambodian friends and teachers in the Boston area. Issues of language maintenance and educational achievement were consistently raised by my students in the Bilingual/English as a Second Language studies program at the University of Massachusetts who are themselves ethnic Khmer bilingual teachers. This initial contact led me to conduct further ethnographic research in the Khmer community. The study was carried out over a ten-month period, from September of 1988 to June of 1989.

Research relied upon in-depth questionnaires combined with open-ended interviews and carefully recorded observations. The attitudes of Khmer parents were a major focus of inquiry; however, in order to ascertain the degree to which community leaders express and support widely held parental attitudes, interviews were also conducted with a number of ethnic Khmer teachers, ethnic association officials, and religious leaders. Interviews involved both a series of standardized questions to allow for the comparison of responses on key issues, and open-ended discussions to allow interviewees to raise issues of individual concern. These were supplemented by ethnographic observations so that actual patterns of language use and behavior could be assessed. Observations were conducted by myself and a Cambodian assistant in Khmer homes at the time of the interviews, and at various school and community events that took place throughout the year. During the 1988–89 school year, we were invited to, and attended, dinners, weddings, birthday celebrations, school cultural presentations, and religious ceremonies.

Interviews with teachers included all of the Khmer bilingual staff at the Alexander Hamilton Elementary School, site of the largest Cambodian bilingual program in Boston. Of the 71 Khmer families with children enrolled in the school's bilingual and mainstream classrooms, 35 participated in the study. In addition, several families who have recently moved outside of the city and whose children now attend other schools were interviewed. The interviews were conducted in the child's home with the child present for at least the first portion of the interview. In the majority of cases both parents took part. Depending on the language preference of the interviewee, the interviews were conducted in English and/or Khmer, with the assistance of a Cambodian collaborator. A total of 55 formal interviews were conducted in all.

Khmer families were selected at random by the bilingual teachers. Based on teachers' and school administrators' reports, we assumed that a child's placement in a bilingual classroom is not necessarily an indication of parental approval of the program. All Khmer-speaking children are tested when they enter the school system. If they are found to be limited English proficient (designated LEP), they are normally placed in some form of bilingual program. Although parents can refuse to put their child in the program, and can also withdraw their child from it at any time, teachers and bilingual coordinators report that most Khmer parents accept the recommendation of the school personnel.

Research focused on primary school children because the situation of older Khmer children is distorted by a number of complicating issues. Older children have often experienced a lengthy gap in their schooling due to events related to the war, the temporary closing of schools during the Pol Pot era, forced work in the countryside, and the upheaval of escape and of life in refugee camps. Early on in the research, it became clear that Khmer parents have different attitudes toward the language and education of their older and younger children. For example, although a significant number of older children have never learned to read and write in Khmer, and are currently receiving no instruction in their native language, parents feel that these children are "like themselves"; that is, their major problem is thought to be an immediate one—quickly acquiring enough English to allow them to get a job and make a living.

By contrast, most Khmer children now in primary school in the United States were born either in the camps or in this country, and are being educated completely in American schools. The parents of these children face a different set of issues and options. As they watch these children rapidly and seemingly effortlessly becoming fluent in English, many Khmer parents are beginning to wonder what is being lost in the process. Issues of language and identity are central to their concern.

THE SOCIOECONOMIC BACKGROUND OF REFUGEES

All of the Cambodians in our study (with the exception of one bilingual teacher who arrived in 1975) had come to this country beginning in the early 1980s as part of the third wave of Southeast Asian immigration. Their social and educational backgrounds reflect their "third wave" status. The majority of parents were from more rural and less well educated backgrounds than those reported for earlier Southeast Asian arrivals. Just over one-third of those interviewed had originated in urban areas of Cambodia; the remainder were from the countryside. Most parents, including some of those reporting urban backgrounds, had come from families of farmers, unskilled laborers, or small merchants (*srae, chamkaa, kammekaa, neaq lueq koncerain*). Assessed in terms of education and occupation, only 25% of the Khmer interviewed (most of them, the bilingual teachers) were from the Khmer middle class.

With the exception of the bilingual teachers, all of whom reported some teacher-training in or after high school in Cambodia, most parents had little formal education. Among the parents interviewed, fathers averaged just over six years of schooling in their country and mothers just over three. Some of the fathers had experienced only three or four years of education at a village temple school, the traditional site of education in Cambodia; nevertheless, 81% of the men reported that they could read and write some Khmer. In comparison, less than half of the mothers reported being literate in Khmer. Another 30% reported semiliteracy; that is, they could read a little bit, but could not write, or had learned how to read and write, but had forgotten. The discrepancy between levels of education and native language literacy for men and women reflects the fact that until 1953 public education was not widely available for women in Cambodia (Ouk, Huffman, and Lewis 1988:30–31;

Steinberg 1959:252), and, even after schools were open to girls, in rural areas many parents continued to believe that schooling was less important for daughters than for sons.

Due to their low levels of education and of literacy in Cambodia and the recentness of their arrival in the United States, the parents in our study are still struggling to learn English. Lack of English language skills is, of course, a significant barrier to employment. In 56% of the families neither spouse is employed and the family is dependent on welfare.

Khmer parents repeatedly cited their own limited educational experience and economic resources in discussing their role in the education of their children. Indeed, interviews and observations showed clearly that the limited educational backgrounds of Khmer adults strongly affect their attitudes and actions in supporting their children's education.

THE LANGUAGE OF BILINGUAL INSTRUCTION

The Alexander Hamilton School in Boston, the site of the present research, has had a bilingual Cambodian program since 1982. At the beginning of the 1988–89 school year, the program had 121 Cambodian children and seven Khmer bilingual teachers.

The Khmer used in the bilingual program is a standard variant of Khmer, similar to that spoken by over 90% of the Cambodian population. By comparison with other Southeast Asian languages, Khmer is relatively homogeneous; there is little dialectal variation by region (Ouk, Huffman, and Lewis 198:67). As elsewhere in Southeast Asia, however, Khmer recognize a range of intradialectal speech markers, and these play an important role in the ascription and evaluation of status.

Cambodians consider hierarchy to be an integral and natural part of their social order (Steinberg 1959:7). Although many say they appreciate the equality of social relations in the United States, among Khmer, the recognition of social distinctions through appropriate speech and behavior is felt to be essential to harmonious social relations. Titles and other terms of address are used to indicate subtle differences in the relative age and social standing of interactants (Center for Applied Linguistics 1981:8; Ehrman 1972:39; Gorgoniyev 1966:73). Different linguistic forms are utilized to address monks, royalty, teachers, and others who are older or highly esteemed. Differences between urban and rural, educated and uneducated populations, are also signaled linguistically. These distinctions are quite salient to members of the Khmer speech community and are often referred to in assessing individuals' character, the quality of their upbringing, and the social deference to which they are entitled.

The role of terms of address and reference, linguistic registers, and special vocabularies in the articulation of Khmer social hierarchy made them a prime target of the Khmer Rouge's revolutionary cultural policies. In an effort to "equalize" social relations, Pol Pot's Khmer Rouge outlawed the use of elements of the polite speech registers, specifically, those terms which were most critical in marking social distinctions among interactants.

When asked about Pol Pot's language policies, parents uniformly responded that it was not an attempt to equalize social relations at all, but an attempt to wipe out "everything good." Especially distasteful to adult Khmer were attempts made by Pol Pot to equalize relationships between parents and children (parents were to be called with the epithet *met* "friend," and unmarked forms like *hoep baay* "eat" replaced polite forms such as *pisaa baay*, normally used in speaking to elders). Many adults reported the continued use of respect-marked forms in their private interactions with their own parents and elder relatives, despite Khmer Rouge policy. One man even claimed that he was so enraged by the policy that he announced his refusal to comply publicly at a weekly village political meeting.

The recognition of the status of one's parents is seen as a first step in the child's understanding of status relationships in the public sphere and beyond.[1] Indeed, one of the most consistent concerns of parents in the study was that their children learn to use respectful terms of address and polite forms of speech. A good deal of parents' efforts at linguistic socialization is focused on teaching just these forms. When guests or elders come to the house, children are instructed to *satuq* or *sampea*, to put their two hands together in front of their face and bow slightly. They are told to say, *cumriep sue*, "respectful greetings," and are supplied with the appropriate term of address, kin term, or title. Other adults present commonly join in the urging, *Monih, monih! Cumriep sue om!* ("Come here, come here! Pay obeisance to older aunt!") and comment on the child's performance, saying, "Very good" or "What a good child." It is at moments such as these that children are taught to pay attention to differences in the age and status of various addressees.

Khmer say that a child's speech and behavior reflect on the child's family. They cite a familiar Khmer saying, *Mieyiet saa pouc* "One's behavior reveals one's roots," by way of explanation. If a Khmer child acts or speaks inappropriately to an adult, it may be reported to the child's parents, and is a source of great shame. Fear of public censure and concomitant loss of face are repeatedly stressed in Khmer conversation, and are also cited as the primary reason for teaching one's children respect forms. "If my child did not know how to call people correctly people would say, *Nih koen caw neaq naa*? 'Whose child is this?' They would say, 'That child's family doesn't know how to raise their kids right!' " For a child, the consequences of such bad behavior can be serious. If reported to a parent by a teacher or neighbor, a child may be beaten for disrespectful speech.

It is because appropriate speech is felt to both express and reinforce Khmer social hierarchy, that an individual's failure to speak properly is interpreted as having larger social repercussions. In anecdotes adults associated children's inability to speak Khmer with other culturally unacceptable behaviors, such as the desire to live away from home and the refusal to care for their parents in old age. One bilingual teacher explained his extreme distress at being called with the disrespectful epithet *a-*, *(a-kruu)*, by his students in this country, saying,

> It's like being called "crazy teacher." To be called like that is so shameful. You lose face. When someone calls you inappropriately like that, you feel yourself come tumbling down from your level, your class. When that happens, everything, everyone, all order, is upset.

Many interviewees linked this emphasis on the role of language in status and hierarchy to the more general problem of maintaining Khmer identity. Parents expressed their sorrow and dismay at those children who had lost or never learned their native language. Not to know Khmer, parents, teachers, and community leaders said, is to risk losing one's identity as a Cambodian.

CAMBODIAN ATTITUDES TOWARD BILINGUAL EDUCATION

When parents, teachers, and community leaders were asked if bilingual education is important (*mien prayaoc, mien samkhan*) for Khmer children, responses were consistently and overwhelmingly positive. Ninety-five percent of those surveyed said they feel very strongly that bilingual education is both important and necessary. Furthermore, the overwhelming majority of Khmer said that just knowing how to speak Khmer is not enough; they want their children to learn how to read and write in Khmer as well. This was true *even of those parents whose children were not enrolled in a Cambodian bilingual program and were, subsequently, not being instructed in Khmer literacy.*

When asked why parents feel that it is important for their children to learn to read and write in Khmer, parents again stressed that knowing Khmer is critical for establishing

and maintaining one's membership in the community. The ability to communicate with relatives by reading and writing letters from Cambodia was cited as of particular importance.

Even more significant, and somewhat unexpected, was the finding that many
Cambodians link the importance of their children learning Khmer to their own hopes of returning one day to Cambodia. As many as 90% of parents interviewed indicated a strong
desire to return home "at least to visit." A number of older parents (those in their 40s and
50s) and many grandparents of children in the study said they hoped to eventually return
to Cambodia to stay—much to the dismay of their children. As word of the pullout of
Vietnamese troops from Cambodia and plans for the formation of a new coalition government have intensified, the possibility of returning to Cambodia has for many Khmer become a lively topic of conversation. Some Khmer expressed the fear that if political events
change, the U.S. government will send them back to their country. One man explained,

> Maybe the law will require that we go back to my country, we're not sure, we don't
> know. Like when Cambodia went to war, we don't know before, we don't know it's
> changing. . . . If I go back to my country, if my children don't study (Khmer), it's hard.

Interestingly, in discussing with parents their reasons for placing their children in the
bilingual program, only two parents cited the issue of their child not being able to understand English. (A number of parents in fact stated that "English is easy for him/her whereas
Khmer is difficult.") Only one parent mentioned (indirectly) the possibility of ease of transfer of skills from Khmer to English. In general, Cambodian parents express the view that
the function of bilingual education is to teach their children Khmer literacy in addition to
English. That is, bilingual education is seen as a means for Khmer children to maintain their
native language and identity. Parents feel that their children will learn English easily because they now live in an English-speaking country and "they use English every day." By
contrast, they insist, without bilingual education their children are unlikely to learn to read
and write in Khmer; one more critical link to their native culture will disappear.

The positive assessment of the bilingual program by Khmer parents is consistent both
with the important role assigned to appropriate language use among Cambodians and with
the high value placed on one's children learning to read and write Khmer. What is curious,
however, is that despite this positive assessment, there is in fact a certain ambivalence
among many parents toward actually placing their children in bilingual classrooms. While
praising the virtues of Khmer language-learning, nearly one-third of the parents in our survey had not enrolled their children in the bilingual program.

A good number of the Khmer bilingual teachers themselves, for example, do not have
their children in bilingual classrooms, or do not keep them there for more than one year.
This pattern seems to be typical of parents from middle-class backgrounds with strong aspirations for upward mobility for their children. Teachers said they feel they can give their
children the English language support necessary for their success in a mainstream classroom and that they plan to teach their children to read and write in Khmer at home when
the children are older. Nevertheless, despite parents' best intentions, many of these children will not in fact learn to read and write in Khmer. One teacher described what is a typical pattern,

> I planned to teach my son Khmer when he got older. But now he is in high school and
> he is too busy studying other subjects. He has no time to study Khmer. I don't think that
> he will ever learn to read and write in Khmer. I feel very bad about that.

Other Khmer parents decided against placing their children in bilingual classrooms
for a variety of less easily categorized reasons. One mother reported that although she
wanted her eight-year-old daughter to attend a school with a bilingual program, her daugh-

ter had answered the questionnaire sent out to parents asking their choice of schools by herself, and she chose a school without a bilingual program. The mother said resignedly, "I don't know anything about that. I want her to learn Khmer and English but she is now at a school without a bilingual program." Another father said that although he wanted his son to learn Khmer, he had enrolled him in the nearby all-English school because the boy kept missing the bus which services children in the bilingual program who do not live within walking distance of the school. Another two parents said their children "were not smart" or "were easily confused" and could not handle learning in two languages at the same time.

This ambivalence toward actually placing one's child in a bilingual classroom is even more surprising in light of the enormous status parents accord to teachers, above all, Khmer teachers, and the very significant role parents expect teachers to play in the education of Khmer children. When Khmer parents were asked who has responsibility for teaching their children to read and write in Khmer, the overwhelming majority of parents, both literate and illiterate, said quite forcefully that it is the teacher's responsibility. Teachers were often referred to as "second mothers, second fathers." Typical comments from parents included, "I give my child to the teacher," and, "I have confidence in the teacher and the teacher has to teach everything to my child." One parent explained that, "The parents' role is only to take care of the child, to feed them when they are hungry and when they are sick, to give them medicine. As for education, it's the teacher who has responsibility for all kinds of knowledge."

Teachers are thus expected to make all decisions regarding the form and content of instruction. But whereas parents repeatedly stressed that teachers are responsible for all aspects of teaching, they also emphasized that ultimate responsibility for *learning* lies with the child.

Several parents in the survey, for example, reported that their children were not doing well in Khmer, that they find it too difficult.

> When Sokhaa is given homework in Khmer, she cries and has headaches and says it is so boring and she doesn't want to do it. She says it is very hard for her to learn Khmer.

> Samnang has difficulty to study Khmer, but English is easy for him.[2]

What is especially interesting is that parents take their children's complaints seriously and, despite their own desires that their children learn to read and write Khmer, reported that they generally accept their children's reluctance and do not push (*cumrueny*).

> You know some children, like Wichet, he doesn't like to study Khmer. But I like. For example, if I push him, maybe he's not going to study good.

> To know how to speak two languages is good for him, but it depends on him. If he doesn't want to study Khmer, it's up to him.

At first sight, these and similar comments seem to contradict parent's overwhelming emphasis on teachers and parents as enforcers of discipline and on adults as the ultimate decision makers for children. In our conversations, for example, parents stressed that children must fear/respect (*klaic*) their teachers. If children do not fear their teachers, said parents, they will not learn. Fear of the teacher is necessary and good, and it is reinforced by frequent parental threats to "tell the teacher" when a child misbehaves. During interviews, many parents underscored this emphasis on discipline for me (and for the children present) by repeating the words traditionally uttered to monks back in Cambodia when parents brought their children to the temple school: "I give you my child. Do whatever you want with him. I ask only that you keep the eyes and the bones for me."[3]

Khmer parents were adamant that children should obey their elders and do what they are told; this, they insisted time and time again, is what distinguishes Khmer children from

Americans. It gradually became clear from our observations and interviews, however, that *whereas a child's failure to speak or behave appropriately and respectfully according to community norms is considered just cause for physical punishment, in matters of academic performance, Khmer parents hesitate to push their children against the child's own interests or desires.*

EDUCATIONAL ATTITUDES AND ACADEMIC ACHIEVEMENT

Parental ambivalence toward placing their children in bilingual classrooms (despite strongly positive evaluations of the program and the expressed desire for native language maintenance) and their reluctance to "push" their children in academic matters are particularly interesting in light of recent research on the academic performance of Khmer children in American schools. Although research has generally confirmed reports in the popular media of the academic success of Southeast Asian children (Caplan, Whitmore, and Choy 1989; Whitmore, Trautmann, and Caplan 1989), a recent study conducted in California (Rumbaut 1989) found significant differences between Southeast Asian groups. By both local and national measures of school achievement, the Vietnamese did best, followed by the Sino-Vietnamese and the Hmong, with the Khmer and the Lao ranking below the majority white population (Rumbaut 1989:169).

The results for the Vietnamese and the Sino-Vietnamese are not completely surprising, since many of these immigrants come from more westernized, urban, and better-educated backgrounds. The educational data for Hmong, Khmer, and Lao, however, are more perplexing. At first sight, for example, one would have expected the Hmong to perform well below the Khmer and the Lao, since Hmong children come from households reporting the lowest levels of literacy and education among all immigrant groups, and they come almost exclusively from rural backgrounds. Acknowledging this anomaly, Rumbaut (1989:181) suggests that although social class and economic differences explain much of the pattern of achievement observed among Indochinese youth, additional factors must be taken into account to explain the lower levels of Khmer and Lao achievement. It is in relation to this point that the Khmer data from the present study are most interesting.

One factor that emerged as a significant and recurrent theme in discussions with Khmer parents regarding their children's education is the degree to which Khmer parents feel they can no longer control their children in this country (cf. Whitmore, Trautmann, and Caplan 1989:133). Parents tend to see this as a result of American laws protecting children against child abuse, which they say prevent them from disciplining their children as they would in Cambodia.[4] Many parents report that their children no longer fear parental threats of discipline and instead now respond with threats of their own. It is because of this, parents say, that they are unable to push their children here to the degree that they would in Cambodia.

More importantly, however, and less widely recognized by Khmer themselves, our observations and interviews revealed that the extent to which parents feel they can control their children in this country is related to Khmer notions of personhood, motivation, and achievement. These notions seem peculiar to the Khmer, moreover, and distinguish them from other Southeast Asian refugee groups.

Many Khmer parents feel that their attempts to direct the course of their children's lives are deeply constrained or limited by the personal character of each child. Indigenous theories of development among Khmer are not strongly environmental: the child's character is not viewed as primarily the product of parental social inputs. Quite the contrary, the child's qualities are thought to emerge from within the child itself. This view of child development influences Khmer attitudes on socialization. Caregivers consistently emphasize that it is important to pay attention to a child's behavior so as to assess that child's character and likely path. "When you see the direction that the child chooses, then you know what she likes."[5] Parents can and do give their children advice and guidance, but feel that, beyond a certain limit, it is not possible to force the child to take it. Emphasizing a nativist view of child development, Khmer parents believe that a child's growth and achievements are strongly influenced by its intrinsic dispositions. As one mother said of her 10-year-old daughter, "Somehow she has interests within her already; pushing her in some other direction is no use."

Focusing on their child's behavior, parents seek to evaluate their child's performance so as to discern this pregiven, intrinsic capability. The effort, and the larger notion of personal development to which it testifies, gives rise to a distinctive interpretation of the parent's role. That role requires a precarious balance of intervention where intervention can succeed, and resignation in the face of a child's inalterably native dispositions. Behavior itself, it is thought, provides the best guide to the child's potential, and her likely achievement. A child who gets good grades "can do it"; a child who does not do well in school, "cannot do it." Children who do not do well in Khmer cannot do well in Khmer.

The important role assigned to behavior and the view that behavior is strongly shaped by the intrinsic dispositions of the child were also evident in parents' virtual refusal to speculate about their children's futures. Here again, Khmer attitudes contrast strongly with those of other Southeast Asian immigrant groups. When asked what they would like their children to become or how far they would like their children to go in school, Khmer parents typically made comments such as,

> I don't know Seyha's future. . . . I don't know what he likes. It depends on him. . . . I don't know my son yet.

> After she grows up she can decide for herself.

> I don't know if he can do it. . . . I have to watch and see the direction he takes.

> We cannot decide or choose for Sitha what she wants to do. It's up to her to choose herself.

Stated quite simply, a child's destiny is fundamentally dependent upon the pregiven nature she brings to its unfolding.

ORIGINS OF KHMER PERSONHOOD

With very few exceptions, the parents in our study were Theravada Buddhists, as are the majority of Cambodians. Virtually all reported that they follow major Buddhist holy days at the Buddhist temple in nearby Lynn. Many parents expressed a strong belief in destiny or fate (*wiesnaa* or *samnang*). Some also cited the influence of reincarnation or the transmigration of the soul (*kaa deng ciet* or *kaut medong tiet*). According to these beliefs, one's present state is determined in part by one's behavior in the past. Good acts done in a past life will result in good things in this life (*twee bon leqaa, baan leqaa*). One parent went so far as to say that the reason he could not learn English and was illiterate in his own language was that he had performed bad acts in a previous life. Another parent said of his son,

> For my son, it doesn't matter what I want. It's up to his previous life. If he did good things, so he can become a policeman or a doctor or a teacher. If his destiny says stop school here, I cannot change it.

A few Khmer parents said they did not place their faith in destiny; they rejected the notion of reincarnation. Nonetheless, native theories of intelligence and achievement seem consonant with these religious concepts—as well as with other traditional beliefs such as the immutability of social categories and the importance of moderation, "the middle road" (*plew kandal*). Taking the middle road, explained one parent, means not aiming too high or too low, but maintaining the present balance, doing the average. For one's children, taking the middle road means not demanding too much of the child, not expecting more than the child can deliver. To push one's child in a particular direction and fail, said another parent, is to risk losing face and one's standing in the community. Parents hope, of course, that given the appropriate moral training when young, their children will choose the right path and achieve great things. Ultimately, however, what the child becomes depends upon forces less easily seen or known.

Given these notions, it is easier to understand the apparently contradictory views of Khmer parents on the language and education of their children. On one hand, most assert quite forcefully, "I don't want my daughter to forget her identity as a Khmer. I want her to learn Khmer reading and writing." On the other hand, parents then go on to concede that actual performance "depends on her to do it or not. I cannot force her to take a particular course." In education as in other domains of social life, achievement is desirable but is ultimately shaped as much by destiny and disposition as it is the urgings of teachers or parents.

DISCUSSION

Studies of the educational achievement of Southeast Asian refugees by both Whitmore et al. (1989) and Rumbaut (1989) found that parental attitudes toward identity and ethnic culture strongly correlate with patterns of achievement among their children. The stronger the sense of ethnic pride among a population, the higher the average GPAs attained by their children.

Among Boston-area Khmer, attitudes toward Khmer language maintenance *are* quite positive and are also linked to a strong desire on the part of parents for ethnic maintenance and, more generally, cultural survival. The exploration of the reasons why, despite these attitudes, not all Khmer place or keep their children in bilingual classrooms suggests in turn some of the reasons why Khmer children are not doing well in American schools.

Socioeconomic considerations certainly come into play in making decisions concerning the education of Cambodian children. The majority of Cambodians living in the Boston area came to the United States in the third wave of Southeast Asian immigration. Most are still struggling to make ends meet, and the desire for native language literacy often cannot compete with the requirements of economic survival. In addition, parents who are themselves illiterate or lacking education have difficulties understanding how American schools work and what their role in their child's education should be. In turning their children over to the teacher, many Khmer parents feel that their job is finished; the rest is up to the schools.

As Rumbaut (1989:181) suggests, however, socioeconomic differences can only partially explain the educational performance of Southeast Asian refugees. Additional factors must be taken into account in explaining the lower levels of Khmer achievement. In the present study, it is Khmer notions of person, intelligence, and motivation that stand out as particularly distinctive.

The Khmer belief that it is not possible to "push" one's children, that one must "look at the child to determine his future" appears in large part to have originated in Theravada Buddhism, or the variant of it practiced among ordinary Khmer. Theravada Buddhism, of course, is not practiced by more than a minority of Vietnamese, nor is it practiced by the Hmong. Accounts of Vietnamese, Sino-Vietnamese, and Hmong refugees, correspondingly, paint a portrait of quite different attitudes toward personhood and achievement.[6] These accounts consistently emphasize parents' clear career or educational goals for their children. They also stress the value placed by parents on children's self-sacrifice for the benefit and prestige of the group, and the strong pressures on the child to succeed against all odds (Caplan, Whitmore, and Choy 1989:87–126; Rumbaut 1989:181–182; Whitmore, Trautmann, and Caplan 1989:131–133).

By contrast, the Khmer parents in our study tend to see their children as individuals with distinctively personal capacities, goals, and frailties. Parents believe that it is as much their role to discover these native dispositions as it is to direct the child. Parents regard their children's success in school programs with great pride, and, to the extent they can do so, they encourage their children to do their best. Nonetheless, a child's failure may in the end be rationalized as inevitable, the result of forces native to the child's character and thus outside of parental control. In such circumstances, parents believe, wisdom lies in adjusting one's demands to the pregiven capacities of the child.

CONCLUSION

According to one current theory, the fact that Southeast Asian refugees share a common social and political categorization as refugees means that they should share similar educational attitudes and patterns of achievement. The cultural ecologists' model (as described by Ogbu and Matute-Bianchi 1986; Ogbu 1987; and Gibson 1987) proposes that those who have undergone similar sociohistorical experiences and a similar pattern of oppression respond to their schooling in a similar manner.

The portrait of Khmer educational attitudes which emerges from the present study, however, suggests that this view is inadequate. The taxonomy proposed by cultural ecologists cannot satisfactorily account for the differential academic success of Southeast Asian immigrants despite the many similar characteristics they share as refugees (Trueba 1988:278). The Khmer example contrasts sharply with the accounts of extraordinary achievement attained by some other Southeast Asian refugee groups. For the Khmer, cultural identity and native notions of personhood and individual development play an important role in shaping Khmer attitudes and achievement. The present study thus supports the contention of Trueba (1988) and others who argue that social structural forces alone cannot fully explain the differential achievement of minority students, and insists on the critical role of culture.

The most important lesson to be drawn from the present study is that the Southeast Asian refugee community is culturally diverse. We cannot assume that because Southeast Asian groups share a status as refugees and as Asians, they are all alike, sharing the same desires and aspirations for the education of their children. The cultural diversity suggested by the Khmer example, moreover, underscores the need for further ethnographic and comparative research on Southeast Asian refugees, as well as other minority groups. A greater understanding of the social, cultural, and psychological characteristics of these groups is vital if we hope to assist more sensitively and successfully in the education and integration of minority children in American schools.

NOTES

Acknowledgments. Funding for research was provided by the Spencer Foundation and by a faculty development grant from the University of Massachusetts. I would like to acknowledge with appreciation the contribution of Kim Nay Biv, who assisted me through the research. I would also like to thank John Molloy, principal of Alexander-Hamilton

School in Boston, for his cooperation in allowing us to base our research in his school. Miwako Yamashina conducted interviews with Boston-area bilingual coordinators and tried to make sense of often contradictory statistics. Saren Eo, Ely Phlek, Margy DeMonchy, David Tedone, and Robert Hefner offered helpful discussion and commentary during various phases of the project. And, of course, research would not have been possible without the very kind cooperation of the Cambodian parents and community members themselves.

1. Children may be reminded by their elders, "Your parents are your first gods" (*qewpuk mdaay cie preah knong pteah*), literally, "Your parents are your god(s) within the house."
2. All names have been changed to protect the identities of the respondents.
3. In Khmer, *Twee qey twee choh tuq tae ceqeng ning pneiq qaoy knyom*, "Do whatever you want, just keep his bones and eyes for me."
4. In questioning parents about their own socialization in Cambodia, almost all could remember having been beaten rather severely on one or more occasions at home or at school, although repeated severe beatings were not common.
5. This is very different from the Javanese, among whom I conducted previous research. Javanese share many cultural features with the Khmer, however, unlike Khmer parents, Javanese expect to "shape" the child into an appropriate adult through molding and modeling, even imposing, appropriate speech and behavior on the child, through gentle, insistent repetition (Smith-Hefner 1990).
6. Lao are also Theravada Buddhists and may share some of the educational attitudes and characteristics of the Khmer. Further research is necessary, however, to determine the extent to which this is in fact the case.

REFERENCES

Caplan, Nathan, John K. Whitmore, and Marcella H. Choy. 1989. *The Boat People and Achievement in America: A Study of Family Life, Hard Work and Cultural Values*. Ann Arbor: University of Michigan Press.

Center for Applied Linguistics. 1981. *Teaching English to Cambodian Students*. Washington, D.C.: Center for Applied Linguistics.

Crawford, James. 1989. *Bilingual Education: History, Politics, Theory and Practice*. Trenton, N.J.: Crane Publishing.

Crossette, Barbara. 1988. After the Killing Fields: Cambodia's Forgotten Refugees. *New York Times Magazine*, 26 June, pp. 17–68.

Ebihara, May M. 1985. Khmer. In *Refugees in the United States: A Reference Handbook*. David W. Haines, ed. Pp. 127–147. Westport, Conn.: Greenwood Press.

Ehrman, Madeline E. 1972. *Contemporary Cambodian: A Grammatical Sketch*. Washington, D.C.: Foreign Service Institute.

Gibson, Margaret. 1987. The School Performance of Immigrant Minorities: A Comparative View. *Anthropology and Education Quarterly* 18(4):262–275.

Gordon, Linda W. 1987. Southeast Asian Refugee Migration to the United States. In *Pacific Bridges: The New Immigration from Asia and the Pacific Islands*. James T. Fawcett and Benjamin V. Carino, eds. Pp. 153–173. New York: Center for Migration Studies.

Gorgoniyev, Iuri A. 1966. *The Khmer Language*. Moscow: Nauka Publishing House.

Haines, David W. 1989. Introduction. In *Refugees as Immigrants: Cambodians, Laotians, and Vietnamese in America*. David W. Haines, ed. Pp. 1–23. Totowa, N.J.: Rowman and Littlefield.

Kelly, Gail P. 1986. Southeast Asians in the United States. In *Dictionary of Asian American History*. Pp. 1–50. New York: Greenwood Press.

Massachusetts Department of Education (MDE). 1976. *Two Way*. Boston: The Commonwealth of Massachusetts, Bureau of Transitional Bilingual Education and the Bureau of Educational Information Services.

————. 1987. *The Condition of Massachusetts*. Boston: The Commonwealth of Massachusetts.

————. 1988. *October 1 Report*. Boston: The Commonwealth of Massachusetts, Bureau of Data Collection.

Massachusetts Office for Refugees and Immigrants (MORI). 1988. *Refugees and Immigrants in Massachusetts: A Demographic Report*. Boston: The Commonwealth of Massachusetts, Executive Office of Human Services.

Ogbu, John U. 1987. Variability in Minority School Performance: A Problem in Search of an Explanation. *Anthropology and Education Quarterly* 18(4):312–334.

Ogbu, John U., and Maria E. Matute-Bianchi. 1986. Understanding Sociocultural Factors: Knowledge, Identity and School Adjustment. In *Beyond Language: Social and Cultural Factors in Schooling Language Minority Students*. Pp. 73–142. Sacramento: Bilingual Education Office, California State Department of Education.

Ouk, Mory, Franklin E. Huffman, and Judy Lewis. 1988. *Handbook for Teaching Khmer-Speaking Students*. Cordova, Calif.: Folsom Cordova Unified School District, Southeast Asia Community Resource Center.

Rumbaut, Ruben G. 1989. Portraits, Patterns and Predictors of the Refugee Adaptation Process: Results and Reflections from the IHARP Panel Study. In *Refugees as Immigrants: Cambodians, Laotians and Vietnamese in America*. David W. Haines, ed. Pp. 138–182. Westport, Conn.: Greenwood Press.

Smith-Hefner, Nancy J. 1988. The Linguistic Socialization of Javanese Children in Two Communities. *Anthropological Linguistics* 30(2):166–198.

Steinberg, David J. 1959. *Cambodia: Its People, Its Society, Its Culture*. New Haven, Conn.: HRAF Press.

Strand, Paul J., and Woodrow Jones, Jr. 1985. *Indochinese Refugees in America: Problems of Adaptation and Assimilation*. Durham, N.C.: Duke University Press.

Trueba, Henry T. 1988. Commentary: Culturally Based Explanations of Minority Student's Academic Achievement. *Anthropology and Education Quarterly* 19(2):270–287.

Whitmore, John K., Marcella Trautmann, and Nathan Caplan. 1989. The Socio-Cultural Basis for the Economic and Educational Success of Southeast Asian Refugees (1978–1982 Arrivals). In *Refugees as Immigrants: Cambodians, Laotians, and Vietnamese in America*. David W. Haines, ed. Pp. 121–137. Westport, Conn.: Greenwood Press.

12 Service Delivery to Asian/Pacific LEP Children: A Cross-Cultural Framework

Li-Rong Lilly Cheng

A MAJOR CONCERN in the field of communicative disorders today is service delivery to Asian/Pacific Islanders whose native languages are not English. Issues regarding service provision are emerging and will continue to grow in magnitude in coming years. The purposes of this article are (1) to present general information on the history, cultures, and languages of the major Asian/Pacific immigrant and refugee groups; and (2) to provide information on the types of knowledge required by professionals if they are to work effectively with Asian/Pacific limited-English-proficient (LEP) students.

HISTORY, CULTURES, AND LANGUAGES OF THE ASIAN/PACIFIC POPULATIONS

The influx of Asians/Pacific Islanders to the United States in the last decade has resulted in an increasing number of non-English-proficient (NEP) and LEP students in schools. Some are landed immigrants, while others are refugees. Immigrants file for an immigrant visa and wait for a period of time ranging from six months to four or five years before the visa interviews and screening procedures. Immigrants must have a U.S. sponsor, either a close relative or an employer. Many Asian immigrants are citizens from Malaysia, China, India, Hong Kong, Taiwan, Japan, and Korea. Refugees, on the other hand, leave their countries because of fear of persecution; many have risked their lives to escape and have left their families behind. For them the time of transition is filled with unrest, separation, anxiety, and fear. Most refugees are taken to camps until their sponsors arrange passage to the United States. Typically refugees speak no English and have never traveled beyond their homeland.

There are four types of Asian in terms of immigration status and education: (1) first-generation immigrants and refugees are those who came to the United States as young adults; (2) the "one and a half" generation were born in Southeast Asia but are being educated in the United States; (3) the second generation (*ni-sei* in Japanese) were born and educated in the United States; and (4) the third generation (*san-sei*) are those whose parents were born and educated in the United States.

The parents of the LEP populations have different levels of education. Among the refugee populations, some have very little schooling, while others have experienced repeated disruptions in schooling. It is not unusual to find a refugee adolescent with minimal formal education.

From *Topics in Language Disorders* 9:3 (1989):1–14. Reprinted with permission of Aspen Publishers, Inc. © 1989.

The refugee population is younger than the general U.S. population (mean age 32.8). Asian Youth Office of Refugee Resettlement (ORR) data indicate that approximately 40% of the more than 800,000 Southeast Asian refugees admitted to the United States from 1975 to 1986 were between the ages of 6 and 20. Furthermore, more than 200,000 Southeast Asian children were born in the United States over the last decade. Youth is the predominant characteristic of the refugee population: It is estimated that half of all Southeast Asians in the U.S. are under 18 years of age. It should also be noted that in recent years more Indochinese have arrived in the United States from Vietnam, Laos, and Cambodia. A large number of Indochinese refugees are ethnic Chinese. The Hmong and the Mien, who come from the mountains of Laos, are ethnic minorities. More than 100,000 Lao people have come to the United States in recent years. Whereas ethnic Lao people make up 50% of the total Lao population, the rest are composed of Khmu, Tai Dam, Hmong, I-Mien (Yao-Mien), and others.

Clearly there are numerous variables that one needs to consider when working with the Asian/Pacific populations. One important variable is the home language(s) of the LEP individual.

LANGUAGE PATTERNS OF THE ASIAN/PACIFIC POPULATIONS

Hundreds of distinct languages and their dialects are spoken in East Asia, Southeast Asia, and the Pacific Islands. They can be classified into five major families, each encompassing several important languages (Ma, 1985):

1. Malayo-Polynesian (Austronesian) family: Chamorro, Ilocano, Tagalog
2. Sino-Tibetan family: Thai, Yao, Mandarin, Cantonese
3. Austro-Asiatic family: Khmer, Vietnamese, Hmong
4. Papuan family: New Guinean
5. Altaic family: Japanese, Korean

The main languages spoken by Asian/Pacific populations in the United States are Mandarin, Cantonese, Taiwanese, Hakka, Tagalog, Ilocano, Japanese, Korean, Vietnamese, Khmer, Lao, Hmong, Mien, Chamorro, Samoan, and Hindi.

Southeast Asians who emigrate to the U.S. have various bilingual and biliterate backgrounds. Some of them are bilingual or trilingual, whereas others are monolingual. As was noted earlier, some come with prior education and others do not. Some read fluently in many languages; others are illiterate. Moreover, some Southeast Asian groups, like the Hmong, did not have a written language until the 1950s. While the Hmong people have a rich oral history, many are unable to read. These distinctions provide practitioners with a tremendous challenge.

Other important variables include the religious beliefs of the individual and family, which may affect their perceptions of both the world and their handicapping conditions.

RELIGIONS

The Asian/Pacific populations have a variety of religious/philosophical beliefs; among the major ones are: Buddhism, Confucianism, Taoism, Shintoism, Animism, Catholicism, and Islamism.

Buddhism, an offshoot of Hinduism, began in around the fifth century. Buddha preached kindness and nonviolence. He believed that desire is what causes human misery. Buddhist missionaries first went to Ceylon, which then became the center of Theravada Buddhism. Later, missionaries from Siam, Burma, and Cambodia went to Sri Lanka to seek clarification of the truth (Ma, 1985). Refugees from Laos and Cambodia (now Kampuchea) practice Theravada Buddhism.

Confucianism exerts a strong influence in China and Vietnam. Confucius defined the rules that dictate relationships between father and son, teacher and student, husband and wife, and so forth. His influence spread all the way to Japan and Korea. In another vein, Taoism is derived from the doctrines of Lao Tzu. The basic principle of Taoism, which many Chinese practice, is that one must not interfere with nature but must rather follow its course. Taoism promotes passivity, and those who practice it may display a sense of fatalism about events surrounding them, resulting in resignation and inaction. This basic principle of nonintervention may have a deleterious effect when parents are asked to approve interventions for remediation of language or learning disorders.

Shintoism is the principal religion of Japan, with emphasis upon worship of nature, ancestors, and ancient heroes, and reverence for the spirits of natural forces and emperors. It was the state religion until 1945, before the American occupation.

Animism is another common religion in Southeast Asia. It holds that there are spirits in everything, including one's body, and that demons and spirits exist. Baci, a ritual in animism, is a common practice among the Southeast Asians from Indochina. It is usually performed if one is ill or has to go away on a trip.

The Pacific Islanders have been influenced by Catholicism, and many do practice Catholicism with a mixture of folk beliefs, such as taotaomona/spirits (Chamorro), menehune/spirits (Hawaiian), and the suruhana/healer (Chamorro) (Ashby, 1983). A small portion of Asians are Moslem, scattered from the Malaysian islands to the Philippines. Ancestral worship is a prevailing theme in Asian beliefs, and it is practiced in China, Japan, Korea, and Vietnam. Some Asians may feel that there is nothing that can be done to alter their "karma" (fate) when a family member has a handicapping condition. The Chamorro culture regards the handicapped child as everyone's child and as a gift of God, whereas the Chinese may regard the child as a curse, a result brought about by the wrongdoings of their ancestors.

There are also differences in the child-rearing practices among the various Asian/Pacific cultures. It is not uncommon to find young children taking care of their younger siblings. Discipline may also take a different form. A less active, quiet child is often viewed as a good child. Children generally are not encouraged to explore and take risks but rather to be cautious and observant.

Another key variable is the immigration history of the child and his or her family. It is important to understand the major differences among the refugee and immigrant populations in terms of background, such as those demonstrated by the two major groups of refugees, namely the Vietnamese, Chinese, and Hmong (VCH) and the Lao and Khmer (LK).

IMMIGRATION BACKGROUND: HOME OF ORIGIN

Refugees: The VCH and LK. Researchers in Indochinese studies have observed tremendous differences within the Indochinese group (Rumbaut & Ima, 1987). For example, there is great diversity in social class among the families of Indochinese students attending U.S. schools. Overall, Vietnamese parents are the most educated, followed by the Chinese-Vietnamese, the Khmer, the Lao, and the Hmong, whose average parental education level is just above grade one. About 95% of Vietnamese and Chinese-Vietnamese refugees and 75% of the Lao are from urban backgrounds, while more than 50% of the Khmers and 90% of the Hmong come from rural backgrounds. As with any cultural group, heterogeneity within the population must be recognized even though there may be cultural ties and similarities that also link groups together.

The VCHs have similar cultural traits, including sharing of the patrilineal-extended family systems. Patrilineal-extended families were built on a Confucian cultural model that emphasizes family relationships, duties, discipline, filial piety, obedience, parental authority, and respect for the elderly. VCH languages also share some commonalities, in that they are tonal, noninflectional, and essentially monosyllabic.

LK people have common cultural roots, elements of which are borrowed from Indian culture and languages. For example, the Lao and Khmer languages are derived from Sanskrit and Pali. The LKs share similar customs, such as the same form of Theravada Buddhism. The LK group also has a looser neolocal and bilateral system of nuclear family organization than that of VCHs. The Khmer man lives with the wife's family when they are first married, and then sets up his own household. Both parents have authority over family matters.

Professionals in education and allied health services should be sensitive to, and knowledgeable about, the backgrounds of Indochinese students but should be careful to avoid overgeneralization about presumed similarities. Although they have often been referred to as the "boat people," many Indochinese actually traveled long distances on foot to leave their homelands, while others left with the assistance of the United States. The experiences of Indochinese refugees vary greatly. Some left immediately after the fall of Saigon in 1975; others spent many years in resettlement camps at the Thailand border (Walker, 1985). Some families managed to find sponsors to get their families out of their homelands, whereas others lost their families and have suffered great disruptions in their lives (Rumbaut & Ima, 1987). Those who experienced the Khmer Rouge and the Pol Pot era have been severely traumatized.

The VCH and LK cultural groups have different views and expectations. The diversity comes from differences in socio-economic levels, cultural backgrounds, education, lifestyles, concepts of illness and healing, self-care practices, child rearing practices, and family systems (Ebihara, 1968; Libby, 1984; Luangpraseut, 1987; Mitchell, 1987; Scott, 1986; Smalley, 1984; Te, 1987; Wittet, 1983). Misunderstandings caused by cultural differences often result in feelings of vulnerability, mistrust, alienation, stigma, discomfort, and social distance (Goldstein, 1985).

Nonrefugees. Many immigrants from other parts of Asia come to the United States to further their education and then decide to make it their home. Immigrants may elect to petition for permanent residency in the United States. Some immigrants are fluent speakers of English, whereas others have only a limited familiarity with the English language. Even fluent English speakers may prefer to use their first language to communicate at home. Still others, whose English proficiency may be limited, are often employed in jobs where communication in English is not a requirement. Nonrefugee groups include Pacific Islanders, including the people of Guam and the Micronesian Islands, Samoans, and Filipinos.

Pacific Islanders. An increasing number of Pacific Islanders have migrated to the state of Hawaii and the U.S. mainland in the last two decades. The Chamorro people of Guam hold U.S. passports and can travel freely to the U.S. mainland. People from American Samoa are U.S. residents and travel in large numbers to Hawaii, California, and a few other states.

The people of Guam and the Micronesian Islands. A territory of the United States, Guam lies at the southern end of the Mariana Islands in the western Pacific. It is the largest island in the Pacific Ocean between Hawaii and the Philippines—30 miles long and 4 to 9 miles wide. Chamorro is the native language of Guam and also of Saipan, Rota, and Tinian, which make up the Commonwealth of the Northern Mariana Islands. English and Chamorro are the official languages of Saipan, Rota, and Tinian. Residents of the islands speak a variety of languages including Carolinian, Trukese, Yapese, Marshallese, Palauan, Pohnpeian, and Kosraean. There are eleven languages spoken in Saipan and Guam.

The Samoans. Western Samoa is under the rule of the British government, and American Samoa is part of the U.S. territory. During the 1920s some Samoans left to provide the free labor that built the Mormon temples in Hawaii. It was not until the 1950s that large groups of Samoans left for Hawaii and the U.S. mainland. There are approximately 60,000 Samoans living in the United States, and only 30,000 remain on the island of American Samoa.

The indigenous culture of Samoa is a clan culture with an extended family system. The chief (*Matai*), who is elected by the clan members, is responsible for locating resources that include fish, food, land titles, and housing (Shore, 1986). In the Samoan language there is no word for "person," since in the Samoan culture a person is only a part of the whole group. The social system is patrilineal. The chief has authority over titles, although they can also be inherited. Chiefs speak a high form of Samoan, whereas the rest of the people speak "common Samoan." Among the many reasons why Samoans leave their homeland are a search for a better life, access to health care, better education, and an escape from the traditional authoritarian system.

American Samoa is 25 miles by 5 miles and lies 30 miles from Western Samoa. The schools in Samoa are bilingual, using the official languages of Samoan and English. However, many students from American Samoa have encountered academic problems in school and/or are considered to be LEP. Rumbaut and Ima (1987) report that in San Diego County, Samoan students have the lowest grade point average of all groups. Similar reports can be found in Hawaii, where there are also large groups of Samoans.

The Filipinos. There has been a steady flow of immigration from Philippines since the end of World War II. The 1983 Hawaiian census indicated that the Filipino population in Hawaii was over 11% and growing.

The people of the Philippines, an archipelago of more than 7,200 islands, speak a total of 87 mutually unintelligible languages. The major languages are Tagalog, Ilocano, Cebuano, Visayan, and Pampango. Some immigrants from the Philippines do not speak English at home and have little experience with the English language.

KNOWLEDGE REQUIRED TO BECOME A CROSS-CULTURAL COMMUNICATOR

School systems are challenged by the growing numbers of Indochinese students. In neighborhoods where there are large numbers of refugees, professionals such as speech-language pathologists can rely on the natural support system that includes family and community for advice and help. Where resources such as interpreters are scarce, professionals face significant difficulties when trying to provide adequate services in a cross-cultural context.

The question of denying services to culturally diverse populations because professionals are inadequately prepared warrants close scrutiny. Korman (cited in Sue, 1981) describes the dilemma clearly:

> The provision of professional services to persons of culturally diverse backgrounds not competent in understanding and providing professional services to such groups shall be considered unethical. It shall be equally unethical to deny such persons professional services because the present staff is inadequately prepared. It shall therefore be the obligation of all service agencies to employ competent persons or to provide continuing education for the present staff to meet the service needs of the culturally diverse population it serves. (p. vii)

Obviously professionals need to become cross-cultural communicators in order to provide adequate services when working with such a culturally and linguistically diverse population.

Collecting information: Guidelines for cross-cultural communication

Language learning is affected by many factors. Wong-Fillmore (1985a) indicates that children who are extremely proficient in their home language may not necessarily be the fastest learners of English. In other words, native language proficiency may not be a reliable predictor of success in learning English. Factors leading to successful English acquisition include the number of years devoted to learning English, the amount of English heard, and the kind of English used (Wong-Fillmore, 1985b).

In addition to information regarding the student's language-learning experience, areas such as cultural exposure, educational background, school experience, personal life history, family background, support systems, and health history are essential to a good assessment. A sample questionnaire, presented as an appendix to this article, may be useful for collecting information.

Personal knowledge, skills, and attitudes of professionals

It is of the utmost importance that service providers make a critical examination of their worldview, values, beliefs, way of life, communication style, learning style, cognitive style, and personal life history. One should strive for cultural literacy, described by Bjorkland and Bjorkland (1988) as the "broad working knowledge of the traditions, terminology, folklore, and history of our culture" (p. 144). Through these processes, one can gain insight into one's clinical *modus operandi*.

An appreciation and understanding of cultural diversity and affirmation of cultural differences need to be nurtured. Professionals need to develop greater knowledge of the cultural/ethnic composition of this country in order to affirm the existence of these diverse cultures (Cole & Deal, 1986). (For more information on Asian belief systems, see Anderson [1983], Lieban [1979], Moser [1983], and Muecke [1983].)

Knowledge of cultures, languages, and discourse styles

Clinicians need to identify strategies that are culturally and socially relevant. Understanding the differences between oral and literate cultures is relevant in language intervention; for example, as children become acculturated, the language of the curriculum becomes more meaningful. Mastery of academics may be even more difficult for immigrant children because from the beginning there is an absence of shared background in addition to linguistic differences (Gumperz & Hymes, 1972). For example, a child from the mountains of Laos will not know the significance of a jack-o'-lantern, and a Hmong child may not have had the experience of eating macaroni and cheese for lunch. Chamorro children may be very familiar with typhoons but unacquainted with snow. The Hawaiian student may be quite capable of understanding the details of a volcanic eruption but may fail to appreciate the meaning of a white Christmas.

Speech-language pathologists need to identify "foreground information," or that which is needed to understand the intended meaning of a speaker. Such foregrounding of information may be essential for LEP students in therapy. Highlighting crucial information is the task of the clinician.

Professionals must also question assumptions that are made about what children know (e.g., schema knowledge). Not all students have experienced a birthday party or a family picnic. Furthermore, children may not share assumptions about participant structures (Philips, 1983). Important patterns of verbal and nonverbal behavior learned at home may be quite different from the teacher's expectations. It is rude in the Japanese culture to say "No" in various contexts. One needs to interpret the communicative intent of the answer, since a "Yes" may actually mean "No."

Sociolinguistic rules such as turn-taking, turn-allocation, interruptions, topic shift, topic maintenance, and other conversational rules that underlie the interactions of LEP students must be identified. For example, students from Asia are quiet in the classroom and seldom volunteer information. The classroom is a place where teachers control turn-taking and direct turn-allocations. While these unspoken rules are shared by those who understand them, Asian/Pacific students may need further explanation, exposure, and practice.

Asian/Pacific populations often take meanings literally rather than understanding the implied communicative intent of the speaker. Although LEP students may learn the words and sentences of English, they may operate from a different socio-cultural perspective. For example, to Americans the question "Do you have the time?" actually means "What time is it?" Similarly, "Why don't we go to the park?" means "Let's go to the park," and "You like it, don't you?" means "I think you like it." LEP students may have different interpretations and thus may not respond with the expected answers. They may try to give an answer that they believe to be appropriate, such as "Yes. I have the time," rather than "It's two o'clock."

Appropriate usage of the more ritualized sociolinguistic rules—for example, accepting compliments such as "I like your work"; greetings such as "How are you doing?"; leave-taking phrases such as "Good-bye, have a nice day"; or saying "Excuse me"—may have to be taught explicitly.

Clinicians should also increase their knowledge about the home languages of LEP students and try to learn a few words from those languages (Ruhlen, 1975). Learning words in students' languages may set the tone for better communication. However, clinicians must understand that the LEP child's home language (L_1) may be deteriorating while he or she is attempting to become proficient in English.

The discourse systems of Asian/Pacific children include such rules as "Do not speak when you are eating," "Speak only when spoken to," "Do not speak in class," "Be quiet and obedient in class," and "Do not stare at the person you talk to." Whereas these students in an American school may be told by their teacher to ask questions and to challenge assumptions, the same children may be told by their parents at home to be observant and respectful of authority. The significance of such inconsistencies between home and school cultures must not be minimized (Weade & Green, 1985).

KNOWLEDGE OF FAMILY AND SUPPORT SYSTEMS

Children placed in a new environment must be given time to develop their social circle. Since all encounters are in essence social encounters (Taylor, 1986), children must feel part of a group before they can engage in peer interactions. Fellow students from the same ethnic, linguistic, and cultural backgrounds who tend to be sociable need to be encouraged to work with the newcomers (Erickson, 1979) to show them the rules of the classroom and the school.

Professionals should consult with classroom teachers, who are frequently the best informants about the children's social status. They should also make use of all people who provide support for the child. This may include parents, siblings, friends, neighbors, relatives, and even the community as a whole. For example, to whom does the parent go to seek advice? Who provides assistance when there is a family crisis or emergency? Who makes the decisions about education in the family? Who provides translation for the family if it is needed?

As always, clinicians need to obtain detailed information about the student and his or her family. Once a referral is received, a face-to-face interview with the family should be arranged. If time allows, a home visit by a member of the assessment team should be made. Information should be obtained about what the family is like, how the child is functioning, and what child care needs may exist. Questions such as "What is a typical day like?" "What do you do during the weekends?" and "What does your child like or dislike?" would be appropriate.

During any personal contact with an Asian student's family, clinicians should always keep in mind the cultural values associated with the family's background. Individual family members are expected to submerge behaviors and feelings in a way as to reflect credit on the entire family. Inappropriate behavior on the part of one family member can cause the whole family to be shamed and "lose face." Failure in school may be considered to be shameful behavior; such problems are typically handled within the family as much as possible, without public admission. The same restraint of feelings that is valued in Asian culture may be seen as passive and inhibited behavior in American culture. Professionals need to identify LEP populations, including their language backgrounds, residing in their school district. Especially when only a few students from a particular language group are scattered among different schools in the district, efforts should be made to locate more proficient students who speak the LEP student's language and to enlist their assistance. This may also lead to their families supporting one another. Additionally, service professionals should consider the possibility that peer teaching by more proficient Asian students may be less threatening to the Asian LEP population. Peer instruction may also be more closely matched with the LEP's learning style.

It is imperative that professionals provide assessment and intervention within a cross-cultural framework using all available resources from both cultures.

REFERENCES

Anderson, J. N. (1983). Health and illness in Filipino immigrants. *Western Journal of Medicine*, 139(6). 811–819.

Ashby, G. (1983). *Micronesian customs and beliefs*. Eugene, OR: Rainy Day Press.

Bjorkland, D., & Bjorkland, B. (1988, January). Cultural literacy. *Parents*, p 144.

Cole, I. & Deal, V. (1986). *Communication disorders in multicultural populations*. Rockville, MD: American Speech-Language-Hearing Association.

Ebihara, M. M. (1968). *Svay, a Khmer village in Cambodia*. Unpublished doctoral dissertation. Columbia University.

Erickson, F. (1979). Talking down: Some cultural sources of miscommunication in interracial interviews. In A. Wolfgang (Ed.), *Nonverbal Behavior* (pp. 99–126). New York: Academic Press.

Goldstein, B. I. (1985). *Schooling for cultural transition: Hmong girls and boys in American high schools*. Madison, WI: University of Wisconsin.

Gumperz, J. & Hymes, D. (1972). *Directions in sociolinguistics: The ethnography of communication*. New York: Holt, Rinehart, Winston.

Libby, M. R. (1984). *The self care practices of the Hmong hilltribes from Laos*. Unpublished master's thesis. University of Missouri.

Lieban, R. (1979). Sex differences and cultural dimensions of medical phenomena in a Philippine setting. In P. Morley & R. Wallis (Eds.). *Culture and curing* (pp 99–114). Pittsburgh: University of Pittsburgh Press.

Luangpraseut, K. (1987). *Introduction to Lao culture*. Paper presented at the Southeast Asia Education Fair. Stockton, CA.

Ma, L. J. (1985). Cultural diversity. In A. K. Dutt (Ed.), *Southeast Asia: Realm of contrast*. Boulder, CO: Westview Press.

Mitchell, F. S. (1987). *From refugee to rebuilder: Cambodian women in America*. Unpublished doctoral dissertation, Syracuse University.

Moser, R. (1983). Indochinese refugees and American health care: Adaptive comparisons of Cambodians and Hmong. In J. H. Morgan (Ed.). *Third world medicine and social change* (pp 141–156). Lanham, MD: University Press of America.

Muecke, M. A. (1983). In search of healers—Southeast Asian refugees in the American health care system. *Western Journal of Medicine*. 139(6). 835–840.

Philips, S. (1983). *The invisible culture*. New York: Longman.

Ruhlen, M. (1975). *A guide to the languages of the world (Language Universals Project)*. San Diego: Los Amigos Research Associates.

Rumbaut, T. & Ima, K. (1987). *The adaptation of Southeast Asian refugee youth: A comparative study*. San Diego: San Diego State University

Scott, G. M. (1986). *Migrants without mountains: The sociocultural adjustment among the Lao Hmong refugees in San Diego*. Unpublished doctoral dissertation. University of California, San Diego.

Smore, B. (1986). *Salailua village*. Chicago: University of Chicago Press.

Smalley, W. A. (1984). Adaptive language strategies for the Hmong: From Asian mountains to American ghettos. *Language Science*. 7(2), 241–269.

Sme, D. W. (1981). *Counseling the culturally different: Theory and practice*. New York: John Wiley and Sons.

Taylor, O. (1986). *Treatment of communication disorders in culturally and linguistically diverse populations*. San Diego: College-Hill Press.

Te, H. D. (1987). *Introduction to Vietnamese culture*. San Diego: Multifunctional Resource Center, San Diego State University.

Walker, C. I. (1985). Learning English: The Southeast Asian refugee experience. *Topics in Language Disorders*, 5(4) 53–65.

Weade, R. & Green, J. I., (1985). Talking to learn: Social and academic requirements for classroom participation *Peabody Journal of Education*. 62. 6–19

Wittet, S. (1983). *Information needs of Southeast Asian refugees in medical situations*. Unpublished master's thesis. University of Washington.

Wong-Fillmore, I. (1985a). Learning a second language: Chinese children in the American classroom In J. F. Alatis & J. J. Staczek (Ed.), *Perspectives on bilingualism and bilingual education*, pp. 436–452. Washington, DC: Georgetown University Press.

Wong-Fillmore, I. (1985b). When does teacher talk work as input? In S. M. Gass & C. G. Madden (Eds.). *Input in second language acquisition*, pp 17–30. Rowley, MN: Newbury House.

13 The Education of White, Chinese, Filipino, and Japanese Students: A Look at "High School and Beyond"

Morrision G. Wong

IN RECENT YEARS, a frequent topic of scholarly interest and discussion in the field of education has been the extraordinary educational attainment of the Asian population—the Japanese, Chinese, Filipinos, Koreans, Asian-Indians, and Vietnamese—in the United States. Articles with titles such as "The Triumph of Asian Americans," "Why Asian Students Excel," "A Formula for Success," "Asians: To America with Skills," and "The New Whiz Kids" have also appeared in the popular press regarding the phenomenal educational achievements of the Asian population in general or the extraordinary educational achievements of a member of a particular Asian group (Bell 1985; Brand 1987; Butterfield 1986; Divoky 1988; Doerner 1985; Lee and Rong 1988; Shin 1988; *U.S. News and World Report* 1988; Williams and McDonald 1984).

However, there are two sides to this story. Despite their high educational attainment, Table 1 also reveals that, with the exception of the Japanese, a greater proportion of Asians than whites were at the lower end of the educational spectrum. For example, whereas only about 2.6 percent of the white population completed less than five years of education, the corresponding figures were 10.3 percent for the Chinese and Vietnamese and 7.0 percent for the Filipinos. Despite the bimodal distribution in educational achievement among these Asian groups, it is usually the high end of the Asian educational spectrum that receives publicity and media attention. More recently, charges of the use of quotas and discrimination in the recruitment and selection of qualified Asian students have been filed against several selective universities such as the University of California at Berkeley, Harvard, Columbia, and Brown (Barinaga 1988; Bunzel and Au 1987; Hsia 1988; Molotsky 1988; Salholz 1987; Shimatsu 1987; Sue 1985; Wilson 1988).

This article examines in greater depth the educational characteristics of the Asian high school seniors. In order to accomplish this task, differences in the social, demographic, and academic characteristics, the degree of participation in extracurricular activities, and the sociopsychological orientations (e.g., educational perceptions, aspirations, expectations, and influences) among Chinese, Filipino, Japanese, and white high school seniors in the United States is examined. Multivariate analyses are conducted to ascertain the impact of the major variables involved in the educational expectations of Asian and white students. Lastly, unresolved issues in the education of Asians are discussed.

From *Sociological Perspectives* 33 (1990): 355–374. Reprinted with permission by JAI Press, Inc.

Table 1. Education Levels, Percent Completed High School, and Median Years of Education of White, Japanese, Chinese, Filipino, Korean, Asian Indian, and Vietnamese Individuals, 25 Years of Age or Older: 1980

Education	White	Japanese	Chinese	Filipino	Korean	Indian	Vietnamese
Elementary							
0–4 years	2.6	2.3	10.3	7.0	4.0	3.1	10.3
5–7 years	5.8	3.4	7.9	7.9	6.5	4.1	10.6
8 years	8.2	4.6	3.0	2.5	3.2	4.1	4.3
High School							
1–3 years	4.6	8.1	7.4	8.4	8.3	8.6	12.6
4 years	35.7	35.7	19.6	18.1	28.6	14.7	29.3
College							
1–3 years	16.0	19.5	15.0	19.0	15.8	13.5	20.0
4-years	17.1	26.4	36.6	37.0	33.7	51.9	12.0
Pct completed high school	68.8	81.6	71.3	74.2	78.1	80.1	62.2
Median years of education	12.5	12.9	13.4	14.1	13.0	16.1	12.4

Source: U.S. Census. 1983. Tables 123 and 160.

DATA AND VARIABLES

The "High School and Beyond" survey, a national longitudinal study of the cohorts of high school seniors and sophomores in the United States in 1980, was utilized (U.S. National Center for Educational Statistics 1980).[1] In this paper I undertake separate analyses of the major Asian groups. Although one could combine all Asians for analytical purposes, this would mask the diverse cultural and ethnic differences among the several Asian groups. Students identifying themselves as Chinese (89), Filipino (96), and Japanese (103) were included in the analyses. Because there were major questions and concerns regarding the representativeness of the Asian Indian sample when compared to the 1980 U.S. Census, they were not included in the analysis. Moreover, Korean (47), Vietnamese (26), Pacific Islander (19), and Other Asian (21) students were not included because of their small sample size. Only white and Asian high school seniors were selected. This sample yielded 11,757 whites and 288 Asians.

Most of the variables are relatively self-explanatory and require no elaboration. However, the variable, Socioeconomic Status (SES) does require some discussion. The "High School and Beyond" data set provides a standard SES variable, which is a composite scale constructed from father's occupation, mother's education, family income, and a set of items that ask whether the student's family receives a daily newspaper, owns an encyclopedia or other reference books, has a typewriter, owns an electric dishwasher, owns two or more cars or trucks, has more than fifty books, owns a pocket calculator, and whether the student has his or her own room. This composite scale of socioeconomic status was then divided into three different ranks—high, middle, and low. Although this socioeco-

---

[1] The "High School and Beyond" survey was conducted by the National Research Center on behalf of the National Center for Educational Statistics. The sample was a two-stage stratified probability sample with schools within a stratum drawn with a probability proportional to their size. Once a school was selected, up to 36 sophomores and 36 seniors were drawn randomly from the students enrolled in each selected school. Overall, approximately 58,000 students at 1,015 schools completed questionnaires. The data set represents a population of 3.8 million sophomores and three million seniors in more than 21,000 schools in spring of 1980.

nomic ranking scale is different from that utilized by Duncan (1961), it is adequate for the descriptive portion of this paper.

SOCIAL AND DEMOGRAPHIC CHARACTERISTICS

Before discussing the academic characteristics of the Asian and white high school seniors, it may be informative to first look at their social and demographic characteristics. Although Asian and white students can be found in every part of the United States, Asian students are more residentially concentrated in certain areas of the United States. Two-thirds to three-fourths of the Chinese, Filipino, and Japanese students live in the West. White students are more geographically dispersed, but about one-third live in the North. Japanese students are the most residentially concentrated of the Asian groups with about 80 percent living on the West Coast. The Chinese are the second most concentrated group with about 88 percent living on the West or East Coast.

Although a majority of fathers of Asian and white students are employed in white-collar occupations, there are important differences among specific occupational categories. Fathers of Chinese students are much more likely to work in management or as proprietors (e.g., small "mom and pop" stores) and less likely to work in the crafts than their white counterparts. Filipino fathers differ from white fathers in being more involved in the professions and the military and less in management and crafts. The occupational distribution of the fathers of Japanese students is very similar to white students. Differences also exist among the Asian groups. Filipino fathers are much more likely to be involved in the professions and the military, Chinese fathers in service and, to a lesser degree, in management, and Japanese fathers in crafts than their Asian counterparts.

Fathers of Asian students had educational achievements that were equal to or higher than the fathers of white students. A larger proportion of fathers of Asian students had graduated from college and possess postgraduate education than their white counterparts. However, it should be noted that over one-third of the fathers of Chinese students had less than a high school education compared to about 20 percent of their white counterparts.

Except for a few differences, the occupational distribution of the mothers of Asian and white students is very similar. One difference is the slightly higher proportion of unemployed white mothers. Mothers of Chinese students are more likely to be managers or proprietors (e.g., small "mom and pop" stores) and less likely to be involved in clerical occupations, and mothers of Filipino students are about twice as likely to be in the professions (e.g., nurses) than their white counterparts. Among the three Asian groups, Chinese mothers are more likely to be employed as managers and proprietors, Filipino mothers in the professions, and Japanese mothers in clerical occupations.

Mothers of Asian students are overrepresented at both extremes of the education continuum when compared with their white counterparts. Mothers of Filipino and Japanese students attained higher educational levels than mothers of white students, being two to two and a half times more likely to have some college, have graduated from college, or have postgraduate education. On the other hand, mothers of Chinese students were the least educated of the Asian groups with close to half having less than a high school education.

The differences in the occupational and educational characteristics between the parents of Asian and white high school students were reflected in their socioeconomic status. A greater proportion of Japanese and Filipino students were at the high end of the socioeconomic continuum compared with white students. On the other hand, Chinese students were almost twice as likely than white students to have lower socioeconomic status. Of the three Asian groups, the Japanese not only have the highest socioeconomic status, but also the lowest proportion with low socioeconomic status—a mere 11 percent.

Table 2. Social and Demographic Characteristics of the White, Chinese, Filipino, and Japanese High School Seniors

Characteristics	White	Chinese	Filipino	Japanese
Region				
West	15.1	64.0	64.9	78.6
East	21.7	23.6	6.4	1.9
North	33.3	7.9	16.0	9.7
South	29.8	4.5	12.8	9.7
Father's occupation				
Professional	20.6	22.4	31.3	21.4
Manager and proprietor	26.9	37.3	10.0	31.0
Clerical	7.8	7.5	10.0	4.8
Crafts	26.9	13.4	16.3	22.6
Service	1.7	16.4	1.3	4.8
Labor	8.8	1.5	11.3	3.6
Farm	5.0	—	2.5	8.3
Military	2.1	—	17.5	3.6
Not Employed	0.2	1.5	—	—
Father's education				
Less than high school	19.7	35.8	11.1	9.5
High school graduate	31.3	19.4	22.8	23.8
Some college	23.0	12.0	27.9	33.3
College graduate	13.5	16.4	19.0	19.0
Post graduate	12.5	16.4	19.0	14.3
Mother's occupation				
Professional	18.0	14.7	33.7	21.7
Manager and proprietor	7.6	16.2	4.8	6.5
Clerical	33.6	14.7	27.7	37.0
Crafts	7.0	13.2	8.4	2.2
Service	10.0	14.7	7.2	10.9
Labor	2.5	10.3	7.2	2.2
Farm	0.6	—	—	2.2
Military	0.1	—	1.2	—
Not Employed	20.7	16.2	9.6	17.4
Mother's education				
Less than high school	15.2	43.9	18.1	7.3
High school graduate	45.7	22.7	14.5	34.1
Some college	23.7	19.7	26.5	42.7
College graduate	10.2	9.1	28.9	11.0
Postgraduate degree	5.1	4.5	12.0	4.9
Socioeconomic status				
Low	23.3	40.2	23.4	10.9
Middle	50.2	39.1	38.2	53.5
High	26.5	20.7	38.3	35.6
Family income				
Less than $7,000	4.5	12.2	8.2	3.2
$7–16,000	25.2	40.5	27.0	18.3
$16–25,000	37.9	29.7	28.2	33.4
$25–38,000	17.9	6.8	20.0	21.5
$38,000+	14.6	10.8	16.5	23.7
Nativity status				
Born in U.S.	97.5	41.6	47.9	78.6
Foreign-born	2.5	58.4	52.1	21.4

Source: High School and Beyond Data Set.

Japanese and Filipino families were more economically advantaged than white families with a greater proportion having incomes at the high end of the income distribution. This may be due to the higher proportion of multiple workers in Asian families (U.S. Census 1983). However, a greater proportion of Filipino than white families were also at the lower end of the income distribution. Chinese families had a greater proportion at the lower end and a smaller proportion at the higher end of the income distribution than white families. One explanation for this finding may be that, despite their greater proportion of multiple workers in the family, Asian workers are involved in jobs which enable them to barely make ends meet (Wong 1983) or serve in the ethnic economy at substandard wages (Light and Wong 1975).

White high school students are overwhelmingly native-born with about 98 percent being born in this country. The majority of Japanese students were also born in the United States. In sharp contrast, the majority of Chinese and Filipino students are foreign-born. Recent studies suggest that, with the exception of the Japanese, the proportion of foreign-born Asian students has increased and projections suggest that it will continue to increase dramatically during the next decade (Bouvier and Agresta 1987; Gardner, Robey, and Smith 1985).

ACADEMIC CHARACTERISTICS

The question which may now be addressed is: how different are the Asian and white high school seniors with regard to such academic characteristics as the type of high school program, courses taken, grades, and hours spent on homework? The most striking finding is that Asian students have equivalent or higher levels of achievement on practically all academic characteristics compared with white students. They were more involved in academic programs and more likely to take college preparatory courses. For example, the proportion of Asian students taking such courses as Algebra I, Algebra II, Geometry, Trigonometry, Calculus, Physics, Chemistry, Advanced English, and Advanced Math was substantially higher than white students. Moreover, Asian students received higher grades in high school than white students. As expected, a greater proportion of Chinese students received A's and B's in math than white students. Unexpected was the greater proportion of Japanese and Filipino students receiving A's and B's in English than white students.

The comparatively larger number of Asian students receiving high grades may be partially accounted for by the fact that they report spending a greater number of hours on homework per week. Filipino and Japanese students were twice as likely—and Chinese students, three and a half times more likely—to spend ten or more hours doing homework than white students. Moreover, they were more likely to spend 5–10 hours per week on homework than white students. Of the three Asian groups, the Chinese spent the most time on homework. An interesting, and for some a discouraging feature of contemporary high school education, is the finding that about 27 percent of the white students as well as from 1 to 8 percent of the Asian students report not doing any homework or spending less than one hour per week on it.

Another indicator of the seriousness with which students view their education is the number of days they are absent from school, but not ill. About one-quarter of the white students had never been absent from school compared with about one-third of the Filipino and Japanese and almost one-half of the Chinese. Moreover, Chinese students were also less likely than whites or other Asians to cut class.

Many teachers consider Asian students "model students" (Wong 1981). Despite this perception, Asian students were just as likely as white students to consider themselves to be a discipline problem. However, they were half as likely than white students to be placed on probation or suspension.

Table 3. Academic Characteristics of White, Chinese, Filipino, and Japanese High School Seniors

Characteristic	White	Chinese	Filipino	Japanese
High school program				
General	36.0	42.7	35.1	28.2
Academic	41.0	43.8	50.0	62.1
Vocational	23.0	13.5	14.9	9.7
Algebra 1	82.3	89.7	88.0	94.1
Algebra 2	53.0	80.7	59.3	78.2
Geometry	61.6	83.0	71.4	78.4
Trigonometry	30.1	64.4	31.4	52.0
Calculus	9.7	19.8	22.6	23.7
Physics	21.7	39.5	28.2	36.8
Chemistry	41.5	62.8	58.1	54.1
Computer	12.5	17.4	18.2	10.0
Advanced English	28.2	33.0	45.2	40.8
Advanced math	24.7	43.2	25.5	39.8
High school grades				
Mostly A	13.7	19.1	17.0	20.4
A & B	44.0	56.2	47.9	47.6
Math grades (A & B)	46.3	62.9	43.6	47.6
English grades (A & B)	52.9	49.4	59.6	66.0
Hours spent on homework				
Don't do homework	7.4	1.1	2.1	7.7
Less than 5 hours	67.0	48.3	57.4	48.6
5–10 hours	18.8	24.7	30.1	
10 + hours	6.9	25.8	13.8	13.6
Absent from school, not ill				
0 days	26.6	45.5	31.9	34.0
1–4 days	53.9	43.1	40.5	52.4
5–10 days	13.2	5.7	17.0	8.7
11–20 days	5.0	5.6	5.4	3.9
21 + days	1.3	—	5.3	1.0
Cut class	42.7	32.2	40.9	40.2
Discipline problem	12.2	15.1	12.9	9.8
Probation or suspension	11.5	5.7	5.4	6.9

Source: High School and Beyond Data Set.

The above findings suggest that Asian students take their education much more seriously than white students—being more involved in academic high school programs and more likely to enroll in college preparatory courses. They spend more time doing homework, and, probably as a consequence, achieve higher grades. Chinese students tend to be more involved in college preparatory courses, spend more time on homework, are absent from school less, and are less likely to cut class than other Asian students.

EXTRACURRICULAR ACTIVITIES

In documenting the high educational achievements of Asians, one might ask if there is correspondingly high participation in other arenas of high school life. A common stereotype of Asians is that they show considerable intellectual aptitude, especially in the technical fields, and that they are model students. A related perception is that they are socially inept and do not fit very well into the overall school social structure or general environment. Table 4 looks at the proportion of white, Chinese, Filipino, and Japanese seniors involved in selected high school extracurricular activities. The data shown in Table 4 suggest that

Table 4. Extracurricular Activities of White, Chinese, Filipino, and Japanese High School Seniors

Activities	White	Chinese	Filipino	Japanese
Varsity	35.4	28.1	31.9	35.3
Other sports	41.5	30.3	36.5	46.1
School activities	15.6	4.5	21.5	11.9
Debate	15.6	12.4	11.9	7.0
Band	15.3	7.8	19.8	17.7
Choir	20.7	13.8	27.8	11.0
Honor clubs	18.8	11.2	25.5	26.8
School newspaper	21.0	18.0	22.8	17.8
Subject clubs	23.6	21.4	23.6	26.8
Student government	18.6	17.1	24.2	19.0

Source: High School and Beyond Data Set.

white-Asian differences in participation in selected extracurricular activities depends upon differences within the Asian group.

Chinese students are less likely than whites to involve themselves in the ten selected extracurricular activities. This is particularly true for "other sports" and "school activities." But even for activities such as varsity, band, choir, and honor clubs, there is a much greater involvement by whites than by Chinese.

Filipino students show a different pattern. They are more involved in school activities, choir, and honor clubs than whites. No basic differences were found for the other extracurricular activities.

Of the ten extracurricular activities, Japanese students are more involved in honor clubs and less in choir, and to a lesser degree, in debate than white students.

In sum, the data suggest that the stereotype of Asians as socially inept and not actively involved in the high school social environment may be applicable only to Chinese students. Except for a few instances, differences among the participation rates of Filipino, Japanese, and white students are minimal. Separate analyses controlling for nativity suggest that much of the similarity in involvement in extracurricular activities is due to the overparticipation of the native-born Asian students.

SOCIOPSYCHOLOGICAL DIFFERENCES

What are the sociopsychological differences between Asian and white students that may account for differences in education? Table 5 compares the educational perceptions, aspirations, expectations, and influences of white and Asian high school seniors. One major difference is that Asian students are more likely than whites to be interested in academics and enjoy working hard at school and feel that their school should place a greater emphasis on academics, such as basic math, science, and English. Asian students were about as equally satisfied with their education as white students. There were basically no differences among the Asian groups in their attitudes toward education.

Asian students report having higher educational expectations and aspirations than white students. From 76 to 91 percent of the Asian students say they would be disappointed if they did not attend college, as compared with about 62 percent of the white students. Compared with whites, a higher proportion of Asian students are planning on attending a four-year college and feel themselves able to complete college. Moreover, Asian students, more so than white students, expect to graduate from college and/or receive a graduate degree. They are also more likely than white students to say that the lowest acceptable level

Table 5. Educational Perceptions, Aspirations, Expectations, and Influences of White, Chinese, Filipino, and Japanese High School Seniors

Activities	White	Chinese	Filipino	Japanese
Interested in school	73.1	82.0	87.1	82.4
Like working hard in school	51.0	73.6	70.7	59.8
More academic emphasis	70.3	80.3	84.7	81.6
Satisfied with education	70.2	69.3	61.7	73.3
Disappointed if not a college graduate	62.3	87.6	91.3	75.7
Plan to attend a four-year college	31.4	56.2	42.6	39.8
Have the ability to complete college	81.9	88.8	83.0	92.2
Educational expectation				
Less than high school	0.3	—	—	—
High school graduate	18.9	3.5	10.1	3.9
Some college	33.5	14.0	20.2	19.6
College graduate	26.7	38.4	36.0	34.3
Postgraduate degree	20.5	44.2	33.7	42.2
Lowest education acceptable				
Less than high school	1.2	—	1.1	—
High school graduate	34.4	8.0	14.0	13.6
Some college	34.8	37.9	38.7	38.8
College graduate	22.8	41.4	30.1	36.9
Postgraduate	6.8	12.6	16.1	10.7
Occupational aspiration				
Professional	52.0	63.2	62.6	67.6
Manager and proprietor	12.6	16.1	13.2	13.7
Sales and clerical	11.6	8.0	11.0	4.9
Crafts and operatives	10.4	5.7	4.4	5.9
Service	3.3	2.3	3.3	2.0
Labor	1.9	1.1	2.2	2.0
Farm	2.2	—	—	3.9
Military	1.8	2.3	1.1	—
Not employed	4.2	1.1	2.2	—

Table 5. *Continued on next page*

of education was some college, college graduation, or a postgraduate degree. Of the three Asian groups, Chinese students have the highest educational expectations.

The high educational aspirations and expectations of Asian students are also reflected in their higher occupational aspirations compared with whites. Although the majority of white and Asian students aspire to professional occupations, the proportion is much higher for the Asian groups. About half of the white students compared to about two-thirds of the Asian students aspire to professional occupations.

A common perception of Asian students is that they tend to concentrate in specific college programs, especially premed studies, engineering, computer science, and the natural and physical sciences. Do Asian high school students anticipate studying in these fields in college? The answer is "yes and no." As expected, the proportion of students who anticipate majoring in some technical field reveals some differences between white and Asian students. Japanese students are slightly more likely and Chinese students twice as likely than white students to anticipate studying in a technical field. Interestingly, the proportion of white students who anticipate majoring in the physical sciences is equal to Chinese and Filipino students and slightly higher than Japanese students. Filipino students are much

Table 5. *Continued*

Activities	White	Chinese	Filipino	Japanese
Anticipated field of study in college				
Agriculture	3.3	—	—	2.1
Technical	16.0	38.7	16.7	22.9
Humanities	28.1	12.0	20.8	29.2
Physical sciences	12.8	12.0	12.5	9.4
Business	22.5	22.7	29.2	19.8
Preprofessional	6.7	10.7	16.7	9.7
Vocational	5.4	4.0	—	4.2
Other	5.1	—	4.2	3.1
Father monitors high school work	29.3	42.5	30.5	30.3
Mother monitors high school work	15.8	25.2	18.5	20.5
Father's influence after high school	82.1	80.0	88.1	81.5
Mother's influence after high school	87.9	88.6	90.3	89.3
Father's plans for student after high school				
College	63.1	89.2	81.1	83.7
Job	12.4	—	2.2	1.0
Trade	9.2	3.6	3.3	6.1
Military	3.3	—	7.8	2.0
Don't know	12.1	7.2	5.6	7.1
Mother's plans for student after high school				
College	67.6	86.9	91.3	88.3
Job	12.0	1.2	2.2	1.0
Trade	9.5	6.0	1.1	6.8
Military	2.3	1.2	3.3	—
Don't know	8.6	4.8	2.2	3.9

Source: High School and Beyond Data Set.

more likely to major in a professional field and Chinese students half as likely to major in the humanities than white students. Among the Asian groups, the Chinese are much more likely to major in the technical fields, Filipinos students in business, and Japanese students in the humanities than their Asian counterparts.

It is commonly believed that Asian families are much more tightly knit than their white counterparts; that due to tradition and customs, Asian parents exert a greater influence and have a greater impact on the life choices and life chances of their children than white parents (Wong 1988). If this is the case, then one would expect a greater proportion of Asian than white parents monitoring their children's work, having an influence on their work, and having expressed specific plans for their children's future. However, of the three Asian groups, only Chinese parents monitor their children's work to a greater extent than the white parents. There were basically no differences between Asian and white parents in parental influence after high school. However, Asian parents are more likely than white parents to plan that their child go to college after high school.

In sum, there were some major differences in sociopsychological characteristics between Asian and white students. Asian students tend to be more interested in school, have higher educational expectations and aspirations, and were more likely to aspire to professional careers than white students. Although Asian students were found to be slightly more likely to anticipate majoring in a technical field, they are just as likely to major in the physical sciences as white students. Moreover, a greater proportion of Asian parents have made plans for their child to go to college than white parents.

DETERMINANTS OF EDUCATIONAL EXPECTATIONS

The findings of the previous section suggest that Asian students have much higher educational expectations than white students. A greater proportion of Asian students expect to graduate from college than white students. Even more dramatic and important is that about 44 percent of the Chinese, 34 percent of the Filipino, and 42 percent of the Japanese students expect to attain some postgraduate degree compared with only 20 percent of the white. What accounts for these differences in educational expectations between the Asian and white students?

In order to assess the impact of educational expectations, multivariate regression analysis was performed. Ethnicity was recorded into three dummy variables: foreign-born Asian students, native-born Asian students, and white students. The reference group are the white students. The variable "Socioeconomic Status" posed a slight problem. In order to get a more accurate indicator of socioeconomic status than the three-category scale provided by the data set, the sixteen categories of occupation were reassigned a mean score derived from the 1980 U.S. Census occupational codes (Stevens and Cho 1985). The variables "Father's Plans for Child After High School" and "Mother's Plans for Child After High School" were recoded "0" to represent "Not College" and "1" to represent "College." The "Educational Expectations" variable also posed a minor problem as it was operationalized by type of education (i.e., high school graduate, some college, vocational education, Ph.D, etc.). The mean number of years for each of these categories was selected with a range from 10 (less than high school education) to 22 years of education (Ph.D). The Chinese, Filipino, and Japanese students were analyzed separately. Table 6 displays the results of this analysis.

Looking first at the general patterns or relationships between educational expectations and selected variables, the findings first confirm that Asian students have higher educational expectations than white students. This was especially true for the native-born Japanese students. All the variables in the model—Socioeconomic Status, Father's Plans for Child After High School, Mother's Plans for Child After High School, High School Grades, and Hours Spent on Homework per Week—had a significant effect on the educa-

Table 6. Determinants of Educational Expectations of White, Chinese, Filipino, and Japanese High School Seniors

Variable	Beta		
	Chinese	Filipino	Japanese
Foreign-born asian	.0136	.0145	−.0043
Native-born asian	.0047	.0170	.0255**
Socioeconomic status	.1569***	.1572***	.1570***
Father's plans	.2127***	.2137***	.2113***
Mother's plans	.1678***	.1663***	.1678***
High-school grade	.1952***	.1952***	.1951***
Hours spent on homework	.1760***	.1764***	.1774***
Adjusted R2	.3729	.3732	.3728

Source: High School and Beyond Data File.
Notes: $*p < .05$; $**p < .01$; $***p < .0001$

tional expectations of Asian and white students. About 37 percent of the variance was explained by these seven variables.

The variables differed in their impact on the educational expectations of Asian and white students. As indicated by the beta weights, the father's plans for the child after high school had the greatest impact on the educational expectations of the students. This was followed by high-school grades and the number of hours spent on homework per week. Mothers' plans for the child after high school also had a significant impact on the students' educational expectations, but it was not as great as that of the fathers' expectations. Socioeconomic status, although significant, had a lesser impact on the educational attainment of the students than the other variables.

The educational process, at least in terms of educational expectations, is governed by both ascriptive characteristics (parental socioeconomic status and the parental plans after high school for the student) and achieved characteristics (the number of hours spent on homework per week and grades in high school). The implications of these findings are discussed in the next section.

ISSUES IN ASIAN EDUCATION

One of the basic tenets of the American educational system is that it serves as the great equalizer; that regardless of social and economic background, anyone can "make it" to the top, can go as high or as far as they wish. It is presumed that the educational system is a meritocratic system based strictly on ability, hard work, and rugged individualism. Many Asian parents, especially from the lower or working class or of immigrant background, believe in the verity of these espoused characteristics and are willing to forego luxuries and undergo extreme economic and social sacrifices so that their children can obtain a college education, and hopefully, have more comfortable lives than they have had. Although this study, as well as many others (Bowles and Gintis 1976), questions the purely meritocratic nature of our educational system, the fact still remains that many Asian parents believe in this aspect of the American Dream. To them, education is the only available channel of social mobility. However, their consequent substantial investment in their children's college education at a disproportionate sacrifice to family finances and social well-being causes one to question whether a college education should be regarded necessarily as a sign of success (Chun 1980:3).

This study, as well as others (Endo 1980, 1984; Schwartz 1971), has found that Asian parents have a significant influence and place considerable pressure on their children to achieve academically. Although such influence and pressure may encourage many Asian students to reach their full potential, it may not be without consequences. The lack of superior academic performance by Asian students may lead to feelings of personal guilt that they are failing or not living up to parental expectations. These feelings of guilt or failure may become even more intense if the students believe that their parents had undergone great financial burden and sacrifice so that they may receive a college education. Each year, there are reports from colleges and universities on the West Coast of suicides or attempted suicides by Asian students. Although conjectural, it may be that some of these Asian students were guilt-ridden by their lack of academic success and felt that they had disgraced or failed their parents and family (Caudill 1962; DeVos 1960; Fischer 1988).

Despite their college education or their advanced degrees, many Asian students fail to develop adequate oral or written communication skills in English. With the changes in immigration policies implemented by the Immigration Act of 1965 (Hirschman and Wong 1981; Wong 1985, 1986; Wong and Hirschman 1983), the demography of the Asian population and Asian students is rapidly changing (Gardner et al. 1985). They are becoming increasingly foreign-born. Despite the lack of facility with the English language, many of these Asian immigrant students are able to gain entrance to colleges, universities, graduate, or professional schools through a "risk aversive strategy" (Hsia 1988). For Asian high school students, this strategy usually entails an over-concentration in advanced courses in science and mathematics and a minimal concentration of English courses. The short-term benefit to this strategy is that the grade point averages of these Asian students go up and their scores on the quantitative section of college entrance examinations are, on the average, higher than white students, allowing them admission into colleges and universities. When in college, the same "risk aversive strategy" is employed. Asian students tend to concentrate in such fields as business, mathematics, science, and engineering. This allows them to gain entrance into graduate or professional schools. Although such a strategy may allow many Asian students to obtain short-term goals (e.g., entrance into college and graduate or professional school), their long-term goals may be severely curtailed. Their lack of facility with the English language, whether involving written and/or oral communication skills, may place an insurmountable barrier to their further socioeconomic and career advancement.

A similar argument has been proposed by Suzuki (1977), who argues that Asian students, partly because of their concentration in the technical fields, are being educated and socialized to be robots, to work in lower white-collar positions such as computer or systems analysts, draftspersons, and lower-level technicians and engineers. They are not educated or trained for decision-making, administrative positions. In essence, they are perceived as good technocrats, but not persons capable of decision-making or supervisory responsibilities. Moreover, as the character of Asian immigration to the United States changes—from those possessing scarce skills to those being reunited with their families—the educational character of the Asian population will surely change. Further research is needed to document these changes.

One last issue which deserves mention is the dramatic increase in qualified Asian applicants to major universities within recent years. In many cases, the Asian applicant pool is much greater than their population would warrant. Yet, Asian students are finding that the gates to higher education are beginning to close. At the same time, there has been a corresponding increase in the number of charges or accusations by various members of the Asian community of unequal treatment, insensitivity, racism, bias in the college entrance examinations, differential and additional admission criteria, and the specter of quotas. It has been charged that the university's defense of "diversity" is another, subtler form of racism (Bunzel and Au 1987; Greene 1987). If such exclusionist policies exist, they call into question the cherished foundation of equality of educational opportunity. How universities resolve this dilemma of diversity vs. meritocracy will have tremendous implications for the future of higher education in American society and the educational future of Asian Americans.

References

Barinaga, Marcia. 1988. "Enrollment Mix Raises Ethnic Issue at Berkeley, California." *Nature* 331:4.
Bell, David A. 1985. "The Triumph of Asian Americans." *The New Republic* (July 14 and 22):24–31.
Bouvier, Leon F. and Anthony J. Agresta. 1987. Pp. 285–301 in *Pacific Bridges: The New Immigration from Asia and the Pacific Island*, edited by James T. Fawcett and Benjamin V. Carino. Staten Island, New York: Center for Migration Studies.
Bowles, Samuel and Herbert Gintis. 1976. *Schooling in Capitalist America: Educational Reform and the Contradictions of Economic Life*. New York: Basic Books.
Brand, David. 1987. "The New Whiz Kids: Why Asians Are Doing So Well and What It Costs Them." *Time* (August 31):42–51.

Bunzel, John H. and Jeffrey K. D. Au. 1987. "Diversity or Discrimination: Asian Americans in College." *Public Interest* 87:49–63.

Butterfield, Fox. 1986. "Why Asian Students Excel." *The New York Times* (August 3):22–25.

Caudill, William. 1962. "Patterns of Emotion in Modern Japan." Pp. 115–131 in *Japanese Culture*, edited by Robert J. Smith and Richard K. Beardsley. Chicago: Aldine.

Chun, Ki-Taek. 1980. "The Myth of Asian American Success and Its Educational Ramifications." *IRCD Bulletin* 15:1–12.

DeVos, George. 1960. "The Relation of Guilt toward Parents to Achievement and Arranged Marriages Among the Japanese." *Psychiatry* 23:287–301.

Divoky, Diane. 1988. "The Model Minority Goes to School." *Phi Delta Kappa* 70:219–222.

Doerner, William R. 1985. "Asians: To America with Skills." *Time* (July 8):42–44.

Duncan, Otis Dudley. 1961. "A Socioeconomic Index for All Occupations." Pp. 109–138 in *Occupations and Social Status*, edited by A. J. Reiss, Jr. New York: Free Press.

Endo, Russell. 1980. "Asian Americans and Higher Education." *Phylon* 41:367–378.

———. 1984. "Race and Educational Ambitions: The Case of Japanese Americans." *Pacific/Asian American Mental Health Research Center Research Review* 3:1–3.

Fischer, Bill. 1988. " 'Whiz Kid' Image Masks Problem of Asian Americans." *NEA Today* 6:14–15.

Fogel, Walter. 1966. "The Effects of Low Educational Attainment on Income: A Comparative Study of Selected Ethnic Groups." *Journal of Human Resources* 1:22–40.

Gardner, Robert W., Bryant Robey, and Peter C. Smith. 1985. "Asian Americans' Growth, Change and Diversity." *Population Bulletin* 40(4):1–44.

Greene, Elizabeth. 1987. "Asian Americans Find U.S. Colleges Insensitivities, Form Campus Organizations to Fight Bias." *Chronicle of Higher Education* 34:38–40.

Hirschman, Charles and Morrison G. Wong. 1981. "Trends in Socioeconomic Achievement Among Immigrant and Native-Born Asian Americans, 1960–1976." *Sociological Quarterly* 22:495–513.

———. 1984. "Socioeconomic Gains of Asian Americans, Blacks, and Hispanics: 1960–1976." *American Journal of Sociology* 90:584–607.

———. 1986. "The Extraordinary Educational Attainment of Asian Americans: A Search for Historical Evidence and Explanations." *Social Forces* 65:1–27.

Hsia, Jayjia. 1988. *Asian Americans in Higher Education and at Work.* Hillsdale, NJ: Lawrence Erlbaum Associates.

Hurh, Won Moo and Kwang Chung Kim. 1984. *Korean Immigrants in America: A Structural Analysis of Ethnic Confinement and Adhesive Adaptation.* Madison, NJ: Fairleigh Dickinson University Press.

Institute for Social Research. 1985. "Working Toward Self-Sufficiency." *ISR Newsletter* Spring Summer:4–7.

Kitano, Harry H. L. 1976. *Japanese Americans: The Evolution of a Subculture.* Englewood Cliffs, NJ: Prentice-Hall.

Kitano, Harry H. L. and Roger Daniels. 1988. *Asian Americans: Emerging Minorities.* Englewood Cliffs, NJ: Prentice-Hall.

Lee, Everett S. and Xue-lan Rong. 1988. "The Educational and Economic Achievement of Asian Americans." *The Elementary School Journal* 88:545–560.

Levine, Gene N. and Darrel M. Montero. 1973. "Socioeconomic Mobility Among Three Generations of Japanese Americans." *Journal of Social Issues* 29:33–48.

Light, Ivan and Charles Choy Wong. 1975. "Protest or Work: Dilemmas of the Tourist Industry in American Chinatowns." *American Journal of Sociology* 80:1342–1368.

Lyman, Stanford M. 1974. *Chinese Americans.* New York: Random House.

Molotsky, Irvin. 1988. "Harvard and U.C.L.A. Facing Inquiries on Quotas for Asians." *The New York Times* (November 20) A1:18, 35.

Montero, Darrel and Ronald Tsukashima. 1977. "Assimilation and Educational Achievement: The Case of the Second-Generation Japanese American." *Sociological Quarterly* 18:490–503.

Petersen, William. 1971. *Japanese-Americans: Oppression and Success.* New York: Random House.

Salholz, Eloise. 1987. "Do Colleges Set Asian Quotas? Enrollments Are Up, But They Could Be Higher Still." *Newsweek* (February 9):60.

Schmid, Calvin F. and Charles E. Nobbe. 1965. "Socioeconomic Differentials Among Non-White Races." *American Sociological Review* 30:909–922.

Schwartz, Audrey James. 1970. *Traditional Values and Contemporary Achievement of Japanese American Pupils*. University of Southern California: California Center for the Study of Evaluation.

———. 1971. "The Culturally Advantaged: A Study of Japanese American Pupils." *Sociology and Social Research* 55:341–351.

Shimatsu, Yoichi. 1987. "Whiz Kids' Have a Right to Excel Too." *East/West* (October 1):3.

Shin, Frank H. 1988. "Asian American Students on College Campuses." *Education Digest* 54:59–62.

Stevens, Gillian and Joo Hyun Cho. 1985. "Socioeconomic Indexes and the New 1980 Occupational Classification Scheme." *Social Science Research* 14:142–168.

Sue, Stanley. 1985. "Asian Americans and Educational Pursuits: Are the Doors Beginning to Close?" *Pacific/Asian American Mental Health Research Center Research Review* 4:25.

Suzuki, Bob H. 1977. "Education and the Socialization of Asian Americans: A Revisionist Analysis of the 'Model Minority' Thesis." *Amerasia Journal* 4:23–51.

U.S. Bureau of the Census. 1983. *1980 Census of the Population*. Volume I. *Characteristics of the Population*. Chapter C. General Social and Economic Characteristics. U.S. Summary. PC80-1-C1. Washington, DC: U.S. Government Printing Office.

U.S. Commission on Civil Rights. 1978. *Social Indicators of Equality for Minorities and Women*. Washington, DC: Commission on Civil Rights.

U.S. National Center for Educational Statistics. 1980. *High School and Beyond, 1980: A Longitudinal Survey of Students in the United States*. [MRDF] National Opinion Research Center (producer) Ann Arbor: Inter-university Consortium for Political and Social Research (distributor).

U.S. News and World Report. 1988. "What Puts the Whiz in Whiz Kids?" March 14, pp. 48–53.

Vernon, Philip E. 1982. *The Abilities and Achievements of Orientals in North America*. New York: Academic.

Williams, Dennis A. and Dianne H. McDonald. 1987. "A Formula for Success: Asian American Students Win Academic Honors—and Cope with the Mixed Blessings of Achievement." *Newsweek* (April 23):77–79.

Wilson, Robin. 1988. "U.S. Studies Policies at Harvard, UCLA on Admitting Asians; Public Concern Over Quotas Cited; Universities Vehemently Deny Bias." *The Chronicle of Higher Education* (November 30):A1–A2.

Wong, Morrison G. 1980a. "Changes in Socioeconomic Status of the Chinese Males in the United States from 1960 to 1970." *International Migration Review* 14:511–524.

———. 1980b. "Model Students?: Teachers' Perceptions and Expectations of Their Asian and White Students." *Sociology of Education* 53:236–246.

———. 1983. "Chinese Sweatshops in the United States: A Look at the Garment Industry." Pp. 212–225 in *Research in the Sociology of Work*, Volume II, edited by Ida H. Simpson and Richard L. Simpson. Greenwich, CT: JAI Press.

———. 1985. "Post-1965 Immigrants: Demographic and Socio-economic Profile." Pp. 51–71 in *Urban Ethnicity: New Immigrants and Old Minorities*, edited by Lionel A. Maldonado and Joan W. Moore. *Urban Affairs Annual Review*. Volume 29. Beverly Hills, CA: Sage Publishers.

———. 1986. "Post-1965 Asian Immigrants: Where Do They Come From, Where Are They Now, and Where Are They Going?" *The Annals of the American Academy of Political and Social Science* 487:150–168.

———. 1988. "The Chinese American Family." Pp. 230–257 in *Ethnic Families in America: Patterns and Variations*, edited by Charles H. Mindel, Robert W. Habenstein, and Roosevelt Wright, Jr. New York: Elsevier.

Wong, Morrison G. and Charles Hirschman. 1983. "The New Asian Immigrants." Pp. 381–403 in *Culture, Ethnicity, and Identity: Current Issues in Research*, edited by William C. McCready. New York: Academic.

14 Barriers to Higher Education for Asian/Pacific-American Females

Rosalind Y. Mau

THIRTY YEARS AGO a high school diploma was a means of getting a good job and a better societal status. Today, a college diploma is necessary for pursuing high-paying jobs and upward social mobility. Immigrants seek a better life in the United States through a dream of education for their children. Many realize their dream, but others see their children struggling in school and not entering higher education.

Immigrants and native-born Asian/Pacific Americans (APA) are great believers in education as a way to achieve equality of occupational opportunity. Demographically, the APA population is a growing, predominantly immigrant group living in urban areas of the United States (U.S. Bureau of the Census, 1983). This heterogeneous population—Asian Indians, Chinese, Filipinos, Guamanians, Hawaiians, Japanese, Koreans, Samoans, Vietnamese, and others—differs in ethnicity, language, culture, history, values, and behavior norms.

The assumption is Asian/Pacific Americans have no problems in school and achieve well academically. Studies of Asian Americans have supported this assumption: The average mathematics test scores of high school seniors by number of years of mathematics taken, ethnic group, and gender show that Asian/American females in the aggregate are only a few points below white males (College Entrance Examination Board, 1985). The High School and Beyond national study found that Asian American students have higher average test scores in mathematics and science and have more credits in high-level mathematics and science than white students (Peng, Owings, and Fetters, 1984) (see Tables 1 and 2). In another study, Rothman (1988), using a congressionally mandated assessment of a national sample of students, showed that Asian students significantly outperform all other groups at all grade levels in mathematics. Yet in another study, Brandon, Newton, and Hammond (1987) analyzed mathematics subtests of annual statewide Stanford Achievement Tests (SAT) in Hawaii and found that from 1982 to 1984 Japanese American students achieved higher than all other ethnic groups in the study.

With the arrival of new immigrants from Southeast Asia, and the inclusion of Pacific Islanders in the census data, the academic achievement of Asian/Pacific Americans has changed. A range of percentiles designed to provide policy makers with information on student achievement supports the notion that APAs are indeed a heterogeneous minority group. For example, percentiles of students in grade 12 show differences in mathematics achievement among different ethnic groups: Chinese (71.2), Filipino (53.3), Japanese (72.1),

From *The Urban Review* 22 (1990): 183–197. Reprinted with permission of Human Sciences Press, Inc.

Table 1. Average Scores on Mathematics and Science in the 10th and 12th Grades, by Racial/Ethnic Group

Racial/Ethnic Group	Mathematics		Science	
	10th	12th	10th	12th
Asian	16.6 (.86)	18.8 (.91)	9.2 (.43)	10.8 (.50)
White	15.5 (.18)	17.6 (.19)	10.3 (.08)	11.3 (.08)
Black	6.5 (.31)	8.2 (.33)	5.6 (.16)	6.4 (.16)
Hispanic	7.7 (.30)	9.1 (.30)	6.5 (.14)	7.5 (.15)
American Indian	7.8 (1.15)	10.3 (1.24)	7.6 (.68)	8.7 (.68)

Source: Peng, Owings, and Fetters (1984).
Figures in parentheses are standard errors.

Korean (74.9), and Southeast Asian (56.9) (California Department of Education, 1986). In a 1986 survey of 8,471 teenagers (grades 7–12) taken in Hawaii, 82.1% of the Asians planned to go to college and 54.6% of the Hawaiian/South Pacific Islanders planned to pursue higher education.

The APA category is institutionalized in most national data systems, which precludes an accurate assessment of subpopulations included in the APA category. For example, the Samoan group is a relatively small subpopulation that is underrepresented in college enrollments (University of Hawaii, 1987). Luce (1985) lamented that Samoan students suffer severe education deprivation because their poor academic achievement is obscured by grouping data on Pacific Islanders with the more urbanized and culturally different Asian Americans who generally do better academically than Samoan students.

In addition to a diversity of ethnicities in the APA category, there is a gender differentiation. APA females face similar cultural and socioeconomic status (SES) barriers to higher education as males, but females also are socialized into traditional roles. Such roles as homemaker, secretary, and other service-oriented jobs do not require a college degree.

This paper examines barriers to higher education for subpopulations of Asian/Pacific-American females, namely Hawaiian, Samoan, and Filipino. Cultural, socioeconomic, gender, and school barriers to higher education are multiplied for these groups of Asian/Pacific Americans. Therefore, research literature on these topics has relevance to the conceptualization of the paper.

CULTURAL DIFFERENCES

For some ethnic groups, values learned in the home culture are different from values rewarded in the school culture. For example, a pattern of behavior learned in the home of nei-

Table 2. Average Number of Credits in High-Level Mathematics and Science, By Racial/Ethnic Group

Racial/Ethnic Group	Mathematics		Science	
Asian	1.65	(1.36)	.84	(1.08)
White	1.09	(1.26)	.46	(.84)
Black	.50	(.89)	.23	(.57)
Hispanic	.48	(.93)	.17	(.49)
American Indian	.38	(.84)	.23	(.62)

Source: Peng, Owings, and Fetters (1984).
High-level mathematics includes geometry, algebra II, advanced algebra, trigonometry, calculus, statistics, and other advanced mathematics.
High-level science includes advanced biology, chemistry, advanced chemistry, physics I, and advanced physics.
Figures in parentheses are standard errors.

ther "showing off" in front of adults nor incurring shame by responding incorrectly is appropriate at home. From a student's point of reference, this behavior is correct, but schoolteachers may misidentify this student as shy or uncooperative. Conversely, competing for academic grades and individual achievement is appropriate in schools but inappropriate in some homes where the focus is on group cooperation (Clark, 1983).

Teaching styles based on competitive standards are not congruent with cooperative learning understood by Pacific Island children. Creativity, competition, individual response, and individual problem solving are encouraged in American schools. By contrast, experiential learning, group problem solving, and learning by rote are stressed at home. Luce (1985) suggested that a lack of knowledge of Pacific Island cultures among educational agencies and teachers contribute to educational problems for many students.

The cultural differences theory espouses that students from cultures with a similar educational orientation as the school culture do better than other ethnic groups with a different orientation. Many school personnel are unfamiliar with student values and nonverbal behaviors of Asian and Pacific Islander cultures. Children who choose an inappropriate response for either home or school context may find themselves in familial conflict or in academic and social difficulty (Hawaii Department of Labor, 1984).

Since a greater proportion of APAs are foreign-born (see Table 3) and not proficient in English, they may also lack high-level sentence structures, concepts, and English vocabulary required to do advanced mathematics and science. Cole and Griffin (1987) indicated that bilingual students have more difficulty than monolinguals in solving mathematics problems requiring semantic processing. Although studies have not directly focused on school performances in mathematics and science courses of limited English-proficient students, understanding and solving problems written in English may be difficult for them.

A disproportionately large number of certain minority groups drop out of the educational pipeline prior to completing high school or entering higher education (Astin, Astin, Green, Kent, McNamara, and Williams, 1982). In the Asian American group proportionately more Filipino Americans than Japanese Americans have poor academic performances and drop out of school. Scholastic Aptitude Test scores of Filipino American, Native Hawaiian, and Samoan American groups were lower by about 75 points on both mathematics and verbal tests than Chinese and Japanese Americans. So while some Asian/Pacific American groups are well represented in college enrollments, the Native Hawaiians, Filipinos, and Samoans are proportionately underrepresented at a state university (University of Hawaii, 1987).

Table 3. 1980 Population of Asian/Pacific Americans in the United States

	Subtotal	Foreign-Born	
		Number	Percent
Chinese	812,178	514,639	59
Filipino	781,894	505,389	63
Japanese	716,331	203,338	28
Asian Indian	387,223	272,617	70
Korean	357,393	292,573	82
Vietnamese	245,025	221,649	90
Hawaiian	172,346	2,812	2
Samoan	39,520	14,082	36
Guamanian	30,695	2,919	10
Other	183,835	152,756	83
Total	3,726,440	2,182,639	

Source: United States Bureau of the Census (1983).

Conflict theorists suggest that the school system based on majority group values prepares children of the majority group to compete for desirable roles in society (Scimecca, 1987; Bowles and Gintis, 1964). Among the Asian/Pacific group, Chinese, Japanese, and Koreans share similar educational values as the majority group. Consequently, these Asian groups generally compete well in the academic context, get college degrees, and obtain professional/managerial jobs (Alu Like, Inc., 1988). Other APA students from Filipino, Native Hawaiian, and South Pacific Islander families are underrepresented in colleges. One explanation is the traditional Polynesian learning in the household with its informal setting is a radical contrast with middle-class American methods of teaching and learning.

Ogbu (1984) suggests that certain ethnic groups are educationally prepared for subordinate roles in society. Many teachers treat racial minorities differently from white students by encouraging minority students to take less challenging, nonacademic courses. Teachers may feel it is better to prepare minority students for jobs they can readily get after schooling. Moreover, a lack of role models in professional and technical fields verify students' belief that they cannot succeed in these fields.

SOCIOECONOMIC STATUS

Recent research on low SES of families has called into question the cultural explanation of educational achievement. Lack of money creates stress during acculturation. It often fosters dissonance, lack of educational and material success, and in many cases, deviant behaviors (Campbell, 1984; Bowker and Klein, 1983). Sources of family stress from poverty, unemployment, and other social problems hamper the ability of students to learn in school. Many adults from the South Pacific and Southeast Asia have limited educational or technical training and have severe difficulty in gaining access to the labor market. One report showed that 25% of the estimated 20,000 Samoans living in Hawaii are on welfare and in public housing (Brewer and Hosek, 1987).

Low SES affects the internal structure of community resource-sharing networks and strategies for meeting current needs (Brewer and Hosek, 1987). APA students in the United States experience less rigid standards of behavior than their parents or grandparents who came from a foreign country. Students seeking rewards from individual initiative threaten the stability of the extended families who traditionally have cooperated and shared resources with one another. Parents who expect obedience from their children and teachers who expect respect within their classrooms are often disappointed. Moreover, parents under pressure to support their families have little time to encourage their children to study academic courses. Children themselves internalize family stress, which may lower their self-esteem and lessen their concentration on school subjects (Franco, 1987). Schorr and Schorr (1988) concluded that children who differ in class, race, education, and family income from those of the school staff may perceive school as the enemy.

A lack of money and support for higher education is a barrier to higher education. A college education is too costly for families who are struggling to meet immediate needs of food, shelter, and clothing. Some minority students are hampered by their parents' diminished aspirations for them, which are a result of the parents' lack of higher education and a need for additional family income from a child working right after high school (Schwartz, 1987).

GENDER

A structural barriers approach is followed when females find themselves in blocked mobility situations. Females in these situations tend to limit their aspirations, take fewer challenging subjects, and seek satisfaction in sociable peer groups. Another approach is a normative barriers one, which suggests that girls are socialized to view professional jobs such as doctors and lawyers as "typically male" occupations and inappropriate for females (Fiorentine, 1987, p. 1126). O'Leary (1974) showed that girls anticipate a conflict in undertaking nontraditional female or male-dominated roles. Also, Lenney (1977) and Deaux (1976) indicated that girls when compared to boys receive less encouragement to achieve from parents and teachers. Girls were found to be less confident in their ability to perform successfully in achievement-oriented situations.

In the school setting, female students are not encouraged to enroll in higher mathematics and science courses. If they do, they are frequently ignored while the teacher concentrates on male students who are assumed to pursue mathematics and science careers (Goleman, 1987).

Research has shown that males generally outperform females in secondary school mathematics and science courses (College Entrance Examination Board, 1985; Kahle, 1983). As girls progress in school, they are registered in less advanced courses. Berryman's (1983) data showed that underrepresentation of black females in quantitative fields is partly a function of their lack of enrollment in science and mathematics courses. Moreover, Wong, Franklin, and Merritt (1987) found that significantly more males felt that mathematics is more appropriate for males than females. About half of the girls in their study felt that mathematics is in a "male domain." Many girls choose not to enroll in higher-level mathematics and science courses which, may in turn, lower their grade point average on applications for college entrance. These girls then exclude themselves from better-paying and prestigious jobs in science, engineering, and high-level computer work. APA females often do not pursue their potential in mathematics and/or science because they lack confidence in their abilities, have few role models in technological fields, and feel discrimination in school. By the time girls reach high school, many have already lost their interest in mathematics and science because of an earlier lack of achievement in these areas and/or social pressure from their family and teachers (Cole and Griffith, 1987).

School grades primarily measure academic performance, but grades are influenced by teachers who assign grades. Some teachers frequently ignore girls in their high-level mathematics and science courses, assuming that female students cannot grasp the subject matter and that males will more likely pursue careers in these fields (Goleman, 1987). Other teachers see few successful Asian/Pacific-American women in technical fields so they may feel that APA girls cannot succeed in these fields. Yet other teachers may not encourage girls to take high-level mathematics and science courses because these students cannot speak English well and may face employment discrimination in the workplace. In addition, teachers from minority groups who could serve as role models are limited. More of these teachers could help minority group students understand opportunities and strategies for improving their life chances (Grant and Gilette, 1987; Badura and Walters, 1963).

In brief, APA parents expect their children to graduate from high school and even pursue postsecondary schooling. Children do realize how important graduating from high school is to their parents yet dropout rates in urban areas are increasing. While APA parents hope their children will go to college. Native Hawaiians who comprise 21% of the public school enrollment, Filipinos 19%, and Samoans 3% are proportionately underrepresented at the state university (University of Hawaii, 1987). Steinberg, Blinde, and Chan (1984) documented that many minority students leave school and consequently experience limited income and career prospects, leading to social costs of billions of dollars for welfare and training programs.

Cultural differences between home and school as well as socioeconomic disparities affect minority groups including Asian/Pacific Americans in the United States. Bias expe-

rienced by Asian/Pacific-American females is not only the result of individual teachers'
and parents' conduct. Bias has been institutionalized in the school setting through tracking
when some groups are steered away from a curriculum of higher-level mathematics and
science. From a review of the literature, it can be surmised that APA females have multiple barriers to higher education. This paper, following a sociocultural approach, further explores these barriers from the point of view of a sample of students from Filipino, Native
Hawaiian, and Samoan families living in Hawaii. One barrier is the difference between
home and school cultures, which interfere with learning. Another barrier is the socialization of APA females into traditional roles in the home and school. In the school higher-
level mathematics and science courses may not be encouraged by teachers. By not
registering and/or completing these courses, the likelihood of having acceptable college entrance examination scores is diminished. Even if a student is accepted to college, a lack of
high-level mathematics and science courses may hinder a satisfactory completion of required college courses.

METHOD

Approximately equal numbers of Filipino-American (15), Native Hawaiian (15), and
Samoan-American (16) girls completed a written questionnaire and an oral history in the
spring of 1987. The hour-long questionnaires and hour-long oral history narratives were
analyzed for socialization patterns in the home and school settings as well as their views
on the traditional role for women. In addition, data on mathematics and science courses and
grade point averages were collected from school records in the registrar's office.

The girls in grades 10, 11, and 12 attended an urban public high school in Hawaii.
Data from this sample of Filipino, Native Hawaiian, and Samoan-American females were
similar to data from a sample taken at two other Hawaii public high schools (Mau, 1988),
and a high school characterized by a selected student body representing a proportionate
number of ethnic and socioeconomic groups in Hawaii (MacDonald, 1987). The cumulative grade point averages for South Pacific and Hawaiian students were lower, and they
were in less demanding mathematics sections than Chinese, Japanese, and Korean groups.

Since national studies sample small numbers of Filipino, Samoan, and Hawaiian females, and since these ethnic groups are combined within the Asian/Pacific category, it is
difficult to establish that patterns of coursework taken by this sample of APA females is
significantly different from coursework taken by other American females.

RESULTS FROM COURSEWORK AND NARRATIVES FROM APA FEMALES

For this sample of APA females, grade point averages ranged from 1.66 to 1.75 on a 4.0
scale. Most of the girls enrolled in low-level mathematics and science courses to meet graduation requirements. Over a quarter were not enrolled in any mathematics class and over
half were enrolled in mathematics courses below algebra (Table 4).

About half of the APA girls in this sample were not enrolled in any science course,
about a fifth were in general science courses, and about a third were enrolled in chemistry,
physics, and biology (Table 5). Nontraditional careers such as engineers, researchers, and
executive-type positions often require more basic science knowledge than traditional positions like secretaries, teachers, and hotel workers. Therefore, many of these girls may indeed be inadvertently self-selecting themselves from successfully competing for college
admission and professional jobs by not enrolling in mathematics and science courses during their high school years.

Table 4. Number of Math Courses Taken in 1986–87 By Girls from Filipino-American, Native Hawaiian, and Samoan-American Families

| | Grades | | | |
Mathematics Courses	10th	11th	12th	Totals
No mathematics courses	5	6	15	26
Courses for Stanines 1–3				
Math Applications	15	7	3	25
Pre-Algebra	6	2		8
Courses for Stanines 3–4				
Math Problem Solving	7	1		8
Business Mathematics	2			2
Courses for Stanines 5–6				
Core Algebra			2	2
Geometry		4	6	10
Courses for Stanines 7–9				
Algebra			2	2
Calculus			2	2
Total				85

Data source in Honolulu high school transcripts of 46 female students from 1986–87. Stanines represent scores on the Stanford Achievement Test taken in the 8th or 10th grade. Stanines range from a low 1 to a high of 9. Prerequisites for mathematics courses are based primarily on stanine scores.

Table 5. Number of Science Courses Taken in 1986–87 By Girls from Filipino-American, Native Hawaiian, and Samoan-American Families

| | Grades | | | |
Science Courses	10th	11th	12th	Totals
No science courses	19	12	19	50
Courses for Stanines 1–3				
Marine Science	2	4		6
Skills in Science	8			8
Biology BSCS SM	12			12
Courses for Stanines 3–4				
Human Physiology			3	3
Zoology			4	4
Courses for Stanines 5–6				
Directed Studies (Science)			2	2
Biology BSCS I			6	6
Courses for Stanines 7–9				
Chemistry			2	2
Physics				6
Total				99

Data source in Honolulu high school transcripts of 46 female students from 1986–87. Stanines represent scores on the Stanford Achievement Test taken in the 8th or 10th grade. Stanines range from a low of 1 to a high of 9. Prerequisites for science courses are based primarily on stanine scores.

TRADITIONAL ROLE SOCIALIZATION IN THE HOME

According to the girls' narratives, they are socialized into traditional roles in the home. Early experiences and responsibilities of many Filipino- and South Pacific-American girls depend substantially on their birth order. Within the home setting, older children care for the younger ones and are responsible for most of the household chores.

The women in the family take care of all the household chores. We get up early in the morning and have breakfast by seven. We then clean up. If school is not in session, we do the same thing for lunch and are expected to clean the house spic and span. Not one speck of dust can remain. The girls prepare dinner and clean up the house before bedtime. I have lots of experience cooking and cleaning. The boys in the family are responsible for the outside of the house. The traditional roles for men and women are carried on in my generation.

A sophomore of Samoan ancestry

"I'm happiest when I am out of the house. I have the responsibility of caring for my brothers. I watch them, cook, and clean for them," shared a Samoan girl born fourth in a family of eight.

Younger children are disciplined by their older siblings and listen to them as they would their parents. Another girl in the study said, "I have a big family. I am the youngest of five sisters and seven bothers. My mother is a grandmother and my older sister was the one who raised me." In addition to caring for their own family members, girls have to cook for and entertain extended family members who visit their home. One girl wrote that she preferred being at school even if she hated it because she could see all her friends there and did not have to work so hard at home.

Since the traditional role for girls is watching younger siblings and cleaning the home, their role at home may interfere with their role as students. The APA girls in this study expressed role conflicts between their home and school settings. Some of the girls in the study felt negatively toward their subordinate role at school. Many of the older girls assumed authority positions over younger children at home, but were in subordinate roles in school. Bossiness observed by teachers in the classroom may be a behavior transferred from the older girls' role in the home.

Another thing the girls expressed was the priority of responsibilities. They said that often their time at home was used to do household tasks rather than studying. As a result, they have less time to study and participate in extracurricular activities.

Like most parents, Asian/Pacific-American parents have high educational expectations for their children. They know that education is a means to good jobs and higher incomes. However, many parents neither understand the workings of the educational system nor how to counsel their children in pursuing higher education. Two girls wrote about their parents' educational expectations for them:

> My parents have encouraged us to do our best in school and not to miss one day. They raised us believing that school is important to survive in life. One of the happiest times of my life has to be when I graduated from high school. I fulfilled my parents' expectations and [I] was so happy that I actually cried. I didn't really care for school, but I knew I finally had accomplished something.

> My parents always told us that we should get a good education. They told my brothers the same thing that they told the girls. I know now that my parents were right. I wish I had taken them a little more seriously. Although I graduated, I I really didn't do as well as I could have.

For parents who realize the importance of education, especially developing high mathematic and science skills, a child's poor grades indicate to them that their child is not smart enough to pursue high-level mathematic and science courses. An eleventh grader in this study said, "My parents have a high regard for education. They expect everyone to graduate from high school and some to go on to college. They already know that I am not college material. I sometimes feel I'm not even high school material."

Traditional Role Socialization in the School

Students who are not fully acculturated into the American school system often face academic and social difficulties in school. Some teachers negatively stereotype students and some students may feel discrimination in their classes. Except for one girl's story about discrimination against her by one of her teachers, no incidents of negative stereotyping by school personnel were revealed in this study. Most of the girls liked school. However, none of the teachers encouraged the girls to take higher-level mathematics and science courses and/or encourage them to attend college.

> I really enjoy math. I have a pretty cool teacher. He makes the class fun and enjoyable. I wish he taught all of my classes or that more teachers were like him. Everyone likes his classes, especially me. . . . If all teachers just added a little excitement, kids would learn more.

> I graduated from high school, but just barely. I had to attend summer school so that I could receive my diploma on time. Another year in school might have made me drop out. I thank God that I made it through high school. . . . I'm working now, but I want to go back to school and get an education that will allow me to make a career for myself.

Most of the girls liked their teachers and a girl wrote how a counselor helped her:

> My school counselor is good. I wanted to take all easy classes next year. It is my last year after all. She told me that she wanted me to take harder classes because I've got the ability to do higher-level work. I have taken computer data processing classes, but I didn't take a math course this year. Next year I will take algebra. I didn't want to but she persuaded me to do it.

The girls in the study thought school personnel were generally helpful. The reason seems to be that the girls could negotiate with adults in schools whereas at home there existed a top-down communication. At home children are taught to follow instructions without questioning the authority of parents. Children make requests of adults indirectly and accept their decisions without arguing. In school, students have the opportunity to confront and challenge teachers.

Of this sample of APA females, only four had plans to pursue higher education: one at the local university and three at a community college. They explained that they can begin working at a full-time job after two years of community college rather than four years at a university. All but four girls in the sample belonged to families who were on welfare.

Conclusion

Asian/Pacific-American parents dream of education as a way for their children to have a better life in terms of more income and status. Access to higher education is based on high school academic performance and the ability to financially and socially pursue higher education. Especially for immigrant APA females, the adjustment and acculturation to a new culture is difficult. Families still rely on females to care of the younger ones and to clean and cook. Teachers in schools do not openly encourage APA females to enroll in coursework to prepare them for college entrance examinations and college classes.

Some APA females have conflict of roles between home and school. At home they tell younger ones what to do, but in school they must listen and follow the teachers' instructions. In addition, many are lured away from their family cultural values by liberal attitudes of their American peers. Behavior considered a normal part of growing up in an American family often becomes an act of rebellion in an Asian/Pacific-American family.

Cultural conflicts emerge between home and school settings that leave many adolescents confused and frustrated.

Besides cultural conflicts, most Asian/Pacific-American females face socialization into traditional roles both at home and school. Responses from the sample of girls indicate that the role of females is to cook, clean, and watch younger brothers and sisters. In school, poor academic performance influences students' enrollment in high school courses. For this sample of APA girls, the cumulative grade point averages were low/average and the mathematics and science courses enrolled in were few and low-level. Usually, students prepare for college by enrolling in a mathematics course each of their four years in high school. Girls who are enrolled in lower levels of mathematics are not preparing themselves to meet minimum standards of college entrance examinations or may not pass examinations for state, federal, or business jobs. Consequently, they are unprepared for college entrance examinations and/or work placement tests. They unknowingly self-select themselves from nontraditional jobs with higher pay and status because of their traditional role socialization in their homes and schools.

Findings from this study show that when Asian/Pacific-American females are examined more closely (focusing on Filipino, Native Hawaiian, and Samoan Americans), then greater proportions do not proceed to higher education. The majority of girls in this sample were in lower-level mathematics and science courses and had aspirations of going on to community colleges or work rather than to the university.

Further research is needed on a longitudinal basis with a larger sample size of Asian/Pacific-American female groups. Case studies could compare home background, school performances, and college enrollment of APA females who pursued higher education with those who did not.

REFERENCES

Alu Like, Inc. (1988). *Native Hawaiian Students at the University of Hawaii: Implications for Vocational and Higher Education*. Honolulu, Hawaii: University of Hawaii Department of Sociology and Social Science Research Institute.

Astin, A., Astin, H., Green, D., Kent, L., McNamara, P., and Williams, M. (1982). *Minorities in Higher Education*. San Francisco: Jossey-Bass.

Badura, A., and Walters, R. (1963). *Social Learning and Personality Development*. New York: Holt, Rinehart and Winston.

Berryman, Sue E. (1983). *Who Will Do Science?* New York: The Rockefeller Foundation.

Bowker, L., and Klein, M. (1983). The etiology of female juvenile delinquency and gang membership: A test of psychological and social structural explanations. *Adolescence* 18:739–751.

Brandon, P., Newton, B., and Hammond, O. (1987). Children's mathematics achievement in Hawaii: Sex differences favoring girls. *American Educational Research Journal* 24:437–461.

Brewer, N., and Hosek, L. (1987). Samoans' budget woes erode the old traditions. *Honolulu Star Bulletin*, July 14, p. A-1.

California Department of Education (1986). Twelfth grade CAP results, 1985–86, percentile rank by language groups. In L. Olsen, ed., *Crossing the Schoolhouse Border*. San Francisco: California Tomorrow, p. 86.

Campbell, A. (1984). *The Girls in the Gang: A Report from New York City*. New York: Basil Blackwell, Inc.

Clark, R. (1983). *Family Life and School Achievement*. Chicago: University of Chicago Press.

Cole, M., and Griffith, P. (eds.) (1978). *Contextual Factors in Education: Improving Science and Mathematics for Minorities and Women*. Madison: Wisconsin Center for Education Research.

College Entrance Examination Board (1985). *Equality and Excellence: The Educational Status of Black Americans*. New York: The College Board.

Deaux, K. (1976). Sex: A perspective on the attribution process. In J. Harvey, W. Ickes, and R. Kidd, eds., *New Directions in Attribution Research*. Hillsdale, NJ: Erlbaum.

Fiorentine, R. (1987). Men, women and the premed persistence gap: A normative alternatives approach. *American Journal of Sociology* 92: 1118–1139.

Franco, R. (1987). *Samoans in Hawaii: A Demographic Profile*. Honolulu: East-West Center.

Goleman, D. (1987). Girls and math: Is biology really destiny? Education Supplement to the *Sunday New York Times*, pp. 42–43.

Grant, C., and Gilette, M. (1987). The Holmes Report and minorities in education. *Social Education* 4: 517–521.

Hawaii Department of Labor (1984). Study of Unemployment Poverty and Training Needs of American Samoans. *Final Report*.

Kahle, J. (1983). The disadvantaged majority: Science education for women. AETS outstanding paper for 1983. ERIC ED 242 561.

Lenney, E. (1977). Women's self confidence in achievement settings. *Psychological Bulletin* 84: 1–13.

Luce, P. (1985). The educational needs of American Samoan students. ERIC ED 257 886.

MacDonald, S. (1987). Educational opportunity and Samoan students in Hawaii: A case study. Dissertation. Honolulu, Hawaii: University of Hawaii at Manoa.

Mau, R. (1988). Some explanations for unfilled aspirations among minority group females. *Pacific Educational Research Journal* 4: 5–14.

Ogbu, J. (1978). *Minority Education and Caste: The American System in Cross-cultural Perspective*. New York: Academic Press.

O'Leary, V. (1974). Some attitudinal barriers to occupational aspirations in women. *Psychological Bulletin* 81: 809–826.

Peng, S., Owings, J., and Fetters, W. (1984). School experience and performance of Asian American high school students. Paper presented at the 1984 American Educational Research Association in New Orleans.

Rothman, R. (1988). English fluency, attainment linked in new NAEP study. *Education Week* 8: 1, 19.

Schorr, L., and Schorr, D. (1988). *Within Our Reach: Breaking the Cycle of Disadvantage*. New York: Anchor Press/Doubleday.

Schwartz, W. (1987). Teaching science and mathematics to at risk students. *ERIC Clearinghouse on Urban Education Digest*, Number 36.

Steinberg, L., Blinde, P., and Chan, K. (1984). Dropping out among language minority youth. *Review of Educational Research* 54: 113–132.

Tharpe, R., Jordan, C., Speidel, G., Au, K., Klein, T., Calkins, R., Sloat, K., and Gallimore, R. (1984). Product and process in applied developmental research: Education and the children of a minority. *Advances in Development Psychology*, vol. 3. Hillsdale, NJ: Lawrence Erlbaum Associates.

United States Bureau of the Census (1983). *1980 Census of Population, Volume 1, Characteristics of the Population, Chapter C, General Social and Economic Characteristics, Part I, United States Summary*. Report Number PC80-1-C1. Washington, DC: Bureau of the Census, U.S. Department of Commerce.

University of Hawaii (1987). Requesting a study to improve access to public higher education programs and support services for minority students. Report to the 1987 Legislature, SR 114, SD 1, 1986 Session.

Wong, E., Franklin, M., and Merritt, N. (1987). Reaching math potential: Parents' and students' attitudes toward math. Report by Research and Educational Planning center, University of Nevada, Reno.

IV HIGHER EDUCATIONAL ISSUES AND EXPERIENCES: ACCESS, REPRESENTATION, AND EQUITY

15 The Demographics of Diversity:
Asian Americans and
Higher Education

Jayjia Hsia & Marsha Hirano-Nakanishi

TODAY'S MEDIA attention to Asian American talent and college-going—the stories about Westinghouse talent-search winners, allegations of bias in Ivy League admissions—is best understood in a shifting demographic context. Asian Americans this decade have been the nation's fastest-growing group of college-goers. In 1976, there were 150,000 Asian American undergraduates in U.S. higher education. A decade later, in fall of 1986, there were almost three times as many—448,000. If this phenomenal growth had *not* drawn attention, one might be surprised.

Beyond the headlines, though, there has been too thin an information base for higher education policymakers as they plan services for a set of students remarkable for its commitment to education—and striking diversity.

THE NUMBERS

The number of Asian American college-goers tripled in no small measure because of growth in the larger Asian American population. The 1980 census reported a total of 3.5 million Asian Americans; they constituted a mere 1.5 percent of the total U.S. population. The 1980 count, however, represented more than a doubling of the previous Asian American count in 1970. The rate of growth of Asian Americans (141 percent) over that decade exceeded increases recorded among Hispanic (39 percent) and black (17 percent) persons—and for the population as a whole (11 percent).

Population estimates for Asian Americans *after* 1980, unlike those for larger minority groups, are at best informed approximations. None of the inter-decennial national surveys of population collect enough sampled Asian Americans to provide statistically reliable estimates. Population projections of Asian American growth by researchers from the East-West Population Institute in Honolulu put the total figure for Asian Americans at 5 million in 1985, making Asian Americans about 2 percent of the total U.S. population. Some estimate that the 1990 Asian American population will number about 6.5 million, or just under 3 percent of the total U.S. population. Some demographers postulate that ethnic Asians could become as much as 10 percent of the U.S. population by the year 2080.

Projections aside, we address the more modest question: How did the number of Asian

From *Change* (November/December 1989):20–27. Reprinted with permission of the Helen Dwight Reed Educational Foundation. Published by Heldref Publications, 1319 Eighteenth St., N.W., Washington, D.C. 20036-1802. Copyright © 1989.

Americans escalate so dramatically between 1970 and 1980? It did not come about through what demographers call "natural increase," wherein recorded live births exceed recorded deaths. Asian American women of child-bearing age recorded lower fertility rates than white, black, and Hispanic women. U.S.-born Asian American women, aged 25 to 34, recorded only 951 children per 1,000 women, while the foreign-born averaged 1,268 children. The equivalent figure among white women was 1,404. By ethnic group, fertility was highest among Vietnamese women, predominantly newcomers whose rate of 1,785 approached those reported for Hispanic and black women. Native-born Japanese and Chinese American women, who tend to be well-educated professionals living in urban centers, recorded the lowest fertility rates of all groups, with 768 and 669 children per 1,000 respectively. (For a group to "naturally increase," fertility rates need to approach 2,000 births per 1,000 women of child-bearing age.) In short, Asian Americans have not given birth to enough children to maintain their numbers, let alone explain the explosive growth among Asians.

That growth has been due principally to a steady stream of Asian immigrants and refugees. It must be noted that the last 20 years of Asian immigration have been unlike any other in the history of Asians in America. Beginning with the Chinese Exclusion Act of 1882, a series of racially motivated, restrictive immigration laws, such as the 1924 National Origins Act, virtually halted immigration from Asia. The year 1968 is a landmark in changing that situation: it was the year the Immigration Act of 1965 took effect. The 1965 law abolished the national-origins quota system and classified immigrants according to whether they originated from the Eastern or Western hemispheres. The annual quota for the Eastern hemisphere, which included Asia, was set at 170,000, with no more than 20,000 permitted to emigrate from any single country.

A preference system for ranking potential immigrants also was established, which emphasized reunification of families of U.S. citizens. Since 1980, the family-reunification preference has been the driving force for admission among all Asian immigrant groups. In earlier years, the third preference, which favored specified professionals, scientists, and artists of exceptional ability, and the sixth preference, which focused on skilled and unskilled workers in occupations that suffered from labor shortages in the U.S., were important vehicles for Asian immigration. As examples, one out of five immigrants from the Philippines was admitted under the third or sixth preference in 1970; 19 percent of Asian Indian immigrants in 1975 entered under an occupational preference.

For perspective, it is worth noting that, from 1971 to 1980, Asian immigration totaled about 1.6 million; this was the first time Asian immigration ever exceeded 500,000 in any 10-year period. For immigrants from the Americas the figures were higher. Asian and other immigration remained much lower than the historic inflow from Europe. In the decades between 1841 and 1971, the median decade-long immigration figure for Europeans to the U.S. was a little over 2 million.

Current U.S. immigration policy, then, may be viewed as one that seeks to remediate past imbalances and that recognizes that Asian peoples constitute over half of the world population. The figures continued to rise from fiscal 1981 through 1988. According to the Immigration and Naturalization Service, 1.75 million East, Southeast, and South Asian immigrants were admitted legally to the U.S., with Asians now constituting the largest group of legal immigrants annually. (The numbers of illegal Asian immigrants in this country are quite small.) Perhaps the most remarkable point that can be made here is that the number of Asian immigrants coming to the U.S. during '80s exceeded all Asian Americans counted in the 1970 census.

Parallel with immigrants, Southeast Asian *refugees* have also been admitted under a series of parole authorizations granted by the U.S. Attorney General since 1975, with the flow enhanced by events abroad and a broadened definition for "refugees" in the 1980 Refugee Act. Refugees can take new steps to become permanent residents after a year's residence in this country; most eventually acquire U.S. citizenship through naturalization. In the 1980 census, just over 300,000 Vietnamese, Laotians, and Cambodians were counted in the U.S. From 1980 to May 30, 1989, a total of 657,000 refugees identified as Vietnamese, Khmer, Cambodian, Laotian, or Highlanders were admitted, with the trendline decreasing in successive years from a high of 168,000 in FY 1981 to 26,000 during the first half of FY 1989. Thus, even before we get to the 1990 census count, we know there are more than a million Southeast Asians in the United States today—a substantial new addition to the mix called Asian Americans.

In the 1990 census, which begins in April, we can expect that the Asian American population will have lost some individuals through death, emigration, or repatriation and gained others through birth, immigration, refugees, and asylees. Asylees? Refugees come from abroad; asylees are already in the U.S., or at a port of entry, when they seek shelter. Recent events in Tiananmen Square and the response of U.S. leaders suggest that some fraction of the 26,000 students and additional numbers of political dissidents from the People's Republic of China may be granted asylum. The uncertain political climate in Hong Kong as of 1997 also may increase emigration; some U.S. legislators have urged that the current quota of 5,000 from Hong Kong be increased several-fold. Indeed, political or economic instability in any of the Asian nations can act as a push to increase future migration.

Finally, it should be noted that definitional changes in the 1980 census also increased the count of Asian Americans. Asian Indians have been treated historically as Asians—indeed, they were barred for decades from migrating to the U.S., and were denied U.S. citizenship through naturalization until 1965. Somewhat startlingly, through 1970 the Census Bureau generally classified Asian Indians as Caucasians. The contradictory categorizations occurred despite, or perhaps because of, the fact that India is the second most populous nation in the world and has enormous racial, ethnic, and linguistic diversity. Some of the discrepancy here, of course, stems from the use of forced choices about race, which until recently were limited to Caucasoid, Mongoloid, and Negroid. Given the social, economic, and political uses of the census, Asian Indian organizations lobbied effectively to be counted as Asian Americans for the 1980 census, a step that increased the count of Asian Americans by over 200,000.

CHANGE AND DIVERSITY

Until the recent influx of immigrants and refugees, the structure of the Asian American population had remained relatively stable for decades. Chinese, Japanese, and Filipino Americans comprised the three largest ethnic groups. In the decades up to 1970, the Asian American population became increasingly U.S.-born.

The new influx changed the picture. By 1980, the proportion of foreign-born Asian Americans had jumped to 62 percent. That census, for the first time, counted six specific Asian ethnic groups. In descending numerical order, these were Chinese (812,178), Filipino (781,894), Japanese (716,331), Asian Indian (387,223), Korean (357,393), and Vietnamese (245,025). Chart 1 shows the changing ethnic Asian demographics across the last three census counts. According to demographers, Filipinos will have surpassed Chinese as the largest group by 1990, and the number of Japanese probably will have fallen below those of Vietnamese and Korean Americans.

The proportion of foreign-born among Asian American groups varies widely, from 28 percent among Japanese Americans to 91 percent among the Vietnamese. Chart 2 shows the relative proportions of foreign-born among the six groups.

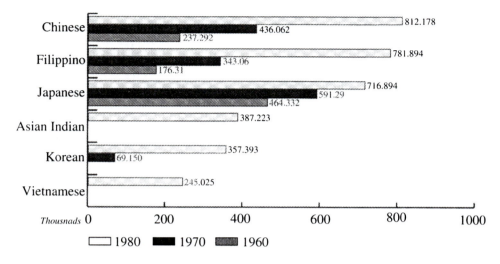

Source: Gardner, Robey & Smith (1985)

Chart 1 Asian American Population Growth from 1960–1980: Six Largest Ethnic Groups as of 1980

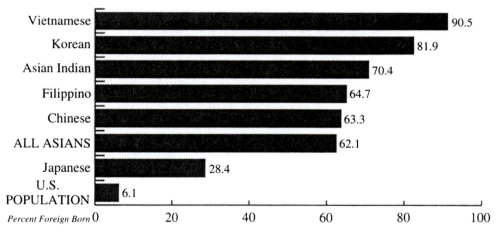

U.S. Census Bureau (1980)

Chart 2 Percent of Six Largest Asian Ethnic Groups in 1980 Who Were Born in Foreign Countries

With the exception of scholars, bureaucrats, and political activists, Americans of Asian ancestry rarely think of themselves first and foremost as "Asian American." Most ethnic Asians, particularly newcomers, are more likely to identify with their specific national or regional identities: Vietnamese, Korean, Hmong, Punjabi Sikh, Cantonese or Taiwanese, Visayan or Ilocano. A third-generation Japanese American typically would be fluent in English and well assimilated in the mainstream society, but have only passing knowledge of Japanese language or culture. A first-generation Asian Indian—admitted under the third preference—with a good job, possessing advanced degrees, and proficient in several languages including English, typically would fit with ease into a professional milieu and live in a middle class neighborhood. By contrast, a Laotian refugee who disembarked from a jumbo jet after years in refugee camps might have considerable trouble communicating in English and find life in the U.S. almost as alien as Alice found Wonderland. Yet, all are classified "Asian American," and are too often treated as members of a homogeneous population.

Beyond the six groups reported by the 1980 census, 166,000 persons were counted in a catch-all "other Asian" category. The designation included 22 specified ethnic groups. Laotian, Thai, Kampuchean (Cambodian), Pakistani, Indonesian, and Hmong people were each counted in the thousands. The remainder consisted of more than 26,000 East, Southeast, and South Asians who identified themselves as everything from Bangladeshi and Bhutanese to Singaporean and Sri Lankan.

Asian newcomers speak hundreds of mutually unintelligible languages and dialects. They transmit their diverse cultures by means as ancient as the oral traditions of pre-literate societies and as modern as the weekend classes for Korean students in Hangul, an orthography developed by a royal commission in the fifteenth century, but officially adopted by the Korean government only at the end of World War II. In short, when most Asian American ethnic groups communicate across subgroup lines, the only real language of common communication is—as one should expect in America—English.

Along other dimensions that define ethnicity and cultural identity, there are Asian Americans affiliated with virtually all the world's faiths, from Buddhist to Zoroastrian. And while country of origin often is the manner by which people identify themselves, country of *ancestry* is the choice of many, such as people from Vietnam of Chinese ancestry.

Finally, striking variations abound *within* each Asian American ethnic group. These are associated with a panoply of factors—time or generation in the U.S., origin from regions at peace or strife, socioeconomic status in the country of origin and in the U.S., and the transferability of skills and foreign credentials to the U.S. As an example, the early Vietnamese refugees were predominantly of the educated, urban, middle-to-upper class, with a working knowledge of English, having lived in the United States for many years now. The more recent wave of Vietnamese "boat people" consisted of people much less advantaged in almost every way upon entry into the United States. Their trek to our shores was harrowing and tragic. Unfortunately, bringing so little with them, their days here have also been fraught with stress and pain. In 1980, 9.6 percent of U.S. families lived below the poverty line; the proportions of Vietnamese (33.5 percent), Cambodian (48.7 percent), Hmong (62.8 percent), and Laotian (65.9 percent) families living at poverty level were many times greater.

PARTICIPATION IN HIGHER EDUCATION

Differences notwithstanding, there are characteristics shared by most of the groups that magnify impact upon higher education.

The most important of these characteristics is that education has long been associated with status and respect in most Asian societies. For early waves of Asian immigrants, heavy investments in education provided one of the only avenues of mobility in an otherwise restrictive environment. That value is strong, too, among Asian newcomers. Between 1976 and 1986, while the Asian population doubled, its post-secondary participation rose threefold—accounting, in the process, for a big chunk in higher education's total growth over those years.

This valuing of education is demonstrated also in the superior levels of educational attainment held by almost every older-adult Asian subgroup in 1980. Chart 3 indicates that, with the exception of Vietnamese, Asians (25 and older) held high school degrees in higher proportions than the U.S. average. Significantly greater proportions of Asians over 25 (with the exception of Vietnamese) hold the equivalent of at least a four-year college degree. Over 50 percent of older-adult Asian Indians have college degrees—more than triple the national average.

Chart 3 also indicates the apparent *under*attainment of Japanese Americans in higher education in comparison to Asian peers. Among Japanese American older adults, over 70 percent of whom are native-born, the lower rate reflects the fact that many were prevented from attending college by various restrictive policies, not the least by their wholesale incarceration in concentration camps during World War II.

Depressed as degree-earning is among the Nisei, it is high when compared with the proportion of college graduates among the older-adult Hmongs (2.9 percent), Cambodians (7.7 percent), and Laotians (5.6 percent), most of whom found no opportunity for advanced study in their homelands—and precious little here.

Asians' educational commitment translates into the phenomenon that the children—newcomers and native Asian Americans alike—enter *and* stay in school. In every age range, from kindergarten to young adult, higher proportions of Asian Americans enroll in school than their white, black, and Hispanic peers. Asian American high school sophomores and seniors, followed for six years by the 1980 High School and Beyond (HS&B) survey, recorded the lowest high school dropout rates and the highest cumulative grade point av-

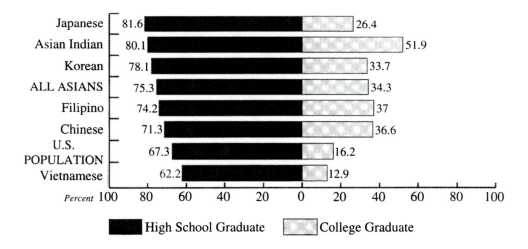

U.S. Census Bureau (1980)

Chart 3 High School and College Graduates in Asian Subgroups Who Were 25 or Older in 1980

erages among all groups. A higher proportion of Asian high school graduates went right on to college than graduating peers. Among Asian American seniors who enrolled in four-year colleges, 86 percent persisted, and 12 percent transferred to a different institution, only 2 percent reporting they had completed a short-term program or withdrawn. Among all students, 75 percent persisted, 15 percent transferred, and 10 percent completed a short course or withdrew. The persistence and transfer figure for Asian Americans attending two-year colleges was 91 percent, compared with 75 percent among all community college students.

In the jargon of higher educational research, there is little "leakage" of Asian Americans from the U.S. educational pipeline.

Note, however, that the sample of Asian American students in HS&B was inadequate for analysis by subgroups. But there is growing evidence that all is not uniformly rosy for Asian ethnics, especially for the growing segment of Southeast Asian refugees and immigrants. There have been reports of higher dropout rates among students from some Southeast Asian refugee groups in urban areas. Public schools in Boston and a number of Midwestern cities report high school dropout rates of Khmer, Hmong, and Laotian students that approach the rates of other disadvantaged minority students. To the extent that these phenomena are validated, Asian-ethnic students may be polarized over time into two segments, one in grave need of all forms of special assistance, the other a group appearing at first blush to exceed all expectations. Worse, the former may be lumped with the latter and lose sorely needed help.

Besides Asian cultural traditions of support for education, practical reasons for investing in higher education have always been a driving force for Asians. The socioeconomic position of ethnic Asian families in American society has improved markedly in recent decades, accomplished in no small measure by the Asian family's "over-investment" in higher educational credentials—that is, getting the highest degrees possible even while earning less than white counterparts with equivalent qualifications. Asians also tend to pool resources by living in larger households and having more family members work (Chart 4).

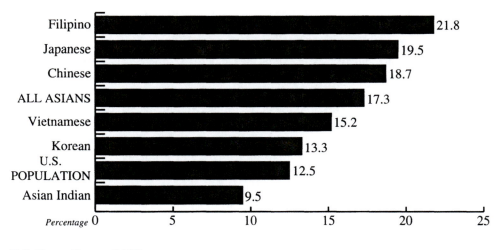

U.S. Census Bureau (1980)

Chart 4 Percent of Families with Three or More Workers in Six Largest Asian Ethnic Groups

Over-investment in education, with family members sharing the earnings load, has been a principal strategy of Asian Americans to gain entry to good jobs and a more comfortable life.

A common strategy, too, has been to optimize academic strengths in choosing a college major. First-generation and children of first-generation Asian Americans generally have shown above-average quantitative skills and compiled enviable high school records, but many have yet to achieve ease in speaking or writing English. For them, majors of choice have been those that take advantage of their mathematical reasoning abilities and minimize the need for eloquence. Thus, as first-generation students, Asians have focused on engineering, computer science, the physical sciences, and mathematics. Often coupled with this optimization strategy is the pragmatic view that study in technical fields will provide marketable skills and entry to secure, high-status, well-paying jobs.

Given these strategies, and the fact that future increases in Asian American college enrollment will come from immigrant families, it doesn't take a crystal ball to make reasonable guesses about the major fields that enrollment will head for. An important key to steering these talented students into broader fields will be to find ways of addressing their limited English proficiency.

We know also that Asian Americans choose public over private institutions. In 1986, 83 percent enrolled in public colleges and universities, compared with 77 percent of all college students. Financially limited, predominantly urban newcomers take advantage of community colleges. While 63 percent of all postsecondary students are enrolled in four-year colleges, only 58 percent of Asian Americans did so.

Demographic factors help explain the generally heightened participation of Asian Americans in higher education, but that participation is not spread evenly across institutions. According to Dr. Sam Peng of NCES, this 2 percent of the U.S. population accounted for 37 percent of the 23,000 students at the City College of San Francisco (fall of 1986), 25 percent of all students at UC-Irvine, 20 percent of Cooper Union, and 12 percent of the women at Wellesley. How could there be 758 Asian Americans out of 9,757 students at MIT, but only 427 Asian Americans out of 100,000 students in the entire state of Mississippi?

The short answer is, as Chart 5 shows, that Asian Americans are concentrated geographically. In 1980, 56 percent lived in the West and only 12 percent in the Midwest. There are, of course, differences among ethnic groups. In 1980, the Japanese (80.3 percent), Filipinos (68.8 percent), and, to a lesser extent, the Chinese (52.7 percent) lived in the West. Proportionately more Asian Indians (34 percent) and Chinese (27 percent) lived in the Northeast than Asian Americans in general (17 percent). Southeast Asians are more widely distributed as a result of a dispersal policy in the refugee resettlement program. But there has been migration over time, with resulting clusters of Southeast Asians in Texas, Louisiana, Northern Virginia, and California. Six out of 10 Asian Americans live in California, Hawaii, or New York. Nine out of 10 live in urban areas. Seven states had 100,000 or more Asian Americans, and 20 standard metropolitan statistical areas had 25,000 or more, as shown in Chart 5.

An examination of recent higher education enrollment shows parallel concentrations of students in specific regions, states, and institutions. In fall of 1986, there were a total of 12.5 million students enrolled in higher education institutions. About 448,000, or 3.6 percent, were Asian or Pacific Islander Americans. Asian enrollments were highest in the three states with large Asian American populations: California (192,837 students), Hawaii (36,478 students), and New York (32,532 students). In California, for example, with its pyramidal system of 106 community colleges, 19 campuses of California State University (CSU), and nine campuses of the University of California (UC), Asian students in 1987 constituted about 9 percent of all high school graduates (20,640 Asians), 7.3 percent of all

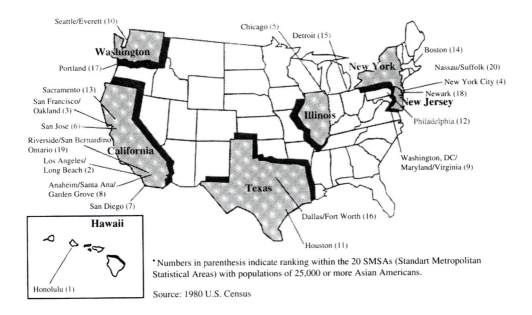

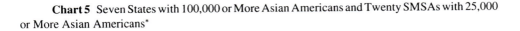

* Numbers in parenthesis indicate ranking within the 20 SMSAs (Standart Metropolitan Statistical Areas) with populations of 25,000 or more Asian Americans.

Source: 1980 U.S. Census

Chart 5 Seven States with 100,000 or More Asian Americans and Twenty SMSAs with 25,000 or More Asian Americans*

community college first-time freshmen (5,439 Asians), 16 percent of all CSU freshmen (3,574 Asians), and 20 percent of all UC first-time freshmen (3,578 Asians).

When some observers see these figures, they are quick to point out that Asian Americans are *not* primarily attending the "flagship" UC campuses—that over 40 percent attend the basic level of postsecondary education, the community colleges. In the hands of others, the same figures are used to raise questions of Asian "over-representation" in the more-selective CSU and UC sectors. Others still, who know that 26 percent of Asian high schools graduates are academically eligible for the UC (double the eligibility of the total high school graduate pool) and that 49 percent are academically eligible for CSU (about 1.7 times the eligibility rate of the total high school graduate pool), wonder if Asian Americans are under-represented, given their qualifications. Suffice it to say here that the increase in the Asian American college-age population in California, coupled with its strong educational record and propensity to participate in higher education, have created tension and placed Asian admissions in the political spotlight.

In 1985, a sample survey of students was undertaken by the CSU system across its campuses. Overall and on individual campuses, Asian American students were uniformly more critical of academic programs and practices than students of any other ethnic group. They wanted a greater variety of course offerings, enhanced instruction, improved career guidance, and personal counseling. Cognizant that the "model minority" image of Asian/Pacific students conceals real problems that students face, CSU has a system-wide committee at work to assess needs and recommend ways of more effectively meeting them.

This review of demographic trends highlights the striking diversity of the nation's Asian American population. In years to come, that diversity will increase—somewhat unpredictably, given pending changes in immigration policies and political instabilities around the Pacific Rim. One certainty is that the nation and its colleges must increase assistance for the current and coming waves of refugees and immigrants from Southeast Asia—people who sink under the poverty line and leak along our educational pipeline.

At the other end of the distribution, it will be increasingly important for educational decisionmakers to be mindful that Asian Americans have believed in the meritocracy that is part of the American promise. Asian Americans have not only invested in education, they have invested in that promise. All evidence points to the observation that Asian American students work hard on studies and on the job, do well on tests, and, despite allegations to the contrary, participate in extracurricular activities. They seek stronger academic programs, courses, guidance, and counseling. The tensions over Asian American participation in higher education must and eventually will be settled, for more is at stake than a seat in a class.

16 Asian Americans in Higher Education:
Trends and Issues

Eugenia Escueta and Eileen O'Brien

ASIAN AND PACIFIC Islander Americans[1] are now the country's fastest growing racial/ethnic group. Just as the Asian American population has doubled in size over the past two decades, so has its representation in college enrollments. The media has labeled Asian students in America as "the model minority," yet research indicates that this stereotype has hidden the academic difficulties faced by many Asian Americans—particularly members of certain groups.

In this research brief, we will review trends in both population and higher education, and their implications for the Asian American population. We will determine the status of Asian American students and faculty compared with other ethnic groups and identify the issues and problems connected with Asian Americans in academe. Finally, we will examine how this group's participation has changed and affected overall trends in higher education.

HIGHLIGHTS

- The Asian American population in the United States has reached almost 7.3 million, according to the 1990 Census, and Asian Americans now represent almost 3 percent of the total U.S. population.
- The Census Bureau also found that in 1990, 80 percent of the Asian population 25 years and older were high school graduates—very close to the 81 percent rate recorded for whites.
- However, Asian ethnic groups showed significantly different high school completion rates in the 1980 Census: only 22 percent of the Hmong population and 43 percent of Cambodians finished high school, compared with more than 80 percent of Asian Indian, Japanese, Indonesian and Pakistani individuals.
- Census data show increasingly higher levels of college participation for Asian Americans: in 1980, 33 percent of Asian Americans aged 25 and above had at least four years of college. By 1990, the proportion rose to 40 percent, almost double the figure for whites (23 percent).
- The number of Asian Americans enrolled in all higher education institutions rose from 198,000 in 1976 to 497,000 in 1988. Asian American women, whose enrollment doubled during this period, contributed significantly to this increase. The

From *Research Briefs* 2:4 (1991):1–11. Reprinted with permission by the American Council on Education.

overall representation of Asian Americans in higher education grew from 2 percent in 1976 to 4 percent in 1988.

- Most Asian American students (82 percent) attend public institutions, and almost half of these (39 percent) were enrolled in public, two-year colleges in 1988.
- From 1979 to 1989, the number of bachelor's degrees conferred to Asian Americans more than doubled (from 15,400 to 38,200), and the number of master's degrees earned by Asian Americans nearly doubled (from 5,500 to 10,700).
- Overall, Asian Americans earn a high proportion of their degrees in business and the sciences, and compared with all students, earn a much smaller number of degrees in the humanities and the social sciences. However, these trends are not as marked for Asian American women.
- Of all ethnic and racial groups, including whites, Asian Americans recorded the biggest increase (46 percent) in the number of Ph.D.s earned between 1979 and 1989. This gain coincided with a doubling of the number of doctorates earned by Asians who are not U.S. citizens.
- Almost 5 percent of all full-time faculty in U.S. colleges and universities are Asian, and 40 percent of Asian faculty are foreign nationals.
- Only 41 percent of Asian faculty are tenured; more than 30 percent are in non-tenure track positions.
- One out of 100 executive and managerial positions in higher education is held by an Asian American.

IMPLICATIONS

While much has been made of the success of Asians in U.S. higher education, combining more than 28 different Asian and Pacific Island groups into the single category "Asian American" has caused the educational needs of specific groups to be masked by the group's overall academic achievement. Although Asian Americans appear to be overrepresented in higher education, some groups are underrepresented.

The quality and quantity of data on Asian Americans is diminished by research categorizations that provide racial and ethnic breakdowns using only three or four groups: white, African American, Hispanic and "other." Researchers need to design studies and data-gathering strategies that provide basic information on Asian Americans and information on racial and ethnic subgroups—not just for Asian Americans, but for all minority groups.

Results of standardized tests show that the verbal skills of Asian American students (as a group) are underdeveloped. This may narrow their career options, and hence, influence their choice of degree fields and programs. Colleges and universities need to improve language skills assessment for Asian American students, and should also study whether academic advisors need to encourage Asian Americans to pursue a wider variety of fields.

Colleges and universities should examine their tenure and promotion practices to determine the causes for the low tenure rate of Asian faculty, their concentration in non-tenure track positions, and their underrepresentation among higher education administrators.

INTRODUCTION

Most research on Asian Americans in higher education has focused on the achievement and status of the entire group, yet the population known as "Asian and Pacific Islander American" is extremely diverse. Individuals from 28 countries of origin identified themselves as members of the Asian American/Pacific Islander category of the 1980 Census.

Asian groups vary widely according to educational attainment, average income levels, cultural origins, and year of entry into the United States.

Because data is rarely collected or disaggregated by Asian ethnic group or by citizenship or generation (whether individuals are first, second, third, etc., generation in the U.S.), the diversity within the Asian American population typically is not recognized. This brief will focus primarily on the educational experiences of Asians who are U.S. citizens, and will provide as much specific Asian ethnic group information as possible.

DEMOGRAPHIC TRENDS

- The Asian American population in the United States reached almost 7.3 million, according to data released from the 1990 Census.[2] Asian Americans now represent 2.9 percent of the total U.S. population, and this has more than doubled from the 3.5 million individuals who identified themselves as Asian or Pacific Island Americans just ten years ago in the 1980 Census (table 1).
- In 1980 and 1990, the six largest Asian groups were from China, the Philippines, Japan, India, Korea and Vietnam (figure 1). However, some of these groups grew more rapidly than others during the 1980s; Asian Indian, Korean, and Vietnamese populations more than doubled, while the Japanese population increased by 20 percent.
- The Population Reference Bureau projects that by the year 2000, the Asian American population could reach almost 11 million and comprise almost 4 percent of the total U.S. population.[3]

IMMIGRATION

- Increased immigration from Asian countries accounted for a sizable portion of the growth in the Asian American population; in the 1980s, almost 2.9 million new Asian immigrants came to the United States.[4] Vietnamese, Cambodian, Hmong and Laotian refugees and immigrants accounted for a significant portion of this growth.
- In 1980, 59 percent of the Asian American population was born in foreign countries, compared with 6 percent of the total U.S. population.

AGE

Because of the youthfulness of the overall Asian American population and the tendency of many Asian Americans to invest heavily in postsecondary education, the increase in the Asian American population has and will continue to greatly impact higher education.

Table 1. U.S. Population Estimates, 1980 and 1990

Race/Ethnicity	1980		1990	
	Number	Percent	Number	Percent
Total U.S. Population	227,757,000	100.0	248,709,873	100.0
White	195,571,000	85.9	199,686,070	80.3
African American	26,903,000	11.8	29,986,060	12.1
Asian/Pacific Islander	3,834,000	1.7	7,273,662	2.9
American Indian	1,420,400	0.6	1,959,234	0.9
Hispanic Origin*	14,608,673	6.4	22,354,059	9.0

*Persons of Hispanic origin can be of any race.

Note: The 1990 figures are subject to possible correction for undercount or overcount and have not been statistically adjusted to account for persons who identified themselves as "other race."

Source: Census Bureau, Preliminary Population Estimates, unpublished data, 1991.

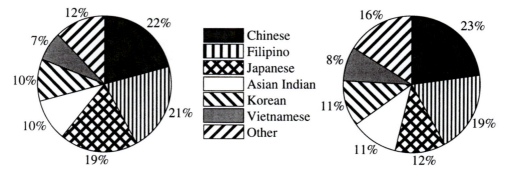

Note: Percentages may not add to 100 due to rounding.
Source: Census Bureau. Preliminary Population Estimates, unpublished data, 1991.

Figure 1 Composition of Asian American Population, 1980 and 1990.

- The median age of Asians in the 1980 census was 28.4 years, compared with an overall median age of 30.0 for the nation. The Japanese represent the eldest group, with a median age of 33.5 years. At the opposite end, the median age for the Vietnamese population is 21.5 years.

EDUCATIONAL ATTAINMENT

As a group, Asian Americans have reached high educational levels, yet the diversity within the Asian American population is manifested in its varied educational attainment levels.

- In 1990, 80 percent of Asian Americans who were 25 years and older were high school graduates—equal to the 81 percent rate recorded for whites (O'Hare and Felt, 1991).
- The 1990 Current Population Survey (CPS) indicated high college attendance levels for Asian Americans (O'Hare and Felt, 1991). Forty percent of Asian Americans aged 25 and above had at least four years of college, almost double the figure for whites (23 percent).

The Decennial Census is the best source for educational data on Asian American subgroups; yet, this data will not be available from the 1990 Census until 1992. This leads us to rely primarily on 1980 data for subgroup analysis, which shows educational attainment levels varied widely among different Asian groups.

- For example, in 1980, only 22 percent of the Hmong population above 25 years of age had a high school diploma or equivalent, and only 3 percent had four or more years of college. Similarly, 43 percent of Cambodians finished high school, and 8 percent had four or more years of college.
- Yet more than 80 percent of Asian Indian, Japanese, Indonesian and Pakistani individuals completed high school. More than one-quarter of Japanese and Indonesian adults and more than one-half of Asian Indian and Pakistani adults attended four or more years of college.

Asian American high school graduation rates differed somewhat based on gender, according to the 1980 Census.

- While 79 percent of Asian American men graduated from high school, only 71 percent of Asian American women did.

- These differences were even more striking within certain subgroups. Nine out of ten Korean men completed high school, compared with seven out of ten women, and Vietnamese males were much more likely to finish high school (71 percent) than were Vietnamese women (54 percent).
- Although Asian Americans as a group have the lowest high school dropout rate of any racial and ethnic group (including whites), there is growing evidence that dropout rates of Southeast Asian refugee students are increasing at an alarming pace (Hsia, 1988). A summary report from the Boston Public Schools showed that the dropout rate had almost doubled from 14 percent in 1982 to 27 percent in 1985 for students from Southeast Asia.[5]

ASIAN AMERICANS IN HIGHER EDUCATION

PREPARATION FOR COLLEGE

In a study of 1988 eighth graders, the National Center for Education Statistics (NCES) found that Asian Americans had higher educational aspirations than their non-Asian peers.[6]

- Thirty-seven percent of Asian American eighth graders planned to take a college preparatory high school program, compared with 29 percent of all students.
- Almost forty percent of Asian American eighth graders expected to finish college and attend graduate school, compared with all students, 43 percent of whom expected to finish college, and 23 percent of whom expected to attend graduate school.
- The Scholastic Aptitude Test (SAT) Mathematics scores of Asian Americans are normally above the national average.[7] In 1990, the national average was 476, while Asian Americans scored an average of 528 (College Board, 1990).
- However, Asian Americans consistently have had below-average verbal SAT scores—their 1990 average score of 410 contrasts with the national average of 424.

An analysis of 1984 University of California freshmen (Sue and Abe, 1988) showed important differences in SAT scores and high school grade point averages among different Asian groups (table 2).

- Of the six Asian groups studied, only Filipino students had lower high school GPAs than the white students; Chinese, Indian/Pakistani, Japanese, Korean, and students in the "other" Asian American group had higher GPAs than white students.

Table 2. SAT Scores and High School GPAs of University of California Freshmen, 1984

Students' Ethnicity	High School GPA	SAT, Verbal	SAT, Mathematics
White	3.59	512	577
All Asian American	3.69	456	584
Chinese	3.73	473	612
Filipino	3.56	448	520
Indian/Pakistani	3.80	520	606
Japanese	3.75	510	604
Korean	3.64	418	594
Other Asian Americans	3.72	373	556

Note: The Scholastic Aptitude Test is scored on a scale of 200 to 800 for each of the two sections, and the grade point averages are reported based on a 4.0 scale.
Source: The College Board, *Predictors of Academic Achievement Among Asian American and White Students*, 1988.

- Only Indian/Pakistani students had higher SAT verbal scores than white students. Asian students in the "other" category had the lowest average score, 373, almost 140 points lower than the average score for white students.
- However, most Asian groups had significantly higher marks than white students on the math section of the SAT. Only Filipinos and "other" Asian Americans scored below that of white students, while Chinese students scored the highest.

The lower scores Asian Americans earn on the verbal sections of the SAT and other standardized tests can be correlated with the large number who speak English as a second language.

- In 1985, 27 percent of Asian American college-bound high school seniors reported English was not their best language, compared with only 4 percent of all college-bound seniors (Ramist and Arbeiter, 1986).

ENROLLMENT TRENDS

- Asian American enrollment in higher education is increasing dramatically. From 1976 to 1988, the number of Asian Americans enrolled in all higher education institutions increased twofold from 198,000 to 497,000, and their overall representation doubled from about 2 percent to 4 percent.
- During the same time period, data on Asian Americans also show comparable increases in undergraduate and graduate enrollments, while their enrollment in first professional programs more than tripled from 1976 to 1988.
- Between 1978 and 1988, the proportion of Asian American women in higher education stayed the same—almost 50 percent of Asian undergraduates and slightly more than 40 percent of Asian graduate students (first professional women students did increase their numbers from 31 to 40 percent).
- However, the number of women students soared. At the undergraduate level, their numbers more than doubled; at the graduate level, their representation grew by 75 percent; and at the first professional level, their numbers almost quadrupled.
- With 82 percent of all Asian Americans enrolled in higher education attending public institutions in 1988, their enrollment in public colleges and universities is slightly above the national average of 78 percent.
- In 1988, 39 percent of all Asian American college students were enrolled in public, two-year colleges. This proportion has remained stable since 1978.
- The 1980 Census showed some significant enrollment differences among Asian ethnic groups in the 20–24 age group: for example, Chinese Americans had the highest enrollment rate (60 percent), while Filipino Americans had the lowest (27 percent) of the six largest Asian groups.[8] This compared with an enrollment rate of 24 percent for whites and 21 percent for African Americans.

DEGREES CONFERRED AND FIELD OF STUDY

Asian Americans' growth in the overall population has been matched by a comparable increase in their representation among those who earned college degrees (table 3). From 1979 to 1989, the number of bachelor's degrees conferred to Asian Americans more than doubled from 15,400 to 38,200, and the number of master's degrees they earned almost doubled, from 5,500 to 10,700 (figure 2).

- In 1979, Asian Americans accounted for 1.7 percent of all bachelor's degrees awarded. By 1989, Asian Americans had earned just under 4 percent of all conferred baccalaureates.

Table 3. Degrees Conferred to Asian American and All Students, 1979 and 1989

Degree	1979	1989	Percentage Increase
Bachelor's			
Total	919,540	1,015,239	11%
Asian American	15,407	38,219	148%
Master's			
Total	300,255	308,872	3%
Asian American	5,496	10,714	95%
Doctorate's			
Total	31,239	34,319	10%
Asian American	428	624	46%

Sources: National Center for Education Statistics, "Integrated Postsecondary Education Data System (IPEDS)," unpublished tabulations, 1990, and National Research Council, *Summary Report 1989: Doctorate Recipients from United States Universities*, 1990.

- During the same period, the proportion of Asian Americans earning master's degrees rose from 1.8 percent to 3.5 percent.
- Asian American women's increases fueled this growth between 1979 and 1989: the number of women earning bachelor's degrees rose from 7,000 to almost 19,000, and the number earning master's degrees jumped from 2,000 to 4,000.

The stereotype of Asian Americans might suggest that they pursue degrees in science-based fields, such as engineering or physical sciences, and to some extent this is true. However, similar to trends for students overall, Asian Americans earn the highest number

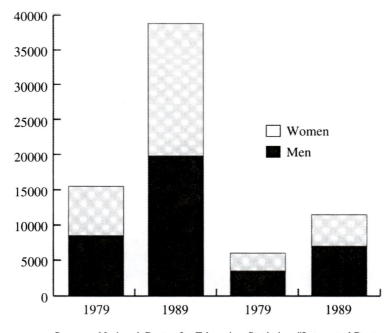

Sources: National Center for Education Statistics, "Integrated Postsecondary Education Data System (IPEDS)," unpublished tabulations, 1990.

Figure 2 Bachelor's and Master's Degrees Earned by Asian Americans, 1979 and 1989.

of their bachelor's and master's degrees in business. In addition, the preference for careers in science-based fields does not extend to Asian American women.

- In 1989, the top three broad subject fields in which Asian Americans earned their bachelor's degrees were business, engineering, and social sciences, also the top three fields for all students. At the master's level, Asian Americans' top three field choices also paralleled those of all students: business, engineering and education.
- Asian Americans are less likely than white and other ethnic minority students to pursue degrees in education. Education degrees represented 10 percent of bachelor's earned by all students, yet only 3 percent of Asian Americans earned education degrees in 1989. At the master's level, education degrees accounted for 27 percent of degrees awarded to all students, but only 10 percent of those conferred to Asian Americans.

Engineering is a very popular field for Asian Americans—it ranks second in both bachelor's and master's degrees awarded to Asians in 1989. However, when broken down by gender, the data reveal a different pattern:

- More than 25 percent of all bachelor's and master's degrees conferred to Asian American men were earned in engineering.
- Engineering accounted for only 6 percent and 7 percent, respectively, of the bachelor's and master's degrees earned by Asian American women.

Differences in choice of field also were displayed among the top three degree fields for Asian American men and women.

- At the bachelor's level, engineering, business and social sciences were the top fields for men, while business, social sciences and life sciences were the top choices for women.
- At the master's level, Asian American women's top fields were business, education and the health professions, compared with men's choices of business, engineering and computer sciences.
- Recent baccalaureate trends indicate that Asian Americans, especially women, may be diversifying, moving away from physical sciences and computer science, and branching out into social sciences, psychology and health professions. Although the primary field for Asian American men may remain engineering, there are signs that they, too, are earning degrees in a greater variety of fields.
- If current trends continue, it appears that the popularity of master's degrees in business among Asian American men and women will continue to grow, as will the choice of education master's degrees.

DOCTORATE PRODUCTION

Data from the National Research Council (NRC, 1990) indicate that the increases Asian Americans have shown at the doctoral level have not been as impressive as their gains at the bachelor's and master's level. In addition, the number of doctorates earned by Asians studying under permanent and temporary visas has far surpassed the number of Ph.D.s awarded to Asian U.S. citizens during the past ten years.

- From 1979 to 1989, the number of Asian Americans (U.S. citizens only) earning doctorates each year rose from 428 to 624, a 46 percent increase. This compares with an overall increase of 10 percent for all Ph.D.s.
- This was the biggest increase in earned doctorates of any ethnic group from 1979 to 1989. The number of African Americans and whites earning Ph.D.s actually de-

clined by 23 percent and 6 percent, respectively, while Hispanics and American Indians increased their number of doctorates by 23 percent and 15 percent, respectively.

- Asian American doctorates increased their proportion of all Ph.D.s earned by U.S. citizens from 1.7 percent in 1979 to 2.7 percent in 1989.
- However, the number of Asian doctorates who were not U.S. citizens more than doubled during that same time (from 2,137 to 4,508), and their proportion of doctorates awarded to all Asians increased to 88 percent in 1989.
- Three-fourths of Asian doctorates were temporary residents, representing a steady increase of nearly 1.5 percent per year since 1978.
- NRC data indicate that Asian women still lag behind Asian men with respect to Ph.D. numbers. Women accounted for only 29 percent of the Asian Ph.D.s who were U.S. citizens (women represented 43 percent of all doctorates earned by U.S. citizens). In addition, only 18 percent of the Asian doctorate recipients on temporary and permanent visas were women.
- Almost 70 percent of the doctorates awarded to Asian Americans were in the areas of engineering, life sciences and physical sciences, yet less than half of all doctorates was awarded in these fields. Asian Americans earned the least number of Ph.D.s in professional fields and the humanities.

NRC data show a trend away from employment in academe and toward employment in industry for Asian American doctorates.

- In 1973, 45 percent of Asian American doctorates reported employment commitments to academe, compared with only 39 percent in 1989; similarly, the proportion of whites with Ph.D.s who planned to work in academe dropped from 64 percent in 1973 to 52 percent in 1989.
- A larger proportion of Asian Americans had commitments to enter industry jobs: 41 percent in 1973 and 46 percent in 1989. This compares with an increase from 12 percent to 20 percent for white doctorates committed to industry work.

FACULTY AND STAFF IN HIGHER EDUCATION

Preliminary analyses might indicate that the proportion of Asian Americans employed by higher education is equal to the overall population proportion; however, Asian American women have not reached parity with the overall population, and a high percentage of Asian faculty are in non-tenure track positions.

- Most reports on the composition of full-time faculty in U.S. colleges and universities show that between 4 and 5 percent are Asian American (EEOC, 1991; NCES, 1990).
- According to the Equal Employment Opportunity Commission (EEOC), 24,252 of a total of 514,662 full-time faculty were Asian American in 1989.
- This represents a considerable growth from 1975, when Asian faculty totaled 9,763, or 2 percent, of all full-time faculty.[9]
- In 1989, EEOC data indicate that 40 percent of Asian faculty were foreign nationals (not U.S. citizens). Most Asian foreign nationals (81 percent) are male.
- Although men outnumber women among all faculty (70 percent vs. 30 percent), Asian American men are even more disproportionately represented among faculty (78 percent vs. 22 percent).

With respect to tenure, the EEOC data[10] indicate Asian faculty have not reached parity with other groups (figures 3 and 4).

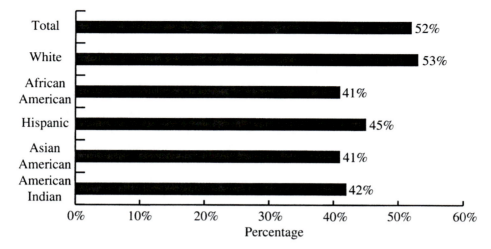

Source: Equal Employment Opportunity Commission, 1989 EEO-6 Detail Summary
Report, U.S. Summary, unpublished data, 1991.

Figure 3 Faculty Tenure Rates by Race/Ethnicity, 1989.

- Looking at all full-time faculty (including those not on a tenure track), Asian faculty have one of the lowest tenure rates of all minority groups: 41 percent (African
  American faculty also have a rate of 41 percent). The overall tenure rate is 52 percent.
- Women faculty overall have lower tenure rates than men (38 percent compared
  with 58 percent), and Asian Americans are no exception—31 percent of Asian
  American women and 44 percent of Asian American men are tenured.
- As with other minority groups, a large segment of the Asian faculty is found in
  non-tenure track positions; three out of every ten Asian faculty members are in
  non-tenure track positions (table 4).
- The EEOC survey also indicates that as of 1989 only 1 out of 100 executive or
  managerial positions in higher education administration were filled by Asian
  Americans.

IMPLICATIONS

The aggregation of more than 28 different Asian and Pacific Island groups into the single
category "Asian American" has led to educational needs and problems of the subgroups
being masked by the overall academic achievement record of Asian Americans. As a group,
Asian Americans appear to be slightly overrepresented in higher education, even though
some groups are underrepresented.

Compounding the problem of aggregating data on Asian Americans are research categorizations that provide racial and ethnic breakdowns using only three or four groups:
white, black, Hispanic, and "other," which may include Asian Americans, American Indians
and non–U.S. citizens. To indicate that the U.S. population consists only of three ethnic
groups ignores the nation's diversity and diminishes the quality and quantity of data on all
minority groups.

Researchers and policymakers need to design studies and data-gathering strategies
that provide basic information on Asian Americans and provide information on subgroups—

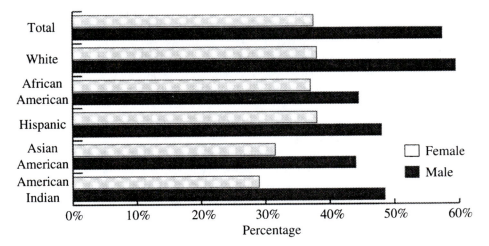

Source: Equal Employment Opportunity Commission, 1989 EEO-6 Detail Summary Report, U.S. Summary, unpublished data, 1991.

Figure 4 Tenure Rates for Faculty, by Gender, 1989.

not just for Asian Americans, but for all minority groups. This may require oversampling, but the paucity of basic data on all subgroups warrants it.

With the Census Bureau now including Asian Americans in the Current Population Surveys, and considering oversampling to provide a better dataset, more information will be available. Also, when detailed racial and ethnic information on education and income from the 1990 Census are released in 1992, the data will provide a rich, comprehensive source for new research. A careful analysis of the differences among Asian American subgroups, rather than a simple study of the trends of the overall group, is warranted.

Since immigration from Asian and Pacific Island countries is projected to increase, research comparing recent immigrants to second-and third-generation Asian American students and faculty is essential (currently, such research is practically nonexistent). Some scholars say that there are important differences in the educational achievement levels of these groups, and Census data support their assertion: the Hmong and Cambodian populations, two groups with high percentages of immigrants, have extremely low high school completion rates. As the number of Asian immigrants entering the nation's educational system grows, educators need more research to understand the particular educational strengths and needs of the Asian students from various ethnic groups.

Table 4. Tenure Status of Full-Time Faculty, by Race/Ethnicity, 1989

Race/ Ethnic Group	Tenure Track		Non- Tenure Track
	Tenured	Not Tenured	
All	52%	21%	27%
Asian American	41	28	31
White	53	21	26
African American	41	26	33
Hispanic	45	25	30
American Indian	42	21	37

Source: Equal Employment Opportunity Commission, Higher Education Staff Survey, *1989 EEO-6 Detail Summary Report*. Unpublished data, 1991.

Research shows that the underdevelopment of verbal skills of certain Asian ethnic groups persists, and may influence their choice of degree fields and programs. Colleges and universities should assess the needs of Asian Americans and recent Asian immigrants with respect to developing verbal and language skills. Institutions might also study whether academic advisors can ensure that Asian Americans' choices of major fields of study are not overly influenced by any perceived language barriers, and encourage Asian students to pursue a wider variety of fields.

Overall, Asian Americans have recorded impressive gains in enrollment and earned degrees at all levels over the last decade. However, at the doctorate level, women continue to earn a significantly smaller number of Ph.D.s than men, and this may correlate with the smaller proportion of Asian women faculty. Research on why fewer Asian American women than men are earning doctoral degrees and becoming faculty members is recommended. In addition, because Asians who are not U.S. citizens far outnumber Asian Americans in terms of earned Ph.D.s, research on the experience of Asian doctorates who study under temporary or permanent visas might offer important insight into these trends.

Although the number of Asian faculty has grown, these faculty have not achieved the same tenure rates as other groups. Colleges and universities should examine their tenure and promotion practices to determine the causes for the low tenure rates of Asian faculty, their concentration in non-tenure track positions, and their vast underrepresentation among higher education administrators.

Recently, many Asian Americans in higher education, both students and faculty, have formed new organizations and coalitions to increase awareness and address issues that are of immediate importance to Asian Americans. By collaborating with these groups, institutions could develop ways to improve the campus climate for Asian Americans.

How higher education responds to these concerns will greatly affect the perceptions and progress of Asian Americans in the future. Our primary recommendation is for educators to recognize that there are differences among Asian American groups, and to seek out undetected but damaging weaknesses in a record that may seem laudatory overall.

BIBLIOGRAPHY

The College Board. *College Bound Seniors: 1990 Profile of SAT and Achievement Test Takers*. New York: The College Board, 1990.

Robert Gardner, Bryant Robey, and Peter Smith. *Asian Americans: Growth, Change and Diversity. Population Bulletin*. Washington, D.C.: Population Reference Bureau, 1985.

Jayjia Hsia. *Asian Americans in Higher Education and at Work*. Hillsdale, N.J.: Lawrence Erlbaum Assoc., 1988.

Institute of International Education. *Open Doors, 1989–90: Report on International Educational Exchange*. New York: Institute of International Education, 1990.

National Research Council, Office of Scientific and Engineering Personnel. *Summary Report 1989: Doctorate Recipients from United States Universities*. Washington, D.C.: National Academy Press., 1990.

William P. O'Hare and Judy Felt. *Asian Americans: America's Fastest Growing Minority Group*. Washington, D.C.: Population Reference Bureau, 1991.

Leonard Ramist and Solomon Arbeiter. *Profiles, College-Bound Seniors, 1985*. New York: College Entrance Examination Board, 1986.

Stanley Sue and Jennifer Abe. *Predictors of Academic Achievement Among Asian American and White Students*. New York: College Entrance Examination Board, 1988.

U.S. Department of Commerce, Bureau of the Census. *We, the Asian and Pacific Islander Americans*. Washington, D.C.: U.S. Government Printing Office, 1988.

———. *Preliminary Population Estimates*, unpublished tabulations, 1991.

U.S. Department of Education, National Center for Education Statistics. *Digest of Education Statistics, 1990* Report No. NCES 89–643. Washington, D.C.: U.S. Government Printing Office, 1990.

————. "Integrated Postsecondary Education Data System (IPEDS)," unpublished tabulations, 1990.

————. *National Education Longitudinal Study of 1988: A Profile of the American Eighth Grader.* Washington, D.C.: U.S. Government Printing Office, 1990.

U.S. Equal Employment Opportunity Commission, Higher Education Staff. 1989 EEO-6 Detail Summary Report, U.S. Summary. Unpublished data, 1991.

Reginald Wilson and Deborah Carter. *Seventh Annual Status Report on Minorities in Higher Education.* Washington, D.C.: Office of Minorities in Higher Education, American Council on Education, 1988.

RESOURCES

1. Data from the Census Bureau's Decennial Census provides the most comprehensive national statistics on Asians and Asian ethnic groups living in the United States. However, statistics on racial and ethnic groups covering such areas as education, place of birth, citizenship, labor force participation, income, etc., will not be available from the Racial Statistics Division until 1992. The division is planning to update the 1988 publication, *We, the Asian and Pacific Islander Americans*, which offers a statistical snapshot of the U.S. Asian population based on the 1980 Census. The expected publication date is 1993. For more information, contact the Racial Statistics Division, U.S. Bureau of the Census, Washington, D.C. 20233, (301) 763-7572.

2. The November/December 1989 issue of *Change* magazine, published by the American Association for Higher Education, was devoted to Asian and Pacific Americans. Edited by Paula Bagasao and Bob H. Suzuki, the issue features articles on the "model minority" stereotype, demographics of Asian Americans, student activism, admissions quotas, affirmative action, and other areas. Many of the articles are based on anecdotal information, but the magazine provides a comprehensive look at the issues facing Asian Americans in higher education. A limited number of copies are available for $7.50 from Heldref Publications, *Change* Magazine, 1319 18th Street, NW, Washington, D.C. 20036.

3. Another comprehensive view of Asian American issues, also written by Bob H. Suzuki, appears as a chapter in the 1989 Jossey-Bass Inc. publication, edited by Arthur Levine, *Shaping Higher Education's Future: Demographic Realities and Opportunities*, 1990-2000. The chapter, titled "Asian Americans in Higher Education: Impact of Changing Demographics and Other Social Forces," provides a historical review of Asian immigration, as well as a thorough examination of the socioeconomic status and educational trends of Asian Americans. The book is available for $23.95 from Jossey-Bass Inc., 350 Sansome Street, San Francisco, CA 94104.

ENDNOTES

1. In this brief, the phrase "Asian Americans" refers to U.S. citizens who trace their ancestry to South Asia, Southeast Asia, East Asia, and the Pacific Islands. This term does not include non-U.S. citizens or foreign nationals.

2. The Census Bureau does not distinguish between Asians who are U.S. citizens and Asians who are foreign nationals.

3. Conversation with Judy Felt, Research Demographer, Population Reference Bureau.

4. Based on data in *Asian Americans: America's Fastest Growing Minority Group*, 1991,

(Washington, D.C.: Population Reference Bureau), 2.

5. Study cited in Hsia, Jayjia, *Asian American in Higher Education and at Work*, 1988, (Lawrence Erlbaum Assoc.: Hillsdale, N.J.), 57.

6. U.S. Department of Education, National Center for Education Statistics, *National Education Longitudinal Study of 1988: A Profile of the American Eighth Grader*, 1990, pp. 66 and 71.

7. The College Board combines foreign Asian students' scores with Asian American students' scores in the category of "Asian American."

8. Most enrollment data on Asian ethnic groups comes from the Decennial Census; the Education Department does not provide subgroup breakdowns. This information is based on 1980 Census data cited in *Asian Americans: Growth, Change and Diversity*, 1985, (Washington, D.C.: Population Reference Bureau), 27.

9. EEOC data as reported in *Seventh Annual Status Report on Minorities in Higher Education*, 1988, (Washington, D.C.: Office of Minorities in Higher Education, American Council on Education), pp. 32–35.

10. Some reviewers pointed out limitations to EEOC data: 1) Although EEOC recently began collecting data on faculty who are foreign nationals, only counts are available. Tenures rates and faculty ranks are not disaggregated by foreign national status, and therefore, all data on rank and tenure also include foreign nationals. 2) EEOC does not collect information on faculty by field of study. Data on both of these variables might show interactions such as lower tenure rates for Asian foreign nationals or Asian faculty members' concentration in certain fields.

17

A Quota on Excellence?
The Asian American
Admissions Debate

Don T. Nakanishi

ALLEGATIONS OF POSSIBLE quotas or limitations in the admission and enrollment of Asian American applicants to some of the country's most selective public and private colleges are fueling one of the hottest educational policy controversies in recent years. From the White House to the California State House, from Berkeley to Cambridge, and from New York's Chinatown to Los Angeles's Koreatown, the so-called "Asian American admissions issue" has been the focus of extensive media scrutiny, unprecedented bipartisan political intervention, and prolonged protests by Asian American students, professors, and civil rights groups. And although some colleges have responded by formally apologizing to the Asian American community, by launching fact-finding studies, and by revising admissions procedures, it is highly likely that this issue will be with us for some time. The major competing social forces as well as perspectives of change and tradition that gave rise to this controversy still remain in an uneasy tug-of-war.

For over five years—beginning in 1983 at Brown and other private Ivy League colleges in the Northeast, and shortly after at the Berkeley and Los Angeles campuses of the public, taxpayer-supported University of California system—this admissions controversy has placed Asian Americans on an unexpected collision course with their most prized vehicle for social mobility. Indeed, despite the growth and heterogeneity of the Asian American population during the past two decades—with respect to national origin, religion, social class, and generation—there is unmistakeable unanimity in the belief that higher education is the *sine qua non* for individual and group survival and advancement in American society. Consequently, it is not surprising that the admissions debate has elicited powerful emotional responses from Asian American students and parents alike, and has been an ongoing front-page news story in the Asian American ethnic press for several years. It also now occupies the top rung of the leadership agenda of Asian American civil rights and educational groups across the country.

However, probably not so obvious is why this admissions issue has escalated far beyond a simple tête-à-tête between Asian Americans and college administrators. Why, for example, have Presidents Reagan and Bush joined an unusually diverse group of liberals and conservatives from both political parties in Congress and in state legislatures—like Democratic U.S. Senators Paul Simon and Thomas Daschle, Republican U.S.

From *Change* (November/December 1989):38–47. Reprinted with permission of the Helen Dwight Reed Educational Foundation. Published by Heldref Publications, 1319 Eighteenth St., N.W., Washington, D.C. 20036-1802. Copyright © 1989.

Representatives Patricia Saiki and Dana Rohrabacher, and top Democratic California state legislators Tom Hayden, Willie Brown, David Roberti, and Art Torres—in embracing this admissions issue, denouncing "exclusionary racial quotas," and spearheading numerous hearings in Washington and across the country?

Why is the Office of Civil Rights of the Department of Education conducting full-scale Title VI anti-bias compliance investigations of potentially discriminatory admissions practices and policies toward Asian American applicants at UCLA and Harvard? And why is it highly likely that other colleges will be targeted in the future? Why has almost every major newspaper and magazine in the nation, many television news programs, as well as just about every syndicated columnist from left to right on the political spectrum—including Doonesbury—found this controversy to be so newsworthy and symptomatic of much of what is wrong with American education?

Above all, why does the Asian American admissions debate represent a serious challenge to a number of long-standing institutional goals and practices of American higher education, whether the goal is socially engineering a "diverse" or "balanced" undergraduate student body or seeking the meritocratic ideal of choosing the best of the brightest? And what, if anything, can be done to resolve this issue?

The answers to these questions, I believe, require an understanding of not only the specific points of contention regarding possible bias and unfairness in evaluating Asian American applicants, but also the social and political context within which this controversy has emerged.

THE EMERGENCE OF THE DEBATE

The Asian American admissions debate probably could not have been foreseen. Until recently, the Asian American college-going population received little media, policy, or scholarly attention, because of their relatively small numbers nationally and their seemingly strong academic performance levels. In two of the more highly regarded comparative studies of minority students—Alexander Astin's *Minorities in Higher Education* (1982) and John Ogbu's *Minority Education and Caste* (1978)—Asian Americans were not included in the data collection and analysis because they were not considered to be "educationally disadvantaged" like other non-white minority groups. Indeed, there is much to suggest that the admissions debate might not have become so explosive if there had been a body of empirical knowledge that all parties to the dispute could have used to test or verify their largely unfounded assumptions and assertions about Asian American students. (One major point of contention has focused on the predictive value of admissions criteria—high school GPA, SAT verbal and math, and achievement tests—in explaining future college performance of Asian American and other groups of students. Contrary to conventional wisdom, a comparative study of University of California students found that the SAT math score was a better predictor of first-year grades than the SAT verbal for Asian Americans. For whites, the SAT verbal score remained the stronger predictor. Similarly, math achievement was a better predictor than English composition for Asian Americans, while the opposite was true for whites. The study served to challenge the common admissions practice of placing greater weight on verbal rather than math scores. See Stanley Sue and Jennifer Abe, "Predictors of Academic Achievement Among Asian American and White Students," *College Board Report*, No. 88–11, 1988.) Instead, much of this controversy has evolved in a virtual scholarly vacuum.

Beginning in the early 1980s, the national press became increasingly interested in the Asian American college-going population. They initially wrote stories touting the individual academic achievements of some of the most gifted Asian American students—such as the winners of the Westinghouse Talent Search—and what appeared to be their dramatic rise in enrollment at many of the country's most selective institutions. *U.S. News and World Report* wrote that "Asians are, in fact, flocking to top colleges. They make up about 10 percent of Harvard's freshman class and 20 percent of all students at the Juilliard School. In California, where Asians are 5.5 percent of the population, they total 23.5 percent of all Berkeley undergraduates." And *Newsweek* asked rhetorically: "Is it true what they say about Asian American students, or is it mythology? They say that Asian Americans are brilliant. They say that Asian Americans behave as a model minority, that they dominate mathematics, engineering, and science courses—that they are grinds who are so dedicated to getting ahead that they never have any fun."

Beginning in 1985, however, journalists and syndicated columnists began portraying Asian American undergraduates not only as "Whiz Kids," as *Time* magazine boldly proclaimed in a major cover story, but also as possible victims of racially discriminatory admissions practices. In a highly influential 1986 *Chronicle of Higher Education* article, Lawrence Biemiller wrote, "Charges that some elite colleges and universities may be purposefully limiting the admission of persons of Asian descent continue to worry students and parents. . . . The allegations come at a time when reports of racially motivated violence against Asians are increasing and talk of 'trade wars' with Asian countries continues, prompting concern about a possible resurgence of anti-Asian sentiment."

Historical analogies often were drawn to the situation facing American Jewish students before World War II when invidious, discriminatory policies and procedures officially were adopted to limit their access to many of the same selective institutions now concerning Asian/Pacific Americans. As *Los Angeles Times* reporter Linda Mathews wrote, "There may be a parallel between what is happening to Asian Americans now and what happened to Jews in the 1920s and 1930s at some Ivy League schools. . . . To keep a lid on the number of Jewish students—denounced as 'damned curve raisers' by less talented classmates—the universities imposed quotas, sometimes overt, sometimes covert. . . . Today's 'damned curve raisers' are Asian Americans, who are winning academic prizes and qualifying for prestigious universities in numbers out of proportion to their percentage of the population. And, like Jews before them, the members of the new model minority contend that they have begun to bump up against artificial barriers to their advancement."

Conservative and liberal commentators alike also joined the fray, linking the Asian American admissions issue to their ongoing ideological donneybrooks on a range of such unsettled policy topics as affirmative action programs, the nation's competitiveness with foreign economic powers, or recent educational reform measures. George F. Will, writing in April 1989, shortly after Berkeley Chancellor Ira Michael Heyman apologized to the Asian American community for his administration's past admissions policies that "indisputably had a disproportionate impact on Asian Americans," declared that liberalism was to blame for the admissions controversy. In echoing the highly controversial views expressed a few months earlier by former Assistant Attorney General William Bradford Reynolds, columnist Will argued that the discrimination that Asian American students encountered was due to affirmative action policies, one of the major cornerstones of the liberal social agenda. He wrote, "Affirmative action discriminated against Asian Americans by restricting the social rewards open to competition on the basis of merit. We may want a modified meritocracy, but it should not be modified by racism and the resentment of excellence. . . . At a time of high anxiety about declining educational standards and rising competition from abroad, and especially from the Pacific Rim, it is lunacy to punish Asian Americans—the nation's model minority—for their passion to excel."

Clarence Page was one of many liberal commentators, along with major Asian American community leaders, who denounced the conservatives' attack on affirmative action and their attempt to connect it with the situation facing Asian American students at Berkeley. As Page wrote, "Since this announcement offers ammunition in their relentless fight against affirmative action programs, some political conservatives applaud it. Conservatives often offer the success of Asian Americans as evidence that the American system is so fair to all that blacks and other minorities jolly well better look to themselves, not to the government or 'reverse discrimination,' for solutions to their problems. But the Berkeley problem was not 'reverse discrimination.' It was plain, old-fashioned discrimination of a sort affirmative action programs were intended to remedy, not create. The big difference this time is that it penalizes a people who have a reputation for over-achievement."

During the past decade, the media's changing portrayal of Asian American college students may have appeared to reflect a zealous search for not only good, but provocative news stories rather than focusing on policy. However, beyond the catchy headlines and one-line history lessons, a new and potentially far-reaching controversy about undergraduate admissions was gradually, and unexpectedly, unfolding. In many respects, the points of contention appeared quite familiar, and somehow *seemed* to be settled, especially in the aftermath of *Bakke*. Like other recent conflicts dealing with access and representation of women or historically under-represented racial minorities in America's institutions of higher education, the Asian American admissions debate eventually focused on the potential bias and arbitrariness of selection criteria procedures, and policies that might limit equal educational opportunities. Broad philosophical concepts (like meritocracy) and seemingly widely shared, long-standing institutional goals (like the deliberate social engineering of a "diverse" or "balanced" undergraduate student body) were again debated, and their procedural role in the admissions process was both questioned and justified.

And yet not anticipated was that this new admissions controversy would involve Asian Americans, a group that had not figured prominently in the earlier policy and legal disputes over admissions, and a group that did not have a reputation for being particularly assertive, visible, or efficacious in the political or other decision-making arenas. However, during the 1980s, a new and different Asian American population emerged as a result of unprecedented demographic, economic, and political trends. Higher education officials, like others who were not population specialists, probably could not have foreseen the dramatic changes that were occurring among Asian Americans, nor could they have fully realized how these trends would seriously challenge their seemingly well-established institutional practices and policies.

Contrary to the media's interpretation, the extraordinary rise in Asian American enrollment in many of the country's most competitive institutions starting in the early 1980s probably had far less to do with Asian American students' suddenly becoming more academically motivated and qualified than it did with their phenomenal demographic growth. According to the 1980 U.S. Census, Asian Americans were America's fastest-growing group. Between 1970 and 1980, they increased nationally by 128 percent from 1.5 million to 3.5 million. Recent projections estimate that Asian Americans will again double in size to 7 million by 1990 because of the continued large influx of refugees and immigrants from East and Southeast Asia, along with the Pacific Islands.

By extension, Asian Americans also are the fastest-growing group in the American college-going population, and the large increases in enrollment that the media reported with such surprise and awe for the most competitive private colleges were simultaneously occurring at other, less selective institutions as well. In the fall of 1976, there were 150,000 Asian American undergraduates in American higher education nationwide. A decade later, in fall of 1986, there were almost three times as many—448,000 Asian Americans in colleges and universities across the country, with almost half enrolled in two-year institutions.

All demographic projections of the Asian American college-age sector indicate that this exceptionally fast growth pattern will continue well into the next century.

Coinciding with this demographic upsurge during the '80s was the Asian American population's growing political maturity and influence at both the national and local levels. Perhaps at no other period in the over 150-year history of Asians in the United States have so many individuals and organizations participated in such a wide array of political and civil rights activities, not only in relation to the American political system, but also to the affairs of their ancestral homelands in Asia. In traditional electoral politics, what had come to be taken as a common occurrence in Hawaii—namely the election of Asian Americans to public office—suddenly became a less than surprising novelty in the so-called mainland states with the election and appointment of Asian Americans to federal, state, and local positions in California, Washington, New York, and elsewhere. And perhaps most significantly, the Asian American population came to demonstrate that it, too, had resources and talents—organizational, financial, or otherwise—to advance its specific concerns in a variety of political arenas, and to confront political issues that potentially are damaging to its group interests. Two widely reported grassroots campaigns illustrate this new collective determination: the successful drive by Japanese Americans to gain redress and reparations for their World War II incarceration, and the effective national movement to appeal and overturn the light sentences given to two unemployed Detroit auto workers who, in 1982, used a baseball bat to kill Chinese American Vincent Chin. (The two men mistook Chin for a Japanese and, therefore, someone who was viewed as having taken away their jobs).

The Asian American population's enhanced political participation during the '80s had several idiosyncratic features, with peculiar consequences for the Asian American admissions controversy. For example, other ethnic groups register and vote in overwhelming proportions for one or the other of the two major political parties—for example, blacks and American Jews for the Democratic party—which makes them largely beholden to the electoral success of that one party. Asian Americans, however, began during the '80s to exhibit a very different pattern of political affiliations at both the mass and elite levels. In numerous studies I conducted for the UCLA Asian/Pacific American Voter Registration Project, Asian Americans were almost evenly divided between Democrats and Republicans in their registration and voting behavior. Both political parties, especially the Republicans, have attempted to register the hundreds of thousands of recent Asian immigrants and refugees who annually become naturalized citizens—most notably in key electoral states like California. At the same time, Asian Americans have been cultivating a strong reputation as major financial contributors to Republican and Democratic candidates alike. Their estimated $10 million in contributions to the 1988 presidential election were divided almost equally between George Bush and Michael Dukakis. This 1980s pattern of supporting both parties at the voting and campaign fund-raising levels will likely continue. In turn, Democratic and Republican leaders, attempting to appeal to their growing and valued Asian American constituents, are addressing issues of special concern to them.

This unusual pattern of bipartisan affiliations among Asian Americans might well explain why the Asian American admissions issue is gaining the support of top leaders from both political parties. In California, for example, the state legislature's foremost liberal Democratic leaders—like Tom Hayden, Art Torres, David Roberti, and Willie Brown— have actively monitored the admissions controversy at the public University of California campuses for close to five years. They held numerous fact-finding hearings, intervened by bringing together university officials and Asian American community leaders, passed special resolutions on admissions, and had the state Auditor General undertake an unprecedented audit of admissions procedures at Berkeley. When addressing local Asian American communities, these politicians—along with other key municipal leaders like Mayor Tom

Bradley of Los Angeles—have frequently spoken out against potentially discriminatory admissions practices. At the national level, in Washington, where politics often do make for very strange bedfellows, the issue has been championed by liberals like Senator Paul Simon and conservatives like Congressman Dana Rohrabacher. Simon and Rohrabacher, on separate occasions, both expressed a keen interest in the current Title VI compliance investigations by the Office of Civil Rights at UCLA and Harvard, and indicated they may request that other institutions be formally reviewed in the future.

Rohrabacher, whose Southern California congressional district has a large number of Asian American voters, and Hawaiian representative Patricia Saiki, a Japanese American, introduced a bill in Congress last June dealing with bias against Asian American applicants. Hearings were held in cities across the nation. And although many Asian American liberals fear that conservative Republicans like Rohrabacher will attempt to use the Asian American issue to dismantle or discredit affirmative action programs and policies in higher education, it also is evident that Republican leaders are attempting to address one of the foremost concerns raised by their own constituents and the increasingly influential group of Asian American leaders in the Republican party.

For Asian Americans, then, the admissions controversy has gone beyond party or ideological differences, and has come to rest at the top of the leadership agenda for Asian Americans of all political persuasions. It is highly likely, therefore, that Republican and Democratic Asian American leaders, working together or independently, will continue pushing officials from both parties to resolve this issue.

The Asian American admissions controversy evolved out of the largely unexpected convergence of dramatic demographic and political changes among the Asian American population during the 1980s. Although higher education officials probably could not have anticipated these extraordinary social trends, it was their general reluctance and inability to fully and expeditiously address the complaints raised initially by Asian American students and professors on their own campuses that dramatically escalated this controversy.

Some commentators speculate that university administrators were fully convinced their customary policies and procedures were sound and fair and did not believe there were compelling reasons to change them. Writing in *The New Republic*, David Bell said, "The universities, however, consider their idea of the academic community to be liberal and sound. They are understandably hesitant to change it because of a demographic shift in the admissions pool."

Still others suggest that university administrators simply did not believe the admissions debate involving Asian Americans would get out of control or receive such prominent national media and political attention. These observers speculate that higher education officials were blinded by stereotypic images of Asian Americans as being politically passive and ineffectual, and did not anticipate how a new and more assertive Asian American population would use its many resources and alliances to confront a potentially discriminatory situation.

Whatever the case, the Asian American admissions controversy emerged and continues to be played out in this broader social context. Specific points of contention of the ongoing debate must be considered in terms of the interplay of these larger social forces and perspectives.

THE PROS AND CONS

All parties to the controversy—the critics as well as the admissions officers—agree that Asian American applicants to many of the nation's most selective undergraduate Ivy League institutions, as well as Stanford and the flagship Berkeley and Los Angeles campuses of the UC system, now have lower rates of admission than other groups of applicants, including whites (see Tables 1 and 2 for Harvard and Berkeley).

Although disparities have existed and been acknowledged officially for several years, data for the fall 1985 entering class are illustrative. At Princeton, 17 percent of all applicants and 14 percent of the Asian American applicants were admitted. At Harvard, 15.9 percent of all applicants and 12.5 percent of the Asian Americans were accepted. And at Yale, 18 percent of all applicants and 16.7 percent of Asian Americans were admitted. Put another way, Asian American applicants to Princeton were admitted at a rate that was only 82.4 percent of that for other applicants; to Harvard at 78.6 percent; and to Yale at 92.6 percent. Likewise, a study undertaken by a Standard University Academic Senate committee found that, between 1982 and 1985, "Asian American applicants to Stanford had admission rates ranging between 66 percent and 70 percent of admission rates for whites."

Similarly, in perhaps the most exhaustive external investigation of the admissions controversy performed to date (at the time this article was being written, the Office of Civil Rights of the U.S. Department of Education had not completed its Title VI compliance investigations of potentially biased admissions practices toward Asian American applicants at Harvard and UCLA), the California State Auditor General, at the State Senate's request, conducted a full-scale audit of white and Asian/Pacific American freshman applicants to the UC-Berkeley campus. Academic records for applicants to Berkeley's seven different undergraduate colleges and programs from 1981 through 1987 were examined, producing a total of 49 different categories of comparison between Asian/Pacifics and whites. In 37 of the 49 cases, whites had higher admission rates than Asian/Pacifics, even though Asian/Pacific applicants were found to have higher academic qualifications in practically all comparison groups.

Indeed, the academic qualifications of Asian American applicants have never been an issue, nor have they been used in rebuttal to explain lower admission rates. Every campus that launched its own *ad hoc* inquiry to examine and resolve this debate—Brown, Princeton, Harvard, Berkeley, and Stanford, among others—has found that Asian/Pacific applicants have stronger group-level academic profiles as measured by high school grades and standardized tests, and that those who are ultimately admitted usually have far stronger academic qualifications than other groups of admits.

Bunzel and Au wrote in *Public Interest* that, of the students who were admitted to Harvard in 1982, "Asian Americans had average verbal and math scores of 742 and 725, respectively, for an average combined score of 1467, while the scores for Caucasians were 666 and 689, for a total of 1355, or 112 points lower." An official letter sent by Harvard's admissions office to its alumni recruiters nationwide challenged these figures while ac-

Table 1. 1978–87 Admission Rates at Harvard for Asian Americans and Whites

	1978	1979	1980	1981	1982	1983	1984	1985	1986	1987
Asian Americans	12%	15%	15%	14%	13%	14%	13%	12%	11%	12%
Whites	17%	16%	15%	16%	18%	19%	18%	17%	18%	16%

Harvard University, Office of Admissions.

Table 2 1981–87 Admission Rates at U.C. Berkeley for Asian Americans and Whites

	1981	1982	1983	1984	1985	1986	1987
Asian Americans	50.4%	60.3%	66.8%	45.0%	44.4%	28.4%	27.7%
Whites	54.3%	64.5%	70.5%	56.4%	52.3%	32.7%	31.4%

University of California, Berkeley, Chancellor's Report.

knowledging that Asian/Pacific admits usually had higher test scores than whites: "The actual difference for the year cited in the article was 50 points, and the typical difference in a given year is 40 points for the verbal and mathematics SATs combined."

The findings by these individual campuses are consistent with other formal studies. The California Postsecondary Education Commission's periodic investigations of eligibility rates for the UC system consistently show that Asian/Pacific Americans have the largest proportion of "academically eligible" students of any group and, thus, should have the highest admission rate if grades and test scores were the *only* selection criteria. In the most recent study, based on the state's 1986 high school graduating class, 32.8 percent of the Asian American graduates were found to be eligible for the University of California, in contrast to 15.8 percent for whites, 5 percent for Latinos, and 4.5 percent for blacks. Similar patterns of university eligibility by ethnic group have been found in previous years.

Several major explanations have been offered to account for these disparities in admission rates. Critics contend that admissions officers at both highly selective public and private institutions are engaging in intentionally discriminatory practices to limit the representation of Asian/Pacific students—who tend to be the fastest-growing group of applicants at these campuses. For example, over 20 percent of the fall 1987 entering class at Berkeley was Asian American. Given that Asian Americans make up approximately 2 percent of the nation's population and 6 percent of California's population, at first glance this figure might provide credence to the claim that Asian Americans were "over-represented." However, what is not apparent is that Asian/Pacific Americans now represent an increasingly sizeable proportion of the total applicant pools at these colleges. Of the 16,318 applicants who competed for regular admissions slots at Berkeley for the fall 1987 class, 5,032—or 30.8 percent—were Asian Americans.

Critics also contend that public institutions like the UC campuses have secretly, without adequate public and legislative discussion, deviated from their long-standing academic, merit-based admissions policies by giving weight to a variety of subjective criteria in the selection process. They also argue that Asian/Pacific American faculty and administrators at the institutions are systematically excluded from participating in decision-making committees and activities dealing with undergraduate selection policies and procedures.

Admissions officers, on the other hand, deny that quotas, informal or formal, exist for Asian/Pacific Americans or any other group, especially in the post-*Bakke* era. They contend that admission rates are simplistic indicators of discrimination and do not fully describe the highly professional, multi-level process of admissions review that all applicants receive. They further argue that privacy laws, like the so-called Buckley Amendment of 1974, prevent access to all the relevant materials that are reviewed in an applicant's file, especially personal essays and letters of recommendation that can play a far more decisive role in highly competitive admissions situations than is generally recognized.

Finally, admissions officers at private institutions, and increasingly at public colleges as well, have argued that their admissions policies are not entirely meritocratic, but encompass other significant institutional goals and traditions. A common explanation offered to account for lower admission rates among Asian/Pacific American applicants is that they are less likely to be proportionately represented among a range of criteria that underlie a broad and flexible interpretation of the goal of seeking undergraduate diversity. Ironically, current officials at many of the nation's most prestigious research universities, like their predecessors who dealt with the upsurge in American Jewish applicants, have found themselves defending their institutional need to enroll good football players and the siblings of loyal and wealthy alumni rather than a meritocratic ideal of choosing the best of the brightest.

Geographic diversity, for example, is a well-established and widely accepted goal of private elite institutions, which is explicitly routinized in the admissions process. Recruiting in certain cities and states, specific admissions officers not only identify, but are advocates for, the top students in admissions committee deliberations, which systematically reflect geographic considerations rather than a random review of the entire applicant pool. As a result, only a few of the many applicants from any particular geographic area can be admitted. Thus, the various talents and characteristics of student diversity, or other institutional priorities, must be encompassed within this formal geographic quota.

Admissions officers argue that Asian Americans are at a disadvantage because the vast majority of their applicants are from New York, California, or the western states, and, as a result, their representation in the entering class is a function of the size and strength of their local applicant pools. Ironically, this goal of geographic diversity was first instituted by many of these same undergraduate institutions to limit indirectly the enrollment of American Jews before World War II, who were concentrated mainly in New York and other parts of the Northeast.

However, the geographic skewing of the Asian Americans and American Jewish applicant pools may not be unique. Indeed, New York probably provides more applicants and matriculants overall to the Ivy colleges than any other state. California, the site of intensive recruiting campaigns by institutions from across the nation, usually ranks second or third in its overall representation of these student bodies. For example, during the 1985–86 academic year, there were 1,094 students from New York, 747 from Yale's home state of Connecticut, and 455 Californians among Yale's total undergraduate enrollment of 5,190. Together, these three three top feeder states accounted for 44.2 percent of Yale's undergraduate student body. Similarly, Harvard's entering class of 1985 had 290 students from New York, 279 from its home state of Massachusetts, and 168 from California. Although all 50 states were represented among the 1,525 domestic freshman students, Harvard's top three feeder states of New York, Massachusetts, and California accounted for 48.3 percent of its entering class.

Admissions officers at the nation's selective institutions, public and private, also argue that Asian American applicants show a disproportionate interest in specific future college programs, especially pre-med studies, engineering, and the natural and physical sciences. For example, an official faculty and student committee investigating Asian American admissions at Princeton in 1985 argued that "Asian American applicants have not been strongly represented in those subgroups tending to have higher than average rates of admission (e.g., alumni children, athletes); on the other hand, Asian Americans are strongly represented in the one applicant group with a somewhat lower rate of admission (engineering school candidates)." Similarly, L. Fred Jewitt, former dean of admissions at Harvard, made an analogous assessment: "A terribly high proportion of Asian students are heading toward the sciences. In the interests of diversity, then, more of them must be left out."

Admissions to these majors, of course, tends to be extremely competitive because of the oversupply of highly qualified applicants and the formal and informal restrictions placed on the number of potential admits by specific departments. Thus, university administrators argue that the lower admission rate for Asian American applicants is due to their overconcentration in particular majors of choice that are designated when filing applications. Put another way, they believe that if Asian Americans were less homogeneous and were equally distributed among a range of majors, then there would be no disparities in admission rates.

A comparative analysis of data on the characteristics of California SAT test-takers in 1977 and 1985 tends to support the notion of "lack of diversity of major." Approximately 70 percent of the state's Asian/Pacific American males and over 50 percent of the females who took the test in 1985 indicated at the time that they intended to major in engineering, the sciences, or mathematics. For the males, interest in majoring specifically in engineering or computer science jumped from 26.1 percent to 46.1 percent from 1977 to 1985, while for females there was an increase from 5.3 percent to 15.8 percent. Interest in being a pre-med major declined slightly for Asian American males from 8.6 percent to 7.8 percent, and rose slightly for females from 6.2 percent to 8.6 percent (Table 3).

However, admissions data from UC's Los Angeles and Berkeley campuses, as well as Stanford, empirically support the more important hypothesis that there are disparities in admit rates across fields. As Table 4 illustrates, Asian American applicants to UCLA from 1983–85 had lower overall admission rates than other applicants, including white applicants, that cannot be explained by analyzing separate admissions statistics for the institution's three undergraduate colleges. Aside from the College of Fine Arts, which accounts for a small proportion of applicants and admits for all groups, Asian Americans consistently had lower rates than whites and other applicants in engineering, as well as letters and science at UCLA. Similarly, as noted earlier, the situation at the Berkeley campus for applicants to the seven different undergraduate colleges and programs from 1981–87 demonstrated comparable differences in admission rates for Asian and white applicants in engineering, the sciences, and the liberal arts. A Stanford University Academic Senate report found that for *every* category of intended majors, Asian Americans had a lower admission rate than whites.

Finally, another common argument for explaining away admission rate disparities is that Asian Americans are less likely than whites to be among specific categories of applicants who receive, by tradition or official decree, special consideration in the admission process—alumni children and athletes. Applicants from these "special" groups usually are admitted at twice or more the rate of other applicants and tend to be largely white at Ivy League and other private elite institutions. For example, the overall admission rate for Brown's entering class in fall of 1987 was an extremely competitive 18.5 percent for all who applied. The admission rates, on the other hand, for alumni legacies and athletes, were 46.1 percent and 56 percent, respectively. The rationale for giving such added preference to special groups of applicants is usually embedded in long-standing institutional policies and practices.

Admissions officers argue that differences in admit rates would not be apparent if Asian Americans were proportionately represented among applicants with alumni and athletic preferences. They also believe that such disparities will vanish in the future as those who are currently enrolled become alumni and urge their own siblings to apply to their alma maters. For example, as Harvard's admissions office wrote, "Today, relatively few Asian Americans are the children of alumni/ae, although the recent dramatic increases in the percentages of Asian Americans in the college will obviously change this significantly in the coming years."

Table 3. Changes in Intended Undergraduate Majors for Asian/Pacific American Students*

Intended Major	Males		Females	
	1977 N=3,699	1985 N=6,730	1977 N=3,738	1985 N=7,008
All sciences and engineering combined**	2,325 (62.9%)	4,672 (69.4%)	1,876 (50.2%)	3,590 (51.2%)
Engineering and computer science only	966 (26.1%)	3,104 (46.1%)	200 (5.3%)	1,106 (15.8%)

*Based on SAT data tapes for California test-takers. 1977 and 1985.
**Includes all test-takers who indicated a preference for majoring in the biological sciences, computer science, engineering, health and medicine, mathematics, physical sciences, and psychology.
Source: UCLA Project on Asian/Pacific Americans in Higher Education.

Table 4. 1983–85 Applicants and Admits to the UCLA School of Engineering, College of Letters and Science, and College of Fine Arts

	1983			1984			1985		
	Appli-cants	Admits	Admit Rate	Appli-cants	Admits	Admit Rate	Appli-cants	Admits	Admit Rate
School of Engineering									
All Applicants	655	368	56.2%	1,665	596	35.8%	1,780	712	40.0%
Asian Americans	174	94	54.0%	617	145	23.5%	719	241	33.5%
Whites	350	161	46.0%	807	281	34.8%	860	319	37.0%
College of Letters and Science									
All Applicants	7,184	4,826	67.2%	8,271	4,787	57.9%	8,426	4,620	54.8%
Asian Americans	1,296	804	62.0%	1,356	647	47.7%	1,325	595	44.9%
Whites	3,903	2,480	63.5%	4,479	2,362	52.7%	4,496	2,137	47.5%
Colleges of Fine Arts									
All Applicants	514	231	45.0%	614	319	51.9%	680	299	44.0%
Asian Americans	63	25	40.0%	72	42	58.3%	97	46	47.4%
Whites	374	165	44.1%	437	220	50.3%	478	211	44.1%
Combined Total									
All Applicants	8,852	5,508	63.2%	10,550	5,782	53.9%	10,889	5,631	51.7%
Asian Americans	1,533	923	60.2%	2,047	834	40.7%	2,141	882	41.2%
Whites	4,627	2,806	60.6%	5,727	2,863	50.0%	5,834	2,667	45.7%

Source: UCLA Planning Office

WHAT SHOULD BE DONE?

Since the Asian American admissions issue evolved out of an extraordinary historical convergence of social, political, and demographic changes among the Asian American population—a pattern projected to continue for many more years—positive steps must be taken to resolve the major points of the dispute. If they are not resolved, it is highly likely we will witness further intervention by legislative bodies and governmental compliance agencies; more protests by Asian American students, professors, and civil rights leaders; and continued attention by the news media. There might also be an individual or class-action lawsuit. (In the January 1989 issue of the *Yale Law Journal*, attorney Grace Tsuang provided the necessary legal foundation for a possible future lawsuit, which might be filed by an Asian American who is denied admission to either a public or private college because of an upper-limit quota on Asian Americans.)

The Asian American admissions controversy represents only the most recent dispute focusing on issues of equal and fair access and representation in higher education. If the Asian American applicant pool continues to increase in the future, two complex policy issues will become increasingly significant and controversial. First, how large a difference in admission rates between Asian Americans and other groups of applicants will be tolerated by university administrators before they take, or are compelled by others to take, corrective measures? As indicated earlier, the present disparities in admission rates are not closely guarded secrets, but rather are openly and publicly acknowledged facts. Although several campuses have initiated fact-finding studies, most admissions officers have only speculated on the causes of what they perceive to be less than compelling differences. What would be compelling? If Asian American applicants to a college were 75 percent, 50 percent, or 25 percent as likely as other applicants to gain admission, would this constitute sufficient cause for university administrators to address the issue more rigorously? Would such disparities lead to further external intervention or perhaps legal challenges?

The second issue relates directly to the first, and it deals with the broader issue of how much of an Asian American presence will be accepted and tolerated by institutions of higher learning. University officials usually do not maintain an inflexible and predetermined score card on how much varied representation they seek from different groups. However, they do not seem to have given sufficient thought and attention to relating institutional goals of academic-based meritocracy and valued diversity to the Asian American representation on their campuses. Indeed, it seems that Asian American applicants are evaluated exclusively with the non-minority, regular admission pool and tend to be strong candidates. Their presence in the pool, and ultimately in the college, strengthens the academic profile of the university's entering class. However, because Asian American applicants are counted as minorities, university officials also can boast about the racial diversity of their entering class. There is something at least peculiar, and perhaps insidious, about this relationship that demands closer and more serious attention.

The continuation of an adversarial relationship is not in the best interests of any of the parties involved in the Asian American admissions debate. There is definitely more to be gained by seeking a mutually advantageous partnership between the new and growing Asian American population and institutions of higher education. Berkeley Professor L. Ling-Chi Wang, a major national spokesperson for fair and equal admissions practices toward Asian Americans, best summarized what should be done. "Universities, public or private, should allow full access to their admissions policies and data to avoid suspicion and abuse of power. Asian Americans are not asking for numerical increases in their enrollments, nor are they challenging the merit of existing affirmative action programs. Not unlike whites, they are asking only for fair and equal treatment and demanding equal participation in decision-making processes. In other words, Asian Americans want only equality and justice, no more and no less."

18

Meritocracy and Diversity in Higher Education:
Discrimination Against Asian Americans in the Post-*Bakke* Era

L. Ling-Chi Wang

NOT SINCE the U.S. Supreme Court decision in the case of *Bakke* v. *The University of California* in 1978 has a controversy in higher education been given as much media and political attention as the issue of discrimination against highly qualified Asian Americans seeking admissions, through regular, competitive channels, into the nation's most prestigious public and private universities. The issue was initially identified and raised as a regional concern in a study completed in 1983 by a group of Asian American college students attending elite private universities in the Northeast (Ho and Chin, 1983). Although it received only scant public attention in the media and in the Asian American community, the issue became the sustained focus of growing national attention following the release in June 1985 of the widely publicized report of the Asian American Task Force on University Admissions (ATFUA, 1985a). In its report, ATFUA, a broadly based community group cochaired by two Asian American judges in northern California, accused the University of California at Berkeley (UCB) of abruptly changing its admission policies and practices to slow down, if not to reverse, rising Asian American and declining white enrollments. The report reignited the earlier concern of Asian American students attending East Coast universities and stimulated others to look into previously unsuspected elite universities such as Stanford University and MIT. Two federal law enforcement agencies—the U.S. Department of Justice and the Office for Civil Rights of the U.S. Department of Education—openly expressed interest in looking into the allegations of racial discrimination (Bennett, 1985; Manzagal, 1986). With the publication of a major article in the *Chronicle of Higher Education* (Biemiller, 1986), what began modestly as a regional concern in 1983 rapidly emerged into a national debate (Hassan, 1986–87), prompting President Ronald Reagan to warn the nation on May 3 that "the use of informal exclusionary racial quotas or any practice of racial discrimination against any individual violates the law, is morally wrong and will not be tolerated" (*Asian Week*, 1988, p. 1). Ironically, this debate over "overrepresentation" and possible admissions "quotas" for Asian Americans is occurring amidst a national celebration in the media of Asian Americans as a successful "model minority" on the one hand, and, on the other, an avalanche of blue-ribbon studies urging the nation's schools and colleges to return to the pursuit of academic excellence to help maintain the U.S. competitive edge in technology and trade (Gross and Gross, 1985).

The purpose of this paper is to examine recent changes in the admissions patterns and

From *The Urban Review* 20 (1988):189–209. Reprinted with permission of Human Sciences Press, Inc.

policies of some of the most prestigious institutions of higher education in the U.S., with particular reference to the University of California system. More specifically, the paper focuses on recent moves away from the application of strict meritocratic admissions criteria toward an increasing reliance on subjective or nonacademic criteria, as well as an emerging, but vaguely defined, concept of "diversity." Additionally, this paper assesses the impact of these changes on both the admission of Asian American students in these institutions and on the time-honored principle of meritocracy upon which these so-called world-class universities have built their reputations of academic excellence. The scope of this study is severely limited by the closely guarded data and documents available to date, as well as by the fact that the issue is complex and still unfolding. As a consequence, this study should be considered a contribution to an ongoing public policy debate and its conclusions considered tentative.

MERITOCRACY AND THE STRUCTURE OF PRIVILEGE

In an essay published during national debates over the meanings of *Bakke* and charges of "reverse discrimination," Duster (1976, p. 73) persuasively argues that the universalistic criterion of merit used in selection procedures for admission actually "(1) *varies* in time, (2) is *socially defined*, and (3) is *intrinsically interconnected with the social structure of privilege and its maintenance*." As an example, he cites the use of the quota systems against Jews for nearly a century by the nation's top medical schools. According to Duster, the quota system was introduced as "an additional criterion" for admission to limit effectively the number and proportion of academically qualified, but "socially undesirable Jews" into these medical schools and to perpetuate the domination and privilege of the white Protestant males in these institutions in the wider society. Here the social and political concerns of the power elite—namely, the perpetuation of the structure of power and privilege—were deemed more important than a rigid adherence to some outdated universalistic meritocratic criterion or standard of academic qualification. In present-day language, the additional criterion used to curb Jewish enrollment—the quota system—was in fact an affirmative action program for the less competitive white Gentile males, disguised as meritocracy. Similar affirmative action programs for whites existed in the worlds of professional sports, entertainment, business, and labor to keep out racial minorities. In other words, the admission criterion, adopted as a universal criterion, was introduced and readily modified over time to help maintain the social and political structure of privilege dominated by the white Protestant elite.

Duster is, of course, not opposed to the use of universalistic and meritocratic criteria in hiring or admissions decisions. Nor is he opposed to the legitimate use of "other criteria" or additional criteria under certain circumstances, such as affirmative action programs designed to break down the cycle of exclusion and privilege, programs erroneously labeled "reverse discrimination." However, he is unequivocally opposed to the use of "other criteria" that are prejudicial, unfair, and discriminatory and whose deployment is for the sole purpose of perpetuating unjustly established power and privilege.

In a related study on the decision to use the quota system and the discretionary power of the admissions offices against highly competitive Jewish applicants between the world wars by the "Big Three"—Harvard, Yale, and Princeton—Karabel (1984, p. 26) calls the decision the "iron law" of admissions at work: "An institution will retain a particular process of selection only so long as it produces outcomes that correspond to perceived organizational interests (of the dominant Protestant upper class)." According to Karabel, the central force behind the decision against the upwardly mobile Jews by the Big Three was the struggle of emerging, competing status groups for scarce resources. (Access to these universities was highly restrictive and selective, and thus was considered a scarce resource.) Since the Big Three were "utterly dependent on the Protestant upper class" for the supply of needed resources, including the administrations of these institutions, "they readily volunteered for service on behalf of its interests and eagerly embraced its fundamental goals." They did so by introducing several nonacademic and subjective criteria to sharply curtail Jewish access to this scarce resource and privileged structure. Among the criteria used were personal character, geographic diversity, religious affiliation, leadership potential, and alumni parentage. Karabel further concludes that the legacy of this period of intense status-group struggle is with us still and that the procedures and criteria developed at that time are used differently today. Echoing Duster, he writes, "Institutional discretion is wielded within the confines of a definition of merit that, albeit now stripped of its more overtly ascriptive trappings, effectively ensures that dominant groups will continue to be its main beneficiaries" (Karabel, 1984, p. 30).

This study uses the concepts of Duster (1976) and Karabel (1984) to clarify the current debate on Asian American admissions among the most selective universities. Moreover, it covers only the competitive channel of admission—not to be confused with the noncompetitive channel through which most leading universities routinely admit athletes, special talents, underrepresented minorities, children of VIPs and wealthy alumni, etc.—through which mostly white and Asian American applicants, supposedly evaluated by strict meritocratic criteria, gain access to these elite institutions. The key questions then for this paper is, In the post-*Bakke* era, have elite universities in the U.S. introduced "other criteria," many of which are nonacademic and subjective, in the name of increasing student diversity in the competitive channel to maintain unjustly the structure of privilege and domination against the emerging, competitive racial group called Asian Americans?

ASIAN AMERICANS IN HIGHER EDUCATION

Measured by several traditional indicators of academic achievement, Asian Americans excel above all other racial groups in the U.S. (Peng, 1988). In fact, it is this extraordinary accomplishment that led the national media to call them the "model minority" (Bell, 1985; Givens et al., 1984; Kasindorf, 1982; McBee et al., 1984; Oxnam, 1986; Whitman, 1987) and "super minority" (Ramirez, 1986). For example, according to the 1980 census, all Asian American groups except the Vietnamese Americans exceeded whites, blacks, and Hispanics in the proportion of the population with a college education (Kan and Liu, 1986; Tsang and Wing, 1985). While only 17.4% of whites 25 years old or over had 4 or more years of college education, 37% of all Chinese Americans 25 years old or over had 4 or more years of college education. Similarly high rates were noted among Japanese Americans (26.3%), Filipino Americans (36.9%), and Korean Americans (33.9%), with only Vietnamese Americans (12%) showing less achievement in this area.

In California, although Asian Americans made up 6.7% of the total population in 1980, they had the lowest school dropout rate and highest school achievements among all racial groups. In 1986, 33% of California's Asian American high school graduates were rated academically eligible for freshman admission to the University of California, compared to only 16% of their white counterparts (California Postsecondary Education Commission, 1985; Curtis, 1988a). In that same year, Asian Americans constituted 13.2% of all students who took the SAT in California, whereas whites made up 56.6%. This impressive record resulted in Asian Americans having the highest college-going rate (California Postsecondary Education Commission, 1987) and is reflected in their enrollment in the nine-campus UC system—18,946, or 18.2%, in 1985 (Office of the President, 1987).

Even more impressive is the ability of this Asian minority (1.6% of the U.S. population in 1980) in just the last 10 years to gain admission to the most prestigious and selective universities—including both the public and private "Ivies"—in percentages far exceeding their population percentage (Bell, 1985; Bunzel and Au, 1987; Hsia, 1988a, b; Hu, 1986, 1987 a,b). For example, Asian Americans made up only 1.95% of Brown's undergraduate pool in 1975 but increased to 10% in 1980. This represents an 848% increase—from 168 students in 1983 to 1,451 students in 1984 (Asian American Students Association, 1983)! Similarly, only 217 Asian Americans applied to Yale in 1976; but in 1987, Asian American applicants increased to 1,597 (Romanoff, 1986). In 1977, UC-Berkeley recorded only 1,936 Asian American applicants, but in 1987, the number shot up to 6,698. To measure the quantum jump with another indicator, between 1976 and 1986, the freshman enrollment of Asian Americans at Harvard rose from 3.6% to 12.8%; at Stanford, from 5.7% to 14.7%; at MIT, from 5.3% to 20.6%; and at UC-Berkeley, from 17.1% to 26.5% (Hu, 1987b).

From this sketchy overview, it is clear that since 1975, Asian Americans have been vigorously pursuing access to one of the nation's scarcest resources: admission into the most prestigious, selective universities. It is important to note that historically this pursuit began only after the black civil rights movement succeeded in opening the doors for racial minorities to these traditionally white-dominated institutions and the coming of age of the children of a significant number of well-educated Asian immigrants after the 1965 change in immigration law (Synnott, 1979). To understand how elite universities have handled the rising Asian American enrollment pressure in this period, I will analyze in some detail the UC-Berkeley example (Gibney, 1988). It is chosen in part because it has attracted the most attention nationally, but more importantly, it is the case upon which we possess reasonably good data.[*]

Recent Developments at UC-Berkeley

To determine possible discrimination, two questions are asked: (1) Have the sudden changes in admissions policy at Berkeley since 1984 had an adverse impact on Asian American applicants in comparison to white applicants? (2) Have these changes in admissions criteria had a racist intent?

The University of California-Berkeley, long considered the flagship campus of the nine-school, state-supported system, has had a total undergraduate student body of about 20,000 in the past decade. In spite of rising demand for admissions, the total undergraduate enrollment over the past 12 years has remained relatively stable. The stability has been maintained largely by steadily and arbitrarily raising the academic standards for admission to UC-Berkeley, by massively redirecting less competitive applicants to other UC campuses—notably UC-Santa Cruz—and by permitting other UC campuses—notably, UC at Santa Cruz, San Diego, Irvine, and Riverside—to expand their enrollments at rates commensurate with the rising demand for access to UC. One result of the rising admission standard in the competitive channel was to make UC-Berkeley extraordinarily competitive for unprotected white and Asian American applicants (Cesa, 1988) and to heighten inadvertently their competition not only for admission but also for access to coveted majors, such

---

[*]In the longer version of this paper that was prepared for the Conference on Comparative Ethnicity (Johnson and Oliver, 1988) I not only analyze the admissions policies and rates of Asian enrollment at UC-Berkeley but also provide an analysis of Asian American admissions at several elite eastern colleges and universities. Those interested in a fuller discussion that goes beyond the case of Berkeley should consult those proceedings.

as engineering and business administration, with a host of unintended consequences, including racial tension (Gibney, 1988).

By virtue of its international reputation as one of the leading public universities in the U.S., and its geographic proximity to San Francisco, which has one of the largest Asian American communities in the U.S., UC-Berkeley has always been the preferred campus for many Asian American parents, dating back to the pre–World War II era. The fact that it is tuition free and readily accessible by public transportation makes it even more attractive to the largely lower-middle- and lower-class Asian American families who simply cannot afford to send their children to more expensive and distant private colleges and other UC campuses (Thomson, 1986). The desirability of this campus can be seen from the huge Asian American applicant pool: 5,713 applied in fall 1987 (28% of all applicants), whereas white applicants registered only 11,190 (54.9% of the total applicant pool). This 2:1 ratio is impressive when one considers the fact that white high school graduates in California outnumbered Asian Americans by 6:1 (140,228 to 22,545). Similar enrollment pressure is found on the UCLA campus because of the surrounding Asian American population.

During the 1975–87 period, the number of Asian American undergraduates (excluding the foreign Asian students) increased rapidly in both absolute and relative terms, from 16.8% (3,410) of all undergraduates to 25.6% (5,665). (By comparison, during the same period the percentage of all undergraduates who were black rose from 4.1% to 6.5% and who were Hispanic, from 3.2% to 9.4%.) Consistent with their demographic decline in California during the same period, white enrollment dropped from 68.2% (13,820) to 51.9% (11,472).

Beyond the steady enrollment gains, the academic qualifications of Asian Americans, measured by their GPA and standardized test scores, also rose at a rate faster than for their white peers. In a recent audit of UC-Berkeley's admission records, for example, the California auditor general reported that the average high school GPA of Asian American applicants rose from 3.10 to 3.72 between 1981 and 1987, whereas the average GPA of whites during the same period rose from 3.27 to 3.62 (California Auditor General, 1987). The report also shows that Asian American applicants proportionately have higher academic index scores—combined scores of GPA, two SAT tests, and three achievement tests—than their white counterparts.

These trends led Roderick Park, the vice chancellor for Academic Affairs, to project in 1985, in his 5-year plan, that the ethnic composition of UC-Berkeley undergraduates by 1990 will be one-third white, one-third Asian American, and one-third for all others (Office of the Chancellor, 1984a). No wonder the Asian American community in the Bay Area was stunned in October 1984, when UC-Berkeley announced that the number of Asian American freshmen, instead of rising from 1,239 in 1983 to possibly about 1,400 in 1984, took a nose dive to 1,008 (ATFUA, 1985a; Gust, 1986). In fact, with the exception of Filipino Americans, who were protected by the affirmative action program, every Asian American subgroup registered a decline. The sharpest reduction occurred among Chinese American freshmen, dropping from 609 in 1983 to 418 in 1984, or by 30%. By comparison, white freshmen admissions declined by only 4%, from 2,425 to 2,327. In short, the decline in the number of Asian American freshmen, in comparison with whites, was disproportionate and significant. Just as significant is the persistence of the disparity in admission rates between Asian Americans and whites over the past several years (see Table 1).

In spite of their superior qualifications vis-à-vis white applicants, from 1985 to 1988, both the number and percentage of Asian American freshmen remained virtually unchanged from the 1984 level. Also alarming to the Asian American community is the fact that the overall undergraduate Asian American enrollment has remained basically stationary at around 25% since 1983. In other words, Vice Chancellor Park's projected annual increase

Table 1. Admission Rates at UC-Berkeley for Whites and Asian Americans, 1981–1987 (Percentages)

	1981	1982	1983	1984	1985	1986	1987
Asian Americans	50.4	60.3	66.8	45.0	44.4	28.4	27.7
Whites	54.3	64.5	70.5	56.4	52.3	32.7	31.4

Source: University of California—Berkeley, 1987a.

in the numbers and percentages of Asian American undergraduates never materialized, convincing many in the Asian American community that UC-Berkeley had a "hidden quota" for Asian Americans (Gust, 1986; Lindsey, 1987; Lye, 1986; Nakao, 1987; Salholz, 1987). The administration steadfastly denied the allegation through press statements and issued studies to refute the findings of ATFUA and to clear the university of any wrongdoing (Office of the Chancellor, 1987).

Following two years of heated public exchanges over the reasons behind the unexpected drop in 1984 and mounting public skepticism over the university's handling of the Asian American concerns, the California auditor general, acting on a request by the California state legislature, conducted an extensive independent audit of UC-Berkeley's admissions records for the period from 1981 to 1987 (California Auditor General, 1987). The auditor general released his 400-page report on October 7, 1987. The report revealed that during the period covered in the audit, whites "gained admission to Berkeley's five colleges at rates that were higher in general than those of Asians" in spite of the superior academic qualifications of Asian American applicants (California Auditor General, 1987, p. 5–2). More specifically, the auditor general stated that "of the 49 Asian admission rates and the 49 Caucasian admission rates that we compared with each other, the Caucasian rates were higher in 37 instances" (ibid., p. 5–4). Without making any allegations of racial discrimination, Deputy Auditor General Kurt Sjoberg said, "I think many would ask why (there are disparities), and I think the university will have to answer why" (p. 5–4). In short, the persistent disparity in the admission rates between whites and Asian Americans uncovered by the auditor general confirmed the earlier findings of ATFUA and provided credence to its allegations of racial discrimination and hidden quotas.

In response to the report, Berkeley's Chancellor Ira M. Heyman claimed, "From all the evidence I have seen, I remain firmly convinced that our methods are sound and that there is no pattern of unfairness" (UCB, 1987a, p. 2). In a measured response, ATFUA firmly rejected the chancellor's claim and called for additional probes by the academic senate, the UC board of regents, and the California state legislature (ATFUA, 1987; Board of Regents, 1987; California State Assembly, 1988; Lye, 1987; Office of the President, 1988).

Two questions remain unanswered: (1) What policy changes were made to cause the disparity between white and Asian American admissions? and (2) What was the motive or intent behind these changes? A careful analysis of the rationales and intents behind the policy changes after 1983 should provide a clue to the main issue raised in this paper. Unfortunately, most of the relevant documents and minutes of meetings are still unavailable. The following analysis is based on what has been disclosed to date.

ADVERSE IMPACT

Sometime in late 1983 or early 1984, a major policy decision was made without public knowledge to redirect Educational Opportunity Program (EOP) applicants "who were not Blacks, Hispanic or Native Americans" to UC-Santa Cruz (Office of the Chancellor, 1984b, p. 2). The program had previously protected UC-eligible, but noncompetitive, applicants who were poor and disadvantaged—regardless of race—from being rejected or redirected to other UC campuses (ATFUA, 1985a). The decision represented a major policy shift from a socioeconomic to a race-based admission program. Subsequent investigation revealed that the decision was made without the participation and approval of the Academic Senate Committee on Admissions and Enrollment, a faculty committee authorized to make admissions policy decisions, and no public announcement of the change was made (Lye, 1986). Since there has always been a larger proportion of Asian American applicants who are from disadvantaged backgrounds in the San Francisco Bay area than whites (377 to 122 in 1983, and 446 to 143 in 1984), the decision disproportionately affected Asian American EOP applicants (Min, 1987; Thomson, 1986). Among the new EOP students in 1983, 62 were whites and 248 were Asian Americans, but in the following year, their numbers dropped to 55 and 136 respectively. In spite of the chancellor's assurance that "students with hardship will be given special consideration during the subjective phase of application review" (ATFUA, 1985a, Attach. 1, p. 3), poor and disadvantaged Asian American students became the major victims of this new policy. Continuing the declining trends, the numbers of new white and Asian American EOP students in 1985 were, respectively, 24 and 83 (Min, 1987). That the decision to change the EOP policy had an adverse impact on Asian Americans is clear.

INTENT

Sometime before the 1984 freshmen class was admitted, a rumor surfaced on the Berkeley campus that the administration had decided to impose a minimum SAT verbal standard on all unprotected applicants (this included, among others, both whites and Asian Americans). When the chancellor was first questioned about this issue by a regent of UC in late 1984, he flatly denied that such a policy decision was ever made and cited evidence to show that the allegation was unfounded (Gibney, 1988, p. 16; Office of the Chancellor, 1984b). ATFUA, however, continued to press for full disclosure of that decision (ATFUA, 1985a, Attach. 3, p. 2). Finally, in a response to ATFUA, Assistant Vice Chancellor Travers wrote, "At one point (in 1984) a minimum 400 Verbal SAT score was set, but shortly after the written directive was issued, it was withdrawn" (ATFUA, 1985a). With this belated admission in March 1985, the university ended several months of repeated denials that such a directive was ever issued in 1984. However, the administration failed to release the memo and did not offer an explanation for the policy decision (Pickell, 1988). Additionally, an investigation was never ordered to find out why and how the decision came to be made. It was not until November 18, 1987, a month after the release of the auditor general's report, that the chancellor agreed to have this matter investigated by a special academic senate committee (Burkhard, 1987; Ipson and Tjoa, 1987; Lye, 1987). On January 26, 1988, Chancellor Heyman publicly apologized to the Asian American community for mishandling its concerns (California State Assembly, 1988; Gordon, 1988). However, it was not until February 1988 that the directive, issued on December 28, 1983, and reaffirmed on January 4, 1984, by Robert L. Bailey, director of the Office of Admissions and Records, was secured by the task force and released to the press (Levine, 1988; Lum, 1988; Tokunaga, 1988).

From the very beginning, the directive was the focus of attention and the "smoking gun" sought by the task force (Tokunaga, 1988). If such a policy in fact existed, it would have provided ATFUA the most direct proof of illegality and racist intent. At no time in the history of UC-Berkeley had there been such a criterion used for rejecting qualified applicants in the competitive channel of admission. In fact, in all published announcements, catalogs, and application forms, the policy had always been to use only the combined SAT verbal and math scores, the combined scores of three achievement tests, and GPA for admissions decisions in the competitive channel. The reliance on a single criterion—a minimal SAT verbal standard—to disqualify an unprotected and unsuspecting applicant, white or Asian American, was unprecedented and in violation of UC-Berkeley's announced policy. Even its validity for predicting Asian American college performance is questionable (Zane, Sue, and Abe, 1988). Worse yet, the decision to use such a criterion was made with the full knowledge that its implementation would have an adverse impact on Asian American applicants who, like their white peers, were not protected by any affirmative action program. What made the policy insidious was the fact that the university administration knew that the national average Asian SAT verbal score in 1984 was 28 points below the national average of 426 (College Board, 1985; Office of the President, 1986, 1987). (Incidentally, the average Asian SAT math score in 1984 was 48 points above the national average of 417.) What is more, the mean SAT verbal score for Berkeley freshmen of immigrant background—overwhelmingly Asian Americans—was at least 100 points lower than the mean for other freshmen between 1978 and 1982—a vital bit of information widely known to the UC-Berkeley decision makers (Tang, 1982). In other words, the unmistakable intent behind the secret decision was to disqualify some UC-eligible Asian American applicants from competition with white applicants, even though they were eligible according to the written policy. The decision made jointly by several key figures in the administration was illegal, and it amounted to an abuse of power and betrayal of public trust (Packer, 1988; Pickell, 1988).

Another important policy change also reveals the intention of the administration. In 1985, an Admission Study Group headed by Leonard Kuhi, provost and dean of the College of Letters and Science (L & S), drew up and put to limited use a set of supplemental admission criteria, most of which did not measure an applicant's competitive excellence and some of which were quite subjective (ATFUA, 1985a, Attach. 4). These nonacademic criteria were modified and more broadly applied in 1986 and again in 1987 to screen applicants in the competitive channel (ATFUA, 1987; California Auditor General, 1987; Hickey, 1987). According to the university, these criteria were introduced to enable the admissions office "to make better distinctions between the various (competitive) applicants [and] to determine qualities considered by the Academic Senate to be relevant to Berkeley students" (Office of the Chancellor, 1987a, p. 8). From these added criteria and the differential weight assigned to each, it is clear that the intent is to admit well-rounded individuals. In other words, beyond competitive excellence, some unprotected applicants, mostly whites and Asian Americans, must compete on nonacademic criteria as well (Lye, 1987).

By this decision, the administration created a secondary channel within the competitive channel to admit a different type of freshmen (Office of the Chancellor, 1987). In promulgating these additional criteria, the administration gave no rationale, conducted no adverse-impact study prior to adoption, solicited no input from Asian American constituencies, and provided virtually no advance notice to the 1985 applicants. As subsequent investigation revealed, the decision was made again without prior participation and approval of the Academic Senate Committee on Admissions and Enrollment; it was approved only retroactively.

These new criteria came to be known as "supplemental criteria" or "selection criteria," and their implementation was first disclosed in a report assembled by Assistant Vice Chancellor Bud Travers in response to mounting public criticism over the Asian admission issue in January 1987 (Office of the Chancellor, 1987). Up to 1,300 points were to be added to an applicant's academic index score under seven criteria: 200 points for California residence, 200 for EOP eligibility, 200 for 4 years of math or 3 years of laboratory science, 100 for 4 years of one foreign language or 2 years of two foreign languages, 100 for exemption for Subject A (remedial English), 100 for attending a high school that does not offer two honors courses in the junior year, and 500 for an essay that demonstrates leadership, character, motivation, and accomplishments in extracurricular activities. Only 1,500 out of over 20,000 applicants were subjected to the additional screening in 1985 and only 3,000 in 1986.

Again, on the surface, the additional criteria appear to be neutral. In actuality, they have built-in bias against the majority of Asian American applicants who are of immigrant and refugee background. For example, those aspects that gave additional points to those applicants who were exempt from remedial English, who had four years of a foreign (European) language, and who demonstrated leadership potential through their extracurricular activities appear designed precisely to make a large number of Asian Americans less competitive than white applicants (Hickey, 1986, 1987; Lye, 1986; Nakao, 1987; Office of the Chancellor, 1982; Office of Student Research, 1980, 1982). (Based on publicly announced admissions criteria, most Asian immigrant parents had discouraged, if not prohibited, their children from participation in extracurricular activities because most of them had assumed such activities to be worthless for gaining access into the most academically selective universities.) In addition, questions could be raised on the use of these criteria for only a small, selected segment of about 18% of the total freshman class. Needless to say, there is no basis for verifying the claims in the required essay, which carries up to 500 points.

The policy changes just described explain in part what has happened since 1983; how these changes adversely affected Asian American admissions; and, by their impact, what the intent was behind the changes. Questions could be raised also about how UC recruited and processed Asian American applicants who qualified under the Special Action program and how UC recruited and admitted Asian Americans who were athletes, veterans, disabled persons, or students with special talents (Cesa, 1988; Office of the Chancellor, 1988). Just as important to the institution committed to academic excellence is how it intends to prevent obviously top-performing students, like Steve Ta and Yat-pang Au, the subjects of two highly publicized cases in 1986 and 1987, from being denied admission (Feist, 1987; Hickey, 1986; Matthews, 1987; Nakao, 1987).

Unfortunately, the Berkeley experience is not unique. The Asian American freshmen and admissions rates at UCLA also started to decline in 1983 (Nakanishi, 1988). The percentage of Asian American freshmen dropped from 19.7% in 1982 to 18.7% in 1983 to 15.9% in 1984 (Siporin, 1984). During the same period, the admission rate for Asian American freshmen declined from 62.1% in 1982 to 40.7% in 1984, while the rate for all freshmen decreased only from 62.1% to 53.9%. The total number of Asian American undergraduates dropped from 4,640 in 1983 to 4,185 in 1985 (Fanucchi, 1985; Ogasawara, 1985, p. 1).

These UCLA figures make sense when placed against a 1984 internal planning paper written by Rae Lee Siporin, UCLA admissions director (California State Assembly, 1988, pp. 13–14; Siporin, 1984). In this confidential paper on issues of undergraduate enrollment, Siporin made it perfectly clear that "race" remains a key concept in the planning process: "This campus will endeavor to curb the decline of Caucasian students. A rising concern will come from Asian students and Asians in general as the number and proportion of Asian students entering at the freshmen level decline—however small the decline may be" (Siporin, 1984). Maintaining a certain racial character of the institution is clearly a top priority.

Overrepresentation of Asian American students is likewise a major preoccupation of nine-campus UC president, David P. Gardner. In an Associated Press story, dated December 12, 1986, Gardner said that "changes [in admissions policy] are needed because Asians comprise more than 20% of the undergraduate enrollment at UC campuses but make up only 6% of the state's population" (Associated Press, 1986; also, see *San Diego Union,*

1986; Scott-Blair, 1986). He labeled this phenomenon "overrepresentation" and "racial imbalance" and claimed that it was having "an adverse effect on the (UC) systems' attempts to increase Hispanic and black enrollment" (Associated Press, 1986). He even candidly admitted that the "overrepresentation" has caused "unrest" among some ethnic groups, "including whites," who had been experiencing a decline in representation. To rectify the situation, he called for new legislation to make UC enrollment "more accurately reflect the population (of California)" (Associated Press, 1986).

By implication, Gardner is suggesting that the overrepresentation of Asian Americans is preventing UC from increasing its underrepresented minorities or that affirmative action is a factor affecting Asian American admissions. Such analysis is hardly correct. Asian American and white applicants do not compete with applicants in the protected categories. By taking this position, Gardner is at odds with what most elite universities accept as principles guiding their admissions practices: academic excellence and egalitarianism. The two principles are not considered contradictory. The two-tier system is designed precisely to accomplish these two principles and to avoid competition between tiers. There are, however, grounds to conclude that Gardner holds a different view. Gardner reiterated his view in a National Public Radio interview in November 1987, in which he directly commented on the two principles: "We are being asked to accomplish society goals and to attain educational objectives that are not wholly, but substantially, contradictory."

In a speech before the Commonwealth club in San Francisco on October 29, 1987, he again stated his position and said that it was UC's policy to admit students of varied backgrounds, rather than simply fill up the freshmen class with straight-A students (Smith, 1987). He said UC should not be defensive about admissions policies that strive for a diverse class of popular campuses, even if it means redirecting (a euphemism for rejecting) qualified students and explaining to Asian Americans that other UC campuses have something to offer, too. In short, it was appropriate for a UC campus to reject academically excellent students, not on meritocratic grounds, but in the name of diversity (Roark, 1986). Diversity, a concept used in *Bakke* to legally justify the university's use of an affirmative action program to bring in historically discriminated, underrepresented racial minorities and to enrich the learning environment suddenly became a basis for setting an unspecified upper limit of enrollment for the "overrepresented" Asian Americans, regardless of their qualifications. The new notion of diversity, however vaguely defined by Gardner, signals a departure from the meritocratic principle. In fact, Gardner succeeded in introducing this notion into a new admissions policy adopted by the regents of the university on May 20, 1988 (Curtis, 1988b). Its implementation is aimed more at preventing overrepresentation of Asian Americans than at admitting underrepresented blacks and Hispanics in accordance with their percentages in the California population. In short, Gardner's objective is to control the rising Asian American and declining white enrollment trends without fully and logically conceding to the principle of proportional representation based on race. Diversity, in this sense, is an affirmative action program for less competitive and declining white applicants and tokenism for the underrepresented minorities.

To prevent the overrepresentation of Asian American students, university administrators use their discretionary power to devise stopgap measures or new selection criteria, without adequate public input and knowledge. The intent of these measures is clearly to slow down or reverse the accelerating rate of Asian American admissions. On the surface, these additional criteria, most of which are nonacademic or subjective, appear to be neutral and fair. In practice, they have adversely impacted Asian American applicants, most of whom have immigrant or disadvantaged backgrounds. The secret manner by which these measures were developed and carried out by a tax-supported institution is questionable, if not illegal. Finally, the callous manner by which university officials have been handling the legitimate concerns raised by Asian American educators and leaders also leaves much to be desired and creates a crisis of public trust in the institution (Lye, 1987).

IMPLICATIONS OF RECENT POLICY CHANGES

From the preceding analysis it is clear that Asian Americans, in light of their diverse class backgrounds, can be considered an emerging, competitive status group in the U.S. (Karabel, 1984). It is the first and only nonwhite minority group to succeed, unassisted, in penetrating the traditional aristocratic strongholds maintained historically and socially with class-biased and allegedly universalistic meritocratic criteria. To maintain their privileged status and to perpetuate their domination in these white citadels of knowledge and power, to use Duster's analysis (1976), they have been forced in the 1980s to modify their admissions criteria in order to slow down the Asian American "invasion," much like what these same institutions had to do from 1918 to 1947 when they discovered the "Jewish problem" (Steinberg, 1981; Synnott, 1979). To these elite institutions, Asian American students constitute a "New Yellow Peril," an upwardly mobile, competitive status group seeking access to tightly controlled, scarce resources, and ultimately, a share in the power and privilege of the dominant elite. After all, these are the traditional institutions from which America recruits her future leaders or elite. The inevitable response is to protect the organizational interests and to make sure the dominant powers will continue to control these institutions and to derive benefit for themselves.

This has been accomplished by redefining the concept of diversity used in *Bakke* to justify the use of affirmative action programs to admit underrepresented minorities through the noncompetitive channel. Under this new and expanded definition, the university now uses the concept of diversity to impose an undisclosed upper limit or ceiling on the highly competitive, but "overrepresented," Asian Americans in the competitive channel, clearly an unintended and unanticipated use—indeed, one prohibited by *Bakke*. In public policy terms, diversity is to be achieved with the introduction of some nonacademic and subjective criteria in the screening process. On the surface, these new criteria appear to be fair and racially neutral. But as the preceding analysis demonstrates, they have had an adverse impact on Asian American applicants and, indeed, were designed to curb the rising Asian American and declining white enrollments. In other words, they are additional criteria incorporated into a new affirmative action program, built on a newly defined principle of diversity, for less competitive white applicants. The elimination of the EOP program for Asians and whites and the admission of larger numbers of whites under various color-blind, but protected, categories in fact account for the disparity between white and Asian American students at UC-Berkeley and other elite private institutions (Office of the Chancellor, 1988).

However, by introducing these new criteria for tier-one admissions, the university also redefines and, indeed, contradicts its earlier universal concept of merit and academic excellence. The rationale for these newly defined universal criteria is the need for diversity, especially ethnic and geographic diversity, and the need to avoid "overrepresentation" of Asian Americans. Diversity, of course, was the concept used for decades by the Ivy League universities to limit Jewish students to a small quota. Now the same concept is being used to curb the "overrepresentation" of Asian American students. UC's President Gardner said he was opposed to any racial quota, but he also made the following statement about UC admissions policy:

> It seems to me that if we continue on the present path [of admitting the highly qualified Asian American students], it inevitably will lead to quotas, so I don't wish to continue on this path. I wish to change paths. . . . I want to build into our admissions process criteria that take account of ethnicity for purposes of assuring a pluralistic student body

responsive to the changing demographics of California, but only as part of a number of
criteria that we apply for the purpose of assuring that an entering freshman class is possessed of the kind of experience, potential, ethnic differences, social differences, rural
and urban differences and so forth to enrich the whole learning environment and experience that these young people have. . . . We will apply some of the criteria the private
institutions routinely apply in making judgments about who to admit so that the freshmen class is diverse. (*San Diego Union*, 1986, p. c-3)

In both language and tone, this statement is reminiscent of what President Lawrence Lowell
of Harvard said some 60 years ago when he was confronted with a large pool of highly
qualified Jewish applicants from the New York area. Lowell made it clear that he wanted
diversity. I am not opposed to the use of additional criteria to bring in promising students,
especially those who were currently underrepresented. However, to follow Duster's (1976)
analysis, the new criteria, introduced in the name of a newly defined diversity, are prejudicial, unfair, and discriminatory to Asian Americans, and their use is designed solely to
provide a competitive edge for white applicants in the tier-one admissions and thereby to
perpetuate the white domination in these institutions.

Even though Gardner expressed his distaste for the use of quotas, what he said about
diversity and what he intends to do—that is, rely heavily on subjective and nonacademic
criteria—will inevitably lead to an arbitrary limit of Asian American access and, hence, a
quota. This, in fact, is what has been happening at UC-Berkeley and at some elite private
universities. This development is perhaps one of the major unintended and certainly unanticipated abuses of the discretionary power authorized by the *Bakke* decision in 1978: setting an upper numerical limit in the competitive admission process solely on the basis of
race and requiring individual applicants to have diverse backgrounds. It is certainly one
legal issue that may have to be resolved in the future by another U.S. Supreme Court decision.

The introduction of nonacademic and subjective criteria to achieve diversity means
also a redefinition of the mission or goal of these research-oriented institutions traditionally committed to the pursuit of academic excellence. There is clearly a limit to the extent
that these new criteria are to be carried out without seriously undermining these institutions' commitment to competitive excellence. Without restraint, this new development
could destroy these institutions and in the process deprive this nation of one of its most
valuable national resources. Unfortunately, for the time being, political expediency takes
priority over thoughtful reflection.

Ironically, this has come about precisely at the time when the political and economic
elite of the nation have been trying to build a national consensus on the need to improve
the nation's schools and to renew our commitment to academic excellence. At the forefront
of this movement is the National Commission on Excellence in Education, led by none
other than David P. Gardner (National Commission on Excellence in Education, 1983, p.
3). In its 1983 final report, *A Nation at Risk*, the commission wrote:

Our Nation is at risk. Our once unchallenged preeminence in commerce, industry, science, and technological innovation is being overtaken by competitors throughout the
world. . . . We report to the American people that while we can take justifiable pride in
what our schools and colleges have historically accomplished and contributed to the
United States and the well-being of its people, the educational foundations of our society are presently being eroded by a rising tide of mediocrity that threatens our very future as a Nation and a people. What was unimaginable a generation ago has begun to
occur—others are matching and surpassing our educational attainments. . . . We have,

in effect, been committing an act of unthinking, unilateral educational disarmament. . . .
If an unfriendly foreign power had attempted to impose on America the mediocre educational performance that exists today, we might well have viewed it as an act of war.
(p. 3)

This is very strong, if not exaggerated, Cold War rhetoric, quite contradictory, both
in language and tone, to the words used to justify the rejection of straight-A Asian American
students and to advocate diversity and use of nonacademic and subjective criteria. By failing to clarify the precise meaning of diversity, excellence, and egalitarianism and setting
the limit for the use of these new criteria, Gardner is in fact exposing the university to mediocrity and committing "an act of unilateral educational disarmament." When a major university president says he does not want to "simply fill up the freshman class with straight-A
students" and when this same university has been rejecting large numbers of the nation's
top students, what kind of message is he conveying to the students of the nation? If the university is prepared to admit eligible students whose GPAs range from 3.3 to 4.0, why not,
to be perfectly fair, simply admit applicants within this range by lottery?

In the late 19th and early 20th centuries, the U.S. Congress enacted a series of exclusionary immigration laws to halt the old "Yellow Peril" and passed discriminatory laws
to permanently disenfranchise and suppress those Asians who chose to remain in the U.S.
During World War II, the U.S. government succumbed to racist hysteria and invoked national security concerns to incarcerate 110,000 innocent Japanese Americans. In the 1980s,
in response to a new "Yellow Peril" syndrome, the liberal and enlightened universities of
America have been busy erecting comparable exclusionary measures to prevent overrepresentation of Asian Americans in these institutions. The only problem is that these new
schemes tend to undermine the traditional rhetoric of meritocracy and to conflict with the
national drive to improve the quality of education.

CONCLUSIONS

In the pre-World War II period, the elite universities solved the "Jewish problem" by imposing a strict quota for Jewish enrollments (10% to 15%) and by redesigning an affirmative action program for white Gentiles that called for, as in the case of Harvard, scholarship,
geographic diversity, and "character and fitness and the promise of the greatest usefulness
in the future as a result of a Harvard education" (Synott, 1986, p. 234). Others added nonacademic criteria—notably religious and social criteria and culturally biased character evaluation—to the existing meritocratic criteria for academic qualifications to effectively prevent
Jews from overrepresentation. Dartmouth even mobilized its alumni to interview, screen,
and reject Jewish applicants. Dartmouth's president defended his action, with liberal
rhetoric, as the only way to prevent anti-Semitism from increasing in the U.S. as it had in
Nazi Germany. Or, as Harvard President Lawrence Lowell told *The New York Times* on
June 17, 1922, "If every college in the country would take a limited proportion of Jews, we
should go a long way toward eliminating race feeling among the students, and, as these students passed out into the world, eliminating it in the community" (Synott, 1986, p. 233).

In light of what happened to the Jewish applicants in the prewar period and what has
been encountered by Asian American applicants in the 1980s, we are compelled to ask if
these same institutions have now discovered an "Asian American problem" in the 1980s
and if their recent changes in admission criteria with added emphasis on nonacademic and
subjective criteria, student body diversity, and well-rounded individuals were calculated
efforts aimed at solving the problem of "overrepresentation" or quelling the racial "unrest"
noted by UC President Gardner.

When Bud Travers, assistant vice chancellor for Undergraduate Affairs at UC-Berkeley, advised Asian Americans in his January 1987 report that "Cal [UC-Berkeley] is only one of eight UC campuses with undergraduate programs, and every student in California who is UC eligible can be accommodated at one of these campuses, but not necessarily at all," we are likewise compelled to ask if he was telling Asian Americans that the Berkeley campus had reached its tolerance level for Asian Americans, much like the presidents of Harvard and Dartmouth did to rationalize, with good intention, their small Jewish quotas (Office of the Chancellor, 1987, p. 3). Whether Asian American applicants are willing and financially able to attend UC campuses away from their homes, which happen to concentrate mostly in the San Francisco and Los Angeles areas, appears to be a problem UC considers immaterial and irrelevant.

In conclusion, the current efforts to limit Asian American access to high-quality education is in fact another manifestation of a very old anti-Asian racism deeply woven into the fabric of our society and embedded in our culture and national consciousness. This anti-Asian sentiment has existed as long as the history of the nation, as Stuart Miller (1969) persuasively demonstrated in his book *The Unwelcome Immigrant*. It surfaced periodically in waves of anti-Asian movements in the second half of the 19th and throughout the 20th centuries (Daniels, 1962; Saniels, 1967; Saxton, 1971). This sentiment has recently surfaced again because of the growing presence, assertiveness, and perceived competition of different classes of Asian Americans across the nation. The proliferation of anti-Asian violence, the demands for more restrictive and selective immigration laws, and the rise of the English-only movement in both public education and the electoral process are some of the latest manifestations of this racist sentiment (Asian American Resource Workshop, 1987; Break the Silence Coalition, 1986; U.S. Commission on Civil Rights, 1986). At the root of these manifestations is a shared conviction or attitude that Asian Americans are simply "foreigners," not Americans; that they are not entitled to have the same rights and privileges as American citizens; that, as an emerging group in the 1980s, they should get only what they are given and understand that what is given can be taken back at will—a prerogative of those in control of the power and distribution of scarce resources, who also have the right and power to redefine values and criteria to perpetuate their domination. Considering their collective contributions to the postwar U.S. economy and development of science and technology, it is ironic that Asian Americans should now become the victims of their own success.

The issue of diversity is a legitimate one that must not be dismissed lightly, even if it is being used as a pretext to limit or exclude any racial minority. It should be discussed, studied, and debated by all affected parties. Whatever meanings and values are attached to the concept and ultimately adopted by universities in the admissions process should be fair and relevant to the higher missions of these universities, and potential students should be given ample time to meet the new requirements.

Finally, universities, public or private, should allow full access to their admissions policies and data to avoid suspicion and abuse of power. Asian Americans are not asking for numerical increases in their enrollment, nor are they challenging the merit of existing affirmative action programs. Not unlike whites, they are asking only for a fair and equal treatment and demanding equal participation in decision-making processes. In other words, Asian Americans want only equality and justice, no more and no less.

REFERENCES

Academic Senate. (1986). Report of the Committee on Admissions and Enrollment. (Minutes). Berkeley: University of California.

Asian American Resource Workshop (1987). To live in peace: Responding to anti-Asian violence in Boston. Boston.

Asian American Students Association (1983). Asian American admissions at Brown University. Providence, RI: Brown University.

Asian American Task Force on University Admissions (ATFUA) (1985a). Task force report. San Francisco.

Asian American Task Force (ATFUA) (1985b). Task force response to UC-Berkeley's comments on ATFUA's report. San Francisco.

Asian American Task Force (ATFUA) (1987). Task force response to the report by the California Auditor General. San Francisco.

Asian Week (1988, May 6). p. 1.

Associated Press (1986, December 12). UC chief wants a better ethnic mix. *Tribune* (Oakland).

Bell, D. A. (1985, July 15, 22). An American success story: the triumph of Asian Americans. *The New Republic* (No. 3677): 24–31.

Bennett, W. J. (1985, October 22). Address by William J. Bennett, U.S. Secretary of Education. A speech delivered to the Vietnamese League of Orange County, Orange County, CA.

Biemiller, L. (1986, November 19). Asian students fear top colleges use quota systems. *Chronicle of Higher Education*, p. 1.

Board of Regents (1987). Minutes of meeting on November 20. Berkeley: University of California.

Brand, D. (1987, August 31). The new whiz kids. *Time* 139(9): 42–51.

Break the Silence Coalition (1986). Break silence: A conference on anti-Asian violence. San Francisco.

Bunzel, J. H., and Au, J. K. D. (1987). Diversity or discrimination? Asian Americans in College. *The Public Interest* 87: 49–62.

Burkhard, M. (1987, October 29). UC admissions group disbands. *Daily Californian*.

California Auditor General (1987). A review of first-year admissions of Asians and Caucasians at the University of California at Berkeley. Sacramento: Office of the Auditor General.

California Postsecondary Education Commission (1985). *Eligibility of California's 1983 High School Graduates for Admission to the State's Public Universities*. Sacramento: Author.

California Postsecondary Education Commission (1987). *California College-Going Rates: 1986 Update*. Sacramento.

California State Assembly. (1988). Asian American admissions at the University of California: Excerpts from a legislative hearing on Jan. 26, 1988. Sacramento.

Cesa, T. A. (1988). The freshman applicant cycle at the University of California at Berkeley for fall 1985 to fall 1987. Berkeley: UC-Berkeley Office of Student Research.

College Board (1985). *ATP Racial/Ethnic Data Report: Comparative Data, 1980–84*. Princeton, NJ: Educational Testing Service.

Curtis, D. (1988a, May 5). State study of university entry standards. *San Francisco Chronicle*.

Curtis, D. (1988b, May 20). UC ethnic policy becoming official. *San Francisco Chronicle*.

Daniels, R. (1962). *The Politics of Prejudice: The Anti-Japanese Movement in California*. Berkeley: University of California Press.

Duster, T. (1976). The structure of privilege and its universe of discourse. *American Sociologist*, 2: 73–78.

Fanucchi, K. J. (1985, July 7). Reasons sought for drop in UCLA Asian enrollment. *The Los Angeles Times*.

Feist, Paul (1987, September 25). Rejection letters from UC miff top students. *Nichi Bei Times*, p. 3.

Gardner, D. P. (1987a). The American university in transition. Speech delivered at the Commonwealth Club of California, San Francisco.

Gibney, J. (1988). The Berkeley squeeze. *The New Republic* 3821: 15–17.

Givens, R., et al. (1984, April). The drive to excel: strong families and hard work propel Asian Americans to the top of the class. *Newsweek on Campus*, pp. 4–13.

Gordon, L. (1988, January 27). UC Berkeley apologizes for handling of bias charges. *The Los Angeles Times*.

Gross, B., and Gross, R., eds. (1985). *The Great School Debate: Which Way for American Education.* New York: Simon & Schuster.

Gust, K. (1986, May 11). Asians say bias in education troubles them. *The Tribune* (Oakland), p. A1.

Hassan, T. E. (1986–87). Asian American admissions: debating discrimination. *The College Board Review* 142: 19–21.

Hickey, S. (1986, December 11). Admissiongate. *East/West* 20: 51.

Hickey, S. (1987, September). Unequal opportunity: Does UC Berkeley's language requirement subtly discriminate against Asians? *San Francisco Focus.*

Ho, D., and Chin, M. (1983). Admissions: impossible. *The Bridge Magazine* 8(3): 7–8, 51.

Hsia, J. (1988a). *Asian Americans in Higher Education and at Work.* Hillsdale, NJ: Lawrence Erlbaum.

Hsia, J. (1988b). Limits of affirmative action: Asian American access to higher education. *Educational Policy* 2(2): 117–36.

Hu, A. (1986, February 14). The changing face of MIT. *The Tech* (MIT).

Hu, A. (1987a). Asian Americans: Model minority or double minority. Unpublished manuscript. Boston, MA: Mosaic Software.

Hu, A. (1987b, February 10). Superstudents or understudents: Asian Americans as the new minority in America's colleges. Unpublished manuscript. Boston, MA: Mosaic Software.

Ipson, Steve, and Tjoa, May (1987, October 12). Professor doubts credibility of faculty Asian panel. *Daily Californian.*

Johnson, J. H., Jr., and Oliver, M. L., eds. (1988). *Ethnic Dilemmas in Comparative Perspective: Proceedings of the Los Angeles Conference on Comparative Ethnicity.* UCLA: Institute for Social Science Research.

Kan, S. H., and Liu, W. T. (1986). The educational status of Asian Americans: An update from the 1980 census. *P/AAMHRC Research Review* 5(3/4): 21–24.

Karabel, J. (1984). Status-group struggle, organizational interests, and the limits of institutional autonomy: The transformation of Harvard, Yale, and Princeton, 1918–1940. *Theory and Society* 13: 1–40.

Kasindorf, Martin (1982, December 6). Asian Americans: A model minority. *Newsweek*, pp. 39–51.

Levine, H. (1988, February 11). '83 UC memo reviews charge of Asian quota. *San Francisco Examiner.*

Lindsey, R. (1987, January 19). Colleges accused of bias to stem Asians' gains. *The New York Times*, p. A10.

Lum, G. (1988, February 4). Memo may have prodded UC chancellor's apology. *East/West* 22(5): 1.

Lye, C. (1986, November). Is there a ceiling under the table? Three years of admissions rules changes seem targeted at Asians. *The Berkeley Graduate* 1(3): 1, 4–5, 7–8.

Lye, C. (1987, December). On the Asian question. *The Berkeley Graduate* 2(2): 3–9).

Manzagal, M. (1986, October 31). Asian enrollment figures subject of federal inquiry. *The Daily Californian*, p. 1.

Matthews, J. (1985, November 14). Asian American students creating new mainstream. *The Washington Post*, A1, A6.

Matthews, L. (1987, July 19). When being best isn't good enough. *The Los Angeles Times Magazine*, pp. 22–28.

McBee, S., et al. (1984, April 2). Asian Americans: Are they making the grade? *US News and World Report* 96(3): 41–47.

Miller, S. C. (1969). *The Unwelcome Immigrant: The American Image of the Chinese*, 1785–1882. Berkeley: University of California Press.

Min, M. (1987). Select statistics: Undergraduate ethnic representation, UC Berkeley, 1976–1987. In *Beyond the Barriers: Affirmative Action, Berkeley, 1987.* Berkeley: Associated Students of the University of California Senate.

Nakanishi, D. T. (1988, Winter). Asian/Pacific Americans and selective undergraduate admissions. *Journal of College Admissions*, 118: 17–26.

Nakao, A. (1987, May 3, 4). Thorny debate over UC: Too many brainy Asians? *San Francisco Examiner*, p. 1.

National Commission on Excellence in Education. (1983). *A Nation at Risk: The Imperative for Educational Reform*. Washington, DC: U.S. Government Printing Office.

Office of the Chancellor (1982). Language Acquisition Skills Task Force. Berkeley: University of California.

Office of the Chancellor (1984a). UCB: Five-Year Academic Plan. Berkeley: University of California.

Office of the Chancellor (1984b). Chancellor Heyman's Response to Regent Yori Wada's Inquiry. Berkeley: University of California.

Office of the Chancellor (1987). Asian Admissions at UC Berkeley. Berkeley: University of California.

Office of the Chancellor (1988). Asian Admissions Briefing Book: 1984 Actions. Berkeley: University of California.

Office of Student Research (1980). Survey of immigrant and refugee students at UC Berkeley. Berkeley: University of California.

Office of Student Research (1982). Language Background Survey of foreign-born Asian undergraduates at UCB. Berkeley: University of California.

Ogasawara, Julie (1985, May 29). UCLA's Asian student enrollment declines. *Bruin News*.

Oxnam, R. B. (1986, November 30). Why Asians succeed here. *The New York Times Magazine*.

Packer, J. (1988, March 25). University appoints new fund-raising chancellor. *Daily Californian*.

Peng, S. S. (1988). Attainment status of Asian Americans in higher education. Paper prepared for a symposium on Asian Americans and Higher Education, Cornell University, Ithaca, NY.

Pickell, D. (1988, April). The "Temporary 400," An exercise in damage decontrol. *The Berkeley Graduate* 2(3): 6–8.

Ramirez, A. (1986, November 24). America's super minority. *Fortune* 114(12): 148–161.

Roark, A. C. (1986, November 23). UCLA to alter student admissions policy next fall. *The Los Angeles Times*, pp. 3, 39.

Romanoff, A. (1986, April). Yale accepts 2,176 to class of 1990. *The Yale Daily*.

Salholz, Eloise (1987, February 9). Do colleges set Asian quotas? *Newsweek*, p. 60.

San Diego Union (1986, December 21) UC fee formula was born of student fear of huge hikes: An interview with UC President David Gardner, pp. c6, c8.

Saniels, J. M., ed. (1967). *Filipino Exclusion Movement*. Quezon City: University of the Philippines Press.

Saxton, A. (1971). *The Indispensable Enemy: Labor and the Anti-Chinese Movement in California*. Berkeley: University of California Press.

Scott-Blair, M. (1986, December 11). Ethnic imbalance shifts at UC. *San Diego Union*. p. A1.

Seligman, Katherine (1987, October 8). Admission of Asians lags at UC. *San Francisco Examiner*.

Siporin, Rae (1984, November 30). Undergraduate admissions and relations with schools: Issues for Undergraduate Enrollment Planning Committee. Los Angeles: Office of Admissions, UCLA.

Smith, J. L. (1987, October 31). Ethnic studies requirement unlikely, UC chief says. *The Sacramento Bee*.

Steinberg, S. (1981). *The Ethnic Myth*. Boston: Beacon.

Synnott, M. (1979). *The Half-Opened Door: Discrimination and Admissions at Harvard, Yale, and Princeton, 1900–1970*. Westport, CT: Greenwood Press.

Synott, M. (1986). Anti-Semitism and American universities: Did quotas follow the Jews? In David A. Gerber (ed), *Anti-Semitism in American History*, p. 234. Urbana, IL: University of Illinois.

Tang, N. M. (1982). Immigrant and refugee students project: Report and recommendations, 1983–84. Berkeley: Office of Undergraduate Affairs, University of California.

Thomson, G. (1986). 1985 entering fall freshmen with low and moderate estimated annual parental income—cumulative percentages by ethnicity and immigrant status. Berkeley: Office of Student Research, University of California.

Tokunaga, R. (1988, February 6). Task Force on UC Admissions says it has "smoking gun." *Hokubei Mainichi*, p. 1.

Tsang, S., and Wing, L. C. (1985). Beyond Angel Island: The Education of Asian Americans. Unpublished manuscript. Oakland, CA: ARC Associates.

U.S. Commission on Civil Rights (1986). *Recent Activities Against Citizens and Residents of Asian Descent*. Washington, DC: U.S. Government Printing Office.

UCB (1987a, October). From the Chancellor. *Cal Report* 4: 2.

UCB (1987b, October 14). Asian audit concluded; Studies continue. *Berkeleyan* 16: 6.

Whitman, D. (1987, February 23). Trouble for America's "model" minority. *US News and World Report* 102(7): 18–19.

Williams, D. (1984, April 23). A formula for success. *Newsweek* 103(17): 77–78.

Zane, Nolan, Sue, Stanley and Abe, Jennifer (1988). Predictors of academic achievement among Asian American university students. Paper presented at a symposium on Asian Americans and Higher Education, Cornell University, Ithaca, NY.

19 Predictors of Academic Achievement Among Asian American and White Students

Stanley Sue and Jennifer Abe

INTRODUCTION

ASIAN AMERICAN students have a wide reputation for extraordinary educational achievement. Their success on college campuses around the country has been the subject of media attention in such popular publications as *Newsweek* (April 23, 1984), *Newsweek*: "On Campus" (April 1984), *U.S. News and World Report* (April 2, 1984), the *New Republic* (July 15 and 22, 1985), the *New York Times* (August 3, 1986), and *Asian Week* (August 8, 1986). As these news features highlight, Asian Americans have the highest level of college education of any ethnic or racial group in this country. Among persons over 24 years of age living in California in 1980, for instance, over 31 percent of Asian Americans had completed four or more years of college compared with 21 percent of whites, 11 percent of blacks, 10 percent of American Indians, and 6 percent of Hispanics (U.S. Department of Commerce 1983).

In addition, the enrollment of Asian Americans at the top universities throughout the nation is increasing. Approximately 10 percent of Harvard's freshman class is Asian American. While no more than 13 percent of California high school graduates are eligible for admission to the University of California (UC) system, about 26 percent of Asian Americans qualify (University of California 1985). The educational performance of Asian Americans has generated considerable interest and controversy. On the one hand, their achievements have stimulated interest in the personality, cultural, child-rearing, and other sociopsychological factors that might account for the high achievement levels. On the other hand, the very success of Asian American students has raised concerns over university admissions policies and over the stereotyping of all Asian Americans as high achievers.

The myth that Asian Americans are a "model minority" (Sue and Sue 1972) tends to perpetuate the view that all Asian American students are high achievers with very few needs within the academic realm. Concerns have been expressed over practices that may, in effect, limit the increasing numbers of Asian Americans enrolling in universities. These practices include the use of subjective or nonacademic criteria (for example, the student's interview behavior, high school background of leadership and participation in social activities, and having parents who are university alumni) and the imposition of new entry requirements that are weighted more heavily with verbal than with quantitative skills

(Butterfield 1986; Sue and Zane 1985). Asian Americans consistently outscore all other groups, including whites, on tests of quantitative skills, although their verbal scores are typically lower than those of whites (Hsia 1985).

PREDICTORS OF SUCCESS

Research suggests that high school academic performance and scores obtained on college entrance examinations such as the College Board's Scholastic Aptitude Test (SAT) and the American College Testing Program (ACT) are the best predictors of college success (Aleamoni and Oboler 1978; Malloch and Michael 1981; Nisbet, Ruble, and Schurr 1982; Passons 1967; Weitzman 1982). Although high school academic performance is the best single predictor of college academic performance (Dispenzier et al. 1971; McCausland and Stewart 1974; McDonald and Gawkoski 1979), the SAT has been used to supplement the school record and other information about the student in assessing his or her competence for college work (Donlon and Angoff 1971). Fincher (1974), in a 13-year analysis of SAT data in a statewide system, found that use of the SAT increased predictive efficiency 46 percent for males and 43 percent for females over the use of high school grades alone. The College Board Commission on Tests (1970) stated that although the use of SAT scores added appreciably to the accuracy of predicting college grades from high school grade-point average (GPA) or class rank, the College Board's Achievement Tests in specific subject areas added only a modest amount of predictive power to that already obtained by the combination of high school GPA and SAT score (Vol. 1, p. 18).

PREDICTORS OF SUCCESS FOR MINORITY STUDENTS

Predictors of college academic success vary by ethnicity. Thomas and Stanley (1969) suggested that academic aptitude and achievement test scores, rather than high school grades, are often better predictors of college performance for blacks than for whites. Pfeifer and Sedlacek (1971) found that the SAT-verbal (SAT-V) score was a better predictor than was the high school GPA for black males. However, other studies indicate that although SAT scores may improve the prediction of the college GPA for blacks, they may add little to the power already obtained through the high school GPA in predicting college performance for Chicanos, Puerto Ricans, and American Indians (Astin 1982).

In an analysis of SAT-verbal and SAT-mathematical (SAT-M) scores as predictors of freshman college grades for black and white students at 19 institutions, Davis and Temp (1971) suggested that prediction equations derived from a white or a combined population would tend to overpredict college performance for blacks. Other studies also reported that the use of regression equations derived from white samples would result in an overprediction of grades for black students (Cleary 1968; Kallingal 1971; Pfeifer and Sedlacek 1971; Temp 1971) and for Chicano/Latino students (Goldman and Richards 1974).

In a series of reports from the University of California, predictors of academic achievement were examined for various ethnic groups (Neville, Scott, and Wakim 1982; Song undated; Song and Scott 1980). In a study of freshmen at the University of California, Berkeley, in 1977, Song found no evidence that high school grades and SAT scores resulted in substantial over- or underprediction of university grades for Asian American students. Using the same data base, Song and Scott reported that for Asian Americans the multiple correlation (R) for freshman GPA, using high school grades and SAT-verbal and SAT-mathematical scores, was .42, similar to that for whites ($R = .41$) but lower than the multiple correlations for blacks ($R = .64$) and Hispanics ($R = .52$). In addition, when these three predictors were compared with some nontraditional predictors (for example, high school rank, honors/awards received, extracurricular activities, parental income, and leadership ability), high school grades and SAT scores still emerged as the best correlates to university grades.

Wilcox (1974), in a study of predictors of academic success for undergraduate foreign students from Vietnam and Hong Kong, found the correlation between high school GPA and freshman performance to be about .50 in each sample. SAT-mathematical scores were found to predict freshman grades equally as well. Interestingly enough, although the combination of these two predictors—high school GPA and SAT-M scores—increased the correlation with freshman grades by about .10 more than either predictor alone, neither verbal scores nor English proficiency contributed to the prediction equation.

In another study of foreign students attending college in the United States, Dizney and Roskens (1964) found a sample of foreign students at Kent State University to have a significantly greater aptitude for mathematics than for English on the American College Test (ACT). Furthermore, although combining mathematical and English aptitude scores significantly improved the prediction of college performance for domestic students, the combination did not significantly affect the prediction of college GPA for foreign students.

In a domestic study of Chinese and white students from three liberal arts colleges, Yang (1978) reported that SAT-verbal scores were a better predictor than SAT-mathematical scores for white students, whereas the reverse was true for Chinese students. However, college GPAs predicted from regression equations for Chinese students did not differ from GPAs predicted for white students, even though the regression equations for the two groups were significantly different. In an investigation of academic performance by University of California, Los Angeles (UCLA), freshman students, Neville, Scott, and Wakim (1982) found an R^2 of .26 between high school grades and UCLA freshman grades for Asian Americans. The addition of SAT-V and then SAT-M scores in a stepwise regression equation yielded R^2s of .31 and .32, respectively. The Rs obtained at UCLA were somewhat lower than those for Asian American students at Berkeley. Furthermore, whereas SAT-M scores were a better predictor at Berkeley, SAT-V scores were superior in predicting college performance by UCLA's Asian American students.

Goldman and Hewitt (1976) have also examined multiple correlations between certain predictors (high school GPA and SAT performance) and the criterion (university freshman grades) for various University of California campuses. For the largest campus in their study, UCLA, the multiple correlations were .42 for Asian Americans, .43 for whites, .33 for blacks, and .38 for Hispanics. For the Asian American students, SAT-M scores were far superior to SAT-V scores in predicting university grades. In contrast, the better predictor among whites and blacks was SAT-V scores; both tests had similar predictive value among Hispanics.

SUMMARY

In summary, the results for Asian American students in the University of California system appear to differ from those found for non-Asian American students in other studies. First, most other studies have reported higher R values for college grades when high school grades and SAT scores were used as predictors (Aleamoni and Oboler 1978; Chissom and Lanier 1975; Larson and Scontrino 1976; Slack and Porter 1980). Second, the SAT-V score has been a superior predictor compared with the SAT-M score in most of these studies.

Our study examined various predictors of academic performance for Asian American students who enrolled as freshmen in any of the eight University of California campuses during fall 1984. The campuses are Berkeley, Davis, Irvine, Los Angeles, Riverside, San Diego, Santa Barbara, and Santa Cruz. The purpose of the study was to determine how well certain variables such as high school grades, SAT scores, and College Board Achievement

Test scores predicted academic performance during the freshman year at a university and to determine whether the predictors varied according to (1) membership within different Asian American groups (Chinese, Japanese, Korean, Filipino, East Indian/Pakistani, and other Asian groups); (2) major (undeclared, professional schools, physical sciences, life sciences, humanities, engineering, or social sciences); (3) language spoken (English best or English not best); and (4) gender. This study is unique in that no other validity investigation has examined differences among various Asian American subgroups on these factors, nor has any other study reported on as many Asian American students.

METHOD

SUBJECTS

From a total freshman student population of 22,105 who enrolled in the eight UC campuses in fall 1984, the records of the 4,113 Asian American domestic (nonforeign) students were examined and compared with those of 1,000 randomly selected white students. Students indicated their ethnicity on the application forms used for admissions. Males constituted about 50 percent of the Asian Americans, while 49 percent of the white sample were males. The Asian American student numbers were, in descending order, Chinese 1,470; Filipinos 712; Japanese 643; Koreans 575; Other Asian Americans, or those not members of the specific groups listed in this study, 525; and East Indians/Pakistanis 170. It should be noted that, in the tables, sample sizes for analysis vary because some students were missing data on some variables. Asian American students were also divided into two groups by presumed English proficiency: those for whom English was probably the best language and those for whom English was probably not the best language. From data in a previous study by Ramist and Arbeiter (1986), SAT scores were compared between Asian American students who indicated that English was their best language and those who said it was not. A discrepancy score of at least 170 points between SAT-M and SAT-V scores was found to reliably identify Asian American students for whom English was not the best language. In fact, no overlap on the verbal score was found between the bottom 25 percent of the students for whom English was the best language and the top 25 percent of the students for whom English was not the best language. By using the discrepancy score procedure, we were able to classify most students as to whether their primary language was or was not English.

VARIABLES EXAMINED

The criterion variable was the university freshman grade-point average, which was the average of all grades received by a student during the academic year. Six predictor variables were used for the GPA:

1. High school grade-point average (HSGPA) calculated from courses such as English, history, mathematics, laboratory science, and foreign language
2. Scholastic Aptitude Test-verbal score
3. Scholastic Aptitude Test-mathematical score
4. English Composition Test (ECT) score from the College Board Achievement Test series
5 Level I or Level II Mathematics Test (MI or MII) score from the College Board Achievement Test series

ANALYSIS

With five predictor variables, it was possible to generate a large number of predictor-criterion combinations. A decision was made to conduct regression analyses with two sets of predictors of the freshman GPA. First, HSGPA, SAT-V score, and SAT-M score were used as predictors. This set of variables has been widely employed in making admissions decisions and was of primary importance in this study. Second, Achievement Test results (ECT and MI or MII) were combined with HSGPA to predict the university GPA.

The regression analyses were performed for each Asian American group, all Asian American students combined, and whites. Analyses were also made for all Asian American and white students according to gender and academic majors. (Female East Indian/Pakistanis were not analyzed because the number of students was too small to reach the size criterion for conducting an analysis.) For the academic major analysis, students were first grouped by their declaration or nondeclaration of a major. Students who declared were further categorized according to field: professional schools (not including engineering), physical sciences, life sciences, humanities, engineering, and social sciences.

RESULTS

MEANS FOR ALL VARIABLES

Means (M) and standard deviations (SD) for each predictor variable and the criterion variable—divided by ethnicity, gender, and English-best/not-best language—are shown in Tables 1, 2, and 3. In view of their large number, not all variables shown in the tables are fully discussed in the text; only the more salient findings are presented below. It should be noted that in the comparisons of means, t-tests were performed; if the two compared values were based on widely discrepant variances, t^1-tests were used.

High School Grades. Asian American students had superior high school grades (Table 1). The mean HSGPA for Asian Americans was 3.69 compared with 3.59 for whites; t^1 (987) = 6.88, with a probability (p) of $p < .001$. Females tended to have higher HSGPAs than did males: For Asian Americans it was 3.71 versus 3.67, respectively; t (4,073) = 6.81, $p < .001$. For whites it was 3.64 versus 3.53; t (943) = 8.46, $p < .001$. Within the Asian American group, East Indians/Pakistanis had the highest mean HSGPA (3.80), while Filipinos had the lowest (3.56). With the exception of the Filipinos, all the Asian American subgroups exceeded the average HSGPA of whites. Dividing students by their proficiency in English failed to reveal differences in HSGPA; note that $M = 3.69$ for both groups, as shown in Table 3.

SAT Scores. Consistent with previous studies, Table 1 shows that Asian Americans achieved higher average SAT-mathematical scores than did whites (584 versus 577); t^1 (1,043) = 2.27, $p < .01$. They received lower average scores than did whites on the SAT-verbal sections (456 versus 512); t^1 (1,117) = 16.59, $p < .001$. The scores for the Asian American students rank favorably with the average scores (SAT-M = 519 and SAT-V = 398) obtained from a national sample of college-bound Asian American seniors (Arbeiter 1984). For both Asian Americans and whites, males had higher SAT-verbal and SAT-mathematical scores than did females. The difference was stronger in SAT-M than in SAT-V scores. Asian American males had an average SAT-M score of 610, while females achieved an average score of 559; t (4,111) = 33.94, $p < .001$. On SAT-V performances, males achieved an average of 462 compared with an average of 450 for females; t (4,113) = 2.96, $p < .01$. The male-female difference for SAT-M scores was also substantial for whites: 607 versus 548; t (958) = 21.35, $p < .001$. White SAT-V scores were 519 versus 506; t (958) = 4.55, $p < .001$. Thus, while females exceeded males in high school grades, their average SAT scores, particularly on the mathematical portion, were lower than those of males. Large differences in SAT performances were found among the Asian American subgroups. East Indians/Pakistanis ($M = 520$) had the highest SAT-V score, while Other Asian Americans

Table 1. Group Means and Standard Deviations for Each Variable by Gender and Ethnicity

	SAT-V		SAT-M		HSGPA	
	M	SD	M	SD	M	SD
Males						
All Asian	462.5	117.5	609.6	92.2	3.67	0.39
American	(2,050)		(2,050)		(2,023)	
Chinese	477.5	116.1	632.4	87.0	3.69	0.38
	(742)		(742)		(724)	
Japanese	516.8	89.9	632.0	75.5	3.72	0.39
	(310)		(310)		(303)	
Korean	432.6	118.2	626.5	84.5	3.63	0.37
	(284)		(284)		(280)	
Filipino	459.2	89.7	547.7	86.6	3.55	0.40
	(321)		(321)		(328)	
East Indian/	538.8	97.2	635.5	84.3	3.79	0.37
Pakistani	(96)		(96)		(99)	
Other Asian	373.2	119.1	572.0	92.9	3.70	0.34
American	(289)		(289)		(281)	
White	519.0	89.5	607.0	84.7	3.53	0.42
	(471)		(471)		(456)	
*Females**						
All Asian	449.8	116.7	559.3	97.8	3.71	0.36
American	(2,063)		(2,063)		(2,052)	
Chinese	469.3	119.6	590.9	92.8	3.77	0.35
	(728)		(728)		(722)	
Japanese	505.1	90.1	577.6	86.6	3.77	0.34
	(333)		(333)		(335)	
Korean	403.4	119.7	562.3	90.8	3.65	0.35
	(291)		(291)		(285)	
Filipino	439.0	92.1	496.3	92.9	3.57	0.38
	(391)		(391)		(390)	
Other Asian	373.5	115.8	535.9	90.7	3.73	0.34
American	(236)		(236)		(235)	
White	506.0	87.4	548.0	86.5	3.64	0.38
	(489)		(489)		(489)	
Totals						
All Asian	456.1	117.3	584.4	98.3	3.69	0.37
American	(4,113)		(4,113)		(4,075)	
Chinese	473.4	117.9	611.8	92.3	3.73	0.37
	(1,470)		(1,470)		(1,446)	
Japanese	510.8	90.1	603.8	85.8	3.75	0.36
	(643)		(643)		(638)	
Korean	417.8	119.8	594.0	93.4	3.64	0.36
	(575)		(575)		(565)	
Filipino	448.1	91.5	519.5	93.6	3.56	0.39
	(712)		(712)		(718)	
East Indian/	520.0	101.1	605.8	93.8	3.80	0.37
Pakistani	(170)		(170)		(175)	
Other Asian	373.3	117.5	555.89	93.6	3.72	0.34
American	(525)		(525)		(516)	
White	512.4	88.6	576.9	90.5	3.59	0.41
	(960)		(960)		(945)	

Note: Figures in parentheses are base *N*s for the adjacent means. Because number of subjects was calculated in different ways, combined Asian American subgroups yield slightly different figures than the "All Asian American" (i.e., total) number of subjects.

*Number of East Indian/Pakistani female students was too small for analysis.

Table 2. Group Means and Standard Deviations for Each Variable by Gender and Ethnicity

	Univ. GPA		ECT		MI		MII	
	M	SD	M	SD	M	SD	M	SD
Males								
All Asian American	2.74 (1,946)	0.69	461.6 (2,003)	99.9	568.6 (1,234)	85.9	669.5 (773)	85.4
Chinese	2.86 (689)	0.68	473.2 (730)	98.9	584.9 (420)	88.5	693.9 (310)	77.7
Japanese	2.68 (295)	0.68	495.7 (307)	96.1	584.5 (193)	78.7	677.3 (114)	75.9
Korean	2.72 (270)	0.69	437.7 (280)	93.7	579.8 (160)	85.5	659.2 (122)	82.8
Filipino	2.47 (321)	0.62	448.9 (308)	86.6	527.2 (233)	77.4	609.3 (75)	91.4
East Indian/Pakistani	2.92 (96)	0.68	534.7 (94)	93.7	—	—	—	—
Other	2.80 (267)	0.68	405.4 (278)	92.0	545.1 (163)	78.2	641.9 (117)	88.2
White	2.72 (441)	0.60	521.9 (454)	92.9	556.3 (331)	79.1	665.7 (124)	72.3
*Females**								
All Asian American	2.73 (1,976)	0.64	470.8 (2,034)	102.9	530.1 (1,563)	86.4	640.1 (472)	84.5
Chinese	2.91 (697)	0.62	489.1 (714)	101.6	560.0 (526)	85.2	661.8 (187)	85.8
Japanese	2.76 (318)	0.61	515.5 (331)	95.4	538.4 (250)	80.2	646.9 (80)	74.6
Korean	2.65 (280)	0.61	433.8 (285)	103.6	527.9 (220)	81.2	628.3 (66)	76.0
Filipino	2.43 (384)	0.60	449.4 (384)	85.5	483.7 (336)	79.2	587.1 (49)	85.7
Other	2.77 (216)	0.63	418.4 (236)	99.4	517.7 (167)	77.7	618.9 (70)	82.2
White	2.78 (461)	0.62	528.8 (480)	90.0	518.2 (404)	80.5	623.9 (75)	82.1
Totals								
All Asian American	2.74 (3,922)	0.66	466.3 (4,037)	101.5	547.0 (2,797)	88.3	658.3 (1,245)	86.2
Chinese	2.89 (1,386)	0.65	481.1 (1,444)	100.5	571.0 (946)	87.5	681.8 (497)	82.3
Japanese	2.73 (613)	0.65	506.0 (638)	96.2	558.5 (443)	82.7	664.7 (194)	76.7
Korean	2.68 (550)	0.65	435.7 (565)	98.7	549.8 (380)	86.8	648.4 (188)	81.6
Filipino	2.44 (705)	0.61	449.2 (692)	85.9	501.5 (569)	81.3	600.6 (124)	89.5
East Indian/Pakistani	2.86 (168)	0.66	529.1 (168)	92.2	—	—	—	—
Other	2.78 (483)	0.66	411.4 (514)	95.6	531.2 (330)	79.0	633.3 (187)	86.5
White	2.75 (902)	0.61	525.4 (934)	91.5	535.3 (735)	82.1	649.9 (199)	78.6

Note: Figures in parentheses are base *N*s for the adjacent means.

Because number of subjects was calculated in different ways, combined Asian American subgroups yield slightly different figures than the "All Asian American" (i.e., total) number of subjects.

*Number of East Indian/Pakistani female students was too small for analysis.

Table 3. Group Means and Standard Deviations for Each Variable by Language

Variable	English best			English not best		
	M	SD	N	M	SD	N
SAT-V	500.30	101.80	2,718	370.0	95.60	1,395
SAT-M	563.20	98.80	2,718	625.80	83.00	1,395
HSGPA	3.69	0.39	2,642	3.69	0.34	1,358
GPA*	2.70	0.67	2,543	2.79	0.64	1,294
ECT	491.60	99.10		417.10	87.10	
MI	533.00	87.70		580.10	80.70	
MII	651.80	88.60		666.60	82.70	

*University freshman-year grade point average.

($M = 373$) had the lowest score. On the SAT-M section, the Chinese ($M = 612$) scored the highest, and Filipinos ($M = 520$) scored the lowest.

Since the English-best/not-best dichotomy (Table 3) was derived from SAT scores, it was not surprising that the mean SAT-V score (500) for Asian American students whose best language was English exceeded that of English-not-best students (370). In the SAT-M section English-best students received a lower average score than did their English-not-best counterparts (563 versus 626); $t^1 (1,815) = 21.43, p < .001$.

University Grades. Overall, the university grade-point averages for Asian American and white students were very similar: $M = 2.74$ and $M = 2.75$, respectively (Table 2). While Asian American males and females were highly similar in GPA, white females ($M = 2.78$) tended to achieve higher grades than white males did ($M = 2.72$); $t (900) = 2.95, p < .01$. Within the Asian American student group, considerable ethnic differences in university GPA were found. In descending order, the mean GPAs were Chinese 2.89, East Indians/Pakistanis 2.86, Other Asians 2.78, Japanese 2.73, Koreans 2.68, and Filipinos 2.44. Asian American students for whom English was not the best language ($M = 2.79$) performed better than did those for whom English was the best language ($M = 2.70$); $t^1 (1,567) = 4.05$, $p < .001$.

College Board Achievement Test Scores. Analysis was made of students who had taken the English Composition Test and either the Mathematics I or II Achievement Tests (Table 2). The comparisons of Asian American and white students yielded results that were highly consistent with those from the analysis of the SAT performances in Table 1. Whites outperformed Asian Americans on the ECT (525 versus 466); $t^1 (1,535) = 17.42, p < .001$. Asian American students tended to achieve higher scores on the mathematics tests: The scores were 547 versus 535 for MI; $t^1 (808) = 3.41, p < .01$. The scores were 658 versus 650 for MII; $t^1 (208) = 1.38, p$ not significant. The average scores of males exceeded those of females: For Mathematics I white males = 556 and white females = 518; $t (733) = 12.93$, $p < .001$. Asian American males = 569 and females = 530 for MI; $t (2,795) = 23.62, p < .001$. For Mathematics II white males = 666 and females = 624; $t^1 (85) = 3.64, p < .01$. For MII Asian American males = 670 and females = 640; $t (1,243) = 12.20, p < .001$. Unlike the SAT results, however, white ($M = 529$) and Asian American ($M = 471$) females had higher scores on the ECT than did their male counterparts. For white males $M = 522$; $t (932) = 2.31, p < .05$. For Asian American males $M = 462$; $t (4,035) = 5.76, p < .001$.

ACADEMIC MAJORS

Fifty-two percent of the Asian American and white students did not declare a major. The fields and percentages of Asian Americans and whites (percentages are shown, respectively, in parentheses) declaring a major were as follows: professional schools (2 percent and 3 percent), physical sciences (6 percent and 5 percent), life sciences (18 percent and 15 percent), humanities (3 percent and 6 percent) engineering (14 percent and 8 percent), and social sciences (5 percent and 11 percent). In general, Asian American students were more likely than white students to major in engineering and less likely to major in the humanities and the social sciences.

HIGH SCHOOL GRADES AND SAT SCORES AS PREDICTORS OF UNIVERSITY GRADES

Overall Comparisons. The zero-order correlations between the predictor variables (HSGPA, SAT-V score, and SAT-M score) and the criterion (university first-year GPA) indicated that for Asian American students the HSGPA was the strongest correlate: $r = .455$, where r is a correlation. The SAT-V score and the SAT-M score were correlated, respectively, .235 and .370 with the GPA. Although the HSGPA achieved the highest correlation with the university GPA for whites ($r = .413$), the correlation of SAT-V score and GPA exceeded that of SAT-M score and GPA (.272 to .194). Since the predictor variables were intercorrelated, it was necessary to examine the multiple correlations (R) between the predictors and the criterion and to note the unique contributions of each predictor to the criterion. Tables 4 and 5 show the multiple correlations between the predictor variables (HSGPA, SAT-V, and SAT-M) and the criterion (university GPA). For all Asian American students the three predictor variables yielded a multiple correlation of .498, which exceeded the multiple correlation of .451 for white students (Table 4). An examination of the beta weights (expressed as proportional contributions of the predictors to the criterion) for the predictor variables revealed interesting ethnic differences that were consistent with the findings on the zero-order correlations. Whereas HSGPA made the largest contribution in the prediction of university grades for both Asian American and white students, considerable differences were found in the contributions made by SAT performances. For Asian Americans the SAT-M score contributed 36 percent and the SAT-V score contributed only 3 percent to the prediction of university grades. For whites the situation was reversed; SAT-M and SAT-V scores contributed, respectively, 3 percent and 32 percent.

Gender and English Proficiency. Dividing the students by ethnicity and gender did not alter the findings presented above. Regardless of gender and ethnicity, HSGPA made the largest contribution to the regression equation. For Asian American males and females, the SAT-M score was a stronger predictor than the SAT-V score, while the opposite was true for white males and females (Table 4). Interestingly, the SAT-M score was superior to the SAT-V score for Asian American students whose best or not-best language was English; however, where English was the best language, the superiority was slight (Table 5).

Asian American Subgroup Differences. Some marked differences emerged when the various Asian American groups were compared. The multiple correlations for the groups ranged from a high of .545 for East Indians/Pakistanis to a low of .391 for Filipinos (Table 4). Thus, high school grades and SAT scores showed only a modest ability to predict the university grades of Filipinos. Furthermore, in contrast to all other groups where the HSGPA made the strongest contribution in the prediction of university grades, the SAT-M score was the strongest predictor for Other Asian Americans. Filipinos and East Indians/Pakistanis were also unlike the other Asian American groups in that SAT-V scores contributed more to the regression equation than did SAT-M scores. These findings reveal a great variability among Asian American subgroups.

Academic Majors. Table 5 shows the multiple correlations and proportions of contributions for Asian American and white students according to academic major categories—undeclared, professional schools, physical sciences, life sciences, humanities, engineering,

Table 4. Proportional Contributions of SAT-V Score, SAT-M Score, and HSGPA to Regression Equation by Gender and Ethnicity

	N	R	SE	SAT-V	SAT-M	HSGPA
Males						
All Asian American	1,842	.498	.59	.01	.38	.61
Chinese	649	.572	.55	.03	.32	.65
Japanese	281	.405	.61	.08	.30	.62
Korean	257	.423	.63	.02	.31	.67
Filipino	308	.389	.58	.32	.09	.59
East Indian/ Pakistani	89	.489	.59	.23	.14	.63
Other Asian American	250	.517	.59	.02	.57	.41
White	411	.443	.53	.27	.05	.68
*Females**						
All Asian American	1,888	.501	.55	.06	.35	.59
Chinese	667	.492	.54	.04	.41	.55
Japanese	304	.492	.53	.14	.20	.66
Korean	262	.396	.55	.11	.06	.83
Filipino	372	.393	.55	.27	.12	.61
Other Asian American	205	.518	.54	.03	.43	.54
White	437	.465	.55	.33	.13	.54
Totals						
All Asian American	3,730	.498	.57	.03	.36	.61
Chinese	1,316	.532	.54	.00	.35	.65
Japanese	585	.442	.57	.13	.20	.67
Korean	519	.408	.59	.03	.27	.70
Filipino	680	.391	.56	.29	.11	.60
East Indian/ Pakistani	159	.545	.56	.29	.11	.60
Other Asian American	455	.515	.57	.01	.54	.45
White	848	.451	.54	.32	.03	.65

Note: Because number of subjects was calculated in different ways, combined Asian American subgroups yield slightly different figures than the "All Asian American" (i.e., total) number of subjects.

*Number of East Indian/Pakistani female students was too small for analysis.

and social sciences. (Since the white sample was composed of 1,000 students, dividing them according to declared majors produced insufficient numbers for data analysis in the professional schools, physical sciences, and humanities.) The HSGPA made the largest contribution to the regression equations except for Asian Americans in engineering. Very striking was the superiority of SAT-M over SAT-V scores as a predictor for Asian Americans in all majors except the social sciences, where the proportion of contribution for SAT-M (.21) was similar to that for SAT-V (.20). For whites the pattern was mixed, and SAT-M scores made a larger contribution to the regression equation than did SAT-V scores in the social sciences; SAT-V was superior for undeclared students and for those majoring in the life sciences. The SAT scores were not a major predictor in the regression equation for white students majoring in engineering, since HSGPA accounted for 95 percent of the contribution. The findings suggest that SAT-M scores are an important predictor of university grades for Asian American students, regardless of their academic majors.

Table 5. Proportional Contributions of SAT-V Score, SAT-M Score, and HSGPA to Regression Equation by Major, Ethnicity, and Language

	N	R	SE	SAT-V	SAT-M	HSGPA
Undeclared						
Asian American	1,958	.492	.57	.07	.34	.60
White	440	.451	.56	.39	.04	.57
*Professional schools**						
Asian American	63	.563	.55	.00	.35	.64
*Physical sciences**						
Asian American	222	.491	.57	.09	.30	.61
Life sciences						
Asian American	690	.560	.57	.01	.36	.62
White	130	.561	.48	.34	.03	.63
*Humanities**						
Asian American	94	.516	.51	.03	.37	.60
Engineering						
Asian American	526	.435	.56	.16	.44	.40
White	69	.563	.51	.01	.04	.95
Social sciences						
Asian American	177	.488	.55	.20	.21	.59
White	96	.534	.50	.12	.21	.67
English best	2,472	.505	.57	.17	.22	.61
English not best	1,258	.490	.56	.11	.38	.50

*Number of white students in sample was too small for analysis.

HIGH SCHOOL GRADES AND ACHIEVEMENT TEST SCORES AS PREDICTORS OF UNIVERSITY GRADES

Overall Comparisons. When high school grades and College Board Achievement Test scores (English Composition Test and Mathematics I and II) were used as predictors (zero-order correlates) of university freshman grades, the results were consistent with those found for high school grades and SAT scores. For Asian American and white students, the best single predictor of the university GPA was the high school GPA. However, the next strongest correlate for Asian Americans was the mathematics score (.348 for MI and .436 for MII); ECT yielded a correlation of .291. For whites mathematics scores were correlated .195 for MI and .164 for MII, while ECT was correlated .286 with the GPA. As indicated in Table 6, the multiple correlation using HSGPA, ECT, and MI was .474 for all Asian Americans, which exceeded the .446 multiple correlation for all whites. For Asian Americans and whites, HSGPA made the largest contribution to the regression equation, accounting for 55 percent and 62 percent, respectively. Among the Asian Americans, MI and ECT accounted for, respectively, 33 percent and 12 percent of the predictive weight. For whites the figures were 31 percent for ECT and 7 percent for MI. Similar findings were obtained when MII rather than MI was used as a predictor (Table 7). The proportions of contribution for the predictors were 52 percent HSGPA, 1 percent ECT, and 47 percent MII for Asian Americans and 69 percent HSGPA, 26 percent ECT, and 5 percent MII for whites. The multiple correlation was higher for Asian Americans than for whites (.542 versus .461). Therefore, the results, when high school grades and Achievement Test scores are used, provide convergent support for the findings when the SAT is used—namely, mathematical skills are better predictors of academic performance than are verbal skills for Asian American but not for white students.

Gender and English Proficiency. Using HSGPA, ECT, and MI as predictors, the multiple correlations were .464 for Asian American males, .487 for Asian American females,

Table 6. Proportional Contributions of HSGPA, ECT, and MI to Regression Equation by Gender and Ethnicity

	N	R	SE	HSGPA	ECT	MI
Males						
All Asian American	1,091	.464	.58	.50	.06	.44
Chinese	358	.557	.56	.58	.03	.40
Japanese	173	.431	.54	.42	.13	.45
Korean	144	.428	.60	.19	.03	.48
Filipino	223	.345	.58	.49	.45	.06
Other Asian American	135	.480	.56	.31	.22	.47
White	294	.427	.52	.71	.26	.03
Females						
All Asian American	1,419	.487	.55	.59	.15	.26
Chinese	476	.443	.55	.60	.16	.23
Japanese	228	.544	.50	.50	.29	.20
Korean	197	.401	.54	.90	.04	.06
Filipino	318	.391	.54	.54	.38	.09
Other Asian American	141	.500	.58	.60	.03	.37
White	357	.462	.55	.56	.36	.09
Totals						
All Asian American	2,510	.474	.57	.55	.12	.33
Chinese	834	.498	.56	.62	.08	.30
Japanese	401	.487	.53	.48	.28	.23
Korean	341	.401	.57	.62	.04	.34
Filipino	541	.371	.56	.51	.41	.08
East Indian/Pakistani	105	.520	.56	.73	.00	.26
Other Asian American	276	.481	.57	.42	.11	.47
White	651	.446	.54	.62	.31	.07

Note: Because number of subjects was calculated in different ways, combined Asian American subgroups yield slightly different figures than the "All Asian American" (i.e., total) number of subjects.

.427 for white males, and .462 for white females (Table 6). Thus, when these variables were used, university grades were predicted more accurately for Asian Americans than for whites, and more accurately for females than for males. For Asian Americans as an aggregate, HSGPA made the largest contribution to the regression equation. Moreover, regardless of gender, MI was a stronger predictor than was ECT for Asian Americans, while the reverse was true for whites. Similar findings emerged when MII rather than MI was used (Table 7). The only striking difference was in the multiple correlations. For all ethnicity-by-gender groups except Japanese and white females, the regression equations involving MII yielded higher multiple correlations than those involving MI. Although MII was a better predictor than MI for white females, the multiple correlation using MII was lower than for MI because HSGPA for white females with an MII score was a relatively poor predictor; it was the lowest contributor among the three predictor variables.

As depicted in Tables 8 and 9, those Asian American students for whom English was the best language showed patterns similar to those for whom English was not the best language: (1) the multiple correlations involving MII were higher than those involving MI; (2) HSGPA was the single largest contributor to the regression equation except for the equation involving MII for English-best students, where HSGPA and MII were similar; and (3) ECT was the weakest contributor in the prediction of university grades.

Asian American Subgroup Differences. The results for the regression equations when the SAT was used revealed that the multiple correlation was highest for East Indians/Pakistanis and lowest for Filipinos (Table 4). Similar results were obtained when Achievement Test scores rather than SAT scores were used as a predictor. In general,

Table 7. Proportional Contributions of HSGPA, ECT, and MII to Regression Equation by Gender and Ethnicity

	N	R	SE	HSGPA	ECT	MII
Males						
All Asian American	708	.534	.57	.54	.05	.41
Chinese	282	.574	.50	.55	.07	.38
Japanese	105	.468	.64	.44	.12	.44
Korean	109	.500	.64	.58	.12	.30
Other Asian American	105	.570	.60	.43	.07	.50
White	102	.494	.57	.78	.18	.04
Females						
All Asian American	445	.565	.51	.41	.05	.54
Chinese	177	.637	.47	.38	.05	.57
Japanese	76	.489	.56	.59	.05	.35
White	70	.432	.53	.28	.37	.35
Totals						
All Asian American	1,153	.542	.55	.52	.01	.47
Chinese	459	.591	.49	.52	.02	.45
Japanese	181	.474	.61	.49	.10	.41
Korean	170	.445	.61	.56	.11	.33
Filipino	120	.422	.51	.65	.09	.26
Other Asian American	169	.574	.55	.43	.06	.51
White	172	.461	.56	.69	.26	.05

Note: Number of East Indian/Pakistani students was too small for MII computation.

Because number of subjects was calculated in different ways, combined Asian American subgroups yield slightly different figures than the "All Asian American" (i.e., total) number of subjects

HSGPA and Achievement Test scores provided the highest multiple correlation for East Indians/Pakistanis and the lowest for Filipinos. (Because of insufficient numbers of East Indians/Pakistanis in the equations involving MII, a multiple correlation was computed only for MI.) For all Asian American groups except Other Asians, the HSGPA accounted for the largest proportions of predictive weight in the regression equation (Table 6). With the exception of Filipinos and Japanese on the MI equations, all Asian American groups had mathematics scores rather than English Composition Test scores as the next-largest contributor to the variance for university grades.

Academic Majors. When those students who completed the Achievement Tests were divided according to declared academic majors, as shown in Tables 10 and 11, the sample sizes in many cases were so small that meaningful analysis could not be performed, especially for whites. If there was an insufficient sample size, the group was not entered in these tables. In general, HSGPA was the largest contributor to the equation except for Asian Americans in engineering, where mathematics Achievement Test scores were superior. For Asian Americans mathematics was a stronger contributor than was the English Composition Test across all majors. There were simply not enough whites in the different majors to permit overall conclusions.

PREDICTION BIAS

Another way of comparing ethnic differences in predictors of academic achievement is to note the prediction bias that occurs when the regression equation derived from one group is applied to the other. In other words, is the regression equation generated by whites accurate in predicting the performances of Asian American students? To conduct the analysis, we used the white regression equation, which predicted the criterion (university freshman grades) with the lowest average squared error possible. By entering into this equa-

Table 8. Proportional Contributions of HSGPA, ECT, and MI to Regression Equation by Language and Ethnicity

	N	R	SE	HSGPA	ECT	MI
English best						
Chinese	578	.514	.57	.68	.14	.19
Japanese	333	.487	.53	.48	.21	.30
Korean	175	.357	.53	.70	.07	.23
Filipino	465	.391	.55	.57	.39	.04
East Indian/Pakistani	84	.570	.55	.71	.04	.24
Other Asian American	128	.512	.60	.29	.37	.34
Total Asian American	1,772	.490	.56	.57	.20	.23
White	573	.451	.54	.61	.37	.01
English not best						
Chinese	253	.467	.54	.51	.11	.38
Korean	166	.459	.61	.52	.05	.43
Other Asian American	146	.459	.54	.49	.03	.48
Total Asian American	725	.437	.58	.53	.01	.46
White	74	.499	.51	.71	.03	.27

Note: Because of small sample sizes, some Asian American groups are not listed but are included in the total Asian American group.

tion the scores received by Asian American students on the predictor variables, we could compare the grades predicted by the white regression equation with those that were actually received by Asian American students. Tables 12 and 13 show the differences between the predicted and the actual grades obtained when the prediction is based on the white regression equation for HSGPA, SAT-M score, and SAT-V score. Asian Americans received actual grades that were .02 higher than the predicted grades. Thus, there is no evidence that the use of the regression equation placed Asian Americans, as an aggregate group, at a major disadvantage.

Some substantial differences occurred, however, when the prediction bias was examined for specific groups. The white regression equation severely underpredicted the performances of Chinese and Other Asian American students. The Chinese received an average grade that was 0.12 higher, while Other Asians performed 0.15 higher than predicted by the white regression equation. Serious overprediction occurred for Filipinos and the Japanese, who achieved average grades 0.19 and 0.09, respectively, lower than predicted.

Table 9. Proportional Contributions of HSGPA, ECT, and MII to Regression Equation by Language and Ethnicity

	N	R	SE	HSGPA	ECT	MII
English best						
Chinese	245	.575	.52	.49	.08	.44
Japanese	134	.485	.62	.46	.06	.48
Filipino	95	.384	.52	.54	.15	.31
Total Asian American	642	.521	.58	.47	.03	.50
White	143	.475	.57	.67	.22	.11
English not best						
Chinese	214	.617	.46	.51	.08	.41
Korean	96	.541	.57	.89	.01	.10
Other Asian American	113	.635	.49	.33	.23	.44
Total Asian American	506	.575	.51	.57	.02	.41

Note: Because of small sample sizes, some Asian American groups are not listed but are included in the total Asian American group.

Table 10. Proportional Contributions of HSGPA, ECT, and MI to Regression Equation by Ethnicity and Major

	N	R	SE	HSGPA	ECT	MI
Undeclared						
Asian American	1,364	.482	.56	.53	.15	.31
White	332	.468	.56	.58	.31	.11
Physical sciences						
Asian American	133	.524	.53	.60	.00	.40
Life sciences						
Asian American	508	.549	.57	.57	.06	.37
White	110	.531	.50	.66	.32	.03
Humanities						
Asian American	215	.497	.53	.49	.11	.40
Engineering						
Asian American	215	.296	.54	.34	.24	.41
Social sciences						
Asian American	157	.506	.55	.49	.23	.28
White	90	.462	.52	.66	.14	.20

This means that the white regression equation was biased in either direction, depending on the particular Asian American group. The white regression equation also severely underpredicted the performance of Asian American students for whom English was not the best language (Table 13). The university grades of these students averaged 2.79 when they were predicted to have an average of 2.62. On the other hand, Asian American students for whom English was the best language were overpredicted by 0.07. The only other striking finding was the underprediction of Asian American students majoring in the humanities. The white regression equation predicted an average grade of 2.65, and these students actually received a GPA of 2.86.

Although the detailed analysis is not presented in this report, the same patterns were found when HSGPA and Achievement Test scores were used as predictors in the white regression equation.

DISCUSSION

The purpose of the study was to examine the validity of predictors of freshman-year university grades for Asian American and white students and to determine the effects of gender, Asian American subgroup, and academic majors on predictive validity. The following

Table 11. Proportional Contributions of HSGPA, ECT, and MII to Regression Equation by Ethnicity and Major

	N	R	SE	HSGPA	ECT	MII
Undeclared						
Asian American	552	.535	.55	.50	.01	.49
White	91	.358	.56	.44	.24	.31
Physical sciences						
Asian American	84	.525	.57	.56	.13	.31
Life sciences						
Asian American	175	.611	.52	.56	.04	.40
Engineering						
Asian American	303	.493	.55	.40	.10	.50

Table 12. Prediction of University Freshman GPA Using White Students' Regression Equations with SAT-V Score, SAT-M Score, and HSGPA

	Predicted	Actual	Difference
Males			
All Asian American	2.71	2.74	−.03
Chinese	2.73	2.86	−.13
Japanese	2.79	2.68	+.11
Korean	2.66	2.72	−.06
Filipino	2.65	2.47	+.18
East Indian/Pakistani	2.85	2.92	−.07
Other Asian American	2.65	2.80	−.15
Females			
All Asian American	2.73	2.73	0
Chinese	2.81	2.91	−.10
Japanese	2.85	2.76	+.09
Korean	2.63	2.65	−.02
Filipino	2.60	2.43	+.17
Other Asian American	2.61	2.77	−.16
Totals			
All Asian American	2.72	2.74	−.02
Chinese	2.77	2.89	−.12
Japanese	2.82	2.73	+.09
Korean	2.64	2.68	−.04
Filipino	2.63	2.44	+.19
East Indian/Pakistani	2.86	2.86	0
Other Asian American	2.63	2.78	−.15

White prediction equations:
Males
Cumulative GPA
$$= .00999(\text{SAT-V}) - .00198(\text{SAT-M}) + .56970(\text{HSGPA}) + .28012$$
Females
Cumulative GPA
$$= .014470(\text{SAT-V}) + .00577(\text{SAT-M}) + .53185(\text{HSGPA}) - .21987$$
Totals
Cumulative GPA
$$= .01237(\text{SAT-V}) + .00116(\text{SAT-M}) + .55925(\text{HSGPA}) + .02262$$

points summarize the major findings: (1) High school grades and SAT or Achievement Test scores can, to a moderate degree, predict university freshman grades of Asian American and white students. (2) For both Asian American and white students, the best single predictor is the high school grade-point average. (3) For Asian American but not for white students, mathematics scores or quantitative skills are a better predictor of university grades than are verbal scores; this ethnic difference persisted even across academic majors declared by students and even for students whose best language was or was not English. (4) No major sex differences emerged to contradict the overall ethnic differences that were found, except that in the regression equation involving the Level II Mathematics Achievement Test, the contribution of the HSGPA was low for white females. (5) The various Asian American groups showed some differences in the regression equations used to predict the university GPA—especially Filipinos, for whom the predictors yielded the lowest multiple correlation among all the subgroups and for whom verbal skills were superior to mathematical skills in predicting first-year university grades. (6) The white regression equation underpredicted the performances of Chinese, Other Asians, and Asian Americans for whom English was not the best language and overpredicted those of Filipinos, Japanese, and Asian Americans for whom English was the best language.

Table 13. Prediction of Asian American Students' University Freshman GPA Using White Students' Regression Equations with SAT-V Score, SAT-M Score, and HSGPA

	Predicted	Actual	Difference
English best	2.77	2.70	+.07
English not best	2.62	2.79	−.17
Undeclared	2.72	2.74	−.02
Professional schools	2.63	2.68	−.05
Physical sciences	2.60	2.65	−.05
Life sciences	2.66	2.68	−.02
Humanities	2.65	2.86	−.21
Engineering	2.89	2.89	0
Social sciences	2.59	2.58	+.01

The findings suggest that high school grades and performance tests have value in predicting future academic performance. Unless better predictors are found, it seems wise to continue their use in estimating academic achievement. The findings also suggest that for Asian American students any changes in admissions criteria that would weigh verbal test scores more heavily are likely to reduce the validity of the prediction equation for those students. Given that most studies have found verbal predictors to be stronger than mathematical predictors for students in general, such changes may have an adverse impact on Asian American students but not on students in general.

The analysis of prediction bias indicated that if the white regression equation is applied to Asian American students, little bias is revealed. However, the findings suggest that applying the equation to Asian American students as an aggregate group masks serious bias toward specific student groups: serious underprediction for Chinese, Other Asian Americans, and Asian Americans for whom English is not the best language; serious overprediction for Japanese, Filipinos, and Asian Americans for whom English is the best language. Since Chinese and Other Asian Americans are more heavily represented than are Japanese and Filipinos among Asian American students for whom English is not the best language, prediction bias for particular subgroups may be influenced by English proficiency.

The strength of this study is the inclusion of a large Asian American student population broken down by particular ethnicity. However, there are some important limitations to consider. First, it was not possible to examine other important variables, such as the socioeconomic class of the students, which may substantially influence the validity of predictors. Second, the sole criterion of overall achievement was first-year university grades. One could argue that other criteria should be used, such as grades in certain courses, grades for more than just the freshman year, or nonacademic indices of achievement. Third, many students were unable to declare their majors or may change majors over time; in retrospect, the sample of 1,000 randomly selected white students was not large enough to permit specific Asian American—white comparisons for some majors. Fourth, the population of Asian American students was highly selective. As noted earlier, the Asian American students enrolled in the University of California system achieved higher SAT scores than did college-bound Asian Americans in the rest of the nation. Furthermore, a student who had low SAT-verbal *and* SAT-mathematical scores was unlikely to be admitted to a UC campus. Thus, a student who had a low SAT score on one subtest must have achieved a high score on the other subtest in order to be admitted. This UC admissions procedure is likely to reduce the correlation between SAT-V and SAT-M scores and to restrict the range of scores of enrolled students. These limitations point to the need for further research in order for us to understand the theoretical and policy-related issues involved in the academic achievement of Asian American students.

REFERENCES

Aleamoni, L. M., and L. Oboler. 1978. ACT versus SAT in predicting first semester GPA. *Educational and Psychological Measurement* 38:393–99.

Arbeiter, S. 1984. *Profiles, college-bound seniors, 1984*. New York: College Entrance Examination Board.

Astin, A. W. 1982. *Minorities in American higher education*. San Francisco: Jossey-Bass.

Butterfield, F. 1986. Why Asians are going to the head of the class. *New York Times*. August 3, pp. 18–23.

Chissom, B. S., and D. Lanier. 1975. Prediction of first quarter freshman GPA using SAT scores and high school grades. *Educational and Psychological Measurement* 35:461–63.

Cleary, T. A. 1968. Test bias: Prediction of grades of Negro and white students in integrated colleges. *Journal of Educational Measurement* 5:115–24.

Commission on Tests. 1970. *Report of the Commission on Tests*. Vol. I, *Righting the balance*. New York: College Entrance Examination Board.

Davis, J. A., and G. Temp. 1971. The cultural context of achievement motivation: Comparative research. In *Socialization for achievement: Essays on the cultural psychology of the Japanese*, ed. G. A. DeVos, pp. 170–86. Berkeley and Los Angeles: University of California Press.

Dispenzier, A., S. Giniger, W. Reichman, and M. Levy. 1971. College performance of disadvantaged students as a function of ability and personality. *Journal of Counseling Psychology* 18:298–305.

Dizney, H., and R. Roskens. 1964. Comparative aptitude and achievement of American and foreign students in an American university. *Journal of College Student Personnel* 5:146–51.

Donloff, T. F., W. H. Angoff. 1971. The Scholastic Aptitude Test. In *The College Board Admissions Testing Program*, ed. W. H. Angoff. New York: College Entrance Examination Board.

Fincher, C. 1974. Is SAT worth its salt? *Review of Educational Research* 44:293–305.

Goldman, R. D., and B. N. Hewitt. 1976. Predicting the success of black, Chicano, Oriental, and white college students. *Journal of Educational Measurement* 13:107–17.

Goldman, R. D., and R. Richards. 1974. The SAT prediction of grades for Mexican-American versus Anglo-American students at the University of California, Riverside. *Journal of Educational Measurement* 11:129–35.

Hsia, J. 1985. The new racism, affirmative discrimination and Asian Americans. Paper presented at meeting of the Asian American Psychological Association, August, Los Angeles.

Kallingal, A. 1971. The prediction of grades for black and white students at Michigan State University. *Journal of Educational Measurement* 8:263–65.

Larson, L. R., and M. P. Scontrino. 1976. The consistency of high school grade point average and of the verbal and mathematical portions of the Scholastic Aptitude Test of the College Entrance Examination Board, as predictors of college performance: An eight-year study. *Educational and Psychological Measurement* 36:439–43.

McCausland, D. F., and N. E. Stewart. 1974. Academic aptitude: Study skills, and attitudes and college GPA. *Journal of Educational Research* 67:8.

McDonald, R. T., and R. S. Gawkoski. 1979. Predictive value of SAT scores and high school achievement for success in a college honors program. *Educational and Psychological Measurement* 39:411–14.

Malloch, D. C., and W. B. Michael. 1981. Predicting student grade point average at a community college from Scholastic Aptitude Tests and from measures representing three constructs in Vroom's expectancy theory model of motivation. *Educational and Psychological Measurement* 41:1127–35.

Neville, P. G., E. L. Scott, and P. G. Wakim. 1982. Predictive study of student performance at the University of California: A comparison between the Berkeley and the Los Angeles campuses. Parts I and II. Unpublished manuscript, University of California, Berkeley.

Nisbet, J., V. E. Ruble, and K. T. Schurr. 1982. Predictors of academic success with high risk college students. *Journal of College Student Personnel* 5(3):227–35.

Passons, W. R. 1967. Predictive validities of the ACT, SAT, and high school grades for first semester GPA and freshman courses. *Educational and Psychological Measurement* 27:1143–44.

Pfeifer, C. M., and W. E. Sedlacek. 1971. The validity of academic predictors for black and white students at a predominantly white university. *Journal of Educational Measurement* 8:253–61.

Ramist, L., and S. Arbeiter. 1986. *Profiles, college-bound seniors, 1985.* New York: College Entrance Examination Board.

Slack, W. V., and D. Porter. 1980. The Scholastic Aptitude Test: A critical appraisal. *Harvard Educational Review* 50:154–75.

Song, H. Undated. Systematic differences in the predictions of student performances among different subgroups of regularly admitted freshman students. Pilot study for Berkeley students who entered in fall 1977. Unpublished manuscript, University of California, Berkeley.

Song, H., E. L. Scott. 1980. Predictive performance studies with nontraditional predictor variables. Unpublished manuscript, University of California, Berkeley.

Sue, D. W., and S. Sue. 1972. Ethnic minorities: Resistance to being researched. *Professional Psychology* 3:11–17.

Sue, S., and N. W. S. Zane. 1985. Academic achievement and socioemotional adjustment among Chinese university students. *Journal of Counseling Psychology* 32(4):570–79.

Temp, G. 1971 Validity of the SAT for blacks and whites in thirteen integrated institutions. *Journal of Educational Measurement* 6:203–15.

Thomas, C. L., and J. C. Stanley. 1969. Effectiveness of high school grades for predicting college grades of black students: A review and discussion. *Journal of Educational Measurement* 6(4):203–14.

University of California. 1985. *University Bulletin* 33(1):1.

U.S. Department of Commerce. 1983. *Detailed population characteristics: California.* Washington, D.C.: U.S. Government Printing Office.

Weitzman, R. A. 1982. The prediction of college achievement by the Scholastic Aptitude Test and the high school record. *Journal of Educational Measurement* 19(3):179–91.

Wilcox, L. O. 1974. The prediction of academic success of undergraduate foreign students. Unpublished doctoral dissertation, University of Minnesota.

Yang, C. 1978. The predictive validity of the Scholastic Aptitude Test for Chinese college students. Ph.D. diss., Teachers College, Columbia University.

20 Opening the American Mind and Body:
The Role of Asian American Studies

Shirley Hune

THIS FALL, Asian American studies entered its third decade in higher education. After suffering some decline and loss of institutional support a number of years ago, it has experienced a renewed interest among students and scholars in the late 1980s and can now be reckoned as a national phenomenon and an accepted part of university life.

The Association for Asian American Studies (AAAS) has doubled its membership over the past three years. Over 500 scholars, students, policymakers, creative artists, and community organization members attended this year's AAAS Conference held in June at Hunter College. They came to New York from as far away as Hawaii and Canada to serve on some 50 panels covering a full range of topics on Asian Americans and Pacific Islanders, with disciplinary contributions from history, social science, law, education, literature, communication, and the arts. This is a remarkable achievement for the field that was begun only 20 years ago by students in social protest. Even so, its contributions to pedagogy and scholarship remain under-recognized and undersupported.

What is Asian American studies? It is the documentation and interpretation of the history, identity, social formation, contributions, and contemporary concerns of Asian and Pacific Americans and their communities. Its activities of research, teaching, and curriculum development relate to the experience of Asian and Pacific peoples in America. While thoroughly academic in its approaches, Asian American studies is also strongly committed to a focus on community issues and social problems.

Asian American studies was born out of the Third World strike of 1968–69 at San Francisco State College and similar events at other institutions, as minority students and white supporters marched, picketed, and took over university buildings to demand ethnic studies programs and open admissions. Its beginnings were an extension of wider protests of the time—Civil Rights, Black Power, Women's Liberation, Anti-War, La Raza, Native American Movement, and so on. Asian Americans, too, came to question American values and institutions.

The war in Vietnam had a particular impact on many Asian Americans, recalling for them earlier and present atrocities done to Asians in America and Asians in Asia. Power relations were changing internationally, especially with the emergence of newly independent Third World countries, some as a result of wars of national liberation, and many advocating alternative forms of social organization, such as the Chinese revolution. American social reformers condemned racism and sexism at home and imperialism and militarism abroad; they sought to create a more socially just and egalitarian nation. To construct a new society, higher education was one institution that had to be changed. Many Asian Americans shared this vision.

The ethnic and women's studies movements begun in the late '60s demanded that university curricula reflect and respond to the diversity of American society, especially racial minorities, women, and the working class. Higher education's organization and course content, it was argued, reflected the power relations of U.S. society in which white males govern hierarchically, Western culture is superior, American values and interests are considered universal, and a Eurocentric view of the world prevails. Asian Americans found themselves selectively represented, closed out of decision making, and nowhere to be seen in the canon.

This backdrop is important because it tells a story of the political, not just academic, origins of ethnic and women's studies. The universities' response in general was to incorporate these programs as forms of *compensatory* education, an aspect of affirmative action. This view lives on but limits the significance of these "new" studies.

Asian American studies should be seen as part of a social movement for educational reform. It is more than "compensatory" or a convenient way to help Asian American students learn their own history and to increase the representation of Asian American students, faculty, and administrators on campuses. Asian American studies is part of an effort to *change* education in all its facets, with an emphasis on making it more equitable, inclusive, and open to alternative perspectives.

Beyond curriculum change, the field has made contributions to pedagogy, research methodology, scholarship, ethics, and critical analysis. It is *transformative* in that Asian American studies looks to both a restructuring of education and an expansion of knowledge. Asian American scholars envision that their teaching and research will play a role in countering the cultural domination of the existing Euro-American knowledge base taught in American colleges; they hope to produce the kind of scholarship and students capable of resolving injustices and creating a more equitable society. In short, Asian American studies seeks to *democratize* higher education.

Higher education is currently paying new attention to Asian American studies. This interest is due in large part to the recent, dramatic increase in Asian American student enrollment at colleges and universities nationwide. Asian American scholars welcome that interest, but point also to needs and conditions quite different from those that gave initial rise to their field.

One such condition comes from the growth and remarkable diversity of Asian American communities, a circumstance that raises complex scholarly agendas. Needs of the newer immigrants and refugees (Koreans, South Asians, Southeast Asians) are woefully unmet. On another flank, Asian American studies faculty have had to keep a wary eye on this decade's retreat from support for social programs and group rights and the consequent opposition to affirmative action, ethnic studies, and bilingual education programs. The rise of anti-Asian violence (and racial violence in general) on college campuses and within the larger society also raises issues that demand inquiry. On still another front, the economic and strategic importance of the Pacific Rim to the United States has led to the creation of another new field—Pacific Rim area studies—engendering mixed feelings among Asian American scholars as to its purpose. These and other issues, even as they bring attention to the field, present its practitioners with a swelling agenda.

What forms does Asian American studies take in higher education today? It can be as small and limited as a course or two on the history and contemporary concerns of Asian Americans, taught by visiting faculty from traditional departments, perhaps with the sponsorship of students or an experimental program (this is typical of Ivy League schools, like Yale). A standard, fuller model is that of a relatively permanent and distinct teaching unit with its own faculty (some with joint appointments) offering credits toward a minor or, in a few cases, a major (this one finds at San Francisco State, in the UC system, and at the Universities of Hawaii and Washington). Increasingly, Asian American studies services the entire college or university by providing courses that meet general education requirements.

Organizationally, some Asian American studies units remain separate entities, while others operate within ethnic studies or comparative cultures units (the latter is true at Washington State, Colorado, and UC-Irvine); and a few institutions combine Asian American studies with Asian studies (e.g., City College of CUNY, California State at Long Beach). To date, UCLA offers the only M.A. degree in Asian American studies; UC-Berkeley has the only Ph.D. program in ethnic studies with a concentration in Asian American studies. Until the formation of the Asian American Center at Queens College, CUNY in 1987, UCLA had the sole research center devoted to Asian Americans (it was founded in 1969).

Asian American studies can be found from Hawaii to New England. Over a 20-year period, a few programs have come and gone, but most have stabilized. During the past two or three years, the field has begun to expand. West Coast institutions, especially in California where Asian American studies is well established and the Asian American student population has grown dramatically, are adding faculty positions to existing programs (e.g., at UC-Berkeley, Davis, and Santa Barbara, and at San Jose State).

New teaching units are being formed at UC-San Diego and at Stanford. Reflecting the influx of Asian immigrants to the East Coast, Asian American courses have been offered with increasing frequency at a number of colleges (e.g., Hunter, U-Mass-Boston, NYU, Haverford, and Tufts). An interesting development is that institutions located in areas lacking historic Asian American communities (although they may now have a significant number of Asian American students) are presently establishing medium-sized Asian American studies programs (e.g., Cornell, UW-Madison).

In the area of scholarship, Asian American studies is part of the "new" history, social science, literature, and education, challenging traditional assumptions, premises, sensibilities, theories, and research methods. Russell Leong's essay in this issue mentions specific works, but here let me suggest themes. Scholars take a bottoms-up (non-elite) view of Asian American history. They retrieve a "buried past" and write national histories of the various Asian and Pacific American groups. They explore neglected areas of research, such as agricultural history, Asian American mental health, women and work. Using new, untapped sources (e.g., Asian language newspapers, coroners' reports, material culture) and methods, including oral history, Asian Americanists are finding a past formerly hidden, one that reveals their active participation in creating private and public lives and institutions and which describes a society's effort to obscure and distort their contributions. In the process, the field has contributed major findings to our understanding of labor history, economic development, women's studies, foreign policy, urban anthropology, community politics, and of race, power, and ethnicity.

In the area of social theory, research in Asian American studies has exposed existing biases (e.g., assimilationist theory) and raised serious questions about the use and misuse of statistical data (e.g., the model minority thesis). Scholars have added new understanding and empirical data to international labor migration theory, race relations (e.g., the internal colonial model, middleman minority thesis), strategies of ethnic survival (e.g., the role of entrepreneurship), resistance, racial formation, socio-psychological adaptation (e.g., reexamining the sojourner and marginal man hypotheses), relationships between race, ethnicity, class, gender, biracial/bicultural identity, and more.

Asian American literature and literary criticism has become a central part of the comparative and ethnic literature field. Asian American writers have come forth with national best-sellers and book award winners. Themes of migration, community, family, and racism permeate that literature. "Lost" works of earlier generations have been retrieved and their sociopolitical context examined.

A number of excellent textbooks in Asian American history, social sciences, and literature are now available for classroom use. Award-winning videos, films, and plays now document aspects of what it is to be Asian American.

Asian American studies closely identifies with current critical theories in education. In the classroom, Asian American studies has brought attention to institutionalized racism (e.g., tracking influenced by stereotype) and issues of class, culture, and language-bias in achievement, and cultural styles in learning and teaching. Most importantly, it has raised the issue of cultural hegemony in course content, organizational structure, classroom management, philosophies of education, and counseling practices.

Asian American studies emphasizes the empowerment of students and teachers and the crucial link between the university and the community. From its inception, Asian American studies has criticized the elitist notion of knowledge as personal property or as a thing required for its own sake, and the notion that education entails an acquisition of skills and credentials for individual aggrandizement. Teachers and researchers made a commitment to community development; students have been encouraged to participate in community activities and find careers that serve community needs. While fulfilling this role has been complicated by the demands of the academy (notably the pressures of publish or perish), the premises of Asian American studies are community service, social responsibility, and accountability.

Ultimately, Asian American studies is about opening the American educational mind and body. So it is not a surprise that *resistance* to Asian American studies persists. The resistance may come in the form of restricting Asian American student enrollment, or the hiring of faculty and administrators, or from a more general anti-Asian climate on campus; there is always the fall-back claim of "limited resources," though institutions usually manage to support that which they deem necessary.

In a larger sense, the resistance to Asian American studies reflects a historic debate about the purpose of American education. On one side there are those who view American education as an agent to conserve and socialize, an instrument of social control to perpetuate the culture and produce the next generation of citizens and workers. The outcome of this approach, however, is usually to maintain an existing social and economic order—and, in an American context, to devalue non-Western peoples and cultures. On the other side are people who view American education as a liberating agent, as an instrument of social change whereby the historically disadvantaged and the newcomer can obtain some measure of equity. To achieve that, curricular reform and institutional restructuring are seen as necessary. It is within the latter ranks, of course, that one finds supporters of Asian American studies and similar programs.

Resistance can be in the form of benign neglect. Too often Asian American studies is seen by university officers as a way to meet the needs or demands of a target group (Asian American students) rather than as an institutional commitment of benefit to all students, the university itself, and the society at large. The result is the occasional course, but rarely a faculty position. At these institutions, Asian American studies always hinges on the concerted efforts of an active but, by definition, transient group of motivated students to push the venture. The outcome is the non-institutionalization of Asian American studies on campuses that appear to be supportive.

Institutional resistance also exists on campuses that do have Asian American studies. Programs may not receive adequate resources nor be given institutional recognition for their services. At the same time, they are expected to fulfill multiple functions beyond teaching and research, such as counseling students, participating on committees, representing the community and university, and so on. (One is all too familiar with the add-on demands made of minority faculty that are not borne by others.) Programs can become marginalized (some would say ghettoized) but tolerated as political necessities. Some may "fail to live up to expectations" (especially for research, even if crowded out by other duties) and hence receive even less support—contributing to a vicious cycle of isolation and decline.

Resistance can also come from Asian (as opposed to Asian American) faculty on a campus, and from the "old" area studies—in this case Asian studies—which are generally well established and respected on campuses and dominated by non-Asians. These parties may feel a need to protect intellectual territory (an unfounded view, since Asian American studies sees itself more a part of American studies than Asian studies), or fear competition for university funds, and often feel discomfort with a field that links itself to other American minority groups and adopts an activist stance.

At the departmental level, resistance centers on issues of recruitment and retention of faculty. Positions assigned to Asian American studies often remain unfilled as "traditional" standards are invoked and questions related to the legitimacy of one's scholarship and teaching interests are raised, which inevitably means that the minority and female candidate is not sufficiently qualified. Duke and the University of Wisconsin-Madison (with its "Madison Plan"), on the other hand, actively support the recruitment of women and minorities and are exceptions to the rule.

There is a terrible irony here: a pool of highly talented Asian Americans with relevant doctorates does indeed exist. But because elite universities were not looking over the years for what they had to offer, most took positions in second- and third-tier institutions, colleges where they had high teaching loads and many extra demands placed upon them. Today, they inevitably have slimmer publication records. And they are at institutions to which the elites seldom look in hiring. So it is that flagship institutions just can't seem to spot "qualified" candidates.

In addition, in an era of bottom lines and a cost-benefit view of education, institutions want assurances about outside sources of program support. Here Asian American studies is decidedly handicapped. Private foundations and key governmental funding agencies have declared flatly that Asian Americans (with small exceptions) are ineligible for various kinds of support, ranging from research funds to fellowships. Asian American objections to this—to their status as so-called "successful minorities" not requiring assistance—have not changed these policies. Thus, having been "defined out" of the funding opportunities open to other minority groups, Asian American scholars are left highly dependent on their own resources and their institutions for support.

The institutionalization of Asian American studies has its supporters. They, for the most part, originally viewed these programs as forms of compensatory education. Many now recognize, as Asian American scholars have argued, that Asian American studies speaks to an integral part of American history. There is a growing consensus about the multicultural origins of American development and an acceptance that *all* students need to know more about the ways that racial and ethnic groups, women, and different classes participated in the shaping of the nation, including its ugly side. Concommitantly, to be a global citizen, today's graduate must be informed about the histories and cultures of other regions of the world.

Multicultural education has grown from the demand in the late '60s for separate programs to today's emphasis on "mainstreaming" or "balancing the curriculum," with readings and courses on the formerly excluded. Increasingly, the content and perspective of ethnic and women's studies are being incorporated into wider coursework, and more institutions are adopting such courses and some aspect of global studies as part of their general requirements. This direction has been wholeheartedly supported by Asian American studies faculty, who view the education of *all* Americans on the history, problems, and aspirations of Asian and Pacific American communities as essential and necessary. Today, being culturally literate includes multicultural competency.

Asian American studies has a solid future. There has even been a debate within the field as to whether some campus programs have become so institutionalized that they have become rigid, created their own standards, and feel a need to protect their legitimacy.

Asian American studies is finding broad potential in its national and international perspectives. In the first two decades, Asian Americanists concentrated on constructing national histories of the older communities, correcting misconceptions, and defining their experiences and cultural expressions. Greater attention is now being given to research on the newer Asian and Pacific American communities and on comparative and global perspectives of the Asian diaspora (this was the theme of the 1989 national conference of the Association for Asian American Studies).

The comparative approach has much to offer in clarifying the influences of culture, social structure, and policy making, not only for the Asian American experience but for development of communities globally. The potential range of studies is unlimited: between generations, regions, men and women, new and old Asian communities, and other Asian American groups. Comparative studies with other groups of Americans, particularly racial and ethnic minorities and women, has led to links with women's studies and other ethnic studies programs. A number of scholars are looking at inter-ethnic relations, including Asian American interactions with African Americans and Hispanic Americans—studies long overdue, given that in major American cities and the state of California these three minority groups together are the new majority.

The global perspective of Asian American studies places any tendency to interpret the Asian American experience as American exceptionalism in a new perspective. Asian Americans become part of international history, interconnected with all human development. The large contemporary Asian emigration (both as immigrants and refugees) and its effects on the politics, economies, and social structures of receiving countries around the world is contributing to a new interest in studying Asians in the diaspora. (There are sizeable overseas Asian communities—some old, some new, some old and new—in Canada, Australia, parts of the Caribbean, Latin America, Southeast Asia, Africa, and now in Britain and the Middle East.)

Cross-national studies are also underway, comparing experiences in such areas as immigration and settlement policies, racial discrimination, aging, and ethnic entrepreneurship. This global dimension, which includes relations between the country of origin and the new home country, brings with it links to international and other area studies programs, such as Asian and Latin American studies. These create new opportunities for joint appointments in support of scholars with broad interests.

What should come next? Comparative studies at the domestic and international level could serve as a basis for doctoral programs. Without sacrificing undergraduate teaching, ethnic studies needs to become an object of graduate-level study. Indeed, much has been made of the lack of minority doctorates and of the shortage of available faculty for the 1990s. Graduate programs in ethnic studies could have a place in preparing the next generation of minority faculty in the humanities and social sciences—people who are needed immediately.

Finally, the demographic changes in America should be apparent to all. The Asian/Pacific American presence is permanent, growing, and diverse; more and more

Americans will work and live alongside Asian/Pacific Americans. Asian American studies has a practical application and fulfills a major societal need. Its courses can help prepare the teachers, social workers, health-care professionals, civil servants, and others whose responsibilities will include sizeable Asian populations. I'm led to this conclusion by the responses from my students (most of whom are non-Asian) in my "Asian Immigrants in the American Educational System" and "Ethnic Issues in Counseling" courses at Hunter College. They tell me that what they learn to understand about the racial and immigrant experience in these and related courses enhances their capabilities in multiracial and multicultural environments.

What Asian American studies cannot do is solve racism, poverty, violence, and the other inequities in American society, nor can it solve America's trade imbalance. What it can do is provide opportunities for students to learn the reasons behind such injustices, and perhaps learn to work together to address some of its consequences. It can support research on some of the nation's most critical issues, and it can work with others to transform education and humanize the university. These are reasons enough for pressing ahead.

21 On the Ethnic Studies Requirement

Sucheng Chan

STANFORD UNIVERSITY made national headlines when its faculty debated whether or not to change the core list of books that first-year students are required to read in its Western Culture Program, in response to faculty and student criticisms that works by non-Europeans and by women were not included in the "canon." Likewise, the University of California at Berkeley received widespread media coverage when its faculty postponed voting on a proposal to add an "American cultures" course to the university's list of graduation requirements. The actions garnered so much publicity because these two institutions rank among the world's leading research universities. But they are by no means the only campuses where such debates are taking place. As more and more institutions begin to grapple with various aspects of ethnic diversity in the coming years, it is important to understand why current efforts at enlarging the curriculum have generated such heated exchanges between supporters and opponents of the proposed reforms.

On the face of it, the very reasonable request that universities require their graduates to learn something about nonwhite peoples and cultures in the United States should not have aroused the intense emotions that it did. The fact that such efforts have been so controversial indicates that something far larger than curriculum reform is at stake. What is being challenged, I think, is the very structure of power within the university—the debate over whether or not to add one little course being only a sign of a more encompassing struggle.

A similar challenge had been mounted in the 1960s and 1970s, when student and faculty activists demonstrated militantly to demand that ethnic studies programs be established. Some were indeed set up, but though quite a number have survived, few have expanded in the last twenty years. The campaign to get a campus-wide ethnic studies requirement passed at various colleges across the nation marks a new stage in the growth of ethnic studies. This development is encountering stiff resistance in some places because no one can predict how the final outcome will affect existing power relations in American higher education. Like their predecessors, today's activists are asking questions about who makes decisions, based on what criteria, about curriculum, personnel, and the distribution of resources, and to whom such decision-makers should be accountable. But beyond these material concerns, they are also raising issues about who gets to define reality. By so doing, they are calling into question the ideological foundations of society in general and of the university in particular.

From *Amerasia Journal*, 15 (1989): 267–280. Reprinted with permission of the Regents of the University of California and the UCLA Asian American Studies Center.

Were this not the case, we would not be witnessing the sound and fury that have so captured public attention in recent months.

In the last three years, students and faculty at four University of California campuses—Santa Cruz, Riverside, Santa Barbara, and Berkeley—have pushed for the establishment of some kind of ethnic studies requirement. While such a requirement is already in force in Santa Cruz and Riverside, the final votes will not be taken at Santa Barbara and Berkeley until the spring of 1989.[1] I shall analyze the efforts to get such a requirement passed at these four UC campuses, as well as at Stanford University, in Part II of this article. In this first segment, I shall reflect on how the classroom dynamics in the ethnic studies courses I have taught that fulfill a campus-wide requirement differ from the situation in classes that do not fulfill one. By analyzing my own reactions to the changes, I hope to clarify some of the commonly held but not always explicitly articulated premises upon which ethnic studies—as both an academic enterprise and a political project—have been built.

I began teaching Asian American Studies at Sonoma State University in 1971. Subsequently, I spent ten years on the Asian American Studies faculty at UC Berkeley. At both institutions, Asian American students comprised at least 97 percent of the enrollment in my classes. (This represents a greater "ethnic concentration" than is found in most Afro-American, Chicano/Latino, or Native American Studies courses, according to colleagues teaching in those areas.) Quite frankly, I rather liked having such an ethnic enclave. My students, on the other hand, have reacted to the ethnic clustering in different ways. Many feel more comfortable in these Asian American Studies classes than they do in other classes. After an initial reluctance, they often learn to talk freely in discussions. Some who have grown up in primarily white neighborhoods or who have purposely avoided contact with fellow Asian Americans, on the other hand, tend to feel very uneasy when they are first surrounded by people who look like themselves. Yet others experience a virtual catharsis when given the chance to come to terms with who they are. The latter often become strongly committed to the Asian American movement. As is true of other teachers, I have been liked by some of my students and disliked by others. But regardless of how they evaluated my teaching, I always felt that teaching primarily Asian American students was a privilege: the rooms in which we held our classes became, however temporarily, *our* space; the lecture hours became *our* time. I did not realize how much this privilege meant to me until I lost it.

At UC Santa Cruz, to which I moved in 1984, the ethnic composition and the atmosphere in my classes did not differ greatly from those at Berkeley. But after the Santa Cruz Academic Senate approved an ethnic/Third World studies requirement in February 1985—a requirement that went into effect in the fall of 1986—things changed in subtle but important ways. I taught the introductory Asian American history course twice that first year. These two classes—though the same course—turned out to be vastly different experiences for me as a teacher. Even though I assigned the same readings and gave more or less the same lectures (my lectures are never *quite* the same from quarter to quarter, since I do not read from notes), the overall ambience of the class changed. The shift was probably perceptible to no one but myself, but it troubled me sufficiently to make me wonder what the difference augured.

The first time around, there were forty-six students in the class. Thirty-five were Asian American, two were Black, two Chicano, one Latino American, and six White. I had no teaching assistants, so we had no scheduled discussion sections. But the class was still small enough for spontaneous discussions to occur. At first, almost everybody was shy and I had to pull words out of many individuals. But by the third week or so, the ice had broken and several talkative students began to say more and more. In time, the class became so eager to talk that I had to set up discussion sections outside of lecture hours, so that we could get through the lecture materials.

In these conversations, the most important discovery we made was that not only do non-Asians hold biased images of Asian Americans—something we have always known and felt angry about—but that Asian Americans *also* have inaccurate perceptions of White, Black, Latino, and other Americans. Moreover, we found that among that group of students, at least, television programs seemed to be the primary source of such stereotypes. A very touching exchange took place one afternoon when several Asian American students talked about how their parents did not love them. Unlike white parents in certain television shows they had watched who hug, kiss, and say nice things to their children, they said, theirs never embraced them. As tears began to glisten in some of their eyes, one of the white students said very gently, "You know, in real life not all white parents express their affection the way you think they do . . . many of our parents are divorced, some of our moms and dads fight a lot and seldom spend time with us . . . my Mom had to work when I was very young so she was never home waiting with a jar of cookies when I came home from school . . . one of the reasons I took this class is that I have always envied Asian Americans who have such close-knit families." The Asian American students who had felt so sorry for themselves just a moment ago looked up, startled. Other students then told about their childhood, many of which were not happy. Although the discussion took time away from the lecture I had planned to give that day, I did not stop the students from talking, because the factual information they missed hearing from me seemed less important than the common bond they were discovering amongst themselves.

As the quarter progressed, I encouraged members of the class to relate the Asian American material to larger issues, particularly their own relationship to the world around them. Like other people, I pointed out, Asian Americans are connected to others through history and a complex web of social interactions in which are embedded unequal power relationships. While some of us accept our lot, others do not. But before we can transform what we do not like, I cautioned, we need to understand clearly how the present situation evolved, why some conditions are so difficult to change, and what the personal and social costs of political action may be. By getting the students to think along these lines, I hoped that even if I did not succeed in goading them to do anything significant to change their lives—much less the world—I could at least help them understand how individual psychology is linked to history and sociology, so that those who felt wounded by life's cruelties no longer suffered alone.

That class was very satisfying to teach. With Asian American students in the majority, it provided a haven in which those who were verbally reticent could slowly learn to express themselves. At the same time, having a small number of students from a variety of ethnic backgrounds made a more probing exchange of views possible. The following quarter, however, more than a hundred students crowded into a room designed to hold forty. As I looked out over the sea of faces—most of them white—my mind began tying itself into knots: "I have no T.A.s, no readers . . . we can't have this kind of class without discussions . . . the students *must* have an opportunity to talk about and 'process' the emotionally charged issues we will be dealing with . . . I cannot possibly lead five discussion sections a week and write more than a hundred narrative evaluations[2] without any help . . . certainly not when I am holding two administrative positions! . . . I *must* do something to reduce the class size . . ."

My virtual panic had nothing to do with a fear of crowds: I not only do not mind teaching large classes, I actually *enjoy* teaching them. However, when I had taught very large classes at Berkeley, I always had T.A.s to work with me. Even though the graduate assistants I hired there often had no training in Asian American Studies *per se*, they learned quickly and were indispensable to the success of the courses. At Santa Cruz, in contrast, no provision had been made for dealing with the sudden rise in the enrollment in courses fulfilling the new requirement; moreover, even if funds were available, few graduate students were to be had, since there are only a few Ph.D. programs outside of the natural sciences.

"There is no way I can accommodate so many students in this class," I began.

"You can't kick us out!" they exclaimed, before I could finish my sentence. "We *have* to get into a class that fulfills the ethnic studies requirement."

"But there are lots of other classes that do," I replied.

"That's not true—there are only five this quarter!"

"The fire marshall won't let you sit all over the aisles . . ."

"Then get a bigger classroom!" they demanded.

"I've already tried, there aren't any available at this hour. You know, there's going to be *lots*, and I mean *lots*, of reading in this course—are you *sure* you want to take this class?"

"We have to! We have no choice."

Well, neither really did I. Having worked so hard to get an ethnic studies requirement established, was I not morally obligated to take all the students who desired to enroll, with or without T.A.s?

We eventually found a larger classroom in an evening time slot. That worked out well since I had a grant that quarter to rent a lot of films. Though only four hours were scheduled for the lectures, the class actually met for six hours a week: I was able to show the films after the lectures without reserving another room for them since there was no other class scheduled in that room after mine. Furthermore, since I felt that it was mandatory that we have some discussions, I arranged voluntary discussion sections in the afternoons. I divided the class into four groups, each of which was to meet every other week. There being no T.A.s, I had to lead all the sections myself. This was a heavy burden. What helped me get through the quarter was that the class had an upbeat atmosphere: attendance was surprisingly good (even though it rained a lot that winter, and dark, wet nights in the redwoods of Santa Cruz can be scary), morale was high, and the students frequently told me how much they were enjoying the course.

But one aspect of the class really bothered me. In the discussion sections, the white students chatted amiably enough, but regardless of how hard I tried, very few of the Asian American students were willing to say anything. Although many of the T.A.s who had worked with me at Berkeley had often wrung their hands over Asian American students who would not talk, I have seldom encountered this problem myself. Somehow, I had always managed to get at least a few of the students to say something. But in this instance, being numerically overwhelmed, the Asian American students felt vulnerable: they could not very well spill their guts in public.

My colleague Wendy Ng, who has also taught at Santa Cruz, has tried heroically to carry on discussions *during lecture hours* in a class with over a hundred students—something I never found the courage to do. Despite her success, she was troubled greatly by the anger that Asian American students felt over the way white students dominated the discussions. My students did not seem particularly angry, but their silence nevertheless spoke volumes. Behind closed doors in my office, I tried to find out why, unlike the group I had the quarter before, these students did not open their mouths.

"Surely it can't be so hard to talk to or in front of white classmates . . . don't you have any non-Asian friends?" I asked.

"Yes, but those are our *friends*."

"Some of the students in this class *could* become your friends . . ."

"It's not the same."

Indeed, it was not. Although I received superb teaching evaluations that quarter—from Asian and non-Asian students—I could not help feeling an immense and inconsolable sense of loss: the circle of trust within which my Asian American students and I had ensconced ourselves in bygone years was no more.

That I should feel disconsolate requires explanation, for I am not normally a sentimental person. Why, then, in this case, in spite of the overwhelmingly positive response to my course, did I feel such nostalgia for the way things used to be? To get to the root of my vexation, I asked myself anew several old questions. First, for whose benefit are we offering ethnic studies courses? Second, what do we actually hope to accomplish in our classes? Third, what undergirds the authority of the faculty teaching such courses? With respect to each question, how does the answer change when our courses become part of a general education requirement? In thinking about these issues, much can be learned about race relations in today's American universities.

At first glance, the answer to the question, "Whom should our courses benefit?" seems simple enough. Since students of color were the primary motive force behind the establishment of the pioneer ethnic studies programs, the courses should of course benefit them. But even a cursory look at the faces in our classrooms will immediately reveal that "students of color" or "minority students" or "Asian American students" are not monolithic terms. Our students come from different national origins and socioeconomic classes. They were born in places near and far. They have been in the United States for varying lengths of time—fifth-generation Chinese Americans mingle with recently arrived refugees from Vietnam. Those who are immigrants came to this country at different ages, which means they encountered mainstream American culture at different stages in their socio-psychological development. They have also grown up in contrasting environments. Some are the children of well-off professionals and business executives, others come from families so poor that they have to send part of their financial aid checks home to help support their parents, grandparents, or siblings. Just because we use the handy label "Asian American" to refer to them collectively, it does not mean they have similar interests or that we should expect our lectures and assigned readings to touch them equally.

On the other hand, heterogeneity does not imply a lack of commonality. I have learned through my teaching that what makes "Asian American" a defensible and meaningful *analytical category* is not so much that we or our ancestors all came from somewhere in Asia, but rather, virtually all individuals of Asian ancestry in the United States know what it feels like to be a member of a minority group. I say this despite the fact that some students of Asian ancestry deny vehemently that they have ever encountered racism or discrimination of any kind. But such denial is often a protective device, a defense mechanism. When placed in a situation—such as an Asian American Studies class—where it is socially *acceptable* to discuss how Asian Americans and other minorities have been treated, the memories of such individuals seem all of a sudden to be triggered. They begin to recall little incidents or disquieting feelings they have long forgotten or repressed—experiences that reveal they *have*, after all, encountered racial and cultural subordination. Whether or not we wish to acknowledge it, we discover that in the end it is our status as members of *American-made* minority groups that binds us.

Asian American students respond well to Asian American Studies because in our courses we *do* dissect the experiences that trouble them. We do so by imparting information about historical and sociological phenomena and by analyzing and interpreting their meaning. It is this cognitive component that differentiates our courses from what goes on in counseling groups: we attempt to link personal experiences to changing social, cultural, economic, and political *structures*, while therapists focus more on *individuals* and their relationship to people closest and most significant to them.

Because I consider efforts to help Asian American students "locate" themselves in society to be so important, I felt as though the rug had been pulled out from under me when my classroom became populated largely by white students. I reacted this way not because I am a "reverse racist" but because I am conscious of the fact that my effectiveness as a teacher of Asian American Studies depends on my ability to keep my finger on the pulse of a majority of my students. I am tuned in to how most Asian American students think and feel, but I do not think the same "fit" exists between me and my non–Asian American students.

"Fit" matters because for me what kind of students are in my class and how they respond to the materials I present affect how I teach. I believe that in every course there is a "text" and a "subtext." The text is what is in our syllabuses, lectures, and readings—the body of knowledge to be transmitted. But since students are not mere receptacles, the manner in which they absorb and react to what we present becomes a subtext. Thus, though we may dish out the same text year after year, the subtext changes every time we encounter a new group of students. Teachers who care about *how* students learn take note of such changes and react to them, whether consciously or subconsciously. I, for example, prefer to lecture without notes because it allows me to sweep my eyes across the room, calibrating the amount of details I should present as well as how I should frame particular issues, depending on what my "antenna" is picking up.

When the composition of my class changed from being largely Asian American to predominately white, I told the students my purpose would remain the same—to help them understand what life has been like for Asian Americans through successive historical periods. But at the same time, I realized that instead of *articulating* the experience of the group—on its behalf, as I had always done—I now had to, instead, *translate* that experience into terms that non–Asian Americans could comprehend.

Articulation is important when some of our students have not yet found words to describe certain facets of their lives. For them, language has not yet become a tool for making the world intelligible, not because their English is inadequate or they lack intelligence, but because in their families and at school, some aspects of reality have never been talked about or are not permitted to be talked about. By helping them to express inchoate feelings and to explore suppressed ideas, I provide them with cognitive maps—in the form of a vocabulary and a set of explanations—that enable them to make better sense of their world. To the extent that my analysis reflects and resonates with their own experiences, I validate their existence and offer them a means to get a handle on whatever has vexed them. "Facts" thus become vehicles for self-discovery and empowerment, as they realize that being different is not the same as being deviant or inferior.

Having a large number of non-Asian students in my class complicates matters enormously because even though I can still articulate the Asian American experience, when I do so now I risk making my Asian American students feel self-consciously naked—as though they are in a fishbowl, for everyone to stare at and possibly to make fun of. As Asian American playwright Philip Kan Gotanda has put it, being a minority person is a real burden because it forces one to constantly "monitor" one's environment. Gotanda tells of an almost magical moment when, after residing in Japan for some years—a period long enough for him to have become fluent in spoken Japanese and to have picked up all the proper body language—he all of a sudden felt he could finally become anonymous, and consequently free.[3] For the same reason, I think many Asian American students prefer not to talk in classes where they are not in the majority because they hope silence will spare them ridicule: "If *I* don't say anything, maybe *they* won't notice that I'm different." But having a teacher express what they themselves might have said is no less disconcerting when it is done in a room full of "strangers." Thus, the very same process of self-delineation—which can be so empowering in an in-group setting—can cause profound discomfort when it occurs in a mixed milieu.

My dilemma is that I feel obligated to cover the same ground even though I know doing so might make the Asian American students embarrassed and their white peers uneasy. I believe that if I eschew talking about the more sensitive issues, I cheat both my Asian American and my non–Asian American students of the very insights they should gain by taking courses such as mine. The challenge then becomes how one can pay equal attention to both subgroups. The solution I found was to translate, instead of articulate. A translator must ensure that *both* sets of communicators understand the messages being conveyed. In this instance, even though we are all speaking English, I still play the role of translator because I am explicating a reality known by one subgroup to the other subgroup, whose members may not be privy to its secrets. However, translation is not a perfect solution. When I could no longer focus exclusively on Asian American students and their needs, the lucidity born of intimacy is lost.

My sense of loss is tied to my understanding of the different perspectives that can be used to study minority groups. I can think of at least four. The oldest approach—an attitude that permeates the scholarly literature published before the 1960s—treats minority groups as deviant or deficient. According to proponents of this view, to become "normal," members of minority groups must assimilate into the majority culture and discard the "dysfunctional" minority one. The second perspective focuses on the "contributions" of various ethnic groups. It is a celebratory stance couched in terms of multicultural enrichment, but it seldom probes the causes of inequality. The third viewpoint defines the minority groups as victims. Its theorists seek to understand how forces of exploitation and oppression are built into the fabric of society. The fourth angle of vision sees members of minority groups as agents of history—people who think and feel and who make decisions even when their lives are severely circumscribed by conditions beyond their control.

I identify most strongly with the fourth perspective. For that reason, getting quiet Asian American students to talk in class is very important to me because I believe self-expression is one means through which individuals can *externalize* their experiences. Unlike the internalization that occurs when new members of a society—be they children or immigrants—are socialized into the values and norms of the community they have to learn to call home, externalization involves an opposite social process: it allows subjective experiences to acquire communal meaning and to become a vocalized, hence tangible, element in the culture that the new members enter. Instead of being passive recipients of the host culture, new members who have a voice can play an active role in shaping that culture. Speech provides a means through which many hitherto quiet Asian American students can learn to become agents of history. But they can acquire such agency only when they overcome a double repression: Asian traditions that train the young (and especially the female) to be quiet, submissive, and obedient *and* American racism that threatens members of minority groups with harm unless they "stay in their place." Staying in their place means keeping silent. Conversely, breaking silence is an act of rebellion—a declaration that a public self now exists.

I believe that those who control decision-making in the university have opposed the growth of ethnic studies courses precisely because they contain such an element of self-discovery and empowerment for students. If all that ethnic studies courses try to do is to impart information *about* the history and "exotic" cultural practices of nonwhite groups, they would not be threatening at all. After all, cultural pluralism in and of itself is innocuous and even colorful; it only becomes ominous when it is used as the ideological justification for changing existing arrangements of privilege and power. On the level of scholar-ship, those academic gatekeepers who determine what kind of work is legitimate some-times dismiss the writings of feminist scholars or minority scholars as "too shrill," "too angry," or "too bitter" precisely because our sharp words puncture the sheath that envelops the still mostly male and mostly white world of academic discourse—discourse that pre-tends it has the sole right to define normalcy, universality, what is human.

Ideally, for ethnic studies courses that enroll a large number of non-minority students to succeed in their purpose, they must help students of color to arrive at the same concep-tual clarity about the history, contemporary manifestation, and meaning of racial inequal-ity that all ethnic studies courses aim to achieve. Second, they must help white students to come to terms with the fact that they may unwittingly be what Kenneth Clark has called "accessories to profound injustice."[4] Third, they must provide all students with an arena in which to explore a new vision—a world where interdependent groups share a common des-tiny. The end we seek is mutual empathy. But we can only hope to reach this goal if we do not assume an accusatory stance. The importance of not "guilt tripping" white students was taught me by a student who had acquired a reputation for disrupting the lectures of minor-ity faculty whenever they talked about racism. This student, however, was very well be-haved in my class. One day I decided to ask him what had caused him to change his attitude.

"It's not my attitude," he explained. "I got angry in the other classes because every time the professors lectured about racism, I felt that they were accusing me *personally* of being racist. But you're very analytical—you try to explain why racism exists and how it has affected Asian Americans—so I don't feel like you are attacking *me* directly."

This observation alerted me to another dilemma: by creating analytical "distance," I avoid alienating white students, but by soft-pedaling racism, I rob my Asian American stu-dents of an important forum in which to express their confusion, hurt, and anger. In the short span of ten weeks—or even fifteen or twenty weeks—it does not seem possible to meet the needs of white and Asian American students simultaneously. There simply is not enough time to work through all the thoughts and feelings that the course material elicits. A more daunting difficulty is that even if faculty may want to help students overcome the interracial tensions that are so deeply rooted in American society, most of us are not up to the task. Which one of us can claim to be completely free of racism, sexism, homophobia, and class and religious prejudice?

Therefore, to avoid disappointment, bitterness, and cynicism, we must be modest in our goals. We should recognize that courses that fulfill an ethnic studies requirement can-not eradicate racism. All we can hope to do, if we are good teachers, is to get our students to listen to us and to each other, to learn a few unpleasant truths, to gain the insight that people who do not look like ourselves nevertheless face similar dilemmas common to the human condition. Even this will not be easy to accomplish: students who have to take a course because it is required often resent doing so.

Faced with a captive, possibly restive, audience, we may wonder if our authority as professors under such circumstances may have become more tenuous. Could the "thresh-old of convincibility"—the amount of evidence needed to convince our audience that this or that assertion is indeed true—now be higher?[5] I worried about such a possibility when I puzzled over why far fewer students challenged all the things I said than I had expected. It was then that I realized that several of the films I had shown contained scenes of white, male scholars discussing the discrimination Asian immigrants had faced (and continue to face). Not only that, these colleagues assert that such discrimination was clearly racist. In Stephen Okazaki's *Unfinished Business*, for example, Peter Irons and Roger Daniels ex-pound on the racism that led to the incarceration of Japanese Americans during World War

II. In Spencer Nakasako's film on Vietnamese refugee fishermen, *Monterey's Boat People*, Sandy Lydon comments on the earlier discriminatory legislation against Chinese and Japanese immigrant fishermen. In *Dollar a Day, Ten Cents a Dance*, a film about Filipino farmworkers by Mark Schwartz and Geoffrey Dunn, Howard DeWitt talks about the racism manifest in the anti-Filipino riot that took place in Watsonville, California, in the early 1930s. Although I had lectured about the same events and their meaning, I could not help but suspect that having Irons, Daniels, Lydon, and DeWitt—who *look and talk* like the white male authority figures with whom all students are familiar—validate my analysis made it easier for my students to accept what they heard. It does not flatter my ego, of course, to think that white male colleagues may have enhanced my credibility; on the other hand, since I want above all else to penetrate the wall of resistance that some students may have unconsciously erected to block out information about the dark, unpleasant "underside of American history," I do not mind using all the means at my disposal.

As we enter a new stage in our struggle for academic legitimacy and more widespread influence, our central task is to convince colleagues and non-minority students that we, too, are educators—educators competent to teach not only students of color but *all* students. Such a claim has to be made because during the last two decades we have justified the existence of ethnic studies programs primarily by arguing that we meet the special, unmet needs of students of color. Critics of such programs, meanwhile, have charged *ad nauseum* that the manner in which we have sought to meet those needs has been "nonacademic," too "political," and therefore unacceptable. But we must point out to them that what we are trying to do is but a variant of what the defenders of a liberal education argue it should do.

Faculty who believe in the importance of a liberal education try to provide an overview of the structure of knowledge and how scholars have divided it into different branches, each dealing with some segment of human experience or natural phenomena. They teach students how to think critically about the information they receive by examining the underlying values that influence the way such information is packaged. They encourage those coming of age in these times of flux to understand the constantly changing world in which we live and our relationship to it. They urge students to use the knowledge they gain to improve the quality of human life.

Faculty teaching ethnic studies, skeptics need to realize, can play a crucial role in a liberal education, though our contributions have so far not yet been recognized, much less rewarded. Our specialty is to make sense of the historical and contemporary experiences of nonwhite peoples in the United States. We broaden the university's offerings first by unearthing (through research and analysis) and then by imparting (through teaching) information not found in the regular curriculum. When we show students how to think critically, we often do so by suggesting competing perspectives on the world—points of view that have sometimes been suppressed because they challenge the status quo way of looking at things. While our stance may threaten colleagues who are insecure about their own standing in the academy, it can, and should, stimulate others to formulate dazzling new theories or promote collaborative efforts that lead to breakthroughs in the state of knowledge about certain phenomena. Hence, our presence within the university should be treated as an exciting addition, not an inconvenient political necessity. Finally, when we give students tools needed to enable them to make the world better, future generations benefit. If those of us who have taught ethnic studies for many years did not believe all this to be true, we certainly would not have devoted the best years of our lives to developing the field.

NOTES

1. The University of California, one of the largest public university systems in the world, consists of nine campuses located at Berkeley, Davis, Irvine, Los Angeles, Riverside, San Diego, San Francisco, Santa Barbara, and Santa Cruz. With the exception of the San Francisco campus, which is a medical school, all the other campuses are comprehensive, research universities, offering the B.A., B.S., M.A., Ph.D. and a variety of professional degrees in a wide range of subjects.

2. The University of California, Santa Cruz, does not have grades. Rather, instructors must write a "narrative evaluation"—ranging from a few sentences to more than a page (single-spaced)—describing and assessing the work each student has done during the quarter. This is a time-consuming task that not all faculty enjoy doing.

3. Philip Kan Gotanda, "Visions of an Asian American Writer," National Asian American Telecommunications Association workshop, San Francisco, 3 December 1988.

4. Kenneth Clark, *Dark Ghetto* (New York, 1965), 75.

5. I borrow this term from Carol Nagy Jacklin, "Feminist Research and Psychology," in *The Impact of Feminist Research in the Academy*, edited by Christie Farnham (Bloomington and Indianapolis, 1988), 99.

22 Prejudicial Studies: One Astounding Lesson for the University of Connecticut

David Morse

BEFORE THE DANCE, the word "semiformal" had the usual romantic connotations for Marta Ho—pretty dresses, corsages, crepe-paper streamers. It also suggested independence.

All through high school, Marta had struggled for acceptance. "I wanted to fit in so badly," she says. Her mother and father, who had emigrated from China by way of Taiwan and South America, would not let her have boyfriends or stay out late. Branford High School was overwhelmingly white, and Marta hadn't gone to dances.

"My father was trying to keep a little China around us. He knew that we were in America, but 'Don't be American . . . Don't live that kind of lifestyle; "Don't start drinking, don't start smoking, don't start having boyfriends. Don't, don't, don't.' " She delivers his remarks in a singsong litany, then laughs. "I hated high school. I don't think I liked myself, either."

Marta is 22 now, a senior at the University of Connecticut. She has been an American citizen for six years. She talks in the breezy post-literate style of her college peers, the softened Chinese "r" the only sign of an accent. Forsaking syntax for verve, she regularly inserts little dialogues in mid-sentence to make a point. She has an expressive face, ready to laugh; hair swept back from her high forehead; hands usually fidgeting.

The college dance that would come to signify a different kind of independence for Marta Ho is almost two years in the past. But her life has been altered irrevocably by the event. So, too, has the university.

Headlines tell a bare-bones story. Eight Asian students step onto a crowded bus bound for a semiformal dance. They are spat upon repeatedly and called names. But headlines and news stories do little to show what it's like to be an Asian American on a college campus, to be the victim of racial harassment. Nor do they reveal the reverberations and deep tremors the incident still sends through the Storrs campus, or the change in Marta Ho.

Last May, just before final exams, Marta sat on a naugahyde chair in the Student Union and talked about growing up as a Chinese-American. She wore pedal pushers in a gold-and-avocado pattern, and a beige top with long sleeves. Her hands kept disappearing inside the cuffs, even as she waved them around to make a point.

"Why?" Marta and her sister had asked their father. "Why no boyfriends?"

" 'Because one boyfriend leads to another, and then that means you're going to have sex, and then maybe marriage; and it's all too young and premature; so don't get into any of those things: just study, study, study.' "

Originally published in The *Hartford Courant*, November 26, 1989, pp 10–15. Copyright© David Morse.

And work. Outside of school, there was the family restaurant. Always, the restaurant the frenetic pace, the steamy kitchen, smoke from the wok, angry customers, spilled tea. Marta and her sister and brother worked six days a week, often from 3 in the afternoon until 1 in the morning. And for most of her high school years, they lived in back of their restaurant; there was no escape. The odor clung to her clothing. Marta wrinkled her nose. "All the other kids smelled of Ivory soap or something, and I'm the only one who smells like food."

Even when the family's circumstances grew more comfortable, the children continued to work at the restaurant. Marta earned a reputation for laughing a lot and teasing the customers. Among the regulars, she was known as "Giggles."

"You have to laugh," her sister says, "or you'll be miserable that you're stuck there working on a Friday night, every single weekend."

The Ho children grew up with the paradox of immigrant parents who want the best for their children but have little time to spend with them. "It's not that they didn't care about us," Marta said. "They were just always working 15 hours a day."

"Their philosophy is when you're young, work hard, accomplish your goal. Then you can relax, take vacations. Maybe I'm Americanized, but—well, I like to work hard, but I think they're workaholics. I know it makes sense to them. But for me, I don't feel every single day of my life has to be spent working. They never relax. I look at my parents and I don't want to be like that."

Her mother, who works a second job as an aide at a nursing home, "only gets two hours' sleep. She still says, 'I'm young, I don't need sleep.' I go, 'Oh, no, I need 10 hours' sleep!' "

Hard work, obedience, modesty. These are the Confucian values. "We knew what we were supposed to do when we got home from school: study, practice piano, write Chinese." But, she confesses, the reality was different. "I was always getting in trouble. I knew where my mother hid her money, so once I bought all these candy bars and sodas for my friends. The whole neighborhood was there . . . I was always the ringleader." Marta said she was punished often. "I always thought my father hated me . . . I keep reminding myself that my father really loved me."

As the middle child, Marta had to compete with her sister Maria, two years older and a kind of surrogate firstborn son in her father's eyes, and with her younger brother, on whom her mother doted. Marta learned to excel in certain areas, such as keeping her room neat, and math.

Her father had taught high school math and science in Taiwan, where the family lived until Marta was 8. They moved to South America then, living mostly in Bolivia and Brazil, and stayed long enough to take advantage of more favorable quotas for immigrating to the United States—which they were able to do in 1978. After making a start in Pennsylvania, her father thought the family would fare better by opening a restaurant in Hawaii. He sent the two girls ahead to check it out.

Marta laughed, remembering the trip. "What is a 13- or 14-year-old going to say about Hawaii? We said, 'Sure, come on!' " After a couple of years there, Marta's father decided Hawaii was "too laid back," Marta said, " 'not conducive to study.' " He explored California. " 'Not conducive.' " He moved them to Connecticut to be closer to Ivy League colleges.

Marta resented moving around. She always felt uprooted. Even today, she feels a barrier in making friends—a fear that if she gets too close, she'll be snatched away. But growing up in that fashion taught her to adapt quickly. "I think I can adjust to almost any environment. I was always the new kid on the block. I was different looking. I discovered if I didn't make the initiative, I'd never have anyone to talk to."

"I always wanted to be one of those people who lived in a house with the white picket fence and friends they've known since kindergarten. Now I wouldn't exchange that for my own experience."

Her sister was the first to rebel against their father's prohibition against dating and makeup. "Maria opened doors for us," Marta said, describing how desperately Maria wanted to go to the school prom. "You know how important it is . . . If you didn't go you felt like a real loser." Marta continued the story, complete with dialogue.

"If you go," their father said to her sister, "I'll disown you. You choose one or the other."

"Why are you making such a big deal?" her sister asked.

"Because you're going with a boy and you're going to be coming home very late; you'll be coming home at 3 o'clock, and what decent girl would be coming home at 3 o'-clock in the morning? And what kind of boy is he? Is he Chinese?"

The boy was Jewish.

"Oh, no! No, no, no! Things happen when you start drinking. And then . . ."

Maria defied their father and went to the prom. He stayed up waiting for her return—and made sure the whole family stayed up, waiting. "She even came home early," Marta recalled. "One o'clock. And he was still mad. He said, 'No decent girl comes home at 1 o'-clock. And why are you made up like that?' "

Marta paused. "My father," she insisted, "is holding values they don't even have in China anymore."

Nowadays, however, he is a little less conservative. She described a recent conversation in which she tried to dissuade him from some of his prejudices. "He's saying I can't marry white or black or Koreans or Japanese; those people are all out. Except for Chinese. And I say, 'Where do you think we are? We're not in China! I'm not exposed to that many Chinese guys. And if I am exposed to them, you expose me to the dweebiest ones!' " The sons of his friends are generally frightened of her, she claimed. "I have too much of a man's trait. I'm too aggressive, and I scare them when I talk too much, like 'Oh, she's scary! She's too fresh!' "

Her father's response, she thought, was more enlightened than it would have been a few years ago. "He said, 'If you get married to a Caucasian or somebody I don't approve, I just won't go to the wedding.' You see? He doesn't say 'No way! You're disowned!' He just says, 'I won't go to the wedding.' And I think once I do get married, and if it happens to be Anglo-Saxon or whatever nationality that person is, I think once we start having children, it all starts changing. My parents love children."

"But," she added, "I don't think I would marry Caucasian." She shook her head, and her slight smile was at once wry and wistful.

On her right ankle was a little bracelet woven from pumpkin-colored gimp by a friend who she insisted was "a boy and a friend, but not a boyfriend."

From the window came the ragged purr of construction equipment, grading the area around the pride of UConn: the $28-million sports center. The shiny, stainless steel geodesic dome filled the view, like an enormous silver breast.

On the evening of December 3, 1987, at about 9:30, Marta and seven other students of Asian descent boarded a bus that was to take them to a semiformal Christmas dance sponsored by two dorms, Belden and Watson, at the Italian-American Club in Tolland. They were dressed up, Marta in a black-and-white, knee-length gown made of silk, which she had borrowed from her sister. Her friend, Feona Lee, was wearing a full-length, blue silk gown that she had brought from her native Hong Kong.

Feona was excited, never having been to a real dance. A business major here on a student visa, she would graduate in January and return to Hong Kong, so for her, it was a kind of prom. It was Feona who had gotten the eight people together, setting Marta up with

Lenny Chow, a senior in engineering. While Lenny was technically her date, as far as Marta was concerned they were just eight people going out to dance.

The crowded bus held between 50 and 60 people, according to Marta—some of them drinking and yelling profanities. With some difficulty, the group of Asians found places scattered toward the rear of the bus.

What occurred next, and throughout the course of the evening, is the subject of dispute. The following account is based on interviews with victims, police officers, and university officials; sworn affidavits contained in police reports; and internal UConn memos. While the students accused of misconduct declined to grant interviews, the father of one defended his son as an innocent person caught in a "scatter-gun approach" to identifying and punishing the guilty parties. Much of the information presented here has not previously been made public. Other details were unavailable because of laws protecting individuals' privacy.

Beyond the events of December 3, the response of the university also came under attack. As a result, far-reaching efforts are being made to change the climate of intolerance on the rural campus. It is a complex task that itself invites criticism: How far can rules and codes go in trying to prohibit harassment before they inhibit free speech?

UConn opened classes this fall armed with a more explicit definition of harassment and toughened penalties, but acts of bigotry continued. None has approached the magnitude of the 1987 episode that began on the bus.

Marta and her friends waited quietly while the bus remained parked in front of Belden Hall. Suddenly Feona, who was sitting on someone's lap, felt something land in her hair. "At first I thought it was just water dripping from the bus," she told UConn police afterward. "Then I felt something warm and slimy hit me in the face." She realized it was spit. As she stood and turned to face her attackers, she was hit again, this time in the eye. "Who did that?" she screamed. "Stop!"

"Shut up!" someone yelled, shouting profanities. "Sit down!"

Daniel Shan, from Hong Kong, rushed over to see what was wrong. Feona was facing a group of a half-dozen young men sitting in the back seats—drinking beer, some of them chewing tobacco—two of whom Shan recognized because their room was next door to his at Belden: Mark Landolfi and Sean Doyle.

Shan knew them vaguely as football players. In fact, Landolfi was a varsity fullback from Hanover, Mass., a recruited player on scholarship. Doyle, a walk-on from North Haven, hadn't made the varsity team. They were wearing sweats and baseball caps and flip-flops. "Why are you looking at me?" one of them demanded.

Danny Shan responded that he was not accusing anybody, he just wanted the spitting to stop. When Feona sat down, both Doyle and Landolfi spat on her, according to Shan, hitting him as well, and yelling slurs such as "Chinks!" and "Oriental faggots!"

Shan and another man in the group of eight, Ron Cheung, approached Doyle and Landolfi, demanding they apologize. Doyle and Landolfi invited them to fight and, according to victims' affidavits, Landolfi threw a punch at Cheung and missed. Someone separated them, and the bus driver yelled at everyone to "Sit down and shut up!" No effort was made to put the spitters off the bus.

The harassment of the eight Asians continued during the drive to Tolland—and was ignored by most of the students on the bus. Marta was sitting two rows forward from the rear. "A few guys eventually stood up," she said, to shield the victims. "They seemed to be friendly with the guys in back. One of them said to me, 'Don't worry, these guys are just drunk. We'll keep things under control.' " But Marta felt something on her hand and looked down to see a globule of brown tobacco spit. A blob of white spittle landed next to her on the seat. The group in back continued yelling racial slurs and began singing "We All Live in a Yellow Submarine." By the time the bus pulled up to the Italian-American Club, the harassment had lasted nearly 45 minutes.

The Asian students tried to salvage the evening by dancing and staying on the opposite side of the room from their antagonists. But Doyle followed them, repeatedly elbowing Marta's dance partner, Ping Szeto, making "animal sounds" and screaming insults. According to Feona's affidavit, Doyle dropped his sweatpants, mooning her and her partner, and then danced with his penis exposed. She said he later urinated on a window and confronted Danny Shan in a stairwell, apparently trying to get him to fight.

According to Marta, the victims complained to three RAs, the upperclass students hired as Resident Assistants, the university's nominal authorities in the dormitories. The group was warned to stay away from their attackers. "They told us not to spoil a good time or we would be written up," Marta said. "We asked permission to leave the dance, and they said we couldn't because they were 'responsible for our safety.' "

Marta and Feona tried to call the police, but dialed the Vernon police department by mistake, thinking the Italian-American Club was in Vernon. Doyle, in the meantime, began to goad Ron Cheung, according to two victims, he spat beer in Cheung's face. At Feona's urging, Marta and two other women hid in a clothes closet near the front door until the threat of violence had seemed to pass.

Finally, a little before midnight, a squad car drove up. The victims thought it was in response to their call. In fact, it belonged to a state trooper responding to another call stemming from an unrelated fight. By this time the dance was coming to an end, and the first bus had arrived to take people home; without making a complaint to the trooper, the group got on the bus and rode back to the UConn campus.

The night had been devastating. A group photograph taken afterward at Shippee Hall shows the young people dressed up and, for the most part, smiling—trying to put a brave face on what had happened. But upon closer inspection, you can see the brown tobacco stains on Feona's blue gown and on her wrist—which she'd been unable to scrub clean in the ladies' room.

Last May, 17 months later, Marta still couldn't talk about what had happened without reliving it. Her eyes welled up with tears when she tried to describe the anger and the hurt—the sense of her human rights being violated. "*And nobody was going to do anything about it.*"

She can't comprehend the hatred behind the attack. "Somebody that didn't even know me. I just didn't understand the mentality . . . not being able to accept me because of my race and how I look." She described the feeling of isolation on the bus. "And like nothing you can do. A whole bus of people. You feel so *vulnerable.*"

Hardest of all to understand was the attitude of the other people on the bus. "If it was happening to a white person, and they were getting beat up or something, would everybody on the bus—50 people—just sit there and not even bother? I always question that. Would they?" Her voice took on an insistent edge. "Maybe they would. Then there's something wrong with this society. How can human life not matter to anyone else?"

She said a black girl she'd known from high school approached her in the bathroom at the dance. "She said, 'I heard what was going on in the back.' "

"I went, 'Yeah.' "

" 'Well, they're just a bunch of jerks.' "

But it was no consolation for Marta. "Everyone justified it by saying, 'They're just a bunch of jerks, and they're jocks, and they're drunk; they didn't really mean to pick on you guys.' I think that it's like a rape victim. You're stripped of everything—your integrity, your pride, your self-identity. You're like, 'What's going on? What am I? I know I'm Chinese, but it's something I don't want to be ashamed of.' And I'm *not*. That hasn't hap-

pened to me." Her voice dropped. "When it's stripped away from you, it's hard to regain
. . ."

On December 4, 1987, the day after the dance, Marta's sister Maria, then a senior at
UConn, was sitting in the lobby of the Homer Babbidge Library, waiting for Marta to show
up at 3:30. They planned to go home to Branford for the weekend to work in the restaurant.

As soon as Maria saw Marta's face, she knew her sister was upset. "What happened?"
she asked when Marta sat down.

Marta told the story. Maria could feel her own anger growing as she listened to Marta's
description of the spit covering Feona's face, the brown and white globs on her dress. "When
she finished telling me the story," Maria recalled, "I looked at her and said: 'Well? What's
going on?' She says, 'nothing.' "

"What do you *mean*, 'nothing'?"

It was Maria who insisted they take the matter to the police. In retrospect, she realizes the others were numb, still trying to comprehend what had happened. "It was much
easier for me to take the leadership position and say, 'This is what we need to get done,'
because I could separate myself from the incident. I felt it personally, as an attack on my
sister, but to me it was bigger than that. It was not because she was my sister, it was because she was Chinese or because she was an Asian that she was treated this way. I saw it
as an issue that affected not just me but all Asians on campus."

Maria Ho is a formidable presence. Physically larger than Marta and accustomed to
making her own way, she rounded up the others to begin an inquiry that would have exhausted most people.

"Where's Feona?" Maria asked Marta told her that Feona played the piano when she
was upset. So they went into the music building and looked through the practice rooms
until they found her.

"Feona," Marta said, "Maria thinks we should go to the police and report this."

Feona looked up from the piano. "OK," she said. "Good idea."

Next they picked up Lenny Chow at his dorm and went to the campus police. By this
time, it was 4 o'clock. Officer Dan Oppert listened to their story, but after conferring with
his supervisor he told them there was nothing he could do because the incident had taken
place in Tolland, outside UConn's jurisdiction. He suggested they take their complaint to
state police.

"Aren't you at least going to take a report?" Maria asked.

Oppert agreed to take a "Miscellaneous" report for future reference—in case of "further problems" with Doyle and Landolfi. He also suggested they visit the affirmative action office on campus when it opened on Monday.

After twice driving to the wrong place—the Vernon police department and the state
police barracks in Stafford Springs—the group arrived at the resident state trooper's office
in Tolland. There they told their story to Officer Michael Guillot. The trooper's response,
according to Marta, was to laugh. "He said something like, 'Boy, this guy must have been
drunk out of his mind.' "

Guillot denies laughing or making the comment. He says he did, however, discourage the students from seeking an arrest in Tolland and advised them to go back to campus
police because the incident had begun on UConn property.

It was nearly 10 o'clock by the time the students talked to Guillot; they were already
tired and discouraged. Feona recalls being put off by the trooper's attitude. "He asked me,
did I see Sean Doyle pull his pants down, and did I see his penis? I said I did, and he asked
me, do I really know what a penis looks like?"

Guillot is adamant that he never asked the last question. In an interview last April, he explained that his questions about Doyle's antics were pertinent to Connecticut law—which does not penalize spitting on people, but does prohibit indecent exposure. To qualify as "indecent," the act must be committed in a public place and must be done "with intent to arouse or satisfy sexual desire." Guillot decided from their description that Doyle had not attempted to arouse. The students failed to mention the other acts of harassment—the name-calling and spitting of beer—which had also taken place in Toll and, Guillot said. "Based on the information I was given, I didn't feel they had a case in Tolland."

It was 11 p.m. when the students finally went home. They had been shunted back and forth for seven hours.

The following Monday, December 7, Maria called the university's Office of Affirmative Action Programs and made an afternoon appointment. When she, Marta, and six of the seven other victims showed up, they were told the case lay outside the office's jurisdiction because it involved charges of students against students. They were referred to Dean of Students Frank Ardaiolo.

By this time, things were moving entirely too slowly for Maria. "We wanted justice," she said. "We wanted these people to be taught a lesson so that they won't do this kind of thing again."

When she called Ardaiolo's office Tuesday for an appointment, she learned the dean was out. His assistant, Joanne Quiñones, offered to schedule them for later in the week. Maria replied that if they did not receive prompt attention, they would tell their story to the newspapers. Quiñones invited the students to come to the office to give oral testimony. After listening to five victims who showed up, Quiñones asked them to file written statements.

Word of the students' threat to go to the press was passed quickly up the UConn hierarchy along with a summary of the incident. In a December 8 memo, Thomasina Clemons, director of the affirmative action office, warned Dean Ardaiolo's boss, Vice President of Student Affairs Carol Wiggins, "I am forwarding a copy to President Casteen, also, because the students are angry enough to go to the press."

Racism was not an issue widely talked about on the UConn campus in the early 1980s. But racist threats against a Vietnamese RA at Middlesex Hall got so ugly during the spring of 1987 that all 29 students on one floor were removed and reassigned to other dorms.

The number of Asian students had doubled between 1982 and 1987, and the isolated campus in Storrs was struggling to deal with its growing cultural diversity. The problem was by no means unique to UConn; Asian enrollment had was talk of a "new racism" on campuses nationwide.

During the tenure of President John T. Casteen III, UConn had taken steps to accommodate the changing makeup of its student body. Included in the training program for RAs was a component designed to sensitize students to the needs of minorities. The freshmen orientation program featured workshops on diversity. And, like most large universities, UConn had a number of international programs designed to foster cross-cultural learning experiences.

Still, the bulk of UConn's predominantly white undergraduate population had little contact with minority students. And the problem of harassment was "so deep-seated on campus," a special subcomittee observed later, "that in some instances people do not even realize that their behavior could be considered as harassing."

Moreover, a gap existed between the university's stated goals and its achievements. Programs that looked good on paper often missed their targeted constituencies: Workshops designed to teach pluralism in the dorms were poorly attended; a requirement that all acts of harassment be reported to the office of affirmative action was widely ignored; and, as a survey later revealed, the very existence of the affirmative action office was unknown to 60 percent of Asian American undergraduates.

Often, cases of racial harassment were routinely reported as "disorderly conduct" or "vandalism." Even the overt bigotry at Middlesex Hall—which had included racist graffiti in the halls and rest rooms and a dead bird fastened to the RA's door—was identified in some reports to and from the vice president of student affairs as "threatening" and "derogatory" without making reference to its racial content.

Contributing to this climate was the university's failure to keep up with the needs of foreign graduate students who worked as teaching assistants, or TAs. These students, assigned to run labs or teach classes while working on advanced degrees, received little support in coping with the complex task of adjusting to a new culture. Some arrived on a Friday and were expected to teach the following Monday. And because of a paucity of courses in English as a Second Language (ESL), many had problems being understood by undergraduates. In an interview last spring, Arthur Abramson, professor of linguistics and a former chairman of the department, expressed the need for a full-scale language program. "It's disgraceful that they have to go somewhere else."

Bigotry began to surface in the campus newspaper. In 1985, a cartoon in the *Daily Campus* portrayed international TAs as illiterate and stupid.

But problems involving minorities had begun to attract attention as early as 1983 at the university's branch in Hartford, which had a higher proportion of minority students and staff—mostly black and Hispanic. Then-president John DiBiaggio responded by appointing the Affirmative Action Advisory Committee for the Greater Hartford campus.

Glenn Chu-Richardson, who oversees the MBA program at the Hartford campus, chaired the committee for two years. "We sent proposal upon proposal, first to DiBiaggio, then to [Anthony] DiBenedetto, while he was temporarily running things, then to Casteen— and literally none of the proposals was acted upon."

By the time Casteen appointed a similar committee in Storrs, to serve the entire university, the Hartford committee was discouraged and talking about dissolving. Members of the Storrs committee urged the group to remain intact. The Hartford proposals would be channeled through Storrs, and it was hoped that the presence of key staff, faculty, and administrators on the Storrs committee would give it more clout.

In July 1987, the affirmative action advisory committee at Storrs recommended to Casteen a number of actions to improve the university's performance as an employer. Among them was the establishment of clear affirmative action goals for each division; strengthening support for professional development of employees, especially women and minorities; offering "sensitivity training" workshops for all employees; and changing the university environment "to make it more conducive to retaining minorities," with emphasis on improving child-care and transportation facilities. Also proposed was a bus link between Hartford and Storrs so the campus in eastern Connecticut would be less isolated from the rich ethnic diversity in Hartford.

The committee was still awaiting Casteen's response when the spitting incident occurred in December. On Feb. 10 of the following year, the president formally replied to their proposal. Glenda Price, dean of the School of Allied Health Professions who chaired the Storrs committee, voiced "frustration" with the slowness of his response.

Eventually, the Hartford group decided to disband. "After the third time the proposals were submitted," said Chu-Richardson, "we decided the committee really had no reason for existing because we couldn't get anything accomplished. People on the committee were very frustrated and angry."

It was against this backdrop of inertia that the drama which had begun on the bus began to find its way into the university hierarchy.

The dean's office moved quickly. On Thursday, December 10, Sean M. Doyle and Mark A. Landolfi were charged with violating the Student Conduct Code. A hearing was scheduled for December 17.

In the meantime, the posture of the UConn police changed. Director of Public Safety Robert Hudd determined that the actions that occurred while the bus was parked on UConn property were, in fact, within his jurisdiction. Officer Oppert summoned the victims back and took sworn affidavits. Warrants were obtained for Landolfi's and Doyle's arrest on charges of disorderly conduct.

The group began to have hope. Marta was grateful for her sister's support. Her own numbness, the sense of helplessness and isolation she had felt on the bus, was ameliorated by the efforts they were making to obtain justice. It helped to be *doing something*. Feona Lee delayed her return to Hong Kong so she could testify at the hearing.

Some of the victims were more reticent; they faded into the background, carrying their hurt with them. The young men found it especially difficult to talk about their feelings. None of the parents became involved.

Marta went through a period of blaming herself. "I think as the victim, you do that. And a lot of people *did* blame us. Our parents asked us, 'Did you dress funny? Did you all wear, like, *gangster outfits* or something? Eight of you? Why so many? Were you guys intimidating? Why did you sit on the bus? Why did you have to go to the dance?' "

The group met frequently while they waited for the hearing, and began "net-working" with the Chinese Association and other campus groups. One contact led to another. The Korean Student Association sent them to the minority recruiter, who sent them to the campus ombudsman. The dean of students' assistant, Joanne Quiñones, seemed nervous about the meetings, Maria said, "Like, 'It's finals, and you guys should be studying.' She seemed to be offended that we didn't trust the way they were handling it. And she asked me to stop coming around, since I wasn't a victim."

Maria had been acting as spokesperson for the group. Under the Student Conduct Code, students have the right to bring someone with them to disciplinary hearings. Marta said, "I want my sister there."

The hearing began on the afternoon of December 17 and continued until 10:30 or 10:45 that night, according to University Ombudsman Charles Oliver, who agreed to accompany the Asian students as a neutral observer.

While Landolfi and Doyle were permitted to sit through most of the testimony, the victims were called in separately—effectively denying their right, under the Student Conduct Code, to be present during the entire fact-finding portion of the hearing. In a later interview, Ardaiolo said he called the victims in separately because they were functioning as witnesses, who are allowed in the hearing room only to give testimony. Maria was asked to sit outside.

"They made us feel like we were the ones accused," Marta said.

Around 10 or 10:30 that night, Oliver said, the dean brought the hearing to a halt. "I thought we were just stopping to go to the bathroom. But then it seemed to be over." The victims, too, thought the hearing had been concluded.

The following afternoon, Ping Szeto received a phone call asking that he and Danny Shan report to the dean's office immediately. When Szeto and Shan arrived at 8:30, they found neither Oliver nor their fellow victims there—only Ardaiolo, Quiñones, Landolfi, and Doyle.

According to Shan, when he and Szeto sat down, Ardaiolo informed them, "We consider this a very serious case. It will affect both gentlemen's future." Doyle "is no longer a student of this university," he said, explaining his decision to suspend him. Then, turning his attention to Landolfi, Ardaiolo asked them to consider how their judgment would "affect this young man's future." Ardaiolo then asked Landolfi, "Do you have anything to say to these gentlemen?" Landolfi apologized, apparently attributing all of the spitting to Doyle.

"Do you mean you didn't do anything or spit at anyone?" Shan asked Landolfi.

Before Landolfi could respond, according to Shan, the dean interrupted to announce that the hearing was about to begin.

Shan and Szeto later expressed shock. This was the first indication they had that another bearing was taking place.

Shan said the dean began by asking him to step outside, and that Szeto was then questioned for 20 minutes. According to Shan, when his turn came, Ardaiolo badgered him: *Did you actually see him spit directly at you? Is it possible that you made a mistake? Could he have been spitting elsewhere? Could he have just been gargling or clearing his throat? Did you really see the spit coming out of his mouth? It was very dark on the bus, do you think you made a mistake in perception? Do you think perhaps you didn't actually see it, but you only thought you saw it?*

Ardaiolo's demeanor had changed from the day before, according to Shan and Szeto. Earlier, in the ombudsman's presence, he had appeared impartial—"like a judge hearing a case," Shan said. Now he seemed to be taking Landolfi's side.

"By repeatedly asking me whether it was possible to misperceive Mark's actions," Shan said the next day, "I feel that the dean was trying to lead me to say that I was not sure what I saw. Eventually, he succeeded." Shan said the dean apologized on behalf of Landolfi—who now seemed remorseful—and then played on Shan's sympathies to get him to recommend a softer punishment. Szeto, in a separate interview, reported similar efforts by Ardaiolo. Both Shan and Szeto finally agreed, under repeated questioning, that it was theoretically possible Landolfi had not spat at them—that they might have been mistaken. Marta thinks that, in the end, they went along with the dean's urging on Landolfi's behalf partly because of the intimidating situation, but also because of the importance the two Asians attached to studies. "To them," she said, "suspension was a big deal."

The final outcome was that while Doyle was suspended from school for a year, Landolfi would simply be barred from living in a campus dormitory and placed on disciplinary probation. Although the latter action could have included restrictions on participating in university activities or events, Aradiolo chose to allow Landolfi to continue playing football.

In a letter to President Casteen dated January 9, 1989, 13 months later, when his handling of the matter came under official investigation, Ardaiolo said the December 18 meeting was a continuation of the first hearing. The victims, he said, had left the evening of December 17 while the hearing was still in progress. In the same letter, Ardaiolo defended his actions as follows:

"I had ended the hearing on the night of December 17 (after five hours) about midnight, having decided to suspend Doyle and Landolfi. I told Landolfi that night he was guilty of threatening, harassing through racial epithets, and intimidating the students who confronted him. The next day, December 18, Landolfi requested to see me and started to defend himself and provide new information which did not come out the previous night. He explained he did not fully defend himself the night before because he believed he was innocent, having been provoked and a victim of circumstance. Doyle, who was his roommate, was sitting next to him on the bus, and both were similarly dressed with hats on. Landolfi always maintained he never spit on anyone and never called anyone a 'Chink' or 'Gook' and that the two witnesses who said so the night before were confused."

In the letter, Ardaiolo also addressed widespread accusations that Landolfi had received special treatment because he was an athlete.

"The difference in sanctions in Landolfi and Doyle," he wrote, "can only be attributed to their different level of involvement in the violations and my judgment as to what sanctions were appropriate. . . . I would typically only deny an athlete the playing of the sport if the violation was related to the sport. Thus, Landolfi was removed from the halls (in addition to being placed on disciplinary probation) because the violation was related to a hall social event. Landolfi's father, a school principal in Massachusetts, tried to get me to reduce his son's sanctions, and at one point I thought he might sue the university."

In an interview last August, Ardaiolo said there was "absolutely no contact" between his office and the athletic department during the hearing process. He said in his letter to Casteen, "I thought both students were football players when I sanctioned them." But he contradicted himself in a report to the university subcommittee five weeks later, saying, "I did not know if athletes were involved in the hearing." Todd Turner, director of athletics, also said there was no contact between his office and Ardaiolo's.

Mark Landolfi declined repeated requests for an interview. But his father, Michael Landolfi, said, "I think a lot of people are guilty of a lot of things on both sides. I think the administration made some mistakes. The Asian people, I think they overreacted. And the administration was looking for a scapegoat, and they found one. The Asian people were right to protect their rights, but they did it at the expense of an innocent person."

He did not deny trying to get his son's punishment softened; and while he said he did not threaten to sue the university, he allowed that he "may have led them to believe that. I did say I was going to appeal it. . . . There was an incident. But as far as Mark was concerned, it wasn't a racial incident."

Dean Ardaiolo refused to answer questions regarding the substance of Mark Landolfi's testimony. Asked why he chose to call Shan and Szeto back to testify, while ignoring the two young women, Aradiolo said that only Shan and Szeto had offered "clear and convincing testimony" relevant to Landolfi's role in the incident. "What Marta Ho said about Mr. Landolfi was not relevant." As for Feona Lee, he would say only that "people's perceptions of the reality become skewed because of the emotions involved."

Ardaiolo also denied pressuring Szeto and Shan, either to return to his office or, once there, to soften their accusation. He expressed surprise upon being told that they were unhappy with the outcome.

In his January letter to Casteen, the dean said, "By the conclusion of the December 18 phase of the hearing, there was a genuine reconciliation between Landolfi and the two male victims. There was even an embrace and tears in peoples' eyes."

Shan and Szeto say they recall no tears and certainly no embrace. Shan says he shook hands in a formal way.

In the interview, the dean said Maria and Marta Ho later reported that the two male victims were "very pleased" with the way he had handled that part of the hearing—a contention the Ho sisters vehemently deny.

If there was any lingering uncertainty in Danny Shan's mind after the December 18, 1987, hearing, it was settled late that night at the dorm, where—in the room he shared with Cheung and Szeto—Shan was awakened by what sounded like a celebration next door. Landolfi and Doyle apparently had their window open, and voices carried into the night. Shan said he heard someone, who he believed to be Doyle, yelling racial slurs, and then another voice saying, "Shut up, those kids are sleeping."

Shan, whose bed was closest to the commotion, said someone then asked Doyle what sentence he had been given. Doyle replied, "The dean just told me to take it as a vacation."

As far as the university was concerned, the case was closed. A December 29 memo described the Asian students as "satisfied that their complaint was handled in a serious and solemn manner," and suggested that the opportunity to tell their stories might even have been "cathartic." Two months later, Doyle and Landolfi pleaded guilty to disorderly conduct and were granted accelerated rehabilitation, which would allow them, if they kept their records clear, to have the charges erased.

To the Asian and Asian American students, the administration's treatment of them was as bad as the original incident. Perhaps worse.

One day, shortly after the hearings, Feona, Marta, and Maria were sitting around the dining room table trying to figure out what they were going to do before they went home— Marta and Maria back to Branford for the Christmas holidays, Feona back to Hong Kong to stay.

"Hey," said Maria, "there's got to be an Asian association of some kind in Boston." They dialed information and found a listing for the Asian American Resource Workshop, which led them to the East Coast Asian Student Union. During the months that followed, Marta and Maria attended conferences at Cornell University, and talked to people at Yale and Brown. "We got not just ideas," Maria said, "but support, having people say, 'I understand what you're going through. How can we help?' We didn't get anything like that at UConn."

One of the people who helped them was Peter Kiang, a lecturer in American Studies at the University of Massachusetts/Boston who is active in Asian American affairs.

Kiang debunks the "myth of the model minority"—the stereotype of Asian Americans as successful, hardworking, obedient, and uncomplaining. The danger of the myth, he said in an interview last spring, is that it is used to manipulate Asians and other minorities, as well as the public at large. On the surface, it appears positive—preferable to the older stereotypes of Asians as laundry workers or coolie laborers. But a look at its history shows that the model minority image, promoted heavily in the national media in the 1960s, during riots in Watts and Detroit, and again in the 1970s and early 1980s, was used by some to undermine affirmative action programs. It sent "a message to the blacks . . . to say 'Why can't you be like the Asians?' . . . a way of disciplining blacks in their demands for social equality."

Kiang noted that the image breeds resentment. In the Greater Boston area, scarcely a week goes by without cars parked in Asian neighborhoods being vandalized—covered with anti-Asian graffiti, their windshields smashed. But statistics supporting the upbeat view of the status of Asians are often misleading, Kiang said. Median family income is relatively high among Asians, for instance, even compared to whites, but more people work in the typical Asian family, so the income per person is, in fact, much lower. Even the gains in education are deceptive, he said, because Asians continue to earn less per year of education than whites.

Kiang observed that on the one hand the myth of the model minority is "praising Asian Americans for 'making it' in American society, on the other hand, it can also be interpreted as a warning. 'Watch out for the Asians; they're taking over.' And that harkens back to another set of images, of Asians as invading—the Yellow Peril of the 1860s and 1870s, Pearl Harbor, Japanese imports during the trade wars of the late 1970s and early 1980s." This is the underside of the myth, and Kiang relates it directly to the incident on the bus.

Harassment of the sort encountered on the night of December 3 is not uncommon for Asian Americans, Kiang said. "What was particularly distressing about the UConn incident, really, was the failure of the administration to respond in any meaningful way afterward"—perhaps, he said, because of a general feeling that "Asians don't have problems and that they shouldn't complain."

Kiang's advice to Marta and the others is appropriate to anyone who suffers harassment: First, "Don't blame yourself; you have to understand that it's tied to a larger social and structural reality." Second, "Get support. Talk to people about it and hopefully get organized and respond to it, because it is not just an isolated incident and happening just to you." But he warned that the first hurdle—getting past self-blame—is often the most difficult.

"Some people are able to rise to the occasion and respond in a righteous manner the way that Marta did; others, it leaves such deep scars it affects them for the rest of their life—how they relate to other people, and their academic and professional performance."

The Ho sisters followed Kiang's advice during the spring semester. They began to organize. They started an Asian American Student Association. Maria became its first president; Marta was vice president. Paul Bock, a professor of hydrology, acted as their faculty sponsor and also formed an Asian American Faculty Association—reportedly the first on the East Coast.

Marta depended on her sister for much of her support. "The incident brought us closer, because of what we had to do. My sister was a stronger person, and I was feeling very hurt." At first, Marta didn't want to talk about the incident. She remembers that when they were scheduled to speak at a rally at Yale, she was afraid. "I felt really alone, and I didn't want to break out in tears, talking in front of all these people that I don't know. I wanted someone I could lean on. And that was my sister." When Marta's voice started to break, Maria was there to carry on.

They became a team. Maria was the organizer: She could run meetings, use a computer, confront officials fearlessly. Marta's great gift was that, alone among the victims, she was vocal; she was willing to talk about her feelings, and it was her firsthand testimony that brought the reality of what had happened home to audiences. Maria was the head; Marta was the heart. Together, they began to chip away at what they saw as a wall of indifference.

In February 1988, President Casteen issued a public statement defining various forms of harassing behavior and reaffirming that such acts were unacceptable at the university. It prohibited not only physically abusive acts directed toward individuals or groups because of race, gender, religion, sexual preference, age and other attributes, but extended to "derogatory names, inappropriately directed laughter, inconsiderate jokes, anonymous notes or phone calls, and conspicuous exclusion from conversation and/or classroom discussion." Although he refrained from mentioning the incident directly, the statement seemed to be in response to the events of December 3.

For the Asian Americans, the new definition of harassment appeared too late. After all, most of the perpetrators had escaped punishment and Mark Landolfi was still on the football team. There was a feeling that Casteen should intervene or in some sense apologize. As the months wore on, the president's public silence on the incident became intolerable.

The Ho sisters wanted to press for concrete changes—an Asian American center, counselors with multi-cultural backgrounds, classes in Asian American studies. Paul Bock began agitating for the university to expand its recruitment of faculty and students with Asian backgrounds, and for the University Senate to investigate the administration's handling of the December 3 incident.

In May 1988, Bock asked the president if he would wear a button at the commencement ceremony saying "Please reduce racism at UConn." When he did, along with members of the Board of Trustees, "it was the happiest day of my life," Bock said.

For Casteen, too, the occasion was a moving one, because Bock took the opportunity to introduce the Ho sisters. It was the first time Casteen had met any of the victims.

That summer, Casteen initiated two exploratory studies. One would assess the desirability and feasibility of establishing an Asian American studies program. The other would survey what was being done to meet the needs of Asian American students on other campuses.

Another proposal was submitted to Casteen around this time—one that had grown directly out of concern about the spitting incident. Drafted by an ad hoc committee organized by the Women's Center and chaired by Thomasina Clemons, head of the affirmative action office, this proposal called for a "comprehensive multi-cultural training effort" that would be mandatory for administrators, faculty, and employees who have regular contact with students—from library personnel to campus police, from recruiters to counselors. Casteen referred the proposal to his newly appointed provost, Thomas Tighe. Months passed.

With the arrival of summer, the students were afraid they would lose their momentum. Maria complained of feeling "burnt out." Marta was feeling like an errand girl for Maria. The organization of Asian American students they had founded was already divided between those who wanted to continue to pursue a "political" course and those who feared the group's activism would only isolate them further from the mainstream campus.

Paul Bock, in the meantime, was undergoing something he would later describe as much like a religious conversion. In August, Bock pitched a pup tent on the commons and went on a hunger strike to call attention to the Asian American demands. The tactic worked: By fall, 700 people had signed a petition seeking an investigation.

When the University Senate met in September 1988, President Casteen's address focused on racial intolerance. And it was on this occasion—nearly a year after the fact—that he first referred publicly and directly to the December 3 incident. During the same session, the Senate passed a resolution directing an investigation into the spitting incident and the university's response.

A special subcommittee made up of faculty, students, and one dean was formed with instructions to report back in April 1989. The probe, however, got off to a rough start. The group would not be given access to the transcripts of the hearings conducted by Ardaiolo.

The ruling came from Paul Shapiro, the assistant attorney general assigned to UConn, who cited the Family Education Rights and Privacy Act of 1974, also known as the Buckley amendment, which was instituted to protect individuals' records from unwarranted snooping. Even the victims were denied access to the transcripts, lest this violate the rights of the accused. Nor could they even learn officially what sanctions the dean had imposed on Landolfi and Doyle. A "curious shroud," as it was called in the subcommittee's later report, was thrown over the whole inquiry.

Early last spring, while the subcommittee worked to conclude its investigation, Bock, with support from a handful of faculty, began pressing for Ardaiolo's suspension or removal—accusing the dean of carrying out a "campaign of racism." The dean, they said, had mishandled the hearings and violated the victims' rights.

On April 4, 1989—the day before the subcommittee was to issue its official report—Bock succeeded in getting a resolution through the College of Liberal Arts and Sciences accusing Ardaiolo and Quiñones of "malfeasance," and requesting that President Casteen investigate the allegations. The personal tone of the attacks against Ardaiolo, however, was beginning to generate a backlash within the faculty. The Ho sisters, too, tried to distance themselves from Bock.

When the subcommittee's report was released the following day, it referred to serious causes for concern at the Storrs campus deep-seated intolerance, a perceived absence of leadership at the top, an atmosphere "altogether too permissive of harassing behavior," lack of trust in the administration, and inadequate support for foreign students. The subcommittee made 32 recommendations to Casteen. Some would strengthen the rights of victims and the penalties for harassment; others would address background causes of tension between majority students and minorities.

Among the causes of tension was UConn's lack of support for international students, in particular "the lack of an ESL program" and a shortage of minorities and "culturally skilled counselors" among the RAs and professional staff.

Casteen and administrators "will have to find quicker, stronger, more direct and more creative approaches to issues of diversity and harassment," the report said. It noted that "for many members of the university community, there is a fatalistic sense that at UConn things change little if at all."

The committee supported the victims' allegation that the office of the dean was "more careful in protecting the rights of the accused than protecting their rights." It found that Ardaiolo violated university procedure when he resumed the hearing without informing the other victims. But because of the Buckley amendment, it could not determine if the dean pressured the students to soften their testimony; nor was it able to determine whether preferential treatment was given an athlete. The committee urged changes in the code that would clarify the process for reporting and documenting cases of harassment, articulate the role of the ombudsman as an advocate, provide better support for victims, and resolve the conflict between the Buckley amendment and the hearing process.

Casteen acknowledged that he should have responded more quickly to the incident. "In hindsight," he told reporters, "if I had known more of the incident, I would have or should have acted differently. I would have taken a fairly strong posture."

Shortly afterward, he announced two changes in the Student Conduct Code. One prevents students found guilty of harassment from playing sports or taking part in other activities for at least one semester. In addition, every student accused of discriminatory harassment faces suspension or expulsion as a possible punishment.

Last June, Frank Ardaiolo resigned to become Vice President of Student Life at Winthrop College in South Carolina. Efforts to persuade him to stay drew expressions of outrage from Asian Americans.

The president continues to defend Ardaiolo, who he says "did his best under difficult circumstances." He said that whatever regrets he has about the incident—which he called "egregious"—the sanctions against Landolfi and Doyle were "appropriate and strict, considering the procedures and penalties that were in place at the time."

Asked why he remained publicly silent for so long, Casteen said that the impact on the victims had not made a strong impression on him until he met the Ho sisters for the first time in May 1988, when Bock introduced them. "Their firsthand reports were much more affecting." Casteen said, "when I realized the trauma they had undergone, and their obvious need for counseling."

"But," he added, "if what you're asking is why have I not pitched tents on the lawn or carried out a vendetta against Frank Ardaiolo, the answer is that I have chosen to focus on positive steps—on persuading people that it is time for change."

In reporting back to the College of Liberal Arts and Sciences last August, Casteen found no evidence that the dean deprived the victims of their rights or intimidated them. He called the attack on Ardaiolo "bitterly personal and poorly documented." Others, including many who have championed minority rights on campus, have defended Ardaiolo's record—noting that since his arrival at UConn in 1972, the dean had one of the best records for hiring minorities in his own office.

Some see Ardaiolo as another victim. Peter Halvorson, the geography professor who co-chaired the Senate subcommittee, feels that when Casteen finally spoke out about the incident it was "too late." This view is shared by Gail Mellow, former head of the Women's Center and now a dean at Quinnebaug Valley Community College. She believes Ardaiolo became a "scapegoat."

"What was difficult for me, in watching events unfold," said Mellow, "was the inability of some of the faculty members, who I believe cast him in that role, to understand that they needed to look at the system. This didn't happen because one person at the university responded inappropriately; it happened because the university—like so many universities—hasn't been able to deal in a rich and complex way with racism and sexism, and their combined impact on the lives of students."

Ardaiolo himself comes from a multi-cultural background, having grown up speaking several languages in West Africa and the Azores. "I've been arrested twice in my life because I was a white American," he said earlier this year. "I understand what it is, to a limited degree, to be subjugated to repression because you're different from the majority."

He continues to insist that at UConn "the discipline system worked." Asked why events had seemed to spiral out of control, he observed with obvious bitterness that "people were trying to use the situation to fulfill their own political agendas. It's gone way beyond the facts, way beyond the incident. It's taken up an inordinate amount of time. It's whipped this institution around like it should not have been whipped around."

Sean Doyle also believes the incident has been blown out of proportion. "It was a mistake," he said earlier this year. "I'm putting it behind me. It happened a long time ago."

Tina Chin, one of the quieter victims, disagrees. "Some good has come," she said, "from such a terrible thing."

The university has moved to implement most of the recommendations contained in the subcommittee's report. Courses in Asian American studies are now being offered; more funds are being made available to recruit minority students; a course is being planned to teach "multi-cultural awareness" to undergraduates; and a new dean has been hired to address the needs of UConn's international population.

Casteen also has asked for a review of the role of deans at the university—not just the dean of students, whose office he says is "understaffed"—but "the role of all deans in relation to the educational process." The dean of students, he has said, is unreasonably burdened in disciplining students, being put in the position of "prosecutor, judge, and jury with regard to complex, highly public cases."

Meanwhile, the stance of the campus police has also changed. Last spring, they arrested two UConn basketball players who verbally harassed gay visitors attending a gay-lesbian conference.

Casteen called for an overhaul of the Student Conduct Code last August and appointed a committee to redraft it so it carefully spells out the standards and conduct expected of students, and clearly states the penalties for breaking the code.

A federal lawsuit filed by a student in October, however, has shifted that issue into federal court. The student, Nina Wu, claims the university violated her right to free speech by expelling her from her dormitory after a student conduct hearing acted on complaints that a sign on her door said "homos" would be "shot on sight." In an agreement forged by U.S. District Judge Peter C. Dorsey, the two sides are working together to redraft the code so it protects students' rights to free speech and still gives the university power to punish those who harass or intimidate others.

Casteen says part of his charge last summer to the committee revising the code was to reconcile victims' rights with individual rights, and that the suit raised no surprising issues. "The way I've come to think of it is as a continuum," he said, "and not absolutes of right and wrong. The question is, what is harassment or abuse? In the incident involving Ms. Ho and the others, what you had was several kinds of abuse. For example, they were called names. The attorney general is telling us there is a legal way to deal with verbal abuse, something known as 'fighting words,' that are not defensible constitutionally." Nonverbal forms of abuse—such as shoving or spitting—are more clearly prohibitable, he said. "We're working to deal with a social evil, and the problem is to do that and still adhere to the most fundamental law."

Ann Huckenbeck, acting director of admissions, notes that the spitting incident has "forced the university to look at the educational issues involved. If the Ho sisters did nothing else," she said, "they raised awareness of the complaint procedure." But she cautions against "overreaction." Not all Asian Americans favor the creation of an Asian American Center, and the needs of Asian graduate students are very different from those of Asian Americans. Even the push to educate white undergraduates carries the danger of a backlash. This year's freshman orientation, which she helped design, contained a "very strong multi-cultural component"—so strong, she said, that some parents complained it was "too long and set too serious a tone."

Casteen appears eager to change his stance from reactive to a more "pro-active" style. In September, following three cases of harassment, he personally visited one of the dorms to lecture students and condemned the actions in a letter to students in the college newspaper. And when Chinese graduate students complained to him last summer that UConn had done nothing to respond to the bloody crackdown on student protesters in Beijing. Casteen was already in motion. Telecommunication links were set up between students at UConn and their friends and families in China; efforts were made to rally community support; video and audio tapes were collected to document what had happened. Now plans are being made to set up a permanent archive which might someday help prosecute the perpetrators of the massacre.

Today Casteen is embracing the "comprehensive multi-cultural training effort" proposed in July 1988, as well as some of the recommendations that came out of the Affirmative Action Advisory Committee in July 1987 and the Hartford committee as early as 1984. Whether dollars will be committed to long-term efforts to make UConn more hospitable to minorities will depend in part on support from the board of trustees and the state legislature.

"Every one of us should feel a sense of urgency about building a multi-cultural institution," says Glenn Chu-Richardson. "The burden of accountability shouldn't fall on Casteen or any other administrator. We are all complicit, every one of us. Institutionalized racism is rarely overt. It takes the form of resistance, lack of support, inertia, inactivity."

Marta seems unable, for now, to put the incident aside. There is a part of her that has not yet healed. Her voice rises whenever she talks about what happened that night—especially when she describes how other Asians implied that she did something wrong. "I had every right to be on that bus, like anyone else, so that is not wrong! And my parents were saying, 'Why did you go to the dance? You know better; when you're in school, you go to school, not dances!' And this graduate student would say, 'Oh, well, why didn't you just go to a Chinese party? You know, we have a lot of Chinese graduate dances.' And I go, 'Well, why don't I just not live in America, then?' You know? 'If I'm just going to hang out with Chinese people, then I might as well not stay in America.' He says, 'That's not the point. You shoulda not gone to places like that.' Which is like, 'OK, I'm sick of it.' There's too many excuses of what I should've done and what I shouldn't have done, and I don't think any of them are right. You know, I had every legitimate reason to be there."

Even if she knew it was going to happen again, she says, she would get on that bus.

In her quieter moments, she talks about the positive changes that have taken place in the past two years. She has become more assertive, more conscious of her identity as an Asian American. She calls the experience "valuable" because it helped her clarify her values. Even the "paranoia" she experienced for several months was ultimately clarifying. "I was oversensitive at first to everything. You know, we'd walk down campus and if some girl was just looking at us and staring, I'd yell and tell my sister, 'I can't stand this! What are they looking at me for? What are they gawking at? I'm just a person!' "

Next, she says, she went through a period of "reverse-discrimination," of looking down on whites. "I was overproud of myself. I was overproud of our accomplishments, of my culture. I thought that we were superior. I caught myself all the time. You know, *this* isn't right. What makes *me* any better than Sean Doyle or Mark Landolfi? You know? And when I catch myself I realize that I'm going through a problem stage . . . I was beginning to think and talk like my father!"

Both stages, however, helped her assimilate the experience in healthy ways, and understand her own process of assimilation into American society. "In high school I tried so hard for everyone to like me, to be well-rounded in my personality . . . Now, I'm making less of an effort. Nothing I do, nothing I say, the way I dress, is ever going to change [some people's] impression of Asian Americans. I realized that no matter how hard I try, people are always going to look at me because of my skin color. People are always going to say, 'Oh I'm surprised you speak English so well.' " Now, however, she realizes that "I come first and not what whites think of me."

This past summer, she worked part-time at a Japanese restaurant. She and her two roommates had talked about backpacking through southern Europe, but the plan had fallen through for lack of money. She found herself depressed, asking her boss at the restaurant for more hours—escaping into work. Then she talked to one of her teachers, Grace Yun—who taught UConn's first course in Asian American studies, as a visiting professor. The talk helped. Grace Yun understood. Marta made some decisions—about her role in the Asian American Student Association this fall, about her own needs, apart from politics. The trip to Europe ended up happening. In Rome, the three befriended an Italian who spoke Chinese, and Marta was amazed to discover that Italian families are "real tight." She laughs. "Just like Chinese!"

Over her father's protests, Marta has switched her major from math—which she has always found easy—to the humanities, where she has to struggle, especially with English. Somewhere in that choice, she supposes she may be fighting what she calls the "stereotype of Asians as big superachievers and technocrats." But the course she took last spring from Grace Yun—a course she and her sister helped bring into being—seemed to confirm the rightness of her choice. It was, she says, the best course she's had in college.

"Before the incident," she says, "I thought I was either Chinese or I was American. I'm very Chinese when I'm home with my parents, and when I'm at school it's like I'm American. And those two never met together." Now, however, she describes a process of picking and choosing the best from both worlds. She finds herself favoring Chinese morality, especially in relationships; yet she likes the freedom and assertiveness that she experiences as an American woman.

"I never wanted to deny the fact that I was Chinese. I'm very proud of being Chinese. But I've accepted that I'm never going to lose that. I thought I was going to have to give up one or the other. Now I'm comfortable knowing that I can maintain that heritage, but also be very comfortable being American. Being American doesn't necessarily mean that you have to be white. I thought that eating and dressing and talking correct English, that was American. But being American is not that; it's not blond hair and blue eyes. I realize now that I don't have to try with anybody, as long as I'm comfortable with myself."

She has a few white friends, but she's most comfortable around Asians. "I still don't know what Anglo-Saxons eat," she confesses.

What advice does she have for Asian Americans starting college?

"Don't deny your ethnicity. Don't be a banana or a Twinkie [someone who is Asian on the outside, but white inside]. You've got to like yourself. Your hair, your flat nose, slanted eyes. If you don't like yourself, I don't think anybody else will; and you'll never even understand why when somebody else does like you. You'll always have doubts, like,

'Oh, I'm so weird. Why do they like me?' That's something you need when you come to college, because there's enough insecurity around."

"And if you think your rights are being violated, do something about it; don't just complain. That's what Asians do all the time; we sit around and complain. You know, if you want some difference, make the difference."

Last year, Marta and Maria were joint recipients of an award from the UConn Women's Studies program, for work reflecting "a dedication to the understanding and advancement of minority women in the U.S." The award is named in honor of Gladys Tantaquidgeon, a Mohegan Indian who spent a lifetime acquainting Connecticut scholars and schoolchildren with her Native-American culture.

Marta's father attended the ceremony, wearing a dark suit and a red shirt. He was beaming.

23 Guerilla War at UCLA: Political and Legal Dimensions of the Tenure Battle

Dale Minami

PROFESSOR DON NAKANISHI'S three-year fight for tenure is probably best described as "institutional guerrilla warfare"—a classic David and Goliath struggle, pitting an emerging minority community and its allies against a massive institution. The whole story, combining elements of intrigue, espionage, double-agents, internal bickering, back-door politics and secret deals is, unfortunately, beyond the scope of this article. Nevertheless, the tortuous journey taken by Don and his supporters illustrates the difficulties in fighting Goliath and the rewards in winning.

This struggle, begun in 1986, took on a life of its own, becoming a virtual movement. The battlefield shifted from campus to the community, to the media, then to the California State Legislature, and finally to the UCLA Chancellor's office—with each arena engaging different players and tactics. In the end, victory brought Asian/Pacific Americans to a new understanding of our political power.

Overall, this struggle shows why a legal case combined with a political campaign, increases the odds of success against a public institution. We achieved victory because we were able to develop a sound legal argument as well as a larger political strategy, capable of mobilizing thousands of allies nationwide. The following discussion begins with a description of the academic context in which Don's case arose, followed by an explanation of the legal alternatives, and ending with an analysis of the legal/political strategy that we adopted.

THE UNIVERSITY OF CALIFORNIA: LARGE, RICH AND POWERFUL

The University of California is not an institution to trifle with. It is large, rich and powerful, and commands enormous respect in the State of California. Its allies include sympathetic legislators, wealthy businessmen, and influential alumni. Even its legal status is "special." As an agency created by the California Constitution, it enjoys privileges not given to other governmental bodies.

This "special" status sets the context for understanding how the University selects its permanent professors. The tenure review process is complex, convoluted and secretive, with each level of review insulated from outside influence. The faculty who make recommendations to the Chancellor ferociously guard their review prerogative from interference

From *Amerasia Journal* 16 (1990): 81–107. Reprinted with permission of the Regents of the University of California and the UCLA Asian American Studies Center.

by the Chancellor and "outside" forces. Deliberations are conducted in secret, and every twist and turn allows for ambush by unknown enemies.

In brief, the system functions as follows: Tenure candidates submit dossiers containing their resumé, copies of publications, and list of accomplishments to the department chair. The department then appoints an ad hoc committee which solicits letters from experts outside the university and makes a recommendation to the department. Next, the tenured faculty of the department vote on the candidate and submit a recommendation to a secret campus-wide ad hoc committee. Because a university is divided into jealously protected and powerful fiefdoms known as departments, a departmental recommendation is probably the most important factor in the granting of tenure.

In the next phase, publications are reviewed, and accomplishments appraised by the ad hoc committee. Another recommendation is submitted to a larger campus committee, known as the Committee on Academic Personnel (CAP) at UCLA, which reviews the reports and submits its own recommendation to the Chancellor. The Chancellor makes the final decision, but rarely rejects the campus-wide committee's recommendation.

The whole process is conducted in secret: Tenure candidates do not have the right to know the specific content of committee recommendations concerning their candidacy or the identity of members of review committees or external reviewers. The process is governed by a set of rules embodied in the Academic Personnel Manual (APM) as well as additional rules which each department and campus establishes. The process is complicated further by customs and traditions unique to each department and campus.

The theory behind this review process is that multiple levels of review, conducted without inhibitions, will allow for the fair appraisal of each candidate's performance. In reality, every level is fraught with the potential for arbitrary, subjective decisions and the injection of impermissible political criteria. Thus, a candidate outside the dominant clique of a department may be sabotaged by unknown hostile reviewers appointed to the ad hoc committee by the chair of the department. (This is like hiring a lawyer who is committed to losing your case to argue your side in court.) Later in the process, the campus-wide ad hoc committee can be stacked against the candidate by an antagonistic Chancellor.

The ostensible criteria for tenure include teaching, university and public service, professional activities and research. But in institutions such as the University of California, "superior academic achievement" in research is indispensable for obtaining tenure. "Publish or perish" is still the controlling rule in tenure decisions. Within this framework, subjective interpretations are often used against an unpopular, threatening, or simply "different" candidate. Because each candidate's rating necessarily depends to some degree on the interpretation of their work, it is quite easy to erect subjective arguments as artificial barriers to a favorable recommendation.

The requirement shielding the decision-making process from outside scrutiny has recently been successfully challenged in the United States Supreme Court. In *University of Pennsylvania* v. *Equal Employment Opportunity Commission*, Rosalie Tung at the University of Pennsylvania was denied tenure. She filed a charge of discrimination based on race, sex and national origin. The Equal Employment Opportunity Commission attempted to obtain confidential letters written by her evaluators, documents reflecting the internal deliberations of faculty committees and comparable portions of tenure review files involving five white males who recently gained tenure in her department. The University refused to produce the requested materials. On appeal to the Supreme Court, the Court ordered them produced, denying University claims of privilege and the First Amendment right to "academic freedom."

The Court ruled that no special privilege existed for such documents in common law and that the costs of disclosure were outweighed by the need to determine whether illegal discrimination has taken place. As the Court aptly observed, "Indeed, if there is a 'smoking gun' to be found that demonstrates discrimination in tenure decision, it is likely to be tucked away in peer review files."

This decision will probably not alter the *result* of tenure reviews, only the *manner* in which information is presented. Rather than alter their opinions, opponents of a minority or female candidate will simply document their biased opinions better. The decision will significantly change, however, the chances of winning complaints and lawsuits based on sex and race discrimination, because dismantling the confidentiality shield will expose biased decisions.

Some universities, such as UCLA, permit a candidate more access to confidential information than other campuses. The UCLA rules require a summary of the deliberations of the campus ad hoc and full committees and allow a candidate to submit rebuttals to the file. Summaries, however, can still be expertly slanted to hide discriminatory intent. Other campuses will not even offer this synopsis, so candidates are usually left shooting in the dark at unknown enemies.

ACADEMIC ATTITUDES: THE IMPACT OF BIAS, ENVY, AND ARROGANCE

The tenure system operates from the premise that reviewers will apply their best objective judgments, free from the bias or petty animosities which characterize many decisions outside the academe. This premise, of course, is a fiction. From my experience, professors are at least as biased, envious, petty and pusillanimous as your everyday Six-Pack Joe. Two additional qualities of professors, however, stand out—intelligence and arrogance. Professors are smart enough to murder a tenure candidate with daggers instead of machetes. But their arrogance sometimes leads them to mistakes, such as leaving fingerprints on the corpse.

Because of confidentiality, the professors who negatively evaluate a candidate know (or knew, before the recent *University of Pennsylvania* decision) they could never get caught. For example, in one tenure denial case I handled, I interviewed a seemingly sympathetic department representative to the campus ad hoc committee who expressed dismay that his colleagues had voted against my client. Later, at a deposition, I discovered that he, in fact, was the primary opponent of my client. He had wielded the dagger that killed my client's chances for tenure. When I confronted this man with the facts, his response was incredulity as to how I discovered the information. I learned early on that it is essential in challenging tenure decisions to find sympathetic reviewers who can provide information as to what occurred in secret deliberations.

As mentioned above, Don Nakanishi was not the first academic I had represented. I previously sued the University of California at Davis for denial of tenure to a Korean American professor, Dr. Kenne Chang. The case eventually ended up in the California Court of Appeals (*Chang* v. *Regents of California*, 135 Cal. App. 3d 88, 1982), where the Court held that Dr. Chang had no expectation of continued employment despite assurances of such throughout his career. I had also represented others in tenure or promotion disputes and many clients in employment-related cases.

Among my Asian American clients in these situations, I have noticed a common attitude. Invariably, they believe in the merit system: If you work hard, you will be duly rewarded. And when faced with an adverse decision based on something other than merit, they have difficulty accepting that reality. All too often, they never understand that politics and racism may have as much to do with a particular decision as merit.

The academic institution is not immune from political considerations in tenure decisions. Although we tend to idealize universities as centers of enlightenment, the level of racism and fierce politicking is numbing. Thus, candidates who do not socialize with other professors, who have many interests outside the university, who study subjects not considered significant or not well understood by their colleagues, and who do not play the game of courting favor with those in power in their department may find themselves out of a job at tenure time. Moreover, departments dominated by white males usually select for tenure those like themselves, i.e., other white males. There is good reason why universities are called "Ivory Towers." In practice, it is similar to other employment situations where Asian/Pacific Americans confront a glass ceiling in promotional decisions.

LEGAL ALTERNATIVES: A LAWYER'S NIGHTMARE

Challenging an adverse tenure decision is a lawyer's nightmare. An attorney taking a case must wade through an arcane thicket of university rules and regulations, unwritten customs and traditions, internal politics and academic terminology. Because the cases are usually fought in an academic context, tenure cases typically generate documents stacked several feet high, and usually single-spaced. Often, the subject matter is so abstruse that most lawyers and judges—and professors, for that matter—can comprehend but a fraction of the subject area.

The defendant is usually a powerful, wealthy institution with infinite resources, including smart, arrogant, shrewd administrators and professors. Your plaintiff is a person who is losing a job, probably a bit depressed, and usually has little resources to pay legal fees. And he/she may also feel some conflict about the decision to retain an attorney to take the institution to court.

While most aggrieved persons believe they can obtain justice, the reality of academic lawsuits is sobering. In a recent study of tenure cases, George R. LaNoue and Barbara A. Lee analyzed cases involving discrimination against college institutions from the 1960s through the 1980s. They found that judges were not familiar with these complex cases and were reluctant to second-guess university evaluators. The attorney costs were enormous, averaging $52,000 per case. The authors suggest that even this figure underestimates the actual costs. Psychological costs were high as well, with one-half of the plaintiffs dissatisfied with their attorneys, and two-thirds dissatisfied with the entire process. Not surprisingly, attorneys who took such cases expressed reluctance at accepting any more cases.

Despite such dismal findings, there are a number of legal options a wronged professor can undertake. They are as follows:

COURT

In this litigious society, the first reaction to a real or imagined injustice is often: "I'll see you in court!" This reaction is understandable—most people would hire any attorney from McKenzie Brackman of "LA Law" because they never lose a case. Sadly, the real world is quite different from the video world. As indicated above, courts have great difficulty with academic cases, and professors have even greater difficulty with courts. The drawbacks are many: Courts are expensive, emotionally and financially draining and slow. Even worse, professors do not often win, and when they do, full relief is not always granted.

The scope of wrongs a professor can allege is quite limited. If a case is based on a university's violation of its own rules or arbitrary action in rejecting tenure, a professor may be required to file and win an internal grievance first (*Westlake Community Hospital v. Superior Court*, 17 Cal.3d 465, 1976). Further, the type of relief afforded by courts is usually restricted. Rarely will a court order that tenure be granted to a plaintiff. Generally, the relief will be restricted to a re-review, which means only that a tenure candidate is given another chance at bat in front of the same biased umpires. Emotional distress and punitive damages are generally unavailable if based on a breach of contract claim (*Foley* v. *Interactive Data*, 47 Cal.3d 654, 1988). And in some breach of contract claims, the courts have required the professor to seek relief from the National Labor Relations Board rather than the court (*McGough* v. *University of San Francisco*, 214 Cal.App.3d 1577, 1989).

In contexts other than tenure cases, professors have prevailed and obtained reinstatement (not tenure) when procedural irregularities have been demonstrated (see *Apte* v. *Regents of the University of California*, 198 Cal.App.3d 1084, 1988; *Brown* v. *State Personnel Board*, 166 Cal.App.3d 1151, 1985; *Adelson* v. *Regents of University of California*, 128 Cal.App.3d 891, 1982).

Professors denied tenure still have some legal claims available. A charge that a professor has been punished for exercise of the First Amendment right to freedom of speech is legally recognized. For example, as part of Don Nakanishi's claim, we alleged that he was denied tenure for his outspoken role in exposing admissions quotas against Asian/Pacific students at UCLA. This punishment violated his right to freedom of speech as guaranteed by both the State and Federal Constitutions (see *Franklin* v. *Leland Stanford Junior University*, 172 Cal.App.3d 322, 1985).

Breach of contract claims are still available when a university breaks an oral, implied or written promise. The shortcoming in this cause of action is that relief will probably be limited to monetary compensation, not tenure, and the amount of compensation will be quite limited.

Full relief can be available, however, in cases alleging discrimination under Federal Title VII or the State Fair Employment and Housing laws. In Federal courts, a victorious plaintiff can receive tenure, backpay and attorneys' fees and costs; in cases brought under California State law, the plaintiff can obtain tenure, backpay, attorneys' fees and costs, compensation for emotional distress and, in appropriate cases, punitive damages.

But tenure cases based on race discrimination are very difficult to win. In *Academics in Court: The Consequences of Faculty Discrimination Litigation* (Ann Arbor: University of Michigan Press, 1989), George R. LaNoue and Barbara A. Lee found that up to 1989, women and minorities won only thirty-four of 160 cases. Of those "victories," however, white women won four out of four cases against black colleges, white males won eight out of twelve cases against black colleges, and the racial minorities almost always lost. These cases will be even more difficult to win in the future with the United States Supreme Court's assault against past civil rights' rulings. For example, in *Patterson* v. *McLean Credit Union*, 109 S.Ct. 2363, 1986, the Court reversed a long-standing line of authority, suggesting that employees could not sue under the Civil Rights Acts for promotional discrimination (see also, *Jett* v. *Dallas Independent School District*, 109 S.Ct. 2702, 1989). In class actions, the Supreme Court made it more difficult to prove classwide discrimination by establishing new and more stringent rules of proof of discrimination (*Antonio* v. *Wards Cove Packing*, 109 S.Ct.2115, 1989).

As the statistics demonstrate, discrimination is always difficult to prove. Rarely, if ever, do cases have a "smoking gun," and thus the connection between improper motive based on race or sex and denial of tenure turns on circumstantial evidence. The leeway given subjective criteria in tenure decisions permits the masking of discrimination by offering plausible reasons for a candidate's inadequacy. With the recent *University of Pennsylvania* decision, however, the comparison among candidates' files opens the door to new challenges to decisions. Before, these were shielded by confidentiality; now, the plaintiff can obtain files, compare qualifications among tenure candidates and determine whether disparate treatment occurred. The recent case of *Clark* v. *Claremont Colleges* in which a black professor who was denied tenure was awarded one million dollars is a hopeful sign. But the full impact remains to be seen.

Virtually every university incorporates a grievance process into its rules or policies. With variations, these committees are deputized to accept complaints of rule violations, and can call witnesses, obtain documents and make recommendations to higher officials. Grievance committees usually consist of professors who volunteer their time and are usually inexperienced in legalistic procedures.

Because formal grievances are uncommon in the civilized academic world, both the APM and grievance rules tend to be untested, underdeveloped and vague. The quality of justice you get depends to a great degree on the quality of the judges—i.e., members of the grievance committee—so luck is a significant factor. Obtaining the services of an attorney is also important as assistant professors are not trained to identify issues, marshal facts in support of their arguments, find witnesses and develop documentation. And because the committee can only make recommendations, it wields no real power, although it can recommend a wide range of remedies, including re-review, disqualification of hostile witnesses, an extra year of employment for the grievant. Filing grievances does offer advantages over court actions. They are cheaper, faster and adjudicated by persons knowledgeable about academic matters.

Other institutional agencies can assist those with grievances by obtaining information and providing lobbying assistance within the university. Candidates must look through institutional rules to discover possible allies, such as a university ombudsman or a Vice-Chancellor for Faculty Relations. But most of these offices, even when sympathetic, can help in only limited ways.

EEOC/DFEH

In the aftermath of the civil rights struggles of the 1960s, the federal government and most states established agencies to investigate complaints of discrimination. The federal agency charged with this responsibility is the Equal Employment Opportunity Commission. State agencies go by various names, but in California this agency is named the Fair Employment and Housing Commission. In general, these offices are understaffed and overworked and have trouble with complex cases such as tenure disputes. Because filing a complaint with one of these agencies is a prerequisite for filing a suit in court, grievants often look to these offices for help. These offices provide free services and can obtain case information and documents and collect witness statements. They can issue findings and order full relief, although they rarely make findings on behalf of Asian/Pacific Americans.

As I suggested earlier, the legal approach to winning relief in tenure cases has inherent drawbacks. Nevertheless, in many cases the legal challenge is all that is left for an aggrieved professor and thus becomes a necessary step for resolving a case. In Don Nakanishi's case, however, we were able to identify and draw upon other strengths. We were able to pursue a coordinated legal-political strategy toward gaining tenure. Our strategy was neither easy nor simple, but the principles that we developed could well serve others facing similar situations.

DIVERSITY AT UCLA: THE CONTEXT FOR THE TENURE BATTLE

The University of California at Los Angeles is the most populous campus in the UC system. Residing on 411 acres of prime real estate, with 34,400 students, it has long been known for its athletic programs and surfer image. In recent years, however, UCLA has emerged as a world-class university, and the composition of its student body has changed dramatically. Asian/Pacific Americans now comprise more than 20 percent of the undergraduate population.

During the period that Don Nakanishi fought for tenure, UCLA came under a cloud of accusations. Asian/Pacific Americans challenged UCLA for allegedly setting quotas on admissions. State Senator Art Torres began an inquiry and scheduled public hearings. The Office of Civil Rights of the U.S. Department of Education began investigating UCLA and other universities. And despite UC President David Gardner's exhortation to Chancellors, in his letter of September 18, 1989, to hire more minorities to "reaffirm our commitment to encompass the cultural, ethnic and racial richness of our state . . .," tenured minority faculty were an endangered species at UCLA.

As of 1988, only 10 percent of the tenured professors at UCLA were persons of color. Twenty-seven departments had no tenured Asian/Pacific American professors, and nearly three-quarters of the tenured Asian/Pacific professors were concentrated in the Engineering and Physical Sciences departments. In the social sciences, only four Asian/Pacific Americans held tenured positions, accounting for 1.7 percent of the total professors. In Don Nakanishi's department, the Graduate School of Education, three Asian/Pacific professors had previously been denied tenure, although one had finally received tenure after a lengthy grievance struggle. Ultimately, she chose not to remain at UCLA. By 1988, no Asian/Pacific American served as a tenured professor at the GSE, and only three of fifty-one tenured professors at the GSE were racial minorities.

Don Nakanishi's tenure odyssey began on June 25, 1986, when he received a letter from department chair Norma Feshbach requesting submission of his tenure "package" for consideration by the department. Having met with the three-person departmental ad hoc committee and having received no criticisms of his work, Don felt confident that tenure would be granted. However, the department meeting scheduled to consider his application was postponed twice, while members met to consider other candidates less senior. This was the first sign of a problem.

When Don's file was finally discussed, a secret letter opposing tenure was read to the department by Chair Norma Feshbach. The letter was submitted by the chair of the ad hoc committee and was shielded from the other members and from Don. In a split vote, the department voted against tenure.

The secret letter violated University policies but was not revealed to Don Nakanishi by Chair Feshbach prior to the departmental meeting. Nevertheless, when he learned of this deceit, he contacted two University officials to protest this procedural violation: Professor Anne Spence, Chair of the Committee on Grievance and Disciplinary Procedures, and Vice-Chancellor Harold Horowitz. Horowitz denied him any relief, but Spence recommended that another departmental meeting be held.

In the meantime, Don was able to review summaries of the criticisms of his file and offer rebuttals. His ability in teaching and university and public service were considered exceptional, but his research was considered equivocal by certain department members, despite outstanding letters from outside reviewers. The second departmental vote—this time occurring without any secret letters—was held on March 16, 1987, and resulted in a two-thirds plurality in favor of tenure.

This recommendation was forwarded to the campus ad hoc committee of the Committee on Academic Personnel (CAP). This powerful body, charged with making a recommendation to the Chancellor, is almost never overruled. Influenced by Dean Solmon, the ad hoc and full committees recommended against tenure, based primarily on Don's research record. This was predictable because the quality of his research had been evaluated subjectively. The reasons proffered were also predictable. In fact, I had heard almost identical reasons in previous tenure and promotion denial cases I had handled.

The committee and other reviewing agencies denigrated Don's research as "primarily descriptive" and "journalistic rather than scholarly" with "little or no impact on the relevant academic community." The condescension was breathtaking: His work was said to be pathbreaking but then anything in Asian American Studies, as a new field, could be considered pathbreaking. One agency argued that the positive votes for tenure arose out of a "well motivated concern for affirmative action." The reasons offered were also striking in their contradictions. In one part of the summary of the CAP recommendation, Don's work was recognized as the first of its kind, a pioneering work, but was also criticized for being unoriginal and "very ordinary in its conception." At another point, the summary praised Don's work for exploring "important questions" and for making a "valuable contribution to the field of Asian Studies" but chided the work for not being "exciting."

I had heard the same old song before. In another University of California case involving a promotion, the reviewing agencies slapped themselves in the face with contradictions. My client's work was considered the first study ever done, but not "original"; it was described as "pathbreaking" but not "exciting." (These were virtually the same reasons given for Don Nakanishi's denial of tenure.) After an appeal, my client eventually received a promotion with backpay.

A strong minority report was appended to the summary, arguing that Don Nakanishi made substantial, original contributions. The report also noted the favorable external letters in his file, which had been discounted because no one on the reviewing committees had expertise in Asian American Studies. The minority report also criticized the majority report for neglecting Don's substantial university and public service and his administrative responsibilities in the Asian American Studies Center and charged the reviewing agencies with "relentless prejudgment" and an "arrogant mindset" in dismissing his work. Don himself composed a rebuttal, pointing out inaccuracies and misquotes in the majority report and inadequacies in the committee's review of his work. One example: His five most significant published works were not analyzed in any depth.

The file returned to the department for a third vote, as required by the rules. At the departmental meeting, GSE Dean Lewis Solmon, a vocal opponent of Don Nakanishi, sat in on the discussion, an unprecedented action, since he had already been allowed independent comments on Don's work to CAP. Intimidated by the Dean's presence, department members voted against tenure. The recommendation against tenure was accepted by the Chancellor in a decision issued June 30, 1987. Thus, with his candidacy for tenure denied, Don would be leaving the University in one year.

DON NAKANISHI AS A SYMBOL OF THE "NEW CALIFORNIA"

Don Nakanishi first contacted my office by way of a single-spaced letter on February 17, 1987. After reading his documentation of procedural irregularities, I had no doubt that he had become another casualty of academic apartheid. I felt at that time, however, that his strategy should focus on lobbying within his department to obtain a favorable endorsement of his candidacy. It was not until sometime later that we discovered evidence of the incredible bias which resulted in his first tenure denial.

As with all clients, I analyzed Don Nakanishi as a person. I asked myself a series of questions: Is this guy smart? Is he competent as a professor? Is he tough enough to endure an oppressive tenure fight? Does he get the picture quickly, or is he a draw-by-the-numbers kind of person? Will he pay his legal bills? As in all employment cases, I also asked the most important question: Does he have witnesses who would be willing to testify? The answer to this question is critical because without witnesses, a case tends to become one person's word against another's. And even with witnesses, many are afraid to testify in employment cases for fear of losing their jobs or the next promotion.

I knew very little about him at the start, and he seemed too low-key and non-aggressive to wage a protracted struggle against a large institution. I always hope for the fiery heart and cool brain rather than vice versa, but I discovered soon enough that his calm exterior belied a strength of principles which would serve him well in the years to come. I also wondered why this seemingly gentle person could be so dangerous to the University. But after reading some of his materials, I realized that he was quite subversive in his own way. His research dealt with significant issues in minority communities, areas virtually unknown to "pathbreaking" mainstream scholars. He published articles about discrimination in admissions at UCLA *before* being considered for tenure, earning a reputation in some circles as a troublemaker.

Perhaps most significantly, Don Nakanishi was a symbol of a New California where due to changing demographics, the majority of inhabitants would soon be people of color. Don represented this next wave, and many in the Ivory Tower, subconsciously or consciously, feared this. Also, his educational background was impeccable—Harvard and Yale—and his academic record exceptional. This was not *any* person of color, but a person who could compete with anyone. He was also fortunate to have in place an extensive support network, starting with his wife, Marsha, who may be the toughest person in the family, his son, Tommy, and a panoply of community activists cultivated over the years through his own commitment to progressive causes. In tenure fights, one needs all the help available, and psychological support is crucial for the long-term struggle.

THE FIRST GRIEVANCE: BUYING TIME TO ORGANIZE POLITICALLY

Just before the first decision denying tenure, we had uncovered numerous procedural irregularities in the tenure process. These irregularities became the basis for our first grievance filed on October 26, 1987, with the Committee on Privilege and Tenure. Although this committee did not have authority to grant relief and could only make recommendations to the Chancellor, we saw it as an important step in our long-range strategy.

Our strategy centered on mobilizing pressure against UCLA. Based on our understanding of the "political" nature of Don's situation, we ruled out a lawsuit as too expensive, too slow and incapable of achieving tenure. Although the public is predisposed to believe that lawsuits are the appropriate means to settle disputes, my experience is that they are often ineffective by themselves. All too often, attorneys file lawsuits without assessing their role in the larger political context, which results in dissipating all the political energy of supporters. Rather than taking the initiative and acting, the supporters are left watching a proxy battle in court with well-recognized rules of engagement and predetermined scope of relief.

Further, lawsuits do not scare the University. It simply hands the complaint to its lawyers knowing it will take years before a case is resolved. Political activity, however, does scare the University because such actions can inject a devastating uncertainty into the decision-making equation. Will the activists demonstrate or riot? Attract bad publicity? Sit in at offices? Stop funding from alumni or the legislature? No one knows the answer to these questions and this creates a measure of power.

Obviously, Don's strength was his political contacts. Thus, we needed to enlarge the battlefield to take advantage of this strength. But first, we needed to buy time to publicize the case, enlist allies and delay Don's departure from UCLA. We decided to file a grievance with the Committee on Privilege and Tenure, believing that its findings could add credibility to our claims and create a media focus by exposing the unfairness of reviewing agencies. We would use the grievance to stake a moral claim against UCLA and wage war in its own backyard.

Diane Matsuda, a law clerk from Hastings College of the Law, first scoured the

Academic Personnel Manual to identify any violation of the rules. I then drafted a grievance consisting of a forty-six-page brief and 124 pages of appendix. We asserted that Don Nakanishi had been treated in a manner unprecedented in UCLA history. We alleged procedural improprieties, biases, and failures to conduct a fair review. We charged hostility to Asian American Studies as well as race discrimination. The grievance was then critiqued by Don and Bill Lee, a volunteer attorney from the Center for Law in the Public Interest in Los Angeles and old friend of Don's. Bill consented to act as co-counsel throughout the case and offered valuable suggestions.

As in all legal cases, luck plays an important role. Lawyers tend not to admit this, unless they lose a case due to Bad Luck. In this case, we were fortunate to have an impartial, hardworking and experienced Committee on Privilege and Tenure, chaired by Dr. Sidney Roberts, a Professor Emeritus from the School of Medicine, who had been at UCLA for forty years and had experience hearing grievances. Roberts was widely respected at UCLA, and he would later be elected president of the campus Academic Senate. As significantly, we also had witnesses. More than ten tenured professors from the Graduate School of Education had broken with confidentiality and agreed to testify in Don's favor, so great was their perception of unfairness in this case.

The investigating committee had seven volunteer members, all professors at UCLA. They interviewed witnesses, reviewed documents, discussed the evidence, and on January 11, 1988, concluded that Don Nakanishi had proven a *prima facie* case of unfairness. This meant that we had presented enough evidence for a preliminary finding of misconduct sufficient to warrant a full hearing. The committee recommended resolution of the grievance by selection of a new campus ad hoc professors (out of fifty-one) at the Graduate School of Education who either could not be fair or who did not have expertise in Don's field. We also named fifteen other persons who we felt could not be fair or impartial. We sent the long list to the administration, hoping to put them in a box: If they rejected our request and chose anyone from our disqualification list as a departmental representative, they would appear to perpetuate the bias already at issue in our grievance and give us grounds for an additional grievance. If they acceded to our request, one of Don's allies would become the representative.

THE SECOND GRIEVANCE AND DISCOVERY OF A "SMOKING GUN"

During the course of the first grievance, we discovered new and disturbing instances of misconduct by Don's nemesis, Dean Lewis Solmon. We learned, for example, of his attendance at the departmental vote, a clear breach of departmental custom. We also found out that he had not only tried to influence the vote but had sent an unsolicited letter to the campus ad hoc committee voicing his opposition to tenure. As GSE Dean, he had already had the opportunity to comment in writing on Don's candidacy. Thus, his attempt to influence two other "independent" review committees was both unprecedented and inequitable. To its credit, the Committee on Academic Personnel rejected outright the Dean's letter, citing the impropriety of its submission. This amounted to a critical error by the Dean, because his fingerprints were on that letter.

Through our network of "friends," we discovered that Dean Solmon had previously chosen a prominent and vocal adversary of Don Nakanishi, a person with little expertise in Don's area of research, to be the departmental representative to the campus ad hoc committee. Most surprisingly, we were told that he had used a racial epithet in referring to Don. This racial insult was the "smoking gun" we lawyers dream about, and we could not wait to showcase this evidence in a new grievance. Unfortunately, we were not able to reveal the witness as he/she requested anonymity. Dying inside, we respected this request, even though it possibly meant losing tenure. We were allowed, however, to publicize the facts but without the source.

With new evidence of misconduct, we filed a second grievance with the Committee on Privilege and Tenure on April 28, 1988. The grievance highlighted what we had been saying all along: The tenure review process for Don was indelibly tainted with bias and could not be reformed to offer a fair review. The grievance also turned up the political heat on the University, exposing the defects in the tenure process. With the impartiality of the Committee on Privilege and Tenure assured, we knew we would not suffer from Bad Luck.

The grievance painted in broad brush a picture of conspiracy to deny tenure through prejudgment by the Dean and departmental Chair. It highlighted their attempts to influence both the department and CAP in violation of customs and rules. It also stressed racial bias and the selection of departmental review representatives who were hostile to Don and who lacked expertise in his field of research. We demanded that the Dean be shut out from any further participation in the review process, that certain prejudicial documents be excised from the file, and that the usual tenure procedure be altered to adjust for the prior improprieties.

On June 1, 1988 the committee found in our favor, stating that:

> . . . you have also made a *prima facie* case with regard to your allegations concerning Dean Solmon's conduct during and prior to the formal review of your qualifications for promotion to tenure.

The committee did not find similar evidence to support our allegations against Chair Feshbach.

This ruling effectively chopped up the Dean's credibility and established persuasively to the public that Don Nakanishi was the victim of a vendetta. The tenure review process stopped in its tracks because new rules of review had to be negotiated with us before a final decision could be made. At least in the eyes of the public and many faculty, the University's tenure process was a mockery.

For the next four months, we negotiated over the terms of the findings. The administration simply would not remove the Dean, claiming that a definitive ruling had not been made. Its resistance was both the mark of the Dean's power and the University's defense of its "Old Boys' Club" at the expense of fairness.

On October 11, 1988, a compromise was finally achieved. Negative recommendations would be excised from the file, Don Nakanishi would have the right to respond to any comment made by the Dean to CAP; the CAP would agree not to meet with the Dean, as was his right; Don Nakanishi's representatives would be allowed to meet with the Chancellor before the final decision to set forth their position on tenure; the Dean would not participate in the departmental meeting; and Don would get an additional year of employment if the tenure decision were negative.

The field of battle then shifted back to the campus ad hoc committee which would review Don again. We had eliminated those evaluators less sympathetic to Don, as the administration honored our long disqualification list. We also demanded and received appointment of a representative from the Asian American Studies faculty on the ad hoc CAP review committee. Nevertheless, we learned that the campus ad hoc committee's vote was split, equally pro and against tenure. The full committee's recommendation was likewise divided, which required a return to the GSE for another vote and a rebuttal of the CAP recommendation. Then, the decision was in the Chancellor's hands.

In early 1989, before the department's re-review, Don was called to the Chancellor's house for a meeting. I was convinced he was prepared to announce a decision in Don's favor. Instead, he urged Don to accept a permanent lectureship, the equivalent of second-class status. Don flatly rejected sitting in the back of the university bus.

Don now travelled the well-worn path back to his department for a final vote. In the department, faculty members were well versed about Don's case. They had discussed the file fives times; they had been lobbied by undergraduate students, graduate students, colleagues, and the Dean. They knew about the two grievances and the two findings in Don's favor, and they had read almost weekly in the campus newspaper about some new issue relating to Don's tenure fight. They were probably very tired of this file. Due to the publicity, the grievance findings and some strong persuasion by Don's allies in the department, I believe most senior faculty became convinced that Don had been viciously victimized. The last vote seemed to reflect this sentiment, resulting in the largest plurality for tenure of the five department reviews.

The last battlefield was in the Office of the Chancellor. On May 25, 1989, Chancellor Young granted Don Nakanishi tenure. The three-year ordeal was over.

MOBILIZING POLITICAL PRESSURE

From the beginning, we realized that achieving tenure was dependent on the political pressure we could bring on the University. We could not expect a fair appraisal of Don's work because the criteria for tenure—"superior academic achievement"—was subjective, especially as applied to research in "non-traditional" fields such as Asian American Studies. Nor could we expect any help from sympathetic administrators because Don was a well-known troublemaker. Recognizing these weaknesses, we decided to work toward obtaining the strongest recommendation possible within Don's department and within CAP. Knowing that Don would probably not receive a unanimous endorsement from either group, we hoped for enough positive votes that the Chancellor could not reject Don summarily and could justify his decision for tenure to the faculty. We would then concentrate our pressure on the Chancellor to make a positive decision.

Throughout the struggle, the political and legal pressure varied with each battlefield. Initially, we had to fight in the legal arena through grievances to reverse the adverse recommendation and obtain a re-review. At the same time, we had to begin organizing political support outside the University through media and community contacts and inside the University through sympathetic colleagues and students. Later, the focus would be on influencing the department faculty to vote for Don's tenure. Although we initially targeted the University rather than any one individual for political pressure, in the end all attention was focused on Chancellor Young because he had the authority to make the final decision.

As we began our mobilization, we learned that Don's political strengths were enormous. At UCLA, he was well-liked as a professor, mentor and counsellor. He had many supporters within his own department and maintained a strong political base in the Asian American Studies Center. Through his work, he had contacts with instructors throughout the country. But he was no egghead academic either, having cultivated friends over the years in city government and community organizations. Beyond the Asian/Pacific community, he knew people in the Hispanic, Black, Jewish and labor communities. He should have been a politician.

The timing of the case was also a political strength. The Redress issue had galvanized the nascent Japanese American community to intense political activity, liberating it from the wartime burden of incarceration. In a sense, Japanese Americans had reclaimed their political birth-right and were no longer afraid to challenge authority. Also, other Asian/Pacific communities had grown, not only in size but political savvy. And student activism revived after the "Me Decade" of the 1980s. People were ready to fight.

A network of political contacts was also in place. Over the years, Asian/Pacific Americans had moved into levels of influence in the State legislature, alumni associations, city politics, the Board of Regents, media, and educational groups. These networks enlarged the battlefield by bringing in new constituencies, creating larger pools of allies.

Demographics also favored us. Not only had the number of Asian/Pacific American students increased at UCLA, but the growth of our communities in Los Angeles and California created a moral justification for tenure for an Asian/Pacific professor, especially in the field of education. The changing demographics had to be recognized by UCLA.

The moral justification was also strengthened by recent charges of admissions irregularities toward Asian/Pacific applicants at UCLA. Ironically, the investigation by the federal government was precipitated by the very same Don Nakanishi, who now reaped the benefit of this public scrutiny.

However, there were weaknesses in our political position as well. Anti-Asian sentiment was and is a cancer growing in this state, and UCLA professors and administrators are not immune. Don's nemesis was a powerful dean who controlled, to a great degree, the review process and who used all his influence to deny tenure. Perhaps most significantly, we were confronting an intransigent institution and a system of departmental fiefdoms.

Throughout the struggle, a mind-boggling cast of characters leaned on UCLA for Don's tenure. Institutions as large as UCLA do not usually respond to threats unless they reach atomic bomb proportions. Because one rarely has "nuclear weapons" at his/her disposal, any available ammunition must be deployed and hopefully the cumulative firepower can represent a credible threat. Thus, we organized support wherever we could find it. While I cannot mention all who helped, a sample of the players in this drama offer some glimpse of its breadth and depth.

Initially, however, we did not tap the reservoir of support available to us. We made a fairly significant mistake in declaring war without an organized army. What we needed was a steering committee and a spokesperson/organizer to develop and carry out a coherent campaign against the University. Specifically, we needed a committee that could analyze our strengths and weaknesses and those of the University, identify allies and enemies, devise a timetable, distribute tasks and develop media and fund-raising plans. Our legal tactics would be one part of this overall strategy.

While we attempted to create a steering committee, it did not come together until much later, and its effectiveness demonstrated its necessity at a much earlier time. At the start, then, Stewart Kwoh of the Asian/Pacific American Legal Center filled in as spokesperson. John Saito of Japanese American Citizens League (JACL) became treasurer, and Lloyd Inui of Long Beach State played an active role. Karen Umemoto, Gann Matsuda and Ed Pai were the student liaisons. Glenn Omatsu of the Asian American Studies Center came on shortly to compose press releases but eventually became a main organizer in the steering committee. Both he and Karen functioned brilliantly to guide the committee during the final push for tenure.

After declaring war, we recruited our army. We contacted as many allies as possible. Yori Wada, a UC Regent, lobbied Chancellor Young incessantly. Professors stepped forward to assume aggressive advocacy roles. Rod Skager, Julia Wrigley, John McNeil, Gordon Berry, Val Rust, Sol Cohen, and John Hawkins, among many others in the department, joined with several from Asian American Studies—Harry Kitano, Alexander Saxton and Lucie Cheng—to urge the administration to grant tenure.

State legislators sent letters, and their support became critical for the final decision. State Senator Art Torres held public hearings on the Asian admissions issue and demanded tenure for Don. Assemblyman John Vasconcellos, chair of the powerful Ways and Means Committee, privately lobbied UCLA officials. David Roberti, Willie Brown, Tom Hayden,

Dick Floyd lent legislative aides to the effort. In all, twenty-seven California State legislators endorsed Don's candidacy for tenure.

During this phase, local politicians such as Mayor Bradley sent letters pressing for tenure. Los Angeles Unified School Board Member Warren Furutani and Jack Fujimoto, an administrator in the Los Angeles Community College District, met with Chancellor Young. Ron Wakabayashi, then JACL Executive Director, and Melinda Yee of the Organization of Chinese Americans also sent letters. And Asian/Pacific professors throughout the country added their voices for tenure.

Throughout this battle, students were a consistently dedicated force. They were the first to raise Don's issue publicly and organized rallies, forums, demonstrations and candlelight vigils to pressure the University. Using their political power, students lobbied the UCLA Undergraduate Student Association Council and Graduate Student Association to pass resolutions. They also lobbied professors and administrators, submitted petitions, demanded explanations and kept the spirit of the struggle alive.

Another organization also aggressively pushed the University. The Asian/Pacific Alumni had formed during Don's battle and was trying to develop a cooperative relationship with the administration. Don's issue placed the group in an awkward position, but APA actively supported tenure. APA President Ernest Hiroshige, a Los Angeles Superior Court judge, demanded meetings with the Chancellor, wrote scathing letters, and suggested suspending activities of APA if Don were denied tenure. He and Stewart Kwoh also were prepared to resign from the Chancellor-appointed Community Advisory Board if tenure were denied.

Others joined this rag-tag, multi-hued, cross-generational, non-partisan army— Japanese American Bar Association, Korean American Bar Association, Southern California Chinese Lawyers' Association, National Coalition for Redress and Reparations, Native American, Latino and Black groups, labor unions, educational commissions, and influential Japanese American Republicans. The Japanese Chamber of Commerce of Southern California under Kenji Ito even called for Chancellor Young to remove himself from the tenure case, causing quite a controversy within the community when a newspaper columnist interpreted Ito's letter as demanding the Chancellor's resignation.

Publicity was central to our case. We needed media exposure to build political support, raise money, and educate the public. Glenn Omatsu took responsibility for the press releases and did a prolific, masterful job. Sympathetic coverage emerged from the *Daily Bruin*, especially by reporter Shana Chandler, and from Larry Gordon of the *Los Angeles Times*.

At the very end when the Chancellor was considering the final decision, we found an atom bomb in the California State Legislature's Ways and Means Subcommittee where a proposal to fund a multimillion-dollar building for the UCLA Graduate School of Management was just waiting for pro forma approval. Through allies in the Sacramento offices of Elihu Harris, Willie Brown, John Vasconcellos and Robert Campbell, Chair of the Subcommittee, we shut the door on the bill until a final decision on tenure was made.

It was at this time that Chancellor Young requested a meeting with Don and myself. At this meeting in San Francisco, he railed about the unfair publicity he and UCLA had received and his outrage over the political pressure. He decried holding the Management School's building bill hostage and talked about all he had done for minorities and ethnic studies. In response, we expressed outrage too—outrage that our best and brightest could not get a fair review; outrage that the same type of arbitrary authority which took our parents to concentration camps still existed to deny their children equal opportunity. We told the Chancellor that our community had recently fought and won Redress; never again would we sit passively while racism and injustice threatened our people. Further, the University had given us no choice: even if we lost the fight, we would make it pay a price, so it would think twice about doing this again to another Asian/Pacific American. The Chancellor listened to our concerns respectfully and also stated his regret that this issue had spiraled out of control.

Because we were there to promote Don's candidacy, Don discussed his recent achievements, including new publications and awards. The Chancellor seemed genuinely interested, as this was new information to him. The meeting was not without some humor. At one point, Don mentioned that I was a graduate of the University of Southern California. The Chancellor pounded his fist on the table and yelled, "No wonder!!!"

It was clear he was caught in the middle of two difficult political choices. As he explained it, he grants tenure to Don and incurs criticism for having sold out to political pressure. He denies tenure and becomes a racist in the eyes of the community. While we had some sympathy for him, we knew what he had to do. We had raised the stakes to the point that denying tenure was clearly more painful an alternative than granting it. Even he recognized the level of pressure, stating at one point, "I have never seen so much pressure brought to such an issue."

His decision to grant tenure was not quite as simple as balancing the power on each side and choosing the heavier weight. I believe the Chancellor sincerely wanted to grant tenure earlier but was given bad advice by his aides. He was more sympathetic than portrayed in the media and did not become tuned in to the significance of Don as a symbol until it was too late. Had he become engaged in the process earlier, I believe he may have granted tenure earlier.

THE TENURE BATTLE IN THE CONTEXT OF OUR TIMES

In all honesty, the level of support Don attracted surprised me. It was not until I realized what he had come to symbolize that I began to understand how this gentle, unassuming man could command an army of adherents clamoring for tenure. He became a symbol to many different groups. For Asian/Pacific Americans, he represented a victim of racism as well as the emerging political power of our communities. To other minorities, he was seen as another victim of academic apartheid and represented the need to integrate the Ivory Tower. He also represented the legitimacy of Ethnic Studies and other "non-traditional" research fields. He was an underdog, a David fighting the bully with a slingshot.

Don's struggle is best seen in the context of our times: the confluence of the Redress Movement, the anti-Lungren campaign, the revival of the student movement, the growth of the Asian/Pacific American community and our rising political empowerment. Don's case became a test of whether our aspirations would be considered seriously or cast aside as inconsequential. It was also a test of whether we could effectively coalesce different groups and coordinate a coherent strategy to achieve justice. Finally, it was also a test for the University—not of its strength to withstand our concerted offensive, but of its commitment to its own rhetoric of diversity. On this question, I give the University a grade of "D"—passing, but just barely.

For me, the *process* of networking, building coalitions and educating the public was as important as the *result*. By creating a power base not just for Don but for future issues, by educating the community about racism, by motivating people to take action against injustice, and by building coalitions and gaining experience in political mobilizations, we have added to the collective storehouse of knowledge to prepare for future struggles.

So I believe we did not gain just another Asian/Pacific American professor out of this battle. Nor did we achieve just a "victory" over an invincible institution. What we gained was more intangible and also more significant. We gained a sense of empowerment, a sense of confidence that we can fight and we can win, even against great odds.

Selected Annotated Bibliography on Asian/Pacific Americans and Education

Tina Yamano Nishida

CONCURRENT WITH the remarkable recent growth of the Asian and Pacific American population, the body of literature on Asian/Pacific Americans has gained more attention and has begun to reflect the diversity among the array of Asian/Pacific American groups in education. Many articles and other publications have attempted to counter the stereotyping, misunderstanding, and neglect of these groups and their educational problems and needs. However, it is clear that much more empirical, theoretical, and practical research needs to be done to fill many substantive gaps in our understanding of the educational experiences of Asian/Pacific Americans. We hope this book, as well as this bibliography, will assist scholars, students, teachers, administrators, parents, and other educational officials in acquainting them with many of the most important, useful, and provocative recent works on Asian/Pacific American educational topics. We also hope this publication serves to stimulate further scholarly, policy, and practical research on Asian/Pacific American education.

This is a selective annotative bibliography. We believe we have selected works that address the major educational issues of Asian/Pacific Americans, while also being accessible to most of our potential readers. The organization of the bibliography generally follows the section headings of this book. In order to make the bibliography as useful as possible, we selected articles and books that were published between 1980 and 1993. We have included materials available through the Educational Resources Information Center, but we have eliminated all dissertations, theses, and most reports because we felt they might not be readily accessible to many of our readers. Finally, I would like to acknowledge *Amerasia Journal* for its extensive coverage of the literature on Asian Americans which assisted me in the production of this bibliography, and Dr. Don Nakanishi, who provided me with invaluable guidance to help make this bibliography comprehensive.

HISTORICAL PERSPECTIVES ON THE SCHOOLING OF ASIAN/PACIFIC AMERICANS

Hawkins, John N. "Politics, Education, and Language Policy: The Case of Japanese Language Schools in Hawaii." *Amerasia Journal* 5:1 (1978):39–56. Focuses on the political struggle of the Japanese immigrant community to maintain their autonomous Japanese-language schools in strong opposition from the Hawaiian Territorial Government in the early twentieth century.

James, Thomas. *Exile Within: The Schooling of Japanese Americans 1942–1945*. Cambridge, Mass.: Harvard University Press, 1987. Embodies the camps as educational institutions. Addresses what sort of education took place, what educators felt they were accomplishing in camp, and how the children adjusted and reacted. Asserts education for the children interned continued despite inadequate resources.

———. "Life Begins with Freedom: The College Nisei, 1942–1945." *History of Education Quarterly* 25 (Spring/Summer 1985):155–74. Explores the history of the college Nisei (median age was 17) and how more than four thousand students were allowed to leave the camps to pursue higher education outside of the restricted zone. Attempts to understand the experience of the Nisei college age group.

———. "The Education of Japanese Americans at Tule Lake, 1942–1946." *Pacific Historical Review* 41:1 (February 1987):25–58. Maintains Tule Lake Relocation Center was an educational institution, and utilizes the politics of education in the camp to interpret the conflict of social meanings that characterized all wartime camps for Japanese Americans. Divides the educational history of Tule Lake into three institutional periods that reflect resistance in the camp.

Lai, Him Mark, bibliographer, edited by Jean Pang Yip and Russell Leong. *A History Reclaimed: An Annotated Bibliography of Chinese Language Materials on the Chinese of America.* Los Angeles: Asian American Studies Center, University of California, Los Angeles, 1986. Annotations from over fifteen hundred works (including archival collections) classified under selected categories. The core of the bibliography focuses on the Chinese in the United States; however, it also includes works on the overseas Chinese.

Wang, Ling-Chi. "*Lau v. Nichols*: History of a Struggle for Equal and Quality Education," in *Counterpoint* by Emma Gee, et al. (eds.) Los Angeles: Regents of the University of California and the UCLA Asian American Studies Center (1976):240–59. Provides a brief historical overview of the issues leading to the Supreme Court victory and the important contributions toward recognizing the rights of non-English-speaking Americans. Includes insight to the struggle of the Chinese American students and their parents in San Francisco, and the importance of fighting for equal and quality education.

Yu, Renqiu. "Chinese American Contributions to the Educational Development of Toisan, 1910–1940." *Amerasia Journal* 10 (1983):47–72. Chinese in the United States contribute by launching fund-raising campaigns, and by sending remittances to support their schools in China. Believes historical research on Chinese Americans can be expanded by considering political, economic, and social factors that exist in China and the United States.

ACADEMIC ACHIEVEMENT AND THE MODEL MINORITY DEBATE

Barringer, H. R. "Education, Occupational Prestige, and Income of Asian Americans." *Sociology of Education* 63 (January 1990):27–43. Analyzes the 1990 U.S. census data on Asian Americans, and makes a socioeconomic, educational, and status comparison with whites, blacks, and Hispanics. Concludes that although occupational prestige of Asian Americans correlates with their high levels of education, their income does not.

Brand, David. "The New Whiz Kids: Those Asian Americans." *Time* (31 August 1987):42–51. Examines post-secondary education, and addresses ethnic stereotypes, particularly those attached to Asian Americans. Finds that they are setting the educational pace by simply working harder to achieve. Concludes that these "whiz" kids are not a threat to society, but a challenge.

Brandon, P. R. "Gender Differences in Young Asian Americans' Educational Attainment." *Sex Roles* 25 (July 1991):45–61. Findings suggest that young Asian American females reach high levels of educational attainment more quickly than young Asian American males and that the difference may be due to the differential effect of their immigrant status and ethnicity.

Butterfield, F. "Why Asians are Going to the Head of the Class." *New York Times* (3 August 1986):18–23. Analyzes the academic success of Asian Americans and attempts to find out what lies behind their success.

Caplan, Nathan et al. "Indochinese Refugee Families and Academic Achievement." *Scientific American* (February 1992):36–42. Examines the fact that children of the Southeast Asian boat people excel in U.S. schools, especially in the areas of mathematical sciences. Suggests that the reasons may be social, rather than academic.

Chun, Ki-Taek. "The Myth of Asian American Success and Its Educational Ramifications." *IRCD Bulletin* (Winter/Spring 1980):1–12. Examines the empirical basis of the widely shared belief that Asian Americans are worthy of emulation by other minority groups. Explores its historical background and stresses the need for reassessment by educators.

Crystal, David. "Asian Americans and the Myth of the Model Minority." *Social Casework* 70:7 (September 1989):405–13. Argues that the model minority label masks serious social and psychological problems that exist in many Asian American communities. Analyzes the myth and makes recommendations for mental health specialists and educators.

Divoky, Diane. "The Model Minority Goes to School." *Phi Delta Kappan* 70:3 (November 1988):219–22. Addresses the stereotype "model" minority of Asian Americans outperforming their native-born peers in college. Discusses the real problems they face in school.

Greene, Elizabeth. "Asian Americans Find U.S. Colleges Insensitive, Form Campus Organizations to Fight Bias." *Chronicle of Higher Education* 34:12 (18 November 1987):38–40. Asian Americans face discrimination and resentment due to the "model minority" myth, trade war concerns, language barriers, and other stereotypes.

Hartman, Joan S., and Anna C. Askounis. "Asian American Students: Are They Really a 'Model Minority'?" *School Counselor* 37:1 (November 1989):109–12. Addresses the need for special counseling techniques that are adapted to Asian American students. Effective counseling of these students includes knowledge and recognition of their unique cultural background as well as a sensitivity for their individual differences.

Henkin, William A. "Toward Counseling the Japanese in America: A Cross-Cultural Primer." *Journal of Counseling and Development* 63:8 (April 1985):600–6. Asserts that Japanese Americans view mental illness as shameful and therefore cope rather than seek counseling. Consequently, the view of Japanese Americans as a model minority is purported by the low number of reported mental disturbances.

Hu, Arthur. "Asian Americans: Model Minority or Double Minority?" *Amerasia Journal* 15:1 (1989):243–57. Family resources and acculturation are also influential factors when "generalizing" about Asian Americans. Using averages from quantitative data may be misleading.

Humphreys, Lloyd G. "Trends in Level of Academic Achievement of Blacks and Other Minorities." *Intelligence* 12:3 (July-September 1988):231–60. A review of trends in measurement of achievement since 1960s (including data on Asian Americans). Some discussions on the theoretical issues.

Hurh, Won Moo, and Kwang Chung Kim. "The 'Success' Image of Asian Americans: Its Validity and Its Practical and Theoretical Implications." *Ethnic and Racial Studies* 12:4 (October 1989):512–38. Presents historical data to analyze the success stereotype of Asian Americans. Examines how the model minority image affects Asian Americans, other minorities, and majority Americans. Practical and theoretical implications are provided.

Lee, Everett S., and Xue-Ian Rong. "The Educational and Economic Achievement of Asian Americans." *The Elementary School Journal* 88:5 (May 1988):545–60. Supports the model minority stereotype and provides explanations for the remarkable achievements of Asian American students. Findings suggest that no other group has excelled upward in the United States and purports that there has been a movement of highly educated immigrants into the United States.

Li, Wen Lang. "Two Generations of Chinese Americans: Differentials in Education and Status Attainment Process." *Plural Societies* 17:1 (May 1987):95–107. Asserts that despite past discrimination and exclusion from immigration, Chinese Americans have achieved impressive gains in socioeconomic status. Elaborates on the differences between immigrants and natives and concludes that the Chinese American community cannot be viewed as a whole but as two immigrant groups: the old and the new.

Liu, In-Mao. "A Distinction between Early and Late Educational Achievements." *American Psychologist* 46:8 (August 1991):876–77. Argues that perceived limitations in certain career areas may account for Asian Americans' later educational achievements, but does not account for their early educational achievements.

Mathews, Jay. "Alhambra High Leads as Super School." *Rice* (October 1988):6–9. Asian American achievement at a high school in Los Angeles County.

Nagasawa, R., and D. J. Espinosa. "Educational Achievement and the Adaptive Strategy of Asian American College Students: Facts, Theory, and Hypotheses." *Journal of College Student Development* 33: (March 1992):137–42. Presents a theory on the behavioral patterns of Asian Americans as the determining force behind their success in college.

Sanchirico, Andrew. "The Importance of Small-Business Ownership in Chinese American Educational Achievement." *Sociology of Education* 64:4 (October 1991):293–304. A study of the Chinese-American families in small businesses concerning educational mobility and the intergenerational transmission of parental aspirations.

Stanley, Julian C. "Do Asian Americans Tend to Reason Better Mathematically than White Americans?" *Gifted Child Today* 11 (March-April 1988):32. Stresses that Asian Americans outperform all other racial and ethnic groups, especially scoring higher than whites on the Scholastic Aptitude Test mathematical section.

Sue, S., and Nolan W. S. Zane. "Academic Achievement and Socioemotional Adjustment Among Chinese University Students." *Journal of Counseling Psychology* 32:4 (October 1985):570–79. Study of 177 Chinese college students and their academic performance, majors, study habits, and socioemotional adjustment. The study found that although Chinese Americans have been considered high achievers, many of the recent immigrants had less socioemotional adjustment and used certain strategies to compensate for their limited English proficiency.

Sue, Stanley, and Sumie Okazaki. "Asian American Educational Achievements: A Phenomenon in Search of an Explanation." *American Psychologist* 45:8 (August 1990):913–20. Investigates the two most common hypotheses to explain achievement patterns of Asian Americans: hereditary intelligence and Asian cultural values. Findings suggest that Asian Americans perceive and have experienced restrictions in upward mobility in careers that are unrelated to education.

Suzuki, Bob H. "Asian Americans as the 'Model Minority': Outdoing Whites? or Media Hype?" *Change* (November/December 1989):12–19. Addresses when and why the image evolved. Discusses the consequences of its acceptance by the general public, and focuses particularly on how the label has affected Asians in higher education. Concludes Asian Americans have suffered significantly from this stereotype.

Toupin, Elizabeth A., and Linda Son. "Preliminary Findings on Asian Americans: 'The Model Minority' in a Small Private East Coast College. Annual Conference of the Society for the Study of Psychiatry and Culture (1987, Quebec, Canada)." *Journal of Cross-Cultural Psychology* 22:3 (September 1991):403–17. Only factor supporting the Asian American "model minority" stereotype was that the Asian Americans were more likely to major in the sciences. In other academic achievements, they were not superior to matched comparisons.

Vost, Lynn A., *et al.* "Explaining School Failure, Producing School Success: Two Cases." *Anthropology and Education Quarterly* (December 1987):276–86. Focuses on Hawaiians and school failure rates. Discusses the KEEP program developed for Native Hawaiian children and how the same program is not effective for Navajo children. Found cultural compatibility is a credible explanation for school success.

Yee, Albert H. "Asians as Stereotypes and Students: Misperceptions that Persist." *Educational Psychology Review* 4:1 (March 1992):95–132. The stereotypical notion that all Asians are outstanding is scrutinized. Article examines factors that are considered to explain their achievement. Idea that their high achievement was due to inherited cognitive abilities was not supported.

Yee, Barbara W. "Gender and Family Issues in Minority Groups." *Generations* 14:3 (Summer 1990):39–42. Looks at Asian and Pacific Islander as well as other minority groups and asserts that there is increasing diversity within each minority group due to physiological aging and residency in the United States.

ELEMENTARY AND SECONDARY EDUCATIONAL ISSUES

Berman, David M. "Every Vietnamese Was a 'Gook': My Lai, Vietnam, and American Education." *Theory and Research in Social Education* 16:2 (Spring 1988):141–59. Evaluates the social studies curriculum textbook and instruction, and argues that the instructional effectiveness is biased by the U.S. worldview.

Bernson, Mary Hammond, and Tarry L. Lindquist. "What's in a Name? Galloping Toward Cultural Insights: Appreciating Cultural Diversity in the Upper Grades." *Social Studies and the Young Learner* 1:4 (March–April 1989):13–16. Focuses on cultural naming patterns in China as a way of heightening student awareness of social and political attitudes in their own and other cultures.

Biederman, Patricia Ward. "Why Teach?" *Los Angeles Times Magazine* (26 November 1989):10–18+. Describes teachers in Los Angeles public schools, with a focus on Mark Takano.

Blakely, Mary Margaret. "Southeast Asian Refugee Parents: An Inquiry into Home-School Communication and Understanding." *Anthropology and Education Quarterly* 14:1 (Spring 1983):43–68. An evaluative report of an ethnographic study of Southeast Asian refugee families' adjustment to American schools. Looks at their educational needs, parent-school-relatedness, and involvement in bilingualism.

Bowler, Rosemarie, Stephen Rauch, and Ralf Schwarzer. "Self-Esteem and Inter-Racial Attitudes in Black High School Students: A Comparison with Five Other Ethnic Groups." *Urban Education* 21 (1986):3–19. Examines self-esteem, racial tension, ethnic identity, interethnic contact and open-mindedness. Statistics show that Indochinese were found to lack self-esteem.

Chang, Ye-Ling, and Dorothy J. Watson. "Adaptation of Prediction Strategies and Materials in a Chinese-English Bilingual Classroom." *Reading Teacher* 42:2 (October 1988):36–44. Looks at the effects of curriculum materials on Chinese elementary school children in the United States, and their learning acquisition of Chinese.

Chattergy, Virgie, and Belen C. Ongteco. "Educational Needs of Filipino Immigrant Students." *Social Process in Hawaii* 33 (1991):143–52. Educators of Filipino immigrant students have identified problems in the areas of language learning, motivation and classroom interaction, which leads to low academic achievement. Offers ways to assist these students to adjust to a new school environment.

Cheng, Li-Rong L. "Service Delivery to Asian/Pacific LEP Children: A Cross-Cultural Framework." *Topics in Language Disorders* 9:3 (June 1989):1–14. Assesses language implications from an Asian/Pacific perspective on communication and intervention with LEP children. Provides general information on the history, cultures, and languages of immigrant and refugee groups.

Cheung, King Kok. "Drawing Out the Silent Minority." *College Composition and Communication* 35 (December 1984):452–54. Provides insight on how to encourage participation among Asian American students. Advises instructors to be patient with students who have heavy accents, provide positive reinforcement, call on quiet students without forcing them to speak, and to help students articulate their ideas.

Chew, Kenneth S. Y., David J. Eggebeen, and Peter Uhlenberg. "American Children in Multiracial Households." *Sociological Perspectives* 32:1 (1989):65–85. Findings include that the largest proportion of children live in Asian-white households, and that about 60 percent reside in households headed by mixed-race couples.

Chin, Carol. "Asian Americans and California State Textbooks." *Social Studies Review* 23:3 (Spring 1984): 46–48. An evaluation of the social studies textbooks used in the State of California shows that the books fail to include the Asian American experience, past or present.

Christensen, Carole Pigler. "The Perceived Problems and Help-Seeking Preferences of Chinese Immigrants in Montreal." *Canadian Journal of Counseling* 21:4 (October 1987):189–99. Looks into the help-seeking preferences of Canadian Chinese and found that family and friends played an important role.

Clark, E. Audrey, and Hanisee, Jeanette. "Intellectual and Adaptive Performance of Asian Children in Adoptive American Settings." *Developmental Psychology* 18:4 (July 1982):595–99. Investigates adopted Asian children and their levels of social adjustment and intellectual competence. Findings suggest that they were high on performance levels.

Coker, Dolores Muga. "The Asian Student in the Classroom." *Education and Society* 1:3 (Fall 1988):19–20. Addresses the educational needs of Asian American students. Suggests directive, rather than group counseling to reflect sensitivity to their cultural differences.

Curtis, Stuart, and Robin Millar. "Language and Conceptual Understanding in Science: A Comparison of English- and Asian-Language-Speaking Children." *Research in Science and Technological Education* 6:2 (1988):61–77. Discusses conceptual understanding of English-speaking and Asian languages–speaking children in classrooms teaching science. Suggests that their differences in understanding scientific concepts are due to the language of instruction, rather than textbook curriculum.

Davis, D. G., and J. L. McDaid. "Identifying Second-Language Student's Needs: A Survey of Vietnamese High School Students." *Urban Education* 27:(April 1992):32–40. Although Vietnamese students possess positive school perceptions and high expectations for post–high school education, there is a need for guidance and counseling assistance in the areas of high school graduation requirements, post–high school options, and financial aid sources.

Dorfman, Ron. "From the 'Yellow Peril' to the Model Minority." *Quill* 76 (June 1988):10–11. Suggests that the success stereotype glosses over the serious problems of anti-Asian discrimination, which is often accompanied by violence. The notion directs conflict between Asian Americans and other minority communities.

Dunn, Rita, Josephine Gemake, Fatimeh Jalali, Robert Zenhausern, et al. "Cross-Cultural Differences in Learning Styles of Elementary-Age Students from Four Ethnic Backgrounds." *Journal of Multicultural Counseling & Development* 18:2 (April 1990):68–93. Examines the learning styles of elementary school children of different ethnic backgrounds and discusses the need for effective, alternative teaching method.

Eisenbruch, Maurice. "The Mental Health of Refugee Children and Their Cultural Development." *International Migration Review* 22:2 (Summer 1988):282–300. Explores the refugee experience of personal as well as cultural bereavement as a vital element in the later socioemotional development and mental health of refugee children. Suggests that culturally appropriate school-based programs will help a child's cultural identity formation as well as provide early detection and prevention of mental disturbances.

Emblen, Valerie. "Asian Children in Schools: Part Two." *Mathematics in School* 16:1 (January 1987):7–9. Discusses the learning styles of Asian students in mathematics. Addresses the role of communicative skills in the classroom.

Felice, Marianne E. "Reflections on Caring for Indochinese Children and Youth." *Journal of Developmental & Behavioral Pediatrics* 7 (April 1986):124–28. Provides a historical overview of medical issues concerning Indochinese children and asserts that improvements can be made in the areas of patient education programs, multicenter studies, and continuity of care.

Garner, Barbara. "Southeast Asian Culture and Classroom Culture." *College Teaching* 37:4 (Fall 1989):127–30. A descriptive guide for teachers to better meet the special needs of Southeast Asian students. Cultural traits that can affect students' participation in the classroom are presented.

Gersten, Russell, *et al.* "Alternative Educational Models for Language Minority Students: Research on Structured Immersion." *Equity and Excellence* 23:4 (Summer 1988):14–16. Cites the success of the "immersion" programs for low-income Hispanic and Asian children, in response to the claim that these programs fail.

Gersten, Russell. "Structured Immersion for Language Minority Students: Results of a Longitudinal Evaluation." *Educational Evaluation and Policy Analysis* 7:3 (Fall 1985):187–97. This study shows the effectiveness of a structured immersion approach in acquisition of academic skills and proficiency in English for low-income Asian students compared with a transitional bilingual approach.

Gibson, Margaret A., and Parminder K. Bhachu. "Ethnicity and School Performance: A Comparative Study of South Asian Pupils in Britain and America." *Ethnic and Racial Studies* 11:3 (July

1988):239–62. Focuses on how the educational strategies and school adaptation patterns of minority students are directly influenced by cultural models of their ethnic community. Special considerations are provided to the interplay of gender, class, and ethnicity.

Gibson, Margaret A. "Collaborative Educational Ethnography: Problems and Profits." *Anthropology and Education Quarterly* 16:2 (Summer 1985):124–48. Study of the socially disadvantaged immigrant (Punjabi Sikh) children's success in the U.S. schools. Asserts the need to look into the social factors that cause this difference in school performance between the immigrant and non-immigrant children.

Glynn, Ted, and Vin Glynn. "Shared Reading by Cambodian Mothers and Children Learning English as a Second Language: Reciprocal Gains." *Exceptional Child* 33:3 (November 1986):159–72. The introduction of "shared reading" between immigrant mothers and their children: a case study of five Cambodian mothers in New Zealand.

Goldstein, Beth L. "In Search of Survival: The Education and Integration of Hmong Refugee Girls." *Journal of Ethnic Studies* 16:2 (1988):21–27. Examines self-concept, acculturation, and ethnicity among Hmong girls in American high schools.

Hirano-Nakanishi, Marsha, and Elizabeth Osthimer. *The Right of Language Minority Students to a Fair Shot at a High School Diploma: A Legal Analysis* (NCBR Report). Los Alamitos, California: National Center for Bilingual Research Communication/Dissemination Office, 1983.

Hirayama, Kasumi K. "Asian Children's Adaptation to Public Schools." *Social Work in Education* 7:4 (Summer 1985):213–30. Findings suggest that the increasing number of Asian immigrant and refugee children adapt well to American public schools. Offers suggestions to educators on potential problem areas.

Hornberger, Nancy H. "Biliteracy Contexts, Continua, and Contrasts: Policy and Curriculum for Cambodian and Puerto Rican Students in Philadelphia." *Education and Urban Society* 24:2 (February 1992):196–211. A descriptive report of Cambodian and Puerto Rican students in two public elementary schools.

Ima, Kenji, and Ruben G. Rumbaut. "Southeast Asian Refugees in American Schools: A Comparison of Fluent–English Proficient and Limited–English Proficient Students." *Topics in Language Disorders* 9:3 (1989):54–75. Explores the differences and similarities between FEP and LEP Southeast Asian students as a basis for understanding their particular learning contexts and cultural, as well as socioemotional, factors affecting their academic progress.

Johnson, Ronald C., and Craig T. Nagoshi. "Parental Ability, Education and Occupation as Influences as Offspring Cognition in Hawaii and Korea." *Personality & Individual Differences* 6:4 (1985):413–23. Results indicate that although there are substantial variations across groups, parental ability and parental status each independently influence offspring performance in general. However, the influences of status generally are far weaker than the influence of parental cognitive ability.

Jordan, Cathie. "Translating Culture: From Ethnographic Information to Educational Program." *Anthropology and Education Quarterly* 16:2 (Summer 1985):104–23. A descriptive study on a multi-disciplinary educational research and development effort among Hawaiian children.

Keirstead, Carol. "Lowell Looks for Answers." *Equity and Choice* 3:2 (Winter 1987):28–33. Describes the Massachusetts bilingual education program to cope with the influx of Southeast Asian pupils.

Kiang, Peter N., and Vivian Wai-Fun Lee. "Exclusion or Contribution? Education K-12 Policy." In LEAP Asian/Pacific American Public Policy Institute and UCLA Asian American Studies Center, *The State of Asian/Pacific America A Public Policy Report: Policy Issues to the Year 2020* (pp. 25–48). Los Angeles: LEAP and UCLA AASC, 1993. Discusses demographic changes into the twenty-first century. Focuses on specific educational policy areas such as curriculum transformation, improving school climate, teacher training and recruitment, language and culture shift issues, support services, parent empowerment, and serving Asian/Pacific American students.

Kim, S. Peter. "Self-Concept, English Language Acquisition, and School Adaptation in Recently Immigrated Asian Children." *Journal of Children in Contemporary Society* 15:3 (Spring

1983):71–79. Explores the relationship among the level of self-concept, the degree of linguistic proficiency, and school adaptation and achievement through a preliminary study of twelve Korean immigrant children. Results indicate a positive correlation between the above three variables.

Lee, Esther-Yao. "Working Effectively with Asian Immigrant Parents." *Phi-Delta-Kappan* 70:3 (November 1988):223–25. Asian Americans defy stereotypes. Recommends educators to re-examine their personal feelings, prejudices, and expectations concerning immigrant parents.

Lee, Evelyn. "Cultural Factors in Working with Southeast Asian Refugee Adolescents." *Journal of Adolescence* 11:2 (June 1988):167–79. Addresses the cultural adaptation of East Asian adolescents in the United States and their implications for mental health treatment.

Lee, Everett S., and Xue Lan Rong. "The Educational and Economic Achievement of Asian Americans. Special Issue: Minorities." *Elementary School Journal* 88:5 (May 1988):545–60. Evaluates the academic achievement of Asian American immigrants and suggests that family structure, as well as middleman theory, may explain their success.

Leong, Frederick T., and Shiraz P. Tata. "Sex and Acculturation Differences in Occupational Values among Chinese-American Children." *Journal of Counseling Psychology* 37:2 (April 1990):208–12. Study indicates high-acculturation children value self-realization more than low-acculturation children and that boys value object orientation more than girls.

Levin, Paula. "The Impact of Preschool on Teaching and Learning in Hawaiian Families." *Anthropology and Education Quarterly* 23:1 (March 1992):59–72. Examines the daily living skills, family interaction, and school effectiveness among low-income Hawaiian children.

Lewis, Judy, Lue Vang, and Li-Rong Lilly Cheng. "Identifying the Language-Learning Difficulties of Hmong Students: Implications of Context and Culture." *Topics in Language Disorders* 9:3 (1989):21–37. Examines language assessment and intervention with LEP Hmong children: a case study of a hearing-impaired Hmong boy and the process involved in identifying his disabilities.

Marlowe, John, and Katharyn Culler. "How We're Adding Racial Balance to the Math Equation." *Executive Educator* 9:4 (April 1987):24–25. Describes an Albany, California, high school program addressing racial imbalances in remedial and advance math courses.

Matute-Bianchi, Maria Eugenia. "Ethinic Identities and Patterns of School Success and Failure among Mexican-Descent and Japanese-American students in a California High School: An Ethnographic Analysis." *American Journal of Education* 95:1(November 1986):233–55. Points out the interrelatedness of school performance, ethnic identity, and adults' perception of minority status as affecting high school students' performance. Findings suggest Japanese Americans have accommodated themselves linguistically and culturally to the white middle-class mainstream culture, and do not call attention to themselves in an ethnically explicit manner.

Miura, Irene T. "Mathematics Achievement as a Function of Language." *Journal of Educational Psychology* 79:1 (March 1987):79–82. Study of mathematical abilities of Japanese Americans. A study to correlate the cognitive learning-style of mathematics with the linguistic structure of the primary language of Americans and Japanese.

Morrow, Robert D. "Southeast Asian Child-Rearing Practices: Implications for Child and Youth Care Workers." *Child and Youth Care Quarterly* 18:4 (Winter 1989):273–87. Provides cross-cultural differences and emphasizes the issue of culture as well as parent-child relationships for educators and workers of Southeast Asian children.

Morrow, Robert D. "Southeast-Asian Parental Involvement: Can It Be a Reality?" *Elementary School Guidance and Counseling* 23:4 (April 1989):289–97. Explains how Southeast Asian parents' school participation can be inhibited due to their cultural values and background. Discusses various cultural values and implications for educators.

Mortland, Carol A., and Maura G. Egan. "Vietnamese Youth in American Foster Care." *Social Work* 32:3 (May 1987):240–45. Study involving formal and informal interviews of Vietnamese children and their foster parents regarding their adjustment difficulties to the United States.

Nakanishi, Don T., and Hirano-Nakanishi, Marsha, eds. *The Education of Asian and Pacific Americans: Historical Perspectives and Prescriptions for the Future*. Phoenix: Oryx Press,

1983. Includes articles by Bob Suzuki, Florence Yoshiwara, Kenyon S. Chan and Sau-Lim Tsang, Bok-Lim C. Kim, Federico M. Macaranas, Vuong G. Thuy, and Bella Zi Bell. Addresses various issues such as the education of Asian and Pacific Americans, the future of Korean-American children, the socioeconomic issues that affect the education of Filipino Americans, as well as myths concerning Japanese Americans.

Nguyen, Nga A., and Harold L. Williams. "Transition from East to West: Vietnamese Adolescents and Their Parents." *Journal of the American Academy of Child & Adolescent Psychiatry* 28:4 (July 1989):505–15. Analyzes questionnaire data based on parental and adolescent attitudes of family values. Differences between them place strain on Vietnamese refugee families.

Olsen, Laurie. *Crossing the School House Border.* San Francisco: California Tomorrow, 1988. Reports that at least one in six California schoolchildren is an immigrant—two and a half times the proportion ten years ago.

Omizo, Michael M., and Sharon A. Omizo. "Counseling Hawaiian Children." *Journal of Elementary School Guidance and Counseling* 23:4 (April 1989):282–88. Discusses the cultural difference in group orientation, concept of time, and communicative organization. Recommends strategies for counseling Hawaiian children.

Pang, Valerie O. *et al.* "Self-Concepts of Japanese-American Children." *Journal of Cross-Cultural Psychology* 16:1 (March 1985):99–109. A comparative study of Japanese-American and Anglo-American children on their self-perception. Findings show that the Japanese-Americans have a higher self-concept in the areas of behavior and popularity than Anglo-American children, but a lower self-concept in physical characteristics.

Pang, Valerie Ooka. "Asian American Children: A Diverse Population." *The Educational Forum* 55:1 (Fall 1990):49–65. Asserts the term "Asian Americans" encompasses a highly diverse group and criticizes the inaccurate model minority stereotype to be one which limits the development of educational programs that addresses their various needs.

"Pilipino/English Bilingual Materials." El Monte, California: Greenshower Corporation, 1989. Catalog of primary language, bilingual materials, and dictionaries for Pilipino students, kindergarten through twelfth grade.

Ramirez, Bruce A., *et al.* "Culturally and Linguistically Diverse Children: Black Children, Hispanic Children, Asian Children, and Young American Indian Children." *Teaching Exceptional Children* 20:4 (Summer 1988):45–51. Addressing the needs for parental involvement, curriculum change, and "intervention" measures for children with cultural and linguistically diverse background: Blacks, Hispanics, Asians, and American Indians.

Rescorla, Leslie, and Sachiko Okuda. "Modular Patterns in Second Language Acquisition." *Applied Psycholinguistics* 8:3 (1987):281–308. Studies acquisition of English as a second language by a Japanese five-year-old.

Rundall, R. A., and F. Fernandez. "Asian Teachers: A New Dimension." *Clearing House* 60 (October 1986):91–92. Recommends bilingual Asian teachers to meet the needs of native and second-language performance in the schools.

Saeki, Kaeko, Florence A. Clark, and Stanley P. Azen. "Performance of Japanese and Japanese-American Children on the Motor Accuracy-Revised and Design Copying Tests of the Southern California Sensory Integration Tests." *American Journal of Occupational Therapy* 39:2 (February 1985):103–9. A cross-cultural study investigating the effects of cultural differences on a child's sensory-motor skills. Findings suggest that Japan-born children performed better than the American-born children on given performance tests.

Sokoloff, Burton, Jean Carling, and Hien Pham. "Five-Year Follow-Up of Vietnamese Refugee Children in the United States." *Clinical Pediatrics* 23:10 (October 1984):565–70. A survey on Vietnamese refugee children placed in adoptive and foster families show marked improvement in the children's psycho-social adjustment in school after the first year. Comments that school and social problems were minimal, in particular for students who were adopted or had advanced preparation and guidance from agencies.

Speidel, Gisela E., Roland G. Tharp, and Linda Kobayashi. "Is There a Comprehension Problem for Children Who Speak Nonstandard English? A Study of Children with Hawaiian-English Backgrounds." *Applied Psycholinguistics* 6:1 (March 1985):83–96. A descriptive study of parental involvement in Chinese-American families and their value of effort over innate ability to explain their children's academic achievement.

Spencer, David. "Traditional Bilingual Education and the Socialization of Immigrants." *Harvard Educational Review* 58:2 (May 1988):133–53. Suggests the socialization process of bilingual education as preventing the immigrant children from attaining educational fluency in either their own language or English.

Stevenson, Harold *et al.* "Cognitive Performance and Academic Achievement of Japanese, Chinese, and American Children." *Child Development* 56:3 (June 1985):716–34. The testing of cognitive differences in mathematics and reading among children in the elementary grades.

Stone, B. J. "Prediction of Achievement by Asian American and White Children." *Journal of School Psychology* 30:1 (Spring 1992):91–100. A comparative analysis of Asian Americans and white children, ages six to seventeen, using different assessment scales. Findings show that white children's scores were overpredicted on basic number skills, and Asian Americans were underpredicted when common regression lines were used.

Strouse, Joan. "Educational Responsibility: The Hmong Experience." *Equity and Excellence* 22 (1986):115–18. A report on the U.S. educational system's response to the needs of an agriculturally based tribal group, the Hmongs.

Sung, Betty. "Bicultural Conflicts in Chinese Immigrant Children." *Journal of Comparative Family Studies* 16:2 (Summer 1985):255–69. Investigates problems of Chinese immigrant students such as culture shock, school adjustment, and assimilation to values and customs. Argues that children are immobilized when faced with situations that require drastic modification of their values and behavior, and school counselors should instill a healthy respect for cultural differences in immigrant children.

Takaki, Ronald. "The Myth of Ethnicity: Scholarship of the Anti-Affirmative Action Backlash." *Journal of Ethnic Studies* 10:1 (Spring 1982):17–42. School personnel need sensitivity training to cope with the influx of Hispanic and Asian students in the public schools.

Tollefson, James W. *Alien Winds: The Reeducation of America's Indochinese Refugees.* New York: Praeger Publishers, 1989. Contains an in-depth examination of U.S. refugee educational programs. Provides recommendations for both overseas centers and domestic resettlement programs.

Tomine, Satsuki. "*Jan Ken Po Gakko*: A Japanese-American Cultural Education Program." *Journal of Multicultural Counseling and Development* 13:4 (October 1985):164–69. Evaluates a cultural enrichment program as a counseling technique to increase the self-concept of the Japanese-American children.

Tran, My Luong T. "Maximizing Vietnamese Parent Involvement in Schools." *NASSP Bulletin* 76:540 (January 1992):76–79. Surveys show that older Vietnamese had more problems with language acculturation than the younger generation, and women had more language-learning problems than men.

Tsang, Sau-lim. "The Mathematics Education of Asian Americans." *Journal for Research in Mathematics Education* 15:2 (March 1984):114–22. Reveal that most studies have identified the problems faced by immigrant students in taking mathematics tests. Research has looked into the cognitive differences between immigrant students and students educated entirely in the United States.

Walker, Constance L. "Learning English: The Southeast Asian Refugee Experience." *Topics in Language Disorders* 5:4 (September 1985):53–65. Examines the language-learning process among Southeast Asians. Emphasizes the teaching of survival skills, vocabulary, and grammar, rather than pronunciation.

Weaver, Brenda, and Diane J. Sawyer. "Promoting Language and Reading Development for Two Vietnamese Children." *Reading Horizons* 24, no. 2 (Winter 1984):111–18. A case study of two Vietnamese students' attainment toward linguistic instructional goals.

Wehrly, Bea. "Cultural Diversity from an International Perspective: Special Issue: Cross-Cultural Counseling." *Journal of Multicultural Counseling and Development* 16:1 (January 1988):3–15. Investigates the backgrounds of Indochinese refugees students. Limitations of Western monocultural counseling are delineated. Suggests school counselors to be aware of cross-cultural differences.

Yao, Esther Lee. "Roles of Federal Government for Asian LEP Students." *Contemporary Education* 59 (Spring 1988):169–72. In order to meet the needs of culturally diverse Asian American LEP students, the role of the government has to alter the direction of bilingual education. Recommendations such as parent education for Asian parents, more reliable research on Asian LEP students and proper representation of Asian staff and personnel are among those presented.

Yao, Esther-Lee. "Adjustment Needs of Asian Immigrant Children." *Elementary School Guidance and Counseling* 19:3 (Feb 1985): 222–27. Discusses parent-child relationships and learning styles of Asian children. Suggests intervention strategies for school personnel to help these children. Findings include that children tend to be efficient when given definite goals and are in a well-structured, quiet learning environment.

Yao, E.L. and C.C. Hwang. "Teaching English to Asian Immigrant Children." *Educational Horizons* 66 (Fall 1987):43–45. Examines problems encountered by Asian immigrant children and verifies the need for teachers to become sensitive to the underlying reasons for student errors.

Yoon, Keumsil-Kim, and Gladys Nussenbaum. "Assessment of Linguistic Needs of Korean American Students in Northern New Jersey: Implications for Future Directions." *NABE, The Journal for the National Association for Bilingual Education* 12 (Fall 1987):51–63. Suggests an Asian Resource Center to cope with the cost-effective means of meeting Korea-American children's language proficiency in both English and Korean. Addresses the need to educate Korean-American parents about the school system.

HIGHER EDUCATIONAL ISSUES

"Asian American Students." *East Wind* 2:2 (Fall/Winter 1983):19–49. Short articles written by thirteen students discussing major concerns of Asian American students today.

Atkinson, Donald R., Joseph G. Ponterotto, and Arthur R. Sanchez. "Attitudes of Vietnamese and Anglo-American Students toward Counseling." *Journal of College Student Personnel* 25:5 (1984):448–52. Compares their attitudes toward counseling and their preferences for help providers by way of questionnaires. Findings reveal that Anglo-American students held more positive feelings towards counseling than Vietnamese students.

Bagasao, Paula Y., and Bob H. Suzuki, eds. "Asian and Pacific Americans: Behind the Myths." *Change: The Magazine of Higher Learning* (November/December 1989). Special theme issue with articles by Bob H. Suzuki, Jayjia Hsia and Marsha Hirano-Nakanishi, Paula Y. Bagasao, Don T. Nakanishi, Sucheng Chan, Ninotchka Rosca, Shirley Hune, Russell C. Leong, Rosemary Park, and Roy H. Saigo. Interviews college counselors, administrators, and students to understand the real Asian and Pacific American experience. Defies myths such as the "whiz kid" and "model minority" and contends that many students have unmet educational and counseling needs.

Biemiller, L. "Asian Students Fear Top Colleges Use Quota Systems." *Chronicle of Higher Education* 33 (19 November 1986):33. Discusses the charges that U.S. colleges discriminate against Asian students on racial grounds. Also adds that competition in the sciences is high because Asian students have a high academic interest in that area.

Bunzel, John, and Jeffrey K. D. Au. "Diversity or Discrimination? Asian Americans in College." *Public Interest* (Spring 1987):49–63. Asian college admissions blocked by "institutional barriers." Discusses admission rate of Asian Americans and access to higher education. Results indicate that the rate is below the average admission rate. Reasons are provided.

Bunzel, John H. "Affirmative-Action Admissions: How It 'Works' at UC Berkeley." *Public Interest* 93 (Fall 1988):111–29. Efforts to increase hiring minority faculties in California colleges have been concentrated on proportional representation, rather than helping students succeed in school.

Bunzel, John H. "Minority Faculty Hiring: Problems and Prospects." *American Scholar* (Winter 1990):39–52. Efforts to increase faculty recruitment of minorities through affirmative action have been insufficient due to the university's preferential hiring.

Cablas, Amando. "Pilipino Americans and the Scholastic Aptitude Test at the University of Hawaii at Manoa: A Review of Literature." *Social Process in Hawaii* 33 (1991):91–106. Reviews the current literature on the SAT Pilipino American academic performance at the university, and discusses whether the SAT is a useful measure for ethnic minorities. Concludes that despite low SAT verbal scores, Pilipino Americans are able to succeed at the university level.

Cadieux, Ron A. "Advising and Counseling the International Student." *New Directions for Student Services* 36 (Winter 1986):51–63. Discusses problems encountered by foreign students and suggests that college counselors have cultural awareness and sensitivity. Provides advice for school counselors.

Carmody, Deirdre. "Secrecy and Tenure: An Issue for High Court." *New York Times* (6 December 1989):B8. U.S. Supreme Court to hear tenure denial case of Rosalie Tung alleging discrimination due to sex and national origin.

Carter, Lindy. Keane. "Minority Interest." *Currents* 14:4 (April 1988):46–48. Describes Brown University's Third World Alumni Activities Program. A descriptive report that addresses the need to involve Asian Americans in alumni activities, student recruitment, public relations, and fund-raising. Discusses available programs.

Castillo, Cristy Alicuben, and Sandilee Bunda Minamishin. "Filipino Recruitment and Retention at the University of Hawai'i at Manoa." *Social Process in Hawaii* 33:(1991):130–41. Seeks to identify various obstacles that Filipino students face in seeking higher education and to develop recommendations to overcome these obstacles.

Cohon, J. Donald, *et al. Primary Prevention and the Promotion of Mental Health in the ESL Classroom: A Handbook for Teachers*. New York: American Council for Nationalities Service, 1986. Provides ESL teachers with strategies for coping with stress felt by refugees, especially through the use of community resources.

College Board. *Scholastic Aptitude Test Scores*, 1987. Princeton: Educational Testing Service, 1987. Asian American students accounted for highest scores in mathematics on SAT college entrance tests, but their verbal scores in California dipped below last year's scores.

"College Enrollment by Ethnic and Racial Group." *Chronicle of Higher Education* 38:28 (18 March 1992):A35. Provides data on Asian American's college enrollment for 1980 and 1990, which includes gender data and educational level upon graduation.

Cummings, William K., and Wing-Cheung So. "The Preference of Asian Overseas Students for the United States: An Examination of the Context." *Higher Education* 14:4 (August 1985):403–23. Discusses the factors that influence overseas Asian students' choice of U.S. schools of higher education, including U.S. immigration quota and opportunities for financial help.

Dao, M. "Designing Assessment Procedures for Educationally At-Risk Southeast Asian American Students." *Learning Disabilities* 24:10 (December 1991):594–601. Asserts the need to help Southeast Asian American refugee college students with acculturation difficulties (also with basic skills in reading and writing) before they can benefit from instruction.

Dion, Kenneth L., and Paul H. Yee. "Ethnicity and Personality in a Canadian Context." *Journal of Social Psychology* 127:2 (April 1987):175–82. Analyzes 635 college students (data on Japanese and Chinese students included) and found a greater gender role differentiation among Asians than Europeans.

Endo, Russell. "Asian Americans and Higher Education." *Phylon* 14:4 (Winter 1980):367–78. Contends the nature of Asian American involvement in higher education is often misunderstood. Addresses problem areas in higher education: (1) the reluctance of universities to hire qualified Asian American administrators, (2) stress resulting from pressures for high levels of school achievement by family and community, and (3) the lack of oral and writing ability among Asian Americans.

Escueta, Eugenia, and Eileen O'Brien. "Asian Americans in Higher Education: Trends and Issues." *Research Briefs* 2:4 (1991):1–11. Presents trends in both population and higher education and their implications for Asian Americans. In addition to identifying major problems connected with Asian Americans in education, it investigates the status of Asian American students and faculty in relation to other ethnic groups.

"Fact-File: Minority Enrollments at More Than 3,100 Colleges and Universities." *Chronicle of Higher Education* 29:15 (5 December 1984): 13–14; 16–18; 20–22; 24. Data collected by the

Department of Education on students enrolled in the U.S. colleges and universities and their ethnic origins, including foreign students.

Farrell, Charles S. "Institutions Deny Setting Quotas for Asian American Admissions." *Black Issues in Higher Education* 6:3 (13 April 1989):10–11. The case of elite colleges' setting admission quotas on Asian students. Blame now on high schools for failing to prepare Asian students to be more actively involved in extracurricular activities.

Farrell, Walter C., Jr., and Cloyzelle K. Jones. "Recent Racial Incidents in Higher Education: A Preliminary Perspective." *Urban Review* 20:2 (Fall 1988):211–26. Discusses race relations and the resurgence of campus violence in predominantly white colleges.

Fernandez, M. A. "Issues in Counseling Southeast Asian Students." *Journal of Multicultural Counseling and Development* 16 (October 1988):157–66. Delineates factors that bring about culture shock for Southeast Asian students. Some generalizations are made in regard to their socialization to the United States.

Flaskerud, Jacquelyn H., and Adeline M. Nyamathi. "An AIDS Education Program for Vietnamese Women." *New York State Journal of Medicine* 88:12 (December 1988):632–37. A acquired immune deficiency syndrome educational program delivered by a Vietnamese educator to 316 Vietnamese revealed that a didactic program can create changes in attitude, behavior, and knowledge levels in the participants.

Gordon, Larry. "Cal State L.A. Seeks Role as Gateway for Community." *Los Angeles Times* (19 May 1990):A1+. Out of an enrollment of 20,804 students, 28.5 percent are Asian, 30 percent Latino, and 11.5 percent African American—the highest representation of any major university in California.

Gust, Kelly. "Asians Say Bias in Education Troubles Them." *The Tribune* (11 May 1986):D9. States that University of California has been trying to cut back on Asian enrollments. Suggests that Asian Americans demand their fair and equitable treatment in education.

Hassan, Thomas E. "Asian American Admissions: Debating Discrimination." *College Board Review* 142 (Winter 1987):42–45. Discusses the problem of quotas on Asian Americans' admissions to U.S. colleges.

Hess, Robert D., Chih-mei Chang, and Teresa M. McDevitt. "Cultural Variations in Family Beliefs about Children's Performance in Mathematics: Comparisons among People's Republic of China, Chinese-American, and CaucAsian American Families." *Journal of Educational Psychology* 79:2 (June 1987):179–88. Interviews of mothers and their sixth-graders concerning achievement in mathematics in the People's Republic of China, and in the United States.

Hsia, Jayjia, and Marsha Hirano-Nakanishi. "The Demographics of Diversity: Asian Americans and Higher Education." *Change* (November/December 1989):20–27. Reviews demographic trends highlighting the tremendous diversity of the nation's Asian American population, and examines recent higher education enrollment. Discusses tensions over Asian American participation in higher education.

Hune, Shirley. "Opening the American Mind and Body: The Role of Asian American Studies." *Change* (November/December 1989):56–63. Purports that Asian American studies should be seen as part of a social movement to change education in all its facets. It helps to shed light on institutional racism, issues of class and culture. It emphasizes the empowerment of students and teachers and the crucial link between the universities and the larger community.

Hvifeldt, Christina. "Traditional Culture, Perceptual Style, and Learning: The Classroom Behavior of Hmong Adults." *Adult Education Quarterly* 36:2 (Winter 1986):65–77. Discusses how cultural factors affect adult Hmong learning behavior in the classroom. Focuses on Hmong interaction with other classmates and their use of classroom materials.

James, Thomas. "Life Begins with Freedom: The College Nisei, 1942–1945." *History of Education Quarterly* 25 (Spring/Summer 1985): 155–74. A report on the 4,000 Japanese Americans who were allowed to enter higher education in the United States during the internment years.

Jaschik, Scott. "The Year Ahead: Minorities." *Chronicle of Higher Education* 34:2 (2 September 1987):A88–91. Asserts Asian Americans are misunderstood by college officials because many use the term "Asian" and do not understand the vagueness of the term. Differentiates between

Southeast Asians who came in 1975, Laotians who have come in the past few years, and the Chinese and Japanese Americans who have come generations ago.

———. "Conservative Lawmaker Attracts Interest and Ire with Crusade for Asian American Students." *Chronicle of Higher Education* (15 November 1989):A27, A32–33. Focus on Congressman Dana Rohrabacher of Southern California and whether he is an advocate for Asian American college students. Discusses how many Asian American leaders believe his real motivation is to assault the affirmative action programs they support.

———. "U.S. Finds Harvard Did Not Exclude Asian Americans." *The Chronicle of Higher Education* (17 October 1990):A1, A26. Investigation of Harvard's admission policies and found no evidence of bias against Asian Americans or the use of quotas to limit their access to higher education.

Justus, Joyce Bennet. *The University of California in the Twenty-first Century: Successful Approaches to Faculty Diversity.* San Francisco: Office of the President, University of California, 1987. "Ethnographic" study of UC campuses as compared to fourteen other institutions, including Columbia, Stanford, Michigan, North Carolina State, and Yale.

Katayama, Mary. "Doing the Right Thing: The Critical Role of Students in the Tenure Campaign." *Amerasia Journal* 16:1 (1990):109–17. Special theme issue with articles by Glenn Omatsu, Dale Minami, Mary Katayama, John Chien, M. Dick Osumi, Karen Umemoto, Don T. Nakanishi, and Gann Matsuda. Tenure campaign of UCLA Professor Don Nakanishi and its effects on the larger issues of justice and equal representation for Asian/Pacific Americans.

Kember, David, and Lyn Gow. "A Challenge to the Anecdotal Stereotype of the Asian Student." *Studies in Higher Education* 16:2 (1991):117–28. This report challenges the stereotypical notion that Asian university students' rely heavily on rote learning.

Kossoudji, S. A. "English Language Ability and the Labor Market Opportunities of Hispanic and East Asian Immigrant Men." *Journal of Labor Economics* 6 (April 1988):205–28. Findings in the labor market of the high cost of Hispanics having a language deficiency than most East Asians.

Kraska, Marie F. "Vocational Education and Bilingual Education Addressing the Needs of Indochinese Students in Vocational Classrooms." *Journal for Vocational Special Needs Education* 13:3 (Spring 1991):27–31. Addresses the need for vocational teachers to develop educational strategies to better serve Indochinese "Limited-English-Speaking" students.

Kuo, Shih-yu, and Spees, Emil R. "Chinese-American Student Life-styles: A Comparative Study." *Journal of College Student Personnel* 24:2 (March 1983):111–17. An analysis of the differences in goal-orientation between Chinese students and American college students in Taiwan.

Leong, Frederick T., Brent Mallinckrodt, and Mary M. Kralj. "Cross-Cultural Variations in Stress and Adjustment among Asian and Caucasian Graduate Students." *Journal of Multicultural Counseling & Development* 18:1 (January 1990):19–28. Findings on stress management show that Asian graduate students experience fewer stressful life events and report fewer chronic health problems than Caucasian graduate students.

Li, Victor Hao. "Asian Discrimination: Fact or Fiction?" *College Board Review* 149 (Fall 1988):20–23+. Discusses the problems in admission procedure for Asian American students in U.S. institutions of higher education.

Loo, Chalsa, M., and Garry Rolison. "Alienation of Ethnic Minority Students at a Predominantly White University." *Journal of Higher Education* 57:1 (January/February 1986):58–77. Addresses the issue of alienation among minority students in an undergraduate college and identifies the factors that may reduce the ethnic "clustering."

Maeda, Sharon. "Activist to Educator: Warren T. Furutani." *Tozai Times* (March 1987):1+. Suggests developing multicultural activities to enhance cultural awareness of diverse ethnic groups, including the Asian/Pacific Islanders.

Mathews, Linda. "When Being Best Isn't Good Enough." *Los Angeles Times Magazine* (19 July 1987):22–28. Discrimination against Asian American college applicants.

Matsuda, Gann. " 'Only the Beginning': Continuing Our Battle for Empowerment." *Amerasia Journal* 16:1 (1990):159–69. Chronology of the tenure campaign of UCLA Professor Don Nakanishi.

Mau, Rosalind Y. "Barriers to Higher Education for Asian/Pacific-American Females." *Urban Review*

22:3 (1990):183–97. Although Asian/Pacific Americans do not follow "model minority" stereotype, many have scored high on mathematics and sciences. Asian-Pacific females, however, generally are not academically prepared for higher education.

Marsella, Anthony J., and Charles J. Golden. "The Structure of Cognitive Abilities in Americans of Japanese and of European Ancestry in Hawaii." *Journal of Social Psychology* 112 (October 1980):19–30. A comparative study of 118 American college students of Japanese and north European ancestry. Suggests that structure of cognitive skills may be a function of heredity and cultural experiences.

Menez, Herminia Q. "Agyu and the Skyworld: The Philippine Folk Epic, and Multicultural Education." *Amerasia Journal* 13 (1986–87):135–49. Suggests including folk epic of the Philippinos to enrich a multicultural curriculum.

Meredith, G. M. "Ethnicity and Sex Differences in the Concept of the Ideal College Teacher." *Psychological Reports* 63 (August 1988):332–34. A comparative study on the ratings of an ideal teacher by 1,186 Japanese-American and 594 CaucAsian American college students. Examines college teacher characteristics, ethnic and racial differences.

Minami, Dale. "Guerrilla War at UCLA: Political and Legal Dimensions of the Tenure Battle." *Amerasia Journal* 16:1 (1990):81–107. Describes the struggle of Professor Don Nakanishi's three-year tenure battle and what he had come to symbolize.

Minatoya, Lydia Yuriko and William E. Sedlacek. "Another Look at the Melting Pot: Perceptions of Asian American Undergraduates." *Journal of College Student Personnel* (July 1981):328–36. A study of Asian American college students in terms of demographics and their attitudes on self-expression, familial responsibilities, racial conspicuousness, and racial discrimination.

Mohan, B. A., and W. A. Y. Lo. "Academic Writing and Chinese Students: Transfer and Developmental Factors." *TESOL Quarterly* 19 (September 1985):515–34. Discusses the organizational skills in expository writing by Chinese students of English as a Second Language (ESL) to be comparable to native speakers.

Mooney, Carolyn J. "Affirmative-Action Goals, Coupled with Tiny Number of Minority Ph.D.'s, Set off Faculty Recruiting Frenzy." *Chronicle of Higher Education* 35:47 (2 August 1989): 10–11. Affirmative action in hiring minority faculty members has steered attention away from improving undergraduate and graduate programs.

Moore, Thomas H. "Some Top Colleges Admit More Asian Americans, but Deny that the Increase Is Result of Pressure." *Chronicle of Higher Education* 35:42 (28 June 1989):A21–22. A denial of allegation of racial discrimination by elite colleges in light of the high record of admission of Asian American students.

Morales, Royal F. "Filipino American Studies: A Promise and an Unfinished Agenda." *Amerasia Journal* 13:1 (1986–87):119–24. Provides a teacher's perspective on the development of a Filipino American studies program.

Nakanishi, Don T. "Asian/Pacific Americans and Selective Undergraduate Admissions." *Journal of College Admission* 118 (Winter 1988):17–26. A four-year data collection of the undergraduate admission rates of Asian/Pacific Americans to private and public colleges in California, and the Northeast.

———. "A Quota on Excellence? The Asian American Admissions Debate." *Change* (November/December 1989):38–47. Discusses the emergence of the debate, and the issue of quotas on Asian American applicants to selective universities. Purports that Asian Americans only desire equality and justice.

———. "Why I Fought." *Amerasia Journal* 16:1 (1990):139–58. Personal reflections on a three-year tenure battle at UCLA. The fight to gain tenure in the University of California system is an important step toward the realization of self-identity for other Asian Americans.

Ng, Johnny. "Connecticut Prof Takes Asians' Fight to Feds." *Asian Week* (20 July 1990):1+. Prof. Paul Bock's struggle against anti-Asian racism at University of Connecticut.

Njeri, Itabari. "Academic Acrimony: Minority Professors Claim Racism Plays Role in Obtaining Tenure." *Los Angeles Times* (20 September 1989). Includes discussion of Don Nakanishi and Halford Fairchild tenure cases at UCLA.

Okamura, Jonathan Y. "Filipino Educational Status and Achievement at the University of Hawai'i."

Social Process in Hawaii 33 (1991):107–29. Provides a demographic and educational background characteristics of Filipino freshman students at the University of Hawai'i at Manoa between 1979 and 1986. Examines their academic achievement in terms of their grade point average, attrition rate and academic status, and also at institutional constraints that restrict their access to higher education.

Okutsu, James K. "Pedagogic `Hegemonicide' and the Asian American Student." *Amerasia Journal* 15:1 (1989):233–42. A study on understanding the needs and goals of Asian American students from their points of view, including their college experience. The survey included students of Japanese, Korean, Southeast Asian, and Pacific Islander descent.

Oliver, Melvin L., and James H. Johnson, Jr. "The Challenge of Diversity in Higher Education." *Urban Review* 20:2 (Fall 1988):139–45. Cites four papers of recent research on ethnic diversity in higher education and their failure to address group-specific and comparative approaches to ethnic issues on campus.

Ong, Paul M., with assistance from Paul Schimek, Yuko Aoyama, and Glen Kitayama. "California's Asian Population: Past Trends and Projections for the Year 2000." Los Angeles: UCLA Graduate School of Architecture and Urban Planning, May 1989. An analysis of demographic factors provide insights into the challenges facing educational policymakers. Findings suggest that there is a lack of meaningful public education for Asian immigrants as well as unfair competition for admissions to colleges.

Osumi, M. Dick. "No Middle Ground: A Personal View of the Tenure Campaign." *Amerasia Journal* 16:1 (1990):123–29. Tenure campaign of UCLA Professor Don Nakanishi. Discusses civil rights issue and racial discrimination against Asian Americans and Pacific Americans since the 1970s and 1980s.

Pak, Anita Wan-Ping, Kenneth L. Dion, and Karen K. Dion. "Correlates of Self-Confidence with English among Chinese Students in Toronto." *Canadian Journal of Behavioral Science* 17:4 (October 1985):369–78. Study of Chinese college students and their degree of assimilation, psychological adjustment and confidence with English through self-reports.

Pang, Valerie Ooka. "About Teachers and Teaching; Ethnic Prejudice: Still Alive and Hurtful." *Harvard Educational Review* 58 (August 1988):373–79. Naive beliefs and inaccurate information about the homogeneity of Asian Americans have obstructed a change in curriculum, counseling, and instructional strategies toward Asian American students.

Powers, Stephen, Melisa Choroszy, Peggy Douglas, and Brent A. Cool. "Attributions for Success and Failure in Algebra Among Men and Women Attending American Samoa Community College." *Psychological Reports* 60:1 (February 1987):47–51. Analyzes attribution patterns of Samoan community college students and discovered that both sexes attributed success in math to human effort and did not attribute failure to the complexity of the subject matter.

Powers, Stephen, Melisa Chroszy, and Peggy Douglas. "Attributions for Success and Failure of Japanese-American and Anglo-American University Students." *Psychology: A Quarterly Journal of Human Behavior* 24:3 (1987):17–23. Assesses academic achievement of 195 Japanese-American and Anglo-American college students and their attributions for academic success and failure. Findings include cultural variation between the two groups.

Powers, Stephen, Melisa Choroszy, Peggy Douglas, and Brent A. Cool. "Attributions for Success and Failure in Algebra of Samoan Community College Students: A Profile Analysis." *Journal of Instructional Psychology* 13:1 (March 1986):3–9. Examines Samoan community college students and their attribution patterns in math. Looks at measures of motivation, self-esteem, and anxiety levels. Findings include no differences in attribution for success and failure between gender groups.

Quan, D. "Asian Americans and Law: Fighting the Myth of Success." *Journal of Legal Education* 38 (December 1988):619–28. The parity of Asian Americans entering the law profession must be overcome by a change in attitude and role perception by both Asian Americans and Americans involved in mainstream economy.

"Racial and Ethnic Makeup of College and University Enrollments." *Chronicle of Higher Education* 32:21 (23 July 1986):25–34. Quantitative data on minority enrollment, including foreign students, in American colleges and universities.

Sanai, Cyrus M. "No One Benefits When a Law School Turns Out Lawyers Who Have Marginal Qualifications." *Chronicle of Higher Education* (8 June 1988):2. Essay opposing law school special admissions programs for minority groups.

Shih, Frank H. "Asian American Students on College Campuses." *Education Digest* 54 (October 1988):59–62. Examines how Asian American students cope with emotional, social, and academic stresses. Supports the fact that these students are experiencing greater levels of emotional and social adjustment difficulties despite the perception of Asian Americans as the model minority.

Shizuru, Lanette S., and Anthony J. Marsella. "The Sensory Processes of Japanese-American and CaucAsian American Students." *Journal of Social Psychology* 114 (August 1981):147–58. Study of 171 Japanese American and white American male college students and their visual, auditory, and kinesthetic-tactile perception. Findings include data on Japanese Americans and their tendency to rely heavily on spatial-kinesthetic information.

"Student Resource List." *Z Magazine* (July-August 1990):68. Addresses of student organizations, including national Asian American and Pacific Islander formations.

Sue, David, Steve Ino, and Diane M. Sue. "Nonassertiveness of Asian Americans: An Inaccurate Assumption?" *Journal of Counseling Psychology* 30:4 (October 1983):581–88. Investigates whether Asian Americans are nonassertive and if race of the individual with whom they mostly interact is an influential variable on assertion level. Suggests that Chinese Americans were as assertive as Caucasian Americans on all behavioral levels and that race was not an important variable in their degree of assertiveness.

Sue, David. "Sexual Experience and Attitudes of Asian American Students." *Psychological Reports* 51:2 (1982):401–2. Findings suggest that over 80 percent of both sexes of Asian American students (17 male and 19 female) had engaged in premarital sex.

Sue, Stanley, and Jennifer Abe. "Predictors of Academic Achievement Among Asian American and White Students." College Board Report No. 88-11. New York: College Board Publications, 1988. Asserts predictors of college academic success varies by ethnicity. Examined predictors for Asian American students enrolled as freshmen in any of the eight University of California campuses, and determined whether the predictors varied according to membership within different Asian American groups, major, language spoken, and gender.

Taborek, Elizabeth, and Leanor Adamowski. "To Seal Up One's Mouth Three Times: Understanding the Education and Linguistic Differences That Confront Chinese Students in ESL Writing Classes." *TESL Talk* 15:3 (Summer 1984):88–95. Discusses Chinese students' problem with English-writing skills in Canadian universities. Suggests dealing with the problem by way of understanding the Chinese culture and language.

Takagi, Dana Y. *The Retreat from Race: Asian American Admissions and Racial Politics.* New Brunswick: Rutgers University Press, 1992. Maintains that changes in affirmative action grew out of discourses on racial minorities in higher education. Argues that the shift in the organizing principle of affirmative action should be viewed as evidence of a profound crisis in how educational policymakers battle with racial differences in academic achievement.

Umemoto, Karen. "Victory on the Tenure Front: A Summary of Lessons." *Amerasia Journal* 16:1 (1990):131–38. Tenure campaign of UCLA Professor Don Nakanishi. Describes key issues and social movements among Asian Americans following Professor Don Nakanishi's battle for tenureship.

Wang, L. Ling-Chi. "Meritocracy and Diversity in Higher Education: Discrimination against Asian Americans in the Post-*Bakke* Era." *Urban Review* 20:3 (1988):189–209. Studies recent changes in admissions and policies of prestigious universities and assesses the impact on Asian Americans. Concludes that current efforts to limit Asian American admissions are a manifestation of racial bias deeply woven into the fabric of society.

Wang, L. Ling-Chi. "Trends in Admissions for Asian Americans in Colleges and Universities: Higher Education Policy." In LEAP Asian/Pacific American Public Policy Institute and UCLA Asian American Studies Center, *The State of Asian/Pacific America: A Public Policy Report: Policy Issues to the Year 2020* (pp. 49–59). Los Angeles: LEAP and UCLA AASC, 1993. Provides a historical background and analysis of patterns of Asian enrollment in higher education.

Addresses the controversies over the "overrepresentation of Asian American students," the "model minority" and "reverse discrimination." Presents what Asian Americans must do to protect their rights.

CAREER

Amparano, Julie, *et al.* "Ethnicity Can Be a Plus." *Social Education* 53:3 (March 1989):169–71. A descriptive report that includes interview data of three journalists who discuss how their cultural background has enriched their job performances.

Evanoski, Patricia Orsatti, and Florence Wu Tse. "Career Awareness Program for Chinese and Korean American Parents." *Journal of Counseling and Development* 67 (April 1989):472–74. Addresses the issue of community awareness of bilingual careers for American Chinese and American Koreans. Provides strategies that may be effective in working with other ethnic minorities.

Hsia, Jayjia. *Asian Americans in Higher Education and at Work.* Hillsdale, N.J.: Lawrence Erlbaum Associates, 1988. Synthesizes the issues that confront Asian Americans with diverse backgrounds and aspirations. Summarizes the overall achievement of Asian Americans in the United States postsecondary education institutions, and current information about Asian Americans and their work (with a closer look at newcomers with limited English ability).

Leong, F. T. L. "Career Development of Asian Americans." *Journal of College Student Personnel* 26 (November 1985): 539–46. Identifies the important social factors relevant to the career advancement of Asian Americans: process of acculturation; societal barriers to occupational aspirations; and personality traits.

Konrad, Allison M., and Jeffrey Pfeffer. "Understanding the Hiring of Women and Minorities in Educational Institutions." *Sociology of Education* 64:3 (July 1991):141–57. Addresses the gender issue of employment practices. Selection is positively affected by previous employees' gender.

Leong, Frederick T., and William E. Sedlacek. "Academic and Career Needs of International and United States College Students." *Journal of College Student Development* 30:2 (March 1989):106–11. A comparative analysis of incoming international students with U.S. students on educational and career needs. Findings reveal that international students expressed greater academic and career needs than American students.

Schwartz, John. "A 'Superminority' Tops Out." *Newsweek* (11 May 1987):48–49. Discusses job discrimination against Asian Americans, and how promotions into upper management are rare for Asian Americans. Asserts cultural conditioning pressures "Asians" to avoid confrontation. Found that cultural backgrounds of Asian Americans are resources too important to leave untapped.

Vertiz, Virginia C., and Jim C. Fortune. "An Ethnographic Study of Cultural Barriers to Employment among Indochinese Immigrant Youth." *College Student Journal* 18:3 (Fall 1984):229–35. Suggests that Indochinese students' backgrounds present cultural barriers to employment and education. Strategies to bridge the cultural gap as well as recommendations for developing programs are provided.

Notes on Contributors

Jennifer Abe is a professor in the Department of Psychology, Loyola-Marymount University.

Herbert R. Barringer is a professor in the Department of Sociology, University of Hawaii at Manoa.

Sucheng Chan is a professor in the Department of History, and director, Asian American Studies program, University of California, Santa Barbara.

Li-Rong Lilly Cheng is coordinator of the Bilingual/Multicultural Program, Department of Communicative Disorders, San Diego State University.

Ki-Taek Chun is on the staff of the United States Commission on Civil Rights.

Eugenia Escueta is a former research assistant at the American Council on Education.

John N. Hawkins is a professor in the Graduate School of Education, and dean of International Studies and Overseas Programs, University of California, Los Angeles.

Marsha Hirano-Nakanishi is director of Analytical Studies, Office of the Chancellor, California State University.

Jayjia Haia is senior research scientist emeritus at the Educational Testing Service.

Shirley Hune is a professor in the Department of Urban Planning, and associate dean, Graduate Programs, University of California, Los Angeles.

Kenji Ima is a professor in the Department of Sociology, San Diego State University.

Rosalind Y. Mau is a lecturer in the Multifunctional Resource Center, College of Education, University of Hawaii, Manoa.

Dale Minami is an attorney in private practice in San Francisco.

David Morse is a freelance writer.

Don T. Nakanishi is a professor in the Graduate School of Education, and director of the Asian American Studies Center, University of California, Los Angeles.

Tina Yamano Nishida is executive director of the Yamano College of Aesthetics and Yamano Beauty College of Los Angeles and Tokyo.

Eileen O'Brien is a research analyst at the American Council on Education.

Sumie Okazaki is a postdoctoral research fellow in the Department of Psychology, University of California, Los Angeles.

Valerie Ooka Pang is a professor in the School of Education, San Diego State University.

Rubén G. Rumbaut is a professor in the Department of Sociology, Michigan State University.

Nancy J. Smith-Hefner is a professor in the BIL/ESL Studies program, Department of English, University of Massachusetts, Boston.

Stanley Sue is a professor in the Department of Psychology, and director of the National Research Center on Asian/Pacific American Mental Health, University of California, Los Angeles.

Bob H. Suzuki is president of California Polytechnic University, Pomona.

David T. Takeuchi is a professor in the Department of Psychiatry and the Neuropsychiatric Institute, University of California, Los Angeles.

Ling-Chi L. Wang is a professor in the Department of Ethnic Studies, University of California, Berkeley.

Charles M. Wollenberg is an instructor in the Department of History and Government, Vista College.

Morrison G. Wong is a professor in the Department of Sociology, Texas Christian University.

Peter Xenos is a professor in the Department of Sociology, University of Hawaii at Manoa.

Rengiu Yu is a professor in the Department of History, State University of New York, Purchase.

Index

Abramson, Arthur, 346

Academics in Court: The Consequences of Faculty Discrimination Litigation (LaNoue & Lee), 362

acculturation, studies of, 107–108. *See also* Americanization; assimilation

adaptation, theories of, 146–48

administration, school: Asian/Pacific Americans and admissions policies, 280; implications of *Lau v. Nichols* for, 81–82; percentage of Asian Americans in higher education, 260, 268

admissions, university: discrimination against Asian American students, 221, 273–84, 285–98, 303–304

affirmative action programs: ethnic and women's studies movement, 323; "model minority" myth and, 350; political context of Asian American admissions debate, 275–76, 278, 292; racial harassment incidents at University of Connecticut, 339–57

age: and English proficiency of Southeast Asian refugees, 193; Asian American population and secondary education, 261–63; recency of immigration and correlation between education and income, 153–54

Aguirre, Edward, 88n.56

American College Testing Program (ACT), 304

American Federation of Labor, 14, 116

Americanization: Japanese language schools in California, 22–24; Japanese language schools in Hawaii, 35–38; myth of Asian American success, 100, 107; and nativist movement, 122. *See also* assimilation

animism, 214

Anti-Japanese League, 14, 15, 18

Aoki v. Deane (1907), 13, 19–20

Ardaiolo, Frank, 345, 347–49, 352, 353–54

Asian American studies: and ethnic studies requirement, 329–37; role of in higher education, 322–28

Asian American Task Force on University Admissions (ATFUA), 285, 290, 291

Asian Indians: definitional changes in 1980 census, 251; educational levels of, 254, 262

Asian/Pacific Americans: diversity of and educational needs of children, 167–77; education, occupation, and income of, 146–62; education and socialization of, 113–28; explanations of educational achievements, 133–42; higher education and demography of, 249–58; predictors for academic achievement of, 303–19; quotas for and discrimination against in university admissions, 221, 273–84, 285–98; use of term, 129n.9; and trends in higher education, 259–70; violence against on college campuses, 339–57. *See also* Chinese-Americans; Japanese-Americans; model minority, myth of; Pacific-Americans; Southeast Asian refugees; success, myth of

Aspira v. Board of Education of City of New York (1974), 85n.21

assimilation: correlation between education and income, 148–49, 158, 160, 161; interracial marriages and, 128; intragroup conflicts and pressures of, 169–70; of Japanese-American students after World War II, 27; and myth of Asian American success, 100, 107–108; philosophy of Japanese-language schools, 22–23; as theory of adaptation, 146. *See also* Americanization

Assimilation in American Life (Gordon), 139

Association for Asian American Studies (AAAS), 322